# Introduction to Management Science

# Introduction to
# Management
# Science

### Bernard W. Taylor III
Virginia Polytechnic Institute
and State University

ωɔb
**Wm. C. Brown Company Publishers**
Dubuque, Iowa

**wcb**
**group**
**Wm. C. Brown** Chairman of the Board
**Mark C. Falb** Corporate Vice President/Operations

**Book Team**
**Roger L. Ross** Editor
**Julie A. Kennedy** Production Editor
**Julia A. Scannell** Designer
**James M. McNeil** Design Layout Assistant
**Faye Schilling** Visual Research Editor

**wcb**
**Wm. C. Brown Company Publishers, College Division**
**Lawrence E. Cremer** President
**Raymond C. Deveaux** Vice President/Product Development
**David Wm. Smith** Assistant Vice President/National Sales Manager
**David A. Corona** Director of Production Development and Design
**Matthew T. Coghlan** National Marketing Manager
**Janis M. Machala** Director of Marketing Research
**William A. Moss** Production Editorial Manager
**Marilyn A. Phelps** Manager of Design
**Mary M. Heller** Visual Research Manager
**Mavis M. Oeth** Permissions Editor

*To the memory of my grandfather,*
*Bernard W. Taylor, Sr.*

# Contents

Contents

Contents ix

# Illustrations

## Figures

# Tables

## A Note to the Student

Prior to writing this book I tried to recall the reasons I did not like many of my quantitatively oriented textbooks when I was a student. One prominent reason that came to mind was that many of the texts I used consisted of long, sprawling chapters that tried to explain everything about a quantitative technique without the benefit of very many examples. As a result, I have written short, concise chapters that are centered around simple, straightforward examples that demonstrate in detail the fundamentals of the techniques. I have also presented these examples in such a way that it will be easy to apply the same solution steps to homework and test problems.

I have also attempted to write this book so it can be understood by an individual with a limited mathematical background or someone who hasn't had a math course for several quarters (or semesters). Thus, when I begin to cover a particular quantitative technique, I do not automatically assume that one understands the mathematical underpinnings of the technique. And this consideration is not limited to just the easier topics in this text. I have followed the same policy in chapters dealing with what are often perceived as more complex management science techniques—integer programming and dynamic programming. As you read those chapters dealing with topics you thought would be very hard, you will find they are presented in such a way that they are not that difficult.

It is often difficult for a student to perceive the usefulness of quantitative courses in general, like the one for which you will be using this text. I know that when I was a student I did not always foresee how I would use such material in any job I might take. (One reason for this feeling is that the examples used in texts often do not appear to be realistic. However, it must be remembered that simple examples are used to facilitate the learning process. More realistic examples reflecting actual applications would be so complex that they would not be very helpful in learning a technique.) Let me assure you, though, that the techniques presented in this text are already used extensively in the real world and their use is increasing rapidly.

Therefore, the chances of using the techniques you have learned from this text in a future course or job are very high.

Even if you do not use these techniques when you get a job, it should be understood that management science consists of more than just a collection of techniques. Management science also involves a philosophy of approaching a problem in a logical manner, as does any science. This logical approach to problem solving embodied in management science or quantitative methods is valuable for all types of jobs in all types of organizations. Thus, this course and text does not only teach you specific techniques, but also a method for approaching problems that will be very useful in your future endeavors.

## A Note to the Instructor

I wrote this text with two primary objectives in mind. First, I wanted the text to be thoroughly comprehensive, containing all of the topics normally attributed to the field of management science. Second, I wanted the text to be readable.

Regarding the first objective, this text contains twenty-five chapters that encompass the major topics in the field of management science. As such, it can be employed in a variety of course structures. The organization of the various techniques presented in this text is shown in the front endpaper.

The second objective, readability, has primarily been accomplished by creating chapters that are direct and succinct and that avoid rambling discussions of the subleties and nuances of a technique. I have concentrated on the fundamentals of one specific topic (or several closely related topics) in a chapter rather than several areas of coverage combined into a single chapter. In addition, the techniques presented in each chapter are explained within the context of straightforward examples that avoid lengthy written explanations. These examples are organized in a logical step-by-step solution approach that the student can subsequently apply to homework problems. An attempt has been made to avoid complex mathematical notation and formulas wherever possible. The combined effect of these various factors help to ensure student assimilation of the material.

There are many aids to the student in *Introduction to Management Science*. Each chapter begins with a chapter outline, which gives the student a brief overview of topics covered in the chapter. *Marginal notes* are also used to help the student quickly locate specific topics. As an additional aid to the student, a complete *glossary* of all key terms is included at the end of the text.

A criticism of many quantitative methods or management science texts is that they contain a limited number of homework problems. There are over 500 end-of-chapter problems in this text, many with multiple parts. These problems are organized to coincide with the order of presentation of the material in the chapter. In addition, the problems range from very easy to very challenging. The *instructor's manual* that accompanies this text contains the detailed solutions of all homework problems.

Also accompanying this text is a *study guide* (authored by Connie and Bruce McLaren of Indiana State University) to aid the student. The study guide contains a corresponding chapter for every chapter in the text. These study chapters consist of an outline of the text chapter, quizzes (answers are given in the back of the study guide), problems (different from those in the text) that are solved in detail, and cases (solutions are contained in a separate case solutions manual).

The text and its accompaniments comprise a comprehensive package that is flexible enough to accommodate a broad range of management science course structures. The textual material in this package should provide the student with a thorough understanding of the individual management science techniques and an overall comprehension of the management science process.

## Acknowledgments

As with any large project, the completion of a textbook is not achieved without the help of many people. This book is no exception, and I would like to take this opportunity to thank those individuals. First, I would like to thank my friend and colleague, Larry Moore, for his help in developing the organization and approach of this book. We spent many hours discussing what an introductory text in management science should consist of, and his ideas appear in these pages. Larry also served as a sounding board for many ideas regarding content, design, and preparation, as well as reading and editing many portions of the text, for which I am very grateful. Mildred Massey (California State University, Los Angeles), Richard Gunther (California State University, Northridge), and Lisa Sokol performed yeoman duty during the review process of the text, reading and rereading many portions. Their suggestions and comments markedly improved many chapters. At Virginia Tech, Robin Russell was indispensable. She reread all proofs in addition to editing the instructor's solution manual. I am also grateful to Gerry Chenault and Vicki Owen at Virginia Tech for their typing and editorial assistance. Finally, I would like to thank my editor at Wm. C. Brown, Roger Ross, whose patience and encouragement, and the organization he lent to the project are greatly appreciated.

Preface

# Introduction to
# Management
# Science

# 1
Management
Science

## The Management Science Approach to Problem Solving

Observation
Definition of the Problem
Model Construction
Model Solution
Implementation of Results
Management Science as an Ongoing Process

## Management Science Techniques

Linear Mathematical Programming Techniques
Probabilistic Techniques
Inventory Techniques
Network Techniques
Other Linear and Nonlinear Techniques

## Summary

*Management science* is the application of a scientific approach to management problems in order to help managers make better decisions. As implied by this definition, management science encompasses a number of mathematically oriented techniques that have either been developed within the field of management science or adapted from other disciplines, such as the natural sciences, mathematics, statistics, and engineering. It is the purpose of this text to provide an introduction to those techniques that comprise management science and to demonstrate their applications to management problems.

Management science, although rather young, is a recognized and established discipline in the field of business administration. The applications of management science techniques are widespread, and they have been frequently credited with increasing the efficiency and productivity of business firms. In a survey responded to by 275 firms, approximately 50 percent indicated that they used management science techniques, and 80 percent rated the results to be very good.[1] The increasing popularity of management science is reflected in the number of colleges and universities offering undergraduate courses and degree programs in management science. Management science (also referred to as *operations research, quantitative methods, quantitative analysis,* and *decision sciences*) is now part of the fundamental curriculum of most programs in business administration.

As we proceed through the presentations of the various management science models and techniques contained in this text, several items should be remembered. First, management science techniques can be applied to solve problems in a variety of different types of organizations. Management science can be applied to problems in government, military, business and industry, and health care, among others. However, the predominant number of examples presented in this text will be for business organizations, since businesses represent the main users of management science. Second, the mathematical techniques that will be presented require manual solution. However, in every case, computerized solution is possible. Although computerized solutions are the norm rather than the exception in the real business world, they are absent in this text, since the purpose of the text is to teach techniques and how they are applied (a natural prerequisite for subsequent computer application).

*A scientific approach to management*

*Management science can be used in a variety of organizations*

1. Gaither, "The Adoption of Operations Research Techniques by Manufacturing Organizations," *Decision Sciences* 6, no. 4 (October 1975): 797–813.

Finally, as the various management science techniques are presented in the text, it should be remembered that management science consists of more than just a collection of techniques. Management science also involves the philosophy of approaching a problem in a logical manner (i.e., a scientific approach). The logical, consistent, and systematic manner of problem solving employed in management science can be as useful (and valuable) as the knowledge of the mechanics of the mathematical techniques themselves. This is an especially important thought to keep in mind for those readers who do not always see the immediate benefit of studying mathematically oriented disciplines such as management science.

*Management science encompasses a logical approach to problem solving*

## The Management Science Approach to Problem Solving

As indicated in the previous section, management science encompasses a logical, systematic approach to problem solving, which closely parallels what is known as the *scientific method* for attacking problems. This approach to problem solving as shown in figure 1.1 follows a generally recognized, ordered set of steps: (1) observation, (2) definition of the problem, (3) model construction, (4) model solution, and (5) implementation of solution results. We will analyze each of these steps individually.

*The scientific method*

**Figure 1.1** The management science process.

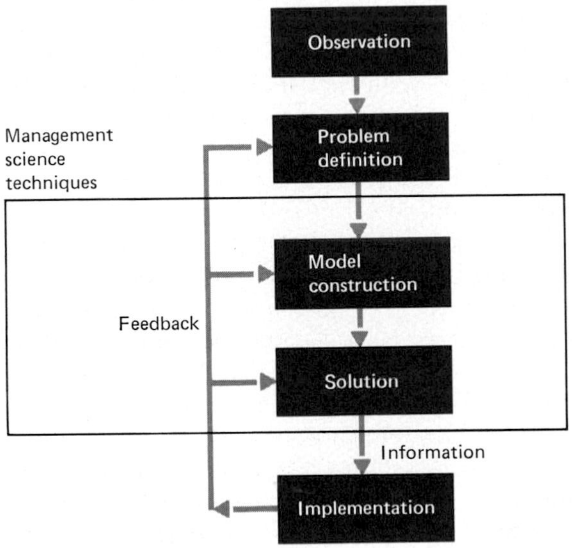

## Observation

The first step in the management science process is the identification of a problem that exists in the system (organization). This requires that the system be continuously and closely observed so that problems can be identified as soon as they occur. The person who normally identifies a problem is the manager, since the manager is the one who works in the vicinity of places where problems might occur. However, problems can often be identified by an individual known as a *management scientist*. This is a person who is skilled in the techniques of management science and trained to identify problems and who has been hired specifically to solve problems using management science techniques.

*Identifying the problem*

*The management scientist*

## Definition of the Problem

Once it has been determined that a problem exists, it must be clearly and concisely *defined*. An improperly defined problem can easily result in no solution or an inappropriate solution. The problem definition must include the limits of the problem and the degree to which it pervades other units of the organization. Since the existence of a problem implies that the objectives of the firm are not being met in some way, a requirement of problem definition is that the goals (or objectives) of the organization must also be clearly defined. A stated objective helps to focus attention on what the problem actually is.

*Defining the objectives of the organization*

## Model Construction

A management science *model* is an abstract representation of an existing problem situation. It can be in the form of a graph or chart, but most frequently, a management science model consists of a set of mathematical relationships. These mathematical relationships are made up of numbers and symbols.

As an example, consider a business firm that sells a product. The product costs $5 to produce and sells for $20. A model that computes the total profit that will accrue from the items sold is

$$Z = \$20x - 5x$$

In this equation $x$ represents the number of units of the product that are sold and $Z$ represents the total profit that will result from the sale of the product. The *symbols, $x$ and $Z$,* are referred to as *variables*. The term *variable* is used because no set numerical value has been specified for those items. The number of units sold and profit can be any amount (within limits); they can vary. However, these two variables can be further distinguished. $Z$ is known as a *dependent variable* because its value is dependent on the number of units sold. Alternatively, $x$ is an *independent variable*, since the number of units sold is dependent upon nothing else (in this equation).

*Variables*

*Dependent variable*
*Independent variable*

*Parameters*    The numbers $20 and $5 in the equation are referred to as *parameters*. Parameters are constant values that are generally coefficients of the variables (symbols) in an equation. Parameters usually remain constant for the process of solving a specific problem.

*Functional*    The equation as a whole is known as a *functional relationship* (also
*relationships*  called function and relationship). The term is derived from the fact that profit, $Z$, is a *function* of the number of units sold, $x$. As such, the equation *relates* profit to units sold.

*The model*    Since only one functional relationship exists in this example, it is also the *model*. In this case the relationship is a model of the determination of profit for the firm. However, this model does not really replicate a problem. Therefore, we will expand our example in order to create a problem situation.

Let us now assume that the product is made from steel and that the business firm has 100 pounds of steel available. If it takes 4 pounds of steel to make each unit of the product, then we can develop an additional mathematical relationship to represent steel utilization:

$$4x = 100 \text{ pounds of steel}$$

This equation represents the fact that for every unit produced, 4 of the available 100 pounds of steel will be used up. Now our model consists of two relationships:

$$Z = \$20x - 5x$$
$$4x = 100$$

*Objective function*    In this new model we say that the profit equation is an *objective*
*Constraint*  *function* and the resource equation is a *constraint*. In other words, the objective of the firm is to achieve as much profit, $Z$, as possible, but it is constrained from achieving an infinite profit by the steel available. To signify this distinction between the two relationships in this model, we will add the following notation.

$$\text{maximize } Z = \$20x - 5x$$
$$\text{subject to } 4x = 100$$

This model now represents the manager's problem of determining the number of units to produce. You will recall that we previously defined the number of units to be produced as $x$. Thus, when we determine what $x$ actually is, it represents a potential (or recommended) *decision* for the
*Decision variable*  manager. As such, $x$ is also known as a *decision variable*. The next step in the management science process is to solve the model to determine the value of the decision variable.

## Model Solution

Once models are constructed in management science, they are solved using the management science techniques to be presented in this text. Actually it is difficult to separate model construction and solution in most cases, since a management science solution technique usually applies to a specific type of model. Thus, the model type and solution method are both part of the management science technique.

*The solution technique*

We are able to say that *a model is solved*, since the model represents a problem. When we refer to model solution we also mean problem solution.

For our example model developed in the previous section,

$$\text{maximize } Z = \$20x - 5x$$
$$\text{subject to } 4x = 100$$

the solution technique is simple algebra. Solving the constraint equation for $x$,

$$4x = 100$$
$$x = 100/4$$
$$x = 25 \text{ units}$$

Substituting the value of 25 for $x$ into the profit function results in the total profit:

$$Z = \$20x - 5x$$
$$= 20(25) - 5(25)$$
$$= \$375$$

Thus, if the manager makes a decision to produce 25 units of the product, the business firm will receive $375 in profit. However, the value that the decision variable equals is not an actual decision, but rather a recommendation or guideline. It is *information* that can help the manager make a decision.

*Information to aid in making a decision*

Some management science techniques do not generate an *answer* or a recommended *decision*. Instead, they provide what is known as *descriptive results*, which are results that describe the system being modeled. For example, suppose the business firm of our example desires to know the average number of units sold each month during a year. The monthly *data* (i.e., sales) for the past year are

*Descriptive results*

| Month | Sales |
|---|---|
| January | 30 |
| February | 40 |
| March | 25 |
| April | 60 |
| May | 30 |
| June | 25 |
| July | 35 |
| August | 50 |
| September | 60 |
| October | 40 |
| November | 35 |
| December | 50 |
| Total | 480 units |

The average monthly sales is 40 units (480 ÷ 12). This result is not really a decision, but a value that describes what is happening in the system. For the management science techniques in this text, the results are of the two types shown in this section: solution/decisions or descriptive results.

## Implementation of Results

*Insuring that management science results are used*

The results of a management science technique are information that can aid the manager in making a decision. However, if the manager does not use this information, then we say the results are not *implemented* (i.e., they are not put to use). If the results are not implemented, then the effort and resources that went into problem definition, model construction, and solution are wasted. As such, this last step in the management science process cannot be ignored. An effort must be made to insure that results will be used (assuming that the results are applicable).

## Management Science as an Ongoing Process

*Model feedback*

Once the five steps described above are completed, it does not necessarily mean that the management science process is completed. The model results and the decisions based on the results provide *feedback* to the original model. The original management science model can be changed to test different conditions and decisions the manager thinks might occur in the future. The results may indicate that a different problem exists that had not been thought of previously, thus the original model is altered or reconstructed. As such, the management science process can be continuous rather than simply consisting of one solution to one problem.

# Management Science Techniques

*Focusing on model construction and solution*

In this text we will focus primarily on only two of the five steps of the management science process: model construction and solution. These two steps encompass the actual use of the management science technique. In a textbook, it is difficult to show how an unstructured real world problem is identified and defined, since the problems must be written out. However, once a problem statement is given then we can show how a model is constructed and a solution derived.

*Model classification*

The techniques presented in this text can be loosely classified into five categories, as shown in figure 1.2.

**Figure 1.2** Classification of management science techniques.

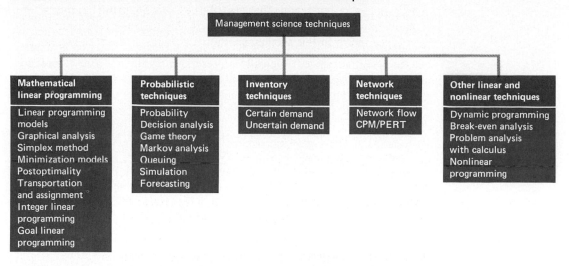

## Linear Mathematical Programming Techniques

Chapters 2 through 9 present the techniques that comprise *linear mathematical programming*. (The first example used to demonstrate model construction earlier in this chapter was a very rudimentary linear programming model). The term *programming* used to identify this technique does not mean computer programming, but rather a predetermined set of mathematical steps used to solve a problem. This particular class of techniques holds such a predominant position in this text because it includes some of the more frequently used and popular techniques in management science.

*Programming as a predetermined set of mathematical solution steps*

## Probabilistic Techniques

The next category, probabilistic techniques, are presented in chapters 10 through 16. These techniques are distinguished from the mathematical programming techniques in that the results are probabilistic. The mathematical programming techniques assume that all the parameters in the models are known with *certainty*. Therefore, the solution results are assumed to be known with certainty with no probability that other solutions might exist. This type of technique where there is no uncertainty in the solution is referred to as *deterministic*. Alternatively, the results from a probabilistic technique do contain uncertainty with some possibility that alternative solutions can occur. In the model solution section presented earlier in this chapter, the result of the first example ($x = 25$ units to produce) is deterministic, while the result of the second example (an average of 40 units sold each month) is probabilistic.

*Model parameters that are not known with certainty*

*Deterministic solution results*

## Inventory Techniques

Inventory techniques are presented in chapters 17 and 18. These techniques are specifically designed for the analysis of inventory problems frequently encountered by business firms. This particular business function is singled out for attention, since it typically represents a significant area of cost for almost every business. Notice that this category is divided into probabilistic and deterministic techniques. As such, at least part of this class of management science techniques could be included in the category of probabilistic techniques. This is why we said at the first of this discussion that figure 1.2 is a *loose* classification of techniques. Many of the techniques cross over between classifications.

## Network Techniques

*A pictorial representation of a system*

Networks, the topic of chapters 19 and 20, consists of models that are represented as diagrams rather than strictly mathematical relationships. As such, these models offer a pictorial representation of the system under analysis. These models can represent either probabilistic or deterministic systems.

## Other Linear and Nonlinear Techniques

*Calculus-based models*

Chapters 21 through 24 include management science techniques that have linear and/or nonlinear components. Dynamic programming presented in chapter 21 is a form of mathematical programming that employs a different modeling and solution logic than linear programming. The models in chapters 22 through 24 employ *calculus* as part of the solution method. Because calculus is employed in these models, they should be considered the most advanced topics in the text. (The preceding chapters require only a knowledge of algebra.) An exception is chapter 22 on break-even analysis, which does not include calculus in its most elementary form. However, an extension of break-even analysis provides an excellent example of a calculus-based model. As such, it is included at this point in the text.

*Management information systems*

*Implementation*

The final topics in this text presented in chapter 25 are *management information systems* and *implementation*. These two topics do not actually encompass specific management science techniques. Instead these topics characterize ways in which management science models and results interface with the manager.

## Summary

In the chapters to follow, the model construction and solutions that comprise each management science technique will be presented in detail and illustrated with examples. In fact, the primary method of presenting the techniques will be through examples. As such, the text will offer the reader a broad spectrum of knowledge of the mechanics of management science techniques. However, the ultimate test of a management scientist or the manager who uses management science techniques is the ability to transfer textbook knowledge to the real business world. In such instances there is an *art* to the application of management science, but it is an art predicated on practical experience and sound textbook knowledge. The first of these necessities is beyond the scope of textbooks; however, the second is the objective of this text.

*Management science as an art*

## References

Ackoff, Russell L., and Sasieni, Maurice W. *Fundamentals of Operations Research.* New York: John Wiley and Sons, 1968.

Beer, Stafford. *Management Sciences: The Business Use of Operations Research.* New York: Doubleday, 1967.

Churchman, C. W.; Ackoff, R. L.; and Arnoff, E. L. *Introduction to Operations Research.* New York: John Wiley and Sons, 1957.

Fabrycky, W. J., and Torgersen, P. E. *Operations Economy: Industrial Applications of Operations Research.* Englewood Cliffs, N.J.: Prentice-Hall, 1966.

Hillier, F. S., and Lieberman, G. J. *Operations Research.* 3rd ed. San Francisco: Holden-Day, 1980.

Lee, Sang M.; Moore, Laurence J.; and Taylor, Bernard W. *Management Science.* Dubuque, Iowa: Wm. C. Brown Company Publishers, 1981.

Taha, Hamdy A. *Operations Research.* 2d ed. New York: Macmillan Co., 1976.

Teichroew, P. *An Introduction to Management Science.* New York: John Wiley and Sons, 1964.

Wagner, Harvey M. *Principles of Operations Research.* Englewood Cliffs, N.J.: Prentice-Hall, 1975.

Wagner, Harvey M. *Principles of Management Science.* Englewood Cliffs, N.J.: Prentice-Hall, 1975.

## Problems

1. Define what management science is.

2. Discuss what the management science approach to problem solving encompasses.

3. What are the steps of the scientific method for solving problems?

4. What is a management scientist?

5. How is problem definition related to the objectives of an organization?

6. Explain what a model is and how it is used in management science.

7. Distinguish between dependent variables, independent variables, and decision variables.

8. Define what a functional relationship is.

9. What are model parameters?

10. Discuss how constraints, the objective function, and decision variables are related in a management science model.

11. Distinguish between model results that recommend a decision and results that are descriptive.

12. A company makes tables from wood. The company sells each table for $100 and it costs $40 to make a table. The company has 500 pounds of wood and each table requires 25 pounds of wood. The company wants to know how many tables to make. Develop a model for this problem situation and solve it to determine the number of tables to produce.

13. Why is management science an ongoing process?

14. What does implementation mean?

15. Outline the different categories of techniques presented in this chapter.

# 2

# Introduction
# to Linear
# Programming
## Model Formulation

**Model Formulation**

**A Product Mix Example**

**An Ingredients Mixture Example**

**An Investment Example**

**A Chemical Mixture Example**

**A Marketing Example**

**A Transportation Example**

**Summary**

Many of the major decisions faced by a manager of a business enterprise are centered around the best way to achieve the objectives of the firm subject to the restrictions placed on the manager by the operating environment. These restrictions can take the form of limited resources, such as time, labor, energy, material, or money, or they can be in the form of restrictive guidelines, such as a recipe for making cereal or engineering specifications. For business firms, in general, the most frequent objective is to gain the most profit possible or, in other words, to *maximize* profit. Alternatively, for individual organizational units within a firm (such as a production or packaging department) the objective is often to *minimize* cost. The general type of problem where an objective is sought subject to restrictions placed on the manager can frequently be solved using a management science technique called *linear programming*.

*Objectives of the business firm*

The linear programming technique consists of, first, identifying the problem as being solvable by linear programming; second, formulating the unstructured problem as a mathematical model; and, third, solving the model using established mathematical techniques. It derives its name from the fact that the functional relationships in the mathematical model are *linear* and the solution technique consists of predetermined mathematical steps, i.e., a *program*. In this chapter we will be primarily concerned with the formulation of the mathematical model, which represents the problem. In subsequent chapters the various solution techniques will be presented.

*Linear programming steps*

## Model Formulation

A linear programming model consists of certain common components and characteristics. The model components include decision variables, an objective function, and model constraints, both of which consist of decision variables and parameters. *Decision variables* are mathematical symbols that represent levels of activity by the firm. For example, an electrical manufacturing firm desires to produce $x_1$ radios, $x_2$ toasters, and $x_3$ clocks, where $x_1$, $x_2$, and $x_3$ are symbols representing unknown variable quantities of each item. The final values of $x_1$, $x_2$, and $x_3$, as determined by the firm, constitute their *decision* (i.e., $x_1 = 10$ radios is a decision by the firm to produce 10 radios.)

*Decision variables*

The *objective function* is a linear mathematical relationship that describes the objective of the firm in terms of the decision variables. The objective function always consists of either *maximizing* or *minimizing* some value (i.e., maximize the profit or minimize the cost of producing radios).

The *model constraints* are also linear relationships of the decision variables, which represent the restrictions placed on the firm by the operating environment. The restrictions can be in the form of limited resources or restrictive guidelines. For example, there may be only forty hours of labor available to produce radios during production. The actual numerical values in the objective function and constraints such as the 40 hours of available labor are *parameters*.

In this section several examples are presented that demonstrate how a linear programming model is formulated. Although these examples are simplified, they are realistic and represent the type of problem to which linear programming can be applied. In each example the model components will be distinctly identified and described. By carefully studying each of these examples, the reader should become familiar with the process of formulating linear programming models.

## A Product Mix Example

The Colonial Pottery Company produces two products daily—bowls and mugs. The company has limited amounts of two resources used in the production of these products—clay and labor. Given these limited resources, the company desires to know how many bowls and mugs to produce each day in order to maximize profit. The two products have the following resource requirements for production and profit per item produced (i.e., the model parameters).

| | Resource Requirements | | |
| --- | --- | --- | --- |
| Product | Labor (hours/units) | Clay (lbs./unit) | Profit ($/unit) |
| Bowl | 1 | 4 | 4 |
| Mug | 2 | 3 | 5 |

There are 40 hours of labor and 120 pounds of clay available each day for production. We will formulate this problem as a linear programming model by defining each component of the model separately and then combining the components into a single model.

## Decision Variables

The decision confronting management in this problem is how many bowls and mugs to produce. As such, there are two decision variables that represent the number of bowls and mugs to be produced on a daily basis. The quantities to be produced can be represented symbolically as,

$x_1$ = the number of bowls to produce
$x_2$ = the number of mugs to produce

## The Objective Function

The objective of the company in this problem is to maximize total profit. *Maximizing profit* The company's profit is the sum of the individual profits gained from each bowl and mug. As such, profit from bowls is determined by multiplying the unit profit for each bowl, $4, by the number of bowls produced, $x_1$. Likewise, profit derived from mugs is the unit profit of a mug, $5, multiplied by the number of mugs produced, $x_2$. Thus, total profit, which we will define symbolically as $Z$, can be expressed mathematically as

maximize $Z = 4x_1 + 5x_2$
where
$Z$ = total profit per day
$4x_1$ = profit from bowls
$5x_2$ = profit from mugs

By placing the term *maximize* in front of the profit function, the relationship expresses the objective of the firm—to maximize total profit.

## Model Constraints

This problem has two resources used for production, which are limited, labor and clay. Production of bowls and mugs require both labor and clay. For each bowl produced, one hour of labor is required. Therefore, the labor used for the production of bowls is $1x_1$ hours. Similarly, each mug requires *Labor constraint* two hours of labor, thus, the labor used to produce mugs every day is $2x_1$ hours. The total labor used by the company is the sum of the individual amounts of labor used for each product,

$1x_1 + 2x_2$

However, the amount of labor represented by "$1x_1 + 2x_2$" is limited to 40 hours per day, thus, the complete labor constraint is

$1x_1 + 2x_2 \leq 40$ hours

The "less than or equal to (≤)" inequality is employed instead of an equality (=) because the forty hours of labor is a maximum limitation than *can be used,* but not an amount *that must be used.* This allows the company more flexibility in that it is not restricted to use the 40 hours exactly, but whatever amount necessary to maximize profit up to and including forty hours. This means that the possibility of "idle or excess capacity" (i.e., the amount under forty hours not used) exists.

The constraint for pottery clay is formulated in the same way as the labor constraint. Since each bowl requires four pounds of clay, the amount of clay used daily for the production of bowls is $4x_1$ pounds, and since each mug requires three pounds of clay, the amount of clay used for mugs daily is $3x_2$. Given that amount of clay available for production each day is 120 pounds, the material constraint can be formulated as

*Material constraint*

$$4x_1 + 3x_2 \leq 120 \text{ pounds}$$

A final restriction is that the number of bowls and mugs produced be either zero or a positive value, since it would be impossible to produce negative items. These restrictions are referred to as *nonnegativity constraints* and are expressed mathematically as

*Nonnegativity constraints*

$$x_1 \geq 0, x_2 \geq 0$$

*The formulated model*

The complete linear programming model for this problem can now be summarized as

$$\text{maximize } Z = \$4x_1 + 5x_2$$
$$\text{subject to}$$

$$1x_1 + 2x_2 \leq 40$$
$$4x_1 + 3x_2 \leq 120$$
$$x_1, x_2 \geq 0$$

*An example solution*

The solution of this model will result in numerical values for $x_1$ and $x_2$, which will maximize total profit, $Z$. As *one possible* solution, consider $x_1 = 5$ bowls and $x_2 = 10$ mugs. First we will substitute this hypothetical solution into each of the constraints in order to make sure that the solution does not require more resources than the constraints show are available.

$$1(5) + 2(10) \leq 40$$
$$25 \leq 40$$

and

$$4(5) + 3(10) \leq 120$$
$$50 \leq 120$$

*A feasible solution*

Thus, neither one of the constraints is violated by this hypothetical solution. As such, we say the solution is *feasible* (i.e., it is possible). Substituting these solution values in the objective function gives $Z = 4(5) + 5(10) = \$70$. However, for the time being we do not have any way of knowing if this is the *maximum* profit.

Now consider a solution of $x_1 = 10$ bowls and $x_2 = 20$ mugs. This would result in a profit of

$$Z = \$4\ (10) + 5\ (20)$$
$$= 40 + 100$$
$$= \$140$$

While this is certainly a better solution in terms of profit, it is also *infeasible* (i.e., not possible) because it violates the resource constraint for labor:

$$1\ (10) + 2\ (20) \le 40$$
$$50 \not\le 40$$

*An infeasible solution*

Thus, the solution to this problem must both maximize profit and not violate the constraints. The actual solution to this model which achieves this objective is $x_1 = 24$ bowls and $x_2 = 8$ mugs, with a corresponding profit of $136. The determination of this solution will be shown in chapters 3 and 4.

## An Ingredients Mixture Example

A cereal company produces a cereal called Fortified Munchies, which they advertise as meeting the minimum daily requirements for vitamins A and D. The mixing department of the company uses three main ingredients in making the cereal—wheat, oats, and rice, all three of which contain amounts of vitamin A and D. Given that each box of cereal must contain minimum amounts of vitamin A and D, the company has instructed the mixing department to determine how many ounces of each ingredient should go into each box of cereal in order to minimize total cost. As such, this problem differs from the previous one in that its objective is to *minimize* cost, rather than maximize profit. Each ingredient has the following vitamin contribution and requirement per box.

*A minimization problem*

| Vitamin | Vitamin Contribution | | | |
| --- | --- | --- | --- | --- |
| | Wheat (mg./oz.) | Oats (mg./oz.) | Rice (mg./oz.) | Milligrams Required/Box |
| A | 10 | 20 | 8 | 100 |
| D | 7 | 14 | 12 | 70 |

The cost of one ounce of wheat is $.04, the cost of an ounce of oats is $.06, and the cost of one ounce of rice is $.02.

## Decision Variables

*Formulating the model* This problem contains three decision variables for the number of ounces of each ingredient in a box of cereal:

$x_1$ = ounces of wheat
$x_2$ = ounces of oats
$x_3$ = ounces of rice

## The Objective Function

*Minimizing cost* The objective of the mixing department of the cereal company is to minimize the cost of each box of cereal. The total cost is the sum of the individual costs resulting from each ingredient. Thus, the objective function that is to minimize total cost, $Z$, is expressed as

minimize $Z = \$.04x_1 + .06x_2 + .02x_3$
where
$Z$ = total cost per box
$\$.04x_1$ = cost of wheat per box
$.06x_2$ = cost of oats per box
$.02x_3$ = cost of rice per box

## Model Constraints

In this problem the constraints reflect the requirements for vitamin consistency of the cereal. Each ingredient contributes a number of milligrams of the vitamin to the cereal. The constraint for vitamin A is

$10x_1 + 20x_2 + 8x_3 \geq 100$ milligrams
where
$10x_1$ = vitamin A contribution (in mg.) for wheat
$20x_2$ = vitamin A contribution (in mg.) for oats
$8x_3$ = vitamin A contribution (in mg.) for rice

*≥ constraints* Notice that rather than a $\leq$ inequality, as used in the previous example, this constraint requires a $\geq$ (greater than or equal to) inequality. This is because the vitamin content is a minimum requirement specifying that *at least* 100 mg of vitamin A must be in a box. If a minimum cost solution results so that more than 100 mg is in the cereal mix, that is acceptable, however, the amount cannot be less than 100 mg.

The constraint for vitamin D is constructed like the constraint for vitamin A.

$7x_1 + 14x_2 + 12x_3 \geq 70$ milligrams

As in the previous problem there are also nonnegativity constraints indicating that negative amounts of each ingredient cannot be in the cereal.

$$x_1, x_2, x_3 \geq 0$$

In the future the nonnegativity constraints will not be specifically described but will be assumed to exist unless otherwise stated.

The linear programming model for this problem can be summarized as

*The formulated model*

$$\text{minimize } Z = \$.04x_1 + .06x_2 + .02x_3$$
subject to
$$10x_1 + 20x_2 + 8x_3 \geq 100$$
$$7x_1 + 14x_2 + 12x_3 \geq 70$$
$$x_1, x_2, x_3 \geq 0$$

## An Investment Example

An individual investor has $70,000 to invest in several alternatives. The alternative investments are municipal bonds with an 8.5% return, certificates of deposit with a 10% return, treasury bills with a 6.5% return, and income bonds with a return of 13%. Each alternative has the same time until maturity. In addition, each investment alternative has a different perceived risk to the investor, thus creating a desire to diversify. The investor wants to know how much to invest in each alternative in order to maximize the return.

The following guidelines have been established for diversifying the investments and lessening the risk perceived by the investor:

1. No more than 20% of the total investment should be in income bonds.
2. The amount invested in certificates of deposit should not exceed the amount invested in the other three alternatives.
3. At least 30% of the investment should be in treasury bills and certificates of deposit.
4. The ratio of the amount invested in municipal bonds to the amount invested in treasury bills should not exceed one to three.

The investor wants to invest the entire $70,000.

## Decision Variables

There are four decision variables in this model representing the monetary amount invested in each investment alternative.

*Formulating the model*

$x_1$ = the amount ($) invested in municipal bonds
$x_2$ = the amount ($) invested in certificates of deposit
$x_3$ = the amount ($) invested in treasury bills
$x_4$ = the amount ($) invested in income bonds

## The Objective Function

*Maximizing return*

The objective of the investor is to maximize the return from the investment in the four alternatives. The total return is the sum of the individual returns from each separate alternative. Thus, the objective function is expressed as

maximize $Z = \$.085x_1 + .100x_2 + .065x_3 + .130x_4$
where

$$Z = \text{the total return from all investments}$$
$$\$.085x_1 = \text{the return from the investment in municipal bonds}$$
$$.100x_2 = \text{the return from the investment in certificates of deposit}$$
$$.065x_3 = \text{the return from the investment in treasury bills}$$
$$.130x_4 = \text{the return from the investment in income bonds}$$

## Model Constraints

*Formulating the investment guidelines as constraints*

In this problem the constraints are the guidelines established by the investor for diversifying the total investment. Each guideline will be transformed into a mathematical constraint separately.

Guideline one states that no more than 20% of the total investment should be in income bonds. Since the total investment will be $70,000 (i.e., the investor desires to invest the entire amount), then 20% of $70,000 is $14,000. Thus, this constraint is

$x_4 \leq \$14,000$

The second guideline indicates that the amount invested in certificates of deposit should not exceed the amount invested in the other three alternatives. Since the investment in certificates of deposit is $x_2$ and the amount invested in the other alternatives is $x_1 + x_3 + x_4$, the constraint is

$x_2 \leq x_1 + x_3 + x_4$

*Standard constraint form*

However, the solution technique for linear programming problems will require that constraints be in a standard form so that all decision variables are on the left side of the inequality (i.e., $\leq$) and all numerical values are on the right side. Thus, by subtracting, $x_1 + x_3 + x_4$, from both sides of the $\leq$ sign, this constraint in proper form becomes

$x_2 - x_1 - x_3 - x_4 \leq 0$

The third guideline specifies that at least 30% of the investment should be in treasury bills and certificates of deposit. Given that 30% of the $70,000 total is $21,000 and the amount invested in certificates of deposit and treasury bills is represented by $x_2 + x_3$, the constraint is,

$x_2 + x_3 \geq \$21,000$

The fourth guideline states that the ratio of the amount invested in municipal bonds to the amount invested in treasury bills should not exceed one to three. This constraint is expressed as

$$x_1/x_3 \leq 1/3$$

This constraint is not in standard linear programming form because of the fractional relationship of the decision variables, $x_1/x_3$. It is converted as follows:

$$x_1 \leq 1x_3/3$$
$$3x_1 \leq x_3$$
$$3x_1 - x_3 \leq 0$$

Finally, the investor wants to invest all of the $70,000 in the four alternatives. Thus, the sum of all the investments in the four alternatives must *equal* $70,000,

$$x_1 + x_2 + x_3 + x_4 = \$70,000$$

This last constraint differs from the $\leq$ and $\geq$ inequalities previously developed, in that a specific requirement exists to invest an *exact amount*. Thus, the possibility of investing more than $70,000 or less than $70,000 is not considered.

*An equality constraint*

This problem contains all three of the types of constraints that are possible in a linear programming problem: $\leq$, $=$, and $\geq$. Further, note that there is no restriction on a model containing any mix of these types of constraints as demonstrated in this problem.

The complete linear programming model for this problem can be summarized as

*The formulated model*

$$\text{maximize } Z = .085x_1 + .100x_2 + .065x_3 + .130x_4$$
$$\text{subject to}$$
$$x_4 \leq 14,000$$
$$x_2 - x_1 - x_3 - x_4 \leq 0$$
$$x_2 + x_3 \geq 21,000$$
$$3x_1 - x_3 \leq 0$$
$$x_1 + x_2 + x_3 + x_4 = 70,000$$
$$x_1, x_2, x_3, x_4 \geq 0$$

## A Chemical Mixture Example

A chemical corporation produces a chemical mixture for a customer in 1,000-pound batches. The mixture contains three ingredients—zinc, mercury, and potassium. The mixture must conform to formula specifications (i.e., a recipe) supplied by the customer. The company wants to know the amount of each ingredient to put in the mixture that will meet all the requirements of the mix and minimize total cost.

The formula for each batch of the mixture consists of the following specifications:

1. The mixture must contain at least 200 lbs. of mercury.
2. The mixture must contain at least 300 lbs. of zinc.
3. The mixture must contain at least 100 lbs. of potassium.

The cost per pound for mercury is $4; for zinc, $8; and for potassium, $9.

## Decision Variables

*Formulating the model*  The model for this problem contains three decision variables representing the amount of each ingredient in the mixture:

$x_1$ = the number of lbs. of mercury in a batch
$x_2$ = the number of lbs. of zinc in a batch
$x_3$ = the number of lbs. of potassium in a batch

## The Objective Function

*Minimizing cost*  The objective of the company is to minimize the cost of producing a batch of the chemical mixture. The total cost is the sum of the individual costs of each ingredient:

minimize $Z = \$4x_1 + 8x_2 + 9x_3$
where
$Z$ = the total cost of all ingredients
$\$4x_1$ = the cost of mercury in each batch
$8x_2$ = the cost of zinc in each batch
$9x_3$ = the cost of potassium in each batch

## Model Constraints

In this problem the constraints are derived from the chemical formula.

*Formulating the mixture requirements*  The first specification indicates that the mixture must contain at least 200 lbs. of mercury,

$x_1 \geq 200$ lbs.

The second specification is that the mixture must contain at least 300 lbs. of zinc,

$x_2 \geq 300$ lbs.

The third specification is that the mixture must contain at least 100 lbs. of potassium,

$x_3 \geq 100$ lbs.

Introduction to Linear Programming

Finally, it must not be overlooked that the whole mixture relates to a 1,000-lb. batch. As such, the sum of all ingredients must exactly equal 1,000 lbs.,

$$x_1 + x_2 + x_3 = 1,000 \text{ lbs.}$$

The complete linear programming model can be summarized as

*The formulated model*

minimize $Z = 4x_1 + 8x_2 + 9x_3$
subject to

$$x_1 \geq 200$$
$$x_2 \geq 300$$
$$x_3 \geq 100$$
$$x_1 + x_2 + x_3 = 1,000$$
$$x_1, x_2, x_3 \geq 0$$

## A Marketing Example

The Biggs Department Store chain has contracted with an advertising firm to determine the types and amount of advertising it should have for its stores. The three types of advertising available are radio and television commercials and newspaper ads. The retail chain desires to know the number of each type of advertisement it should purchase in order to maximize exposure. It is estimated that each ad and commercial will reach the following potential audience and cost the following amount.

| Type of Advertisement | Exposure (people/ad or commercial) | Cost |
|---|---|---|
| Television commercial | 20,000 | $15,000 |
| Radio commercial | 12,000 | 6,000 |
| Newspaper ad | 9,000 | 4,000 |

The following resource constraints exist:

1. There is a budget limit of $100,000 available for advertising.
2. The television station has enough time available for four commercials.
3. The radio station has enough time available for ten radio commercials.
4. The newspaper has enough space available for seven ads.
5. The advertising agency has enough time and staff to produce at most a total of fifteen commercials and/or ads.

## Decision Variables

*Formulating the model*

This model consists of three decision variables representing the number of each type of advertising produced:

$x_1$ = the number of television commercials
$x_2$ = the number of radio commercials
$x_3$ = the number of newspaper ads

## The Objective Function

The objective of this problem is different from the objectives in the previous examples in which only profit was maximized (or cost minimized). In this problem profit is not maximized, but rather the audience exposure is maximized. As such, this objective function demonstrates that although a linear programming model must either maximize or minimize some objective, the objective itself can be in terms of any type of activity or valuation.

*Maximizing audience exposures*

For this problem the objective of audience exposure is determined by summing the audience exposure gained from each type of advertising.

maximize $Z = 20{,}000x_1 + 12{,}000x_2 + 9{,}000x_3$
where

$Z$ = the total number of audience exposures
$20{,}000x_1$ = the estimated number of exposures from television commercials
$12{,}000x_2$ = the estimated number of exposures from radio commercials
$9{,}000x_3$ = the estimated number of exposures from newspaper ads

## Model Constraints

The first constraint in this model reflects the limited budget of $100,000 allocated for advertisement,

$\$15{,}000x_1 + 6{,}000x_2 + 4{,}000x_3 \leq 100{,}000$
where
$\$15{,}000x_1$ = the amount spent for television advertising
$6{,}000x_2$ = the amount spent for radio advertising
$4{,}000x_3$ = the amount spent for newspaper advertising

The next three constraints represent the fact that television and radio commercials are limited to four and ten, respectively, while newspaper ads are limited to seven.

$x_1 \leq 4$ commercials
$x_2 \leq 10$ commercials
$x_3 \leq 7$ ads

The final constraint specifies that the total number of commercials and ads cannot exceed fifteen due to the limitations of the advertising firm:

$$x_1 + x_2 + x_3 \leq 15 \text{ commercials and ads}$$

The complete linear programming model for this problem is summarized as

*The formulated model*

$$\text{maximize } Z = 20,000x_1 + 12,000x_2 + 9,000x_3$$
subject to
$$\$15,000x_1 + 6,000x_2 + 4,000x_3 \leq \$100,000$$
$$x_1 \leq 4$$
$$x_2 \leq 10$$
$$x_3 \leq 7$$
$$x_1 + x_2 + x_3 \leq 15$$
$$x_1, x_2, x_3 \geq 0$$

## A Transportation Example

The Zephyr Television Company produces and ships televisions from three warehouses to three retail stores on a monthly basis. Each warehouse has a fixed supply per month and each store has a fixed demand per month. The manufacturer wants to know the number of television sets to ship from each warehouse to each store in order to minimize the total cost of transportation.

Each warehouse has the following supply of televisions available for shipment each month.

| Warehouse | Supply (sets) |
|---|---|
| 1. Cincinnati | 300 |
| 2. Atlanta | 100 |
| 3. Pittsburgh | 200 |
| | 600 |

Each retail store has the following monthly demand for television sets:

| Store | Demand (sets) |
|---|---|
| A. New York | 150 |
| B. Dallas | 250 |
| C. Detroit | 200 |
| | 600 |

The cost for transporting television sets from each warehouse to each retail store are different as a result of different modes of transportation and distances. The shipping cost per television set for each route are,

| From Warehouse | To Store A | B | C |
|---|---|---|---|
| 1 | $6 | $8 | $1 |
| 2 | 4 | 2 | 3 |
| 3 | 3 | 5 | 7 |

## Decision Variables

*Formulating the model*

The model for this problem consists of nine decision variables representing the number of television sets transported from each of the three warehouses to each of the three stores,

$$x_{ij} = \text{the number of television sets shipped from warehouse "i" to store "j" where } i = 1, 2, 3, \text{ and } j = A, B, C.$$

*Double subscripted variables*

$x_{ij}$ is referred to as a *double subscripted* variable. However, the subscript, whether double or single, simply gives a "name" to the variable (i.e., distinguishes it from other decision variables). As such, the reader should not view it as more complex than it actually is. For example, the decision variable $x_{3A}$ represents the number of television sets from warehouse 3 in Pittsburgh to store $A$ in New York.

## The Objective Function

*Minimizing shipping costs*

The objective function of the television manufacturer is to minimize the total transportation costs for all shipments. Thus, the objective function is the sum of the individual shipping costs from each warehouse to each store.

$$\text{minimize } Z = \$6x_{1A} + 8x_{1B} + 1x_{1C} + 4x_{2A} + 2x_{2B} + 3x_{2C} + 3x_{3A} + 5x_{3B} + 7x_{3C}$$

## Model Constraints

The constraints in this model are the available television sets at each warehouse and the number of sets demanded at each store. As such, six constraints exist—one for each warehouse's supply and one for each store's

*Supply constraints*

demand. For example, warehouse 1 at Cincinnati is able to supply 300 television sets to any of the 3 retail stores. Since the amount shipped to the three stores is the sum of $x_{1A}$, $x_{1B}$, and $x_{1C}$ the constraint for warehouse 1 is

$$x_{1A} + x_{1B} + x_{1C} = 300$$

This constraint is an equality (=) for two reasons. First, more than 300 television sets cannot be shipped, because that is the maximum available at the warehouse. Second, less than 300 cannot be shipped, because all 300 are needed to meet the total demand of 600. That is, total demand equals total supply, which equals 600. To meet all that is demanded at the three stores, all that can be supplied must be supplied by the three warehouses. Thus, since the total shipped from warehouse 1 cannot exceed 300 or be less than 300 the constraint is an equality. Similarly, the other two supply constraints for warehouse 2 and 3 are also equalities,

$$x_{2A} + x_{2B} + x_{2C} = 100$$
$$x_{3A} + x_{3B} + x_{3C} = 200$$

The three demand constraints are developed in the same way except *Demand constraints* that television sets can be supplied from any of the three warehouses. Thus, the amount shipped to one store is the sum of the shipments from the three warehouses:

$$x_{1A} + x_{2A} + x_{3A} = 150$$
$$x_{1B} + x_{2B} + x_{3B} = 250$$
$$x_{1C} + x_{2C} + x_{3C} = 200$$

The complete linear programming model for this problem is summarized as: *The formulated model*

$$\text{minimize } Z = \$6x_{1A} + 8x_{1B} + 1x_{1C} + 4x_{2A} + 2x_{2B}$$
$$+ 3x_{2C} + 3x_{3A} + 5x_{3B} + 7x_{3C}$$

subject to

$$x_{1A} + x_{1B} + x_{1C} = 300$$
$$x_{2A} + x_{2B} + x_{2C} = 100$$
$$x_{3A} + x_{3B} + x_{3C} = 200$$
$$x_{1A} + x_{2A} + x_{3A} = 150$$
$$x_{1B} + x_{2B} + x_{3B} = 250$$
$$x_{1C} + x_{2C} + x_{3C} = 200$$
$$x_{ij} \geq 0$$

## Summary

In this chapter 6 example problems were formulated as linear programming models in order to demonstrate the modeling process. All of these problems were similar in that they were concerned with achieving some objective subject to a set of restrictions (i.e., resource constraints, a formula for blending, investment guidelines, etc.). As such, the linear programming *Characteristics of* models of those problems exhibited certain common characteristics: *linear programming*

An objective function to be maximized or minimized
A set of constraints
Decision variables to measure the level of activity
Linearity among all constraint relationships and the objective function

The two chapters that follow are concerned with the solution of linear programming models. Although the simplex solution method to be discussed in chapter 4 is the most traditional and commonly used technique, a graphical solution approach will be discussed first in chapter 3. While the graphical method has limitations as a solution approach (which will be discussed in chap. 3), it does have the advantage of representing the solution process pictorially.

# References

Charnes, A., and Cooper, W. W. *Management Models and Industrial Applications of Linear Programming.* New York: John Wiley and Sons, 1961.

Hadley, G. *Linear Programming.* Reading, Mass.: Addison-Wesley, 1962.

Hiller, F. S., and Lieberman, G. J. *Introduction to Operations Research.* 3rd ed. San Francisco: Holden-Day, 1980.

Kwak, N. K. *Mathematical Programming with Business Applications.* New York: McGraw-Hill, 1973.

Lee, Sang M.; Moore, Laurence J.; and Taylor, Bernard W. *Management Science.* Dubuque, Iowa: Wm. C. Brown Company Publishers, 1981.

Llewellyn, R. W. *Linear Programming.* New York: Holt, Rinehart and Winston, 1964.

Pfaffenberger, R. C., and Walker, D. A. *Mathematical Programming for Economics and Business.* Ames, Ia.: Iowa State University Press, 1976.

Phillips, D. T.; Ravindran, A.; and Solberg, J. J. *Operations Research.* New York: John Wiley and Sons, 1976.

Taha, H. A. *Operations Research.* 2d ed. New York: The Macmillan Co. 1976.

# Problems

1. The Southern Sporting Goods Company makes basketballs and footballs. Each product is produced from two resources—rubber and leather. The resource requirements for each product and the total resources available are:

| Product | Resource Requirements Per Unit | |
|---|---|---|
| | Rubber (lbs.) | Leather (ft.$^2$) |
| Basketball | 3 | 4 |
| Football | 2 | 5 |
| Total Resources Available | 500 lbs. | 800 ft.$^2$ |

Each basketball produced results in a profit of $12 while each football earns $16 in profit. Formulate a linear programming model to determine the number of basketballs and footballs to produce that will maximize profit.

2. A company produces two products, *A* and *B*, which have profits of $9 and $7 respectively. Each unit of product must be processed on two assembly lines for a required production time, as follows.

|  | Hours/Unit | |
| Product | Line 1 | Line 2 |
| --- | --- | --- |
| A | 12 | 4 |
| B | 4 | 8 |
| Total Hours | 60 | 40 |

Formulate a linear programming model to determine the optimal product mix that will maximize profit.

3. A hospital dietician must prepare breakfast menus every morning for the hospital patients. Part of the dietician's responsibility is to make sure that minimum daily requirements for vitamins A and B are met. At the same time, the menus must be kept at the lowest possible cost. The main breakfast staples providing vitamins A and B are eggs, bacon, and cereal. The vitamin requirements and vitamin contributions for each staple are:

| | Vitamin Contributions | | | Minimum Daily |
| Vitamin | mg/Egg | mg/Bacon Strip | mg/Cereal Cup | Requirements |
| --- | --- | --- | --- | --- |
| A | 2 | 4 | 1 | 16 |
| B | 3 | 2 | 1 | 12 |

The cost of an egg is four cents, the cost of a bacon strip is three cents, and cup of cereal costs two cents. The dietician wants to know how much of each staple to serve per order in order to meet the minimum daily vitamin requirements while minimizing total cost. Formulate a linear programming model for this problem.

4. Moore's Meat Packing Company produces a wiener mixture in 1,000-pound batches. The mixture contains three ingredients—chicken, beef, and cereal. These ingredients have the following costs per pound.

| Ingredient | Cost / lb. |
|---|---|
| Chicken | $3 |
| Beef | 5 |
| Cereal | 2 |

Each batch is mixed according to the following specifications:

1. The mix must contain at least 200 lbs. of chicken.
2. The mix must contain at least 400 lbs. of beef.
3. The mix cannot contain more than 300 lbs. of cereal.

The company wants to know the optimal mixture of ingredients that will minimize cost. Formulate a linear programming model for this problem.

5. The Pyrotec Company produces three electrical products—clocks, radios, and toasters. These products have the following resource requirements.

| Product | Resource Requirements | |
|---|---|---|
| | Cost / Unit | Labor Hours / Unit |
| Clock | $7 | 2 |
| Radio | 10 | 3 |
| Toaster | 5 | 2 |

The manufacturer has a daily production budget of $2,000 and a maximum of 660 hours of labor. Maximum daily customer demand is for 200 clocks, 300 radios, and 150 toasters. Selling prices are $15 for a clock, $20 for a radio, and $12 for a toaster. The company desires to know the optimal product mix that will maximize profit. Formulate a linear programming model for this problem.

6. Betty Malloy, owner of the Eagle Tavern in Pittsburgh, is preparing for Super Bowl Sunday, and she must determine how much beer to stock. Betty stocks three brands of beer: Yodel, Shotz, and Rainwater. The cost per gallon (to the owner) of the three brands are:

| Brand | Cost / Gallon |
|---|---|
| Yodel | $1.50 |
| Shotz | .90 |
| Rainwater | .50 |

The tavern has a budget of $2,000 for beer for Super Bowl Sunday. Betty sells Yodel at a rate of $3.00 per gallon; Shotz for $2.50 per gallon, and Rainwater at $1.75 per gallon. Based on past football games, Betty has determined the maximum customer demand to be 400 gallons of Yodel, 500 gallons of Shotz, and 300 gallons of Rainwater. The tavern has the capacity for 1,000 gallons of beer, which Betty wants to completely stock. Formulate a linear programming model to determine the number of gallons of each brand of beer to order that will maximize profit.

7. The Kalo Fertilizer Company produces two brands of lawn fertilizer, Super Two and Green Grow, at plants in Fresno, California, and Dearborn, Michigan. The plant at Fresno has resources available to produce 5,000 pounds of either brand daily, while the plant at Dearborn has enough resources to produce 6,000 pounds daily. The cost per pound of producing each brand at each plant is:

| | Plant | |
| Product | Fresno | Dearborn |
| --- | --- | --- |
| Super Two | $2 | $4 |
| Green Grow | 2 | 3 |

The company has a daily budget for both plants of $45,000. Based on past sales, the company knows the maximum demand (converted to a daily basis) is 6,000 pounds for Super Two and 7,000 pounds for Green Grow. The selling price of Super Two is $9 per pound and the selling price of Green Grow is $7 per pound. The company wants to know the number of pounds of each brand of fertilizer to produce at each plant in order to maximize profit. Formulate a linear programming model for this problem.

8. The United Aluminum Company of Cincinnati produces 3 grades (high, medium, and low) of aluminum at two mills. Each mill has a different production capacity (in tons per day) for each grade, as follows.

| Aluminum | Mill | |
| Grade | 1 | 2 |
| --- | --- | --- |
| High | 6 | 2 |
| Medium | 2 | 2 |
| Low | 4 | 10 |

The company has a contract with a manufacturing firm to supply at least 12 tons of high-grade aluminum, 8 tons of medium grade, and

5 tons of low-grade aluminum. It costs United $6,000 per day to run mill 1 and $7,000 per day to operate mill 2. The company wants to know the number of days to operate each mill in order to meet the contract at the minimum cost. Formulate a linear programming model for this problem.

9. Fred Friendly owns an automobile dealership in Tampa, Florida. Fred is presently attempting to determine how many cars to order from the factory in Detroit. He stocks three different styles: the Eagle (a full sized car), the Hawk (a medium sized car), and the Sparrow (a compact). Fred has a budget of $210,000 to purchase new cars, and each car costs Fred the following amount.

| Car | Cost |
| --- | --- |
| Eagle | $8,000 |
| Hawk | 5,000 |
| Sparrow | 4,500 |

Fred sells Eagles for $11,000, Hawks for $8,500, and Sparrows for $7,000. Based on past sales, Fred knows the maximum demand for Eagles to be 80 cars, while the maximum demand for Hawks is 175 cars, and for Sparrows it is 250 cars. Fred has 8,000 square feet available on his lot to store new cars. An Eagle takes up 50 square feet, a Hawk requires 35 square feet, and a Sparrow requires 25 square feet. Fred wants to know how many cars of each style to order from the distributor in order to maximize his total profit. Formulate a linear programming model for this problem.

10. The Hickory Cabinet and Furniture Company produces sofas, tables, and chairs at its plant in Greensboro, North Carolina. The plant uses three main resources to make furniture—wood, upholstery, and labor. The resource requirements for each piece of furniture and the total resources available weekly are given, as follows.

| Furniture Product | Resource Requirements | | |
| --- | --- | --- | --- |
| | Wood (lbs.) | Upholstery (yds.) | Labor (hrs.) |
| Sofa | 7 | 12 | 6 |
| Table | 5 | — | 9 |
| Chair | 4 | 7 | 5 |
| Total Available Resources | 2,250 | 1,000 | 240 |

The furniture is produced on a weekly basis and stored in a warehouse until the end of the week when it is shipped out. The warehouse has enough capacity for 650 total pieces of furniture. Each sofa earns $400 in profit, each table $275, and each chair $190. The company wants to know how many pieces of each type of furniture to make per week in order to maximize profit. Formulate a linear programming model for this problem.

11. The Bradley family owns a 410-acre farm in North Carolina on which they plant corn and tobacco. Each acre of corn costs $105 to plant, cultivate, and harvest, while each acre of tobacco costs $210. The Bradleys have a budget of $52,500 for next year. The government limits the acres of tobacco that can be planted to 100 acres. The profit from each acre of corn is $300, while each acre of tobacco results in $520 in profit. The Bradleys want to know how many acres of each crop to plant in order to maximize their profit. Formulate a linear programming model for this problem.

12. The Avalon Cosmetics Company is attempting to determine the number of salespeople it should allocate to its three regions—the East, the Midwest, and the West. The company has 100 salespeople that it wants to assign to the three regions. The annual profit achieved by a salesperson in each region is:

| Region | Profit per Salesperson |
|--------|------------------------|
| East | $25,000 |
| Midwest | 18,000 |
| West | 31,000 |

Because of varying travel distances, costs of living, etc., in the three regions the annual expense involved of having a salesperson in the East is $5,000, $11,000 in the Midwest, and $7,000 in the West. The company has $700,000 budgeted for expenses. In order to insure nationwide exposure for its product the company has decided that each region must have at least ten salespeople. The company wants to know how many salespeople to allocate to each region in order to maximize profit. Formulate a linear programming model for this problem.

13. In a recently passed bill, a congressman's district has been allocated $4 million dollars for programs and projects in the district. However, it is up to the congressman to decide how to distribute the money. There are four presently ongoing programs to which the congressman has decided to allocate the money because of their importance to his district—a job training program, a parks project, a sanitation project, and a mobile library. However, the congressman wants to distribute the money in a manner that will please the most voters, or in other words, gain him the most votes in the upcoming election. His staff has estimated that each dollar spent per program will result in the following number of votes.

| Program | Votes per $ |
|---|---|
| Job Training | .02 |
| Parks | .09 |
| Sanitation | .06 |
| Mobile Library | .04 |

In order to also satisfy several local influential citizens who financed his election, he has the following obligatory guidelines.

(1) None of the programs can receive more than 40% of the total allocation.

(2) The amount allocated to parks cannot exceed the total of the amount allocated to the sanitation project and mobile library.

(3) The amount allocated to job training must be at least as much as the amount spent on the sanitation project.

Of course, since any money not spent in the district is returned to the government, the congressman wants to spend it all. The congressman wants to know the amount to allocate to each program in order to maximize his votes. Formulate a linear programming model for this problem.

14. The Grady Tire Company recaps three types of tires—automobile, truck, and heavy-duty earth-moving equipment. Each type of the recap requires the following amounts of labor and rubber.

| Tire | Labor (hrs.) | Rubber (lbs.) |
|---|---|---|
| Car | 1.2 | 23 |
| Truck | 2.3 | 56 |
| Heavy-Duty | 4.0 | 250 |

The company has 2,000 pounds of rubber available daily to recap. The company has 6 recappers and each works 8 hours per day. The demand for heavy-duty recaps averages only 5 per day. The profit gained from recapping is $8 per car tire, $23 per truck tire, and $145 per heavy-duty tire. The company wants to know how many tires of each type they need to recap in order to maximize profit. Formulate a linear programming model for this problem.

15. The manager of a Burger Doodle franchise wants to determine how many sausage biscuits and ham biscuits to prepare each morning for breakfast customers. Each type of biscuit requires the following amounts of resources.

| Biscuit | Labor (hrs.) | Sausage (lbs.) | Ham (lbs.) | Flour (lbs.) |
|---------|-------------|----------------|------------|--------------|
| Sausage | .010 | .10 | — | .04 |
| Ham | .024 | — | .15 | .04 |

The franchise has 6 hours of labor available each morning. The manager has a contract with a local grocer for 30 pounds of sausage and 30 pounds of ham each morning. The manager also purchases 16 pounds of flour. The profit for a sausage biscuit is $0.60 while the profit for a ham biscuit is $0.50. The manager wants to know the number of each type of biscuit to prepare each morning in order to maximize profit. Formulate a linear programming model for this problem.

16. The Neptune Fish Market in Denver advertises fresh seafood. Its three main items are shrimp, lobster, and crabs, which it must fly in to Denver from Florida, Maine, and Baltimore, respectively. The maximum amount of seafood that can be flown in per day is 200 pounds. The shipping costs per pound for shrimp, lobster, and crabs are $3, $6, and $4, respectively, and the market has $500 available for shipping each day. Once the seafood is received by the market it must be cleaned and packaged. A pound of shrimp requires 15 minutes of preparation, a pound of lobster 5 minutes, and a pound of crab 4 minutes. The market has 3 hours available daily to prepare the seafood. A pound of shrimp earns the market $9 in profit, a pound of lobster $12, and a pound of crab $7. The manager of the market wants to know how many pounds of each type of seafood to order each day in order to maximize profit. Formulate a linear programming model for this problem.

17. The Morris and Taylor Office Supply Company gets a lot of its business by guaranteeing prompt deliveries. Its three most demanded items are binders, file folders, and paper clips, all of which it sells by the case. The company believes it is imperative that these orders be filled immediately. In order to do so, the company estimates that it must stock 100 cases of binders, 70 cases of file folders, and 175 cases of paper

clips at all times. The company does not expect to make a lot of profit off of its instant delivery policy, as it is mainly viewed as customer service that will result in more lucrative orders. However, they do want to at least break even, which means they must sell enough of the three items to make at least $3,500 per week. The profit per case of binders is $35, of file folders $20, and of paper clips $12. The cost to the company of purchasing and keeping these items in stock are $10 for binders, $16 for file folders, and $7 for paper clips. The company wants to know how many of each item to keep in stock in order to minimize cost. Formulate a linear programming model for this problem.

18. The Southfork Feed Company makes a feed mix from four ingredients—oats, corn, soybeans, and a vitamin supplement. The company has 200 pounds of oats, 300 pounds of corn, 150 pounds of soybeans, and 50 pounds of vitamin supplement available for the mix. The company has the following recipe for the mix.

    (1) At least 30% of the mix must be soybeans.
    (2) At least 20% of the mix must be the vitamin supplement.
    (3) The ratio of corn to oats cannot exceed 2 to 1.
    (4) The oats cannot exceed the amount of soybeans.
    (5) The mix must be at least 500 pounds.

    A pound of oats costs $.50, a pound of corn $1.20, a pound of soybeans $.60, and a pound of vitamin supplement $2.00. The feed company wants to know the number of pounds of each ingredient to put in the mix in order to minimize cost. Formulate a linear programming model for this problem.

19. The United Charities annual fund-raising drive is to take place next week. Donations are collected during the day and night, and by telephone and personal contact. Each type of contact results in the following average donation.

| | Phone | Personal |
|---|---|---|
| Day | $2 | $4 |
| Night | $3 | $7 |

The charity group has enough donated gasoline and cars to make at most 300 personal contacts during one day and night. The volunteer minutes required to conduct each type of interview are given as follows.

|        | Phone | Personal |
|--------|-------|----------|
| Day    | 6     | 15       |
| Night  | 5     | 12       |

The charity has 20 volunteer hours available each day and 40 volunteer hours available each night. The chairman of the fund-raising drive wants to know how many different types of contacts to schedule in a 24-hour period (i.e., day and night) in order to maximize the total donations. Formulate a linear programming model for this problem.

20. Jean Brooks, a young attorney, has accumulated $175,000 and is seeking advice from an investment counselor on how to invest some or all of the money. With the aid of the counselor, she has decided to invest among the following alternatives—treasury bills, AAA bonds, common stock, and negotiable certificates of deposit. The counselor, after careful analysis, has determined the yield and risk rating (on a scale of 1 to 4, where 4 is the most risky) for each alternative.

| Investment Alternative | Expected Annual Yield | Risk Rating |
|------------------------|-----------------------|-------------|
| Treasury Bill          | 6.50                  | 1           |
| AAA Bond               | 8.50                  | 3           |
| Common Stock           | 12.00                 | 4           |
| Negotiable CD          | 8.00                  | 2           |

Each treasury bill costs $1,000, each AAA bond costs $5,000, each stock certificate costs $200, and each certificate of deposit costs $500. Jean has determined that she does not want her average risk factor associated with the total investment to exceed 2.5. In addition she has decided that not more than 50% of the total investment should be in treasury bills. Jean wants to know how much to invest in each alternative in order to maximize the expected annual yield. Formulate a linear programming model for this problem.

21. Iggy Olweski is a professional football player who is retiring and is thinking about going into the insurance business. In order to ascertain the feasibility of the venture, he wants to know how many insurance policies will have to be sold per year. He plans to sell three main types of policies—homeowner's insurance, auto insurance, and life insurance. Each type of insurance policy will return the following average amount of profit per year.

| Policy | Yearly Profit per Policy ($) |
| --- | --- |
| Homeowner's | $35 |
| Auto | 20 |
| Life | 58 |

Each homeowner's policy will cost $14 to sell and maintain, each auto policy will cost $12 to sell and maintain, and each life insurance policy will cost $35 to sell and maintain. Iggy has projected a budget of $35,000 per year. In addition, the sale of a homeowner's policy will require 6 hours, the sale of an auto policy will require 3 hours, and the sale of life insurance will require 12 hours. Based on his own planned working hours and the hiring of several employees, Iggy has projected 20,000 available hours per year. Iggy wants to know the number of insurance policies of each type to sell each year to maximize profit. Formulate a linear programming model for this problem.

22. A publishing house publishes three weekly magazines: *Daily Life, Agriculture Today,* and *Surf's Up.* Each issue of the magazine requires the following amounts of production time and paper to publish.

| Magazine | Production (hrs.) | Paper (lbs.) |
| --- | --- | --- |
| *Daily Life* | .01 | .2 |
| *Agriculture Today* | .03 | .5 |
| *Surf's Up* | .02 | .3 |

The publisher has 50 hours available each week for production and 3,000 pounds of paper available each week. In order to keep their advertisers, the total circulation for all three magazines must exceed 5,000 issues per week. The selling price per issue is $.75 for *Daily Life,* $1.50 for *Agriculture Today,* and $.40 for *Surf's Up.* Based on past sales, the publisher knows that the maximum weekly demand for *Daily Life* is 3,000 issues; for *Agriculture Today,* 2,000 issues; and for *Surf's Up,* 6,000 issues. The manager wants to know the number of issues of each magazine to produce weekly in order to maximize total sales revenue. Formulate a linear programming model for this problem.

23. A department store in Seattle is attempting to decide on the types and amounts of advertising it should use. The store has invited representatives from the local radio station, television station, and newspaper to make a presentation indicating their potential audience. The results are given as follows.

(1) The television station indicated that a TV commercial, which costs $15,000, would reach 25,000 potential customers. The breakdown of the audience is:

|       | Male  | Female |
|-------|-------|--------|
| Old   | 5,000 | 5,000  |
| Young | 5,000 | 10,000 |

(2) The newspaper representative claimed an audience of 10,000 potential customers (at a cost of $4,000) per ad, broken down as follows:

|       | Male  | Female |
|-------|-------|--------|
| Old   | 4,000 | 3,000  |
| Young | 2,000 | 1,000  |

(3) The radio station said that the audience for one of their commercials is 15,000 customers, at a cost of $6,000. The breakdown of customers is:

|       | Male  | Female |
|-------|-------|--------|
| Old   | 1,500 | 1,500  |
| Young | 4,500 | 7,500  |

The store has the following advertising policy:

(1) There must be at least twice as many radio commercials as newspaper ads.
(2) The campaign must reach at least 100,000 customers.
(3) The store wants to reach at least twice as many young people as old.
(4) At least 30% of the customers reached should be women.

Available space limits the number of newspaper ads to 7. The store wants to know the optimal number of each type of advertising to purchase in order to minimize total cost. Formulate a linear programming model for this problem.

24. The Rucklehouse Public Relations firm has been contracted to do a survey following a primary in New Hampshire. The firm must assign interviewers to do the survey. The interviews are conducted both by telephone and in person. One person can conduct 80 telephone interviews or 40 in-person interviews in a day. The following criteria have been established by the firm to insure a representative survey:

(1) There must be at least 3,000 total interviews.
(2) At least 1,000 interviews must be by telephone.
(3) At least 800 interviews must be personal.

An interviewer will conduct only one type of interview the entire day. It costs $50 per day for a telephone interviewer and $70 per day for a personal interviewer. The firm wants to know the minimum number of interviewers to hire in order to minimize the total cost of the survey. Formulate a linear programming model for this problem.

25. The Big Pup Dog Food Company makes two brands of dog food, Chowtime and Big Pup. A batch of each brand of dog food contains two main ingredients, meat and cereal fillers. The company has a maximum of 500 pounds of meat and 700 pounds of cereal. A batch of each brand is mixed according to the following specifications.

| Brand | Mixing Specifications |
|-------|----------------------|
| Chowtime | At least 30% meat. Not more than 40% cereal |
| Big Pup | At least 10% but not more than 60% cereal |

A pound of meat costs $1, while a pound of cereal costs $0.35. A pound of Chowtime sells for $4, while a pound of Big Pup sells for $3. The company wants to know the number of pounds of each brand of dog food to make in order to maximize profit. Formulate a linear programming model for this problem.

26. Joe Henderson runs a small metal parts shop. The shop contains three main machines—a drill press, a lathe, and a grinder. Joe has three operators who are certified to work on all three machines. However, each operator performs better on some machines than on others. The shop has contracted for a big job that requires all three machines. The times it takes for each operator to perform the operations on each machine are summarized below.

| Operator | Drill Press (min.) | Machine Lathe (min.) | Grinder (min.) |
|----------|--------------------|-----------------------|----------------|
| 1 | 22 | 18 | 35 |
| 2 | 41 | 30 | 28 |
| 3 | 25 | 36 | 18 |

Joe Henderson wants to assign one operator to each machine so that the total operating time for all three operators is minimized. Formulate a linear programming model for this problem.

27. Green Valley Mills produces carpet at plants in St. Louis and Richmond. They ship the carpet to two outlets in Chicago and Atlanta. The cost per ton of shipping carpet from each of the two plants to the two warehouses is given as follows.

| From | To | |
| --- | --- | --- |
| | Chicago | Atlanta |
| St. Louis | $40 | $65 |
| Richmond | 70 | 30 |

The plant at St. Louis can supply 250 tons of carpet per week, while the plant at Richmond can supply 400 tons per week. The Chicago outlet has a demand of 300 tons per week, while the outlet at Atlanta demands 350 tons per week. The company wants to determine the number of tons of carpet to ship from each plant to each outlet in order to minimize the total shipping cost. Formulate a linear programming model for this problem.

28. The Bluegrass Distillery produces custom blended whiskey. A particular blend consists of rye and bourbon whiskey. The company has received an order for a minimum of 400 gallons of the custom blend. The customer has specified that the order must contain at least 40% rye and not more than 250 gallons of bourbon. The customer also specified that the blend should be mixed in the ratio of two parts rye to one part bourbon. The distillery can produce 500 gallons per week regardless of the blend, and they desire to complete the order in one week. The blend is sold for $5 per gallon. The distillery company's cost per gallon for rye is $2 and $1 for bourbon. The company wants to determine the blend mix that will meet customer requirements and maximize profits. Formulate a linear programming model for this problem.

29. A bathroom fixtures manufacturer produces fiberglass bathtubs in an assembly operation consisting of three processes—molding, smoothing, and painting. Each process can complete the following number of units in an hour:

| Process | Output (units/hr.) |
|---|---|
| Molding | 7 |
| Smoothing | 12 |
| Painting | 10 |

The labor costs per hour are $8 for molding, $5 for smoothing, and $6.50 for painting. The company's labor budget is $3,000 per week. The total available labor hours for all three processes is limited to 120 hours per week. Each completed bathtub requires 90 pounds of fiberglass, and the company has a total of 10,000 pounds of fiberglass available each week. (Note: In this problem the three processes are continuous and sequential, thus no more units can be smoothed or painted than molded.) Each bathtub earns a profit of $175. The manager of the company wants to know how many hours to run each process in a week in order to maximize profit. Formulate a linear programming model for this problem.

30. A manufacturing firm located in Chicago wants to ship its product by railroad to Detroit. However, there are several different routes available, as shown in the following diagram.

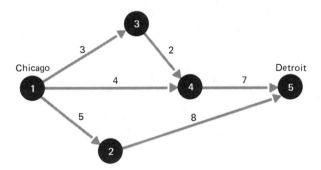

Each circle in the above diagram (which is also referred to as a network) represents a railroad junction. Each arrow is a railroad branch between two junctions. The numbers above each arrow are the shipping times per ton in hours to travel from junction to junction. The firm wants to ship 5 tons of its product from Chicago to Detroit in the minimum amount of time. Formulate a linear programming model for this problem.

# 3
## Graphical Illustration of Linear Programming

## Graphical Illustration of a Linear Programming Model

The Solution Point
The Graphical Solution
Summary of the Graphical Solution Steps

## Graphical Solution of a Minimization Problem

## Summary

Following the formulation of a mathematical model, the next stage in the application of linear programming to a decision-making problem is the solution of the model. The most common solution approach is to solve the set of mathematical relationships that form the model, algebraically, thus determining the values for the decision variables. However, because the relationships are *linear,* some models and their solution can be illustrated *graphically.*

The graphical method is realistically limited to models with only two decision variables, which convert into a graph of two dimensions. Although models with three decision variables can be graphed in three dimensions, it is quite cumbersome, and models of more than three decision variables cannot be graphed at all.

*Limitations of the graphical solution method*

While the graphical method is limited as a solution approach, it is very useful at this point in our presentation of linear programming, in that it gives us a "picture" of how a solution is derived. This, in turn, will result in a clearer understanding of how the mathematical solution approaches presented in subsequent chapters work, and will result in a better understanding of the solutions themselves.

## Graphical Illustration of a Linear Programming Model

In order to demonstrate the graphical interpretation of a linear programming problem, the "product mix" model developed in chapter 2 will be employed. Recall that the problem consisted of the Colonial Pottery Company attempting to decide how many bowls and mugs to produce daily, given limited amounts of labor and clay. The complete linear programming model was formulated as

maximize $Z = \$4x_1 + 5x_2$
subject to
$\quad x_1 + 2x_2 \leq 40$ hours of labor
$\quad 4x_1 + 3x_2 \leq 120$ pounds of clay
$\quad\quad x_1, x_2 \geq 0$
where
$\quad x_1 =$ number of bowls produced
$\quad x_2 =$ number of mugs produced

Further, recall that the values of \$4 and \$5 in the objective function are the profits for a bowl and mug, respectively; the values 1 and 2 in the first constraint are the hours of labor required to produce each bowl and mug, respectively; and the values 4 and 3 in the second constraint represent the pounds of clay required to produce each bowl and mug.

Figure 3.1 is a set of coordinates for the decision variables $x_1$ and $x_2$ on which the graph of our model will be drawn. Note that only the positive quadrant is drawn (i.e., the quadrant where $x_1$ and $x_2$ will always be positive) because of the nonnegativity constraints, $x_1 \geq 0$ and $x_2 \geq 0$.

**Figure 3.1** Coordinates for graphical analysis.

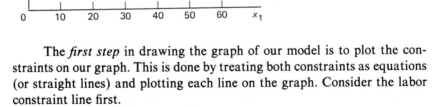

*Graphically plotting
the constraint lines*
The *first step* in drawing the graph of our model is to plot the constraints on our graph. This is done by treating both constraints as equations (or straight lines) and plotting each line on the graph. Consider the labor constraint line first.

$$x_1 + 2x_2 = 40$$

A simple procedure for plotting this line is to determine two points that are on the line and then draw a straight line through the points. One point can be found by letting $x_1 = 0$ and solving for $x_2$,

$$(0) + 2x_2 = 40$$
$$x_2 = 20$$

Thus, one point is at the coordinates $x_1 = 0$, $x_2 = 20$. A second point can be found by now letting $x_2 = 0$ and solving the equation for $x_1$,

$$x_1 + 2(0) = 40$$
$$x_1 = 40$$

Now we have a second point, $x_1 = 40$, $x_2 = 0$. The line on our graph representing this equation is drawn by connecting these two points as shown in figure 3.2. However, this is only the graph of the constraint *line* and does not reflect the entire constraint, which also includes the values "less than or equal to" ($\leq$) this line. This *area* representing the entire constraint is shown in figure 3.3.

*The constraint area*

**Figure 3.2** Graph of the labor constraint line.

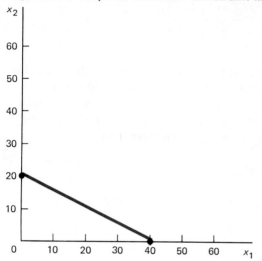

**Figure 3.3** The labor constraint area.

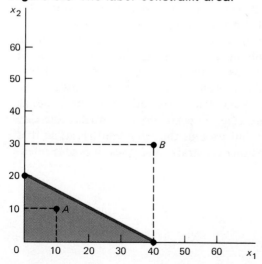

In order to test the correctness of the constraint area, check any two points—one inside the constrained area and one outside. For example, point $A$ in figure 3.3 is formed at the intersection of $x_1 = 10$ and $x_2 = 10$. Substituting these values into the labor constraint,

$$10 + 2(10) \leq 40$$
$$30 \leq 40 \text{ hours}$$

shows that point $A$ is indeed within the constraint area, as these values for $x_1$ and $x_2$ do not exceed the limit of 40 hours. Next check point $B$, which is at $x_1 = 40$ and $x_2 = 30$,

$$40 + 2(30) \leq 40$$
$$100 \nleq 40 \text{ hours}$$

This point is obviously outside the constrained area, as the values for $x_1$ and $x_2$ yield a quantity (100) that exceeds the limit of 40 hours.

The second constraint for clay is drawn in the same way as the labor constraint—by finding two points on the constraint line and connecting them with a straight line. First, let $x_1 = 0$ and solve for $x_2$.

$$4(0) + 3x_2 = 120$$
$$x_2 = 40$$

This results in a point, $x_1 = 0$, $x_2 = 40$. Next, let $x_2 = 0$ and solve for $x_1$.

$$4x_1 + 3(0) = 120$$
$$x_1 = 30$$

This yields our second point, $x_1 = 30$, $x_2 = 0$. Plotting these points on our graph and connecting them with a line gives the constraint line and area for clay as shown in figure 3.4. By combining the two individual graphs for labor and clay (figs. 3.3 and 3.4) we have a graph of the model constraints, as shown in figure 3.5. The darker shaded area in figure 3.5 is the area on the graph that is common to both model constraints. Therefore, this is the only area on the graph that contains points (i.e., values for $x_1$ and $x_2$) that will satisfy both constraints simultaneously. For example, consider the points $R$, $S$, and $T$ in figure 3.6. Point $R$ satisfies both constraints, and, as such, we say that it is a *feasible* solution point. Point $S$ satisfies the clay constraint ($4x_1 + 3x_2 \leq 120$), but exceeds the labor constraint, so it is not feasible. Point $T$ satisfies neither constraint and, thus, it is also infeasible.

*Feasible and infeasible solution points*

**Figure 3.4** The constraint area for clay.

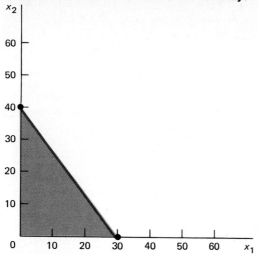

**Figure 3.5** Graph of both model constraints.

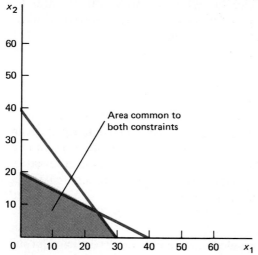

**Figure 3.6** The feasible solution area.

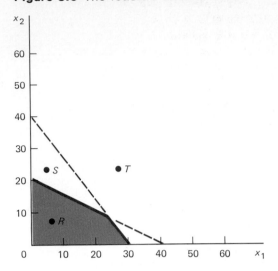

*Feasible solution area*

The entire shaded area in figure 3.6 is referred to as the *feasible solution area,* since all the points in this area satisfy both constraints. Therefore, the solution to the Colonial Pottery Company model exists somewhere within this area. It is a point within the feasible solution area that will result in the *maximum profit.* Our next step in the graphical solution approach is locating this point.

## The Solution Point

*Determining the point in the feasible solution area that will result in maximum profit*

The *second step* in the graphical solution method is to locate the point in the feasible solution area that will result in the greatest total profit. To begin the solution analysis we will first plot the objective function line on our graph for an *arbitrarily* selected level of profit. For example, if profit, $Z,$ is $80, then the objective function is

$$\$80 = 4x_1 + 5x_2$$

*Plotting the objective function line*

Plotting this line just as we plotted the constraint lines results in the graph shown in figure 3.7. Every point on this line is in the feasible solution area and will result in a profit of $80 (i.e., every combination of $x_1$ and $x_2$ on this line will give a $Z$ value of $80). However, let us see if *more* profit can be derived and still have a feasible solution. For example, consider profits of $120 and $160, as shown in figure 3.8.

*Moving the objective function line through the feasible area*

While a portion of the objective function line for a profit of $120 is outside of the feasible solution area, part of the line remains within the area, and, thus, the points on this portion of the line are all feasible. As such, this profit line indicates there are solution points that are feasible, yet also give a greater profit than $80. Now, let us increase profit again to

$160. This profit line, also shown in figure 3.8, is completely outside of the feasible solution area. As such, there are no points on this line that are feasible, thus, a profit of $160 is not possible.

**Figure 3.7** Objective function line for $Z = \$80$.

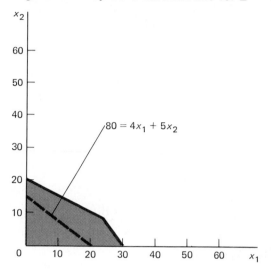

**Figure 3.8** Alternative objective function lines for profits, $Z$, of $80, 120, and 160.

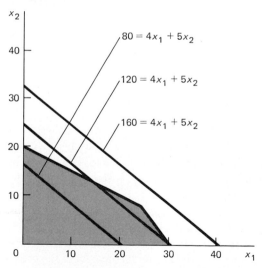

Since a profit of $160 is shown to be too great for the constraint limitations, as shown in figure 3.8, the question remains as to what the maximum profit value actually is. However, the one thing that can be noticed from figure 3.8 is that profit increases as the objective function line moves away from the origin (i.e., the point $x_1 = 0$, $x_2 = 0$). Given this characteristic, the maximum profit will be attained at the point where the objective function line is farthest from the origin *and* still touching a point in the feasible solution area. This point is shown as point $B$ in figure 3.9.

**Figure 3.9** Identification of optimal solution point.

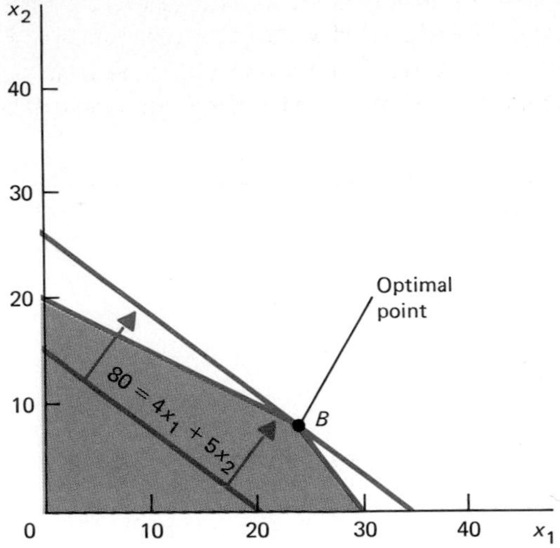

*The optimal solution point*   Point $B$ can be found by moving a straight edge parallel to the objective function line of $\$80 = 4x_1 + 5x_2$ in figure 3.8, outward from the origin until it is moved as far as possible yet still maintains contact with the feasible solution area. Point $B$ is referred to as the *optimal* (e.g., best) solution.

## The Graphical Solution

The *third step* in the graphical solution approach is to solve for the values of $x_1$ and $x_2$ once the *optimal* solution point has been found. We could locate the $x_1$ and $x_2$ coordinates of point $B$ in figure 3.9. However, the solution can be determined mathematically, but first a few characteristics regarding the solution should be pointed out.

*Characteristics of the optimal solution point*   In figure 3.9 as the objective function was increased, the last point it touched in the feasible solution area was on the boundary of the feasible solution area. It will always happen that the solution point is on this boundary because the boundary contains the points farthest from the origin (i.e., the greatest profit). This reduces the possible solution points considerably, from all points in the solution area to just those points on the boundary. However, the possible solution points can be reduced even more by noticing another characteristic.

In figure 3.10 notice the three arrows emanating from the origin. Arrow $L$ represents a distance (and an amount of profit) from the origin. However, both arrows $K$ and $M$ represent greater distances. Thus, if you have a solution at the point where arrow $L$ touches the boundary, you could increase profit by going in either direction, toward point $A$ or $B$. Figure 3.10 demonstrates that the solution point is not only on the boundary *but also at the corners on the boundary where the constraint lines intersect.* These corners (points $A$, $B$, and $C$ in fig. 3.10) represent *extremes* in the feasible solution area, which are the farthest points from the origin. These points are called *extreme points,* and in a linear programming model the optimal solution will always occur at an extreme point. Therefore in our example, the possible solution points are limited to the three extreme points.

*Corners on the solution space boundary*

*Extreme points*

---

**Figure 3.10** Corner point solutions.

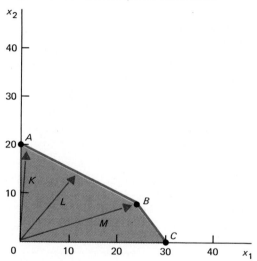

From the graphical analysis in figure 3.9, we already know that the optimal solution point is at point $B$. Since point $B$ is formed by the intersection of two constraint lines, then these two lines are *equal* at point $B$. Thus, the values of $x_1$ and $x_2$ at that intersection can be found by solving these two equations *simultaneously.*

*Solving simultaneous equations to determine the variable values at the optimal solution point*

First, convert both equations to functions of $x_1$:

$$x_1 + 2x_2 = 40$$
$$x_1 = 40 - 2x_2$$

and

$$4x_1 + 3x_2 = 120$$
$$4x_1 = 120 - 3x_2$$
$$x_1 = 30 - 3x_2/4$$

Now let $x_1$ in the first equation equal $x_1$ in the second equation, or

$$40 - 2x_2 = 30 - 3x_2/4$$

*The optimal solution values* and

$$5x_2/4 = 10$$
$$x_2 = 8$$

Substituting $x_2 = 8$ into either one of the original equations will give us $x_1$:

$$x_1 = 40 - 2x_2$$
$$x_1 = 40 - 2(8)$$
$$x_1 = 24$$

Thus, the optimal solution at point $B$ in figure 3.9 is $x_1 = 24$ and $x_2 = 8$. Substituting these values into the objective function gives us the maximum profit,

$$Z = \$4x_1 + 5x_2$$
$$Z = \$4(24) + 5(8)$$
$$Z = \$136$$

*Interpreting the solution* Interpreting the solution in terms of the original problem, if the pottery company produces 24 bowls and 8 mugs, it will receive the maximum daily profit possible (given the resource constraints) of $136.

*An alternative way to find the optimal solution point* Since we now know that the optimal solution will be at one of the extreme corner points $A$, $B$, or $C$, the solution could have been found by testing each of the three points to see which resulted in the greatest profit, rather than graphing the objective function as in figure 3.9, and seeing which point it last touched as it moved out of the feasible solution area. Figure 3.11 shows the solution values for all three points, $A$, $B$, and $C$, and the amount of profit, $Z$, at each point.

**Figure 3.11** Solutions at all corner points.

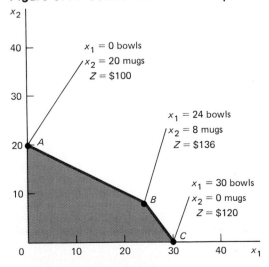

$x_1 = 0$ bowls
$x_2 = 20$ mugs
$Z = \$100$

$x_1 = 24$ bowls
$x_2 = 8$ mugs
$Z = \$136$

$x_1 = 30$ bowls
$x_2 = 0$ mugs
$Z = \$120$

**Graphical Illustration of Linear Programming**

It should be noted that some problems do not have a single extreme point solution. This occurs when the objective function line is parallel to one of the constraint lines. This will result in an entire line segment bounded by two adjacent corner points being optimal, rather than a single extreme point. This is referred to as *multiple optimal solutions*. This case, as well as several other irregular types of solution outcomes in linear programming, is discussed in detail in chapter 5.

*Multiple optimal solutions*

## Summary of the Graphical Solution Steps

Let us briefly summarize the steps for solving a graphical linear programming model.

1. Plot the model constraints as equations on the graph then, considering the inequalities of the constraints, indicate the feasible solution area.
2. Plot the objective function as an edge and moving the edge out from the origin, locate the optimal solution point.
3. Solve simultaneous equations at the solution point to find the optimal solution values.

or

2. Solve simultaneous equations at each corner point to find the solution values at each point.
3. Substitute these values into the objective function to find the set of values that results in the maximum $Z$ value.

# Graphical Solution of a Minimization Problem

The graphical solution for a minimization problem is found the same way as a maximization problem, except for a few minor differences. In order to demonstrate the graphical solution of a minimization problem the following example problem will be used.

A farmer is preparing to plant a crop in the spring and desires to fertilize a field. There are two brands of fertilizer to choose from, Super-gro and Crop-quik. Each brand yields a specific amount of nitrogen and phosphate, as follows

| | Chemical Contribution | |
| --- | --- | --- |
| Brand | Nitrogen (lbs./bag) | Phosphate (lbs./bag) |
| Super-gro | 2 | 4 |
| Crop-quik | 4 | 3 |

The farmer's field requires at least 16 pounds of nitrogen and 24 pounds of phosphate. The cost of a bag of Super-gro is $6 and a bag of

Crop-quik costs $3. The farmer wants to know how many bags of each brand to purchase in order to minimize the total cost of fertilizing.

This problem is formulated as

minimize $Z = \$6x_1 + 3x_2$
subject to
$$2x_1 + 4x_2 \geq 16 \text{ pounds of nitrogen}$$
$$4x_1 + 3x_2 \geq 24 \text{ pounds of phosphate}$$
$$x_1, x_2 \geq 0$$

*Graphically plotting the constraint lines*     The *first step* is to graph the two model constraints as equations as shown in figure 3.12. Next, the $\geq$ nature of the two constraints is considered to give the feasible solution area as shown in figure 3.13.

**Figure 3.12** Constraint lines for fertilizer model.

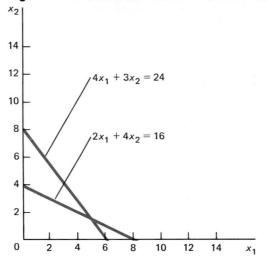

**Figure 3.13** Feasible solution area.

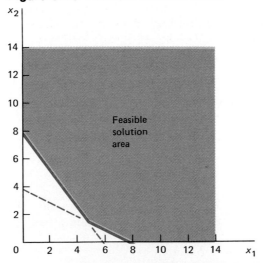

60     **Graphical Illustration of Linear Programming**

Now that the feasible solution area has been determined, the *second step* in the graphical solution approach is locating the optimal point. Recall that in the maximization problem the boundary of the feasible solution area contained the optimum solution because it contains those points *farthest* from the origin. While the optimal solution point is also on the boundary of the feasible solution area in this problem, it is because the boundary contains those points *closest* to the origin (i.e., "0" is the lowest cost possible).

*The feasible solution area*

Like the maximization problem, the optimal solution will be located at one of the extreme corner points along the boundary. In this case the corner points represent extremities in the boundary of the feasible solution area that are *closest* to the origin. Figure 3.14 shows the three corner points, *A, B,* and *C,* and the objective function line.

*Locating the optimal solution point closest to the origin*

**Figure 3.14** The optimal solution point.

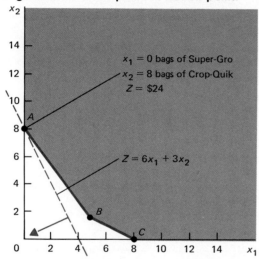

$x_1 = 0$ bags of Super-Gro
$x_2 = 8$ bags of Crop-Quik
$Z = \$24$

$Z = 6x_1 + 3x_2$

As the objective function edges *toward* the origin, the last point it touches in the feasible solution area is *A*. This indicates that point *A* is the closest the objective function can get to the origin (i.e., the lowest cost that can be attained) without encompassing only infeasible points.

The *final step* in the graphical solution approach is to solve for the values of $x_1$ and $x_2$ at point *A*. Since point *A* is on the $x_2$ axis, $x_1 = 0$, and thus,

$$4(0) + 3x_2 = 24$$
$$x_2 = 8$$

*The optimal solution*   Given the optimal solution, $x_1 = 0$, $x_2 = 8$, the minimum cost, $Z$,
　　　　　　is

$$Z = \$6x_1 + 3x_2$$
$$Z = 6(0) + 3(8)$$
$$Z = \$24$$

This means the farmer should purchase no Super-gro and 8 bags of Crop-quik, and the total cost of fertilizer will be \$24.

## Summary

The graphical approach to the solution of linear programming problems is not a very efficient means for solving problems. Not only is drawing accurate graphs tedious, but the graphical approach is limited to models with only two decision variables. However, the analysis of the graphical approach has provided insight into linear programming problems and their solution in general, which will be valuable in subsequent chapters.

Recall that after the feasible solution area and the optimal solution point was determined from the graph, simultaneous equations were solved in order to determine the values of $x_1$ and $x_2$ at the solution point.

The solution of simultaneous equations forms the basis of the *simplex* method for solving linear programming problems to be presented in the next chapter. However, instead of determining the location of the optimal solution point graphically, it is located mathematically through a defined set of mathematical steps that comprise the simplex method.

## References

Dantzig, G. B. *Linear Programming and Extensions.* Princeton, N.J.: Princeton University, 1963.

Gass, S. *Linear Programming.* 4th ed. New York: McGraw-Hill, 1975.

Gottfried, B. S., and Weisman, J. *Introduction to Optimization Theory.* Englewood Cliffs, N.J.: Prentice-Hall, 1973.

Hadley, G. *Linear Programming.* Reading, Mass.: Addison-Wesley, 1962.

Hillier, F. S., and Lieberman, G. J. *Operations Research.* 3rd ed. San Francisco: Holden-Day, 1980.

Kim, C. *Introduction to Linear Programming.* New York: Holt, Rinehart and Winston, 1971.

Lee, Sang M.; Moore, Laurence J.; and Taylor, Bernard W. *Management Science.* Dubuque, Iowa: Wm. C. Brown Company Publishers, 1981.

Moskowitz, H., and Wright, G. P. *Operations Research Techniques for Management.* Englewood Cliffs, N.J.: Prentice-Hall, 1979.

Rothenberg, R. I. *Linear Programming.* New York: Elsevier North-Holland, 1979.

Wagner, H. M. *Principles of Operations Research.* Englewood Cliffs, N.J.: Prentice-Hall, 1969.

# Problems

1. A company makes two products, which we will label products 1 and 2. The company makes the products from two resources. The linear programming model for determining the amounts of product 1 and 2 to produce (i.e., $x_1$ and $x_2$) is given as follows.

maximize $Z = 8x_1 + 2x_2$ (profit, $)
subject to
$$4x_1 + 5x_2 \leq 20 \text{ (resource 1, lbs.)}$$
$$2x_1 + 6x_2 \leq 18 \text{ (resource 2, lbs.)}$$
$$x_1, x_2 \geq 0$$

Solve this model graphically.

2. A company produces two products that are processed on two assembly lines. Assembly line 1 has 100 available hours and assembly line 2 has 42 available hours. The company has formulated the following linear programming model for determining the number of each product ($x_1$ and $x_2$) to produce.

maximize $Z = 6x_1 + 4x_2$ (profit, $)
subject to
$$10x_1 + 10x_2 \leq 100 \text{ (line 1, hrs.)}$$
$$7x_1 + 3x_2 \leq 42 \text{ (line 2, hrs.)}$$
$$x_1, x_2 \geq 0$$

Solve this model graphically.

3. The Munchies Cereal Company makes a brand of cereal from several ingredients. Two of the ingredients, oats and rice, provide vitamins A and B. The company wants to know how many ounces of oats and rice ($x_1$ and $x_2$) must be in each box of cereal in order to meet minimum requirements of vitamins A and B and minimize cost. The following linear programming model has been formulated for this problem.

minimize $Z = .05x_1 + .03x_2$ (cost, $)
subject to
$$8x_1 + 6x_2 \geq 48 \text{ (vitamin A, mg.)}$$
$$x_1 + 2x_2 \geq 12 \text{ (vitamin B, mg.)}$$
$$x_1, x_2 \geq 0$$

Solve this model graphically.

4. The Kalo Fertilizer Company makes a fertilizer using two chemicals. The chemicals provide nitrogen, phosphate, and potassium. The company wants to know how many pounds of each chemical ingredient ($x_1$ and $x_2$) to put into a bag of fertilizer in order to meet minimum requirements of nitrogen, phosphate, and potassium while minimizing cost. The following linear programming model has been developed.

minimize $Z = 3x_1 + 5x_2$ (cost, $)
subject to
$$10x_1 + 2x_2 \geq 20 \text{ (nitrogen, oz.)}$$
$$6x_1 + 6x_2 \geq 36 \text{ (phosphate, oz.)}$$
$$x_2 \geq 2 \text{ (potassium, oz.)}$$
$$x_1, x_2 \geq 0$$

Solve this model graphically.

5. The Pinewood Furniture Company produces chairs and tables. The primary resources used in the production of these items are labor and wood. The company has 80 hours of labor and 36 pounds of wood available each day. Demand for chairs is limited to 6 per day. The company has developed the following linear programming model to determine the number of chairs and tables ($x_1$ and $x_2$) to produce each day in order to maximize profit.

maximize $Z = 400x_1 + 100x_2$ (profit, $)
subject to
$$8x_1 + 10x_2 \leq 80 \text{ (labor, hrs.)}$$
$$2x_1 + 6x_2 \leq 36 \text{ (wood, lbs.)}$$
$$x_1 \leq 6 \text{ (demand, chairs)}$$
$$x_1, x_2 \geq 0$$

Solve this model graphically.

6. The Crumb and Custard Bakery makes cakes and pies. The main ingredients are flour and sugar. The following linear programming model has been developed in order to determine the number of cakes and pies ($x_1$ and $x_2$) to produce each day that will maximize profit.

maximize $Z = x_1 + 5x_2$ (profit, $)
subject to
$$5x_1 + 5x_2 \leq 25 \text{ (flour, lbs.)}$$
$$2x_1 + 4x_2 \leq 16 \text{ (sugar, lbs.)}$$
$$x_1 \leq 5 \text{ (demand for cakes)}$$
$$x_1, x_2 \geq 0$$

Solve this model graphically.

7. Given the following linear programming model:

maximize $Z = 3x_1 + 6x_2$
subject to
$$3x_1 + 2x_2 \leq 18$$
$$x_1 + x_2 \geq 5$$
$$x_1 \leq 4$$
$$x_1, x_2 \geq 0$$

Solve this model graphically.

8. Given the following linear programming model:

maximize $Z = 8x_1 + 7x_2$
subject to
$$10x_1 + 8x_2 \geq 40$$
$$6x_1 + 14x_2 \leq 48$$
$$x_2 \geq 1$$
$$x_1, x_2 \geq 0$$

Solve this model graphically.

9. The Elixer Drug Company produces a drug from two ingredients. Each ingredient supplies an antibiotic to the drug. The company has formulated the following linear programming model to determine the number of grams of each ingredient ($x_1$ and $x_2$) that must go into the drug in order to meet the antibiotic requirements at the minimum cost.

minimize $Z = 80x_1 + 50x_2$ (cost, $)
subject to
$$3x_1 + x_2 \geq 6 \text{ (antibiotic 1, units)}$$
$$x_1 + x_2 \geq 4 \text{ (antibiotic 2, units)}$$
$$2x_1 + 6x_2 \geq 12 \text{ (antibiotic 3, units)}$$
$$x_1, x_2 \geq 0$$

Solve this model graphically.

10. A jewelry store makes necklaces and bracelets from gold and platinum. The store has developed the following linear programming model to determine the number of necklaces and bracelets ($x_1$ and $x_2$) to make in order to maximize profit.

maximize $Z = 300x_1 + 400x_2$ (profit, $)
subject to
$$3x_1 + 2x_2 \leq 18 \text{ (gold, oz.)}$$
$$2x_1 + 4x_2 \leq 20 \text{ (platinum, oz.)}$$
$$x_2 \leq 4 \text{ (demand, bracelets)}$$
$$x_1, x_2 \geq 0$$

Solve this model graphically.

11. A clothier makes coats and slacks. The two main resource requirements are wool cloth and labor. The clothier has developed a linear programming model to determine the number of coats and pairs of slacks ($x_1$ and $x_2$) to make that will maximize profit, as follows:

maximize $Z = 50x_1 + 40x_2$ (profit, \$)
subject to
$$3x_1 + 5x_2 \leq 150 \text{ (wool, yd.}^2\text{)}$$
$$10x_1 + 4x_2 \leq 200 \text{ (labor, hrs.)}$$
$$x_1, x_2 \geq 0$$

Solve this model graphically.

12. Given the following linear programming model:

maximize $Z = 1.5x_1 + x_2$
subject to
$$x_1 \leq 4$$
$$x_2 \leq 6$$
$$x_1 + x_2 \leq 5$$
$$x_1, x_2 \geq 0$$

Solve this model graphically.

13. Given the following linear programming model:

maximize $Z = 5x_1 + 8x_2$
subject to
$$3x_1 + 5x_2 \leq 50$$
$$2x_1 + 4x_2 \leq 40$$
$$x_1 \leq 8$$
$$x_2 \leq 10$$
$$x_1, x_2 \geq 0$$

Solve this model graphically.

14. Given the following linear programming model:

maximize $Z = 6.5x_1 + 10x_2$
subject to
$$2x_1 + 4x_2 \leq 40$$
$$x_1 + x_2 \leq 15$$
$$x_1 \geq 8$$
$$x_1, x_2 \geq 0$$

Solve this model graphically.

15. Given the following linear programming model:

maximize $Z = 5x_1 + x_2$
subject to
$$3x_1 + 4x_2 = 24$$
$$x_1 \leq 6$$
$$x_1 + 3x_2 \leq 12$$
$$x_1, x_2 \geq 0$$

Solve this model graphically.

16. Given the following linear programming model:

maximize $Z = 2x_1 + 5x_2$
subject to
$$7x_1 + 5x_2 \leq 70$$
$$2x_1 + 3x_2 \leq 24$$
$$x_2 \leq 5$$
$$3x_1 + 8x_2 \leq 48$$
$$x_1, x_2 \geq 0$$

Solve this model graphically.

17. Given the following linear programming model:

minimize $Z = 10x_1 + 20x_2$
subject to
$$x_1 + x_2 \geq 12$$
$$2x_1 + 5x_2 \geq 40$$
$$x_2 \leq 20$$
$$x_1, x_2 \geq 0$$

Solve this model graphically.

18. Given the following linear programming model:

minimize $Z = 8x_1 + 2x_2$
subject to
$$2x_1 - 6x_2 \geq 12$$
$$5x_1 + 4x_2 \geq 40$$
$$x_1 + 2x_2 \geq 12$$
$$x_2 \leq 6$$
$$x_1, x_2 \geq 0$$

Solve this model graphically.

19. A manufacturer produces motorized and manual hand trucks in two shop processes. In shop 1 the hand trucks are assembled, while in shop 2 finishing operations are done. The manufacturer has developed the following linear programming model to determine the number of each type of hand truck to produce in order to maximize profit.

maximize $Z = 200x_1 + 300x_2$ (profit, $)
subject to
$$2x_1 + 5x_2 \leq 180 \text{ (shop 1, hrs.)}$$
$$3x_1 + 3x_2 \leq 135 \text{ (shop 2, hrs.)}$$
$$x_1, x_2 \geq 0$$

Solve this model graphically.

20. Given the following linear programming model:

minimize $Z = .06x_1 + .10x_2$
subject to
$$4x_1 + 3x_2 \geq 12$$
$$3x_1 + 6x_2 \geq 12$$
$$5x_1 + 2x_2 \geq 10$$
$$x_1, x_2 \geq 0$$

Solve this model graphically.

21. The Copperfield Mining Company owns two mines, which produce 3 grades of ore—high, medium, and low. The company has a contract to supply a smelting company with 12 tons of high-grade ore, 8 tons of medium-grade ore, and 24 tons of low-grade ore. Each hour one of the mines is operated, it produces a certain amount of each type of ore. The company has developed the following linear programming model to determine the number of hours to operate each mine ($x_1$ and $x_2$) in order to meet their contractural obligations at the lowest cost.

minimize $Z = 200x_1 + 160x_2$ (cost, $)
subject to
$$6x_1 + 2x_2 \geq 12 \text{ (high-grade ore, tons)}$$
$$2x_1 + 2x_2 \geq 8 \text{ (medium-grade ore, tons)}$$
$$4x_1 + 12x_2 \geq 24 \text{ (low-grade ore, tons)}$$
$$x_1, x_2 \geq 0$$

Solve this model graphically.

22. A canning company produces two sizes of cans—regular and large. The cans are produced in 10,000-can lots. The cans are processed through a stamping operation and a coating operation. The company has 30 days available for both stamping and coating. Due to a prior trucking contract, the company must produce at least 9 lots. The following linear programming model has been developed in order to determine the number of lots to produce of each size can ($x_1$ and $x_2$) in order to maximize profit.

maximize $Z = 800x_1 + 900x_2$ (profit, \$)
subject to
$$2x_1 + 4x_2 \leq 30 \text{ (stamping, days)}$$
$$4x_1 + 2x_2 \leq 30 \text{ (coating, days)}$$
$$x_1 + x_2 \geq 9 \text{ (lots)}$$
$$x_1, x_2 \geq 0$$

Solve this model graphically.

23. A manufacturing firm produces two products. Each product must go through an assembly process and a finishing process. There is also a limitation of the number of items that can be stored in the warehouse. The following linear programming model has been developed to determine the quantity of each product to produce in order to maximize profit.

maximize $Z = 30x_1 + 70x_2$ (profit, \$)
subject to
$$4x_1 + 10x_2 \leq 80 \text{ (assembly, hrs.)}$$
$$14x_1 + 8x_2 \leq 112 \text{ (finishing, hrs.)}$$
$$x_1 + x_2 \leq 10 \text{ (inventory, units)}$$
$$x_1, x_2 \geq 0$$

Solve this model graphically.

24. A California grower has a 50-acre farm on which strawberries and tomatoes are planted. The grower has 300 hours of labor, 800 tons of fertilizer, and contracted shipping space for a maximum of 26 acres of strawberries and 37 acres of tomatoes. The following linear programming model has been developed to determine the number of acres of strawberries and tomatoes ($x_1$ and $x_2$) the farmer should plant in order to maximize profit.

maximize $Z = 400x_1 + 300x_2$ (profit, \$)
subject to
$$x_1 + x_2 \leq 50 \text{ (available land, acres)}$$
$$10x_1 + 3x_2 \leq 300 \text{ (labor, hrs.)}$$
$$8x_1 + 20x_2 \leq 800 \text{ (fertilizer, tons)}$$
$$x_1 \leq 26 \text{ (shipping space, acres)}$$
$$x_2 \leq 37 \text{ (shipping space, acres)}$$
$$x_1, x_2 \geq 0$$

Solve this model graphically.

25. Solve problem 1 from chapter 2 graphically.

26. Solve problem 2 from chapter 2 graphically.

27. Solve problem 11 from chapter 2 graphically.

28. Solve problem 15 from chapter 2 graphically.

29. Solve problem 24 from chapter 2 graphically.

30. Solve problem 28 from chapter 2 graphically.

# 4
# The Simplex
# Solution Method

The Simplex Solution Method

In chapter 3 it was demonstrated how a linear programming model solution could be derived from a graph of the model. As such, it provided valuable insight into linear programming and linear programming solutions in general. However, it was also noted that this solution method was limited to problems with only two decision variables, thus limiting its usefulness as a *general* solution technique. In this chapter, a mathematical approach for solving linear programming problems will be presented, which is a general technique. This approach is called the *simplex method*. In the simplex method the model is put into the form of a table, and then a number of mathematical steps are performed on the table. These mathematical steps, in effect, replicate the process of moving from one solution point on the feasible solution space boundary to another. However, unlike the graphical method where we could simply search through all the solution points to find the best one, the simplex method moves from one *better* solution to another until the best one is found, and then it stops.

*A tabular solution method with specific mathematical steps*

In this chapter we will present the general simplex method only as it applies to a *maximization* model. Since the application of the simplex method to a minimization model requires a few alterations, that will be covered in chapter 5 along with several special cases, which include multiple optimum solutions, infeasible problems, and unbounded problems.

## Converting the Model Constraints

The first step in applying the simplex method is to transform the model constraints into equations—a requirement for solving simultaneous equations on which the simplex method is based.

Recall the Colonial Pottery Company example modeled in chapter 2 and graphically solved in chapter 3:

maximize $Z = \$4x_1 + 5x_2$
subject to
$$x_1 + 2x_2 \leq 40 \text{ hours of labor}$$
$$4x_1 + 3x_2 \leq 120 \text{ pounds of clay}$$
$$x_1, x_2 \geq 0$$

where

$$x_1 = \text{the number of bowls produced}$$
$$x_2 = \text{the number of mugs produced}$$

The graph of this model is shown in figure 4.1.

**Figure 4.1** Graph of the pottery company example.

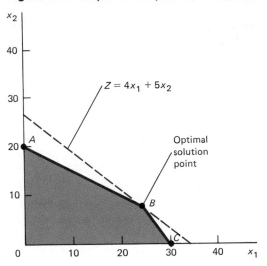

*The simplex method is partially based on the solution of simultaneous equations*

Further recall that once the optimal solution was found to be at point B, simultaneous *equations* were solved to determine the values of $x_1$ and $x_2$. The simplex method for solving linear programming problems is based, at least partially, on the solution of simultaneous equations. As such, the model constraints must all be in *equation* ($=$) form, rather than $\leq$ or $\geq$ inequalities.

*Transforming $\leq$ constraint inequalities into equations*

The simplex method includes a standard procedure for transforming $\leq$ inequality constraints into equations. This transformation is achieved by adding a new variable to each constraint. This new variable is called a *slack variable*. For the pottery company example, the model constraints

*Slack variables* are

$$x_1 + 2x_2 \leq 40 \text{ hours of labor}$$
$$4x_1 + 3x_2 \leq 120 \text{ pounds of clay}$$

The addition of unique slack variables ($s_i$) to each of these inequalities results in the following equations.

$$x_1 + 2x_2 + s_1 = 40 \text{ hours of labor}$$
$$4x_1 + 3x_2 + s_2 = 120 \text{ pounds of clay}$$

The slack variables, $s_1$ and $s_2$, in these equations will take on any value necessary to make the left-hand side of the equation equal to the right-hand side. For example, consider a hypothetical solution of $x_1 = 5$ and $x_2 = 10$. Substituting these values into the above equations,

$$x_1 + 2x_2 + s_1 = 40 \text{ hours of labor}$$
$$5 + 2(10) + s_1 = 40 \text{ hours of labor}$$
$$s_1 = 15 \text{ hours of labor}$$

and

$$4x_1 + 3x_2 + s_2 = 120 \text{ pounds of clay}$$
$$4(5) + 3(10) + s_2 = 120 \text{ pounds of clay}$$
$$s_2 = 70 \text{ pounds of clay}$$

In the above example, $x_1 = 5$ bowls and $x_2 = 10$ mugs represents a solution that does not utilize the total available amount of labor and clay. For example, in the labor constraint, 5 bowls and 10 mugs require only 25 hours of labor. This leaves 15 hours left over that are not used. Thus, $s_1$ represents the amount of *unused labor*.

In the clay constraint, 5 bowls and 10 mugs require only 50 pounds of clay. This leaves 70 pounds of clay left over that are not used. Thus, $s_2$ represents the amount of *unused clay*. In general, a slack variable represents the amount of *unused resource*.

*A slack variable represents unused resources*

The ultimate instance of unused resources is at the origin where $x_1 = 0$ and $x_2 = 0$. Substituting these values into the equations yields,

$$x_1 + 2x_2 + s_1 = 40$$
$$0 + 2(0) + s_1 = 40$$
$$s_1 = 40 \text{ hours of labor}$$

and

$$4x_1 + 3x_2 + s_2 = 120$$
$$4(0) + 3(0) + s_2 = 120$$
$$s_2 = 120 \text{ pounds of clay}$$

This demonstrates that at the origin where no production takes place all of the resources are unused, thus the slack variables equal the total available amounts of each resource: $s_1 = 40$ hours of labor and $s_2 = 120$ pounds of clay.

The next concern is the effect of these new slack variables on the objective function. The objective function for our example represents the profit gained from the production of bowls and mugs,

$$Z = 4x_1 + 5x_2$$

The coefficient, \$4, is the contribution to profit of each bowl, while \$5 is the contribution to profit from each mug. What, then, do $s_1$ and $s_2$ contribute? The answer is that slack variables contribute *nothing* to profit. If labor or clay are not being used, they cannot contribute to profit. Profit

*The effect of slack variables on the objective function*

is made only after the resources are put to use in making bowls and mugs. With slack variables the objective function can be written as

$$\text{maximize } Z = 4x_1 + 5x_2 + 0s_1 + 0s_2$$

As in the case of decision variables ($x_1$ and $x_2$), slack variables can have only nonnegative values since negative resources are not possible. Therefore, for this model formulation, $x_1$, $x_2$, $s_1$, and $s_2 \geq 0$.

## The Solution of Simultaneous Equations

*Solving two equations with four unknowns*

Now that both model constraints have been transformed into equations, these same equations should be solved simultaneously to determine the values of the variable at every solution point. However, notice that in our example problem there are *two* equations and *four* unknowns (i.e., two decision variables and two slack variables), a situation that makes direct simultaneous solution impossible. The simplex method alleviates this problem by assigning some of the variables a value of zero. The number of variables assigned values of zero is $n - m$, where $n$ equals the number of variables and $m$ equals the number of constraints. For this model, $n = 4$ variables and $m = 2$ constraints, therefore, two of the variables are assigned a value of zero (i.e., $4 - 2 = 2$).

For example, let $x_1 = 0$ and $s_1 = 0$. This results in the following set of equations.

$$x_1 + 2x_2 + s_1 = 40$$
$$4x_1 + 3x_2 + s_2 = 120$$

and

$$0 + 2x_2 + 0 = 40$$
$$0 + 3x_2 + s_2 = 120$$

Solving first for $x_2$ in the first equation,

$$2x_2 = 40$$
$$x_2 = 20$$

then solving for $s_2$ in the second equation,

$$3x_2 + s_2 = 120$$
$$3(20) + s_2 = 120$$
$$s_2 = 60$$

This solution corresponds with point $A$ in figure 4.2. The graph in figure 4.2 shows that at point $A$, $x_1 = 0$, $x_2 = 20$, $s_1 = 0$, and $s_2 = 60$, the exact solution obtained by solving simultaneous equations. This solution is referred to as a *basic feasible solution*. In general terms, a basic feasible solution is any solution, not necessarily optimal, that satisfies the constraints. The basic feasible solution will contain as many variables with nonzero values as there are model constraints, that is, $m$ variables with values greater than zero and $n - m$ variables equal to zero.

*A basic feasible solution*

**Figure 4.2** Solutions at points *A, B,* and *C.*

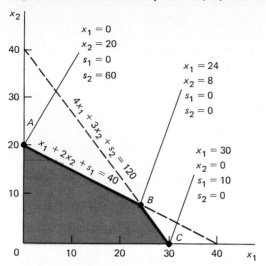

Consider a second example where $x_2 = 0$ and $s_2 = 0$. This results in the following set of equations.

$$x_1 + 2x_2 + s_1 = 40$$
$$4x_1 + 3x_2 + s_2 = 120$$

and

$$x_1 + 0 + s_1 = 40$$
$$4x_1 + 0 + 0 = 120$$

Solving for $x_1$,

$$4x_1 = 120$$
$$x_1 = 30$$

and for $s_1$,

$$30 + s_1 = 40$$
$$s_1 = 10$$

This basic feasible solution corresponds to point $C$ in figure 4.2, where $x_1 = 30$, $x_2 = 0$, $s_1 = 10$, and $s_2 = 0$.

Finally, consider an example where $s_1 = 0$ and $s_2 = 0$. This results in the following set of equations.

$$x_1 + 2x_2 + s_1 = 40$$
$$4x_1 + 3x_2 + s_2 = 120$$

and

$$x_1 + 2x_2 + 0 = 40$$
$$4x_1 + 3x_2 + 0 = 120$$

*Solving a set of
equations using row
operations*

These equations can be solved using *row operations*. In row operations, the equations can be multiplied by constant values and then added or subtracted from each other without changing the values of the decision variables. First multiply the top equation by 4,

$$4x_1 + 8x_2 = 160$$

and then subtract the second equation,

$$
\begin{array}{r}
4x_1 + 8x_2 = 160 \\
-4x_1 - 3x_2 = -120 \\
\hline
5x_2 = 40 \\
x_2 = 8
\end{array}
$$

Next, substitute this value into either one of the constraints,

$$x_1 + 2(8) = 40$$
$$x_1 = 24$$

This solution corresponds to point $B$ on the graph where $x_1 = 24$, $x_2 = 8$, $s_1 = 0$, and $s_2 = 0$, which was previously identified in chapter 3 as the optimal solution point.

All three of these example solutions meet our definition of *basic feasible solutions*. However, several questions are raised by the identification of these solutions:

1. In each example, how was it known which variables to set equal to zero?
2. How is the optimal solution identified?

The answer to both of these questions can be found by using the simplex method. The simplex method is a set of mathematical steps that determines at each step which variables should equal zero and when an optimal solution is reached.

## The Simplex Method

The steps of the simplex method are conducted within the framework of a table or *tableau*. This is a means of organizing the model into a form that makes applying the mathematical steps easier. To demonstrate the simplex tableau and method, the Colonial Pottery Company example will be employed again.

maximize $Z = \$4x_1 + 5x_2 + 0s_1 + 0s_2$
subject to
$$x_1 + 2x_2 + s_1 = 40 \text{ hours}$$
$$4x_1 + 3x_2 + s_2 = 120 \text{ pounds}$$
$$x_1, x_2, s_1, s_2 \geq 0$$

The initial simplex tableau for this model showing the various column and row headings is shown in table 4.1.

**Table 4.1** The Simplex Tableau

| $c_i$ | | | | | | |
|---|---|---|---|---|---|---|
| | basic variables | quantity | $x_1$ | $x_2$ | $s_1$ | $s_2$ |
| | | | | | | |
| | $z_i$ | | | | | |
| | $c_i - z_i$ | | | | | |

*Tableau notation*

The first step in filling in table 4.1 is to designate the variables in the model across the second row from the top. The two decision variables are listed first in the order of the magnitude of their subscript, and the slack variables are listed next, also in the order of the magnitude of their subscript. This results in the row with $x_1$, $x_2$, $s_1$, and $s_2$ in table 4.1.

*The basic feasible solution in the initial simplex tableau*

The next step is to determine a basic feasible solution to start the simplex method with. In other words, which two variables will form the basic feasible solution and which will be assigned a value of zero? Instead of arbitrarily selecting a point (as we did with points *A, B,* and *C* in the examples in the previous section) the simplex method selects the origin as the initial basic feasible solution because the values of the decision variables are always known for all linear programming problems. At that point $x_1 = 0$ and $x_2 = 0$, thus the variables in the basic feasible solution are $s_1$ and $s_2$,

$$x_1 + 2x_2 + s_1 = 40$$
$$0 + 2(0) + s_1 = 40$$
$$s_1 = 40 \text{ hours}$$

and

$$4x_1 + 3x_2 + s_2 = 120$$
$$4(0) + 3(0) + s_2 = 120$$
$$s_2 = 120 \text{ pounds}$$

In other words, at the origin where there is no production, everything is slack or unused resources. The variables $s_1$ and $s_2$, which form the initial basic feasible solution are listed in table 4.2 under the column "basic variables," and their respective values of "40" and "120" are listed under the column "quantity."

*At the initial basic feasible solution at the origin only slack variables have a numerical value other than zero*

**Table 4.2** The Basic Feasible Solution

| $c_i$ | | | | | | |
|---|---|---|---|---|---|---|
| | basic variables | quantity | $x_1$ | $x_2$ | $s_1$ | $s_2$ |
| | $s_1$ | 40 | | | | |
| | $s_2$ | 120 | | | | |
| | $z_i$ | | | | | |
| | $c_i - z_i$ | | | | | |

*The quantity column in the simplex tableau*

The initial simplex tableau always begins with the solution at the origin where $x_1$ and $x_2$ equal zero. Thus, the basic variables at the origin are the slack variables, $s_1$ and $s_2$. The "quantity" values in the initial solution are always the "right-hand side" values of the constraint equations so that they can be read directly from the original constraint equations.

*The number of rows in a tableau*

The top two rows and bottom two rows are standard for all tableaus, however, the middle rows depend on the number of constraints in the model. For example, this problem has two constraints and there are two rows corresponding to $s_1$ and $s_2$. (Recall that $n$ variables minus $m$ constraints equals the number of variables in the problem with values of zero. This also means that the number of basic variables with values other than zero will be equal to $m$ constraints.)

*The number of columns in a tableau*

Similarly, the three columns on the left side of the tableau are standard, while the remaining columns depend on the number of variables. Since there are four variables in this model, there are four columns on the right of the tableau corresponding to $x_1$, $x_2$, $s_1$, and $s_2$.

*The $c_i$ values in the simplex tableau*

The next step is to fill in the "$c_i$" values. $c_i$ represents the *contribution to profit* (or *cost*) for each variable, $x_j$ or $s_j$ in the objective function. Across the top row the $c_i$ values 4, 5, 0, and 0 are inserted for each variable in the model, as shown in table 4.3.

**Table 4.3** The Simplex Tableau with "$c_i$" Values

| $c_i$ | | | 4 | 5 | 0 | 0 |
|---|---|---|---|---|---|---|
| | basic variables | quantity | $x_1$ | $x_2$ | $s_1$ | $s_2$ |
| 0 | $s_1$ | 40 | | | | |
| 0 | $s_2$ | 120 | | | | |
| | $z_i$ | | | | | |
| | $c_i - z_i$ | | | | | |

The values for $c_j$ on the left side of the tableau are the contributions to profit of only those variables in the basic feasible solution, in this case $s_1$ and $s_2$. These values are inserted at this location in the tableau so that they can be used at a later point to compute the values in the $z_j$ row.

*Row values in the simplex tableau*

The columns under each variable (i.e., $x_1$, $x_2$, $s_1$, and $s_2$) are filled in with the coefficients of the decision variables in the model constraint equations. The $s_1$ row represents the first model constraint, thus the coefficient for $x_1$ is 1, the coefficient for $x_2$ is 2, the coefficient for $s_1$ is 1, and the coefficient for $s_2$ is 0. The values in the $s_2$ row are the second constraint equation coefficients, 4, 3, 0, and 1. These are shown in table 4.4.

**Table 4.4** The Simplex Tableau with Model Constraint Coefficients

| $c_j$ | basic variables | quantity | 4 | 5 | 0 | 0 |
|---|---|---|---|---|---|---|
| | | | $x_1$ | $x_2$ | $s_1$ | $s_2$ |
| 0 | $s_1$ | 40 | 1 | 2 | 1 | 0 |
| 0 | $s_2$ | 120 | 4 | 3 | 0 | 1 |
| | $z_j$ | | | | | |
| | $c_j - z_j$ | | | | | |

This completes the process of filling in the initial (i.e., starting) simplex tableau. The remaining values in the $z_j$ and $c_j - z_j$ rows, as well as subsequent tableau values, are computed mathematically using simplex formulas.

Let us summarize the steps of the simplex method (for a maximization model) that have been presented so far.

*The initial steps in the simplex method*

1. First, transform all inequalities to equations by the addition of slack variables.

2. Develop a simplex tableau with a number of columns equaling the number of variables plus three, and a number of rows equaling the number of constraints plus four.

3. Set up table headings including listing the model decision and slack variables.

4. Insert the initial basic feasible solution—the slack variables and their quantity values.

5. Assign $c_j$ values for the model variables in the top row and the basic feasible solution variables on the left side.

6. Insert the model constraint coefficients into the body of the table.

## Computing the $z_j$ and $c_j - z_j$ Rows

So far the simplex tableau has been set up using values taken directly from the model. From this point on the values are determined computationally.

First, the values in the $z_j$ row are computed by multiplying each $c_j$ *column value* (on the left side) by each variable column value (under $x_1$, $x_2$, $s_1$, and $s_2$) and then summing each of these sets of values. These $z_j$ values are shown in table 4.5.

**Table 4.5** The Simplex Tableau with $z_j$ Row Values

| $c_j$ | | | 4 | 5 | 0 | 0 |
|---|---|---|---|---|---|---|
| | basic variables | quantity | $x_1$ | $x_2$ | $s_1$ | $s_2$ |
| 0 | $s_1$ | 40 | 1 | 2 | 1 | 0 |
| 0 | $s_2$ | 120 | 4 | 3 | 0 | 1 |
| | $z_j$ | 0 | 0 | 0 | 0 | 0 |
| | $c_j - z_j$ | | | | | |

For example, the value in the $z_j$ row under the "quantity" column is found by

$$c_j \quad quantity$$
$$0 \times 40 = 0$$
$$0 \times 120 = \underline{0}$$
$$z_q = 0$$

The value in the $z_j$ row under the $x_1$ column is found similarly.

$$c_j \quad x_1$$
$$0 \times 1 = 0$$
$$0 \times 4 = \underline{0}$$
$$z_1 = 0$$

All other $z_j$ row values will also be zero *for this tableau* when computed using this same formula.

Now the $c_j - z_j$ row must be computed by subtracting the $z_j$ row values from the $c_j$ (top) row values. For example, in the $x_1$ column the $c_j - z_j$ row value is computed as $4 - 0 = 4$. This value, as well as other values, are shown in table 4.6.

**Table 4.6** The Complete Initial Simplex Tableau

| $c_j$ | | | 4 | 5 | 0 | 0 |
|---|---|---|---|---|---|---|
| | basic variables | quantity | $x_1$ | $x_2$ | $s_1$ | $s_2$ |
| 0 | $s_1$ | 40 | 1 | 2 | 1 | 0 |
| 0 | $s_2$ | 120 | 4 | 3 | 0 | 1 |
| | $z_j$ | 0 | 0 | 0 | 0 | 0 |
| | $c_j - z_j$ | | 4 | 5 | 0 | 0 |

Table 4.6 is the complete initial simplex tableau with all values filled in. This represents the solution at the origin where $x_1=0$, $x_2=0$, $s_1=40$, and $s_2 = 120$. The profit generated by this solution (i.e., the $Z$ value) is given in the $z_j$ row under the quantity column—0 in table 4.6. This solution is obviously not optimal, since no profit is being made at all. Thus, we want to move to a solution point that will give a *better* solution. In other words, we want to produce either some bowls ($x_1$) or mugs ($x_2$). As such, one of the *nonbasic* variables (i.e., variables not in the present basic feasible solution) will enter the solution and become basic.

*The completed initial tableau*

## The Entering Nonbasic Variable

As an example, suppose it is decided to produce some bowls; that is, $x_1$ will become a basic variable. For every unit of $x_1$ we produce (i.e., each bowl) profit will be increased by \$4, since that is the profit contribution of a bowl. However, when a bowl ($x_1$) is produced, some previously unused resources will be used. For example,

if $x_1 = 1$

then

$$x_1 + 2x_2 + s_1 = 40 \text{ hours of labor}$$
$$1 + 2(0) + s_1 = 40$$
$$s_1 = 39 \text{ hours of labor}$$

and

$$4x_1 + 3x_2 + s_2 = 120 \text{ pounds of clay}$$
$$4(1) + 3(0) + s_2 = 120$$
$$s_2 = 116 \text{ pounds of clay}$$

In the labor constraint we see that the amount of slack or unused labor is *decreased* by *one hour*. In the clay constraint the amount of slack has been *decreased* by *four pounds*. If these increases (for $x_1$) and decreases (for slack) are substituted into the objective function we have

$$
\begin{array}{cc}
\underline{\phantom{xx}c_j\phantom{xx}} & \underline{\phantom{xx}z_j\phantom{xx}} \\
\end{array}
$$
$$Z = 4(1) + 5(0) \; + \; 0(-1) + 0(-4)$$
$$Z = \phantom{4}4 - 0$$
$$Z = \$4$$

The first part of this objective function relationship represents the values in the $c_j$ row, while the second part represents the values in the $z_j$ row. Verbally, this relationship means that to produce some bowls we must give up some of the profit already earned from the items they replace. In this case the production of bowls replaced only slack, so no profit was lost. In general, the $c_j - z_j$ row values are the *net increase per unit of entering a nonbasic variable into the basic solution.* Naturally, we always want to

*Selecting the nonbasic variable with the greatest positive $c_j - z_j$ value as the entering variable*

make as much money as possible (remember the objective is to maximize profit), so we will enter the variable that will have the greatest net increase in profit per unit. Observing table 4.7, variable $x_2$ is selected as the entering basic variable because it has the greatest net increase in profit per unit, $5—the highest positive value in the $c_j - z_j$ row.

**Table 4.7** Selection of the Entering Basic Variable

| $c_j$ | | | 4 | 5 | 0 | 0 |
|---|---|---|---|---|---|---|
| | basic variables | quantity | $x_1$ | $x_2$ | $s_1$ | $s_2$ |
| 0 | $s_1$ | 40 | 1 | 2 | 1 | 0 |
| 0 | $s_2$ | 120 | 4 | 3 | 0 | 1 |
| | $z_j$ | 0 | 0 | 0 | 0 | 0 |
| | $c_j - z_j$ | | 4 | 5 | 0 | 0 |

*Pivot column*

The $x_2$ column is referred to as the *pivot column* (the operations used to solve simultaneous equations have often been referred to in mathematical terminology as "pivot operations") and it is highlighted in table 4.7.

*Moving to an adjacent solution point*

The selection of the entering basic variable is also demonstrated by the graph in figure 4.3. At the origin nothing is produced. In the simplex method we move from one solution point to an *adjacent* point (i.e., *one*

**Figure 4.3** Selection of which item to produce—the entering basic variable.

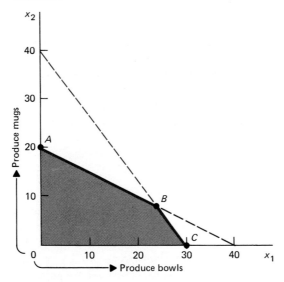

The Simplex Solution Method

variable in the basic feasible solution is replaced with a variable that was previously zero). In figure 4.3 we can move up the $x_1$ axis or the $x_2$ axis in order to seek a better solution. Since $x_2$ will result in a greater profit, it was selected.

## The Leaving Basic Variable

Since each basic feasible solution will contain only two variables with nonzero values; one of the present two basic variables, $s_1$ or $s_2$, will have to leave the solution and become zero. Since we have already decided to produce mugs ($x_2$), we naturally want to produce as much as possible or, in other words, as much as our resources will allow. First, in the labor contraint we will use all the labor to make mugs (since no bowls are produced, $x_1 = 0$, and since we will use all the labor possible and $s_1 =$ unused labor resources, $s_1 = 0$ also).

$$1x_1 + 2x_2 + s_1 = 40 \text{ hours}$$
$$1(0) + 2x_2 + 0 = 40$$
$$x_2 = \frac{40 \text{ hours}}{2 \text{ hours/mugs}}$$
$$x_2 = 20 \text{ mugs}$$

In other words, enough labor is available to produce 20 mugs. Next, we observe the constraint for clay and perform the same analysis.

$$4x_1 + 3x_2 + s_2 = 120 \text{ pounds}$$
$$4(0) + 3x_2 + 0 = 120$$
$$x_2 = \frac{120 \text{ pounds}}{3 \text{ pounds/mugs}}$$
$$x_2 = 40 \text{ mugs}$$

This indicates that there is enough clay to produce 40 mugs but only enough labor to produce 20 mugs. As such, we are limited to the production of only 20 mugs, since we do not have enough labor to produce any more than that. This analysis is shown graphically in figure 4.4. Since we are moving out the $x_2$ axis, we can move to point $A$ or $R$. We select point $A$ because it is the *most constrained* and, thus, feasible, while point $R$ is infeasible.

*The most constrained adjacent solution point*

This analysis is performed in the simplex method by dividing the "quantity" values of the basic solution variables by the pivot column values. For this tableau,

| *basic variables* | *quantity* | $x_2$ |
|---|---|---|
| $s_1$ : | 40 | $\div\ 2 = 20 \leftarrow$ leaving basic variable |
| $s_2$ : | 120 | $\div\ 3 = 40$ |

The leaving basic variable is the variable that corresponds to the minimum positive quotient, which is 20 in this case. Therefore, $s_1$ is the leaving variable. (At point $A$ in fig. 4.4, $s_1$ equals zero since all the labor is used to make the 20 mugs.) The $s_1$ row is also referred to as the *pivot row* and it is highlighted in table 4.8.

*Pivot row*

**Figure 4.4** Determination of the basic feasible solution point.

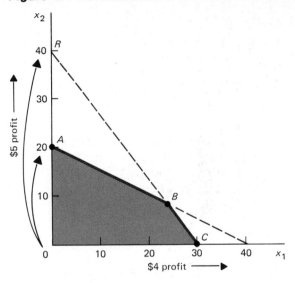

**Table 4.8** Pivot Column, Pivot Row, and Pivot Number

| $c_i$ | | | 4 | 5 | 0 | 0 |
|---|---|---|---|---|---|---|
| | basic variables | quantity | $x_1$ | $x_2$ | $s_1$ | $s_2$ |
| 0 | $s_1$ | 40 | 1 | 2 | 1 | 0 |
| 0 | $s_2$ | 120 | 4 | 3 | 0 | 1 |
| | $z_i$ | 0 | 0 | 0 | 0 | 0 |
| | $c_i - z_i$ | | 4 | 5 | 0 | 0 |

The value of "2" at the intersection of the pivot row and pivot column is called the "pivot number." The pivot number, row, and column are all instrumental in developing the next tableau. We are now ready to proceed to the second simplex tableau and a *better* solution.

*Pivot number*

## Developing a New Tableau

Table 4.9 shows the second simplex tableau with the new basic feasible solution variables of $x_2$ and $s_2$ and their corresponding $c_j$ values.

**Table 4.9** The Basic Variables and $c_j$ Values for the Second Simplex Tableau

| $c_j$ | | | 4 | 5 | 0 | 0 |
|---|---|---|---|---|---|---|
| | basic variables | quantity | $x_1$ | $x_2$ | $s_1$ | $s_2$ |
| 5 | $x_2$ | | | | | |
| 0 | $s_2$ | | | | | |
| | $z_j$ | | | | | |
| | $c_j - z_j$ | | | | | |

The various row values in the second tableau are computed using several simplex formulas. First, the $x_2$ row, which we will call the *new tableau pivot row,* in the new tableau is computed by dividing every value in the pivot row of the first (old) tableau by the pivot number. The formula for these computations is

*Computing the new tableau pivot row values*

$$\text{new tableau pivot row values} = \frac{\text{old tableau pivot row values}}{\text{pivot number}}$$

The new row values and their computation are shown in table 4.10.

**Table 4.10** Computation of the New Pivot Row Values

| $c_j$ | | | 4 | 5 | 0 | 0 |
|---|---|---|---|---|---|---|
| | basic variables | quantity | $x_1$ | $x_2$ | $s_1$ | $s_2$ |
| 5 | $x_2$ | 20 | 1/2 | 1 | 1/2 | 0 |
| 0 | $s_2$ | | | | | |
| | $z_j$ | | | | | |
| | $c_j - z_j$ | | | | | |

To compute all remaining row values (and in this case there is only one other row) another formula is used:

*Computing all remaining row values*

$$\begin{array}{l} \text{new tableau} \\ \text{row values} \end{array} = \begin{array}{l} \text{old tableau} \\ \text{row values} \end{array} - \left( \begin{array}{l} \text{corresponding} \\ \text{coefficients in} \\ \text{pivot column} \end{array} \times \begin{array}{l} \text{corresponding} \\ \text{new tableau} \\ \text{pivot row} \\ \text{value} \end{array} \right)$$

Thus, this formula requires the use of both the old tableau and the new one. The $s_2$ row values are computed in table 4.11.

**Table 4.11** Computation of New $s_2$ Row Values

| Column | Old Row Value | $-$ | (Corresponding Coefficient in Pivot Column | $\times$ | New Tableau Pivot Row Value ) | $=$ | New Tableau Row Value |
|--------|---------------|-----|--------------------------------------------|----------|-------------------------------|-----|------------------------|
| quantity | 120 | $-$ | (3 | $\times$ | 20) | $=$ | 60 |
| $x_1$ | 4 | $-$ | (3 | $\times$ | 1/2) | $=$ | 5/2 |
| $x_2$ | 3 | $-$ | (3 | $\times$ | 1) | $=$ | 0 |
| $s_1$ | 0 | $-$ | (3 | $\times$ | 1/2) | $=$ | $-3/2$ |
| $s_2$ | 1 | $-$ | (3 | $\times$ | 0) | $=$ | 1 |

These values are substituted in the simplex tableau in table 4.12.

**Table 4.12** The Second Simplex Tableau with Row Values

| $c_j$ | | | 4 | 5 | 0 | 0 |
|-------|--------------------|----------|-------|-------|--------|--------|
| | basic variables | quantity | $x_1$ | $x_2$ | $s_1$ | $s_2$ |
| 5 | $x_2$ | 20 | 1/2 | 1 | 1/2 | 0 |
| 0 | $s_2$ | 60 | 5/2 | 0 | $-3/2$ | 1 |
| | $z_j$ | | | | | |
| | $c_j - z_j$ | | | | | |

This solution corresponds to point $A$ in the graph of this model in figure 4.4. The solution at this point is $x_1 = 0, x_2 = 20, s_1 = 0, s_2 = 60$. In other words, 20 mugs are produced and 60 pounds of clay are left unused. No bowls were produced and no labor hours remain unused.

The second simplex tableau is completed by computing the $z_j$ and $c_j - z_j$ row values in the same way that they were computed in the first tableau. The $z_j$ rows are computed by summing the products of the $c_j$ column and all other column values.

*Column*
quantity : $z_q = (5)(20) + (0)(60) = 100$
$\quad x_1 :\ z_1 = (5)(1/2) + (0)(5/2) = 5/2$
$\quad x_2 :\ z_2 = (5)(1) + (0)(0) = 5$
$\quad s_1 :\ z_3 = (5)(1/2) + (0)(-3/2) = 5/2$
$\quad s_2 :\ z_4 = (5)(0) + (0)(1) = 0$

The $z_j$ row values and the $c_j - z_j$ row values are added to the tableau to give the completed second simplex tableau shown in table 4.13.

**Table 4.13** The Completed Second Simplex Tableau

| $c_j$ | basic variables | quantity | 4 $x_1$ | 5 $x_2$ | 0 $s_1$ | 0 $s_2$ |
|---|---|---|---|---|---|---|
| 5 | $x_2$ | 20 | 1/2 | 1 | 1/2 | 0 |
| 0 | $s_2$ | 60 | 5/2 | 0 | −3/2 | 1 |
| | $z_j$ | 100 | 5/2 | 5 | 5/2 | 0 |
| | $c_j - z_j$ | | 3/2 | 0 | −5/2 | 0 |

The value of 100 in the $z_j$ row is the value of the objective function (profit) for this basic feasible solution.

The computational steps that we followed to derive the second tableau in effect accomplish the same thing as *row operations* in the solution of simultaneous equations. These same steps are followed to derive each subsequent tableau (also called *iterations*).

*Simplex iterations*

## The Optimal Simplex Tableau

The steps that we followed to derive the second simplex tableau are repeated to develop the third tableau. First, the pivot column or entering basic variable is determined. Since "3/2" in the $c_j - z_j$ row represents the greatest positive net increase in profit, $x_1$ is the entering nonbasic variable. Dividing the pivot column values into the "quantity" column indicates that $s_2$ is the leaving basic variable *and* corresponds to the pivot row. The pivot row, pivot column, and pivot number are indicated in table 4.14.

**Table 4.14** The Pivot Row, Pivot Column, and Pivot Number

| $c_j$ | basic variables | quantity | 4 $x_1$ | 5 $x_2$ | 0 $s_1$ | 0 $s_2$ |
|---|---|---|---|---|---|---|
| 5 | $x_2$ | 20 | 1/2 | 1 | 1/2 | 0 |
| 0 | $s_2$ | 60 | 5/2 | 0 | −3/2 | 1 |
| | $z_j$ | 100 | 5/2 | 5 | 5/2 | 5 |
| | $c_j - z_j$ | | 3/2 | 0 | −5/2 | 0 |

It might be questioned at this point why 3/2 (i.e., $1.50) is the net increase in profit per bowl ($x_1$), rather than the original profit of $4. It is because the production of bowls ($x_1$) will require some of the resources previously used to produce mugs ($x_2$) only. Hence, we are producing some bowls while not producing as many mugs; thus, we are giving up some of the profit gained from producing mugs in order to gain even more by producing bowls. This difference is the *net increase* of $1.50.

*The net increase in profit resulting from entering a variable*

The new tableau pivot $(x_1)$ row in the third simplex tableau is computed using the same formula used previously. Thus, all old pivot row values are divided through by 5/2, the pivot number. These values are shown in table 4.16. The values for the other $(x_2)$ row are computed as shown in table 4.15.

**Table 4.15** Computation of the $x_2$ Row for the Third Simplex Tableau

| Column | Old Row Value | − | Corresponding Coefficient in Pivot Column | × | New Tableau Pivot Row Value | = | New Tableau Row Value |
|--------|---------------|---|-------------------------------------------|---|------------------------------|---|-----------------------|
| quantity | 20 | − | (1/2 | × | 24) | = | 8 |
| $x_1$ | 1/2 | − | (1/2 | × | 1) | = | 0 |
| $x_2$ | 1 | − | (1/2 | × | 0) | = | 1 |
| $s_1$ | 1/2 | − | (1/2 | × | −3/5) | = | 4/5 |
| $s_2$ | 0 | − | (1/2 | × | 2/5) | = | −1/5 |

These new row values as well as the new $z_j$ row and $c_j - z_j$ row are shown in the completed third simplex tableau in table 4.16.

**Table 4.16** The Completed Third Simplex Tableau

| $c_j$ | | | 4 | 5 | 0 | 0 |
|-------|--------------------|----------|-------|-------|-------|-------|
| | basic variables | quantity | $x_1$ | $x_2$ | $s_1$ | $s_2$ |
| 5 | $x_2$ | 8 | 0 | 1 | 4/5 | −1/5 |
| 4 | $x_1$ | 24 | 1 | 0 | −3/5 | 2/5 |
| | $z_j$ | 136 | 4 | 5 | 8/5 | 3/5 |
| | $c_j - z_j$ | | 0 | 0 | −8/5 | −3/5 |

*Determining if an optimal solution exists*

Observing the $c_j - z_j$ row to determine the entering variable, we see that there is no nonbasic variable that would result in a positive net increase in profit. All values in the $c_j - z_j$ row are zero or negative. This means that the optimal solution has been reached (which corresponds to point $B$ in fig. 3.11 in chapter 3 and fig. 4.4.) The solution is

$x_1 = 24$ bowls
$x_2 = 8$ mugs
$Z = \$136$ profit

*Integer values are not guaranteed*

An additional comment should be made regarding this solution and any simplex solution. Although this solution resulted in *integer* values for the variables (i.e., 24 and 8), this is *not guaranteed* by the simplex method. That is, it is possible to get a fractional solution for decision variables when the variables reflect items that should be only integers, such as airplanes, television sets, bowls, mugs, etc. As such, in order to apply the simplex method it is necessary to accept this limitation. However, linear programming models can be solved using a method that insures integer solutions, which is the topic covered in chapter 8.

## Summary of the Simplex Method

The simplex method demonstrated in the previous section consists of the following steps:

1. Transform the model constraint inequalities into equations.
2. Set up the initial tableau for the basic feasible solution at the origin and compute the $z_j$ and $c_j - z_j$ row values.
3. Determine the pivot column (entering nonbasic solution variable) by selecting the column with the highest positive value in the $c_j - z_j$ row.
4. Determine the pivot row (leaving basic solution variable) by dividing the quantity column values by the pivot column values and selecting the row with the minimum positive quotient.
5. Compute the new pivot row values using the formula:

$$\text{new tableau pivot row value} = \frac{\text{old tableau pivot row value}}{\text{pivot number}}$$

6. Compute all other row values using the formula:

$$\begin{matrix} \text{new tableau} \\ \text{row value} \end{matrix} = \begin{matrix} \text{old row} \\ \text{value} \end{matrix} - \left( \begin{matrix} \text{corresponding} \\ \text{coefficient in} \\ \text{the pivot} \\ \text{column} \end{matrix} \times \begin{matrix} \text{new tableau} \\ \text{pivot row} \\ \text{value} \end{matrix} \right)$$

7. Compute the new $z_j$ and $c_j - z_j$ row.
8. Determine if the new solution is optimal by checking the $c_j - z_j$ row. If all $c_j - z_j$ row values are zero or negative, the solution is optimal. If a positive value exists, return to step 3 and repeat the simplex steps.

## Summary

In this chapter the general simplex method was presented as it applies to a linear programming maximization model. Although the steps of the method are generally applicable to both maximization *and* minimization models, a minimization model requires some slight changes in the way model constraint inequalities are converted to equations and in the simplex tableau. As such, the application of the simplex method to a minimization problem will be considered as a separate topic in chapter 5. In chapter 5 the special cases of multiple optimum solutions, infeasible problems, and unbounded solutions will also be discussed.

*This chapter is limited to the simplex solution of maximization models*

# References

Dantzig, G. B. *Linear Programming and Extensions*. Princeton, N.J.: Princeton University, 1963.

Gass, S. *Linear Programming*. 4th ed. New York: McGraw-Hill, 1975.

Gottfried, B. S., and Weisman, J. *Introduction to Optimization Theory*. Englewood Cliffs, N.J.: Prentice-Hall, 1973.

Hadley, G. *Linear Programming*. Reading, Mass.: Addison-Wesley, 1962.

Hillier, F. S., and Lieberman, G. J. *Operations Research*. 3rd ed. San Francisco: Holden-Day, 1980.

Kim, C. *Introduction to Linear Programming*. New York: Holt, Rinehart and Winston, 1971.

Lee, Sang M.; Moore, Laurence J.; and Taylor, Bernard W. *Management Science*. Dubuque, Iowa: Wm. C. Brown Company Publishers, 1981.

Moskowitz, H., and Wright, G. P. *Operations Research Techniques for Management*. Englewood Cliffs, N.J.: Prentice-Hall, 1979.

Rothenberg, R. I. *Linear Programming*. New York: Elsevier North-Holland, 1979.

Wagner, H. M. *Principles of Operations Research*. Englewood Cliffs, N.J.: Prentice-Hall, 1969.

# Problems

1. A manufacturer produces two products, $A$ and $B$, from steel. The manufacturer has developed the following linear programming model to determine the quantity of each product ($x_1$ and $x_2$) to produce in order to maximize profit.

   maximize $Z = 5x_1 + 10x_2$ (profit, \$)
   subject to
   $$4x_1 + 5x_2 \leq 40 \text{ (steel, lbs.)}$$
   $$x_1, x_2 \geq 0$$

   (a) Solve this problem graphically.
   (b) Solve this problem using the simplex method.

2. Given the following simplex tableau for a linear programming model:

| $c_j$ | | | 10 | 2 | 6 | 0 | 0 | 0 |
|---|---|---|---|---|---|---|---|---|
| | basic variables | quantity | $x_1$ | $x_2$ | $x_3$ | $s_1$ | $s_2$ | $s_3$ |
| 2 | $x_2$ | 10 | 0 | 1 | −2 | 1 | −1/2 | 0 |
| 10 | $x_1$ | 40 | 1 | 0 | 2 | 0 | 1/2 | 0 |
| 0 | $s_3$ | 30 | 0 | 0 | 8 | −3 | 3/2 | 1 |
| | $z_j$ | 420 | 10 | 2 | 16 | 2 | 4 | 0 |
| | $c_j - z_j$ | | 0 | 0 | −10 | −2 | −4 | 0 |

(a) What is the solution given in this tableau?

(b) Is the solution in this tableau optimal? Why?

(c) What does $x_3$ equal in this tableau? $s_2$?

(d) Write out the original objective function for the linear programming model using only decision variables.

(e) How many constraints are in the linear programming model?

(f) Explain briefly why it would have been difficult to solve this problem graphically.

3. In chapter 3, the following problem (1) was presented to be solved graphically. A company makes two products, 1 and 2, from two resources. The linear programming model for determining the amounts of product 1 and 2 to produce ($x_1$ and $x_2$) is

maximize $Z = 8x_1 + 2x_2$ (profit, $)
subject to:
$$4x_1 + 5x_2 \leq 20 \text{ (resource 1, lbs.)}$$
$$2x_1 + 6x_2 \leq 18 \text{ (resource 2, lbs.)}$$
$$x_1, x_2 \geq 0$$

Solve this model using the simplex method.

4. In chapter 3, the following problem (2) was presented to be solved graphically. A company produces two products that are processed on two assembly lines. Assembly line 1 has 100 available hours and assembly line 2 has 42 available hours. The company has formulated the following linear programming model for determining the number of each product ($x_1$ and $x_2$) to produce.

maximize $Z = 6x_1 + 4x_2$ (profit, $)
subject to
$$10x_1 + 10x_2 \leq 100 \text{ (line 1, hrs.)}$$
$$7x_1 + 3x_2 \leq 42 \text{ (line 2, hrs.)}$$
$$x_1, x_2 \geq 0$$

Solve this model using the simplex method.

5. In chapter 3, the following problem (5) was presented to be solved graphically.The Pinewood Company produces chairs and tables from two resources—labor and wood. The company has 80 hours of labor and 36 pounds of wood available each day. The demand for chairs is limited to 6 per day. The company has developed the following linear programming model to determine the number of chairs and tables ($x_1$ and $x_2$) to produce each day in order to maximize profit.

maximize $Z = 400x_1 + 100x_2$ (profit, \$)
subject to
$$8x_1 + 10x_2 \leq 80 \text{ (labor, hrs.)}$$
$$2x_1 + 6x_2 \leq 36 \text{ (wood, lbs.)}$$
$$x_1 \leq 6 \text{ (demand, chairs)}$$
$$x_1, x_2 \geq 0$$

Solve this model using the simplex method.

6. In chapter 3, the following problem (6) was presented to be solved graphically. The Crumb and Custard Bakery makes cakes and pies from flour and sugar. The following linear programming model has been developed in order to determine the number of cakes and pies ($x_1$ and $x_2$) to produce each day that will maximize profit.

maximize $Z = x_1 + 5x_2$ (profit, \$)
subject to
$$5x_1 + 5x_2 \leq 25 \text{ (flour, lbs.)}$$
$$2x_1 + 4x_2 \leq 16 \text{ (sugar, lbs.)}$$
$$x_1 \leq 5 \text{ (demand for cakes)}$$
$$x_1, x_2 \geq 0$$

Solve this model using the simplex method.

7. In chapter 3, the following problem (10) was presented to be solved graphically. A jewelry store makes necklaces and bracelets from gold and platinum. The store has developed the following linear programming model to determine the number of necklaces and bracelets ($x_1$ and $x_2$) to make in order to maximize profit.

maximize $Z = 300x_1 + 400x_2$ (profit, \$)
subject to
$$3x_1 + 2x_2 \leq 18 \text{ (gold, oz.)}$$
$$2x_1 + 4x_2 \leq 20 \text{ (platinum, oz.)}$$
$$x_2 \leq 4 \text{ (demand, bracelets)}$$
$$x_1, x_2 \geq 0$$

Solve this model using the simplex method.

8. A sporting goods company makes baseballs and softballs on a daily basis from leather and yarn. The company has developed the following linear programming model to determine the number of baseballs and softballs to produce ($x_1$ and $x_2$) in order to maximize profits.

maximize $Z = 5x_1 + 4x_2$ (profit, \$)
subject to
$$.3x_1 + .5x_2 \leq 150 \text{ (leather, ft.}^2\text{)}$$
$$10x_1 + 4x_2 \leq 2,000 \text{ (yarn, yds.)}$$
$$x_1, x_2 \geq 0$$

Solve this model using the simplex method.

9. A clothing shop makes suits and blazers. The three main resources are material, rack space, and labor. The shop has developed the following linear programming model to determine the number of suits and blazers to make ($x_1$ and $x_2$) in order to maximize profits.

maximize $Z = 100x_1 + 150x_2$ (profit, \$)
subject to
$$10x_1 + 4x_2 \leq 160 \text{ (material, yd.}^2)$$
$$x_1 + x_2 \leq 20 \text{ (rack space)}$$
$$10x_1 + 20x_2 \leq 300 \text{ (labor, hrs.)}$$
$$x_1, x_2 \geq 0$$

Solve this model using the simplex method.

10. Given the following linear programming model:

maximize $Z = 100x_1 + 20x_2 + 60x_3$
subject to
$$3x_1 + 5x_2 \leq 60$$
$$2x_1 + 2x_2 + 2x_3 \leq 100$$
$$x_3 \leq 40$$
$$x_1, x_2, x_3 \geq 0$$

Solve using the simplex method.

11. Given the following linear programming model:

maximize $Z = 3x_1 + 4x_2$
subject to
$$3x_1 + 2x_2 \leq 18$$
$$2x_1 + 4x_2 \leq 20$$
$$x_1 \leq 5$$
$$x_1, x_2 \geq 0$$

(a) Solve graphically.
(b) Solve using the simplex method.

12. The Cookie Monster Store at South Acres Mall makes three types of cookies—chocolate chip, pecan chip, and pecan sandies. The three main ingredients are chocolate chips, pecans, and sugar. The store has 120 pounds of chocolate chips, 40 pounds of pecans, and 300 pounds of sugar. The following linear programming model has been developed to determine the number of batches of chocolate chip cookies ($x_1$), pecan chip cookies ($x_2$), and pecan sandies ($x_3$) to make in order to maximize profit.

maximize $Z = 10x_1 + 12x_2 + 7x_3$ (profit, \$)
subject to

$$20x_1 + 15x_2 + 10x_3 \leq 300 \text{ (sugar, lbs.)}$$
$$10x_1 + 5x_2 \leq 120 \text{ (chocolate chips, lbs.)}$$
$$x_1 + 2x_3 \leq 40 \text{ (pecans, lbs.)}$$
$$x_1, x_2, x_3 \geq 0$$

Solve this model using the simplex method.

13. The Eastern Iron and Steel Company makes nails, bolts, and washers from leftover steel and zinc (for coating). The company has 24 tons of steel and 30 tons of zinc. The following linear programming model has been developed to determine the number of batches of nails $(x_1)$, the number of batches of bolts $(x_2)$, and the number of batches of washers $(x_3)$ to produce in order to maximize profit.

maximize $Z = 6x_1 + 2x_2 + 12x_3$ (profit, \$1,000s)
subject to

$$4x_1 + x_2 + 3x_3 \leq 24 \text{ (steel, tons)}$$
$$2x_1 + 6x_2 + 3x_3 \leq 30 \text{ (zinc, tons)}$$
$$x_1, x_2, x_3 \geq 0$$

Solve this model using the simplex method.

14. The Valley Wine Company produces two kinds of wine—Valley Nectar and Valley Red. The wines are produced from grapes, and the company has 64 tons of grapes this season. However, the company production is limited by both storage space for aging (50 cubic yards) and processing time (120 hours). The following linear programming model has been developed to determine the number of 1,000-gallon batches to produce of Nectar $(x_1)$ and Red $(x_2)$ in order to maximize profit.

maximize $Z = 9x_1 + 12x_2$ (profit, \$1,000s)
subject to

$$4x_1 + 8x_2 \leq 64 \text{ (grapes, tons)}$$
$$5x_1 + 5x_2 \leq 50 \text{ (storage space, yd.}^3)$$
$$15x_1 + 8x_2 \leq 120 \text{ (processing time, hrs.)}$$
$$x_1 \leq 7 \text{ (demand, Nectar)}$$
$$x_2 \leq 7 \text{ (demand, Red)}$$
$$x_1, x_2 \geq 0$$

Solve this model using the simplex method.

15. Given the following linear programming model:

maximize $Z = 100x_1 + 75x_2 + 90x_3 + 95x_4$
subject to
$$3x_1 + 2x_2 \leq 40$$
$$4x_3 + x_4 \leq 25$$
$$200x_1 + 250x_3 \leq 2,000$$
$$100x_1 + 200x_4 \leq 2,200$$
$$x_1, x_2, x_3, x_4 \geq 0$$

Solve using the simplex method.

16. Given the following linear programming model:

maximize $Z = 60x_1 + 50x_2 + 45x_3 + 50x_4$
subject to
$$x_2 \leq 20$$
$$x_4 \leq 15$$
$$10x_1 + 5x_2 \leq 120$$
$$8x_3 + 6x_4 \leq 135$$
$$x_1, x_2, x_3, x_4 \geq 0$$

Solve using the simplex method.

17. Given the following linear programming model:

maximize $Z = 5x_1 + 7x_2 + 8x_3$
subject to
$$x_1 + x_2 + x_3 \leq 32$$
$$x_1 \leq 20$$
$$x_2 \leq 15$$
$$x_3 \leq 18$$
$$x_1, x_2, x_3 \geq 0$$

Solve using the simplex method.

18. Given the following linear programming model:

maximize $Z = 600x_1 + 540x_2 + 375x_3$
subject to
$$x_1 + x_2 + x_3 \leq 12$$
$$x_1 \leq 5$$
$$80x_1 + 70x_2 + 50x_3 \leq 750$$
$$x_1, x_2, x_3 \geq 0$$

Solve this problem using the simplex method.

19. Given the following linear programming model:

   maximize $Z = 9x_1 + 7x_2$
   subject to
   $$12x_1 + 4x_2 \leq 60$$
   $$4x_1 + 8x_2 \leq 40$$
   $$x_1, x_2 \geq 0$$

   Solve using the simplex method.

20. Given the following linear programming model:

   maximize $Z = 200x_1 + 300x_2$
   subject to
   $$2x_1 + 5x_2 \leq 180$$
   $$3x_1 + 3x_2 \leq 135$$
   $$x_1, x_2 \geq 0$$

   Solve using the simplex method.

21. Solve problem 1 from chapter 2 using the simplex method.

22. Solve problem 5 from chapter 2 using the simplex method.

23. Solve problem 7 from chapter 2 using the simplex method.

24. Solve problem 10 from chapter 2 using the simplex method.

25. Solve problem 19 from chapter 2 using the simplex method.

# 5

The Minimization
Problem and
Irregular Types
of Linear
Programming
Problems

The Minimization Problem and
Irregular Types of Linear Programming Problems

In the previous chapter the simplex method for solving linear programming problems was demonstrated for a maximization problem. In general, the steps of the simplex method outlined in chapter 4 are used for any type of linear programming problem. However, a minimization problem requires a few changes in the normal simplex process. In this chapter these changes will be discussed and demonstrated.

Also, in this chapter several exceptions to the typical linear programming problem will be presented. These include problems with mixed constraints ($=$, $\leq$, and $\geq$), problems with more than one solution, problems with no feasible solution, problems in which the solution is unbounded, problems with a tie for the pivot column, problems with a tie for the pivot row, and problems with constraints with negative quantity values. None of these items really causes the simplex method to be altered. They are basically unusual results in individual simplex tableaus that the reader should know how to interpret.

## A Minimization Problem

In order to demonstrate the application of the simplex method to a minimization problem, the following example model, first introduced as a graphical example in chapter 3, will be used. In this problem a farmer is trying to determine how many bags of two kinds of fertilizer (Super-gro and Crop-quik) to purchase in order to meet minimum nitrogen and phosphate requirements of a field. Each type of fertilizer provides a specific nitrogen and phosphate content. The model was formulated as

*A minimization example*

minimize $Z = \$6x_1 + 3x_2$
subject to
$\quad 2x_1 + 4x_2 \geq 16$ lbs. of nitrogen
$\quad 4x_1 + 3x_2 \geq 24$ lbs. of phosphate
$\quad\quad\quad x_1, x_2 \geq 0$

where
$\quad x_1 =$ bags of Super-gro fertilizer
$\quad x_2 =$ bags of Crop-quik fertilizer
$\quad Z =$ farmer's total cost (\$) of purchasing fertilizer

In chapter 4 the first step of the simplex process was to convert all the model $\leq$ constraint inequalities to equations. This same general step is required for a minimization model. However, this problem has $\geq$ constraints as opposed to the $\leq$ constraints of the Colonial Pottery Company maximization example in chapter 4. The $\geq$ constraints are converted to equations a little differently than $\leq$ constraints.

Instead of adding a slack variable, a $\geq$ constraint first requires that a *surplus* variable be subtracted. While a slack variable is added and reflects unused resources, a surplus variable is subtracted and reflects the excess above a minimum resource requirement level. Like the slack variable, a surplus variable is represented symbolically by $s_i$ and must be nonnegative.

For the nitrogen constraint the subtraction of a surplus variable gives us

$$2x_1 + 4x_2 - s_1 = 16$$

As an example consider the hypothetical solution, $x_1 = 0$ and $x_2 = 10$. Substituting these values into the above equation,

$$2(0) + 4(10) - s_1 = 16$$
$$-s_1 = 16 - 40$$
$$s_1 = 24 \text{ lbs. of nitrogen}$$

$s_1$ can be interpreted in this equation as the *extra* amount of nitrogen above the minimum requirement of 16 lbs., obtained by purchasing 10 bags of Crop-quik fertilizer. For this solution the surplus variable, $s_1$, successfully transforms the nitrogen constraint into an equation.

However, the simplex method requires that the initial basic feasible solution be at the origin where $x_1 = 0$ and $x_2 = 0$. Testing these solution values,

$$2x_1 + 4x_2 - s_1 = 16$$
$$2(0) + 4(0) - s_1 = 16$$
$$s_1 = -16$$

The existence of "negative excess lbs. of nitrogen" is illogical and violates the nonnegativity restriction of linear programming. The reason the surplus variable does not work is shown in figure 5.1. The solution at the origin is outside the feasible solution space.

In order to alleviate this difficulty and get a solution at the origin, an *artificial* variable ($A_i$) is added to the constraint equation,

$$2x_1 + 4x_2 - s_1 + A_1 = 16$$

The artificial variable, $A_1$, does not really have a meaning like a slack variable or surplus variable. It is inserted into the equation simply to give us a "positive" solution at the origin—we are artificially creating a solution, as follows:

**Figure 5.1** Graph of the fertilizer example.

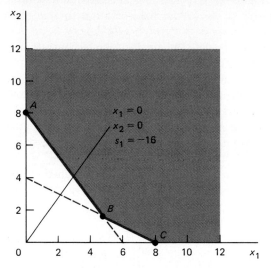

$$2x_1 + 4x_2 - s_1 + A_1 = 16$$
$$2(0) + 4(0) - 0 + A_1 = 16$$
$$A_1 = 16$$

The artificial variable is somewhat analogous to a "booster rocket"—it is there to get us off the ground, but once we get started it has no real use and is discarded. That is, the artificial solution helps us get the simplex process started, but once it does so, we do not want it to end up in the optimal solution, since it has no real meaning.

By subtracting a surplus variable and adding an artificial variable, the phosphate constraint becomes

$$4x_1 + 3x_2 - s_2 + A_2 = 24$$

*The effect of surplus variables on the objective function*

The effect of both surplus and artificial variables on the objective function must now be considered. Like a slack variable, a surplus variable has no effect on the objective function in terms of increasing or decreasing cost. For example, a surplus of 24 lbs. of nitrogen does not contribute to the cost of the objective function, since the cost is determined solely by the number of bags of fertilizer purchased (i.e., the values of $x_1$ and $x_2$). As such, a coefficient of 0 is assigned to each surplus variable in the objective function.

*The effect of artificial variables on the objective function*

By assigning a "cost" of \$0 to each surplus variable, we are not prohibiting it from being in the final optimal solution. It would be quite realistic to have a final solution that showed some surplus nitrogen or phosphate. Likewise, if a cost of \$0 was assigned to an artificial variable in the objective function, it would not be prohibited from being in the final optimal solution. However, what would the artificial variable mean in the solution? The answer is that it would mean nothing and, thus, render the final solution meaningless. The artificial variable was inserted to help the simplex method work, but it has no real meaning. Therefore, we must insure that an artificial variable is *not* in the final solution so that the solution will have meaning.

As previously noted, the presence of a particular variable in the final solution is based on its relative profit or cost. For example, if the cost of a bag of Super-gro was $600 instead of $6 and Crop-quik stayed at $3, it is doubtful that the farmer would purchase Super-gro (i.e., $x_1$ would not be in the solution). Thus, we see that we can prohibit a variable from being in the final solution by assigning it a very high cost. As such, to keep an artificial variable out of the optimal solution it is assigned a *large cost*. Rather than assigning a dollar cost to an artificial variable, a value of $M$, which represents a large positive cost (i.e., $1,000,000) is assigned. This results in the following objective function for our example,

$$\text{minimize } Z = 6x_1 + 3x_2 + 0S_1 + 0S_2 + MA_1 + MA_2$$

The completely transformed minimization model can now be summarized as

$$\text{minimize } Z = 6x_1 + 3x_2 + 0S_1 + 0S_2 + MA_1 + MA_2$$
$$\text{subject to}$$
$$2x_1 + 4x_2 - s_1 + A_1 = 16$$
$$4x_1 + 3x_2 - s_2 + A_2 = 24$$
$$x_1, x_2, s_1, s_2, A_1, A_2 \geq 0$$

## The Simplex Tableau

The initial simplex tableau is developed for a minimization model the same way a maximization model is developed, *except* for one small difference. Rather than computing $c_j - z_j$ in the bottom row of the tableau, $z_j - c_j$ is computed. As such, $z_j - c_j$ represents the *net per unit decrease in cost* and the largest positive value is still selected as the entering variable and pivot column. (Alternatively, the bottom row could be left as $c_j - z_j$ and the largest *negative* value would be selected as the pivot column. However, in order to maintain a consistent rule for selecting the pivot column, $z_j - c_j$ is used.)

The initial simplex tableau for this model is shown in table 5.1. Notice that $A_1$ and $A_2$ form the initial solution at the origin, since that was the reason for inserting them in the first place—to get a solution at the origin. This is not a basic feasible solution, since the origin is not in the feasible solution area in this problem as shown in figure 5.1. As indicated previously, it is an artificially created solution. However, the simplex process will move toward feasibility in subsequent tableaus. Also note that the variables are listed across the top in the order of decision variable first, then surplus variables, and finally artificial variables.

**Table 5.1** The Initial Simplex Tableau

| $c_j$ | | | 6 | 3 | 0 | 0 | M | M |
|---|---|---|---|---|---|---|---|---|
| | basic variables | quantity | $x_1$ | $x_2$ | $s_1$ | $s_2$ | $A_1$ | $A_2$ |
| M | $A_1$ | 16 | 2 | 4 | −1 | 0 | 1 | 0 |
| M | $A_2$ | 24 | 4 | 3 | 0 | −1 | 0 | 1 |
| | $z_j$ | 40M | 6M | 7M | −M | −M | M | M |
| | $z_j - c_j$ | | 6M−6 | 7M−3 | −M | −M | 0 | 0 |

In table 5.1 the pivot column was selected as the $x_2$ column because $7M-3$ is the largest positive value in the $z_j - c_j$ row. $A_1$ was selected as the leaving basic variable (and pivot row), since the quotient of 4 for this row was the minimum positive row value.

*Selecting the pivot column*

*Selecting the pivot row*

The second simplex tableau is developed using the same simplex formulas presented in chapter 4. The second simplex tableau is shown in table 5.2.

**Table 5.2** The Second Simplex Tableau

| $c_j$ | | | 6 | 3 | 0 | 0 | M |
|---|---|---|---|---|---|---|---|
| | basic variables | quantity | $x_1$ | $x_2$ | $s_1$ | $s_2$ | $A_2$ |
| 3 | $x_2$ | 4 | 1/2 | 1 | −1/4 | 0 | 0 |
| M | $A_2$ | 12 | 5/2 | 0 | 3/4 | −1 | 1 |
| | $z_j$ | 12M+12 | 5M/2+3/2 | 3 | −3/4+3M/4 | −M | M |
| | $z_j - c_j$ | | 5M/2−9/2 | 0 | −3/4+3M/4 | −M | 0 |

Notice that the $A_1$ column has been eliminated in the second simplex tableau. Once an artificial variable leaves the basic feasible solution, it will never return because of its high cost, $M$. Thus, like the "booster rocket," once discarded it will not return and can be eliminated from the tableau. However, this is the *only* variable that can be treated this way.

*Eliminating artificial variables that leave the basic solution*

The third simplex tableau with $x_1$ replacing $A_2$ is shown in table 5.3. In table 5.3 both the $A_1$ and $A_2$ columns have been eliminated, since both variables have left the solution. The $x_1$ row is selected as the pivot row, since it corresponds to the minimum positive ratio of 16. In selecting the pivot row, the −4 value for the $x_2$ row was not considered because the minimum *positive* value is selected. Selecting the $x_2$ row would result in a negative quantity value for $s_1$ in the fourth tableau, which is not feasible.

**Table 5.3** The Third Simplex Tableau

| $c_j$ | | | 6 | 3 | 0 | 0 |
|---|---|---|---|---|---|---|
| | basic variables | quantity | $x_1$ | $x_2$ | $s_1$ | $s_2$ |
| 3 | $x_2$ | 8/5 | 0 | 1 | −2/5 | 1/5 |
| 6 | $x_1$ | 24/5 | 1 | 0 | 3/10 | −2/5 |
| | $z_j$ | 168/5 | 6 | 3 | 3/5 | −9/5 |
| | $z_j - c_j$ | | 0 | 0 | 3/5 | −9/5 |

The fourth simplex tableau with $s_1$ replacing $x_1$ is shown in table 5.4.

**Table 5.4** Optimal Simplex Tableau

| $c_j$ | | | 6 | 3 | 0 | 0 |
|---|---|---|---|---|---|---|
| | basic variables | quantity | $x_1$ | $x_2$ | $s_1$ | $s_2$ |
| 3 | $x_2$ | 8 | 4/3 | 1 | 0 | −1/3 |
| 0 | $s_1$ | 16 | 10/3 | 0 | 1 | −4/3 |
| | $z_j$ | 24 | 4 | 3 | 0 | −1 |
| | $z_j - c_j$ | | −2 | 0 | 0 | −1 |

Table 5.4 is the optimal simplex tableau since there are no values in the $z_j - c_j$ row that are positive. The optimal solution is

$x_1$ = 0 bags of Super-gro
$s_1$ = 16 extra lbs. of nitrogen
$x_2$ = 8 bags of Crop-quik
$s_2$ = 0 extra lbs. of phosphate
$Z$ = $24, total cost of purchasing fertilizer

*Summarizing the simplex adjustments for a minimization model*

To summarize, the adjustments necessary to apply the simplex method to a minimization problem are:

1. Transform all $\geq$ inequality constraints to equations by subtracting a surplus variable and adding an artificial variable.
2. Assign a $c_j$ value of $M$ to each artificial variable in the objective function.
3. Change the $c_j - z_j$ row to $z_j - c_j$.

## A Mixed Constraint Problem

*Linear programming models with $\leq$, $\geq$, and = constraints*

So far we have discussed maximization problems with *all $\leq$ constraints* and minimization problems with *all $\geq$ constraints*. However, we have yet to solve a problem with a mixture of "$\leq$," "$\geq$," and "=" constraints.

The Minimization Problem and
Irregular Types of Linear Programming Problems

Further, we have not yet looked at a maximization problem with a $\geq$ constraint. All of these conditions are present in the following example problem.

*A mixed constraint example*

A leather shop makes custom, hand-tooled briefcases and luggage. The shop makes \$400 in profit from each briefcase and \$200 for each piece of luggage. The shop has a contract with a store to provide exactly 30 items per month. The shop has a contract with a tannery that supplies them with at least 80 square yards of leather per month. The shop must use at least this amount, but can order more. Each briefcase requires 2 square yards of leather, while each piece of luggage requires 8 square yards of leather. (The higher profit for briefcases is a result of more hand tooling). From past months experiences the shop knows it cannot make more than twenty briefcases. The shop wants to know the number of briefcases and pieces of luggage to produce in order to maximize profit.

This problem is formulated as

maximize $Z = 400x_1 + 200x_2$
subject to
$$x_1 + x_2 = 30 \text{ contracted items}$$
$$2x_1 + 8x_2 \geq 80 \text{ square yards of leather}$$
$$x_1 \leq 20 \text{ briefcases}$$
$$x_1, x_2 \geq 0$$

where

$x_1$ = briefcases
$x_2$ = pieces of luggage

*Preparing an equality constraint for the simplex method*

The first step in the simplex method is to transform the inequalities to equations. However, the first constraint for the contracted items is already an equation, therefore, it is not necessary to add a slack variable. There can be no slack in the contract with the store, since exactly 30 items must be delivered. While this equation already appears to be in the necessary form for simplex solution, let us test it at the origin to see if it meets the starting requirements.

$$x_1 + x_2 = 30$$
$$0 + 0 = 30$$
$$0 \neq 30$$

Zero does not equal thirty, so this constraint in this form is not feasible. Recall that when a $\geq$ constraint existed it did not work at the origin either, and to make it work an artificial variable was added. The same thing can be done here.

$$x_1 + x_2 + A_1 = 30$$

Now at the origin where $x_1 = 0$ and $x_2 = 0$,

$$0 + 0 + A_1 = 30$$
$$A_1 = 30$$

Thus, any time a constraint is initially an equation an artificial variable is added. However, the artificial variable cannot be assigned a value of $M$ in the objective function of a maximization problem, as this example is. A positive $M$ value would represent a large positive *profit*. Since the objective is to maximize profit, a variable with a large profit contribution, such as \$1,000,000, would definitely end up in the final solution. We have already explained that an artificial variable has no real meaning and it is inserted into the model just to create an initial solution at the origin. Therefore, the existence of an artificial variable in the final solution would render the solution meaningless. To prohibit this occurrence, the artificial variable must be given a large *cost* contribution or $-M$.

*The effect of an artificial variable on the objective function of a maximization model*

The next constraint for leather is a $\geq$ inequality. It is converted to equation form by subtracting a surplus and adding an artificial,

$$2x_1 + 8x_2 - s_1 + A_2 = 80$$

Like the equality constraint, the artificial variable in this constraint must be assigned an objective function coefficient of $-M$.

The final constraint is a $\leq$ inequality and is transformed by adding a slack,

$$x_1 + s_2 = 20$$

*The mixed constraint model in proper form for simplex solution*

The completely transformed linear programming problem can now be summarized as

maximize $Z = 400x_1 + 200x_2 + 0S_1 + 0S_2 - MA_1 - MA_2$
subject to

$$x_1 + x_2 + A_1 = 30$$
$$2x_1 + 8x_2 - s_1 + A_2 = 80$$
$$x_1 + s_2 = 20$$
$$x_1, x_2, s_1, s_2, A_1, A_2 \geq 0$$

The initial simplex tableau for this model is shown in table 5.5.

**Table 5.5** The Initial Simplex Tableau

| $c_j$ | | | 400 | 200 | 0 | 0 | $-M$ | $-M$ |
|---|---|---|---|---|---|---|---|---|
| | basic variables | quantity | $x_1$ | $x_2$ | $s_1$ | $s_2$ | $A_1$ | $A_2$ |
| $-M$ | $A_1$ | 30 | 1 | 1 | 0 | 0 | 1 | 0 |
| $-M$ | $A_2$ | 80 | 2 | 8 | $-1$ | 0 | 0 | 1 |
| 0 | $s_2$ | 20 | 1 | 0 | 0 | 1 | 0 | 0 |
| | $z_j$ | $-110M$ | $-3M$ | $-9M$ | $M$ | 0 | $-M$ | $-M$ |
| | $c_j - z_j$ | | $400+3M$ | $200+9M$ | $-M$ | 0 | 0 | 0 |

*The basic variables for a mixed constraint model*

Notice in table 5.5 that the basic solution variables are a mix of artificial and slack variables. Another item to note that has not been previously encountered is that the third row quotient for determining the pivot row $(20 \div 0)$ equals an undefined value, or $\infty$. As such, this row would never be considered as a candidate for the pivot row.

The second, third, and optimal tableaus for this problem are shown in tables 5.6, 5.7, and 5.8.

**Table 5.6** The Second Simplex Tableau

| $c_j$ | | | 400 | 200 | 0 | 0 | $-M$ |
|---|---|---|---|---|---|---|---|
| | basic variables | quantity | $x_1$ | $x_2$ | $s_1$ | $s_2$ | $A_1$ |
| $-M$ | $A_1$ | 20 | 3/4 | 0 | 1/8 | 0 | 1 |
| 200 | $x_2$ | 10 | 1/4 | 1 | $-1/8$ | 0 | 0 |
| 0 | $s_2$ | 20 | 1 | 0 | 0 | 1 | 0 |
| | $z_j$ | $2,000-20M$ | $50-3M/4$ | 200 | $-25-M/8$ | 0 | $-M$ |
| | $c_j - z_j$ | | $350+3M/4$ | 0 | $25+M/8$ | 0 | 0 |

**Table 5.7** The Third Simplex Tableau

| $c_j$ | | | 400 | 200 | 0 | 0 | $-M$ |
|---|---|---|---|---|---|---|---|
| | basic variables | quantity | $x_1$ | $x_2$ | $s_1$ | $s_2$ | $A_1$ |
| $-M$ | $A_1$ | 5 | 0 | 0 | 1/8 | $-3/4$ | 1 |
| 200 | $x_2$ | 5 | 0 | 1 | $-1/8$ | $-1/4$ | 0 |
| 400 | $x_1$ | 20 | 1 | 0 | 0 | 1 | 0 |
| | $z_j$ | $9,000-5M$ | 400 | 200 | $-25-M/8$ | $350+3M/4$ | $-M$ |
| | $c_j - z_j$ | | 0 | 0 | $25+M/8$ | $-350-3M/4$ | 0 |

**Table 5.8** Optimal Simplex Tableau

| $c_j$ | | | 400 | 200 | 0 | 0 |
|---|---|---|---|---|---|---|
| | basic variables | quantity | $x_1$ | $x_2$ | $s_1$ | $s_2$ |
| 0 | $s_1$ | 40 | 0 | 0 | 1 | $-6$ |
| 200 | $x_2$ | 10 | 0 | 1 | 0 | $-1$ |
| 400 | $x_1$ | 20 | 1 | 0 | 0 | 1 |
| | $z_j$ | 10,000 | 400 | 200 | 0 | 200 |
| | $c_j - z_j$ | | 0 | 0 | 0 | $-200$ |

The solution for the leather shop problem is

$x_1 = 20$ briefcases
$x_2 = 10$ pieces of luggage
$s_1 = 40$ extra square yards of leather
$Z = \$10,000$ profit per month

*Rules for preparing*
*≤, =, and ≥*
*constraints for the*
*simplex method*

It is now possible to summarize a set of rules for transforming all three types of model constraints.

| Constraint | Adjustment | Objective Function Coefficient | |
|---|---|---|---|
| | | Maximization | Minimization |
| ≤ | Add a slack variable | 0 | 0 |
| = | Add an artificial variable | $-M$ | $M$ |
| ≥ | Subtract a surplus variable | 0 | 0 |
| | and add an artificial variable | $-M$ | $M$ |

## Irregular Types of Linear Programming Problems

*Linear programming*
*models for which the*
*general rules do not*
*always apply*

The basic form of a typical maximization problem and a typical minimization problem have been shown in chapter 4 and in this chapter. However, there are several special types of linear programming problems that are atypical. Although these special cases do not occur frequently, they still need to be described so that they can be recognized when confronted. These special types include problems with more than one optimal solution, infeasible problems, problems with an unbounded solution, problems with ties for the pivot column and/or ties for the pivot row, and problems with constraints with negative quantity values.

### Multiple Optimal Solutions

*Models with more*
*than one unique best*
*solution*

Consider the Colonial Pottery Company example with the objective function changed from $Z = 4x_1 + 5x_2$ to $Z = 4x_1 + 3x_2$:

maximize $Z = 4x_1 + 3x_2$
subject to
$$x_1 + 2x_2 \leq 40 \text{ hours of labor}$$
$$4x_1 + 3x_2 \leq 120 \text{ pounds of clay}$$
$$x_1, x_2 \geq 0$$

where

$x_1 = $ bowls produced
$x_2 = $ mugs produced

*An objective function*
*parallel to a*
*constraint line*

The graph of this model is shown in figure 5.2. By changing the objective function slightly, it is now *parallel* to the constraint line, $4x_1 + 3x_2 = 120$. This is because both lines now have the same *slope* of $-4/3$. As a result, as the objective function edge moves outward from the origin, it will touch the whole line segment *BC* before it moves out of the feasible solution area, rather than touching a single extreme corner point.

**Figure 5.2** Graph of the Colonial Pottery Company example with multiple optimal solutions.

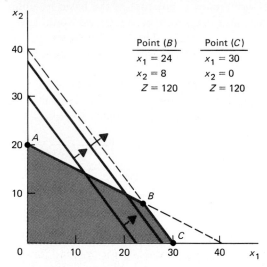

| Point (B) | Point (C) |
|-----------|-----------|
| $x_1 = 24$ | $x_1 = 30$ |
| $x_2 = 8$ | $x_2 = 0$ |
| $Z = 120$ | $Z = 120$ |

This means that every point along this line segment is optimal (i.e., each point results in the same profit of $Z = \$120$). However, the end points of this line segment, B and C, are typically referred to as the *alternate optimal solutions* with the understanding that these points represent the end points of a range of optimal solutions.

*The alternate optimal solution*

To the pottery company this means that it has several options for its decision regarding the number of bowls and mugs to produce. This gives the company greater flexibility in its decision making.

The optimal simplex tableau for this problem is shown in table 5.9.

**Table 5.9** Optimal Simplex Tableau

| $c_j$ | | | 4 | 3 | 0 | 0 |
|---|---|---|---|---|---|---|
| | basic variables | quantity | $x_1$ | $x_2$ | $s_1$ | $s_2$ |
| 0 | $s_1$ | 10 | 0 | 5/4 | 1 | −1/4 |
| 4 | $x_1$ | 30 | 1 | 3/4 | 0 | 1/4 |
| | $z_j$ | 120 | 4 | 3 | 0 | 1 |
| | $c_j - z_j$ | | 0 | 0 | 0 | −1 |

Table 5.9 corresponds to point C in figure 5.2. The fact that this problem contains multiple optimal solutions can be determined from the $c_j - z_j$ row. Recall that the $c_j - z_j$ row values are the net increases in profit per unit for the variable in that column. Thus, $c_j - z_j$ values of zero indicate no net increase in profit *and* no net loss in profit. We would expect

*Using the $c_j - z_j$ (or $z_j - c_j$) row to recognize the existence of multiple optimal solutions*

the basic variables, $s_1$ and $x_1$, to have zero $c_j - z_j$ values because they are already in the solution so they cannot be entered again. However, the $x_2$ column has a $c_j - z_j$ value of zero and it is not part of the basic feasible solution. This means that if some mugs ($x_2$) were produced, we would have a new product mix but the same total profit. Thus, a multiple optimal solution is indicated by a $c_j - z_j$ (or $z_j - c_j$) row value of zero for a nonbasic variable.

*Determining the alternate solution*

To determine the alternate end point solution let $x_2$ be the entering variable (pivot column) and select the pivot row as usual. This results in the $s_1$ row being the pivot row. The alternate solution that corresponds to point $B$ in figure 5.2 is shown in table 5.10.

**Table 5.10** The Alternative Optimal Tableau

| $c_j$ | | | 4 | 3 | 0 | 0 |
|---|---|---|---|---|---|---|
| | basic variables | quantity | $x_1$ | $x_2$ | $s_1$ | $s_2$ |
| 3 | $x_2$ | 8 | 0 | 1 | 4/5 | −1/5 |
| 4 | $x_1$ | 24 | 1 | 0 | −3/5 | 2/5 |
| | $z_j$ | 120 | 4 | 3 | 0 | 1 |
| | $c_j - z_j$ | | 0 | 0 | 0 | −1 |

*Multiple optimal solutions provide greater flexibility to the decision maker*

In certain instances the existence of multiple optimal solutions can benefit the decision maker, since the number of decision options is enlarged. Choosing among the multiple optimal solutions (along the line segment $BC$ in fig. 5.2) allows the decision maker greater flexibility. For example, in the case of the Colonial Pottery Company, it may be easier to sell bowls than mugs, thus the solution shown in table 5.9 (where only bowls are produced) would be more desirable than the solution shown in table 5.10 (where a mix of bowls and mugs is produced).

## An Infeasible Problem

*Problems with no solution*

In some cases a linear programming problem has no feasible solution area, thus there is no basic feasible solution to the problem. An example of an infeasible problem is formulated below and depicted graphically in figure 5.3.

$$\text{maximize } Z = 5x_1 + 3x_2$$
subject to
$$4x_1 + 2x_2 \leq 8$$
$$x_1 \geq 4$$
$$x_2 \geq 6$$
$$x_1, x_2 \geq 0$$

The Minimization Problem and
Irregular Types of Linear Programming Problems

**Figure 5.3** Graph of an infeasible problem.

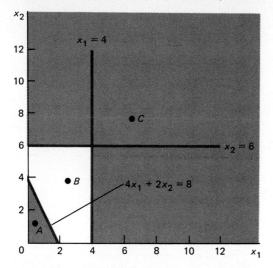

Point $A$ in figure 5.3 satisfies only the constraint $4x_1 + 2x_2 \leq 8$, while point $C$ satisfies only the constraints $x_1 \geq 4$ and $x_2 \geq 6$. Point $B$ satisfies none of the constraints. The three constraints do not overlap to form a feasible solution area. As such, there is no point that satisfies all three constraints simultaneously, and, thus, there is no solution to the problem.

*No feasible solution area*

The final simplex tableau for this problem is shown in table 5.11.

**Table 5.11** Final Simplex Tableau for an Infeasible Problem

| $c_j$ | | | 5 | 3 | 0 | 0 | 0 | $-M$ | $-M$ |
|---|---|---|---|---|---|---|---|---|---|
| | basic variables | quantity | $x_1$ | $x_2$ | $s_1$ | $s_2$ | $s_3$ | $A_1$ | $A_2$ |
| 3 $x_2$ | | 4 | 2 | 1 | 1/2 | 0 | 0 | 0 | 0 |
| $-M$ $A_1$ | | 4 | 1 | 0 | 0 | $-1$ | 0 | 1 | 0 |
| $-M$ $A_2$ | | 2 | $-2$ | 0 | $-1/2$ | 0 | $-1$ | 0 | 1 |
| $z_j$ | | $12-6M$ | $6+M$ | 3 | $3/2+M/2$ | $M$ | $M$ | $-M$ | $-M$ |
| $c_j - z_j$ | | | $-1-M$ | 0 | $-3/2-M/2$ | $-M$ | $-M$ | 0 | 0 |

The tableau in table 5.11 has all zero or negative values in the $c_j - z_j$ row indicating it is optimal. However, the solution is $x_2 = 4$, $A_1 = 4$, and $A_2 = 2$. The existence of artificial variables in the final solution is meaningless, and as a result there is no real solution. In general, any time the $c_j - z_j$ (or $z_j - c_j$) row indicates the solution is optimal yet there are artificial variables in the solution, the solution is infeasible. Infeasible problems do not typically occur, but are usually a result of erroneously defining the problem or formulating the linear programming model.

*Recognizing an infeasible problem in the simplex tableau*

## An Unbounded Problem

*Problems where the objective function increases indefinitely*

In some problems the feasible solution area formed by the model constraints is not a closed boundary. In these cases it is possible for the objective function to increase indefinitely without ever reaching a maximum value, since it never reaches the boundary of the feasible solution area.

An example of this type of problem is formulated below and shown graphically in figure 5.4.

maximize $Z = 4x_1 + 2x_2$
subject to
$$x_1 \geq 4$$
$$x_2 \leq 2$$
$$x_1, x_2 \geq 0$$

*A solution space that is not completely closed in*

In figure 5.4 the objective function is shown to increase without bound, thus a solution is never reached.

**Figure 5.4** An unbounded problem.

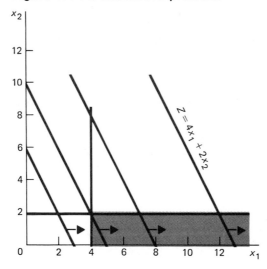

*Identifying an unbounded solution in the simplex tableau*

The second tableau for this problem is shown in table 5.12. In the simplex tableau in table 5.12, $s_1$ is chosen as the entering nonbasic variable and pivot column. However, there is no pivot row or leaving basic variable. One row value is $-4$ and the other undefined. This indicates that there is no "most constrained" point and that the solution is unbounded.

The Minimization Problem and
Irregular Types of Linear Programming Problems

**Table 5.12** The Second Simplex Tableau

| $c_j$ | | | 4 | 2 | 0 | 0 | |
|---|---|---|---|---|---|---|---|
| | basic variables | quantity | $x_1$ | $x_2$ | $s_1$ | $s_2$ | |
| 4 | $x_1$ | 4 | 1 | 0 | -1 | 0 | $4 \div -1 = -4$ |
| 0 | $s_2$ | 2 | 0 | 1 | 0 | 1 | $2 \div 0 = \infty$ |
| | $z_j$ | 16 | 4 | 0 | -4 | 0 | |
| | $c_j - z_j$ | | 0 | 2 | 4 | 0 | |

Since unlimited profits do not occur realistically, an unbounded problem typically is a result of an erroneously defined problem or erroneously formulated model.

## Ties for Pivot Column and Pivot Row

Sometimes when selecting the pivot column, it may occur that there are tied greatest positive $c_j - z_j$ (or $z_j - c_j$) row values, thus creating a tie for the pivot column. When this happens, one of the two tied columns should be selected arbitrarily. It may result that one choice will require less subsequent iterations than the other, but there is no way of knowing beforehand.

*A tie for the entering nonbasic variable*

It can also occur that a tie results for the pivot row—two rows have the lowest positive value. Like a tie for a pivot column, the tie for a pivot row should be broken arbitrarily. However, after the tie is broken, the basic variable that was the *other* tied choice for the leaving basic variable will have a "quantity" value of zero in the next tableau. This condition is often referred to as *degeneracy,* because theoretically it can occur that the subsequent simplex tableau solutions will degenerate into a condition where the objective function value never improves and optimality never results. However, this occurrence is very rare.

*A tie for the leaving basic variable*

*Degeneracy*

In general, tableaus with ties for the pivot row should be treated normally with the simplex steps carried out as usual and the solution will evolve normally.

## Negative Quantity Values

Occasionally a model constraint may be formulated with a negative quantity value on the right side of the inequality sign. The following constraint is an example.

*A negative value on the right-hand side of a model constraint*

$$-6x_1 + 2x_2 \geq -30$$

*Converting a negative*
*quantity value to a*
*positive value*

This condition is improper for the simplex method, as it requires that all quantity values be positive or zero. This difficulty can be alleviated by multiplying the inequality by $-1$, which also changes the direction of the inequality. For example,

$$(-1)(-6x_1 + 2x_2 \geq -30)$$
$$6x_1 - 2x_2 \leq 30$$

Now the model constraint is in proper form for transformation to an equation and the simplex method.

## Summary

In this chapter variations from the general simplex method described in chapter 4 were presented. These variations included a minimization problem, a mixed constraint problem, problems with multiple optimum solutions, problems with no feasible solution, unbounded problems, tied pivot columns and pivot rows, and negative constraint quantities.

The discussion of these exceptional cases of linear programming problems completes the presentation of the simplex method. Over the course of these last four chapters we have learned how to formulate the model, analyze the model graphically, and solve the model regardless of any special conditions. The next chapter will focus on several ways to analyze the final simplex solution, known as the theory of *duality* and *sensitivity analysis*.

## References

Dantzig, G. B. *Linear Programming and Extensions*. Princeton, N.J.: Princeton University, 1963.

Gass, S. *Linear Programming*. 4th ed. New York: McGraw-Hill, 1975.

Gottfried, B. S., and Weisman, J. *Introduction to Optimization Theory*. Englewood Cliffs, N.J.: Prentice-Hall, 1973.

Hadley, G. *Linear Programming*. Reading, Mass.: Addison-Wesley, 1962.

Hillier, F. S., and Lieberman, G. J. *Operations Research*. 3rd ed. San Francisco: Holden-Day, 1980.

Kim, C. *Introduction to Linear Programming*. New York: Holt, Rinehart and Winston, 1971.

Lee, Sang M.; Moore, Laurence J.; and Taylor, Bernard W. *Management Science*. Dubuque, Iowa: Wm. C. Brown Company Publishers, 1981.

Moskowitz, H., and Wright, G. P. *Operations Research Techniques for Management*. Englewood Cliffs, N.J.: Prentice-Hall, 1979.

Rothenberg, R. I. *Linear Programming*. New York: Elsevier North-Holland, 1979.

Wagner, H. M. *Principles of Operations Research*. Englewood Cliffs, N.J.: Prentice-Hall, 1969.

## Problems

1. A livestock feed is produced from soybeans and corn, each of which provide protein. The following linear programming model has been developed to determine how many pounds of soybeans and corn ($x_1$ and $x_2$) should be in the feed mix in order to provide a minimum protein requirement while minimizing cost.

minimize $Z = 10x_1 + 20x_2$ (cost, $)
subject to
$$2x_1 + 6x_2 \geq 18 \text{ (protein, grams)}$$
$$x_1, x_2 \geq 0$$

(a) Solve this model graphically.
(b) Solve this model using the simplex method.

2. Given the following simplex tableau for a linear programming model:

| $c_j$ | basic variables | quantity | 6 $x_1$ | 20 $x_2$ | 12 $x_3$ | 0 $s_1$ | 0 $s_2$ |
|---|---|---|---|---|---|---|---|
| 6 | $x_1$ | 20 | 1 | 1 | 0 | 0 | 0 |
| 12 | $x_3$ | 10 | 0 | 1/3 | 1 | 0 | −1/6 |
| 0 | $s_1$ | 10 | 0 | 1/3 | 0 | 1 | −1/6 |
| | $z_j$ | 240 | 6 | 10 | 12 | 0 | −2 |
| | $z_j - c_j$ | | 0 | −10 | 0 | 0 | −2 |

(a) Is this a maximization or minimization problem? Why?
(b) What is the solution given in this tableau?
(c) Is the solution given in this tableau optimal? Why?
(d) Write out the original objective function for the linear programming model using only decision variables.
(e) How many constraints are in the linear programming model?
(f) Were any of the constraints originally equations? Why?
(g) What does $x_2$ equal in this tableau?

3. In chapter 3, the following problem (3) was presented to be solved graphically. The Munchies Cereal Company makes a brand of cereal from (among other things) oats and rice. These two ingredients provide the cereal with vitamins A and B. The company has developed the following linear programming model to determine how many ounces of oats ($x_1$) and rice ($x_2$) should be in the cereal in order to meet minimum daily requirements of vitamins A and B at the minimum cost.

minimize $Z = .05x_1 + .03x_2$ (cost, \$)

subject to

$$8x_1 + 6x_2 \geq 48 \text{ (vitamin A, mg.)}$$
$$x_1 + 2x_2 \geq 12 \text{ (vitamin B, mg.)}$$
$$x_1, x_2 \geq 0$$

Solve this model using the simplex method.

4. In chapter 3, the following problem (4) was presented to be solved graphically. The Kalo Fertilizer Company makes a fertilizer using two chemical ingredients (1 and 2), which provide nitrogen, phosphate, and potassium. The following linear programming model has been developed to determine the number of pounds of each ingredient ($x_1$ and $x_2$) to put into a bag of fertilizer in order to meet minimum requirements of nitrogen, phosphate, and potassium at the minimum total cost.

minimize $Z = 3x_1 + 5x_2$ (cost, \$)

subject to

$$10x_1 + 2x_2 \geq 20 \text{ (nitrogen, oz.)}$$
$$6x_1 + 6x_2 \geq 36 \text{ (phosphate, oz.)}$$
$$x_2 \geq 2 \text{ (potassium, oz.)}$$
$$x_1, x_2 \geq 0$$

Solve this model using the simplex method.

5. In chapter 3, the following problem (20) was presented to be solved graphically.

minimize $Z = .06x_1 + .10x_2$

subject to

$$4x_1 + 3x_2 \geq 12$$
$$3x_1 + 6x_2 \geq 12$$
$$5x_1 + 2x_2 \geq 10$$
$$x_1, x_2 \geq 0$$

Solve this model using the simplex method.

6. In chapter 3, the following problem (21) was presented to be solved graphically. The Copperfield Mining Company owns two mines (1 and 2), which produce 3 grades of ore—high, medium, and low. The company has a contract to supply a smelting company with 12 tons of high-grade ore, 8 tons of medium-grade ore, and 24 tons of low-grade ore. The company has developed the following linear programming model to determine the number of hours to run each mine ($x_1$ and $x_2$) in order to meet their contractual obligations at the minimum cost.

minimize $Z = 200x_1 + 160x_2$ (cost, $) 
subject to
$$6x_1 + 2x_2 \geq 12 \text{ (high-grade ore, tons)}$$
$$2x_1 + 2x_2 \geq 8 \text{ (medium-grade ore, tons)}$$
$$4x_1 + 12x_2 \geq 24 \text{ (low-grade ore, tons)}$$
$$x_1, x_2 \geq 0$$

Solve this model using the simplex method.

7. A marketing firm has contracted to do a survey on a political issue for a Spokane television station. The firm conducts interviews during the day and at night, and by telephone and in person. Each hour an interviewer works (at each type of interview) results in an average number of interviews. The firm has determined that there must be at least 400 day interviews, 100 personal interviews, and 1,200 interviews overall in order to have a representative survey. The company has developed the following linear programming model to determine the number of hours for telephone interviews during the day ($x_1$), telephone interviews at night ($x_2$), personal interviews during the day ($x_3$), and personal interviews at night ($x_4$) to conduct in order to minimize cost.

minimize $Z = 2x_1 + 3x_2 + 5x_3 + 7x_4$ (cost, $) 
subject to
$$10x_1 + 4x_3 \geq 400 \text{ (day interviews)}$$
$$4x_3 + 5x_4 \geq 100 \text{ (personal interview)}$$
$$x_1 + x_2 + x_3 + x_4 \geq 1,200 \text{ (total interviews)}$$
$$x_1, x_2, x_3, x_4 \geq 0$$

Solve this model using the simplex method.

8. A wood products firm in Oregon plants three types of trees to produce pulp for paper products and wood for lumber—white pines, spruce, and ponderosa pines. The company wants to plant enough acres of each type of tree to produce at least 27 tons of pulp and 30 tons of lumber. The company had developed the following linear programming model to determine the number of acres of white pines ($x_1$), spruce ($x_2$), and ponderosa pines ($x_3$) to plant in order to minimize cost.

minimize $Z = 120x_1 + 40x_2 + 240x_3$ (cost, $) 
subject to
$$4x_1 + x_2 + 3x_3 \geq 27 \text{ (pulp, tons)}$$
$$2x_1 + 6x_2 + 3x_3 \geq 30 \text{ (lumber, tons)}$$
$$x_1, x_2, x_3 \geq 0$$

Solve this model using the simplex method.

9. A baby products firm produces a strained baby food that includes liver and milk, which provide the baby food with protein and iron. Each jar of baby food must have 36 milligrams of protein and 50 milligrams of iron. The company has developed the following linear programming model to determine the number of ounces of liver ($x_1$) and milk ($x_2$) to include in each jar of baby food in order to meet the protein and iron requirements at the minimum cost.

minimize $Z = .05x_1 + .10x_2$ (cost, $)
subject to
$$6x_1 + 2x_2 \geq 36 \text{ (protein, mg.)}$$
$$5x_1 + 5x_2 \geq 50 \text{ (iron, mg.)}$$
$$x_1, x_2 \geq 0$$

Solve this model using the simplex method.

10. Given the following linear programming model:

minimize $Z = 8x_1 + 10x_2 + 4x_3$
subject to
$$x_1 + x_2 + x_3 \geq 40$$
$$2x_1 + 6x_2 \geq 60$$
$$x_3 \geq 100$$
$$x_1, x_2, x_3 \geq 0$$

Solve using the simplex method.

11. Given the following linear programming model:

minimize $Z = 4x_1 + 6x_2$
subject to
$$x_1 + x_2 \geq 8$$
$$2x_1 + x_2 \geq 12$$
$$x_1, x_2 \geq 0$$

Solve using the simplex method.

12. Given the following linear programming model:

minimize $Z = 20x_1 + 16x_2$
subject to
$$3x_1 + x_2 \geq 6$$
$$x_1 + x_2 \geq 4$$
$$2x_1 + 6x_2 \geq 12$$
$$x_1, x_2 \geq 0$$

Solve using the simplex method.

The Minimization Problem and
Irregular Types of Linear Programming Problems

13. A manufacturing firm produces two products (1 and 2) from labor and material. The company presently has a contract to produce 5 of product 1 and 12 of product 2. The company has developed the following linear programming model to determine the number of units of product 1 $(x_1)$ and product 2 $(x_2)$ to produce in order to maximize profit.

maximize $Z = 40x_1 + 60x_2$ (profit, $)
subject to
$$x_1 + 2x_2 \leq 30 \text{ (material, lbs.)}$$
$$4x_1 + 4x_2 \leq 72 \text{ (labor, hrs.)}$$
$$x_1 \geq 5 \text{ (contract, product 1)}$$
$$x_2 \geq 12 \text{ (contract, product 2)}$$
$$x_1, x_2 \geq 0$$

Solve this model using the simplex method.

14. A custom tailor makes pants and jackets from imported Irish wool. In order for the customer to get the wool, at least 25 square feet must be purchased each week. Each pair of pants and each jacket requires 5 square feet of material. The tailor has 16 hours available each week to make pants and jackets. The demand for pants is never more than 5 pairs per week. The tailor has developed the following linear programming model to determine the number of pants $(x_1)$ and jackets $(x_2)$ to make each week in order to maximize profit.

maximize $Z = x_1 + 5x_2$ (profit, $100s)
subject to
$$5x_1 + 5x_2 \geq 25 \text{ (wool, ft.}^2)$$
$$2x_1 + 4x_2 \leq 16 \text{ (labor, hrs.)}$$
$$x_1 \leq 5 \text{ (demand, pants)}$$
$$x_1, x_2 \geq 0$$

Solve this model using the simplex method.

15. A sawmill in Tennessee produces wood for a large furniture manufacturer from cherry and oak. Each month the sawmill must deliver at least 5 tons of wood to the manufacturer. It takes the sawmill 3 days to produce a ton of cherry and 2 days to produce a ton of oak, and the sawmill can allocate 18 days out of a month for this contract. The sawmill can get enough cherry to make 4 tons of wood and enough oak to make 7 tons of wood. The sawmill owner has developed the following linear programming model to determine the number of tons of cherry $(x_1)$ and oak $(x_2)$ to produce in order to minimize cost.

minimize $Z = 3x_1 + 6x_2$ (cost, \$)
subject to

$$3x_1 + 2x_2 \leq 18 \text{ (production time, days)}$$
$$x_1 + x_2 \geq 5 \text{ (contract, tons)}$$
$$x_1 \leq 4 \text{ (cherry, tons)}$$
$$x_2 \leq 7 \text{ (oak, tons)}$$
$$x_1, x_2 \geq 0$$

Solve this model using the simplex method.

16. Given the following linear programming model:

maximize $Z = 4x_1 + 5x_2$
subject to

$$2x_1 + 2x_2 \geq 8$$
$$x_2 = 3$$
$$9x_1 + 3x_2 \leq 27$$
$$x_1, x_2 \geq 0$$

Solve using the simplex method.

17. Given the following linear programming model:

maximize $Z = 10x_1 + 5x_2$
subject to

$$2x_1 + x_2 \geq 10$$
$$x_2 = 4$$
$$x_1 + 4x_2 \leq 20$$
$$x_1, x_2 \geq 0$$

Solve using the simplex method.

18. Given the following linear programming model:

minimize $Z = 4x_1 + 3x_2$
subject to

$$2x_1 + x_2 \geq 10$$
$$-3x_1 + 2x_2 \leq 6$$
$$x_1 + x_2 \geq 6$$
$$x_1, x_2 \geq 0$$

Solve using the simplex method.

19. Given the following linear programming model:

maximize $Z = 10x_1 + 5x_2$
subject to

$$3x_1 + 9x_2 \geq 27$$
$$8x_1 + 6x_2 \geq 48$$
$$-4x_1 + 6x_2 \leq -12$$
$$8x_1 + 12x_2 = 24$$
$$x_1, x_2 \geq 0$$

Solve using the simplex method.

20. Given the following linear programming model:

minimize $Z = 6x_1 + 4x_2$
subject to
$$3x_1 + 2x_2 \geq 18$$
$$2x_1 + 4x_2 = 20$$
$$2x_2 \leq 8$$
$$x_1, x_2 \geq 0$$

Solve using the simplex method.

21. A farmer has a 40-acre farm in Georgia. The farmer is trying to determine how many acres of corn, peanuts, and cotton to plant. Each crop requires labor to plant, fertilizer, and insecticide. The farmer has developed the following linear programming model to determine the number of acres of corn $(x_1)$, peanuts $(x_2)$, and cotton $(x_3)$ to plant in order to maximize profit.

maximize $Z = 400x_1 + 350x_2 + 450x_3$ (profit, $)
subject to
$$2x_1 + 3x_2 + 2x_3 \leq 120 \text{ (labor, hrs.)}$$
$$4x_1 + 3x_2 + x_3 \leq 160 \text{ (fertilizer, tons)}$$
$$3x_1 + 2x_2 + 4x_3 \leq 100 \text{ (insecticide, tons)}$$
$$x_1 + x_2 + x_3 \leq 40 \text{ (acres)}$$
$$x_1, x_2, x_3 \geq 0$$

Solve this model using the simplex method.

22. Given the following linear programming model:

maximize $Z = 3x_1 + 2x_2$
subject to
$$x_1 + x_2 \leq 1$$
$$x_1 + x_2 \geq 2$$
$$x_1, x_2 \geq 0$$

(a) Solve graphically.
(b) Solve using the simplex method.

23. Given the following linear programming model:

maximize $Z = x_1 + x_2$
subject to
$$x_1 - x_2 \geq -1$$
$$-x_1 + 2x_2 \leq 4$$
$$x_1, x_2 \geq 0$$

(a) Solve graphically.
(b) Solve using the simplex method.

24. Given the following linear programming model:

maximize $Z = 7x_1 + 5x_2 + 5x_3$
subject to
$$x_1 + x_2 + x_3 \leq 25$$
$$2x_1 + x_2 + x_3 \leq 40$$
$$x_1 + x_2 \leq 25$$
$$x_3 \leq 6$$
$$x_1, x_2, x_3 \geq 0$$

Solve using the simplex method.

25. Given the following linear programming model:

minimize $Z = 15x_1 + 25x_2$
subject to
$$3x_1 + 4x_2 \geq 12$$
$$2x_1 + x_2 \geq 6$$
$$3x_1 + 2x_2 \leq 9$$
$$x_1, x_2 \geq 0$$

Solve using the simplex method.

26. Given the following linear programming model:

maximize $Z = 5x_1 + 2x_2$
subject to
$$3x_1 + 5x_2 \leq 15$$
$$10x_1 + 4x_2 \leq 20$$
$$x_1, x_2 \geq 0$$

(a) Solve graphically.
(b) Solve using the simplex method.

27. Solve problem 3 from chapter 2 using the simplex method.

28. Solve problem 4 from chapter 2 using the simplex method.

29. Solve problem 24 from chapter 2 using the simplex method.

30. Solve problem 27 from chapter 2 using the simplex method.

The Minimization Problem and
Irregular Types of Linear Programming Problems

# 6
## Postoptimality
## Analysis

## The Dual

Interpreting the Dual Model
Exceptions in Formulating the Dual
A Mixed Constraint Problem
Use of the Dual

## Sensitivity Analysis

Changes in Objective Function Coefficients
Changes in Constraint Quantity Values
Additional Model Parameter Changes

## Summary

Once the solution to a linear programming problem has been determined, there may be a tendency to stop the analysis of the model at that point. However, it is often possible that further analysis of the final optimal solution will result in more useful information than is given by the actual solution. The analysis of the optimal simplex solution in order to gather such additional information, known as *postoptimality analysis,* is the topic of this chapter.

The optimal solution of a linear programming model can be analyzed in two ways. First the *dual* of the model can be formulated and interpreted. The dual is an alternative form of the model that contains useful information regarding the value of the resources that form the constraints of the model. Second, the various numerical coefficients in the model constraints and objective function can be analyzed to see what effect any changes in them might have on the optimal solution. This is known as *sensitivity analysis.* Both topics, duality and sensitivity analysis, are similar in that they consist of an examination of the final optimal simplex solution in order to gain additional information.

## The Dual

Every linear programming model has two forms called the *primal* and the *dual.* The original form of a linear programming model is known as the primal. Thus, all the examples that have been presented in chapters 2 through 5 have been primal models. The dual is an alternative model form that is derived completely from the primal. The usefulness of the dual is that it provides the decision maker with an alternative way of looking at a problem. While the primal gives solution results in terms of the amount of profit gained from producing products, the dual provides information on the *value* of the constrained resources in achieving that profit.

In order to demonstrate how the dual form of a model is derived and what it means, the following example will be employed. The Hickory Furniture Company produces tables and chairs on a daily basis. Each table produced results in $160 in profit, while each chair results in $200 in profit. The production of tables and chairs is dependent upon the availability of limited resources—labor, wood, and storage space. The resource requirements for the production of tables and chairs and the total resources available are as follows.

| | Resource Requirements | | |
|---|---|---|---|
| Resource | Table | Chair | Total Available/Day |
| Labor | 2 hours | 4 hours | 40 hours |
| Wood | 18 pounds | 18 pounds | 216 pounds |
| Storage | 24 ft.$^2$ | 12 ft.$^2$ | 240 ft.$^2$ |

*The primal form of a model*

The company wants to know the number of tables and chairs to produce per day in order to maximize profit. The model for this problem is formulated as

maximize $Z = \$160x_1 + 200x_2$
subject to
$$2x_1 + 4x_2 \leq 40 \text{ hours of labor}$$
$$18x_1 + 18x_2 \leq 216 \text{ pounds of wood}$$
$$24x_1 + 12x_2 \leq 240 \text{ ft.}^2 \text{ of storage space}$$
$$x_1, x_2 \geq 0$$
where
$x_1$ = number of tables produced
$x_2$ = number of chairs produced

*The dual form of a model*

This model represents the primal form. For a primal maximization model, the dual form is a minimization model. The dual form of this example model is

minimize $Z = 40y_1 + 216y_2 + 240y_3$
subject to
$$2y_1 + 18y_2 + 24y_3 \geq 160$$
$$4y_1 + 18y_2 + 12y_3 \geq 200$$
$$y_1, y_2, y_3 \geq 0$$

The specific relationships between the primal and dual demonstrated in this example are:

*Relationships between the primal and dual*

1. The dual variables, $y_1$, $y_2$, and $y_3$, correspond to the model constraints in the primal. For every constraint in the primal there will be a variable in the dual. For example, in the primal there are *three constraints,* thus in the dual there are *three decision variables.*

2. The quantity values on the right-hand side of the primal inequality constraints are the objective function coefficients in the dual. The constraint quantity values, 40, 216, and 240 in the primal, form the dual objective function: $Z = 40y_1 + 216y_2 + 240y_3$.

3. Each set of model constraint coefficients in the primal are the decision variable coefficients in the dual. For example, the labor constraint in the primal has the coefficients of 2 and 4. These values are the $y_1$ variable coefficients in the model constraints of the dual: $2y_1$ and $4y_1$.

4. The objective function coefficients, 160 and 200 in the primal, represent the model constraint requirements (quantity values on the right-hand side of the constraint) in the dual.

5. While the maximization primal model has $\leq$ constraints, the minimization dual model has $\geq$ constraints.

The primal-dual relationships can be observed by comparing the two model forms as follows.

*Comparing the primal and dual models*

**Primal**

$$\max Z_p = 160x_1 + 200x_2$$

subject to

$$2x_1 + 4x_1 \leq 40$$
$$18x_1 + 18x_2 \leq 216$$
$$24x_1 + 12x_2 \leq 240$$
$$x_1, x_2 \geq 0$$

**Dual**

$$\min Z_d = 40y_1 + 216y_2 + 240y_3$$

subject to

$$2y_1 + 18y_2 + 24y_3 \geq 160$$
$$4y_1 + 18y_2 + 12y_3 \geq 200$$
$$y_1, y_2, y_3 \geq 0$$

Now that the dual form of the model has been developed, the next question is, "What does the dual mean?" In other words, it now needs to be determined what the decision variables of $y_1$, $y_2$, and $y_3$ mean, what the $\geq$ model constraints mean, and what is being minimized in the dual objective function.

## Interpreting the Dual Model

The dual model can be interpreted by observing the solution to the primal form of the model. The simplex solution to the primal model is shown in table 6.1.

**Table 6.1** The Optimal Simplex Solution for the Primal Model

| $c_j$ | | | 160 | 200 | 0 | 0 | 0 |
|---|---|---|---|---|---|---|---|
| | basic variables | quantity | $x_1$ | $x_2$ | $s_1$ | $s_2$ | $s_3$ |
| 200 | $x_2$ | 8 | 0 | 1 | 1/2 | −1/18 | 0 |
| 160 | $x_1$ | 4 | 1 | 0 | −1/2 | 1/9 | 0 |
| 0 | $s_3$ | 48 | 0 | 0 | 6 | −2 | 1 |
| | $z_j$ | 2,240 | 160 | 200 | 20 | 20/3 | 0 |
| | $c_j - z_j$ | | 0 | 0 | −20 | −20/3 | 0 |

Interpreting this primal solution,

$x_1$ = 4 tables
$x_2$ = 8 chairs
$s_3$ = 48 ft.² of storage space
$Z$ = \$2,240 profit

This optimal primal tableau also contains information about the dual. In the $c_j - z_j$ row of table 6.1, the negative values of −20 and −20/3 under the $s_1$ and $s_2$ columns indicate that if one unit of either $s_1$ or $s_2$ was

*Interpreting the meaning of $c_j - z_j$ row values for slack variables*

entered into the solution, profit would *decrease* by $20 or $6.67 (i.e., 20/3) respectively.

Recall that $s_1$ represents unused labor and $s_2$ represents unused wood. In the present solution, since $s_1$ and $s_2$ are not basic variables, then they both equal zero. This means that in the present solution all of the material and labor is being used to make tables and chairs, and there are no excess (slack) labor hours or pounds of material left over. Thus, if we enter $s_1$ or $s_2$ into the solution, then $s_1$ or $s_2$ would no longer equal zero—we would be decreasing the *use of labor or wood*. If, for example, one unit of $s_1$ is entered into the solution, then one unit of labor previously used is not being used now, *and this action will reduce profit by $20.*

Let us assume that one unit of $s_1$ has been entered into the solution so that we have one hour of unused labor ($s_1 = 1$). Now let us remove this hour of labor from the solution so that all labor is being used again. Previously it was noted that profit was decreased by $20 by entering one hour of labor, thus it can be expected that if we take this hour back (and use it again), profit will be increased by $20. This is, in effect, analogous to saying that if we could get one more hour of labor, we could increase profit by $20. Therefore, if we could purchase one hour of labor, we would be willing to pay up to $20 for it because that is the amount it would increase profit by.

*The marginal value of resources*
The negative $c_j - z_j$ row values of $20 and $6.67 are the *marginal values* of labor ($s_1$) and wood ($s_2$) respectively. These values are also often referred to as *shadow prices,* since they reflect the maximum "price" one would be willing to pay to obtain one more unit of the resource.

Continuing this analysis, the profit in the primal model was shown to be $2,240. For the furniture company, the value of the resources used to produce tables and chairs must be in terms of this profit. In other words, the value of the labor and wood resources is determined by their contribution toward gaining the $2,240 profit. Thus, if the company wanted to assign a *value* to the resources it used, it could not assign an amount greater than the profit earned by the resources. Conversely, using the same logic, the total *value* of the resources must also be at least as much as the profit they earn. Thus, the value of all of the resources must *exactly equal* the profit earned by the optimal solution.

*The value of resources equals the optimal profit*

*Determining the total value of the resources used to get the optimal solution*
This logic used to determine the *marginal value* of the resources in the model can also be used to analyze the model constraints. For example, the labor constraint is

$$2x_1 + 4x_2 \leq 40 \text{ hours of labor}$$

Recall that the solution to the primal model (from table 6.1) is

$$x_1 = 4 \text{ tables}$$
$$x_2 = 8 \text{ chairs}$$

and that the value of one hour of labor from our previous discussion is $20.

Since one table requires 2 hours of labor, an hour of labor is worth $20, and four tables were produced, we have

($20/hour) (4 tables) (2 hours/table) = $160

as the value of the labor used to *produce tables*.

Looking again at the labor constraint, we see that it requires 4 hours of labor to produce a chair. Since the value of labor is $20 per hour and 8 chairs are produced, we have

($20/hour) (8 chairs) (4 hours/chair) = $640

which is the value of the labor used to *produce chairs*.

Now adding the value of labor used to produce tables and the value of labor used to produce chairs gives us the *total value of labor:*

$160 + $640 = $800, the value of labor

The same type of analysis can be performed to determine the total *value of wood* in producing tables and chairs. Recall that the value of one pound of wood is $6.67, and that the model constraint for wood is

$18x_1 + 18x_2 \leq 216$ pounds of wood

Thus, for tables the value of wood is

($6.67/hour) (4 tables) (18 hours/table) = $480

and for chairs the value of wood is

($6.67/hour) (8 chairs) (18 hours/chair) = $960

Adding the value of wood used to produce both tables and chairs gives us the *total value of wood:*

$480 + $960 = $1,440

Now summing the total value of labor and the total value of wood,

$800 (labor) + $1,440 (wood) = $2,240

which is also the profit, $Z$, shown in the optimal solution to our example.

However, what happened to the third resource, *storage space?* All the resource value in the model appears to have been divided between labor and wood. The answer can be seen in table 6.1. Notice that the $c_j - z_j$ row value for $s_3$ (which represents unused storage space) is zero. This means that storage space has a marginal value of zero, that is, we would not be willing to pay anything for an extra foot of storage space.

*The marginal value of a resource that is not completely used*

The reason more storage space has no value is because storage space was not a limitation in the production of tables and chairs. From table 6.1 it can be seen that 48 ft.$^2$ were left unused (i.e., $s_3 = 48$) after the 4 tables and 8 chairs were produced. Since the company already has 48 square feet of storage space left over, an extra square foot would have no additional value. The company could not use all of the storage space it presently has available.

Now let us look again at the dual form of the model.

$$\text{minimize } Z_d = 40y_1 + 216y_2 + 240y_3$$

subject to

$$2y_1 + 18y_2 + 24y_3 \geq 160$$
$$4y_1 + 18y_2 + 12y_3 \geq 200$$
$$y_1, y_2, y_3 \geq 0$$

*Defining the dual variables*
Given the previous discussion on the value of the model resources, we can now define the decision variables of the dual, $y_1$, $y_2$, and $y_3$, as representing the marginal value of the resources:

$y_1 =$ marginal value of one hour of labor $= \$20.00$
$y_2 =$ marginal value of one pound of wood $= \$6.67$
$y_3 =$ marginal value of one square foot of storage space $= \$0$

*Interpreting the dual constraints*
Now we must consider the dual constraints. For example, the first dual constraint is

$$2y_1 + 18y_2 + 24y_3 \geq \$160 \text{ profit per table}$$

This constraint can be interpreted as meaning that the value of the three resources (labor, wood, and storage space) used in producing *a single table* must be at least as great as the profit obtained from the table. Substituting the values of the dual variables into this constraint,

$$2y_1 = \text{value of labor used to produce a table}$$
$$2(\$20) = \$40$$

$$18y_2 = \text{value of wood used to produce a table}$$
$$18(\$6.67) = \$120$$

$$24y_3 = \text{value of storage space used to produce a table}$$
$$24(0) = \$0$$

and, summing these individual values,

$$2y_1 + 18y_2 + 24y_3 \geq \$160$$
$$2(\$20) + 18(\$6.67) + 24(\$0) \geq \$160$$
$$\$40 + \$120 + \$0 \geq \$160$$
$$\$160 \geq \$160$$

or, $160, the value of the resources used to produce a table, is at least as great or equal to $160, the profit of a table.

The second dual constraint can be analyzed similarly,

$$4y_1 + 18y_2 + 12y_3 \geq \$200, \text{ the profit per chair}$$
$$4(\$20) + 18(\$6.67) + 12(\$0) \geq \$200$$
$$\$80 + \$120 + \$0 \geq \$200$$
$$\$200 \geq \$200$$

or, $200, the value of the resource used to produce a chair, is at least as great or equal to $200, the profit of a chair.

*The dual objective function*

This leaves only the objective function in the dual unexplained. The objective function is

$$\text{minimize } Z_d = 40y_1 + 216y_2 + 240y_3$$

Recall that the objective function coefficients are the total resource quantities available—40 hours of labor, 216 pounds of wood, and 240 square feet of storage space. Thus, if we multiply the marginal value of one unit of resource by the total amount of that resource, we have the *total value* of the resources:

$$Z_d = (40 \text{ hours})(\$20/\text{hour}) + (216 \text{ pounds})(\$6.67/\text{pound}) \\ + (240\text{ft.}^2)(\$0/\text{ft.}^2)$$
$$Z_d = \$800 + 1{,}440 + 0$$
$$Z_d = \$2{,}240, \text{ the value of the resources}$$

Recalling our previous discussion regarding the total value of the resources, $Z_d$, we noted that this value was also equal to the optimal $Z$ value in the primal. Thus,

$$Z_p = \$2{,}240 = Z_d$$

As previously explained, the value of the resources cannot exceed the profit obtained by the use of those resources. Likewise, the value of the resources must be at least as much as that profit. Therefore, the total optimal value of the resources exactly equals the total optimal profit.

The dual model has now been completely defined. Notice that the dual form of the model was developed completely from the primal model. In addition, the solution of the dual was determined completely from the primal solution. As such, in order to determine all information about the dual, it was unnecessary to perform any further simplex operations.

In general, the primal solution and dual solution have the following relationship:

| Primal | Dual |
|---|---|
| $c_j - z_j$ for slack variables, $s_i$ | values for decision variables, $y_i$ |
| $c_j - z_j$ for decision variables, $x_i$ | values for slack variables, $s_i$ |
| $Z_p$, the objective function value | $Z_d$, the objective function value |

*Primal-dual relationships*

## Exceptions in Formulating the Dual

*Formulating the dual of a minimization model*

The Hickory Furniture Company example, which was used to demonstrate how the primal is transformed into the dual, was a maximization problem with all $\leq$ constraints. Now let us consider a minimization primal with $\geq$ constraints. As an example, the fertilizer model first introduced in chapter 3 will be used. This model was formulated as

$$\text{minimize } Z = 6x_1 + 3x_2$$
subject to
$$2x_1 + 4x_2 \geq 16 \text{ pounds of nitrogen}$$
$$4x_1 + 3x_2 \geq 24 \text{ pounds of phosphate}$$
$$x_1, x_2 \geq 0$$
where

$x_1$ = number of bags of Super-gro fertilizer
$x_2$ = number of bags of Crop-quik fertilizer
$Z$ = total cost of purchasing fertilizer

*The dual model*    The dual of this model is formulated as follows.

$$\text{maximize } Z_d = 16y_1 + 24y_2$$
subject to
$$2y_1 + 4y_2 \leq 6, \text{ cost of Super-gro}$$
$$4y_1 + 3y_2 \leq 3, \text{ cost of Crop-quick}$$
$$y_1, y_2 \geq 0$$
where

$y_1$ = marginal value of nitrogen
$y_2$ = marginal value of phosphate

The decision variables in the dual reflect the value of each ingredient, nitrogen and phosphate, used in achieving the minimum cost of fertilizing. The problem specifies certain requirements for nitrogen and phosphate, and as such, these ingredients acquire a value based on the cost of meeting those requirements.

## A Mixed Constraint Problem

We have now formulated the dual for both a maximization and minimization problem; however, we have not yet considered the mixed constraint model. In order to demonstrate how a mixed constraint primal model is transformed into its dual form, the following example will be used.

$$\text{maximize } Z = 10x_1 + 6x_2$$
subject to
$$x_1 + 4x_2 \leq 40$$
$$3x_1 + 2x_2 = 60$$
$$2x_1 + x_2 \geq 25$$
$$x_1, x_2 \geq 0$$

*The standard form of*    One of the conditions necessary for transforming a primal problem
*a primal model*    into a dual is that the primal be in a *standard form*. The standard form for a maximization primal requires that all model constraints be $\leq$, and the standard form for a minimization primal requires that all model constraints be $\geq$. Thus, when a maximization model is confronted with mixed constraints like the one above, the first step is to convert all model constraints into $\leq$ form.

The first constraint,

$$x_1 + 4x_2 \leq 40$$

is already in proper form.

The second constraint, however, is an equation,

*Converting a constraint equation into standard form*

$$3x_1 + 2x_2 = 60$$

and must be converted to a $\leq$ constraint. This equation is equivalent to the following two constraints.

$$3x_1 + 2x_2 \geq 60$$
$$3x_1 + 2x_2 \leq 60$$

In other words, if the constraint values are "greater than or equal to" 60 *and* "less than or equal to" 60, then the only quantity that satisfies both constraints is *equal to* 60.

However, this does not quite complete the conversion, since a $\geq$ constraint still exists. This constraint can be converted by multiplying the constraint by $-1$.

$$(-1)(3x_1 + 2x_2 \geq 60)$$
$$-3x_1 - 2x_2 \leq -60$$

This seemingly violates the simplex restriction that all quantity values must either be zero or positive. However, the constraint is not being converted in order to solve with the simplex method, but to transform into the dual form. In the dual, the quantity (right-hand side) values of the primal forms the coefficients of the objective function and these can be negative.

The last model constraint is in $\geq$ form,

$$2x_1 + x_2 \geq 25$$

It can be converted exactly like the previous constraint, by multiplying by $-1$.

$$(-1)(2x_1 + x_2 \geq 25)$$
$$-2x_1 - x_2 \leq -25$$

The primal form of the model in standard form can now be summarized as

*The primal in standard form*

maximize $Z_P = 10x_1 + 6x_2$
subject to
$$x_1 + 4x_2 \leq 40$$
$$3x_1 + 2x_2 \leq 60$$
$$-3x_1 - 2x_2 \leq -60$$
$$-2x_1 - x_2 \leq -25$$
$$x_1, x_2 \geq 0$$

The dual form of this model is formulated as

minimize $Z_d = 40y_1 + 60y_2 - 60y_3 - 25y_4$
subject to
$$y_1 + 3y_2 - 3y_3 - 2y_4 \geq 10$$
$$4y_1 + 2y_2 - 2y_3 - y_4 \geq 6$$
$$y_1, y_2, y_3, y_4 \geq 0$$

## Use of the Dual

*Using the dual information for decision making*

The importance of the dual to the manager decision maker lies in the information it provides about the model resources. Often the manager is less concerned about profit than about the utilization of resources. This is partially because the manager often has more control over the use of resources than the accumulation of profits. As such, the dual solution informs the manager of the value of the resources, which is important in making the decision to secure more resources and the price to pay for these additional resources.

However, if more resources are secured by the manager, the next question is, "How does this affect the original solution?" The feasible solution area is determined by the values forming the model constraints, and if those values are changed, it is possible for the feasible solution area to change. The effect of changes on the solution to the model is the subject of sensitivity analysis, the next topic to be presented in this chapter.

## Sensitivity Analysis

When linear programming models were formulated in previous chapters, it was implicitly assumed that the *parameters* of the model were known with certainty. These parameters include the objective function coefficients, such as profit per table; model constraint quantity values, such as 40 available hours of labor; and constraint coefficients, such as pounds of wood per chair or pounds of clay per bowl. In all of the examples presented so far,

*Model parameters are estimates*

the models were formulated as if these parameters were known exactly or with certainty. However, rarely does a manager know all of these parameters exactly. In reality the model parameters are simply estimates (or "best guesses") and, thus, subject to change. As such, it is often of interest to the manager to see what effect a "change" in a parameter will have on the solution to the model. These changes may be either a reaction to anticipated uncertainties in the parameters or a reaction to information

*Analyzing the effect of parameter changes on the optimal solution*

gained from the dual. The analysis of parameter changes and their effect on the model solution is known as *sensitivity analysis*.

The most obvious way to ascertain the effect of a change in the parameter of a model is to make the change in the original model, *resolve* the model, and compare the solution results with the original. However, resolving a problem can be very time consuming, and, as we will demonstrate in this chapter, unnecessary. In most cases the effect of changes on the model can be determined directly from the final simplex tableau.

## Changes in Objective Function Coefficients

In order to demonstrate sensitivity analysis for the coefficients in the objective function, the Hickory Furniture Company example developed in the previous section on the dual will be used. The model for this example was formulated as

maximize $Z = 160x_1 + 200x_2$
subject to
$$2x_1 + 4x_2 \leq 40 \text{ hours of labor}$$
$$18x_1 + 18x_2 \leq 216 \text{ pounds of wood}$$
$$24x_1 + 12x_2 \leq 240 \text{ ft.}^2 \text{ of storage space}$$
$$x_1, x_2 \geq 0$$

where
$x_1$ = number of tables produced
$x_2$ = number of chairs produced

The coefficients in the objective function will be represented symbolically as $c_j$ (the same notation used in the simplex tableau). Thus, $c_1 = 160$ and $c_2 = 200$. Now, let us consider a change in one of the $c_j$ values by an amount, $\Delta$. For example, let us change $c_1 = 160$ by an amount, $\Delta = 90$. In other words, we are changing $c_1$ from \$160 to \$250. The effect of this change on the solution of this model is shown graphically in figure 6.1.

*A $\Delta$ change in an objective function coefficient*

---

**Figure 6.1** A change in $c_1$.

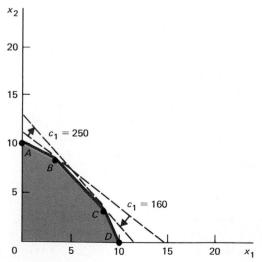

Originally the solution to this problem was located at point $B$ in figure 6.1 where $x_1 = 4$ and $x_2 = 8$. However, by increasing $c_1$ from \$160 to \$250, the slope of the objective function shifts so that point $C$ ($x_1 = 8$, $x_2 = 4$) becomes the optimal solution. This demonstrates that a change in one of the coefficients of the objective function can change the optimal solution. Therefore, when sensitivity analysis is performed, it is to determine the range over which $c_j$ can be changed while the solution remains optimal.

*Determining a range for $c_j$ over which the current solution will remain optimal*

The range of $c_j$ that will maintain the optimal solution can be determined directly from the optimal simplex tableau. The optimal simplex tableau for our furniture company example is shown in table 6.2.

### Table 6.2 Optimal Simplex Tableau

| $c_j$ | | | 160 | 200 | 0 | 0 | 0 |
|---|---|---|---|---|---|---|---|
| | basic variables | quantity | $x_1$ | $x_2$ | $s_1$ | $s_2$ | $s_3$ |
| 200 | $x_2$ | 8 | 0 | 1 | 1/2 | −1/18 | 0 |
| 160 | $x_1$ | 4 | 1 | 0 | −1/2 | 1/9 | 0 |
| 0 | $s_3$ | 48 | 0 | 0 | 6 | −2 | 1 |
| | $z_j$ | 2,240 | 160 | 200 | 20 | 20/3 | 0 |
| | $c_j − z_j$ | | 0 | 0 | −20 | −20/3 | 0 |

*$\Delta$ changes in the optimal simplex tableau*

First, consider a $\Delta$ change for $c_1$. This will change the $c_1$ value from $c_1 = 160$ to $c_1 = 160 + \Delta$, as shown in table 6.3. Notice that when $c_1$ is changed to $160 + \Delta$, it is not only included in the top $c_j$ row, but also in the left-hand $c_j$ column. This is because $x_1$ is a basic solution variable. Since $160 + \Delta$ is in the left-hand column, it becomes a multiple of the column values when computing the new $z_j$ row values and the subsequent $c_j − z_j$ row values, which are also shown in table 6.3.

### Table 6.3 Optimal Simplex Tableau with $c_1 = 160 + \Delta$

| $c_j$ | | | $160 + \Delta$ | 200 | 0 | 0 | 0 |
|---|---|---|---|---|---|---|---|
| | basic variables | quantity | $x_1$ | $x_2$ | $s_1$ | $s_2$ | $s_3$ |
| 200 | $x_2$ | 8 | 0 | 1 | 1/2 | −1/18 | 0 |
| $160 + \Delta$ | $x_1$ | 4 | 1 | 0 | −1/2 | 1/9 | 0 |
| 0 | $s_3$ | 48 | 0 | 0 | 6 | −2 | 1 |
| | $z_j$ | $2,440 + 4\Delta$ | $160 + \Delta$ | 200 | $20 − \Delta/2$ | $20/3 + \Delta/9$ | 0 |
| | $c_j − z_j$ | | 0 | 0 | $−20 + \Delta/2$ | $−20/3 − \Delta/9$ | 0 |

*Solving $\Delta$ inequalities*

The solution shown in table 6.3 will remain optimal as long as the $c_j − z_j$ row values *remain negative*. (If $c_j − z_j$ does become positive the product mix will change and if it becomes zero, there will be an alternate solution.) Thus, for the solution to remain uniquely optimal,

$$-20 + \Delta/2 < 0$$

and

$$-20/3 - \Delta/9 < 0$$

Next, both of these inequalities must be solved for $\Delta$,

$$-20 + \Delta/2 < 0$$
$$\Delta/2 < 20$$
$$\Delta < 40$$

and

$$-20/3 - \Delta/9 < 0$$
$$-\Delta/9 < 20/3$$
$$-\Delta < 60$$
$$\Delta > -60$$

Thus, $\Delta < 40$ and $\Delta > -60$. Now recall that $c_1 = 160 + \Delta$, therefore, $\Delta = c_1 - 160$. Substituting the amount $c_1 - 160$ for $\Delta$ in these inequalities,

$$\Delta < 40$$
$$c_1 - 160 < 40$$
$$c_1 < 200$$

and

$$\Delta > -60$$
$$c_1 - 160 > -60$$
$$c_1 > 100$$

Therefore, the range for $c_1$ over which the solution basis will remain optimal (although the value of the objective function may change) is

$$100 < c_1 < 200$$

*The sensitivity range for $c_1$*

Next, consider a $\Delta$ change in $c_2$ so that $c_2 = 200 + \Delta$. The effect of this change in the final simplex tableau is shown in table 6.4.

*A $\Delta$ change for $c_2$*

**Table 6.4** Optimal Simplex Tableau with $c_2 = 200 + \Delta$

| $c_j$ | | | 160 | $200 + \Delta$ | 0 | 0 | 0 |
|---|---|---|---|---|---|---|---|
| | basic variables | quantity | $x_1$ | $x_2$ | $s_1$ | $s_2$ | $s_3$ |
| $200 + \Delta$ | $x_2$ | 8 | 0 | 1 | 1/2 | $-1/18$ | 0 |
| 160 | $x_1$ | 4 | 1 | 0 | $-1/2$ | 1/9 | 0 |
| 0 | $s_3$ | 48 | 0 | 0 | 6 | $-2$ | 1 |
| | $z_j$ | $2{,}240 + 8\Delta$ | 160 | $200 + \Delta$ | $20 + \Delta/2$ | $20/3 - \Delta/18$ | 0 |
| | $c_j - z_j$ | | 0 | 0 | $-20 - \Delta/2$ | $-20/3 + \Delta/18$ | 0 |

As before, the solution shown in table 6.4 will remain optimal as long as the $c_j - z_j$ row values remain negative or zero. Thus, for the solution to remain optimal,

$$-20 - \Delta/2 < 0$$

and

$$-20/3 + \Delta/18 < 0$$

Solving these inequalities for $\Delta$,

$$\begin{aligned} -20 - \Delta/2 &< 0 \\ -\Delta/2 &< 20 \\ \Delta &> -40 \end{aligned}$$

and

$$\begin{aligned} -20/3 + \Delta/18 &< 0 \\ \Delta/18 &< 20/3 \\ \Delta &< 120 \end{aligned}$$

Thus, $\Delta > -40$ and $\Delta < 120$. Since $c_2 = 200 + \Delta$, we have $\Delta = c_2 - 200$. Substituting this value for $\Delta$ in the inequalities,

$$\begin{aligned} \Delta &> -40 \\ c_2 - 200 &> -40 \\ c_2 &> 160 \end{aligned}$$

and

$$\begin{aligned} \Delta &< 120 \\ c_2 - 200 &< 120 \\ c_2 &< 320 \end{aligned}$$

Therefore, the range for $c_2$ over which the solution will remain optimal is

$$160 < c_2 < 320$$

Summarizing the ranges for both objective function coefficients,

$$100 < c_1 < 200$$
$$160 < c_2 < 320$$

*Determining the* $c_j$
*sensitivity range for*
*a nonbasic variable*

However, these ranges reflect a possible change in either $c_1$ or $c_2$ and not simultaneous changes in both $c_1$ and $c_2$. Both of the objective function coefficients in this example were for basic solution variables. Determining the $c_j$ sensitivity range for a decision variable that is *not basic* is much simpler. Since it is not in the basic variable column, the $\Delta$ change does not become a multiple of the $z_j$ row. Thus, the $\Delta$ change will show up only in one column in the $c_j - z_j$ row. An example of this type of $\Delta$ change when a variable is not basic is shown in the tableau in table 6.5 for the $c_1$ coefficient.

**Table 6.5** The Optimal Simplex Table with $x_1$ Not a Basic Variable

| $c_j$ | | | $4 + \Delta$ | 10 | 0 | 0 |
|---|---|---|---|---|---|---|
| | basic variables | quantity | $x_1$ | $x_2$ | $s_1$ | $s_2$ |
| 10 | $x_2$ | 20 | 1/2 | 1 | 1/2 | 0 |
| 0 | $s_2$ | 60 | 5/2 | 0 | $-3/2$ | 1 |
| | $z_j$ | 200 | 5 | 10 | 5 | 0 |
| | $c_j - z_j$ | | $-1 + \Delta$ | 0 | $-5$ | 0 |

Since the solution shown in table 6.5 will remain optimal if the $c_j - z_j$ row values remain negative or zero, there is only one inequality to solve.

$$-1 + \Delta < 0$$
$$\Delta < 1$$

Since $c_1 = 4 + \Delta$ and $\Delta = c_1 - 4$,

$$\Delta < 1$$
$$c_1 - 4 < 1$$
$$c_1 < 5$$

Thus, as long as $c_1 < 5$, the present solution will remain optimal.

## Changes in Constraint Quantity Values

In order to demonstrate the effect of a change in the quantity values of the model constraints, we will again use the Hickory Furniture Company example.

maximize $Z = 160x_1 + 200x_2$
subject to
$$2x_1 + 4x_2 \leq 40 \text{ hours of labor}$$
$$18x_1 + 18x_2 \leq 216 \text{ pounds of wood}$$
$$24x_1 + 12x_2 \leq 240 \text{ ft.}^2 \text{ of storage space}$$
$$x_1, x_2 \geq 0$$

The quantity values 40, 216, and 240 will be represented symbolically as $q_i$. Thus $q_1 = 40$, $q_2 = 216$, and $q_3 = 240$. Now consider a $\Delta$ change in $q_2$. For example, let us change $q_2 = 216$ by an amount, $\Delta = 18$. In other words, $q_2$ is changed from 216 pounds to 234 pounds. The effect of this change is shown graphically in figure 6.2.

**Figure 6.2** A Δ change in $q_2$.

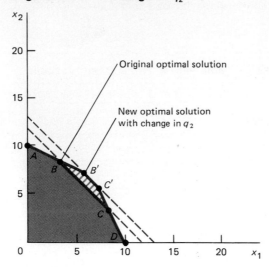

**Figure 6.2** A Δ change in $q_2$.

*The effect of a change in a quantity value on the feasible solution area*

In figure 6.2 a change in $q_2$ is shown to have the effect of changing the feasible solution area from $0ABCD$ to $0AB'C'D$. Originally, the optimal solution point was $B$, however, the change in $q_2$ now causes $B'$ to be the optimal solution point. Thus, a change in a $q_i$ value can change the feasible solution area. Therefore, the purpose of sensitivity analysis is to determine the range for $q_i$ over which the solution *basis* will remain feasible.

*Determining Δ changes in $q_i$ from the optimal tableau*

As in the case of the $c_j$ values, the range for $q_i$ can be determined directly from the optimal simplex tableau. As an example, consider a Δ increase in the number of labor hours. The model constraints become,

$$2x_1 + 4x_2 \leq 40 + 1\Delta$$
$$18x_1 + 18x_2 \leq 216 + 0\Delta$$
$$24x_1 + 12x_2 \leq 240 + 0\Delta$$

Notice in the initial simplex tableau for our example in table 6.6 that the changes in the quantity column are the same as the coefficients in the $s_1$ column.

**Table 6.6** The Initial Simplex Tableau

| $c_j$ | | | 160 | 200 | 0 | 0 | 0 |
|---|---|---|---|---|---|---|---|
| | basic variables | quantity | $x_1$ | $x_2$ | $s_1$ | $s_2$ | $s_3$ |
| 0 | $s_1$ | 40 + 1Δ | 2 | 4 | 1 | 0 | 0 |
| 0 | $s_2$ | 216 + 0Δ | 18 | 18 | 0 | 1 | 0 |
| 0 | $s_3$ | 240 + 0Δ | 24 | 12 | 0 | 0 | 1 |
| | $z_j$ | 0 | 0 | 0 | 0 | 0 | 0 |
| | $c_j - z_j$ | | 160 | 200 | 0 | 0 | 0 |

This duplication will carry through each subsequent tableau so that the $s_1$ column values will duplicate the $\Delta$ changes in the quantity column in the final tableau (table 6.7).

**Table 6.7** The Final Simplex Tableau

| $c_j$ | | | 160 | 200 | 0 | 0 | 0 |
|---|---|---|---|---|---|---|---|
| | basic variables | quantity | $x_1$ | $x_2$ | $s_1$ | $s_2$ | $s_3$ |
| 200 | $x_2$ | $8 + \Delta/2$ | 0 | 1 | $1/2$ | $-1/18$ | 0 |
| 160 | $x_1$ | $4 - \Delta/2$ | 1 | 0 | $-1/2$ | $1/9$ | 0 |
| 0 | $s_3$ | $48 + 6\Delta$ | 0 | 0 | 6 | $-2$ | 1 |
| | $z_j$ | $2{,}240 + 20\Delta$ | 160 | 200 | 20 | $20/3$ | 0 |
| | $c_j - z_j$ | | 0 | 0 | $-20$ | $-20/3$ | 0 |

In general, the $\Delta$ changes represent a separate column identical to the $s_1$ column. As such, it is necessary only to observe the slack ($s_i$) column corresponding to the model constraint quantity ($q_i$) being changed in the final tableau to determine the $\Delta$ change.

Recall that a requirement of the simplex method is that the quantity values not be negative. If any $q_i$ value becomes negative, the solution will no longer be *feasible*. Thus, the following inequalities,

$$8 + \Delta/2 \geq 0$$
$$4 - \Delta/2 \geq 0$$
$$48 + 6\Delta \geq 0$$

*Solving $\Delta$ inequalities*

are solved for $\Delta$,

$$8 + \Delta/2 \geq 0$$
$$\Delta/2 \geq -8$$
$$\Delta \geq -16$$

and,

$$4 - \Delta/2 \geq 0$$
$$-\Delta/2 \geq -4$$
$$\Delta \leq 8$$

and,

$$48 + 6\Delta \geq 0$$
$$6\Delta \geq -48$$
$$\Delta \geq -8$$

Since $q_1 = 40 + \Delta$, then $\Delta = q_1 - 40$. These values are substituted into the inequalities $\Delta \geq -16$, $\Delta \leq 8$, and $\Delta \geq -8$ as follows.

$$\Delta \geq -16$$
$$q_1 - 40 \geq -16$$
$$q_1 \geq 24$$
$$\Delta \leq 8$$
$$q_1 - 40 \leq 8$$
$$q_1 \leq 48$$
$$\Delta \geq -8$$
$$q_1 - 40 \geq -8$$
$$q_1 \geq 32$$

*The sensitivity range for $q_1$*

Summarizing, these inequalities,

$$24 \leq 32 \leq q_1 \leq 48$$

The value of 24 can be eliminated, since $q_1$ must be greater than 32, thus,

$$32 \leq q_1 \leq 48$$

As long as $q_1$ remains in this range, the present basic solution variables will remain positive and feasible. However, the quantity values of those basic variables may change. In other words, while the variables in the basis may remain intact, the values of these variables can change.

In order to determine the range of feasibility for $q_2$ (where $q_2 = 216 + \Delta$), the $s_2$ column values would be used to develop the $\Delta$ inequalities.

$$8 - \Delta/18 \geq 0$$
$$4 + \Delta/9 \geq 0$$
$$48 - 2\Delta \geq 0$$

*Solving $\Delta$ inequalities*

Solving these inequalities,

$$8 - \Delta/18 \geq 0$$
$$-\Delta/18 \geq -8$$
$$\Delta \leq 144$$

$$4 + \Delta/9 \geq 0$$
$$\Delta/9 \geq -4$$
$$\Delta \geq -36$$

$$48 - 2\Delta \geq 0$$
$$-2\Delta \geq -48$$
$$\Delta \leq 24$$

Since $q_2 = 216 + \Delta$, then $\Delta = q_2 - 216$. Substituting this value into the inequalities, $\Delta \leq 144$, $\Delta \geq -36$, and $\Delta \leq 24$:

$$\Delta \leq 144$$
$$q_2 - 216 \leq 144$$
$$q_2 \leq 360$$

$$\Delta \geq -36$$
$$q_2 - 216 \geq -36$$
$$q_2 \geq 180$$

$$\Delta \leq 24$$
$$q_2 - 216 \leq 24$$
$$q_2 \leq 240$$

Summarizing,

$$180 \leq q_2 \leq 240 \leq 360$$

The value, 360, can be eliminated, since $q_2$ cannot exceed 240. Thus, the range over which the basic solution variables will remain feasible is

*The sensitivity range for* $q_2$

$$180 \leq q_2 \leq 240$$

The sensitivity analysis of constraint quantity values can be used in conjunction with the dual solution in order to make decisions regarding model resources. Recall from our analysis of the dual solution of our Hickory Furniture Company example that

*Using the sensitivity ranges for* $q_i$ *in conjunction with the dual for decision making*

$y_1 = \$20$, marginal value of labor
$y_2 = \$6.67$, marginal value of wood
$y_3 = \$0$, marginal value of storage space

Since the resource with the greatest marginal value is labor, the manager might realistically desire to secure some additional hours of labor. How many hours should the manager get? Recalling the range for $q_1$ to be $32 \leq q_1 \leq 48$, the manager could secure up to an additional 8 hours of labor (i.e., 48 total hours) before the solution basis becomes infeasible. If the manager did purchase 8 more hours, the solution values could be found by observing table 6.7 and noticing that the quantity values are

$$x_2 = 8 + \Delta/2$$
$$x_1 = 4 - \Delta/2$$
$$s_3 = 48 + 6\Delta$$

Since $\Delta = 8$,

$$x_2 = 8 + (8)/2$$
$$x_2 = 12$$

$$x_1 = 4 - (8)/2$$
$$x_1 = 0$$

$$s_3 = 48 + 6(8)$$
$$s_3 = 96$$

Total profit will be increased by $20 for each extra hour of labor.

$$Z = \$2,240 + 20\Delta$$
$$= 2,240 + 20(8)$$
$$= 2,240 + 160$$
$$= \$2,400$$

## Additional Model Parameter Changes

Sensitivity analysis is not confined solely to determining ranges for $c_j$ and $q_i$. Other model parameters can also be analyzed to determine their effect on the solution. These additional parameter changes include the constraint coefficients. For example, in our Hickory Furniture Company example, the labor constraint is

$$2x_1 + 4x_2 \leq 40 \text{ hours}$$

*Changes in the constraint coefficients*
The $x_1$ coefficient 2 is the hours required to produce a table. By changing this coefficient to 1 hour per table, the feasible solution area would be changed as shown in figure 6.3. The feasible solution area in figure 6.3 changed from $0ABCD$ to $0AB'CD$ as a result of the change in the $x_1$ coefficient in the labor constraint. As such, the existing solution point will also change from point $B$ to $B'$. However, the determination of a sensitivity range for the model constraint coefficients from the final simplex tableau is beyond the scope of this text, and as such, will not be pursued.

---

**Figure 6.3** A change in the constraint coefficient.

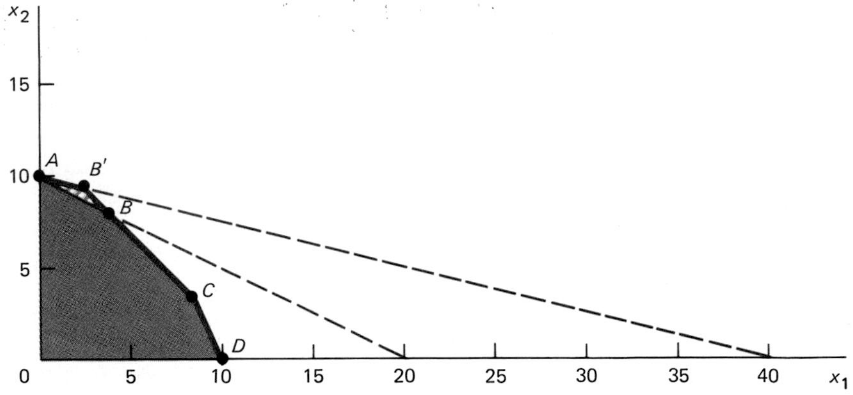

## Summary

In this chapter several different ways to analyze the final simplex solution in order to gather additional information have been examined. First the formulation of the dual was presented and the dual solution was interpreted. The dual solution was shown to contain useful information regarding the economic value of the model resources. Next, sensitivity analysis of various model parameters was presented. It was demonstrated how potential model changes could be examined within the context of the simplex tableau in order to ascertain their effect on the optimal solution.

The topics of duality and sensitivity analysis in this chapter completes the presentation of the *general* linear programming model and the simplex method, but it does not complete the presentation of linear programming.

There are several important variations from the basic linear programming model that will be examined in subsequent chapters. The variations include the transportation and assignment problems, integer programming, and goal programming.

## References

Baumol, W. J. *Economic Theory and Operations Analysis*. Englewood Cliffs, N.J.: Prentice-Hall, 1961.

Dantzig, G. B. *Linear Programming and Extensions*. Princeton, N.J.: Princeton University Press, 1963.

Hadley, G. *Linear Programming*. Reading, Mass.: Addison-Wesley Publishing Co., 1962.

Lee, Sang M.; Moore, Laurence J.; and Taylor, B. W. *Management Science*. Dubuque, Iowa: Wm. C. Brown Company Publishers, 1981.

Loomba, N. P. *Linear Programming: A Managerial Perspective*. 2d ed. New York: Macmillan Co., 1976.

Pfaffenberger, R. C., and Walker, David A. *Mathematical Programming for Economics and Business*. Ames, Ia.: Iowa State University Press, 1976.

Phillips, D. T.; Ravindran, A.; and Solberg, J. J. *Operations Research: Principles and Practice*. New York: John Wiley and Sons, 1976.

Spivey, W. A., and Thrall, R. M. *Linear Optimization*. New York: Holt, Rinehart, and Winston, 1970.

Taha, H. A. *Operations Research: An Introduction*. 2d ed. New York: Macmillan Co., 1976.

## Problems

1. The Old English Metal Crafters Company makes brass trays and buckets. The number of trays $(x_1)$ and buckets $(x_2)$ that can be produced daily are constrained by the availability of brass and labor, as reflected in the following linear programming model.

   maximize $Z = 6x_1 + 10x_2$ (profit, $)
   subject to
   $$x_1 + 4x_2 \leq 90 \text{ (brass, lbs.)}$$
   $$2x_1 + 2x_2 \leq 60 \text{ (labor, hrs.)}$$
   $$x_1, x_2 \geq 0$$

   The final optimal simplex tableau for this model is as follows.

| $c_j$ | | | 6 | 10 | 0 | 0 |
|---|---|---|---|---|---|---|
| | basic variables | quantity | $x_1$ | $x_2$ | $s_1$ | $s_2$ |
| 10 | $x_2$ | 20 | 0 | 1 | 1/3 | −1/6 |
| 6 | $x_1$ | 10 | 1 | 0 | −1/3 | 2/3 |
| | $z_j$ | 260 | 6 | 10 | 4/3 | 7/3 |
| | $c_j - z_j$ | | 0 | 0 | −4/3 | −7/3 |

(a) Formulate the dual of this model.

(b) Define the dual variables and what they mean.

(c) What do the dual variables equal?

2. The Southwest Foods Company produces two brands of chili, Razorback and Longhorn, from several ingredients, including chili beans and ground beef. The number of 100-gallon batches of Razorback chili ($x_1$) and Longhorn chili ($x_2$) that can be produced daily are constrained by the availability of chili beans and ground beef, as shown in the following linear programming model.

maximize $Z = 200x_1 + 300x_2$ (profit, \$)
subject to
$$10x_1 + 50x_2 \leq 500 \text{ (chili beans, lbs.)}$$
$$34x_1 + 20x_2 \leq 800 \text{ (ground beef, lbs.)}$$
$$x_1, x_2 \geq 0$$

The final optimal simplex tableau for this model is as follows.

| $c_j$ | | | 200 | 300 | 0 | 0 |
|---|---|---|---|---|---|---|
| | basic variables | quantity | $x_1$ | $x_2$ | $s_1$ | $s_2$ |
| 300 | $x_2$ | 6 | 0 | 1 | 17/750 | −1/150 |
| 200 | $x_1$ | 20 | 1 | 0 | −1/75 | 1/30 |
| | $z_j$ | 5,800 | 200 | 300 | 310/75 | 70/15 |
| | $c_j - z_j$ | | 0 | 0 | −310/75 | −70/15 |

(a) Interpret the meaning of the $c_j - z_j$ values for this tableau.

(b) Formulate the dual of this model.

(c) What do the dual variables equal and what do they mean?

3. The Agrimaster Company produces two kinds of fertilizer spreaders, regular and cyclone. Each spreader must go through two processes in which parts are made and then assembled. Letting $x_1$ = the number of regular spreaders produced and $x_2$ = the number of cyclone spreaders produced, the problem is formulated as

maximize $Z = 9x_1 + 7x_2$ (profit, $)
subject to
$$12x_1 + 4x_2 \leq 60 \text{ (process 1, production hrs.)}$$
$$4x_1 + 8x_2 \leq 40 \text{ (process 2, production hrs.)}$$
$$x_1, x_2 \geq 0$$

The final optimal simplex tableau for this problem is as follows.

| $c_j$ | | | 9 | 7 | 0 | 0 |
|---|---|---|---|---|---|---|
| | basic variables | quantity | $x_1$ | $x_2$ | $s_1$ | $s_2$ |
| 9 | $x_1$ | 4 | 1 | 0 | 1/10 | −1/20 |
| 7 | $x_2$ | 3 | 0 | 1 | −1/20 | 3/20 |
| | $z_j$ | 57 | 9 | 7 | 11/20 | 12/20 |
| | $c_j - z_j$ | | 0 | 0 | −11/20 | −12/20 |

(a) Formulate the dual to this problem.
(b) Define the dual variables.
(c) Interpret the $c_j - z_j$ values for this tableau.
(d) Allocate profit between the resources to show how much each resource contributed to total profit.

4. The Stratford House Furniture Company makes 2 kinds of tables, end tables ($x_1$) and coffee tables ($x_2$). The manufacturer is restricted by material and labor constraints, as shown in the following linear programming formulation.

maximize $Z = 200x_1 + 300x_2$ (profit, $)
subject to
$$2x_1 + 5x_2 \leq 180 \text{ (labor, hrs.)}$$
$$3x_1 + 3x_2 \leq 135 \text{ (wood, lbs.)}$$
$$x_1, x_2 \geq 0$$

The final optimal simplex tableau for this problem is as follows.

| $c_j$ | basic variables | quantity | 200 $x_1$ | 300 $x_2$ | 0 $s_1$ | 0 $s_2$ |
|---|---|---|---|---|---|---|
| 300 | $x_2$ | 30 | 0 | 1 | 1/3 | −2/9 |
| 200 | $x_1$ | 15 | 1 | 0 | −1/3 | 5/9 |
| | $z_j$ | 12,000 | 200 | 300 | 100/3 | 400/9 |
| | $c_j - z_j$ | | 0 | 0 | −100/3 | −400/9 |

(a) Formulate the dual to this problem.
(b) Define the dual variables.
(c) Allocate profit among the resources to show how much each resource contributed to total profit.

5. An electronics firm produces electric motors for washing machines and vacuum cleaners. The firm has resource constraints for production time, steel, and wire. The linear programming model to determine the number of washing machine motors ($x_1$) and vacuum cleaner motors ($x_2$) to produce has been formulated as follows.

maximize $Z = 70x_1 + 80x_2$ (profit, $)
subject to
$$2x_1 + x_2 \leq 19 \text{ (production, hrs.)}$$
$$x_1 + x_2 \leq 14 \text{ (steel, lbs.)}$$
$$x_1 + 2x_2 \leq 20 \text{ (wire, ft.)}$$
$$x_1, x_2 \geq 0$$

The final optimal simplex tableau for this model is as follows.

| $c_j$ | basic variables | quantity | 70 $x_1$ | 80 $x_2$ | 0 $s_1$ | 0 $s_2$ | 0 $s_3$ |
|---|---|---|---|---|---|---|---|
| 70 | $x_1$ | 6 | 1 | 0 | 2/3 | 0 | −1/3 |
| 0 | $s_2$ | 1 | 0 | 0 | −1/3 | 1 | −1/3 |
| 80 | $x_2$ | 7 | 0 | 1 | −1/3 | 0 | 2/3 |
| | $z_j$ | 980 | 70 | 80 | 20 | 0 | 30 |
| | $c_j - z_j$ | | 0 | 0 | −20 | 0 | −30 |

(a) Formulate the dual to this problem.
(b) What do the dual variables equal and what do they mean?
(c) Allocate profit among the resources to show how much each resource contributes to total profit.

6. A manufacturer produces two products, 1 and 2, from which profits are $9 and $12 respectively. Each product must go through two production processes for which there are labor constraints. There are also material constraints and storage limitations. The linear programming model to determine the number of product 1 to produce $(x_1)$ and the number of product 2 to produce $(x_2)$ is given as follows.

maximize $Z = 9x_1 + 12x_2$ (profit, $)
subject to

$$4x_1 + 8x_2 \leq 64 \text{ (process 1, labor hrs.)}$$
$$5x_1 + 5x_2 \leq 50 \text{ (process 2, labor hrs.)}$$
$$15x_1 + 8x_2 \leq 120 \text{ (material, lbs.)}$$
$$x_1 \leq 7 \text{ (storage space, units)}$$
$$x_2 \leq 7 \text{ (storage space, units)}$$
$$x_1, x_2 \geq 0$$

The final optimal simplex tableau for this problem is as follows.

| $c_j$ | basic variables | quantity | 9 $x_1$ | 12 $x_2$ | 0 $s_1$ | 0 $s_2$ | 0 $s_3$ | 0 $s_4$ | 0 $s_5$ |
|---|---|---|---|---|---|---|---|---|---|
| 9 | $x_1$ | 4 | 1 | 0 | $-1/4$ | $2/5$ | 0 | 0 | 0 |
| 0 | $s_5$ | 1 | 0 | 0 | $-1/4$ | $1/5$ | 0 | 0 | 1 |
| 0 | $s_3$ | 12 | 0 | 0 | $-7/4$ | $-22/5$ | 1 | 0 | 0 |
| 0 | $s_4$ | 3 | 0 | 0 | $1/2$ | $-2/5$ | 0 | 1 | 0 |
| 12 | $x_2$ | 6 | 0 | 1 | $1/4$ | $-1/6$ | 0 | 0 | 0 |
| | $z_j$ | 108 | 9 | 12 | $3/4$ | $6/5$ | 0 | 0 | 0 |
| | $c_j - z_j$ | | 0 | 0 | $-3/4$ | $-6/5$ | 0 | 0 | 0 |

(a) Formulate the dual to this problem.
(b) What do the dual variables equal and what does this dual solution mean?
(c) Allocate profit among the resources to show how much each resource contributed to total profit.

7. A manufacturer produces 3 products (1, 2 and 3) daily. The 3 products are processed through 3 production operations with time constraints and then stored. The following linear programming model has been formulated to determine the number of product 1 $(x_1)$, product 2 $(x_2)$, and product 3 $(x_3)$ to produce.

maximize $Z = 40x_1 + 35x_2 + 45x_3$ (profit, $)
subject to

$$2x_1 + 3x_2 + 2x_3 \leq 120 \text{ (operation \#1, hrs.)}$$
$$4x_1 + 3x_2 + x_3 \leq 160 \text{ (operation \#2, hrs.)}$$
$$3x_1 + 2x_2 + 4x_3 \leq 100 \text{ (operation \#3, hrs.)}$$
$$x_1 + x_2 + x_3 \leq 40 \text{ (storage, ft.}^2)$$
$$x_1, x_2, x_3 \geq 0$$

The final optimal simplex tableau for this model is as follows.

| $c_j$ | | | 40 | 35 | 45 | 0 | 0 | 0 | 0 |
|---|---|---|---|---|---|---|---|---|---|
| | basic variables | quantity | $x_1$ | $x_2$ | $x_3$ | $s_1$ | $s_2$ | $s_3$ | $s_4$ |
| 0 | $s_1$ | 10 | $-1/2$ | 0 | 0 | 1 | 0 | $1/2$ | $-4$ |
| 0 | $s_2$ | 60 | 2 | 0 | 0 | 0 | 1 | 1 | $-5$ |
| 45 | $x_3$ | 10 | $1/2$ | 0 | 1 | 0 | 0 | $1/2$ | $-1$ |
| 35 | $x_2$ | 30 | $1/2$ | 1 | 0 | 0 | 0 | $-1/2$ | 2 |
| | $z_j$ | 1,500 | 40 | 35 | 45 | 0 | 0 | 5 | 25 |
| | $c_j - z_j$ | | 0 | 0 | 0 | 0 | 0 | $-5$ | $-25$ |

(a) Formulate the dual to this problem.

(b) What do the dual variables equal and what do they mean?

(c) How does the fact that this is a multiple optimum solution affect the interpretation of the dual solution values?

8. A school dietician is attempting to determine a lunch that will minimize cost and meet certain minimum dietary requirements. The two main staples in the meal are meat and potatoes, which provide protein, iron, and carbohydrates. The following linear programming model has been formulated to determine the number of ounces of meat $(x_1)$ and the number of ounces of potatoes $(x_2)$ to put in a lunch.

minimize $Z = .03x_1 + .02x_2$ (cost, \$)
subject to
$$4x_1 + 5x_2 \geq 20 \text{ (protein, mg.)}$$
$$12x_1 + 3x_2 \geq 30 \text{ (iron, mg.)}$$
$$3x_1 + 2x_2 \geq 12 \text{ (carbohydrates, mg.)}$$
$$x_1, x_2 \geq 0$$

The final optimal simplex tableau for this problem is as follows.

| $c_j$ | | | .03 | .02 | 0 | 0 | 0 |
|---|---|---|---|---|---|---|---|
| | basic variables | quantity | $x_1$ | $x_2$ | $s_1$ | $s_2$ | $s_3$ |
| .02 | $x_2$ | 3.6 | 0 | 1 | 0 | .20 | $-.80$ |
| .03 | $x_1$ | 1.6 | 1 | 0 | 0 | $-.13$ | .20 |
| 0 | $s_1$ | 4.4 | 0 | 0 | 1 | .47 | $-3.2$ |
| | $z_j$ | .12 | .03 | .02 | 0 | 0 | $-.01$ |
| | $z_j - c_j$ | | 0 | 0 | 0 | 0 | $-.01$ |

(a) Formulate the dual to this problem.

(b) What do the dual variables equal and what do they mean?

9. Given the linear programming problem (problem 6 above),

maximize $Z = 9x_1 + 12x_2$
subject to

$$4x_1 + 8x_2 \leq 64$$
$$5x_1 + 5x_2 \leq 50$$
$$15x_1 + 8x_2 \leq 120$$
$$x_1 \leq 7$$
$$x_2 \leq 7$$
$$x_1, x_2 \geq 0$$

solve the dual model using the simplex method and compare the optimal tableau to the primal optimal tableau.

10. Given problem 5 above,

maximize $Z = 70x_1 + 80x_2$
subject to

$$2x_1 + x_2 \leq 19$$
$$x_1 + x_2 \leq 14$$
$$x_1 + 2x_2 \leq 20$$
$$x_1, x_2 \geq 0$$

solve the dual model using the simplex method and compare the optimal tableau with the primal optimal tableau.

11. Formulate the dual for the following linear programming model.

maximize $Z = 10x_1 + 5x_2 + 8x_3$
subject to

$$6x_1 + 12x_2 + 4x_3 \leq 1,600$$
$$x_1 + 3x_2 + 2x_3 \leq 400$$
$$x_1 + x_2 + x_3 \leq 300$$
$$x_1 \leq 150$$
$$x_2 \leq 200$$
$$x_3 \leq 100$$
$$x_1, x_2, x_3 \geq 0$$

12. Formulate the dual for the following linear programming model.

maximize $Z = 25x_1 + 20x_2 + 10x_3 + 30x_4$
subject to

$$x_1 + x_2 \leq 400$$
$$x_3 + x_4 \leq 600$$
$$50x_1 + 45x_2 \leq 16,000$$
$$40x_3 + 30x_4 \leq 25,000$$
$$2x_1 + 3x_3 \leq 800$$
$$4x_2 + x_4 \leq 900$$
$$x_1, x_2, x_3, x_4 \geq 0$$

13. Formulate the dual for the following linear programming model.

minimize $Z = x_1 + x_2 + x_3 + x_4$
subject to
$$10x_1 + 12x_2 + 7x_3 + 8x_4 \geq 300$$
$$50x_3 + 25x_4 \geq 600$$
$$20x_2 + 30x_4 \geq 800$$
$$x_1 \geq 10$$
$$x_2 \geq 8$$
$$x_3 \geq 10$$
$$x_4 \geq 20$$
$$x_1, x_2, x_3, x_4 \geq 0$$

14. Given the following linear programming model formulate the dual.

maximize $Z = 5x_1 + x_2$
subject to
$$4x_1 + 3x_2 = 24$$
$$x_1 \leq 6$$
$$x_1 + 3x_2 \leq 12$$
$$x_1, x_2 \geq 0$$

15. Given the following linear programming model formulate the dual.

maximize $Z = 2x_1 + 2x_2 - x_3$
subject to
$$x_1 + x_2 - 2x_3 \leq 6$$
$$-2x_1 - x_2 + x_3 \leq 5$$
$$2x_1 + 6x_2 = 10$$
$$x_1, x_2, x_3 \geq 0$$

16. Given the following linear programming model formulate the dual.

maximize $Z = 4x_1 + 10x_2 + 6x_3$
subject to
$$x_1 + 3x_2 + 4x_3 \leq 40$$
$$2x_2 + x_3 \leq 20$$
$$10x_1 + 6x_2 + 20x_3 = 100$$
$$x_1 + 2x_2 = 60$$
$$x_1, x_2, x_3 \geq 0$$

17. Given the following linear programming model formulate the dual.

maximize $Z = x_1 + 2x_2 + 2x_3$
subject to
$$x_1 + x_2 + 2x_3 \leq 12$$
$$2x_1 + x_2 + 5x_3 = 20$$
$$x_1 + x_2 - x_3 \geq 8$$
$$x_1, x_2, x_3 \geq 0$$

18. Given the following linear programming model:

maximize $Z = 4x_1 + 2x_2$
subject to

$$x_1 + x_2 \geq 1$$
$$-4x_1 + x_2 \leq 0$$
$$-x_1 + 4x_2 \geq 0$$
$$-x_1 + x_2 \leq 1$$
$$x_1 + x_2 \leq 6$$
$$x_1 \leq 3$$
$$x_1, x_2 \geq 0$$

formulate the dual for this model.

19. Given the following linear programming model:

maximize $Z = 6x_1 + 2x_2 + 12x_3$
subject to

$$4x_1 + x_2 + 3x_3 \leq 24$$
$$2x_1 + 6x_2 + 3x_3 \leq 30$$
$$x_1, x_2, x_3 \geq 0$$

and the optimal simplex tableau for this model:

| $c_j$ | | | 6 | 2 | 12 | 0 | 0 |
|---|---|---|---|---|---|---|---|
| | basic variables | quantity | $x_1$ | $x_2$ | $x_3$ | $s_1$ | $s_2$ |
| 12 | $x_3$ | 8 | 4/3 | 1/3 | 1 | 1/3 | 0 |
| 0 | $s_2$ | 6 | -2 | 5 | 0 | -1 | 1 |
| | $z_j$ | 96 | 16 | 4 | 12 | 4 | 0 |
| | $c_j - z_j$ | | -10 | -2 | 0 | -4 | 0 |

(a) Find the ranges for all $c_j$ values for which the present solution will remain optimal.
(b) Find the ranges for all $q_i$ values for which the present solution will remain feasible.

20. Given the following linear programming model:

maximize $Z = 10x_1 + 8x_2$
subject to

$$x_1 + 3x_2 \leq 30$$
$$6x_1 + 3x_2 \leq 120$$
$$x_1, x_2 \geq 0$$

and the optimal simplex tableau:

| $c_j$ | basic variables | quantity | 10 $x_1$ | 8 $x_2$ | 0 $s_1$ | 0 $s_2$ |
|---|---|---|---|---|---|---|
| 8 | $x_2$ | 4 | 0 | 1 | 2/5 | −1/15 |
| 10 | $x_1$ | 18 | 1 | 0 | −1/5 | 1/5 |
| | $z_j$ | 212 | 10 | 8 | 6/5 | 22/15 |
| | $c_j - z_j$ | | 0 | 0 | −6/5 | −22/15 |

(a) Find the optimal ranges of all $c_j$ values.
(b) Find the feasible ranges for all $q_i$ values.

21. Given the following linear programming model:

minimize $Z = 3x_1 + 5x_2 + 2x_3$
subject to
$$x_1 + x_2 - 3x_3 \geq 35$$
$$x_1 + 2x_2 \geq 50$$
$$-x_1 + x_2 \geq 25$$
$$x_1, x_2, x_3 \geq 0$$

and the optimal simplex tableau:

| $c_j$ | basic variables | quantity | 3 $x_1$ | 5 $x_2$ | 2 $x_3$ | 0 $s_1$ | 0 $s_2$ | 0 $s_3$ |
|---|---|---|---|---|---|---|---|---|
| 0 | $s_2$ | 15 | 0 | 0 | −9/2 | −3/2 | 1 | −1/2 |
| 3 | $x_1$ | 5 | 1 | 0 | −3/2 | −1/2 | 0 | 1/2 |
| 5 | $x_2$ | 30 | 0 | 1 | −3/2 | −1/2 | 0 | −1/2 |
| | $z_j$ | 165 | 3 | 5 | −12 | −4 | 0 | −1 |
| | $z_j - c_j$ | | 0 | 0 | −14 | −4 | 0 | −1 |

(a) Find the optimal ranges for all $c_j$ values.
(b) Find the feasible ranges for all $q_i$ values.

22. Given the following linear programming model:

maximize $Z = 5x_1 + 7x_2 + 8x_3$
subject to
$$x_1 + x_2 + x_3 \leq 32$$
$$x_1 \leq 20$$
$$x_2 \leq 15$$
$$x_3 \leq 18$$
$$x_1, x_2, x_3 \geq 0$$

and the optimal simplex tableau:

| $c_j$ | | | 5 | 7 | 8 | 0 | 0 | 0 | 0 |
|---|---|---|---|---|---|---|---|---|---|
| | basic variables | quantity | $x_1$ | $x_2$ | $x_3$ | $s_1$ | $s_2$ | $s_3$ | $s_4$ |
| 7 | $x_2$ | 14 | 1 | 1 | 0 | 1 | 0 | 0 | −1 |
| 0 | $s_2$ | 20 | 1 | 0 | 0 | 0 | 1 | 0 | 0 |
| 0 | $s_3$ | 1 | −1 | 0 | 0 | −1 | 0 | 1 | 1 |
| 8 | $x_3$ | 18 | 0 | 0 | 1 | 0 | 0 | 0 | 1 |
| | $z_j$ | 242 | 7 | 7 | 8 | 7 | 0 | 0 | 1 |
| | $c_j - z_j$ | | −2 | 0 | 0 | −7 | 0 | 0 | −1 |

(a) Find the optimal ranges for all $c_j$ values.
(b) Find the feasible ranges for all $q_i$ values.

23. The Sunshine Food Processing Company produces three canned fruit products—mixed fruit ($x_1$), fruit cocktail ($x_2$), and fruit delight ($x_3$). The main ingredients in each product are pears and peaches. Each product is produced in lots and must go through three processes—mixing, canning, and packaging. The resource requirements for each product and each process are shown in the following linear programming formulation.

maximize $Z = 10x_1 + 6x_2 + 8x_3$ (profit, $)
subject to
$$20x_1 + 10x_2 + 16x_3 \leq 320 \text{ (pears, lbs.)}$$
$$10x_1 + 20x_2 + 16x_3 \leq 400 \text{ (peaches, lbs.)}$$
$$x_1 + 2x_2 + 2x_3 \leq 40 \text{ (mixing, hrs.)}$$
$$x_1 + x_2 + x_3 \leq 60 \text{ (canning, hrs.)}$$
$$2x_1 + x_2 + x_3 \leq 40 \text{ (packaging, hrs.)}$$
$$x_1, x_2, x_3 \geq 0$$

The optimal simplex tableau is as follows.

| $c_j$ | | | 10 | 6 | 8 | 0 | 0 | 0 | 0 | 0 |
|---|---|---|---|---|---|---|---|---|---|---|
| | basic variables | quantity | $x_1$ | $x_2$ | $x_3$ | $s_1$ | $s_2$ | $s_3$ | $s_4$ | $s_5$ |
| 10 | $x_1$ | 8 | 1 | 0 | 8/15 | 1/15 | 1/30 | 0 | 0 | 0 |
| 6 | $x_2$ | 16 | 0 | 1 | 8/15 | −1/30 | 1/15 | 0 | 0 | 0 |
| 0 | $s_3$ | 3 | 0 | 0 | 2/5 | −1/40 | −1/10 | 1 | 0 | 0 |
| 0 | $s_4$ | 36 | 0 | 0 | −1/15 | −1/30 | −1/30 | 0 | 1 | 0 |
| 0 | $s_5$ | 8 | 0 | 0 | −3/5 | −1/10 | 0 | 0 | 0 | 1 |
| | $z_j$ | 176 | 10 | 6 | 128/15 | 7/15 | 1/15 | 0 | 0 | 0 |
| | $c_j - z_j$ | | 0 | 0 | −8/15 | −7/15 | −1/15 | 0 | 0 | 0 |

(a) What is the maximum price the company would be willing to pay for additional pears? How much would be purchased at that price?

(b) What is the marginal value of peaches? Over what range of available peaches is this price valid?

(c) The company can purchase a new machine for mixing that would increase the hours available for mixing from 40 to 60. Will this affect the optimal solution?

(d) The company can also purchase a new machine for packaging that will increase the hours available from 40 to 50. Will this affect the optimal solution?

(e) If the manager should attempt to secure additional units of only one of the resources, which should it be?

24. The Evergreen Products Firm produces 3 types of pressed paneling from pine and spruce. The three types of paneling are Western ($x_1$), Old English ($x_2$), and Colonial ($x_3$). Each sheet must be cut and pressed. The resource requirements are given in the following linear programming formulation.

maximize $Z = 4x_1 + 10x_2 + 8x_3$ (profit, $)
subject to
$$5x_1 + 4x_2 + 4x_3 \leq 200 \text{ (pine, lbs.)}$$
$$2x_1 + 5x_2 + 2x_3 \leq 160 \text{ (spruce, lbs.)}$$
$$x_1 + x_2 + 2x_3 \leq 50 \text{ (cutting, hrs.)}$$
$$x_1 + 4x_2 + 2x_3 \leq 80 \text{ (pressing, hrs.)}$$
$$x_1, x_2, x_3 \geq 0$$

The optimal simplex tableau is as follows.

| $c_j$ | | | 4 | 10 | 8 | 0 | 0 | 0 | 0 |
|---|---|---|---|---|---|---|---|---|---|
| | basic variables | quantity | $x_1$ | $x_2$ | $x_3$ | $s_1$ | $s_2$ | $s_3$ | $s_4$ |
| 0 | $s_1$ | 80 | -7/3 | 0 | 0 | 1 | 0 | -4/3 | -2/3 |
| 0 | $s_2$ | 70 | -1/3 | 0 | 0 | 0 | 1 | 1/3 | -4/3 |
| 8 | $x_3$ | 20 | 1/3 | 0 | 1 | 0 | 0 | 2/3 | -1/6 |
| 10 | $x_2$ | 10 | 1/3 | 1 | 0 | 0 | 0 | -1/3 | 1/3 |
| | $z_j$ | 260 | 6 | 10 | 8 | 0 | 0 | 2 | 2 |
| | $c_j - z_j$ | | -2 | 0 | 0 | 0 | 0 | -2 | -2 |

(a) What is the marginal value of an additional pound of spruce? Over what range of available spruce is this value valid?

(b) What is the marginal value of an additional hour of cutting? Over what range is this value valid?

(c) Given a choice between securing more cutting hours or more pressing hours, which should management select? Why?

(d) If the amount of spruce available to the firm is decreased from 160 to 100 lbs., will it affect the solution?

(e) What unit profit would have to be made from Western paneling before management would consider producing it?

(f) Management is considering changing the profit of Colonial paneling from $8 to $13. Would this affect the solution?

25. A manufacturing firm produces four products. Each product requires material and machine processing. The linear programming model formulated to determine the number of product 1 $(x_1)$, product 2 $(x_2)$, product 3 $(x_3)$, and product 4 $(x_4)$ to produce is given as follows.

maximize $Z = 2x_1 + 8x_2 + 10x_3 + 6x_4$ (profit, $)
subject to
$$2x_1 + x_2 + 4x_3 + 2x_4 \le 200 \text{ (material, lbs.)}$$
$$x_1 + 2x_2 + 2x_3 + x_4 \le 160 \text{ (machine processing, hrs.)}$$
$$x_1, x_2, x_3, x_4 \ge 0$$

The optimal simplex tableau is as follows.

| $c_j$ | | | 2 | 8 | 10 | 6 | 0 | 0 |
|---|---|---|---|---|---|---|---|---|
| | basic variables | quantity | $x_1$ | $x_2$ | $x_3$ | $x_4$ | $s_1$ | $s_2$ |
| 6 | $x_4$ | 80 | 1 | 0 | 2 | 1 | 2/3 | -1/3 |
| 8 | $x_2$ | 40 | 0 | 1 | 0 | 0 | -1/3 | 2/3 |
| | $z_j$ | 800 | 6 | 8 | 12 | 6 | 4/3 | 10/3 |
| | $c_j - z_j$ | | -4 | 0 | -2 | 0 | -4/3 | -10/3 |

(a) What is the marginal value of an additional lb. of material? Over what range of material is this value valid?

(b) What is the marginal value of additional hours of processing time? Over what range of hours is this value valid?

(c) How much would the contribution to profit of $x_1$ have to increase before $x_1$ would be produced?

# 7

**Transportation
and Assignment
Problems**

**The Transportation Model**

**Solution of the Transportation Model**

The Northwest Corner Method
The Minimum Cell Cost Method
Vogel's Approximation Method
The Stepping-Stone Solution Method
The Modified Distribution Method
The Unbalanced Transportation Model
Degeneracy
Prohibited Routes

**The Assignment Model**

**Summary**

In this chapter two special types of linear programming problems will be presented that can be solved by methods other than the simplex method: the *transportation problem* and the *assignment problem*. Both of these problem types could be solved using the simplex method, but they would result in rather large simplex tableaus and numerous simplex iterations. However, because of the unique characteristics of each problem, alternative solution methods requiring considerably less mathematical manipulation than the simplex method have been developed. These solution methods for the transportation and assignment problems will be described and demonstrated in this chapter.

## The Transportation Model

The transportation model is formulated for a class of problems that have the following unique characteristics: (1) a product is *transported* from a number of sources to a number of destinations at the minimum possible cost, and (2) each of the sources are able to supply a fixed number of units of the product to each of the destinations, which have a fixed demand for the product. Although, the general transportation model can be applied to a wide variety of problems, it is this particular application to the transportation of goods that is most familiar and from which the problem draws its name.

*Unique characteristics of the transportation model*

    The following example will demonstrate the formulation of the transportation model. Wheat is harvested in the Midwest and stored in grain elevators in three cities, Kansas City, Omaha, and Des Moines. These grain elevators supply three mills that produce flour, located in Chicago, St. Louis, and Cincinnati. Grain is shipped to the mills in railroad cars each capable of holding one ton of wheat. Each grain elevator is able to supply the following number of tons (i.e., railroad cars) of wheat to the mills on a monthly basis.

*A transportation example*

| Grain Warehouse | Supply |
|---|---|
| 1. Kansas City | 150 |
| 2. Omaha | 175 |
| 3. Des Moines | <u>275</u> |
| | 600 tons |

*Supply at each source*

Each mill demands the following tons of wheat per month:

*Demand at each destination*

| Mill | Demand |
|---|---|
| A. Chicago | 200 |
| B. St. Louis | 100 |
| C. Cincinnati | 300 |
| | 600 tons |

*Transportation costs*

The cost of transporting one ton of wheat from each grain elevator (source) to each mill (destination) differs according to the distance and rail system. These costs are:

| Grain Elevator | Mill | | |
| | Chicago A | St. Louis B | Cincinnati C |
|---|---|---|---|
| Kansas City | $6 | 8 | 10 |
| Omaha | 7 | 11 | 11 |
| Des Moines | 4 | 5 | 12 |

For example, the cost of shipping one ton of wheat from the grain elevator at Omaha to the mill at Chicago is $7.

The problem is to determine the number of tons of wheat to transport from each grain elevator to each mill on a monthly basis in order to minimize the total cost of transportation. A diagram of the different transportation routes with supply, demand, and cost figures are shown in figure 7.1.

*The general linear programming model of a transportation problem*

The linear programming model for this problem is formulated as follows.

$$\text{minimize } Z = \$6x_{1A} + 8x_{1B} + 10x_{1C} + 7x_{2A} + 11x_{2B}$$
$$+ 11x_{2C} + 4x_{3A} + 5x_{3B} + 12x_{3C}$$

subject to

$$x_{1A} + x_{1B} + x_{1C} = 150$$
$$x_{2A} + x_{2B} + x_{2C} = 175$$
$$x_{3A} + x_{3B} + x_{3C} = 275$$
$$x_{1A} + x_{2A} + x_{3A} = 200$$
$$x_{1B} + x_{2B} + x_{3B} = 100$$
$$x_{1C} + x_{2C} + x_{3C} = 300$$
$$x_{ij} \geq 0$$

*Variable definitions*

*The objective function*

In this model the decision variables, $x_{ij}$, represent the number of tons of wheat transported from grain elevator, $i$ (where $i = 1, 2, 3$), to mill, $j$ (where $j = A, B, C$). The objective function represents the total cost of transporting for each route. Each term in the objective function reflects the cost of the tonnage transported for one route. For example, if 20 tons are transported from elevator 1 to mill $A$, the cost of $6 is multiplied by ($x_{1A} = 20$), which equals $120.

**Figure 7.1** Network of transportation routes for wheat shipments.

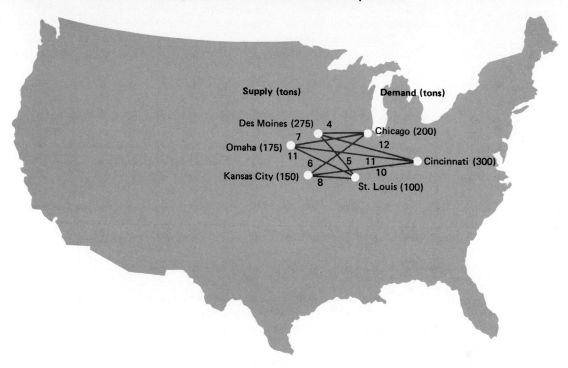

The first three constraints in the linear programming model are for the supply at each elevator, while the last three constraints are for the demand at each mill. As an example, consider the first supply constraint, $x_{1A} + x_{1B} + x_{1C} = 150$. This constraint represents the tons of wheat transported from Kansas City to all three mills: Chicago ($x_{1A}$), St. Louis ($x_{1B}$), and Cincinnati ($x_{1C}$). The amount transported from Kansas City is limited to the 150 tons available. However, this constraint (as well as all others) is an equation (=) rather than a ≤ inequality because all of the tons of wheat available will be needed to meet the *total demand* of 600 tons. In other words, the three mills demand 600 total tons, which is also the exact amount that can be supplied by the three grain elevators. Thus, all that *can* be supplied *will be,* in order to meet demand. This type of model where supply exactly equals demand is referred to as a *balanced* transportation model. The balanced model will be used to demonstrate the solution of a transportation problem.

*Constraint equations*

*A balanced transportation model*

## Solution of the Transportation Model

To this point, linear programming models have been solved with the simplex method. However, simplex solution of the example model developed in the previous section would be very time consuming, since there are nine decision variables and six constraints, and six artificial variables would be added.

This would create a rather large simplex tableau. Fortunately, several alternative solution methods for solving transportation problems are available that require considerably less manual effort than the simplex method.

Transportation models are solved within the context of a *tableau,* as in the simplex method. The tableau for our example "wheat" transportation model is shown in table 7.1.

**Table 7.1** The Transportation Tableau

| From \ To | A | B | C | Supply |
|-----------|-----|-----|-----|--------|
| 1 | 6 | 8 | 10 | 150 |
| 2 | 7 | 11 | 11 | 175 |
| 3 | 4 | 5 | 12 | 275 |
| Demand | 200 | 100 | 300 | 600 |

*Tableau cells*

Each cell in the tableau represents the amount transported from one source to one destination. Thus, the amount placed in each cell is the value of a decision variable for that cell. For example, the cell at the intersection of row 1 and column $A$ represents the decision variable $x_{1A}$. The smaller "box" within each cell contains the transportation cost for that route. For example, in cell $1A$ the value, $6, is the cost of transporting one ton of wheat from Kansas City to Chicago. The values along the outer rim of the tableau are the supply and demand constraint "quantity" values and are referred to as *rim requirements.*

*Rim requirements*

*Transportation model solution methods*

The two methods for solving a transportation model are the *stepping-stone method* and the *modified distribution method* (also known as MODI). Recall, however, that prior to solving a problem with the simplex method, an initial solution had to be established in the initial simplex tableau. This same condition must be met for a transportation model. However, notice in table 7.1 that artificial variables (the initial solution variables for a problem with = constraints) are not included. Thus, in a transportation model the initial solution is not at the origin where the artifical variables would take on all quantity values. In a transportation model an initial solution can be found by several alternative methods, including the *northwest corner method,* the *minimum cell cost method,* and *Vogel's approximation method.*

*Methods for determining an initial basic feasible solution*

## The Northwest Corner Method

In the northwest corner method an initial allocation is made to the cell in the upper left-hand corner of the tableau (i.e., the "northwest corner"). The amount allocated is the most possible, *subject to* the supply and demand constraints for that cell. In our example, we first allocate as much as possible to cell 1A (the "northwest corner"). This amount is 150 tons, since this is the maximum that can be supplied by grain elevator 1 at Kansas City, even though 200 tons are demanded by mill A at Chicago. This initial allocation is shown in table 7.2.

**Table 7.2** The Initial NW Corner Allocation

| From \ To | A | B | C | Supply |
|---|---|---|---|---|
| 1 | 6<br>150 | 8 | 10 | 150 |
| 2 | 7 | 11 | 11 | 175 |
| 3 | 4 | 5 | 12 | 275 |
| Demand | 200 | 100 | 300 | 600 |

The next allocation is made to a cell *adjacent* to cell 1A, in this case either cell 2A or 1B. However, cell 1B no longer represents a feasible allocation, since the total tonnage of wheat available at source 1 (i.e., 150 tons), has already been allocated. Thus, cell 2A represents the only feasible alternative, and as much as possible is allocated to this cell. This amount is either 175 tons, the supply at source 2 (Omaha) or 50 tons, the amount *now* demanded at destination A. (Recall that 150 of the 200 tons demanded at A has already been supplied). Since 50 tons is the most constrained amount, it is allocated to cell 2A, as shown in table 7.3.

*Allocating to an adjacent feasible cell*

**Table 7.3** The Second NW Corner Allocation

| From \ To | A | B | C | Supply |
|---|---|---|---|---|
| 1 | 6<br>150 | 8 | 10 | 150 |
| 2 | 7<br>50 | 11 | 11 | 175 |
| 3 | 4 | 5 | 12 | 275 |
| Demand | 200 | 100 | 300 | 600 |

Notice that the cells in tables 7.2 and 7.3 that are no longer feasible possibilities have been deleted (shaded out).

The third allocation is made in the same way as the second allocation. The only cell adjacent to cell 2A that is feasible is 2B. The most that can be allocated is either 100 tons or 125 tons (175 tons minus the 50 tons allocated to cell 2A). As such, 100 tons are allocated to cell 2B as shown in table 7.4.

**Table 7.4** The Third NW Corner Allocation

| To<br>From | A | B | C | Supply |
|---|---|---|---|---|
| 1 | 150 [6] | [8] | [10] | 150 |
| 2 | 50 [7] | 100 [11] | [11] | 175 |
| 3 | [4] | [5] | [12] | 275 |
| Demand | 200 | 100 | 300 | 600 |

*Meeting all rim requirements*    The fourth allocation is 25 tons to cell 2C and the fifth allocation is 275 tons to cell 3C, both of which are shown in table 7.5. Notice that all of the row and column allocations sum to meet the rim requirements.

**Table 7.5** The Initial Solution

| To<br>From | A | B | C | Supply |
|---|---|---|---|---|
| 1 | 150 [6] | [8] | [10] | 150 |
| 2 | 50 [7] | 100 [11] | 25 [11] | 175 |
| 3 | [4] | [5] | 275 [12] | 275 |
| Demand | 200 | 100 | 300 | 600 |

*The initial solution from the northwest corner method*    The transportation cost of this solution is computed by substituting the cell allocations (i.e., the amounts transported),

$$x_{1A} = 150 \qquad x_{2C} = 25$$
$$x_{2A} = 50 \qquad x_{3C} = 275$$
$$x_{2B} = 100$$

into the objective function.

$$Z = 6x_{1A} + 8x_{1B} + 10x_{1C} + 7x_{2A} + 11x_{2B}$$
$$+ 11x_{2C} + 4x_{3A} + 5x_{3B} + 12x_{3C}$$
$$= 6(150) + 8(0) + 10(0) + 7(50) + 11(100) + 11(25)$$
$$+ 4(0) + 5(0) + 12(275)$$
$$= \$5,925$$

The steps of the northwest corner method can be summarized as:

*Steps of the northwest corner method*

1. Allocate as much as possible to the cell in the upper left-hand corner subject to the supply and demand constraints.
2. Allocate as much as possible to the next adjacent feasible cell.
3. Repeat step 2 until all rim requirements have been met.

## The Minimum Cell Cost Method

In the minimum cell cost method, the initial allocation is made to the cell that has the lowest cost. In the transportation tableau for our example problem, cell 3A has the minimum cost of $4. As much as possible is allocated to this cell, which is either 200 tons or 275 tons. In this case, 200 tons is allocated to cell 3A, since only 200 tons is demanded, even though 275 tons could be supplied. This allocation is shown in table 7.6.

*Allocate as much as possible to the cell with the minimum cost*

**Table 7.6** The Initial Minimum Cell Cost Allocation

| From \ To | A | B | C | Supply |
|---|---|---|---|---|
| 1 | 6 | 8 | 10 | 150 |
| 2 | 7 | 11 | 11 | 175 |
| 3 | 4 <br> 200 | 5 | 12 | 275 |
| Demand | 200 | 100 | 300 | 600 |

Notice that the cells in column A have now been eliminated, since all the tons of wheat demanded at destination A, Chicago, have been supplied by source 3, Des Moines.

The next allocation is made to the cell with the minimum cost that is also feasible. This is cell 3B with a cost of $5. The most that can be allocated is 75 tons (275 tons minus the 200 tons already supplied). This allocation is shown in table 7.7.

**Table 7.7** The Second Minimum Cell Cost Allocation

| From \ To | A | B | C | Supply |
|---|---|---|---|---|
| 1 | 6 | 8 | 10 | 150 |
| 2 | 7 | 11 | 11 | 175 |
| 3 | 4 200 | 5 75 | 12 | 275 |
| Demand | 200 | 100 | 300 | 600 |

The third allocation is made to cell 1B, which has the minimum cost of $8. (Notice that cells with lower costs, such as 1A and 2A, are now infeasible). The amount allocated is 25 tons. The fourth allocation of 125 tons is made to cell 1C, while the last allocation of 175 tons is made to cell 2C. These allocations, which complete the minimum cell cost initial solution, are shown in table 7.8.

**Table 7.8** The Initial Solution

| From \ To | A | B | C | Supply |
|---|---|---|---|---|
| 1 | 6 | 8 25 | 10 125 | 150 |
| 2 | 7 | 11 | 11 175 | 175 |
| 3 | 4 200 | 5 75 | 12 | 275 |
| Demand | 200 | 100 | 300 | 600 |

*A better initial solution than the northwest corner method*

The total cost of this initial solution is $4,550, as compared to the total cost of the northwest corner initial solution ($5,925). The fact that the initial solution cost was lower with the minimum cell cost method is not a coincidence, but a logical occurrence. The northwest corner method does not consider cost at all in making allocations, while the minimum cell cost method does. Since cost is considered by this latter method as a means of allocating, it is natural that a lower initial cost will be attained. As such, the initial solution achieved by using the minimum cell cost method is usually better than that achieved by the northwest corner method. It is better in the sense that since it has a lower cost, it is closer to the optimal solution, and thus will require fewer subsequent iterations to achieve the optimal solution.

The steps of the minimum cell cost method can be summarized as:

*Steps of the minimum cell cost method*

1. Allocate as much as possible to the feasible cell with the minimum transportation cost.
2. Repeat step 1 until all rim requirements have been met.

## Vogel's Approximation Method

The third method for determining an initial solution, Vogel's Approximation Method (also called VAM), is based on the concept of *penalty cost* or *regret*. When a decision maker has several alternative courses of action available, if the wrong decision is made a penalty may be suffered (i.e., the decision maker regrets the decision that was made). For a decision maker solving a transportation problem, the courses of action are the alternative routes to select from and a wrong decision is to allocate to a cell that does not contain the lowest cost.

*Penalty costs*

In the VAM method the first step is to develop a penalty cost for each source and destination. For example, first consider column $A$ in table 7.9. Destination $A$, Chicago, can be supplied by Kansas City, Omaha, and Des Moines. The best decision would be to supply Chicago from source 3 because cell $3A$ has the minimum cost of $4. However, if a wrong decision was made and the next highest cost of $6 was selected at cell $1A$, a "penalty" of $2 per ton would result (i.e., $6 - 4 = $2). This demonstrates how the penalty cost is determined for each row and column of the tableau. The general rule for computing a penalty cost is to subtract the minimum cell cost from the next highest cell cost in each row and column. The penalty costs for our example are shown in table 7.9.

*Developing penalty costs for each row and column*

**Table 7.9** The VAM Penalty Costs

| From \ To | A | B | C | Supply | |
|---|---|---|---|---|---|
| 1 | 6 | 8 | 10 | 150 | 2 |
| 2 | 7 | 11 | 11 | 175 | 4 |
| 3 | 4 | 5 | 12 | 275 | 1 |
| Demand | 200 | 100 | 300 | 600 | |
| | 2 | 3 | 1 | | |

The initial allocation in the VAM method is made in the row or column that has the highest penalty cost. Observing table 7.9, row 2 has the highest penalty cost of $4. We allocate as much as possible to the

*The initial VAM allocation*

feasible cell in this row with the minimum cost. In row 2, cell 2A has the lowest cost of $7, and the most that can be allocated to cell 2A is 175 tons. In this way the greatest penalty cost of $4 has been avoided, since the best course of action has been selected. This allocation is shown in table 7.10.

**Table 7.10** The Initial VAM Allocation

| To<br>From | A | B | C | Supply | |
|---|---|---|---|---|---|
| 1 | 6 | 8 | 10 | 150 | 2 |
| 2 | 7<br>175 | 11 | 11 | 175 | |
| 3 | 4 | 5 | 12 | 275 | 1 |
| Demand | 200 | 100 | 300 | 600 | |
| | 2 | 3 | 2 | | |

*Recomputing all penalty costs*

After making the initial allocation, *all* penalty costs must be recomputed. In some cases the penalty costs will change, in other cases they will not. In table 7.10 we can see that the penalty cost for column C changed from $1 to $2 (i.e., cell 2C is no longer considered in computing penalty cost), while the penalty cost in row 2 was eliminated altogether, since no more allocations are possible for that row.

*Eliminating penalty costs*

Next, we repeat the previous step and allocate to the row or column with the highest penalty cost, which is now column B with a penalty cost of $3 (see table 7.10). The cell in column B with the lowest cost is 3B, and we allocate as much as possible to this cell, 100 tons. This allocation is shown in table 7.11.

**Table 7.11** The Second VAM Allocation

| To<br>From | A | B | C | Supply | |
|---|---|---|---|---|---|
| 1 | 6 | 8 | 10 | 150 | 2 |
| 2 | 7<br>175 | 11 | 11 | 175 | |
| 3 | 4 | 5<br>100 | 12 | 275 | 8 |
| Demand | 200 | 100 | 300 | 600 | |
| | 2 | | 2 | | |

Note that all penalty costs have been recomputed in table 7.11. The highest penalty cost is now $8 for row 3. In row 3 cell 3A has the minimum cell cost of $4, and 25 tons can be allocated to this cell as shown in table 7.12.

**Table 7.12** The Third VAM Allocation

| From \ To | A | B | C | Supply |
|---|---|---|---|---|
| 1 | 6 | 8 | 10 | 150 |
| 2 | 7 175 | 11 | 11 | 175 |
| 3 | 4 25 | 5 100 | 12 | 275 |
| Demand | 200 | 100 | 300 | 600 |

2

Table 7.12 shows the recomputed penalty costs after the third allocation. Notice that only column C presently has a penalty cost. Rows 1 and 3 have only one feasible cell, so a penalty does not exist for these rows. Thus, the last two allocations are made to column C. First, 150 tons are allocated to cell 1C, since it has the lowest cell cost. This leaves only cell 3C as a feasible possibility, and 150 tons are allocated to this cell. Both of these allocations are shown in table 7.13.

**Table 7.13** The Initial VAM Solution

| From \ To | A | B | C | Supply |
|---|---|---|---|---|
| 1 | 6 | 8 | 10 150 | 150 |
| 2 | 7 175 | 11 | 11 | 175 |
| 3 | 4 25 | 5 100 | 12 150 | 275 |
| Demand | 200 | 100 | 300 | 600 |

The total cost of this initial solution is $5,125, which is not as high as the cost obtained by the northwest corner initial solution ($5,925) or as low as the minimum cell cost solution ($4,550). Like the minimum cell cost method, VAM typically results in a lower-cost initial solution than the northwest corner method.

*The VAM initial solution compared to the northwest corner and minimum cell cost initial solutions*

The steps of Vogel's Approximation Method can be summarized as:

*Steps of VAM*

1. Determine the penalty cost for each row and column by subtracting the lowest cell cost in the row or column from the next highest cell cost in the same row or column.
2. Select the row or column with the highest penalty cost.
3. Allocate as much as possible to the feasible cell with the lowest transportation cost in the selected row or column.
4. Repeat steps 1, 2, and 3 until all rim requirements have been met.

## The Stepping-Stone Solution Method

*Solution methods once an initial solution is derived*

Once an initial *basic feasible solution* has been determined by any of the three methods, the next step is to solve the model for the optimal (i.e., minimum total cost) solution. There are two basic solution methods: the stepping-stone method and the modified distribution method (MODI). The *stepping-stone solution method* will be demonstrated first. Since the initial solution obtained by the minimum cell cost method had the lowest total cost of the three initial solutions, we will use it as the starting solution. Table 7.14 repeats the initial solution developed from the minimum cell cost method.

*Using the minimum cell cost initial solution*

**Table 7.14** The Minimum Cell Cost Solution

| From \ To | A | B | C | Supply |
|---|---|---|---|---|
| 1 | [6] | [8] 25 | [10] 125 | 150 |
| 2 | [7] | [11] | [11] 175 | 175 |
| 3 | [4] 200 | [5] 75 | [12] | 275 |
| Demand | 200 | 100 | 300 | 600 |

*Determining if there is an unused route that would lower costs if used*

The basic solution principle in a transportation problem is to determine if there is a transportation route not presently being used (i.e., an empty cell) that would result in a lower total cost if it were used. For example, in table 7.14 there are four empty cells representing unused routes: cell 1A, cell 2A, cell 2B, and cell 3C. Thus, our first step in the stepping-stone method is to evaluate these empty cells to see if the use of any of them would reduce total cost. If we find such a route, then we will allocate as much as possible to it.

*Allocating one ton to cell 1A*

First, let us consider allocating one ton of wheat to cell 1A. If one ton is allocated to cell 1A cost will be increased by $6, the transportation cost for cell 1A. However, by allocating one ton to cell 1A we have increased the supply in row 1 to 151 tons, as shown in table 7.15.

*Maintaining the rim requirements*

Since the constraints of the problem cannot be violated and feasibility maintained, if we add one ton to cell 1A, we must subtract one ton somewhere else where there is already an allocation available to subtract from. Cell 1B is a logical candidate, since it contains 25 tons. By subtracting one ton from cell 1B we now have 150 tons in row 1, and we have satisfied the supply constraint again. At the same time, by subtracting one ton from cell 1B, total cost has been reduced by $8.

However, by subtracting one ton from cell 1B, we now have only 99 tons allocated to column B where 100 tons are demanded, as shown in table 7.16.

**Table 7.15** The Allocation of One Ton to Cell 1*A*

| From \ To | A | | B | | C | | Supply |
|---|---|---|---|---|---|---|---|
| 1 | +1 | 6 | 25 | 8 | 125 | 10 | 150 |
| 2 | | 7 | | 11 | 175 | 11 | 175 |
| 3 | 200 | 4 | 75 | 5 | | 12 | 275 |
| Demand | 200 | | 100 | | 300 | | 600 |

**Table 7.16** The Subtraction of One Ton from Cell 1*B*

| From \ To | A | | B | | C | | Supply |
|---|---|---|---|---|---|---|---|
| 1 | +1 | 6 | −1 | 8 | 125 | 10 | 150 |
| | | | 25 | | | | |
| 2 | | 7 | | 11 | 175 | 11 | 175 |
| 3 | 200 | 4 | 75 | 5 | | 12 | 275 |
| Demand | 200 | | 100 | | 300 | | 600 |

99

*Stepping on stones (i.e., allocated-to cells)*

In order to compensate for this constraint violation, one ton must be added *to a cell already with an allocation.* Since cell 3*B* has 75 tons, we will add one ton to this cell, which again satisfies the demand constraint of 100 tons. A requirement of this solution method is that units can only be added to and subtracted from cells that already have allocations. That is why one ton was added to cell 3*B* and not 2*B*. This, in fact, is where this method derives its name. The process of adding and subtracting units from allocated cells is analogous to a pond an individual is crossing by "stepping" only on stones (i.e., only allocated-to cells).

By allocating one extra ton to cell 3*B* we have increased cost by $5, the transportation cost for that cell. However, we have also increased the supply in row 3 to 276 tons, a violation of the supply constraint for this source. As before, this violation can be remedied by subtracting one ton from cell 3*A,* which contains an allocation of 200 tons. This satisfies the supply constraint again for row 3 and it also reduces the total cost by $4, the transportation cost for cell 3*A.* These allocations and deletions are shown in table 7.17.

**Table 7.17** The Addition of One Ton to Cell 3*B* and the Subtraction of One Ton From Cell 3*A*

| To<br>From | *A* | *B* | *C* | Supply |
|---|---|---|---|---|
| 1 | +1 ⌐6¬ | −1 [8]<br>25 | [10]<br>125 | 150 |
| 2 | [7] | [11]<br> | [11]<br>175 | 175 |
| 3 | −1 ⌐4¬<br>200 | +1 [5]<br>75 | [12]<br> | 275 |
| Demand | 200 | 100 | 300 | 600 |

*The net cost change from allocating to cell 1A*

Notice in table 7.17 that by subtracting one ton from cell 3*A*, the demand constraint for column *A* has not been violated, since we previously added one ton to cell 1*A*.

Now let us review the increases and reductions in costs resulting from this process. We initially increased cost at cell 1*A* by $6, then reduced cost by $8 at cell 1*B*, then increased cost by $5 at cell 3*B*, and, finally, total cost was reduced by $4 at cell 3*A*.

$$1A \Rightarrow 1B \Rightarrow 3B \Rightarrow 3A$$
$$+\$6 - 8 + 5 - 4 = -\$1$$

*The entering nonbasic variable*

In other words, for each ton allocated to cell 1*A*, a route presently not used, total cost will be reduced by $1. This indicates that the solution is not optimal, since a lower cost can be achieved by allocating tons of wheat to cell 1*A*. As such, cell 1*A* represents a possible choice for the *entering nonbasic variable* for this tableau (i.e., analogous to the identification of a pivot column in the simplex method). However, there may be another variable (empty cell) that will result in an even greater decrease in cost than cell 1*A*. If there is such a cell, it will be selected as the entering variable; if not, cell 1*A* will be selected. In order to identify the appropriate entering variable the remaining empty cells must be tested like cell 1*A* was.

*A closed path*

Before testing the remaining empty cells, a few of the general characteristics of the stepping-stone process should be specifically identified. First, we always start with an empty cell and form a *closed path* of cells that presently have allocations. When developing the path, it is possible to "skip over" both unused and used cells. In any row or column there must be *exactly one* addition and *one* subtraction. (For example, in row 1, wheat is added at cell 1*A* and is subtracted at 1*B*).

Let us test cell 2*A* to see if it will result in a cost reduction. The stepping-stone closed path for cell 2*A* is shown in table 7.18.

The path in table 7.18 for cell 2*A* is slightly more complex than the previous path for cell 1*A*. Notice that the path crosses itself at one point, however, this is perfectly acceptable. An allocation to cell 2*A* will reduce cost by $1 as shown in the computation in table 7.18. Thus, we have located another possible entering variable, although it is no better than cell 1*A*.

**Table 7.18** The Stepping-Stone Path for Cell 2A

| To<br>From | A | B | C | Supply |
|---|---|---|---|---|
| 1 | 6 | − ← 8 + <br> 25 | 10 <br> ↑ 125 | 150 |
| 2 | + 7 | 11 − <br> | 11 <br> 175 | 175 |
| 3 | − ← 4 + <br> 200 | 5 <br> 75 | 12 | 275 |
| Demand | 200 | 100 | 300 | 600 |

$$+ \frac{2A}{\$7} - \frac{2C}{11} + \frac{1C}{10} - \frac{1B}{8} + \frac{3B}{5} - \frac{3A}{4} = -\$1$$

The remaining stepping-stone paths for cells 2B and 3C are shown in tables 7.19 and 7.20, respectively.

**Table 7.19** The Stepping-Stone Path for Cell 2B

| To<br>From | A | B | C | Supply |
|---|---|---|---|---|
| 1 | 6 | − ← 8 + <br> 25 | 10 <br> ↑ 125 | 150 |
| 2 | 7 | + 11 − <br> | 11 <br> 175 | 175 |
| 3 | 4 <br> 200 | 5 <br> 75 | 12 | 275 |
| Demand | 200 | 100 | 300 | 600 |

$$+ \frac{2B}{\$11} - \frac{2C}{11} + \frac{1C}{10} - \frac{1B}{8} = +\$2$$

**Table 7.20** The Stepping-Stone Path for Cell 3C

| To<br>From | A | B | C | Supply |
|---|---|---|---|---|
| 1 | 6 | + ← 8 − <br> 25 | 10 <br> ↑ 125 | 150 |
| 2 | 7 | 11 | 11 <br> 175 | 175 |
| 3 | 4 <br> 200 | − 5 + <br> 75 | 12 | 275 |
| Demand | 200 | 100 | 300 | 600 |

$$+ \frac{3C}{\$12} - \frac{1C}{10} + \frac{1B}{8} - \frac{3B}{5} = +\$5$$

Now that all four unused routes have been evaluated, we see that there is a tie for the entering variable represented by cell 1*A* and cell 2*A*. Both show a reduction in cost of $1 per ton allocated to that route. The tie can be broken arbitrarily just as we broke a tie between tied pivot columns in the simplex method. As such, we will select cell 1*A* (i.e., $x_{1A}$) to enter the solution basis.

Since the total cost of the model will be reduced by $1 for each ton we can reallocate to cell 1*A*, we naturally want to reallocate as much as possible. In order to determine how much to allocate, we need to look at the path for cell 1*A* again, as shown in table 7.21.

**Table 7.21** The Stepping-Stone Path for Cell 1*A*

| From \ To | A | B | C | Supply |
|---|---|---|---|---|
| 1 | + ⋯ 6 | − 8 / 25 | 10 / 125 | 150 |
| 2 | 7 | 11 | 11 / 175 | 175 |
| 3 | − 4 / 200 | + 5 / 75 | 12 | 275 |
| Demand | 200 | 100 | 300 | 600 |

On the stepping-stone path in table 7.21, notice that tons of wheat must be subtracted at cells 1*B* and 3*A* in order to meet our rim requirements and satisfy the model constraints. Since we cannot subtract more than is available in a cell, we are limited by the 25 tons in cell 1*B*. In other words, if we allocate more than 25 tons to cell 1*A*, then we must subtract more than 25 tons from 1*B;* however, only 25 tons are available. Therefore, 25 tons is the amount we reallocate to cell 1*A* according to our path. That is, 25 tons are added to 1*A*, subtracted from 1*B*, added to 3*B,* and subtracted from 3*A*. This reallocation is shown in table 7.22.

**Table 7.22** The Second Iteration Stepping-Stone Method

| From \ To | A | B | C | Supply |
|---|---|---|---|---|
| 1 | 6 / 25 | 8 | 10 / 125 | 150 |
| 2 | 7 | 11 | 11 / 175 | 175 |
| 3 | 4 / 175 | 5 / 100 | 12 | 275 |
| Demand | 200 | 100 | 300 | 600 |

The process culminating in table 7.22 represents one *iteration* of the stepping-stone method. The process has been very similar to the simplex method. We selected $x_{1A}$ as the entering variable, and it turned out that $x_{1B}$ was the leaving variable (since it now has a value of zero in table 7.22). Thus, at each iteration one variable enters and one leaves, just as in the simplex method.

*An iteration of the stepping-stone method*

Now the entire process of evaluating unused routes (i.e., empty cells) must be repeated for the solution in table 7.22. The paths for the empty cells (1*B*, 2*A*, 2*B*, and 3*C*) are shown in tables 7.23 through 7.26.

*Repeating the stepping-stone process*

**Table 7.23** The Stepping-Stone Path for Cell 2*A*

| To From | A | B | C | Supply |
|---------|-----|-----|-----|--------|
| 1 | − 6 25 | 8 + | 10 + 125 | 150 |
| 2 | + 7 | 11 | − 11 175 | 175 |
| 3 | 4 175 | 5 100 | 12 | 275 |
| Demand | 200 | 100 | 300 | 600 |

$$\overset{2A}{+\$7} \quad \overset{2C}{-11} \quad \overset{1C}{+10} \quad \overset{1A}{-6} = \$0$$

**Table 7.24** The Stepping-Stone Path for Cell 1*B*

| To From | A | B | C | Supply |
|---------|-----|-----|-----|--------|
| 1 | 6 25 | + 8 | 10 125 | 150 |
| 2 | 7 | 11 | 11 175 | 175 |
| 3 | + 4 175 | − 5 100 | 12 | 275 |
| Demand | 200 | 100 | 300 | 600 |

$$\overset{1B}{+\$8} \quad \overset{3B}{-5} \quad \overset{3A}{+4} \quad \overset{1A}{-6} = +\$1$$

**Table 7.25** The Stepping-Stone Path for Cell 2*B*

| To From | A | B | C | Supply |
|---------|-----|-----|-----|--------|
| 1 | − 6 25 | 8 + | 10 + 125 | 150 |
| 2 | 7 + | 11 | − 11 175 | 175 |
| 3 | + 4 175 | − 5 100 | 12 | 275 |
| Demand | 200 | 100 | 300 | 600 |

$$\overset{2B}{+\$11} \quad \overset{3B}{-5} \quad \overset{3A}{+4} \quad \overset{1A}{-6} \quad \overset{1C}{+10} \quad \overset{2C}{-11} = +\$3$$

179

**Table 7.26** The Stepping-Stone Path for Cell 3C

| From \ To | A | B | C | Supply |
|---|---|---|---|---|
| 1 | + —6— 25 | —8— | —10— 125 | 150 |
| 2 | 7 | 11 | 11 175 | 175 |
| 3 | ←—4— 175 | —5— + 100 | 12 | 275 |
| Demand | 200 | 100 | 300 | 600 |

$$\frac{3C}{+\$12} - \frac{3A}{4} + \frac{1A}{6} - \frac{1C}{10} = +\$4$$

*The optimal solution*

Since the evaluations of all four paths result in no cost reductions, then this solution is optimal. The solution and total minimum cost are

$$x_{1A} = 25 \text{ tons} \qquad x_{3A} = 175 \text{ tons}$$
$$x_{1C} = 125 \text{ tons} \qquad x_{3B} = 100 \text{ tons}$$
$$x_{2C} = 175 \text{ tons}$$

$$Z = \$6(25) + 8(0) + 10(125) + 7(0) + 11(0) + 11(175)$$
$$+ 4(175) + 5(100) + 12(0)$$
$$= \$4,525$$

However, notice that in table 7.23 the path for cell 2A resulted in a cost change of $0. In other words, allocating to this cell would neither increase nor decrease total cost. This occurrence reflects a *multiple optimal solution* (a topic first discussed in chapter 5). Thus, $x_{2A}$ could be entered into the solution and there would not be a change in the total minimum cost of $4,525. To identify the alternative solution we would allocate as much as possible to cell 2A, which in this case is 25 tons of wheat. The alternate solution is shown in table 7.27.

*Multiple optimal solutions*

*The alternate optimal solution*

**Table 7.27** The Alternate Optimum Solution

| From \ To | A | B | C | Supply |
|---|---|---|---|---|
| 1 | 6 | 8 | 10 150 | 150 |
| 2 | 7 25 | 11 | 11 150 | 175 |
| 3 | 4 175 | 5 100 | 12 | 275 |
| Demand | 200 | 100 | 300 | 600 |

The solution in table 7.27 also results in a total minimum cost of $4,525.

The steps of the stepping-stone method can be summarized as:

Steps of the stepping-stone method

1. Determine the stepping-stone paths and cost changes for each empty cell in the tableau.

2. Allocate as much as possible to the empty cell with the greatest net decrease in cost.

3. Repeat steps 1 and 2 until all empty cells have positive cost changes that indicate an optimal solution.

## The Modified Distribution Method

The *modified distribution method* (MODI) is basically a modified version of the stepping-stone method. The difference between the two methods is that in MODI the individual cell cost changes are determined mathematically without having to identify all of the stepping-stone paths for cells with no allocations.

A modified version of the stepping-stone method

In order to demonstrate MODI, we will again use the initial solution obtained by the minimum cell cost method. The tableau for the initial solution with the modifications required by MODI are shown in table 7.28.

**Table 7.28** The Minimum Cell Cost Initial Solution

| $u_i$ | To From | $v_A =$ A | $v_B =$ B | $v_C =$ C | Supply |
|---|---|---|---|---|---|
| $u_1 =$ | 1 | [6] | [8] 25 | [10] 125 | 150 |
| $u_2 =$ | 2 | [7] | [11] | [11] 175 | 175 |
| $u_3 =$ | 3 | [4] 200 | [5] 75 | [12] | 275 |
| | Demand | 200 | 100 | 300 | 600 |

The extra column with the $u_i$ symbols and the extra row on top with the $v_j$ symbols represent row and column values that must be computed in MODI. These values are computed using the following formula for all *used (presently allocated to) cells.*

Adding a $u_i$ column and $v_j$ row

$$u_i + v_j = c_{ij}$$

The value $c_{ij}$ is the transportation cost for cell *ij.* For example, the formula for cell 1B is

Computing $u_i$ and $v_j$ values

$$u_1 + v_B = c_{1B}$$

and, since $c_{1B} = 8$,

$$u_1 + v_B = 8$$

The formulas for the remaining presently allocated to cells are

$$x_{1C} : u_1 + v_C = 10$$
$$x_{2C} : u_2 + v_C = 11$$
$$x_{3A} : u_3 + v_A = 4$$
$$x_{3B} : u_3 + v_B = 5$$

Now there are five equations with six unknowns. In order to solve these equations, it is necessary only to assign one of the unknowns a value of zero. Thus, if we let $u_1 = 0$, then we can solve for all remaining $u_i$ and $v_j$ values.

$$x_{1B} : u_1 + v_B = 8$$
$$0 + v_B = 8$$
$$v_B = 8$$
$$x_{1C} : u_1 + v_C = 10$$
$$0 + v_C = 10$$
$$v_C = 10$$
$$x_{2C} : u_2 + v_C = 11$$
$$u_2 + 10 = 11$$
$$u_2 = 1$$
$$x_{3B} : u_3 + v_B = 5$$
$$u_3 + 8 = 5$$
$$u_3 = -3$$
$$x_{3A} : u_3 + v_A = 4$$
$$-3 + v_A = 4$$
$$v_A = 7$$

Notice that it was necessary to first solve the equation for cell $3B$ before the cell $3A$ equation could be solved. Now all the $u_i$ and $v_j$ values can be substituted into our tableau as shown in table 7.29.

**Table 7.29** The Initial Solution with All $u_i$ and $v$ Values

| $u_i$ | $v_j$ / To From | $v_A = 7$ / A | $v_B = 8$ / B | $v_C = 10$ / C | Supply |
|---|---|---|---|---|---|
| $u_1 = 0$ | 1 | [6] | [8] 25 | [10] 125 | 150 |
| $u_2 = 1$ | 2 | [7] | [11] | [11] 175 | 175 |
| $u_3 = -3$ | 3 | [4] 200 | [5] 75 | [12] | 275 |
| | Demand | 200 | 100 | 300 | 600 |

Next, we use the following formula to evaluate all *empty cells:*

$$c_{ij} - u_i - v_j = k_{ij}$$

where $k_{ij}$ equals the cost increase or decrease that would occur by allocating to a cell.

*Computing the cost change for each unused route*

For the empty cells in table 7.29:

$$x_{1A} : k_{1A} = c_{1A} - u_1 - v_A = 6 - 0 - 7 = -1$$
$$x_{2A} : k_{2A} = c_{2A} - u_2 - v_A = 7 - 1 - 7 = -1$$
$$x_{2B} : k_{2B} = c_{2B} - u_2 - v_B = 11 - 1 - 8 = +2$$
$$x_{3C} : k_{3C} = c_{3C} - u_3 - v_C = 12 - (-3) - 10 = +5$$

This indicates that both cells $1A$ and $2A$ will decrease cost by \$1 per allocated ton. Notice that those are exactly the same cost changes for all four empty cells as computed in the stepping-stone method. The same information obtained by evaluating the paths in the stepping-stone method was obtained in MODI using mathematical formulas.

We can select either cell $1A$ or $2A$ to allocate to since they are tied. If cell $1A$ is selected as the entering nonbasic variable, then the stepping-stone path for that cell must be determined so that we know how much to reallocate. This is the same path previously identified in table 7.21. Reallocating along this path results in the tableau shown in table 7.30 (and previously shown in table 7.22).

*The second iteration of the MODI method*

**Table 7.30** The Second Iteration of the MODI Solution Method

| $u_i$ | $v_j$ To From | $v_A =$ A | $v_B =$ B | $v_C =$ C | Supply |
|---|---|---|---|---|---|
| $u_1 =$ | 1 | 6 <br> 25 | 8 | 10 <br> 125 | 150 |
| $u_2 =$ | 2 | 7 | 11 | 11 <br> 175 | 175 |
| $u_3 =$ | 3 | 4 <br> 175 | 5 <br> 100 | 12 | 275 |
| | Demand | 200 | 100 | 300 | 600 |

The $u_i$ and $v_j$ values for table 7.30 must now be recomputed using our formula for the allocated-to cells.

*Recomputing $u_i$ and $v_j$*

$$x_{1A} : u_1 + v_A = 6$$
$$0 + v_A = 6$$
$$v_A = 6$$
$$x_{1C} : u_1 + v_C = 10$$
$$0 + v_C = 10$$

$$v_C = 10$$
$$x_{2C} : u_2 + v_C = 11$$
$$u_2 + 10 = 11$$
$$u_2 = 1$$
$$x_{3A} : u_3 + v_A = 4$$
$$u_3 + 6 = 4$$
$$u_3 = -2$$
$$x_{3B} : u_3 + v_B = 5$$
$$-2 + v_B = 5$$
$$v_B = 7$$

These new $u_i$ and $v_j$ values are shown in table 7.31.

**Table 7.31** The New $u_i$ and $v_j$ Values for the Second Iteration

| $u_i$ | $v_j$ / From \ To | $v_A = 6$ A | $v_B = 7$ B | $v_C = 10$ C | Supply |
|---|---|---|---|---|---|
| $u_1 = 0$ | 1 | 25 $\lfloor 6$ | $\lfloor 8$ | 125 $\lfloor 10$ | 150 |
| $u_2 = 1$ | 2 | $\lfloor 7$ | $\lfloor 11$ | 175 $\lfloor 11$ | 175 |
| $u_3 = -2$ | 3 | 175 $\lfloor 4$ | 100 $\lfloor 5$ | $\lfloor 12$ | 275 |
| | Demand | 200 | 100 | 300 | 600 |

*Computing the cost change for each unused route*

The cost changes for the empty cells are now computed using the formula $c_{ij} - u_i - v_j = k_{ij}$, as follows.

$$x_{1B} : k_{1B} = c_{1B} - u_1 - v_B = 8 - 0 - 7 = +1$$
$$x_{2A} : k_{2A} = c_{2A} - u_2 - v_A = 7 - 1 - 6 = 0$$
$$x_{2B} : k_{2B} = c_{2B} - u_2 - v_B = 11 - 1 - 7 = +3$$
$$x_{3C} : k_{3C} = c_{3C} - u_3 - v_C = 12 - (-2) - 10 = +4$$

Since none of these values are negative, the solution shown in table 7.31 is optimal. However, as in the stepping-stone method, cell 2A with a zero cost change indicates a multiple optimum solution.

*Steps of MODI*    The steps of the modified distribution method can be summarized as:

1. Develop an initial solution using one of the three methods available.
2. Compute $u_i$ and $v_j$ values for each row and column by applying the formula $u_i + v_j = c_{ij}$ to each cell that has an allocation.
3. Compute the cost change, $k_{ij}$, for each empty cell using the formula $c_{ij} - u_i - v_j = k_{ij}$.

4. Allocate as much as possible to the empty cell that will result in the greatest net decrease in cost $(-k_{ij})$. Allocate according to the stepping-stone path for the selected cell.

5. Repeat steps 2 through 4 until all $k_{ij}$ values are positive or zero.

## The Unbalanced Transportation Model

All of the methods for determining an initial solution and for determining an optimal solution presented so far have been demonstrated within the context of a balanced transportation model. However, realistically, an *unbalanced problem* is a more likely occurrence. Consider our same example for transporting wheat, except that now demand at Cincinnati will be changed to 350 tons. This creates a situation where total demand is 650 tons, while total supply is 600 tons.

*Demand exceeds supply*

In order to compensate for this difference in the transportation tableau, a new "dummy" row is added to the tableau, as shown in table 7.32.

*Inserting a dummy row*

**Table 7.32** An Unbalanced Model (Demand > Supply)

| To / From | A | B | C | Supply |
|---|---|---|---|---|
| 1 | 6 | 8 | 10 | 150 |
| 2 | 7 | 11 | 11 | 175 |
| 3 | 4 | 5 | 12 | 275 |
| Dummy | 0 | 0 | 0 | 50 |
| Demand | 200 | 100 | 350 | 650 |

The dummy row is assigned a supply of 50 tons. This modification serves to balance the model again. The 50 tons that are demanded, but cannot be supplied, will be allocated to a cell in the dummy row. The transportation costs for the cells in the dummy row are zero, since the tons allocated to these cells are amounts not really transported, but the amounts by which demand was not met. These dummy cells are, in effect, *slack variables*.

Now consider our example with supply at Des Moines increased to 375 tons. This increases total supply to 700 tons, while total demand remains at 600 tons. Rather than compensate for this imbalance by adding a dummy row, we now add a dummy column, as shown in table 7.33.

*Supply exceeds demand*

*Inserting a dummy column*

**Table 7.33** An Unbalanced Model (Supply > Demand)

| From \ To | A | B | C | Dummy | Supply |
|-----------|-----|-----|------|-------|--------|
| 1 | 6 | 8 | 10 | 0 | 150 |
| 2 | 7 | 11 | 11 | 0 | 175 |
| 3 | 4 | 5 | 12 | 0 | 375 |
| Demand | 200 | 100 | 300 | 100 | 700 |

The addition of a dummy row or a dummy column has no effect on the initial solution methods or the methods for determining an optimal solution. The dummy row, or column, cells are treated the same as any other tableau cell. For example, in the minimum cell cost method, there would be three cells tied for the minimum cost cell, each with a cost of zero. In this case (as is the case any time there is a tie between cells) the tie should be broken arbitrarily.

## Degeneracy

In all the tableaus showing a solution to our wheat transportation problem, the following condition was met:

$m$ rows $+ n$ columns $- 1 =$ the number of cells with allocations

For example, in any of the balanced tableaus for wheat transportation, the number of rows are 3 (i.e., $m = 3$) and the number of columns are 3 (i.e., $n = 3$), thus,

$3 + 3 - 1 = 5$ cells with allocations

*Violating the $m + n - 1$ condition*

Five cells with allocations always existed for these tableaus, thus our condition for normal solution was met. When this condition is not met and less than $m + n - 1$ cells have allocations, the tableau is said to be *degenerate*.

Consider our wheat transportation example with the supply values changed to the amounts shown in table 7.34. The initial solution shown in this tableau was developed using the minimum cell cost method.

The tableau shown in table 7.34 does not meet our condition,

$m + n - 1 =$ the number of cells with allocations
$3 + 3 - 1 = 5$ cells

*The difficulties resulting from a degenerate solution*

since there are only 4 cells with allocations. The difficulty resulting from a degenerate basic feasible solution is that neither the stepping-stone method or MODI will work unless the above condition is met and the appropriate number of cells with allocations exists. When the tableau is degenerate, a closed path cannot be completed for all cells in the stepping-stone method, *and* all the $u_i + v_j = c_{ij}$ computations cannot be completed in MODI. For example, a closed path cannot be determined for cell $1A$ in table 7.34.

**Table 7.34** The Minimum Cell Cost Initial Solution

| To<br>From | A | B | C | Supply |
|---|---|---|---|---|
| 1 |  | 6<br>100 | 8<br>50 | 10<br>150 |
| 2 |  | 7 | 11<br>250 | 11<br>250 |
| 3 | 4<br>200 | 5 | 12 | 200 |
| Demand | 200 | 100 | 300 | 600 |

In order to compensate for this deficiency, one of the empty cells must be artificially designated as a cell with an allocation. Cell $1A$ in table 7.35 is designated arbitrarily as a cell with an artificial allocation by a "0." This indicates that this cell will be treated as a cell with an allocation when determining our stepping-stone paths or our MODI formulas, although in actuality there is no real allocation in this cell. Notice that the location of "0" was *arbitrary*. There is no general rule for allocating the artificial cell. It is possible to allocate the "0" to a cell so that it will still not be possible to determine all of the stepping-stone paths. For example, if "0" had been allocated to cell $2B$ instead of $1A$, none of the stepping-stone paths could have been determined, even though the tableau would no longer technically be degenerate. In such a case, the "0" must be reallocated to another cell and all paths determined again. This process must be repeated until an artificial cell is selected that will enable the determination of all paths. In most cases, however, there is more than one possible cell location for the "0" to be allocated to.

*Artificially creating an allocated-to cell*

**Table 7.35** The Initial Solution

| To<br>From | A | B | C | Supply |
|---|---|---|---|---|
| 1 | 6<br>"0" | 8<br>100 | 10<br>50 | 150 |
| 2 | 7 | 11 | 11<br>250 | 250 |
| 3 | 4<br>200 | 5 | 12 | 200 |
| Demand | 200 | 100 | 300 | 600 |

The stepping-stone paths and cost changes for this tableau are:

$$
\begin{array}{llcccccccc}
 & & 2A & & 2C & & 1C & & 1A & \\
x_{2A} : & 7 & - & 11 & + & 10 & - & 6 & = & 0 \\
 & & 2B & & 2C & & 1C & & 1B & \\
x_{2B} : & 11 & - & 11 & + & 10 & - & 8 & = & +2 \\
 & & 3B & & 1B & & 1A & & 3A & \\
x_{3B} : & 5 & - & 8 & + & 6 & - & 4 & = & -1 \\
 & & 3C & & 1C & & 1A & & 3A & \\
x_{3C} : & 12 & - & 10 & + & 6 & - & 4 & = & +4 \\
\end{array}
$$

Cell $3B$ shows a \$1 decrease in cost for every ton of wheat allocated to it. 100 tons can be allocated to cell $3B$, which results in the tableau shown in table 7.36.

**Table 7.36** The Second Stepping-Stone Iteration

| To<br>From | A | B | C | Supply |
|---|---|---|---|---|
| 1 | 100 ⌐6 | ⌐8 | 50 ⌐10 | 150 |
| 2 | ⌐7 | ⌐11 | 250 ⌐11 | 250 |
| 3 | 100 ⌐4 | 100 ⌐5 | ⌐12 | 200 |
| Demand | 200 | 100 | 300 | 600 |

Notice that the solution in table 7.36 now meets our condition, $m + n - 1 = 5$. Thus, when applying the stepping-stone method (or MODI) to this tableau, it is not necessary to artificially designate an empty cell as a cell with an allocation. It is quite possible to begin the solution process with a normal tableau and have it become degenerate or vice versa. If it had been indicated that the cell with the "0" should have units subtracted from it, no actual units could be subtracted. What occurs is that the "0" is moved to the cell that represents the entering variable. (The solution shown in table 7.36 is optimal, however, a multiple optimal solution exists at cell $2A$.)

## Prohibited Routes

*A route over which units cannot be transported*

It may occur that one or more of the routes in the transportation model are *prohibited*. That is, units cannot be transported from a particular source to a particular destination. When this situation occurs, it must be insured that no units are allocated to the cell representing this route in the optimal solution. Recall that in the simplex tableau, when we wanted to insure that an artificial variable would not be in the final solution, it was assigned a large coefficient of $M$. This same principle can be used in a transportation model for a prohibited route. A value of $M$ is assigned as the transportation cost for a cell that represents a prohibited route. Thus, when the prohibited cell is evaluated, it will always contain a large positive cost change of $M$, which will keep it from being selected as an entering variable.

*Assigning a cell cost of* M

## The Assignment Model

The assignment model is a special form of linear programming model that is similar to the transportation model. However, in the assignment model, the supply at each source is limited to one unit and the demand at each destination is limited to one unit. In order to demonstrate the assignment model and its special solution method, the following example will be employed.

*A transportation model where the supply at each source and demand at each destination is one*

The Atlantic Coast Conference has four basketball games on a particular night. The conference office wants to assign four teams of officials to the four games in a way that will minimize the total distance traveled by the officials. The distances in miles for each team of officials to each game location are shown in table 7.37.

*An assignment model example*

**Table 7.37** The Travel Distances for Each Team of Officials to Each Game

| | Game Sites | | | |
|---|---|---|---|---|
| Officials | Raleigh | Atlanta | Durham | Clemson |
| A | 210 | 90 | 180 | 160 |
| *B* | 100 | 70 | 130 | 200 |
| *C* | 175 | 105 | 140 | 170 |
| *D* | 80 | 65 | 105 | 120 |

The supply is always one team of officials and the demand at each game is for only one team of officials. Table 7.37 is already in the proper form for the assignment tableau. Since supply and demand are always one, it is not necessary to include supply and demand rows in the tableau.

The first step in the assignment method of solution is to develop an *opportunity cost table.* This is accomplished by first subtracting the minimum value in each row from every other value in the row. These computations are referred to as *row reductions.* A similar principle underlaid the determination of the penalty costs in the VAM method. In other words, the best course of action is determined for each row, and the penalty or "lost opportunity" is developed for all other row values. The *row reductions* for this example are shown in table 7.38.

*Developing an opportunity cost table*

*Row reductions*

**Table 7.38** The Assignment Tableau with Row Reductions

| Officials | Game Sites | | | |
| | Raleigh | Atlanta | Durham | Clemson |
|---|---|---|---|---|
| A | 120 | 0 | 90 | 70 |
| B | 30 | 0 | 60 | 130 |
| C | 70 | 0 | 35 | 65 |
| D | 15 | 0 | 40 | 55 |

*Column reductions*

Next, the minimum value in each column is subtracted from all other column values. These are called *column reductions* and are shown in table 7.39.

**Table 7.39** The Tableau with Column Reductions

| Officials | Game Sites | | | |
| | Raleigh | Atlanta | Durham | Clemson |
|---|---|---|---|---|
| A | 105 | 0 | 55 | 15 |
| B | 15 | 0 | 25 | 75 |
| C | 55 | 0 | 0 | 10 |
| D | 0 | 0 | 5 | 0 |

*Making unique assignments*

Table 7.39 represents the completed opportunity cost table for our example. Assignments are made in this table wherever a zero is present. For example, team *A* can be assigned to Atlanta. An *optimal solution* results when all four teams can be uniquely assigned to a game.

Notice in table 7.39 that by assigning team *A* to Atlanta, no other team can be assigned to that game. This subsequently leaves no zero in row *B*, which indicates that there is not a unique optimal assignment for team *B*. Therefore, table 7.39 does not contain an optimal solution.

*The line test for determining the number of unique assignments available*

A test to determine if four unique assignments exist in table 7.39 is to draw the minimum number of horizontal or vertical lines necessary to cross out all zeros through the rows and columns of the table. For example, table 7.40 shows that three lines were required to cross out all zeros.

**Table 7.40** The Opportunity Cost Table with the Line Test

| Officials | Game Sites | | | |
| | Raleigh | Atlanta | Durham | Clemson |
|---|---|---|---|---|
| A | 105 | 0 | 55 | 15 |
| B | 15 | 0 | 25 | 75 |
| C | 55 | 0 | 0 | 10 |
| D | 0 | 0 | 5 | 0 |

The three lines indicate that there are only three unique assignments, while four are required for an optimal solution. (Note that the three lines could have been drawn differently, however it would not affect the subsequent solution method.) In the solution method for the assignment model the minimum value not crossed through by a line is subtracted from all other values not crossed out by a line, and this minimum value is added to those cells where two lines cross. The minimum value not crossed out by a line in table 7.40 is 15. The second iteration for this model with the appropriate changes is shown in table 7.41.

*An assignment model iteration*

**Table 7.41** The Second Iteration

| Officials | Game Sites | | | |
| --- | --- | --- | --- | --- |
| | Raleigh | Atlanta | Durham | Clemson |
| A | 90 | 0 | 40 | 0 |
| B | 0 | 0 | 10 | 60 |
| C | 55 | 15 | 0 | 10 |
| D | 0 | 15 | 5 | 0 |

No matter how the lines are drawn in table 7.41, at least four are required to cross out all the zeros. This indicates that four unique assignments can be made and that an optimal solution has been reached. Now let us make the assignments from table 7.41.

First, team A can be assigned to either the Atlanta game or the Clemson game. We will assign team A to Atlanta first. This means that team A cannot be assigned to any other game, and no other team can be assigned to Atlanta. As such, row A and the Atlanta column can be eliminated. Next, team B is assigned to Raleigh. (Team B cannot be assigned to Atlanta, since it has already been eliminated.) The third assignment is for team C to the Durham game. This leaves team D assigned to the Clemson game. These assignments and their respective distances (from table 7.37) are summarized as follows.

*The optimal solution*

| | | | *Distance* |
| --- | --- | --- | --- |
| Team A | ⇒ | Atlanta | 90 |
| Team B | ⇒ | Raleigh | 100 |
| Team C | ⇒ | Durham | 140 |
| Team D | ⇒ | Clemson | 120 |
| | | | 450 miles |

Now let us go back and make the initial assignment of team A to Clemson (the alternative assignment we did not initially make). This will result in the following set of assignments.

*An alternate optimal solution*

|        |               |         |     |
|--------|---------------|---------|-----|
| Team A | ⇒ | Clemson | 160 |
| Team B | ⇒ | Atlanta | 70  |
| Team C | ⇒ | Durham  | 140 |
| Team D | ⇒ | Raleigh | 80  |
|        |               |         | 450 miles |

These two assignments represent *multiple optimal solutions* for our example problem. Both assignments will result in a minimum total distance traveled by the officials of 450 miles.

*An unbalanced assignment problem*

As in a transportation problem, an assignment model can be unbalanced when supply exceeds demand or demand exceeds supply. For example, assume that five teams of officials exist instead of four, to be assigned to the four games. In order to compensate for this imbalance a *dummy column* is added to the assignment tableau to balance the model again, as shown in table 7.42.

*Adding a dummy column*

**Table 7.42** An Unbalanced Assignment Tableau with a Dummy Column

| Officials | Raleigh | Atlanta | Game Sites Durham | Clemson | Dummy |
|-----------|---------|---------|--------|---------|-------|
| A | 210 | 90  | 180 | 160 | 0 |
| B | 100 | 70  | 130 | 200 | 0 |
| C | 175 | 105 | 140 | 170 | 0 |
| D | 80  | 65  | 105 | 120 | 0 |
| E | 95  | 115 | 120 | 100 | 0 |

One team of officials would be assigned to the dummy column in the solution to this model. If five games exist and there are only four teams of officials, a *dummy row* would be added instead of a dummy column. The addition of a dummy row or column does not affect the solution method.

*Adding a dummy row*

*Prohibited assignments* are also possible in an assignment problem just as prohibited routes could occur in a transportation model. In the transportation model an $M$ value was assigned as the cost for the cell representing the prohibited route. This same method is used for a prohibited assignment. A value of $M$ is placed in the cell that represents the prohibited assignment.

*Steps of the assignment solution method*

The steps of the assignment solution method can be summarized as:

1. Perform row reductions by subtracting the minimum value in each row from all other row values.

2. Perform column reductions by subtracting the minimum value in each column from all other column values.

3. In the completed opportunity cost table, cross out all zeros with the minimum number of horizontal and/or vertical lines.

4. If less than $m$ lines are required (where $m =$ the number of rows or columns), subtract the minimum uncrossed value from all other uncrossed values, and add this same minimum value to all cells where two lines cross. All other values are unchanged.

5. If $m$ lines are required, the optimal solution exists and $m$ unique assignments are made. If less than $m$ lines are required, repeat step 3.

## Summary

In this chapter two special types of linear programming problems were presented: the transportation problem and the assignment problem. The various solution methods for each type of problem were demonstrated using examples. However, a unique characteristic of the solutions to these problems was that they contained only *integer* values rather than fractional values. The solution methods for these problems were such that they insured integer solutions. Linear programming problems other than transportation problems often occur that also require integer solutions. Since the general simplex solution method does not insure integer solutions, when they are required, other approaches have been developed for generating integer solutions. These integer solution approaches are the subject of chapter 8.

*Integer solution values*

## References

Ackoff, R. L., and Sasieni, M. W. *Fundamentals of Operations Research.* New York: John Wiley and Sons, 1968.

Charnes, A., and Cooper, W. W. *Management Models and Industrial Applications of Linear Programming.* New York: John Wiley and Sons, 1961.

Churchman, C. W.; Ackoff, R. L.; and Arnoff, E. L. *Introduction to Operations Research.* New York: John Wiley and Sons, 1958.

Hillier, F. S., and Lieberman, G. J. *Introduction to Operations Research.* 3rd ed. San Francisco: Holden-Day, 1980.

Hitchcock, F. L. "The Distribution of a Product from Several Sources to Numerous Localities." *Journal of Mathematics and Physics* 20 (1941): 224, 230.

Hoffmann, T. R. *Production: Management and Manufacturing Systems.* Belmont, Calif.: Wadsworth, 1967.

Koopmans, T. C., ed. *Activity Analysis of Production and Allocation.* Cowles Commission Monograph No. 13. New York: John Wiley and Sons, 1951.

Kwak, N. K. *Mathematical Programming with Business Applications.* New York: McGraw-Hill, 1973.

Lee, Sang M.; Moore, Laurence J.; and Taylor, Bernard W. *Management Science.* Dubuque, Iowa: Wm. C. Brown Company Publishers, 1981.

Levin, R. I., and Lamone, R. *Linear Programming for Management Decisions.* Homewood, Ill.: Irwin, 1969.

Llewellyn, R. W. *Linear Programming.* New York: Holt, Rinehart and Winston, 1964.

Orchard-Hays, W. *Advanced Linear Programming Computing Techniques.* New York: McGraw-Hill, 1968.

Taha, H. A. *Operations Research.* 2d ed. New York: Macmillan Co., 1976.

# Problems

1. Given the following transportation tableau determine the initial solution using the northwest corner method, minimum cell cost method, and VAM, and compute the total cost for each.

| To<br>From | A | B | C | Supply |
|---|---|---|---|---|
| 1 | 10 | 9 | 5 | 60 |
| 2 | 6 | 8 | 7 | 30 |
| 3 | 4 | 3 | 2 | 60 |
| Demand | 40 | 40 | 70 | 150 |

2. Given the following transportation tableau and solution determine the optimal solution using the stepping-stone method.

| To<br>From | A | B | C | Supply |
|---|---|---|---|---|
| 1 | 7 | 5<br>30 | 9<br>120 | 150 |
| 2 | 10<br>100 | 12 | 10<br>100 | 200 |
| 3 | 6 | 3<br>50 | 14 | 50 |
| Demand | 100 | 80 | 220 | 400 |

3. The Green Valley Mills produces carpet at plants in St. Louis and Richmond. The carpet is then shipped to two outlets in Chicago and Atlanta. The cost per ton of shipping carpet from each of the two plants to the two warehouses is given as follows.

| From | To | |
|---|---|---|
| | Chicago | Atlanta |
| St. Louis | $40 | 65 |
| Richmond | 70 | 30 |

The plant at St. Louis can supply 250 tons of carpet per week, while the plant at Richmond can supply 400 tons per week. The Chicago outlet has a demand of 300 tons per week while the outlet at Atlanta demands 350 tons per week. The company wants to know the number of tons of carpet to ship from each plant to each outlet in order to minimize the total shipping cost. Solve this transportation problem.

4. Solve the following transportation problem.

| From \ To | 1 | 2 | 3 | Supply |
|---|---|---|---|---|
| A | 7 | 10 | 9 | 35 |
| B | 12 | 5 | 4 | 20 |
| C | 8 | 3 | 11 | 60 |
| Demand | 40 | 45 | 30 | 115 |

5. Given a transportation problem with the following costs, supply, and demand:

| From | To | | | | Supply |
|---|---|---|---|---|---|
| | 1 | 2 | 3 | 4 | |
| 1 | $ 7 | 6 | 2 | 12 | 70 |
| 2 | 3 | 9 | 8 | 7 | 40 |
| 3 | 10 | 4 | 11 | 5 | 100 |
| Demand | 30 | 60 | 90 | 30 | |

(a) Find the initial solution using the northwest corner method, the minimum cell cost method, and Vogel's Approximation Method. Compute total cost for each.

(b) Using the VAM initial solution, find the optimal solution using the stepping-stone method. Compute total minimum cost for the solution.

6. Given a transportation problem with the following costs, supply, and demand:

| From | To 1 | 2 | 3 | 4 | Supply |
|------|------|-----|-----|-----|--------|
| 1 | $500 | 750 | 300 | 450 | 12 |
| 2 | 650 | 800 | 400 | 600 | 17 |
| 3 | 400 | 700 | 500 | 550 | 11 |
| Demand | 10 | 10 | 10 | 10 | |

(a) Find the initial solution using the northwest corner method, the minimum cell cost method, and Vogel's Approximation Method. Compute total cost for each.

(b) Using the VAM initial solution, find the optimal solution using the modified distribution method (MODI).

7. Given the following transportation tableau and solution:

| From \ To | A | B | C | Supply |
|-----------|-----|-----|-----|--------|
| 1 | 12 | 10 | 6 / 600 | 600 |
| 2 | 4 / 400 | 15 | 3 | 400 |
| 3 | 9 / 300 | 7 | M | 300 |
| 4 | 11 | 8 / 500 | 6 / 300 | 800 |
| Dummy | 0 / 200 | 0 | 0 | 200 |
| Demand | 900 | 500 | 900 | 2300 |

(a) Is this a balanced or unbalanced transportation problem? Explain.
(b) Is this solution degenerate? Explain. If it is degenerate show how it would be put into proper form.
(c) Is there a prohibited route in this problem?
(d) Compute the total cost of this solution.
(e) What is the value of $x_{2B}$ in this solution?

8. Solve the following transportation problem.

| From | To 1 | To 2 | To 3 | Supply |
|---|---|---|---|---|
| 1 | $40 | 10 | 20 | 800 |
| 2 | 15 | 20 | 10 | 500 |
| 3 | 20 | 25 | 30 | 600 |
| Demand | 1050 | 500 | 650 | |

9. Given a transportation problem with the following costs, supply, and demand:

| From | To 1 | To 2 | To 3 | Supply |
|---|---|---|---|---|
| A | $ 6 | 7 | 4 | 100 |
| B | 5 | 3 | 6 | 180 |
| C | 8 | 5 | 7 | 200 |
| Demand | 135 | 175 | 170 | |

find the initial solution using the minimum cell cost method and Vogel's Approximation Method (VAM). Is the VAM solution optimal?

10. Given the following transportation problem:

| From | To 1 | To 2 | To 3 | Supply |
|---|---|---|---|---|
| A | $ 6 | 9 | M | 130 |
| B | 12 | 3 | 5 | 70 |
| C | 4 | 8 | 11 | 100 |
| Demand | 80 | 110 | 60 | |

(a) Find the initial solution using VAM and solve using the stepping-stone method.
(b) Formulate this problem as a general linear programming model.

11. Solve the following linear programming problem.

$$\text{minimize } Z = 3x_{11} + 12x_{12} + 8x_{13} + 10x_{21} + 5x_{22}$$
$$+ 6x_{23} + 6x_{31} + 7x_{32} + 10x_{33}$$

subject to
$$x_{11} + x_{12} + x_{13} = 90$$
$$x_{21} + x_{22} + x_{23} = 30$$
$$x_{31} + x_{32} + x_{33} = 100$$
$$x_{11} + x_{21} + x_{31} \leq 70$$
$$x_{12} + x_{22} + x_{32} \leq 110$$
$$x_{13} + x_{23} + x_{33} \leq 80$$
$$x_{ij} \geq 0$$

12. Given the following transportation problem:

| From | To A | B | C | D | Supply |
|---|---|---|---|---|---|
| 1 | $ 5 | 12 | 7 | 10 | 50 |
| 2 | 4 | 6 | 7 | 6 | 50 |
| 3 | 2 | 8 | 5 | 3 | 60 |
| Demand | 40 | 20 | 30 | 70 | |

(a) Find the initial solution using the northwest corner method, the minimum cell cost method, and VAM. Compute the cost for each method.
(b) Solve using the VAM initial solution and MODI.

13. Given the following transportation problem:

| From | To 1 | 2 | 3 | Supply |
|---|---|---|---|---|
| A | $ 6 | 9 | 7 | 130 |
| B | 12 | 3 | 5 | 70 |
| C | 4 | 8 | 11 | 100 |
| Demand | 80 | 110 | 60 | |

(a) Find the initial solution using the minimum cell cost method.
(b) Solve using the stepping-stone method.

14. Steel is produced in three cities:

| Location | Weekly Production (tons) |
|---|---|
| A. Pittsburgh | 150 |
| B. Birmingham | 210 |
| C. Gary | 320 |
| | 680 |

These plants supply steel to markets in four cities, which have the following demand:

| Location | Weekly Demand (tons) |
|----------|----------------------|
| 1. Detroit | 130 |
| 2. St. Louis | 70 |
| 3. Chicago | 180 |
| 4. Norfolk | 240 |
| | 620 |

The following shipping costs/ton have been determined:

| From | To | | | |
|------|------|------|------|------|
| | 1 | 2 | 3 | 4 |
| A | $14 | 9 | 16 | 18 |
| B | 11 | 8 | 7 | 16 |
| C | 16 | 12 | 10 | 22 |

However, due to a trucker's strike, shipments are presently prohibited from Birmingham to Chicago.

(a) Set up a transportation tableau for this problem and determine the initial solution. Identify the method used to find the initial solution.

(b) Solve this problem using MODI.

(c) Are there multiple optimum solutions? Explain. If there are alternative solutions, identify them.

(d) Formulate this problem as a general linear programming model.

15. Tobacco is purchased and stored in warehouses in four cities at the end of each growing season:

| Location | Capacity (tons) |
|----------|-----------------|
| A. Charlotte | 90 |
| B. Raleigh | 50 |
| C. Lexington | 80 |
| D. Danville | 60 |
| | 280 |

These warehouses supply tobacco to companies in three cities that have the following demand:

| Plant | Demand (tons) |
|-------|---------------|
| 1. Richmond | 120 |
| 2. Winston-Salem | 100 |
| 3. Durham | 110 |
| | 330 |

The following railroad shipping costs/ton have been determined:

| From | To 1 | To 2 | To 3 |
|------|------|------|------|
| A | $ 7 | 10 | 5 |
| B | 12 | 9 | 4 |
| C | 7 | 3 | 11 |
| D | 9 | 5 | 7 |

However, due to railroad construction, shipments are presently prohibited from Charlotte to Richmond.
(a) Set up the transportation tableau for this problem and determine the initial solution using VAM and compute total cost.
(b) Solve using MODI.
(c) Are there multiple optimum solutions? Explain. If there are alternative solutions identify them.
(d) Formulate this problem as a linear programming model.

16. Given the following linear programming problem:

$$\text{minimize } Z = 17x_{11} + 10x_{12} + 15x_{13} + 11x_{21} + 14x_{22} + 10x_{23}$$
$$+ 9x_{31} + 13x_{32} + 11x_{33} + 19x_{41} + 8x_{42} + 12x_{43}$$

subject to

$$x_{11} + x_{12} + x_{13} = 120$$
$$x_{21} + x_{22} + x_{23} = 70$$
$$x_{31} + x_{32} + x_{33} = 180$$
$$x_{41} + x_{42} + x_{43} = 30$$
$$x_{11} + x_{21} + x_{31} + x_{41} = 200$$
$$x_{12} + x_{22} + x_{32} + x_{42} = 120$$
$$x_{13} + x_{23} + x_{33} + x_{43} = 80$$
$$x_{ij} \geq 0$$

(a) Set up the transportation tableau for this problem and determine the initial solution using VAM.
(b) Solve using the stepping-stone method.

17. Oranges are grown, picked, and then stored in warehouses in Tampa, Miami, and Fresno. These warehouses supply oranges to markets in New York, Philadelphia, Chicago, and Boston. The following shipping costs/truckload ($100s), supply, and demand exist:

| From | To New York | Philadelphia | Chicago | Boston | Supply |
|------|-------------|--------------|---------|--------|--------|
| Tampa | $ 9 | 14 | 12 | 17 | 200 |
| Miami | 11 | 10 | 6 | 10 | 200 |
| Fresno | 12 | 8 | 15 | 7 | 200 |
| Demand | 130 | 170 | 100 | 150 | |

Due to a distributor's agreement, shipments are prohibited from Miami to Chicago.
  (a) Set up the transportation tableau for this problem and determine the initial solution using the least cost method.
  (b) Solve using MODI.
  (c) Are there multiple optimum solutions? Explain. If there are alternative solutions identify them.
  (d) Formulate this problem as a linear programming model.

18. Given the following transportation problem:

| From | To A | B | C | Supply |
|------|------|---|---|--------|
| 1 | $7 | 10 | 6 | 300 |
| 2 | 4 | 9 | 8 | 150 |
| 3 | 5 | 7 | 5 | 400 |
| Demand | 200 | 400 | 350 | |

  (a) Set up the transportation tableau for this problem and find the initial solution by the northwest corner method, minimum cell cost method, and VAM. Compute the cost for each method.
  (b) Using the VAM initial solution, solve the problem using the stepping-stone method.

19. A manufacturing firm produces diesel engines in four cities—Phoenix, Seattle, St. Louis, and Detroit. The company is able to produce the following engines per month:

| Plant | Production |
|-------|-----------|
| 1. Phoenix | 5 |
| 2. Seattle | 25 |
| 3. St. Louis | 20 |
| 4. Detroit | 25 |

Three trucking firms that purchase the engines have the following demand in their plants in three cities:

| Firm | Demand |
|------|--------|
| A. Greensboro | 10 |
| B. Charlotte | 20 |
| C. Louisville | 15 |

The transportation costs per engine from sources to destinations are ($100s):

| From | To A | B | C |
|---|---|---|---|
| 1 | $ 7 | 8 | 5 |
| 2 | 6 | 10 | 6 |
| 3 | 10 | 4 | 5 |
| 4 | 3 | 9 | 11 |

However, the Charlotte firm will not accept engines made in Seattle and the Louisville firm will not accept engines from Detroit; therefore, these routes are prohibited.

(a) Set up the transportation tableau for this problem. Find the initial solution using VAM.

(b) Solve for the optimal solution using the stepping-stone method. Compute the total minimum cost.

(c) Formulate this problem as a linear programming model.

20. Given the following transportation problem:

| From | To A | B | C | D | Supply |
|---|---|---|---|---|---|
| 1 | $12 | 10 | 9 | 15 | 36 |
| 2 | 10 | 8 | 2 | 10 | 25 |
| 3 | 9 | 5 | 13 | 8 | 30 |
| Demand | 26 | 40 | 25 | 30 | |

(a) Find the initial solution using the northwest corner method.

(b) Solve using the stepping-stone method.

21. A metal parts shop has 3 operators and 3 machines: a drill press, a lathe, and a grinder. Each operator is qualified on each machine. The following table shows the time (in minutes) required by each operator to produce a part on each machine:

| Operator | Press | Machine Lathe | Grinder |
|---|---|---|---|
| 1 | 22 | 18 | 35 |
| 2 | 41 | 30 | 28 |
| 3 | 25 | 36 | 18 |

Determine the optimal assignment that will minimize the total machine time.

22. A plant has 4 operators to be assigned to 4 machines. The time (minutes) required to produce a product by each worker on each machine is:

| Operator | Machine A | B | C | D |
|----------|-----------|------|------|------|
| 1 | 10 | 12 | 9 | 11 |
| 2 | 5 | 10 | 7 | 8 |
| 3 | 12 | 14 | 13 | 11 |
| 4 | 8 | 15 | 11 | 9 |

Determine the optimal assignment and compute total minimum time.

23. A job shop has 4 machinists to be assigned to 4 machines. The hourly cost required to operate each machine by each machinist is:

| Machinist | Machine A | B | C | D |
|-----------|-----------|----|----|----|
| 1 | $12 | 11 | 8 | 14 |
| 2 | 10 | 9 | 10 | 8 |
| 3 | 14 | 8 | 7 | 11 |
| 4 | 6 | 8 | 10 | 9 |

However, due to a lack of experience machinist 3 cannot operate machine B.
   (a) Determine the optimal assignment and compute total minimum cost.
   (b) Formulate this problem as a general linear programming model.

24. The Omega pharmaceutical firm has 5 salespersons, which the firm wants to assign to 5 sales regions. Because of previously acquired contacts, the salespersons are able to cover the regions in different amounts of time. The amount of time (days) required by each salesperson to cover each city is:

| Salesperson | Region A | B | C | D | E |
|-------------|----------|----|----|----|----|
| 1 | 17 | 10 | 15 | 16 | 20 |
| 2 | 12 | 9 | 16 | 9 | 14 |
| 3 | 11 | 16 | 14 | 15 | 12 |
| 4 | 14 | 10 | 10 | 18 | 17 |
| 5 | 13 | 12 | 9 | 15 | 11 |

Which salesperson should be assigned to each region in order to minimize total time? Identify the optimal assignments and compute total minimum time.

25. The Bunker Manufacturing firm has 5 employees and 6 machines, and desires to assign the employees to the machines in a manner that will minimize cost. A cost table showing the cost incurred by each employee on each machine is:

| Employee | Machine | | | | | |
|---|---|---|---|---|---|---|
| | A | B | C | D | E | F |
| 1 | $12 | 7 | 20 | 14 | 8 | 10 |
| 2 | 10 | 14 | 13 | 20 | 9 | 11 |
| 3 | 5 | 3 | 6 | 9 | 7 | 10 |
| 4 | 9 | 11 | 7 | 16 | 9 | 10 |
| 5 | 10 | 6 | 14 | 8 | 10 | 12 |

However, due to union rules regarding departmental transfers, employee 3 cannot be assigned to machine E and employee 4 cannot be assigned to machine B.

Solve this problem, indicate the optimal assignment, and compute total minimum cost.

26. Given the following cost table for an assignment problem:

| Operator | Machine | | | |
|---|---|---|---|---|
| | A | B | C | D |
| 1 | $10 | 2 | 8 | 6 |
| 2 | 9 | 5 | 11 | 9 |
| 3 | 12 | 7 | 14 | 14 |
| 4 | 3 | 1 | 4 | 2 |

Determine the optimal assignment for this problem and compute total minimum cost. Identify all alternative solutions if multiple optimum solutions exist.

27. An electronics firm produces electronic components, which it supplies to various electrical manufacturers. Past quality control records indicate that the number of defective items produced were different for the employees. The average number of defects produced by each employee for each of 6 components is given in the following table.

| Employee | Component | | | | | |
|---|---|---|---|---|---|---|
| | A | B | C | D | E | F |
| 1 | 30 | 24 | 16 | 26 | 30 | 22 |
| 2 | 22 | 28 | 14 | 30 | 20 | 13 |
| 3 | 18 | 16 | 25 | 14 | 12 | 22 |
| 4 | 14 | 22 | 18 | 23 | 21 | 30 |
| 5 | 25 | 18 | 14 | 16 | 16 | 28 |
| 6 | 32 | 14 | 10 | 14 | 18 | 20 |

Determine the optimal assignment that will minimize the total average monthly defects.

28. A dispatcher for the Citywide Taxi Company presently has six taxicabs at different locations and five customers who have called for service. The mileage from each taxi's present location to each customer is:

| Cab | Customer 1 | 2 | 3 | 4 | 5 |
|-----|---|---|---|---|---|
| A | 7 | 2 | 4 | 10 | 7 |
| B | 5 | 1 | 5 | 6 | 6 |
| C | 8 | 7 | 6 | 5 | 5 |
| D | 2 | 5 | 2 | 4 | 5 |
| E | 3 | 3 | 5 | 8 | 4 |
| F | 6 | 2 | 4 | 3 | 4 |

Determine the optimal assignment(s) that will minimize the total mileage traveled.

29. The Southwest Athletic Conference has 6 basketball officials it must assign to 3 conference games. Two officials must be assigned to each game. The conference office desires to assign the officials so that the total distance traveled by all 6 officials will be minimized. The distance each official would have to travel to each game is given in the following table.

| Official | Game Austin | Houston | Lubbock |
|----------|--------|---------|---------|
| 1 | 20 | 45 | 10 |
| 2 | 40 | 90 | 70 |
| 3 | 60 | 70 | 30 |
| 4 | 30 | 60 | 40 |
| 5 | 70 | 15 | 50 |
| 6 | 80 | 25 | 35 |

(a) Should this problem be solved by the transportation method or the assignment method? Explain.
(b) Determine the optimal assignment(s) for this problem that will minimize the total distance traveled by the officials.

30. A university department head has 5 instructors to be assigned to 4 different courses. In the past all of the instructors have taught the courses and have been evaluated by the students. The rating for each instructor for each course is given in the following table (a perfect score is 100).

| Instructor | Course | | | |
|---|---|---|---|---|
| | A | B | C | D |
| 1 | 80 | 75 | 90 | 85 |
| 2 | 95 | 90 | 90 | 97 |
| 3 | 85 | 95 | 88 | 91 |
| 4 | 93 | 91 | 80 | 84 |
| 5 | 91 | 92 | 93 | 88 |

The department head wants to know the optimal assignment of instructors to courses that will maximize the overall average evaluation. The instructor not assigned will be made a grader. Solve this problem using the assignment method.

# 8
Integer
Programming

In the linear programming models that have been formulated and solved in the previous chapters, the implicit assumption has been made that solutions could be fractional (i.e., noninteger). In the Colonial Pottery Company model in chapter 4, although an integer solution of 24 bowls and 8 mugs was generated (table 4.16), in general, an integer solution is not guaranteed by the simplex method. If a noninteger solution, such as 23.73 bowls and 8.51 mugs, had resulted, it would have been difficult to implement the solution by producing 73 percent of a bowl and 51 percent of a mug.

*Problems that require integer solution values*

In cases where the simplex method is applied to a model and noninteger values result, it is sometimes assumed that the solution values can be "rounded off" to the nearest feasible integer values. This method would cause little concern if, for example, $x_1 = 8,000.4$ nails and we rounded off to 8,000 nails, since nails cost only several cents apiece. However, if we are considering the production of jet aircraft and $x_1 = 7.4$ jet airliners, by rounding off we could affect profit (or cost) by millions of dollars. In this case we need to solve the problem so that an *optimal integer solution* is guaranteed. In this chapter, the different forms of integer linear programming models will be presented, and several solution approaches that generate optimal integer solutions will be demonstrated.

*The limitation of rounding off noninteger solutions*

## Integer Programming Models

There are three basic types of integer linear programming models: a total integer model, a 0–1 integer model, and a mixed integer model. In a *total integer* model all of the decision variables are required to have integer solution values. In a *0–1 integer* model all of the decision variables have integer values of zero or one. Finally, in a *mixed integer* model some of the decision variables (but not all) are required to have integer solutions. The following three examples will demonstrate each of these types of integer programming models.

*Three basic types of integer programming models*

## A Total Integer Model Example

*A model where all decision variables must have integer solution values*

The owner of a machine shop is going to expand by purchasing some new machines—presses and lathes. The owner has estimated that each press that is purchased will increase profit by $100 per day, while each lathe will increase profit $150 daily. The number of machines the owner can purchase is limited by the cost of the machines and the available shop floor space. The machine purchase prices and space requirements are as follows:

| Machine | Required Floor Space (ft.$^2$) | Purchase Price |
|---------|-------------------------------|----------------|
| Press   | 15                            | $8,000         |
| Lathe   | 30                            | $4,000         |

The owner has a budget of $40,000 to purchase machines and 200 ft.$^2$ of available floor space. The owner desires to know the number of each type of machine to purchase in order to maximize the daily increase in profit.

The linear programming model for an integer programming problem is formulated exactly the same as the linear programming examples in chapters 2 through 7. The only difference is that in this problem, the decision variables are restricted to integer values, since the owner cannot purchase a fractional portion of a machine. The linear programming model is

maximize $Z = \$100x_1 + 150x_2$
subject to
$$\$8,000x_1 + 4,000x_2 \leq \$40,000$$
$$15x_1 + 30x_2 \leq 200 \text{ ft.}^2$$
$$x_1, x_2 \geq 0 \text{ and integer}$$
where
$x_1$ = the number of presses
$x_2$ = the number of lathes

The decision variables in this model are restricted to whole machines. The fact that *both* decision variables, $x_1$ and $x_2$, can assume any integer value greater than or equal to zero is what gives this model its designation as a total integer model.

## A 0-1 Integer Model Example

*A model where all decision variables must have solution values of either zero or one*

A community council must decide which recreation facilities to construct in its community. Four new recreation facilities have been proposed—a swimming pool, a tennis center, an athletic field, and a gymnasium. The council wants to construct those facilities that will maximize the expected daily usage by the residents of the community subject to land and cost limitations. The expected daily usage, and cost and land requirement for each facility are shown below.

| Recreation Facility | Expected Usage (people/day) | Cost ($) | Land Requirements (acres) |
|---|---|---|---|
| Swimming pool | 300 | $35,000 | 4 |
| Tennis center | 90 | $10,000 | 2 |
| Athletic field | 400 | $25,000 | 7 |
| Gymnasium | 150 | $90,000 | 3 |

The community has a construction budget of $120,000 and a total of 12 acres of land. However, there is also an additional restriction on facility construction. Because the land for the swimming pool and tennis center are in the same area in the community, only one of these two facilities can be constructed.

The council wants to know which of the recreation facilities to construct in order to maximize the expected daily usage.

The model for this problem is formulated as

maximize $Z = 300x_1 + 90x_2 + 400x_3 + 150x_4$
subject to
$$35,000x_1 + 10,000x_2 + 25,000x_3 + 90,000x_4 \leq \$120,000$$
$$4x_1 + 2x_2 + 7x_3 + 3x_4 \leq 12 \text{ acres}$$
$$x_1 + x_2 \leq 1 \text{ facility}$$
$$x_1, x_2, x_3, x_4 = 0 \text{ or } 1$$

where

$x_1$ = construction of a swimming pool
$x_2$ = construction of a tennis center
$x_3$ = construction of an athletic field
$x_4$ = construction of a gymnasium

In this model, the decision variables can have a solution value of either *zero* or *one*. If a facility is not selected for construction, the decision variable representing it will have a value of zero. Alternatively, if a facility is selected, its decision variable will have a value of one.

The last constraint, $x_1 + x_2 \leq 1$, reflects the *contingency* that either the swimming pool ($x_1$) or tennis center ($x_2$) can be constructed, but not both. In order that the sum of $x_1$ and $x_2$ be less than or equal to one, either of the variables can have a value of one or both variables can equal zero.

## A Mixed Integer Model Example

Nancy Smith has $250,000 to invest in three alternative investments— condominiums, land, and municipal bonds. She wants to invest in the alternatives that will result in the greatest monetary return after one year.

*A model where some decision variables must have integer solution values and other variables can be noninteger*

Each condominium costs $50,000 and will return a profit of $5,000 if sold at the end of 1 year; each acre of land costs $12,000 and will return a profit of $1,500 at the end of a year; and each municipal bond costs $8,000 and will result in a return of $1,000 if sold at the end of a year. In addition, there are only 4 condominiums, 30 acres of land, and 20 municipal bonds available for purchase.

The linear programming model for this problem is formulated as follows.

maximize $Z = \$5,000x_1 + 1,500x_2 + 1,000x_3$
subject to
$$50,000x_1 + 12,000x_2 + 8,000x_3 \leq \$250,000$$
$$x_1 \leq 4 \text{ condominiums}$$
$$x_2 \leq 30 \text{ acres}$$
$$x_3 \leq 20 \text{ bonds}$$
$$x_2 \geq 0$$
$$x_1, x_3 \geq 0 \text{ and integer}$$

where
$x_1 =$ condominiums purchased
$x_2 =$ acres of land purchased
$x_3 =$ bonds purchased

Notice that in this model the solution values for condominiums ($x_1$) and municipal bonds ($x_3$) must be integers. It is not possible to invest in a fractional portion of a condominium or purchase part of a bond. However, it is possible to purchase less than a whole acre of land (i.e., a fractional portion of an acre). Thus, two of the decision variables ($x_1, x_3$) are restricted to integer values, while the other variable ($x_2$) can take on any real value greater than or equal to zero.

## Integer Programming Model Solution

*Rounding off fractional solution values*

Several methods exist for solving integer programming models like the examples formulated in the previous section. A frequently suggested and easy solution method is to *round off* fractional solution values to integer values. As an example, consider the total integer "machine shop" model formulated in the previous section.

maximize $Z = 100x_1 + 150x_2$
subject to
$$8,000x_1 + 4,000x_2 \leq 40,000$$
$$15x_1 + 30x_2 \leq 200$$
$$x_1, x_2 \geq 0 \text{ and integer}$$

Solving this model with the simplex method results in the solution shown in table 8.1.

The solution to this model results in a noninteger solution of 2.22 presses and 5.55 lathes. Since the solution values must be integers, let us first round off these two values to the *closest integer value,* which would

**Table 8.1** The Optimal Simplex Solution

| $c_j$ | | | 100 | 150 | 0 | 0 |
|---|---|---|---|---|---|---|
| | basic variables | quantity | $x_1$ | $x_2$ | $s_1$ | $s_2$ |
| 100 | $x_1$ | 2.22 | 1 | 0 | .00016 | −.022 |
| 150 | $x_2$ | 5.55 | 0 | 1 | −.00008 | .044 |
| | $z_j$ | 1,054.5 | 100 | 150 | .004 | 4.4 |
| | $c_j - z_j$ | | 0 | 0 | −.004 | −4.4 |

be $x_1 = 2$ and $x_2 = 6$. However, substituting these values into the second model constraint, we find that this integer solution violates this constraint, and thus is infeasible.

$$15x_1 + 30x_2 \leq 200$$
$$15(2) + 30(6) \leq 200$$
$$210 \nleq 200$$

In a model where the constraints are all $\leq$ (and the constraint coefficients are positive), a feasible solution is always insured by *rounding down*. Thus, an integer solution for this problem, which is also feasible, is

*Insuring a feasible solution by rounding down*

$$x_1 = 2$$
$$x_2 = 5$$
$$Z = \$950$$

However, one of the difficulties of simply rounding down noninteger values, as in this solution, is that there may be another integer solution that will result in a higher profit (i.e., in this problem there may be an integer solution that will result in a profit higher than $950). In order to determine *if* a better integer solution exists, we will analyze the graph of this model shown in figure 8.1.

In figure 8.1 the integer solution points are highlighted as dots, and the point $x_1 = 2$, $x_2 = 5$ is our rounded off solution. However, notice that as the objective function edge moves outward through the feasible solution space, there is an *integer* solution point that yields a greater profit than our rounded off solution. This solution point is $x_1 = 1$ and $x_2 = 6$. At this point, $Z = \$1,000$, which is $50 more profit per day for the machine shop than the rounded down integer solution.

This graphical analysis explicitly demonstrates the error that can result in the solution of an integer programming problem by simply rounding down. In our "machine shop" example, $x_1 = 1$, $x_2 = 6$ is the optimal integer solution instead of the rounded down solution, $x_1 = 2$, $x_2 = 5$ (which is often called the *suboptimal* solution or result). Because erroneous results are caused by rounding down regular simplex solutions, a more direct approach for solving integer problems would be appropriate. The branch and bound method is the most popular general solution approach for integer programming problems.

*A suboptimal solution*

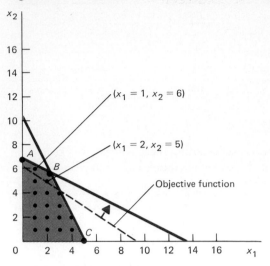

**Figure 8.1** Feasible solution space with integer solution points.

## The Branch and Bound Method

*A solution approach*

The *branch and bound method* is not a solution technique specifically limited to integer programming problems. It is a *solution approach,* which can be applied to a number of different types of problems. The basic principle behind the branch and bound approach is to partition the total set of feasible solutions (such as our feasible area in fig. 8.1) into smaller subsets

*Partitioning the feasible solution space into smaller subsets*

of solutions. These smaller subsets are then evaluated systematically until the best solution is found. When the branch and bound approach is applied to an integer programming problem, it is used in conjunction with the normal simplex method.

In order to demonstrate the branch and bound approach, we will use the "machine shop" example previously used in our graphical analysis. The branch and bound method starts by first solving the problem as a regular

*Relaxing the integer restrictions*

linear programming model without integer restrictions, that is, we say that the integer restrictions are *relaxed.* The linear programming model for the example problem and the optimal relaxed solution obtained by the simplex method are repeated below.

$$\text{maximize } Z = \$100x_1 + 150x_2$$
$$\text{subject to}$$
$$8{,}000x_1 + 4{,}000x_2 \le \$40{,}000$$
$$15x_1 + 30x_2 \le 200 \text{ ft.}^2$$
$$x_1, x_2 \ge 0 \text{ and integer}$$

The branch and bound method employs a diagram consisting of *nodes* and *branches* as a framework for the solution process. The first node of the branch and bound diagram, shown in figure 8.2, contains the *relaxed* linear programming solution shown in table 8.2 *and* the rounded down solution.

*A diagram of nodes and branches*

---

**Figure 8.2** The initial node in the branch and bound diagram.

$UB = 1{,}054.50$ ($x_1 = 2.22$, $x_2 = 5.55$)
$LB = 950$ ($x_1 = 2$, $x_2 = 5$)

---

**Table 8.2** The Optimal "Relaxed" Simplex Solution

| $c_j$ | | | 100 | 150 | 0 | 0 |
|---|---|---|---|---|---|---|
| | basic variables | quantity | $x_1$ | $x_2$ | $s_1$ | $s_2$ |
| 100 | $x_1$ | 2.22 | 1 | 0 | .00016 | −.022 |
| 150 | $x_2$ | 5.55 | 0 | 1 | −.00008 | .044 |
| | $z_j$ | 1,054.5 | 100 | 150 | .004 | 4.4 |
| | $c_j - z_j$ | | 0 | 0 | −.004 | −4.4 |

---

Notice that this node has two designated bounds: an upper bound of 1,054.50 signified by $UB$, and a lower bound, $LB$, of $950. The lower bound is the $Z$ value for the rounded down solution, $x_1 = 2$ and $x_2 = 5$, while the upper bound is the $Z$ value for the relaxed simplex solution of $x_1 = 2.22$ and $x_2 = 5.55$. The *optimal integer solution* will be between these two bounds.

*The upper bound and lower bound at each node*

Recall from our graphical analysis (fig. 8.1) that we were concerned that by rounding down a suboptimal solution would be obtained. In other words, we were hoping that a $Z$ value greater than $950 might be possible. As such, we were not concerned that a value *lower than* $950 might be available. Thus, $950 represents a *lower bound* for our solution. Alternatively, since $Z = 1{,}054.50$ reflects an optimal solution point *on the solution space boundary,* a greater $Z$ value cannot possibly be attained. Point $B$ in fig. 8.1, which corresponds to our table 8.2 solution, is the last point the objective function edge touches in the solution space. Hence, $Z = 1{,}054.50$ is the *upper bound* of our solution.

Now that the possible feasible solutions have been narrowed to values between the upper and lower bounds, we must test the solutions within these bounds to determine the best one. The first step in the branch and bound method is to create *two* solution subsets from the present relaxed

*Partitioning the present relaxed solution*

solution. This is accomplished by observing the relaxed solution value for each variable,

$$x_1 = 2.22$$
$$x_2 = 5.55$$

*Selecting the variable with the greatest fractional part to branch on*

and seeing which one is the farthest from being an integer value (i.e., which variable has the greatest fractional part). For this solution the ".55" portion of 5.55 is the greatest fractional part, thus $x_2$ will be the variable which we will "branch" on.

*Developing two additional constraints*

Since $x_2$ must be an integer value in the optimal solution, the following constraints can be developed.

$$x_2 \leq 5$$
$$x_2 \geq 6$$

In other words $x_2$ can be 0, 1, 2, 3, 4, 5 or 6, 7, 8, etc., but it cannot be a value between 5 and 6, such as 5.55. As such, these two new constraints represent the two solution subsets for our solution approach. Each of these constraints will be added to our linear programming model, which will then be solved by the simplex method to determine a relaxed solution. This sequence of events is shown on the branch and bound diagram in figure 8.3. The solutions at nodes 2 and 3 will be the relaxed solutions obtained by solving our example model with the appropriate constraints added.

**Figure 8.3** Solution subsets for $x_2$.

$UB = 1,054.50\ (x_1 = 2.22, x_2 = 5.55)$
$LB = 950\ (x_1 = 2, x_2 = 5)$

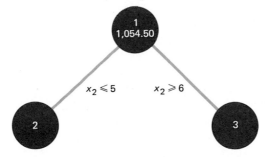

*The node 2 model with one of the branch constraints added*

First, the solution at node 2 is found by solving the following model with the constraint, $x_2 \leq 5$, added.

maximize $Z = \$100x_1 + 150x_2$
subject to
$$8,000x_1 + 4,000x_2 \leq 40,000$$
$$15x_1 + 30x_2 \leq 200$$
$$x_2 \leq 5$$
$$x_1, x_2 \geq 0$$

The optimal simplex solution for this model with integer restrictions relaxed is shown in table 8.3.

**Table 8.3** The Optimal "Relaxed" Solution at Node 2

| $c_j$ | | | 100 | 150 | 0 | 0 | 0 |
|---|---|---|---|---|---|---|---|
| | basic variables | quantity | $x_1$ | $x_2$ | $s_1$ | $s_2$ | $s_3$ |
| 100 | $x_1$ | 2.5 | 1 | 0 | .000125 | 0 | −0.5 |
| 0 | $s_2$ | 12.5 | 0 | 0 | .001875 | 1 | −22.5 |
| 150 | $x_2$ | 5 | 0 | 1 | 0 | 0 | 1 |
| | $z_j$ | 1,000 | 100 | 150 | .0125 | 0 | 100 |
| | $c_j - z_j$ | | 0 | 0 | −.0125 | 0 | −100 |

Next, the solution at node 3 is found by solving our model with $x_2 \geq 6$ added.

*The node 3 model with the second branch constraint added*

$$\text{maximize } Z = \$100x_1 + 150x_2$$

subject to

$$8,000x_1 + 4,000x_2 \leq 40,000$$
$$15x_1 + 30x_2 \leq 200$$
$$\boxed{x_2 \geq 6}$$
$$x_1, x_2 \geq 0$$

The optimal simplex solution for this model with integer restrictions relaxed is shown in table 8.4.

**Table 8.4** The Optimal "Relaxed" Solution at Node 3

| $c_j$ | | | 100 | 150 | 0 | 0 | 0 |
|---|---|---|---|---|---|---|---|
| | basic variables | quantity | $x_1$ | $x_2$ | $s_1$ | $s_2$ | $s_3$ |
| 0 | $s_1$ | 5,352 | 0 | 0 | 1 | −533.3 | 266.6 |
| 100 | $x_1$ | 1.33 | 1 | 0 | 0 | .067 | 2 |
| 150 | $x_2$ | 6.00 | 0 | 1 | 0 | 0 | −1 |
| | $z_j$ | 1,033 | 100 | 150 | 0 | 6.7 | 50 |
| | $c_j - z_j$ | | 0 | 0 | 0 | −6.7 | −50 |

These solutions in tables 8.3 and 8.4 reflect the partitioning of the original relaxed model into two subsets formed by the addition of the two constraints. The resulting solution sets are shown in the graphs in figure 8.4.

**Figure 8.4** Feasible solution spaces for nodes 2 and 3.

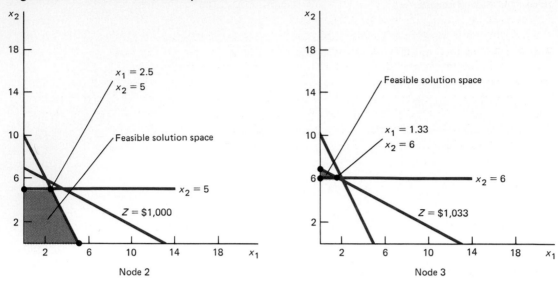

Node 2

Node 3

*Determining the new upper and lower bounds*

Notice that in the "node 2" graph in figure 8.4, the solution point $x_1 = 2.5$, $x_2 = 5$ results in a maximum $Z$ value of $1,000. As such, $1,000 is the upper bound for this node. Next, notice that in the "node 3" graph, the solution point $x_1 = 1.33$, $x_2 = 6$ results in a maximum $Z$ value of $1,033. Thus, $1,033 is the upper bound for node 3. The lower bound at each of these nodes is the maximum *integer* solution. Since neither of these relaxed solutions is totally integer, the lower bound remains $950, the integer solution value obtained at node 1 for the rounded down integer solution. The diagram in figure 8.5 reflects the addition of the upper and lower bounds at each node.

**Figure 8.5** Branch and bound diagram with upper and lower bounds at nodes 2 and 3.

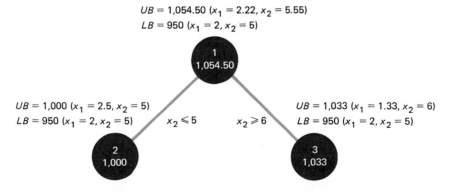

**Integer Programming**

Since we do not have an optimal and feasible integer solution yet, we must continue to branch (i.e., partition) the model, either from node 2 or 3. Observing figure 8.5, if we branch from node 2 the maximum value that can possibly be achieved is $1,000 (the upper bound). However, if we branch from node 3, a higher maximum value of $1,033 is possible. As such, we will branch from node 3. In general, *always branch from the node with the maximum upper bound.*

*Determining the node to branch from*

Now the steps for branching previously followed at node 1 are repeated at node 3. First, the variable that has the value with the greatest fractional part is selected. Since $x_2$ has an integer value, $x_1$ with a fractional part of ".33" is selected by default. Thus, two new constraints are developed from $x_1$,

*Partitioning the solution at node 3*

$$x_1 \leq 1$$
$$x_1 \geq 2$$

This creates the new branch and bound diagram shown in figure 8.6.

**Figure 8.6** Solution subsets for $x_1$.

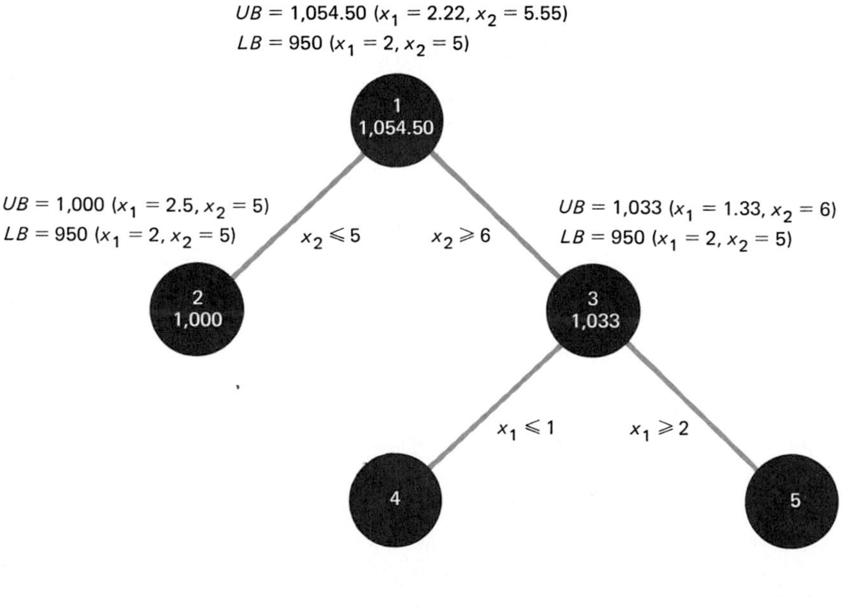

$UB = 1,054.50\ (x_1 = 2.22, x_2 = 5.55)$
$LB = 950\ (x_1 = 2, x_2 = 5)$

$UB = 1,000\ (x_1 = 2.5, x_2 = 5)$
$LB = 950\ (x_1 = 2, x_2 = 5)$

$x_2 \leq 5$     $x_2 \geq 6$

$UB = 1,033\ (x_1 = 1.33, x_2 = 6)$
$LB = 950\ (x_1 = 2, x_2 = 5)$

$x_1 \leq 1$     $x_1 \geq 2$

Next, the relaxed linear programming model with the new constraints added, must be solved at nodes 4 and 5. (However do not forget that the model is not the original, but the original with the constraint, $x_2 \geq 6$, previously added.) Consider the node 4 model first.

*The node 4 model*

$$\text{maximize } Z = 100x_1 + 150x_2$$

subject to

$$8{,}000x_1 + 4{,}000x_2 \leq 40{,}000$$
$$15x_1 + 30x_2 \leq 200$$
$$x_2 \geq 6$$
$$\boxed{x_1 \leq 1}$$
$$x_1, x_2 \geq 0$$

The optimal simplex solution for this model with integer restrictions relaxed is shown in table 8.5.

**Table 8.5** The Optimal "Relaxed" Solution at Node 4

| $c_i$ | | | 100 | 150 | 0 | 0 | 0 | 0 |
|---|---|---|---|---|---|---|---|---|
| | basic variables | quantity | $x_1$ | $x_2$ | $s_1$ | $s_2$ | $s_3$ | $s_4$ |
| 0 | $s_1$ | 7,333.33 | 0 | 0 | 1 | $-133.3$ | 0 | $-6{,}000$ |
| 0 | $s_3$ | .17 | 0 | 0 | 0 | .033 | 1 | $-.50$ |
| 150 | $x_2$ | 6.17 | 0 | 1 | 0 | .033 | 0 | $-.50$ |
| 100 | $x_1$ | 1 | 1 | 0 | 0 | 0 | 0 | 1 |
| | $z_i$ | 1,025.5 | 100 | 150 | 0 | 5 | 0 | 25 |
| | $c_i - z_i$ | | 0 | 0 | $-0$ | $-5$ | 0 | $-25$ |

Next consider the node 5 model.

$$\text{maximize } Z = 100x_1 + 150x_2$$

subject to

$$8{,}000x_1 + 4{,}000x_2 \leq 40{,}000$$
$$15x_1 + 30x_2 \leq 200$$
$$x_2 \geq 6$$
$$\boxed{x_1 \geq 2}$$
$$x_1, x_2 \geq 0$$

The optimal simplex solution for this model is shown in table 8.6.

**Table 8.6** The Optimal "Relaxed" Solution at Node 5

| $c_i$ | | | 100 | 150 | 0 | 0 | 0 | 0 | $-M$ |
|---|---|---|---|---|---|---|---|---|---|
| | basic variables | quantity | $x_1$ | $x_2$ | $s_1$ | $s_2$ | $s_3$ | $s_4$ | $A_2$ |
| 0 | $s_1$ | 5,360 | 0 | 0 | 1 | $-8{,}000$ | $-4{,}000$ | 0 | 0 |
| 100 | $x_1$ | 1.33 | 1 | 0 | 0 | 1 | 2 | 0 | 0 |
| 150 | $x_2$ | 6 | 0 | 1 | 0 | 0 | $-1$ | 0 | 0 |
| $-M$ | $A_2$ | .77 | 0 | 0 | 0 | $-1$ | $-2$ | $-1$ | 1 |
| | $z_i$ | $900 - .77M$ | 100 | 150 | 0 | $100 + M$ | $50 + 2M$ | $M$ | $-M$ |
| | $c_i - z_i$ | | 0 | 0 | 0 | $-100 - M$ | $-50 - 2M$ | $-M$ | 0 |

However, since table 8.6 contains an artificial variable in the final simplex solution, this solution is *infeasible*. As such, no solution exists at node 5, and we only have to evaluate the solution at node 4. Our branch and bound diagram reflecting these results is shown in figure 8.7.

---

**Figure 8.7** Branch and bound diagram with upper and lower bounds at nodes 4 and 5.

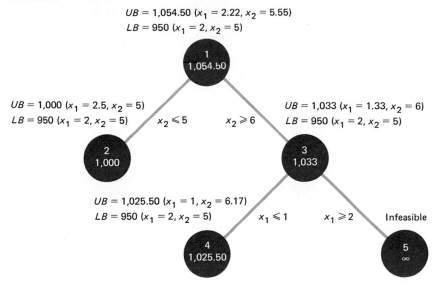

The branch and bound diagram in figure 8.7 indicates that we still have not reached an optimal integer solution, thus we must repeat the branching steps followed earlier. Since a solution does not exist at node 5, there is no comparison between the upper bounds at nodes 4 and 5. We must branch from node 4. Next, since $x_1$ has an integer value, $x_2$ with a fractional part of .17 is selected by default. The two new constraints developed from $x_2$ are

$$x_2 \leq 6$$
$$x_2 \geq 7$$

*Partitioning the solution at node 4*

This creates the new branch and bound diagram in figure 8.8.

The "relaxed" linear programming model with the new constraints added must be solved at nodes 6 and 7. Consider the node 6 model first.

*The node 6 model*

maximize $Z = 100x_1 + 150x_2$
subject to
$$8,000x_1 + 4,000x_2 \leq 40,000$$
$$15x_1 + 30x_2 \leq 200$$
$$x_2 \geq 6$$
$$x_1 \leq 1$$
$$x_2 \leq 6$$
$$x_1, x_2 \geq 0$$

**Figure 8.8** Solution subsets for $x_2$.

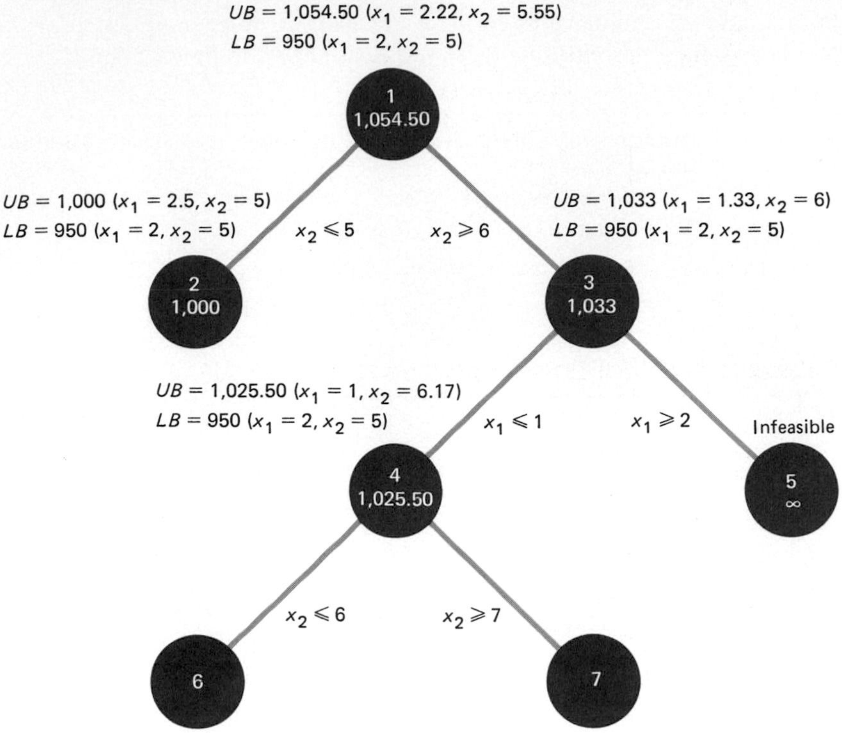
UB = 1,054.50 (x1 = 2.22, x2 = 5.55)
LB = 950 (x1 = 2, x2 = 5)
1
1,054.50
UB = 1,000 (x1 = 2.5, x2 = 5)
LB = 950 (x1 = 2, x2 = 5)
x2 ≤ 5
x2 ≥ 6
UB = 1,033 (x1 = 1.33, x2 = 6)
LB = 950 (x1 = 2, x2 = 5)
2
1,000
3
1,033
UB = 1,025.50 (x1 = 1, x2 = 6.17)
LB = 950 (x1 = 2, x2 = 5)
x1 ≤ 1
x1 ≥ 2
Infeasible
4
1,025.50
5
∞
x2 ≤ 6
x2 ≥ 7
6
7

The optimal simplex solution for this relaxed linear programming model is shown in table 8.7.

**Table 8.7** The Optimal "Relaxed" Solution at Node 6

| $c_j$ | | | 100 | 150 | 0 | 0 | 0 | 0 | 0 |
|---|---|---|---|---|---|---|---|---|---|
| | basic variables | quantity | $x_1$ | $x_2$ | $s_1$ | $s_2$ | $s_3$ | $s_4$ | $s_5$ |
| 0 | $s_1$ | 8,000 | 0 | 0 | 1 | 0 | 0 | −8,000 | −4,000 |
| 0 | $s_2$ | 5 | 0 | 0 | 0 | 1 | 0 | −15 | −30 |
| 150 | $x_2$ | 6 | 0 | 1 | 0 | 0 | 0 | 0 | 1 |
| 100 | $x_1$ | 1 | 1 | 0 | 0 | 0 | 0 | 1 | 0 |
| 0 | $s_3$ | 0 | 0 | 0 | 0 | 0 | 1 | 0 | 1 |
| | $z_j$ | 1,000 | 100 | 150 | 0 | 0 | 0 | 100 | 150 |
| | $c_j - z_j$ | | 0 | 0 | 0 | 0 | 0 | −100 | −150 |

Next, consider the node 7 model.

*The node 7 model*

maximize $Z = 100x_1 + 150x_2$
subject to

$$8,000x_1 + 4,000x_2 \leq 40,000$$
$$15x_1 + 30x_2 \leq 200$$
$$x_2 \geq 6$$
$$x_1 \leq 1$$
$$\boxed{x_1 \geq 7}$$
$$x_1, x_2 \geq 0$$

The final simplex tableau for this model is shown in table 8.8.

**Table 8.8** The Optimal "Relaxed" Solution at Node 7

| $c_i$ | basic variables | quantity | 100 $x_1$ | 150 $x_2$ | 0 $s_1$ | 0 $s_2$ | 0 $s_3$ | 0 $s_4$ | 0 $s_5$ | $-M$ $A_2$ |
|---|---|---|---|---|---|---|---|---|---|---|
| 0 | $s_1$ | 13,333 | 6,000 | 0 | 1 | $-133.3$ | 0 | 0 | 0 | 0 |
| 0 | $s_3$ | .67 | .50 | 0 | 0 | .033 | 1 | 0 | 0 | 0 |
| 150 | $x_2$ | 6.67 | .50 | 1 | 0 | .033 | 0 | 0 | 0 | 0 |
| 0 | $s_4$ | 1 | 1 | 0 | 0 | 0 | 0 | 1 | 0 | 0 |
| $-M$ | $A_2$ | .33 | $-.50$ | 0 | 0 | $-.033$ | 0 | 0 | $-1$ | 1 |
| | $z_i$ | $1,000.5-.33M$ | $75+.5M$ | 150 | 0 | $49.5+.033M$ | 0 | 0 | $M$ | $-M$ |
| | $c_i - z_i$ | | $25-.5M$ | 0 | 0 | $-49.5-.033M$ | 0 | 0 | $-M$ | 0 |

However, table 8.8 contains an artificial variable in the solution, thus the solution is infeasible. As such, no solution exists at node 7. The branch and bound diagram reflecting these results is shown in figure 8.9.

This version of the branch and bound diagram in figure 8.9 indicates that the optimal integer solution, $x_1 = 1$, $x_2 = 6$, has been reached at node 6. The value of 1,000 at node 6 is the maximum integer value that can be obtained, or the upper bound. (It is also the recomputed lower bound, since it is the maximum integer solution achieved to this point.) As such, it is not possible to achieve any higher value by further branching from node 6. Comparing the node 6 solution with nodes 2, 5, and 7, it can be seen that a better solution is not possible. The upper bound at node 2 is 1,000, which is the same upper bound as that obtained at node 6, thus node 2 can result in no greater improvement. The solutions at nodes 5 and 7 are infeasible (and thus further branching will result only in infeasible solutions). By the process of elimination, the integer solution at node 6 is optimal.

*The optimal integer solution*

In general, the optimal integer solution is reached when a feasible integer solution is generated at a node and the upper bound at that node is greater than or equal to the upper bound at any other *ending* node (i.e., a node at the end of a branch).

*Determining when the optimal solution is reached*

**Figure 8.9** The branch and bound diagram with optimal solution at node 6.

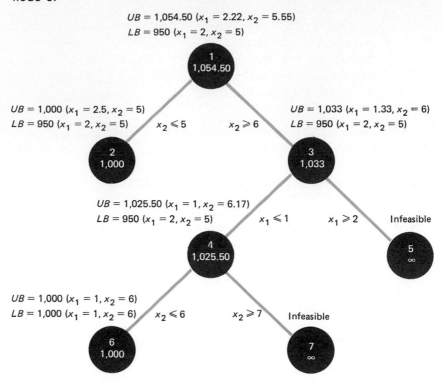

In the context of the original example, this solution indicates that 1 press and 6 lathes should be purchased, and that a daily increase in profit of $1,000 will result. Notice that this solution is the same integer solution achieved graphically in figure 8.1.

*Steps of the branch and bound method*     The steps of the branch and bound method for determining an optimal integer solution for a maximization model can be summarized as follows:

1. Find the optimal simplex solution to the linear programming model with the integer restrictions relaxed.

2. At node 1 let the relaxed simplex solution be the upper bound and the *rounded down* integer solution be the lower bound.

3. Select the variable with the greatest fractional part for branching. Create two new constraints for this variable reflecting the partitioned integer values for this variable. This will result in a new $\leq$ constraint and a new $\geq$ constraint.

4. Create two new nodes; one for the $\geq$ constraint and one for the $\leq$ constraint.

5. Solve the *relaxed* linear programming model with the new constraint added at each of these nodes.

6. The relaxed simplex solution is the upper bound at each node and the *existing* maximum integer solution (at any node) is the lower bound.

7. If a feasible integer solution exists that has the greatest upper bound value of any ending node, the optimal integer solution has been reached. If a feasible integer solution does not exist, branch from the node with the greatest upper bound.

8. Return to Step 3.

For a minimization model, relaxed solutions are rounded up and upper and lower bounds are reversed.

## Solution of the Mixed Integer Model

The mixed integer linear programming problem can also be solved using the branch and bound method. The same basic steps applied to the total integer model in the previous section are used for a mixed integer model with only a few differences.

*Applying the branch and bound method to mixed integer models*

First, at node 1 only those variables with integer restrictions are rounded down to achieve the *lower bound*. Second, in order to determine which variable to branch from, only variables that must be integer are considered. That is, when determining the variable with the greatest fractional part, only variables that must have integer values are considered. All other steps remain the same. The optimal solution is reached when a feasible solution is generated at a node that has integer values for those variables that have integer requirements, and the maximum upper bound of all ending nodes.

## Solution of the 0-1 Integer Model

The $0-1$ integer model can also be solved using the branch and bound method with a few minor changes. First, the $0-1$ restrictions for variables must be reflected as model constraints, $x_j \le 1$. As an example, consider the $0-1$ integer model for selecting recreational facilities formulated earlier in this chapter.

maximize $Z = 300x_1 + 90x_2 + 400x_3 + 150x_4$
subject to
$$35,000x_1 + 10,000x_2 + 25,000x_3 + 90,000x_4 \le \$120,000$$
$$4x_1 + 2x_2 + 7x_3 + 3x_4 \le 12 \text{ acres}$$
$$x_1 + x_2 \le 1 \text{ facility}$$
$$x_1, x_2, x_3, x_4 = 0 \text{ or } 1$$

*Applying the branch
and bound method to
0—1 integer models*

In order to apply the branch and bound method, the following four constraints would have to be added to the model in place of the restriction, "$x_1, x_2, x_3, x_4 = 0$ or 1,"

$$x_1 \leq 1$$
$$x_2 \leq 1$$
$$x_3 \leq 1$$
$$x_4 \leq 1$$

The only other change in the normal branch and bound method is at step 3. Once the variable, $x_j$, with the greatest fractional part is determined, the two new constraints developed from this variable would be $x_j = 0$ and $x_j = 1$. These two new constraints will form the two branches at each node.

*Implicit enumeration*

Another method for solving $0-1$ integer problems is through *implicit enumeration*. In implicit enumeration, obviously infeasible solutions are eliminated and the remaining solutions are evaluated (i.e., enumerated) to see which is the best. We will demonstrate this approach using our original $0-1$ example model above for recreational facility selection (i.e., without the $x_j \leq 1$ constraints).

*Complete enumeration*

The *complete enumeration* (i.e., possible solution sets) for this model is shown as follows.

| Solution | $x_1$ | $x_2$ | $x_3$ | $x_4$ | Feasibility | Z Value |
|---|---|---|---|---|---|---|
| 1 | 0 | 0 | 0 | 0 | Feasible | 0 |
| 2 | 1 | 0 | 0 | 0 | Feasible | 300 |
| 3 | 0 | 1 | 0 | 0 | Feasible | 90 |
| 4 | 0 | 0 | 1 | 0 | Feasible | 400 |
| 5 | 0 | 0 | 0 | 1 | Feasible | 150 |
| 6 | 1 | 1 | 0 | 0 | Infeasible | ∞ |
| 7 | 1 | 0 | 1 | 0 | Feasible | 700 |
| 8 | 1 | 0 | 0 | 1 | Infeasible | ∞ |
| 9 | 0 | 1 | 1 | 0 | Feasible | 490 |
| 10 | 0 | 1 | 0 | 1 | Feasible | 240 |
| 11 | 0 | 0 | 1 | 1 | Feasible | 550 |
| 12 | 1 | 1 | 1 | 0 | Infeasible | ∞ |
| 13 | 1 | 0 | 1 | 1 | Infeasible | ∞ |
| 14 | 1 | 1 | 0 | 1 | Infeasible | ∞ |
| 15 | 0 | 1 | 1 | 1 | Infeasible | ∞ |
| 16 | 1 | 1 | 1 | 1 | Infeasible | ∞ |

*Eliminating
infeasible solutions*

Because of the third constraint, $x_1 + x_2 \leq 1$, solutions 6, 12, 14, and 16 can be initially eliminated since they violate this constraint. Due to the other two constraints, solutions 8, 13, and 15 can also be eliminated for the same reason. This leaves eight possible solution sets (assuming solution 1 can be eliminated) for consideration. Evaluating the objective

*The optimal solution*

function value of these eight solutions shows solution 7, with $x_1 = 1$, $x_2 = 0$, $x_3 = 1$, $x_4 = 0$, to be the best. Interpreting this solution within the context of the example, a swimming pool ($x_1$) and an athletic field ($x_3$) should be constructed, and these facilities will generate an expected usage of 700 people per day.

The process of eliminating infeasible solutions from consideration and then evaluating the feasible solutions to see which is best is the basic principle behind implicit enumeration. However, implicit enumeration generally follows a more systematic process of evaluating solutions with a branching diagram like that used in the branch and bound method, rather than the process of sorting through a complete enumeration as in the example above.

## Summary

In this chapter it was demonstrated that simply rounding off noninteger simplex solution values for models that require integer solutions is not always appropriate. Rounding can often lead to suboptimal results. As such, general solution approaches are needed to solve the three forms of linear integer programming models—total integer models, mixed integer models, and $0-1$ integer models. The most frequently used solution approach, the branch and bound method, was demonstrated as a general solution approach.

By analyzing integer problems and techniques for solving them, we have now presented most of the basic forms of linear programming models and solution techniques. However, one exception is a problem that contains more than one objective. The topic of goal programming to be presented in the next chapter encompasses this type of problem.

## References

Baumol, W. J. *Economic Theory and Operations Analysis.* Englewood Cliffs, N.J.: Prentice-Hall, 1965.

Budnick, F. S.; Mojena, R.; and Vollman, T. E. *Principles of Operations Research.* Homewood, Ill.: Richard D. Irwin, 1977.

Dantzig, G. B. "On the Significance of Solving Linear Programming Problems with Some Integer Variables." *Econometrica* 28 (1960): 30–44.

Gomory, R. E. "An Algorithm for Integer Solutions to Linear Programs." In *Recent Advances in Mathematical Programming,* edited by R. L. Graves and P. Wolfe. New York: McGraw-Hill, 1963.

Hartley, R. W. *Operations Research: A Managerial Emphasis.* Pacific Palisades, Calif.: Goodyear Publishing Co., 1976.

Kwak, N. K. *Mathematical Programming with Business Applications.* New York: McGraw-Hill, 1973.

Lawler, E. L., and Wood, D. W. "Branch and Bound Methods—A Survey." *Operations Research* 14 (1966): 699–719.

Little, J. D. C. et al. "An Algorithm for the Traveling Salesman Problem." *Operations Research,* 11 (1963): 972–89.

McMillan, C., Jr. *Mathematical Programming.* New York: John Wiley and
    Sons, 1970.
Mitten, L. G. "Branch-and-Bound Methods: General Formulation and
    Properties." *Operations Research* 18 (1970): 24–34.
Plane, D. R., and McMillan, C., Jr. *Discrete Optimization.* Englewood Cliffs,
    N.J.: Prentice-Hall, 1971.
Wagner, H. *Principles of Operations Research.* 2d ed. Englewood Cliffs, N.J.:
    Prentice-Hall, 1975.

## Problems

1. Given the following linear programming model:

   maximize $Z = 5x_1 + 4x_2$
   subject to
   $$3x_1 + 4x_2 \leq 10$$
   $$x_1, x_2 \geq 0 \text{ and integer}$$

   (a) Solve using the branch and bound method.
   (b) Demonstrate the solution partitioning graphically.

2. Given the following linear programming model:

   minimize $Z = 3x_1 + 6x_2$
   subject to
   $$7x_1 + 3x_2 \geq 40$$
   $$x_1, x_2 \geq 0 \text{ and integer}$$

   Solve using the branch and bound method.

3. In chapter 3 the following problem (11) was presented. A clothier
   makes coats and slacks from wool cloth and labor. The clothier has
   developed the following linear programming model to determine the
   number of coats and pairs of slacks ($x_1$ and $x_2$) to make in order to
   maximize profit.

   maximize $Z = 50x_1 + 40x_2$ (profit, $)
   subject to
   $$3x_1 + 5x_2 \leq 150 \text{ (wool, yd.}^2)$$
   $$10x_1 + 4x_2 \leq 200 \text{ (labor, hrs.)}$$
   $$x_1, x_2 \geq 0$$

   Although there were no integer restrictions originally placed on this
   model, realistically there should be, since the clothier would not make
   a partial coat or pair of slacks. As such, solve this model with the
   added restriction that $x_1$ and $x_2$ must be integers using the branch and
   bound method.

4. In chapter 3 the following problem (5) was presented. The Pinewood Furniture Company produces chairs and tables from labor and wood. The following linear programming model has been developed to determine the number of chairs $(x_1)$ and tables $(x_2)$ to produce daily in order to maximize profit.

maximize $Z = 400x_1 + 100x_2$ (profit, $) 
subject to
$$8x_1 + 10x_2 \leq 80 \text{ (labor, hrs.)}$$
$$2x_1 + 6x_2 \leq 36 \text{ (wood, lbs.)}$$
$$x_1 \leq 6 \text{ (demand, chairs)}$$
$$x_1, x_2 \geq 0$$

Although there were no integer restrictions originally placed on this model, realistically there should be since the furniture manufacturer could not make a partial table or chair. As such, solve this model with the added restriction that $x_1$ and $x_2$ must be integers using the branch and bound method.

5. A glass blower makes glass decanters and glass trays on a weekly basis. Each item requires 1 pound of glass and the glass blower has 15 pounds of glass available every week. A glass decanter requires 4 hours of labor, while a glass tray requires only 1 hour of labor, and the glass blower works 25 hours during a week. The profit from a decanter is $50, while the profit from a tray is $10. The following linear programming model has been developed to determine the number of decanters $(x_1)$ and trays $(x_2)$ to produce in order to maximize profit.

maximize $Z = 50x_1 + 10x_2$
subject to
$$x_1 + x_2 \leq 15$$
$$4x_1 + x_2 \leq 25$$
$$x_1, x_2 \geq 0 \text{ and integer}$$

The "relaxed" optimal solution to this model is:

| $c_i$ | | | 50 | 10 | 0 | 0 |
|---|---|---|---|---|---|---|
| | basic variables | quantity | $x_1$ | $x_2$ | $s_1$ | $s_2$ |
| 0 | $s_1$ | 8.75 | 0 | $-1/4$ | 1 | $-1/4$ |
| 50 | $x_1$ | 6.25 | 1 | $1/4$ | 0 | $1/4$ |
| | $z_i$ | 312.50 | 50 | $25/2$ | 0 | $25/2$ |
| | $c_i - z_i$ | | 0 | $-5/2$ | 0 | $-25/2$ |

(a) Determine the integer solution to this model using the branch and bound method.
(b) Demonstrate the solution partitioning graphically.

6. The Livewright Medical Supplies Company has a total of 12 sales-people it wants to assign to three regions—the South, the East, and the Midwest. A salesperson in the South earns $600 profit per month for the company, a salesperson in the East earns $540 in profit, while a salesperson in the Midwest makes the company $375 per month. The southern region can have a maximum assignment of 5 salespeople. The company has a total of $750 per day available for expenses for all 12 salespeople. The company has developed the following linear program-ming model to determine the number of salespeople to assign to the South $(x_1)$, the East $(x_2)$, and the Midwest $(x_3)$ in order to maximize profit.

maximize $Z = 600x_1 + 540x_2 + 375x_3$
subject to
$$x_1 + x_2 + x_3 \leq 12$$
$$x_1 \leq 5$$
$$80x_1 + 70x_2 + 50x_3 \leq 750$$
$$x_1, x_2, x_3 \geq 0 \text{ and integer}$$

Solve this model using the branch and bound method.

7. The Audiocorp Company makes stereos and televisions. The company has enough material to produce 9 units daily (stereos and televisions) and 25 hours of labor each day. The company has developed the fol-lowing linear programming model to determine the number of stereos $(x_1)$ and televisions $(x_2)$ to produce each day in order to maximize profit.

maximize $Z = 300x_1 + 400x_2$ (profit, $)
subject to
$$x_1 + x_2 \leq 9 \text{ (material, units)}$$
$$2x_1 + 5x_2 \leq 25 \text{ (labor, hrs.)}$$
$$x_1, x_2 \geq 0 \text{ and integer}$$

Solve this model using the branch and bound method.

8. The Ambrose Bennett Jewelry Store makes custom jewelry to sell at Christmas every year. The store makes necklaces and bracelets, which have profits of $500 and $400 respectively, from gold and labor. The store has developed the following linear programming model to deter-mine the number of bracelets $(x_1)$ and necklaces $(x_2)$ to make in order to maximize profit.

maximize $Z = 500x_1 + 400x_2$
subject to
$$2x_1 + 5x_2 \leq 35$$
$$3x_1 + 2x_2 \leq 20$$
$$x_1, x_2 \geq 0 \text{ and integer}$$

The "relaxed" optimal simplex solution for this model is:

| $c_j$ | | | 500 | 400 | 0 | 0 |
|---|---|---|---|---|---|---|
| | basic variables | quantity | $x_1$ | $x_2$ | $s_1$ | $s_2$ |
| 400 | $x_2$ | 5.91 | 0 | 1 | 3/11 | −2/11 |
| 500 | $x_1$ | 2.73 | 1 | 0 | −2/11 | 5/11 |
| | $z_j$ | 3,729 | 500 | 400 | 200/11 | 1700/11 |
| | $c_j - z_j$ | | 0 | 0 | −200/11 | −1700/11 |

Solve this problem using the branch and bound method.

9. Lynn Fitzgerald has $500,000 to invest in condominium units and land. Lynn has developed the following mixed integer linear programming model to determine how many condominium units ($x_1$) and acres ($x_2$) to purchase in order to maximize the return on the investment.

maximize $Z = 800x_1 + 600x_2$ (annual return, $)
subject to
$$70x_1 + 30x_2 \leq 500 \text{ (capital outlay, \$1,000s)}$$
$$x_1 + 2x_2 \leq 14 \text{ (annual maintenance budget, \$1,000s)}$$
$$x_1 \geq 0 \text{ and integer}$$
$$x_2 \geq 0$$

Solve this model using the branch and bound method.

10. The owner of the Consolidated Machine Shop has $10,000 available to purchase a lathe, a press, or a grinder (or some combination). The following $0 - 1$ integer linear programming model has been developed to determine which of the three machines (lathe $- x_1$, press $- x_2$, or grinder $- x_3$) should be purchased in order to maximize annual profit.

maximize $Z = 1,000x_1 + 700x_2 + 800x_3$ (profit, $)
subject to
$$5,000x_1 + 6,000x_2 + 4,000x_3 \leq 10,000 \text{ (cost, \$)}$$
$$x_1, x_2, x_3 = 0 \text{ or } 1$$

Solve using the branch and bound method.

11. Given the following mixed integer linear programming model:

maximize $Z = 5x_1 + 6x_2 + 4x_3$
subject to
$$5x_1 + 3x_2 + 6x_3 \leq 20$$
$$x_1 + 3x_2 \leq 12$$
$$x_1, x_3 \geq 0$$
$$x_2 \geq 0 \text{ and integer}$$

Solve using the branch and bound method.

12. Solve problem 10 using the implicit enumeration method.

13. A multimillionaire from the Middle East wants to invest \$15 million by purchasing some or all of the following properties: a shopping center, a professional basketball franchise, and a 20-story office building. The cost of the shopping center is \$9 million, the basketball franchise is \$5 million, and the office building is \$10 million. The annual return from the shopping center is \$1 million, the return from the basketball franchise is \$400,000, and the office building will result in a \$1.2 million return annually. The investor has hired a manager who works 50 hours per week. The time required by the manager to oversee operations of the shopping center is 30 hours; the basketball franchise is 10 hours, and the office building is 20 hours. Because of the potential for problems due to traffic conditions at the shopping center and fan reaction to the basketball team, the investor will purchase only one of the two. The investor wants to know which properties to purchase in order to maximize the return. Formulate a linear programming model for this problem and solve using the most convenient method.

14. Given the following linear programming model:

maximize $Z = 20x_1 + 30x_2 + 10x_3 + 40x_4$
subject to
$$2x_1 + 4x_2 + 3x_3 + 7x_4 \leq 10$$
$$10x_1 + 7x_2 + 20x_3 + 15x_4 \leq 40$$
$$x_1 + 10x_2 + x_3 \leq 10$$
$$x_1, x_2, x_3, x_4 = 0 \text{ or } 1$$

(a) Solve using the implicit enumeration method.
(b) What difficulties would be encountered with the implicit enumeration method if this problem were expanded to contain 5 or more variables and more constraints?

# 9

## Goal Programming

## Model Formulation

Labor Goal
Profit Goal
Material Goal
Alternative Forms of Goal Constraints

## Graphical Interpretation of Goal Programming

## The Modified Simplex Method

Summary of the Steps of the Modified Simplex Method

## Applications of Goal Programming

## Summary

In all of the linear programming models presented in chapters 2 through 8, there was a single objective that was either maximized or minimized. However, it often occurs that an organization will have more than one objective, some of which might relate to something other than profit or cost. For example, while a business firm might have an objective to maximize profit, it might also have other objectives, such as minimizing labor layoffs and minimizing pollution. If a strike is imminent or the firm is about to be fined for pollution, these objectives may be more important than profit.

*Organizations with more than one objective*

Given an organizational environment where more than one objective exists, *goal programming* is an appropriate alternative solution technique. Goal programming is very similar to regular linear programming as presented in chapters 2 through 7, except that it includes more than one objective. In fact, goal programming consists entirely of linear functions as in linear programming.

A goal programming model is developed similarly to a linear programming model. Like linear programming, goal programming can be illustrated using a graphical approach. The solution approach for goal programming consists of a simplex process, which is a modified version of the simplex method presented in chapters 4 and 5. As such, some of the material presented in this chapter will seem very familiar, although it relates to a new topic, goal programming.

*Similar to linear programming*

## Model Formulation

In order to demonstrate how a goal programming model is formulated and the differences between a linear programming model and a goal programming model, the Colonial Pottery Company example used in previous chapters will be employed again. Recall that this model was orginally formulated in chapter 2 as

*A goal programming example*

maximize $Z = \$4x_1 + 5x_2$
subject to
$$x_1 + 2x_2 \leq 40 \text{ hours of labor}$$
$$4x_1 + 3x_2 \leq 120 \text{ pounds of clay}$$
$$x_1, x_2 \geq 0$$

where

$x_1$ = number of bowls produced

$x_2$ = number of mugs produced

The objective function, $Z$, represents the total profit to be made from bowls and mugs, where \$4 is the profit per bowl and \$5 is the profit per mug. The first constraint is for available labor. It shows that a bowl requires 1 hour of labor and a mug requires 2 hours and that there are 40 hours available daily. The second constraint is for clay, and it shows that 4 pounds of clay are needed for each bowl and 3 pounds for each mug with a daily limit of 120 pounds of clay.

*Multiple objectives*

This is a standard linear programming model and, as such, it has a single objective function for profit. However, let us suppose that instead of one objective, the pottery company has several objectives that are listed as follows, *in order of importance:*

1. Because of some past labor problems the company wants to avoid using less than 40 hours of labor per day (i.e., avoid layoffs).
2. The company would like to achieve a *satisfactory* profit level of \$160 per day.
3. Since the clay must be stored in a special place to keep it from drying out, the company prefers not to keep more than 120 pounds on hand in a day.
4. Because of high overhead costs for keeping the plant open past normal hours, the company would like to minimize the amount of overtime.

*Goals*

These different objectives of the company are referred to as *goals* in the context of the goal programming technique. The company would, naturally, like to achieve these goals as closely as possible. Since the regular form of the linear programming model that has been presented in previous chapters only considers one objective, we must develop an alternative form of model to reflect these *multiple goals*. The first step in formulating a goal programming model is to transform the linear programming model constraints into goals.

## Labor Goal

*Goal constraints*

The first goal of the pottery company is to avoid using less than 40 hours of labor, which can be referred to as labor *underutilization*. In order to represent the possibility of underutilizing labor the linear programming constraint for labor

$$x_1 + 2x_2 \leq 40 \text{ hours of labor}$$

is reformulated as

$$x_1 + 2x_2 + d_1^- - d_1^+ = 40 \text{ hours}$$

This reformulated equation is now referred to as a *goal constraint*. The two new variables, $d_1^-$ and $d_1^+$, are called *deviational variables*. They represent the amount of labor hours less than 40 ($d_1^-$) and the amount of labor hours exceeding 40 ($d_1^+$). More specifically, $d_1^-$ is labor underutilization while $d_1^+$ is *overtime*. For example, if $x_1 = 5$ bowls and $x_2 = 10$ mugs, then a total of 25 hours of labor have been expended. Substituting these values into our goal constraint,

*Deviational variables*

$$(5) + 2(10) + d_1^- - d_1^+ = 40$$
$$25 + d_1^- - d_1^+ = 40$$

Since only 25 hours were used in production, labor was underutilized by 15 hours ($40 - 25 = 15$). Thus, if we let $d_1^- = 15$ hours and $d_1^+ = 0$ (since there is obviously no overtime) we have

$$25 + d_1^- - d_1^+ = 40$$
$$25 + 15 - 0 = 40$$
$$40 = 40$$

Now consider the case where $x_1 = 10$ bowls and $x_2 = 20$ mugs. This means a total of 50 hours have been used for production, or 10 hours above the "goal" level of 40 hours. This extra 10 hours is, in reality, overtime. Thus, $d_1^- = 0$ (since there is no underutilization) and $d_1^+ = 10$ hours.

Notice that in each of these two brief examples at least one of the deviational variables equaled zero. In the first example, $d_1^+ = 0$, and in the second example $d_1^- = 0$. In other words, it is physically impossible to use less than 40 hours of labor and more than 40 hours of labor *at the same time*. Of course, both deviational variables, $d_1^-$ and $d_1^+$, could have equaled zero if exactly 40 hours were used in production. As such, one of the fundamental characteristics of goal programming is that *at least one or both of the deviational variables in a goal constraint must equal zero*.

*At least one deviational variable in a goal constraint must equal zero*

The next step in our goal programming model formulation is to represent the "goal" of not using less than 40 hours of labor. This is done by creating a new form of objective function,

*The goal programming objective function*

minimize $P_1 d_1^-$

The objective function in all goal programming models is to *minimize* deviation from the goal constraint levels. In this objective function the goal is to minimize $d_1^-$, underutilization of labor. In other words, if $d_1^-$ equaled zero, then we would not be using less than 40 hours of labor. Thus, it is our objective to make $d_1^-$ equal zero or the minimum amount possible. The symbol $P_1$ in the objective function designates the minimization of $d_1^-$ as the *priority one* goal. This means that when this model is solved, the first step will be to minimize the value of $d_1^-$ before any other goal is addressed.

*Minimizing deviation from a goal level*

*Prioritizing goals*

The fourth priority goal in this problem is also associated with the labor constraint. The fourth goal reflected a desire to minimize overtime. Recalling that hours of overtime are represented by $d_1^+$, the objective function becomes

$$\text{minimize } P_1 d_1^-, \quad P_4 d_1^+$$

$P_4$ designates this as the fourth priority goal. As before, the objective is to minimize the deviational variable, in this case $d_1^+$. In other words, if $d_1^+$ equaled zero, there would be no overtime at all. When this model is solved, the possible achievement of this fourth ranked goal will not be attempted until goals one, two, and three have first been considered.

## Profit Goal

*Profit as a goal instead of a single objective function*

The second goal in our goal programming model is to achieve a profit of $160. Recall that the original linear programming objective function was

$$Z = 4x_1 + 5x_2$$

Now we reformulate this objective function as a goal constraint with the following goal level.

$$4x_1 + 5x_2 + d_2^- - d_2^+ = \$160$$

The deviational variables $d_2^-$ and $d_2^+$ represent the amount of profit less than $160 ($d_2^-$) and the amount of profit exceeding $160 ($d_2^+$). The goal of the pottery company to achieve $160 in profit is represented in the objective function as

$$\text{minimize } P_1 d_1^-, \quad P_2 d_2^-, \quad P_4 d_1^+$$

Notice that only $d_2^-$ is being minimized, and not $d_2^+$, since it is logically assumed that the pottery company would be willing to accept all profits in excess of $160 (i.e., they do not desire to minimize $d_2^+$, excess profit). By minimizing $d_2^-$ at the second priority level, the pottery company hopes that $d_2^-$ will equal zero, which results in at least $160 in profit.

## Material Goal

The third goal of the company is to avoid keeping an amount of clay on hand in excess of 120 pounds. The goal constraint is

$$4x_1 + 3x_2 + d_3^- - d_3^+ = 120 \text{ pounds}$$

Since the deviational variables $d_3^-$ and $d_3^+$ represent respectively the amount of clay on hand less than 120 pounds and the amount in excess of 120 pounds, this goal can be reflected in the objective function as

$$\text{minimize } P_1 d_1^-, P_2 d_2^-, \quad P_3 d_3^+, \quad P_4 d_1^+$$

The term $P_3d_3^+$ represents the company's desire to minimize $d_3^+$, the amount of clay in excess of 120 pounds. The $P_3$ designation indicates that it is the third most important goal to the pottery company.

*The complete goal programming model*

The complete goal programming model can now be summarized as

minimize $P_1d_1^-$, $P_2d_2^-$, $P_3d_3^+$, $P_4d_1^+$
subject to
$$x_1 + 2x_2 + d_1^- - d_1^+ = 40$$
$$4x_1 + 5x_2 + d_2^- - d_2^+ = 160$$
$$4x_1 + 3x_2 + d_3^- - d_3^+ = 120$$
$$x_1, x_2, d_1^-, d_1^+, d_2^-, d_2^+, d_3^-, d_3^+ \geq 0$$

*Terms are not summed in the objective function*

Notice that one basic difference between this model and the standard linear programming model is that the objective function terms *are not summed* to equal a total value, $Z$. This is because the deviational variables in the objective function represent different units of measure. For example, $d_1^-$ and $d_1^+$ represent hours of labor, while $d_2^-$ represents dollars and $d_3^+$ represents pounds of clay. As such, it would be illogical to sum hours, dollars, and pounds as we did with just dollars in the linear programming model. The objective function in a goal programming model specifies only that the deviations from the goals represented in the objective function be minimized *individually* in the order of their priority.

## Alternative Forms of Goal Constraints

Let us reconsider our goal programming model above with the following change. Instead of goal number four being to minimize overtime, $d_1^+$, it is now

4. Limit overtime to 10 hours.

Recall that the goal constraint for labor is

$$x_1 + 2x_2 + d_1^- - d_1^+ = 40$$

*A goal constraint with all deviational variables*

In this goal constraint, $d_1^+$ represents overtime. Since the new fourth priority goal is to limit overtime to 10 hours, the following goal constraint is developed.

$$d_1^+ + d_4^- - d_4^+ = 10$$

While this goal constraint looks unusual, it is acceptable in goal programming to have an equation with *all deviational variables*. In this equation, $d_4^-$ represents the amount of overtime less than 10 hours, while $d_4^+$ is the amount of overtime greater than 10 hours. Since the company desires to *limit overtime* to 10 hours, then $d_4^+$ is minimized in the objective function.

minimize $P_1d_1^-$, $P_2d_2^-$, $P_3d_3^+$, $P_4d_4^+$

Now we will consider the addition of a fifth priority goal to this example, as follows:

5. Since the pottery company has limited warehouse space, they can produce no more than 30 bowls and 20 mugs daily, although the company would like to produce these amounts if possible. However, because the profit for mugs is greater than the profit for bowls (i.e., $5 to $4), it is more important to achieve the goal for mugs than bowls.

*A goal constraint with one deviational variable deleted*

This fifth goal requires that two new goal constraints be formulated as follows:

$$x_1 + d_5^- = 30 \text{ bowls}$$
$$x_2 + d_6^- = 20 \text{ mugs}$$

Notice that the positive deviational variables $d_5^+$ and $d_6^+$ have been deleted from these goal constraints. This is because the statement of the fifth goal specifies that "no more than 30 bowls and 20 mugs" can be produced. In other words, positive deviation, or overproduction, is not possible. Thus, in the goal constraints the positive deviational variables are eliminated.

Since the actual goal of the company is to achieve the levels of production shown in these two goal constraints, the negative deviational variables $d_5^-$ and $d_6^-$ are minimized in the objective function. However, recall that it is *more important* to the company to achieve the goal for mugs, since it has the greater profit. This condition is reflected in the objective function as follows.

$$\text{minimize } P_1d_1^-, \ P_2d_2^-, \ P_3d_3^+, \ P_4d_4^+, \ \boxed{4P_5d_5^- + 5P_5d_6^-}$$

*Weighting goals at the same priority level*

Since the goal for mugs is more important than the goal for bowls because the former has the higher profit, the *degree of importance* should be in proportion to the amount of profit. Thus, the goal for mugs is more important than the goal for bowls by a ratio of 5 to 4.

*Weights*

The coefficients of 5 for $P_5d_6^-$ and 4 for $P_5d_5^-$ are referred to as *weights*. In other words, the minimization of $d_6^-$ is "weighted" higher than the minimization of $d_5^-$ at the fifth priority level. When this model is solved, the achievement of the goal for minimizing $d_6^-$ (mugs) will be attempted before the achievement of the goal for minimizing $d_5^-$ (bowls), even though both goals are at the same priority level.

However, also notice that these two weighted goals have been summed. That is because they are at the same priority level. Their sum reflects the desired goal achievement at this one priority level.

The complete goal programming model with both of the new goals for overtime and production is

$$\text{minimize } P_1d_1^-, \ P_2d_2^-, \ P_3d_3^+, \ P_4d_4^+, \ 4P_5d_5^- + 5P_5d_6^-$$
subject to
$$x_1 + 2x_2 + d_1^- - d_1^+ = 40$$
$$4x_1 + 5x_2 + d_2^- - d_2^+ = 160$$

$$4x_1 + 3x_2 + d_3^- - d_3^+ = 120$$
$$d_1^+ + d_4^- - d_4^+ = 10$$
$$x_1 + d_5^- = 30$$
$$x_2 + d_6^- = 20$$
$$x_1, x_2, d_1^-, d_1^+, d_2^-, d_2^+, d_3^-, d_3^+, d_4^-, d_4^+, d_5^-, d_6^- \geq 0$$

## Graphical Interpretation of Goal Programming

In chapter 3, the solution of linear programming models was analyzed using graphical analysis. Since goal programming models are also linear, they can also be analyzed graphically. As an example, the original goal programming model for the Colonial Pottery Company formulated at the beginning of this chapter will be used.

minimize $P_1d_1^-, P_2d_2^-, P_3d_3^+, P_4d_1^+$
subject to
$$x_1 + 2x_2 + d_1^- - d_1^+ = 40$$
$$4x_1 + 5x_2 + d_2^- - d_2^+ = 160$$
$$4x_1 + 3x_2 + d_3^- - d_3^+ = 120$$
$$x_1, x_2, d_1^-, d_1^+, d_2^-, d_2^+, d_3^-, d_3^+ \geq 0$$

In order to graph this model, the deviational variables in each goal constraint are set equal to zero, and each subsequent equation is graphed on a set of coordinates just as we did in chapter 3. Figure 9.1 is a graph of the three goal constraints for this model.

*Graphing the goal constraints*

---

**Figure 9.1** Goal constraints.

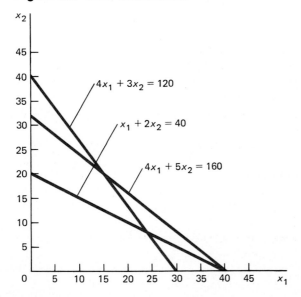

Notice in figure 9.1 that there is no feasible solution space indicated as in a regular linear programming model. The reason is that all three of the goal constraints are *equations*, thus all solution points are on the constraint lines.

*The goal programming solution logic*

The solution logic in a goal programming model is to attempt to achieve the goals in the objective function in order of their priorities. As a goal is achieved, the next highest ranked goal is then considered. However, a higher-ranked goal that has been achieved is never given up in order to achieve a lower-ranked goal.

*Achieving the priority one goal*

In this example we consider the priority one goal of minimizing $d_1^-$ first. In figure 9.2, the relationship of $d_1^-$ and $d_1^+$ to the goal constraint is shown. The area below the goal constraint line $x_1 + 2x_2 = 40$ represents possible values for $d_1^-$, and the area above the line represents values for $d_1^+$. In order to achieve the goal of minimizing $d_1^-$, the area below the constraint line corresponding to $d_1^-$ is eliminated, leaving the shaded area as a possible solution area.

**Figure 9.2** Consideration of first priority goal: minimize $d_1^-$.

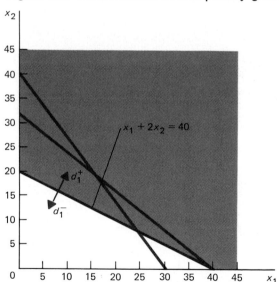

*Achieving the priority two goal*

Next, we consider the second priority goal of minimizing $d_2^-$. In figure 9.3, the area below the constraint line $4x_1 + 5x_2 = 160$ represents the values for $d_2^-$ while the area above the line represents the values for $d_2^+$. In order to minimize $d_2^-$, the area below the constraint line corresponding to $d_2^-$ is eliminated. Notice that by eliminating the area for $d_2^-$, we do not affect the priority one goal of minimizing $d_1^-$ at all.

**Figure 9.3** Consideration of second priority goal: minimize $d_2^-$.

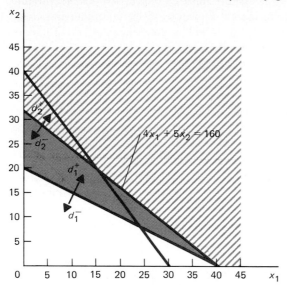

Next, the priority three goal of minimizing $d_3^+$ is considered. Figure 9.4 shows the areas corresponding to $d_3^-$ and $d_3^+$. In order to minimize $d_3^+$, the area above the constraint line $4x_1 + 3x_2 = 120$ is eliminated. After considering the first three goals, we are left with the area between the line segments *AC* and *BC,* which contain possible solution points *and* satisfy the first three goals.

*Achieving the priority three goal*

**Figure 9.4** Consideration of third and fourth priority goals: minimize $d_3^+$ and $d_1^+$.

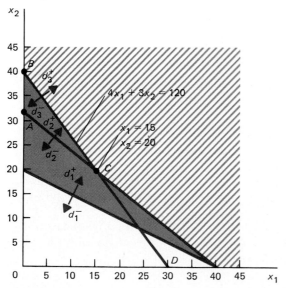

Finally, we must consider the fourth priority goal of minimizing $d_1^+$. In order to achieve this final goal, the area above the constraint line $x_1 + 2x_2 = 40$ must be eliminated. However, if we eliminate this area, then $d_2^-$ and $d_3^-$ both must take on a value. In other words, we cannot minimize $d_1^+$ totally without violating the priority one and two goals. Therefore, we want to find a solution point that still satisfies the first three goals, but achieves as much of the fourth priority goal as possible.

Point $C$ in figure 9.4 is a solution that *satisfies* these conditions. Notice that if we move down the goal constraint line $4x_1 + 5x_2 = 160$ toward point $D$, $d_1^+$ is further minimized, however, $d_2^-$ would take on a value as we moved past point $C$. Thus, the minimization of $d_1^+$ would be accomplished only at the expense of a higher ranked goal.

The solution at point $C$ is determined by simultaneously solving the two equations that intersect at this point. Doing so results in the following solutions.

$$x_1 = 15 \text{ bowls}$$
$$x_2 = 20 \text{ mugs}$$
$$d_1^+ = 15 \text{ hours}$$

Since $d_1^-$, $d_2^-$, and $d_3^+$ all equal zero, then these deviational variables were minimized and the first three goals were achieved. Since $d_1^+ = 15$ hours of overtime, the fourth priority goal was not achieved. The solution to a goal programming model such as this one is referred to as the *most satisfactory* solution rather than an optimal solution, since it satisfies the specified goals as well as possible.

The graphical method suffers the same limitations as a solution approach for a goal programming model as for a regular linear programming model (i.e., limited to two dimensions). However, a more general solution approach exists, which consists of a modified version of the simplex method first presented in chapter 4.

## The Modified Simplex Method

In order to demonstrate the *modified simplex method* for solving a goal programming model, we will use the Colonial Pottery Company example used in the graphical analysis in the previous section.

minimize $P_1 d_1^-$, $P_2 d_2^-$, $P_3 d_3^+$, $P_4 d_1^+$
subject to
$$x_1 + 2x_2 + d_1^- - d_1^+ = 40$$
$$4x_1 + 5x_2 + d_2^- - d_2^+ = 160$$
$$4x_1 + 3x_2 + d_3^- - d_3^+ = 120$$
$$x_1, x_2, d_1^-, d_1^+, d_2^-, d_2^+, d_3^-, d_3^+ \geq 0$$

The simplex tableau presented in chapter 4 must be modified slightly for a goal programming model. The modified version of the initial simplex tableau for this example is shown in table 9.1.

**Table 9.1** The Initial Modified Simplex Tableau

| $P_j$ | basic variables | quantity | $x_1$ | $x_2$ | $P_1$ $d_1$ | $P_2$ $d_2$ | $d_3$ | $P_4$ $d_1$ | $d_2$ | $P_3$ $d_3$ |
|---|---|---|---|---|---|---|---|---|---|---|
| $P_1$ | $d_1$ | 40 | 1 | 2 | 1 | 0 | 0 | $-1$ | 0 | 0 |
| $P_2$ | $d_2$ | 160 | 4 | 5 | 0 | 1 | 0 | 0 | $-1$ | 0 |
|  | $d_3$ | 120 | 4 | 3 | 0 | 0 | 1 | 0 | 0 | $-1$ |
|  | $P_4$ | 0 | 0 | 0 | 0 | 0 | 0 | $-P_4$ | 0 | 0 |
|  | $P_3$ | 0 | 0 | 0 | 0 | 0 | 0 | 0 | 0 | $-P_3$ |
| $z_j - P_j$ | $P_2$ | $160P_2$ | $4P_2$ | $5P_2$ | 0 | 0 | 0 | 0 | $-P_2$ | 0 |
|  | $P_1$ | $40P_1$ | $P_1$ | $2P_1$ | 0 | 0 | 0 | $-P_1$ | 0 | 0 |

In the simplex tableau modified for goal programming, the model variables are listed across the top in the order of decision variables, negative deviational variables, and then positive deviational variables. Rather than assigning the $c_j$ value to each variable across the top row, the priority level $P_j$ is assigned.

*Setting up the tableau*

The initial basic feasible solution variables are always the negative deviational variables for each constraint. The negative deviational variables are analogous to slack variables in a regular linear programming model, and you will recall that slack variables (when present) always formed the initial solution in the simplex method. For this example, $d_1^-$, $d_2^-$, and $d_3^-$ are the initial basic variables. The priority level, $P_j$, for each of these deviational variables is assigned in the left-hand column. In this case minimizing $d_1^-$ is the priority one goal, $P_1$, and minimizing $d_2^-$ is the priority two goal, $P_2$.

*The initial basic feasible solution*

The row values within the body of the tableau are the values corresponding to the goal constraints and are assigned exactly the same way as in the regular simplex method.

*The tableau row values*

Notice that there is not a $z_j$ row or a $z_j - c_j$ now as in the regular simplex method. In the modified tableau the $z_j$ values are completely deleted and there is not a single $z_j - c_j$ row, but four $z_j - P_j$ rows corresponding to the four priority levels. The $z_j - P_j$ rows are computed exactly the same as in the simplex method, except it must be done for each priority level. Although the $z_j$ rows actually exist, they are deleted from the tableau, since their inclusion would make the tableau very large and cumbersome.

*The $z_j$ $-$ $P_j$ rows*

For example, consider the $x_1$ column. Multiplying the $x_1$ column values by the $P_j$ column values results in

$$P_j \quad x_1$$
$$P_1 \times 1 = P_1$$
$$P_2 \times 4 = 4P_2$$
$$0 \times 4 = 0$$

Since $P_j$ for $x_1$ equals zero, the $z_j - P_j$ values are

$$z_j - P_j$$
$$P_1 - 0 = P_1$$
$$4P_2 - 0 = 4P_2$$
$$0 - 0 = 0$$

Instead of listing these values all on one row, they are assigned according to priority. In the $z_j - P_j$ rows in table 9.1, priority one values are listed across the bottom row, priority two values across the next row, etc. For example, this means that the $z_j - P_j$ value of $P_1$ is listed in the bottom row (under the $x_1$ column), and $4P_2$ is listed in the $x_1$ column in the next to the bottom row. All other $z_j - P_j$ values are computed the same way.

*The pivot column*

The next step in the simplex process is to select the *pivot column*. In the modified tableau, the pivot column is determined by choosing the column with the maximum positive $z_j - P_j$ value (just as in the regular simplex method) *in the priority one row*. In other words, we seek to satisfy the priority one goal first. If no positive value exists in the priority one row, we go to the next priority row. In table 9.1, the maximum positive value *The entering* in the priority one row is $2P_1$, thus the $x_2$ column is the pivot column and *nonbasic variable* $x_2$ is the entering nonbasic variable.

The *pivot row* is determined by dividing the quantity values by the $x_2$ column values and selecting the minimum positive value (as in the simplex method). This results in the $d_1^-$ row being selected as the pivot row.

The second modified simplex tableau is shown in table 9.2.

---

**Table 9.2** The Second Modified Simplex Tableau

| $P_j$ | | | | | $P_1$ | $P_2$ | | $P_4$ | | $P_3$ |
|---|---|---|---|---|---|---|---|---|---|---|
| | basic variables | quantity | $x_1$ | $x_2$ | $d_1^-$ | $d_2^-$ | $d_3^-$ | $d_1^+$ | $d_2^+$ | $d_3^+$ |
| | $x_2$ | 20 | 1/2 | 1 | 1/2 | 0 | 0 | −1/2 | 0 | 0 |
| $P_2$ | $d_2^-$ | 60 | 3/2 | 0 | −5/2 | 1 | 0 | 5/2 | −1 | 0 |
| | $d_3^-$ | 60 | 5/2 | 0 | −3/2 | 0 | 1 | 3/2 | 0 | −1 |
| | $P_4$ | 0 | 0 | 0 | 0 | 0 | 0 | −$P_4$ | 0 | 0 |
| | $P_3$ | 0 | 0 | 0 | 0 | 0 | 0 | 0 | 0 | −$P_3$ |
| $z_j - P_j$ | $P_2$ | $60P_2$ | $3P_2/2$ | 0 | −$5P_2/2$ | 0 | 0 | $5P_2/2$ | −$P_2$ | 0 |
| | $P_1$ | 0 | 0 | 0 | −$P_1$ | 0 | 0 | 0 | 0 | 0 |

---

*Computing the new tableau row values*

In table 9.2 the new pivot row values (for the $x_2$ row) are computed the same way as in the simplex method by using the formula

$$\text{new tableau pivot row values} = \frac{\text{old pivot row values}}{\text{pivot number}}$$

All other row values (i.e., $d_2^-$ and $d_3^-$ rows) are also computed the same way as in the simplex method by using the formula new tableau = old tableau − $\begin{pmatrix} \text{corresponding} \\ \text{coefficients in} \\ \text{pivot column} \end{pmatrix} \times \begin{pmatrix} \text{corresponding} \\ \text{new tableau} \\ \text{pivot row} \\ \text{value} \end{pmatrix}$

The new $z_j - P_j$ row values in table 9.2 show that there are no positive values in the priority one row, which means that the priority one goal has been satisfied. Next, observing the priority two row, we see several positive values, the largest of which, $5P_2/2$, is in the $d_1^+$ column. Therefore, the $d_1^+$ column is the pivot column and $d_1^+$ is the entering nonbasic variable. The $d_2^-$ row is selected as the pivot row.

The third modified simplex tableau is shown in table 9.3.

**Table 9.3** The Third Modified Simplex Tableau

| $P_j$ | | | | | $P_1$ | $P_2$ | | | $P_4$ | | $P_3$ |
|---|---|---|---|---|---|---|---|---|---|---|---|
| | basic variables | quantity | $x_1$ | $x_2$ | $d_1^-$ | $d_2^-$ | $d_3^-$ | $d_1^+$ | $d_2^+$ | $d_3^+$ |
| $P_4$ | $x_2$ | 32 | 4/5 | 1 | 0 | 1/5 | 0 | 0 | −1/5 | 0 |
| | $d_1^+$ | 24 | 3/5 | 0 | −1 | 2/5 | 0 | 1 | −2/5 | 0 |
| | $d_3^-$ | 24 | 8/5 | 0 | 0 | −3/5 | 1 | 0 | 3/5 | −1 |
| | $P_4$ | $24P_4$ | $3P_4/5$ | 0 | $-P_4$ | $2P_4/5$ | 0 | 0 | $-2P_4/5$ | 0 |
| | $P_3$ | 0 | 0 | 0 | 0 | 0 | 0 | 0 | 0 | $-P_3$ |
| $z_j - P_j$ | $P_2$ | 0 | 0 | 0 | 0 | $-P_2$ | 0 | 0 | 0 | 0 |
| | $P_1$ | 0 | 0 | 0 | $-P_1$ | 0 | 0 | 0 | 0 | 0 |

Observing the $z_j - P_j$ rows in table 9.3, we see that there are no positive values in the priority one, two, or three rows, which means all the goals at these first three priority levels have been satisfied. However, in the priority four row there are several positive values, the largest of which, $3P_4/5$, is in the $x_1$ column. Thus, the $x_1$ column is the pivot column and the $d_3^-$ row is the pivot row.

The fourth modified simplex tableau is shown in table 9.4.

**Table 9.4** The Optimal Modified Simplex Tableau

| $P_j$ | | | | | $P_1$ | $P_2$ | | $P_4$ | | $P_3$ |
|---|---|---|---|---|---|---|---|---|---|---|
| | basic variables | quantity | $x_1$ $x_2$ | $d_1^-$ | $d_2^-$ | $d_3^-$ | $d_1^+$ | $d_2^+$ | $d_3^+$ |
| $P_4$ | $x_2$ | 20 | 0  1 | 0 | 1/2 | −1/2 | 0 | −1/2 | 1/2 |
| | $d_1^+$ | 15 | 0  0 | −1 | 5/8 | −3/8 | 1 | −5/8 | 3/8 |
| | $x_1$ | 15 | 1  0 | 0 | −3/8 | 5/8 | 0 | 3/8 | −5/8 |
| | $P_4$ | $15P_4$ | 0  0 | $-P_4$ | $5P_4/8$ | $-3P_4/8$ | 0 | $-5P_4/8$ | $3P_4/8$ |
| | $P_3$ | 0 | 0  0 | 0 | 0 | 0 | 0 | 0 | $-P_3$ |
| $z_j - P_j$ | $P_2$ | 0 | 0  0 | 0 | $-P_2$ | 0 | 0 | 0 | 0 |
| | $P_1$ | 0 | 0  0 | $-P_1$ | 0 | 0 | 0 | 0 | 0 |

Observing the $z_j - P_j$ rows in table 9.4, we see that there are no positive values in the priority one, two, or three rows, therefore the goals at these priority levels remain satisfied. Looking at the priority four row, we see that positive values exist in the $d_2^-$ and $d_3^+$ columns. However, notice that there are negative values in these columns at higher priority levels. For example, in the $d_2^-$ column, while a positive value of $5P_4/8$ exists at the priority four level, a negative value of $-P_2$ is at the priority two level. This means that if the deviational variable $d_2^-$ is entered into the solution (by selecting this column as the pivot column), then we will be giving up the priority two goal that is already satisfied in order to satisfy a priority four goal. We have already stated that a higher priority goal is never sacrificed for the sake of achieving a lower-ranked goal. Given this con-

dition, the solution shown in table 9.4 is the *most satisfactory* solution. For this goal programming model

$$x_1 = 15 \text{ bowls}$$
$$x_2 = 20 \text{ mugs}$$
$$d_1^+ = 15 \text{ hours of overtime}$$

Notice that this is the same solution that was achieved previously with the graphical analysis.

## Summary of the Steps of the Modified Simplex Method

1. Set up the initial tableau using negative deviational variables for the initial basic feasible solution. Compute the $z_j - P_j$ rows.

2. Determine the pivot column (entering nonbasic variable) by selecting the column with the maximum positive value at the highest priority level that has not been completely attained.

3. Determine the pivot row (leaving solution variable) by dividing the quantity column values by the pivot column values and selecting the row with either the minimum positive value or zero.

4. Compute the new pivot row values using the formula

$$\text{new tableau pivot row value} = \frac{\text{old pivot row value}}{\text{pivot number}}$$

5. Compute all other row values using the formula

$$\begin{array}{ccc} \text{new tableau} \\ \text{row value} \end{array} = \begin{array}{ccc} \text{old tableau} \\ \text{row value} \end{array} - \left( \begin{array}{c} \text{corresponding} \\ \text{coefficients in} \\ \text{the pivot} \\ \text{column} \end{array} \times \begin{array}{c} \text{corresponding} \\ \text{new tableau} \\ \text{pivot row} \\ \text{value} \end{array} \right)$$

6. Compute the new $z_j - P_j$ row.

7. Determine if the new solution is the most *satisfactory* by checking the $z_j - P_j$ rows. If there are no positive values at any priority level or there is a positive value but with a corresponding negative value at a higher priority, the solution has been reached. If this condition is not met, return to step 2 and repeat the modified simplex steps.

## Applications of Goal Programming

In this chapter we have considered only one example of goal programming, and it was for a business enterprise (the Colonial Pottery Company). However, goal programming is an especially useful technique for organizations, such as government agencies, hospitals, schools, and charitable organizations. Organizations such as these typically do not have an objective such as profit, having instead a variety of other goals. For example, a space agency such as NASA is not concerned with profit, but with several objectives related to space exploration and the research and development of new technology. They would also have a goal related to cost minimization, but it is probably not their most important objective. Similarly the objectives of a school are quality of education, the number of students it can educate, meeting local or state guidelines, and, to a lesser extent, minimizing the cost of running the school. As such, goal programming is a much more applicable technique to the resource allocation problems of these types of organizations than regular linear programming.

*Organizations without profit maximization as a single objective*

## Summary

This chapter presented a variation of linear programming in which more than one objective can exist. Goal programming is especially useful for organizations that do not have a single, clearly defined objective, such as profit maximization or cost minimization. Goal programming is often applicable to decision-making problems in public or governmental organizations where profit or cost are not really the primary consideration, but rather levels of service or efficiency in carrying out numerous goals.

The presentation of goal programming completes the coverage of linear programming. One of the implicit assumptions of linear programming has been that all parameters and values in the model were known with certainty. Upcoming chapters will consider techniques that are probabilistic, or where uncertainty exists.

*Completion of linear programming coverage*

## References

Charnes, A., and Cooper, W. W. *Management Models and Industrial Applications of Linear Programming.* New York: John Wiley and Sons, 1961.

Dyer, J. S. "Interactive Goal Programming." *Management Science* 19,1 (1972): 62–70.

Ignizio, J. P. *Goal Programming and Extensions.* Lexington, Mass.: Lexington Books, 1976.

Ijiri, Y. *Management Goals and Accounting for Control.* Chicago: Rand-McNally, 1965.

Kornbluth, J. S. H. "A Survey of Goal Programming." *Omega* 1, 2 (1973).
Lee, S. M. *Goal Programming for Decision Analysis*. Philadelphia: Auerbach Publishers, 1972.
Lee, S. M., and Clayton, E. R. "A Goal Programming Model for Academic Resource Allocation." *Management Science* 18, 8 (1972):395–408.

## Problems

1. A manufacturing company produces three products, 1, 2, and 3. The three products have resource requirements and profit as follows:

| Product | Labor (hours/unit) | Material (lbs/unit) | Profit ($/unit) |
|---|---|---|---|
| 1 | 5 | 4 | 3 |
| 2 | 2 | 6 | 5 |
| 3 | 4 | 3 | 2 |

At present the firm has a normal labor capacity of 240 available hours daily and a daily supply of 400 pounds of material. The general linear programming formulation for this problem is:

maximize $Z = 3x_1 + 5x_2 + 2x_3$
subject to
$$5x_1 + 2x_2 + 4x_3 \leq 240$$
$$4x_1 + 6x_2 + 3x_3 \leq 400$$
$$x_1, x_2, x_3 \geq 0$$

However, management has developed the following set of multiple goals arranged in order of their importance to the firm.

(1) Due to labor relations difficulties, management desires to avoid underutilization of normal production capacity.
(2) Management has established a satisfactory profit level of $500 per day.
(3) Overtime is to be minimized as much as possible.
(4) Management wants to minimize the purchase of additional materials due to handling and storage problems.

Formulate a goal programming model to determine the number of each product to produce in a way that best satisfies the goals.

2. The Homesaver Appliance Company produces washing machines and dryers. Production of either product requires one hour of production time. The plant has a normal production capacity of 40 hours per week. The maximum number of washers that can be stored per week

is 24, while 30 dryers can be stored per week. The profit for a washer is $80, while it is $40 for a dryer. The manager of the company has established the following goals, arranged in order of their importance:

(1) Minimization of underutilization of normal production capacity.
(2) Production of as many washers and dryers as possible. However, since the profit for a washer is twice that of a dryer, the manager has twice as much desire to achieve the production of washers as dryers.
(3) Minimization of overtime.
   (a) Formulate a goal programming model that will determine the number of washers and dryers to produce in order to satisfy the goals in the best way.
   (b) Reformulate the goal programming model in question (a) with a fourth priority goal of limiting overtime to ten hours per week (if possible).

3. The Bay City Parks and Recreation Department received a federal grant of $600,000 to expand its public recreation facilities. Four different types of facilities have been demanded by the city council representing their constituents—gymnasiums, athletic fields, tennis courts, and swimming pools. In fact, the demand by various communities in the city has been for seven gyms, ten athletic fields, eight tennis courts, and twelve swimming pools. However, each facility costs a certain amount, requires a certain number of acres to build, and has an expected usage, as follows:

| Facility | Cost ($) | Required Acres | Expected Usage (people/week) |
|----------|----------|----------------|------------------------------|
| Gymnasium | $80,000 | 4 | 1,500 |
| Athletic field | 24,000 | 8 | 3,000 |
| Tennis court | 15,000 | 3 | 500 |
| Swimming pool | 40,000 | 5 | 1,000 |

The parks and recreation department has presently located 50 acres of land for construction (although more land could be located if necessary).

The department has established the following list of prioritized goals:

(1) The department must spend the total grant or the amount not spent will be returned to the government.
(2) The department desires that the facilities be used by 20,000 people or more weekly.
(3) The department wants to avoid securing more land than the 50 acres already located.

(4) They would like to meet the demands of the city council for new facilities. However, this goal should be weighted according to the number of people estimated to use each facility.

(5) If the department must secure more land, they desire to limit it to 10 acres.

Formulate a goal programming model to determine the number of each type of facility to construct in order to best achieve the city's goals.

4. A farmer in the Midwest has 1,000 acres of land on which he intends to plant corn, wheat, and soybeans. Each acre of corn costs $100 for preparation, requires 7 worker days of labor, and yields a profit of $30. An acre of wheat costs $120 to prepare, requires 10 worker days of labor, and yields $40 profit. An acre of soybeans costs $70 to prepare, requires 8 worker days, and yields $20 profit. The farmer has taken out a loan of $80,000 for crop preparation and contracted with a union for 6,000 worker days of labor. A midwestern granary has agreed to purchase 200 acres of corn, 500 acres of wheat, and 300 acres of soybeans. The farmer has established the following goals in order of their importance.

(1) The farmer feels that the labor contract must be honored (i.e., use the total labor contracted for) in order to maintain future good relations with the union.

(2) Preparation costs should not exceed the loan amount so that additional loans will not have to be secured.

(3) The farmer desires a profit of at least $105,000 in order to remain in good financial condition.

(4) Contracting for excess labor should be avoided.

(5) The farmer would like to use as much of the available acreage as possible.

(6) The farmer would like to meet the sales agreement with the Chicago firm (weighted according to the profit returned by each crop).

Formulate a goal programming model to determine the number of acres of each crop the farmer should plant in order to satisfy the goals in the best possible way.

5. The Growall Fertilizer Company produces 3 types of fertilizer: Supergro, Dynaplant, and Soilsaver. The company has the capacity to produce a maximum of 2,000 tons of fertilizer in a week. It costs $800 to produce a ton of Supergro, $1,500 to produce Dynaplant, and $500 for Soilsaver. Production requires 10 hours of labor for a ton of Supergro, 12 hours for a ton of Dynaplant, and 18 hours for a ton of Soilsaver. The company has 800 hours of normal production labor available each week. The amount of each brand of fertilizer demanded each week is 800 tons of Supergro, 900 tons of Dynaplant, and 1,100 tons of Soilsaver. The company has established the following goals in order of their priority.

(1) The company does not want to spend over $20,000 per week on production if possible.

(2) They would like to limit overtime to 100 hours per week.

(3) They want to meet demand for all three fertilizers; however, it is twice as important to meet the demand for Supergro as for Dynaplant and it is twice as important to meet the demand for Dynaplant as for Soilsaver.

(4) They want to avoid producing under capacity, if possible.

(5) Because of union agreements they want to avoid underutilization of labor.

Formulate a goal programming model to determine the number of tons of each brand of fertilizer to produce in order to satisfy the goals.

6. The Barrett Textile Mill was inspected by inspectors enforcing the Occupational Safety and Health Act (OSHA). The inspectors found violations in four categories: hazardous materials, fire protection, hand-powered tools, and machine guarding. In each category the mill was not in 100% compliance. Each percent of increase in the compliance level of each category will reduce the frequency of accidents, the accident cost per worker, and progress towards satisfying the OSHA compliance level. However, compliance does cost the mill money to achieve. The following table contains the possible accident frequency reductions, accident cost per worker reductions and costs for achieving a percentage increase in compliance in each category.

| Category | Accident Frequency Reduction (accidents/$10^5$ hours of exposure) | Accident Cost/ Worker Reduction | Cost/ Percentage Point Compliance |
|---|---|---|---|
| 1. Hazardous materials | .18 | $1.21 | $135 |
| 2. Fire protection | .11 | .48 | 87 |
| 3. Hand-powered tools | .17 | .54 | 58 |
| 4. Machine guarding | .21 | 1.04 | 160 |

To achieve 100% compliance in all four categories, the mill must increase compliance in hazardous materials by 60 percentage points (i.e., they are at 40% compliance at present), in fire protection by 28 percentage points, in hand-powered tools by 35 percentage points, and in machine guarding by 17 percentage points. However, the management of the mill faces a dilemma in that they have only a limited amount of funds to spend on safety, $52,000. Any larger expenditure could jeopardize the financial standing of the mill. As such, management hopes to achieve certain levels of accident reduction and compliance within their budget limitation that will satisfy OSHA authorities momentarily and delay punitive action. Therefore, management has established the following goals in the order of importance.

(1) Do not exceed the budget constraint of $52,000.
(2) Achieve the percentage increases in compliance necessary to achieve 100% compliance in each category.
(3) Achieve total accident frequency reduction of 20 accidents/$10^5$ hours of exposure. (This goal denotes managements desire to minimize the frequency of accidents even if 100% compliance cannot be achieved in all categories.)
(4) Reduce the total accident cost/worker to $115.

Formulate a goal programming model to determine the percentage points of compliance needed in each category in order to satisfy the goals.

7. Given the following modified simplex tableau:

| $P_j$ | | | 0 | 0 | 0 | $P_1$ | 0 | $P_2$ | 0 | $P_3$ |
|---|---|---|---|---|---|---|---|---|---|---|
| | basic variables | quantity | $x_1$ | $x_2$ | $d_1^-$ | $d_2^-$ | $d_3^-$ | $d_1^+$ | $d_2^+$ | $d_3^+$ |
| $P_3$ | $d_3^+$ | 48 | 0 | $-4/5$ | $-3/5$ | 4 | $-1$ | 0 | $-4$ | 1 |
| $P_2$ | $d_1^+$ | 40 | 0 | $-12$ | $-4$ | 20 | 0 | 1 | $-20$ | 0 |
| 0 | $x_1$ | 88 | 1 | $-4/15$ | $-3/5$ | 4 | 0 | 0 | $-4$ | 0 |
| $P_3$ | | $48P_3$ | 0 | $4P_3/5$ | $-3P_3/5$ | $4P_3$ | $-P_3$ | 0 | $-4P_3$ | 0 |
| $P_2$ | | $40P_2$ | 0 | $-12P_2$ | $-4P_2$ | $20P_2$ | 0 | 0 | $-20P_2$ | 0 |
| $P_1$ | | 0 | 0 | 0 | 0 | $-P_1$ | 0 | 0 | 0 | 0 |

(a) How many goal constraints are in this goal programming model?
(b) Write out the original objective function.
(c) Write out the solution shown in this tableau.
(d) Is this solution the most satisfactory one that can be achieved? Explain.
(e) Are any of the goals unachieved in this solution? Explain.

8. Given the following goal programming model:

minimize $P_1 d_1^+, P_2 d_2^-, P_3 d_3^-$
subject to
$$4x_1 + 2x_2 + d_1^- - d_1^+ = 80$$
$$x_1 + d_2^- - d_2^+ = 30$$
$$x_2 + d_3^- - d_3^+ = 50$$
$$x_j, d_i^-, d_i^+ \geq 0$$

(a) Solve using the modified simplex method.
(b) Solve graphically.

9. Given the following goal programming model:

minimize $P_1d_1^- + P_1d_1^+, P_2d_2^-, P_3d_3^-, 3P_4d_2^+ + 5P_4d_3^+$
subject to

$$x_1 + x_2 + d_1^- - d_1^+ = 800$$
$$5x_1 + d_2^- - d_2^+ = 2,500$$
$$3x_2 + d_3^- - d_3^+ = 1,400$$
$$x_j, d_i^-, d_i^+ \geq 0$$

(a) Solve using the modified simplex method.

(b) Solve graphically.

10. Solve the following goal programming model using the modified simplex method.

minimize $P_1d_3^+, P_2d_1^-, P_3d_2^-, P_4d_1^+$
subject to

$$x_1 + 2x_2 + d_1^- - d_1^+ = 20$$
$$x_2 + d_2^- = 12$$
$$d_1^+ + d_3^- - d_3^+ = 6$$
$$x_j, d_i^-, d_i^+ \geq 0$$

11. Given the following goal programming model, solve using the modified simplex method.

minimize $P_1d_2^+, P_2d_1^-, P_3d_4^+, P_4d_1^+$
subject to

$$2x_1 + 3x_2 + x_3 + d_1^- - d_1^+ = 300$$
$$5x_2 + 4x_3 + d_2^- - d_2^+ = 400$$
$$x_1 + x_2 + x_3 + d_3^- - d_3^+ = 200$$
$$d_3^+ + d_4^- - d_4^+ = 50$$
$$x_j, d_i^-, d_i^+ \geq 0$$

12. A manufacturer produces two products, A and B, on two production lines. The following goal programming model has been developed to determine the number of product A ($x_1$) and product B ($x_2$) needed in order to meet the manufacturer's goals.

minimize $P_1d_1^-, P_2d_4^+, 4P_3d_2^- + 3P_3d_3^-, 3P_4d_2^+ + 4P_4d_3^+$
subject to

$$2x_1 + 1.5x_2 + d_1^- - d_1^+ = 180 \text{ (material, lbs.)}$$
$$x_1 + d_2^- - d_2^+ = 40 \text{ (line 1 capacity, hrs.)}$$
$$x_2 + d_3^- - d_3^+ = 40 \text{ (line 2 capacity, hrs.)}$$
$$d_2^+ + d_4^- - d_4^+ = 10 \text{ (overtime, hrs.)}$$
$$x_j, d_i^-, d_i^+ \geq 0$$

Solve this goal programming model using the modified simplex method.

13. Solve the following goal programming model using the modified simplex method.

minimize $P_1 d_4^+, P_2 d_2^-, P_3 d_1^-, P_4 d_3^+$
subject to

$$
\begin{aligned}
x_1 + d_1^- - d_1^+ &= 4 \\
x_2 + d_2^- - d_2^+ &= 6 \\
3x_1 + 2x_2 + d_3^- - d_3^+ &= 18 \\
d_3^+ + d_4^- - d_4^+ &= 3 \\
x_j, d_i^-, d_i^+ &\geq 0
\end{aligned}
$$

14. Solve the following goal programming model using the modified simplex method.

minimize $P_1 d_3^-, P_2 d_2^-, P_3 d_1^+, P_4 d_2^+$
subject to

$$
\begin{aligned}
4x_1 + 6x_2 + d_1^- - d_1^+ &= 48 \\
2x_1 + x_2 + d_2^- - d_2^+ &= 20 \\
d_2^+ + d_3^- - d_3^+ &= 10 \\
x_2 + d_4^- &= 6 \\
x_j, d_i^-, d_i^+ &\geq 0
\end{aligned}
$$

15. The Wearever Carpet Company produces two brands of carpet—shag and sculptured. The following goal programming model has been developed to determine the number of yards of shag ($x_1$, in 100-yard lots) and sculptured ($x_2$, in 100-yard lots) to produce daily in order to meet goals for production capacity, daily sales demand, and overtime.

minimize $P_1 d_1^-, 5P_2 d_2^-, 2P_2 d_3^-, P_3 d_4^+$
subject to

$$
\begin{aligned}
8x_1 + 6x_2 + d_1^- - d_1^+ &= 480 \text{ (production capacity, hrs.)} \\
x_1 + d_2^- &= 40 \text{ (demand, 100 yds.)} \\
x_2 + d_3^- &= 50 \text{ (demand, 100 yds.)} \\
d_1^+ + d_4^- - d_4^- &= 20 \text{ (overtime, hrs.)} \\
x_j, d_i^-, d_i^+ &\geq 0
\end{aligned}
$$

Solve this goal programming model using the modified simplex method.

16. The East Midvale Textile Company produces denim and brushed cotton cloth. The average production rate for both types of cloth is 1,000 yards per hour, and the normal weekly production capacity (running 2 shifts) is 80 hours. The marketing department estimates that the maximum demand for denim is 60,000 yards per week and for brushed cotton 35,000 yards per week. The profit is $3.00 per yard for denim and $2.00 per yard for brushed cotton. The following four goals, listed in order of importance, have been determined by the company.

(1) Eliminate underutilization of production capacity in order to maintain stable employment levels.

(2) Limit overtime to 10 hours.

(3) Do not exceed demand for denim and brushed cotton.

(4) Minimize overtime as much as possible.

    (a) Formulate a goal programming model to determine the number of yards (in 1,000-yard lots) to produce in order to satisfy the goals.

    (b) Solve this model using the modified simplex method.

17. The Oregon Atlantic Company produces two kinds of paper: newsprint and white wrapping (butcher) paper. It requires 5 minutes to produce a yard of newsprint and 8 minutes to produce a yard of wrapping paper. The company has 4,800 minutes of normal production capacity available each week. The profit is $.20 for a yard of newsprint and $.25 for a yard of wrapping paper. The demand is 500 yards weekly for newsprint and 400 yards per week of wrapping paper. The company has established the following goals in order of priority.

(1) Limit overtime to 480 minutes.

(2) Achieve a profit of $300 each week.

(3) Achieve the demand for each product in order of importance of their profit.

(4) Avoid underutilization of production capacity.

    (a) Formulate a goal programming model to determine the number of yards of each type of paper to produce weekly in order to satisfy the various goals.

    (b) Solve the goal programming model using the modified simplex method.

# 10
Probability

## Types of Probability

Objective Probability
Subjective Probability

## Fundamentals of Probability

## Statistical Independence and Dependence

Independent Events
Probability Trees
The Binomial Distribution
Dependent Events
Bayesian Analysis

## Expected Value

## The Normal Distribution

## Summary

The techniques that have been presented in chapters 2 through 9 are typically thought of as *deterministic*. The term *deterministic* means that the techniques are not subject to uncertainty. In deterministic techniques the assumption is made that conditions of complete certainty and perfect knowledge of the future exist. In the linear programming models presented in previous chapters, the various parameters of the models and the model results were assumed to be known with certainty. In the model constraints we did not say that a bowl will require 4 pounds of clay "70% of the time." We stated specifically that each bowl would require exactly 4 pounds of clay without any variation (i.e., there was no uncertainty in our problem statement). Similarly, the solutions we derived for the linear programming models contained no variation or uncertainty. It was assumed that the results of the model would occur in the future without any degree of doubt or chance.

*Deterministic techniques*

Alternatively, many of the techniques in management science do reflect information that is *uncertain* and give solutions that are not certain. These techniques are said to be *probabilistic*. This means that there can be more than one outcome or result to a model and that there is some doubt about which result will occur. The solutions generated by these techniques have a probability of occurrence. They may be in the form of *averages* and the actual values that occur will vary over time.

*Uncertainty in management science techniques*

Many of the subsequent chapters in this text present probabilistic techniques. As such, the presentation of these techniques requires that the reader have a fundamental understanding of probability. Thus, the purpose of this chapter is to provide an overview of the fundamentals, properties, and terminology of probability.

## Types of Probability

Two basic types of probability can be defined: *objective probability* and *subjective probability*. First, we will demonstrate what constitutes an objective probability.

*Two types of probability*

### Objective Probability

Consider a referee flipping a coin before a football game to determine which team will kick off and which team will receive. Before the referee tosses the coin, both team captains know that they have a .50 (or 50%) *chance* (or probability) of winning the toss. None of the onlookers in the stands or anywhere else would argue that the probability of a head or a tail is not .50. In this example, the probability of .50 that either a head or a tail will occur when a coin is tossed is called an *objective probability*. More specifically, it is referred to as a *classical* or *a priori* (prior to the occurrence of) probability, one of the two types of objective probabilities.

*Classical probability*　　A classical probability can be defined as follows. Given a set of outcomes for an activity (such as a head and a tail when tossing a coin) the probability of a specific (desired) outcome (such as a head) is the ratio of the number of specific outcomes to the total number of outcomes. For example, in our coin-tossing example the probability of a head is the ratio of the number of specific outcomes (a head) to the total outcomes (a head and a tail), or 1/2. Similarly, the probability of drawing an ace from a deck of 52 cards would be found by dividing 4 (the number of aces) by 52 (the total number of cards in a deck), or 1/13. If we spin a roulette wheel with 50 red numbers and 50 black numbers, the probability of a red number is 50 divided by 100, or 1/2.

*a priori probability*　　The reason these examples are referred to as *a priori* probabilities is because we can state the probabilities *prior to* the actual occurrence of the activity (i.e., ahead of time). This is because we know (or assume we know) the number of specific outcomes and total outcomes prior to the occurrence of the activity. We know, for example, that a deck of cards consists of 4 aces and 52 total cards before we draw a card from the deck and that a coin contains one head and one tail before we toss it. These examples are also known as *classical* probabilities because some of the earliest references in history to probabilities were related to games of chance, which (as shown) these probabilities are readily applicable to.

*Relative frequency*
*probability*　　The second type of objective probability is referred to as the *relative frequency* probability. The definition of this type of objective probability is the relative frequency that a specific outcome has been observed to occur in the long run. It is based on the observation of *past* occurrences. For example, suppose over the past 4 years 3,000 business students have taken the introductory management science course at State University and 300 of them made an A in the course. The relative frequency probability of making an A in management science would be 300/3,000, or .10. Recall that in the case of a classical probability we indicated a probability before an activity (such as tossing a coin) took place, while in this relative frequency case we determined the probability after observing what 3,000 students had done in the past.

*Relative frequency is*
*the more widely*
*accepted definition of*
*objective probability*　　The relative frequency definition of probability is a more general and widely accepted version of objective probability than the classical definition. Actually the relative frequency definition can encompass the classical case. For example, if we flip a coin many times, then in the long run the relative frequency of a head occurring will be .50. However, this illustrates one of the key characteristics of a relative frequency probability. If you toss a coin ten times, it is conceivable that you will get 10 consecutive heads. Thus, the relative frequency (probability) of a head would be 1.0. However, if

the coin is tossed 10,000 times, the relative frequency would approach 1/2 (assuming a fair coin). This illustrates that as the number of tosses is increased, the more accurate the probability becomes. In general the relative frequency probability becomes more accurate as the total number of observations of the activity increases.

## Subjective Probability

When relative frequencies are not available, a probability is often determined anyway. In these cases an individual will rely on personal belief, experience, and knowledge of the situation to develop a probability estimate. Such a probability estimate without the benefit of prior or past evidence is a *subjective probability*. For example, when a meteorologist forecasts a "60% chance of rain tomorrow," the .60 probability is usually based on the meteorologist's expert analysis of the weather conditions and experience. In other words, the meteorologist does not say that these exact weather conditions have occurred 1,000 times in the past and on 600 occasions it has rained, thus there is a 60% probability of rain. Likewise, when a sportswriter says that a football team has an 80% chance of winning, it is not typically because the team has won 8 of its 10 previous games. The prediction is judgmental, based on the sportswriter's knowledge of the teams involved, the playing conditions, etc. If the sportswriter had based the probability estimate solely on the team's relative frequency of winning, then it would have been an objective probability. However, once the relative frequency probability becomes colored by personal belief, then it is subjective.

*A probability estimate based on personal belief, experience, and knowledge of the situation*

Subjective probability estimates are frequently used in making business decisions. For example, consider the case where the manager of the Colonial Pottery Company, which we have referred to in previous chapters, is considering the addition of a third product—plates—besides the bowls and mugs already being produced. In making the decision whether or not to produce plates, the manager will determine the chances of the new product being successful and returning a profit. While the manager can use personal knowledge of the market and judgment to determine a *probability of success,* direct relative frequency evidence is not generally available. The manager cannot observe the frequency with which the introduction of a new product was successful in the past. Thus, the manager must make a subjective probability estimate.

*Use for decision making*

This type of subjective probability analysis is common in the business world. Decision makers are frequently attempting to determine their chances for success or failure, the probability of achieving a certain market share or profit, the probability of a level of demand, etc., without the benefit of relative frequency probabilities based on past observations. While there may not be the consensus of agreement as to the accuracy of a subjective estimate as with an objective probability (i.e., everyone is sure there is a .50 probability of getting a head when a coin is tossed), it is often the only means available for making probabilistic estimates and it is a method frequently used.

A brief warning of caution must be made in regard to the use of subjective probabilities. Different individuals will often arrive at different subjective probabilities; whereas, everyone should arrive at the same objective probability, given the same numbers and correct calculations. As such, when a probabilistic analysis is made of some situation, the use of objective probability will provide more consistent results. In the material on probability in the remainder of this chapter objective probabilities are assumed unless indicated otherwise.

## Fundamentals of Probability

*An experiment*

Recall our example of a referee tossing a coin prior to a football game. In the terminology of probability the coin toss is referred to as an *experiment*. An experiment is an activity (such as tossing a coin) that results in one of several possible outcomes. Our coin-tossing experiment can result in either

*Events*

one of two outcomes, which are referred to as *events:* a head or a tail. The probabilities associated with each event in our experiment are:

| Event | Probability |
|-------|-------------|
| Head | .50 |
| Tail | .50 |
| | 1.00 |

*Two fundamentals of probability*

This simple example highlights two of the fundamental characteristics of probability. First, *the probability of an event is always greater than or equal to zero and less than or equal to one* (i.e., $0 \leq P$ (event) $\leq 1.0$). In our coin-tossing example, each event has a probability of .50, which is in the range of 0 to 1.0. Second, *the probabilities of all the events included in an experiment must sum to one.* Notice that in our example the probability of each of the two events is .50 and that the sum of these two probabilities is 1.0.

*Mutually exclusive events*

The specific example of tossing a coin also exhibits a third characteristic: the events (in a set of events) are *mutually exclusive.* The events in an experiment are mutually exclusive if only one of them can occur at a time. The term *mutually exclusive* in our experiment means that any time the coin is tossed *only one* of the two events can take place—a head

*An example of mutually exclusive events*

or a tail can occur, but not both. Consider a customer who goes into a store to shop for shoes. The store manager estimates that there is a .60 probability the customer will buy a pair of shoes and a .40 probability that the customer will not buy a pair of shoes. These two events are mutually exclusive, since it is impossible to both buy shoes and not buy shoes at the same time. In general, events are mutually exclusive if only one of the events can occur, but not both.

Since the events in our example of obtaining a head or tail are mutually exclusive, we can infer that the probabilities of mutually exclusive events *sum to 1.0.* Also, the probabilities of mutually exclusive events can be added. The following example will demonstrate these fundamental characteristics of probability.

The staff of the dean of the business school at State University has analyzed the records of the 3,000 students who received a grade in management science during the past four years. The dean wants to know the number of students who made each grade (A, B, C, D, or F) in the course. The dean's staff developed the following table of information:

| Event Grade | Number of Students | Relative Frequency | Probability |
|---|---|---|---|
| A | 300 | 300/3,000 | .10 |
| B | 600 | 600/3,000 | .20 |
| C | 1,500 | 1,500/3,000 | .50 |
| D | 450 | 450/3,000 | .15 |
| F | 150 | 150/3,000 | .05 |
| | 3,000 | | 1.00 |

This example demonstrates several of the characteristics of probability. First, the *data* (numerical information) in the second column show how the students are distributed across the different grades (events). Second, the third column shows the relative frequency with which each event occurs for the 3,000 observations. In other words, the relative frequency of a student making a C is 1,500/3,000, which also means that the probability of selecting a student who had obtained a C at random from those students who took management science in the past four years is .50.

This information, organized according to the events in the experiment, is called a *frequency distribution*. The corresponding probabilities for each event in the last column is referred to as a *probability distribution*.

All of the events in this example are mutually exclusive. It is not possible for two or more events to occur at the same time. A student can make only one grade in the course and not two or more grades. As indicated previously, mutually exclusive probabilities of an experiment can be summed to equal one. There are 5 mutually exclusive events in this experiment, the probabilities of which (.10, .20, .50, .15, and .05) sum to equal one.

This example exhibits another characteristic of probability. Since the five events in the example are all that can occur (i.e., no other grade in the course is possible), the experiment is said to be *collectively exhaustive*. Likewise, the coin-tossing experiment is collectively exhaustive, since the only two events that can occur are a head and a tail. In general, when a *set of events* includes all the events that can possibly occur, the set is said to be collectively exhaustive.

In our example, the probability of a single event occurring, such as a student receiving an A in the course, is represented symbolically as $P(A)$. This probability is also called the *marginal probability* in the terminology of probability. For our example, the marginal probability of a student getting an A in management science is

$P(A) = .10$

For mutually exclusive events it is possible to determine the probability that one or the other of several events will occur. This is done by summing the individual marginal probabilities of the events. For example, the probability of a student receiving an *A or a B* is determined as follows.

$$P(A \text{ or } B) = P(A) + P(B)$$
$$= .10 + .20$$
$$= .30$$

*Events that are not mutually exclusive*

Now let us consider the case where two events are *not* mutually exclusive. In this case the probability of *A or B or both* occurring is found as follows.

$$P(A \text{ or } B) = P(A) + P(B) - P(AB)$$

*Joint probability*

where the term $P(AB)$, referred to as the *joint probability* of *A* and *B*, is the probability of *both A* and *B* occurring. For mutually exclusive events, this term would have to equal zero, since both events cannot occur together. Thus, for mutually exclusive events our formula would become

$$P(A \text{ or } B) = P(A) + P(B) - P(AB)$$
$$= P(A) + P(B) - 0$$
$$= P(A) + P(B)$$

which is the same formula we developed previously for mutually exclusive events.

The following example will illustrate the case where two events are *not* mutually exclusive. Suppose it has been determined that 40% of all students in the school of business are presently taking management and 30% of all the students are taking finance. Also, it has been determined that 10% take both subjects. Thus our probabilities are

$$P(M) = .40$$
$$P(F) = .30$$
$$P(MF) = .10$$

The probability of a student taking one or the other of the courses or both is determined as follows.

$$P(M \text{ or } F) = P(M) + P(F) - P(MF)$$
$$= .40 + .30 - .10$$
$$= .60$$

Observing this formulation closely, we can see why the joint probability, $P(MF)$, was subtracted out. The 40% of the students that were taking management also included those students taking both courses. Likewise, the 30% of the students taking finance also included those students taking both courses. Thus, if we add the two marginal probabilities we are *double counting* the percentage of students taking both courses. By subtracting out one of these probabilities (that we added in twice) we derive the correct probability.

# Statistical Independence and Dependence

Events are either statistically independent or dependent. If the occurrence of one event does not affect the probability of the occurrence of another event, the events are *independent*. Alternatively, if the occurrence of one event does affect the probability of the occurrence of another event, the events are *dependent*. We will first turn our attention to a discussion of independent events.

## Independent Events

In our example of tossing a coin the two events, getting a head or tail, are independent. If we get a head on the first toss, this result has absolutely no effect on the probability of getting either a head or tail on the next toss. The probability will still be .50 of getting a head or tail, regardless of the outcomes on previous tosses. As such, the two events are independent.

*A succession of events that do not affect each other*

When events are independent it is possible to determine the probability of both events occurring (in succession) by multiplying the probabilities of each event. For example, if the question is asked, "What is the probability of getting a head on the first toss and a tail on the second toss?" the answer is

*The probability of independent events occurring in succession*

$$P(HT) = P(H) \cdot P(T)$$
where
$P(H) =$ probability of a head
$P(T) =$ probability of a tail
$P(HT) =$ joint probability of both a head and a tail

Therefore,

$$P(HT) = P(H) \cdot P(T)$$
$$P(HT) = (.5)(.5)$$
$$P(HT) = .25$$

As we indicated previously, the probability of both events occurring, $P(HT)$, is referred to as the *joint probability*.

An additional property of independent events relates to *conditional probabilities*. A conditional probability is the "probability that event $A$ will occur given that event $B$ has already occurred. This relationship is expressed symbolically as

*Conditional probabilities*

$$P(A/B)$$

The term in parenthesis, "*A* slash *B*," means "*A given* the occurrence of *B*." Thus, the entire term $P(A/B)$ is interpreted as the probability that $A$ will occur *given* that $B$ has already occurred. If $A$ and $B$ are independent events, then

$$P(A/B) = P(A)$$

Interpreting this result verbally, if *A* and *B* are independent, then the probability of *A*, given the occurrence of event *B*, is simply equal to the probability of *A*. Since the events are independent of each other, then the occurrence of event *B* will have no effect on the occurrence of *A*. Therefore, the probability of *A* is in no way dependent upon the occurrence of *B*.

In summary, if events *A* and *B* are independent, the following two properties exist.

1. $P(AB) = P(A) \cdot P(B)$
2. $P(A/B) = P(A)$

## Probability Trees

*Illustrating the probability of successive independent events*

Consider an example in which a coin is tossed three consecutive times. The possible outcomes of this example can be illustrated using a *probability tree*, as shown in figure 10.1.

---

**Figure 10.1** Probability tree for coin-tossing example.

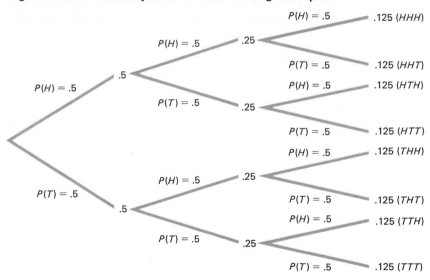

The probability tree in figure 10.1 demonstrates the probabilities of the various occurrences given three tosses of a coin. Notice that at each toss the probability of the two events remain the same, or $P(H) = P(T) = .5$. Thus, the events are independent. Next, the joint probabilities of events occurring in succession are computed by multiplying the probabilities of each event. For example, the probability of getting a head on the first toss, a tail on the second, and a tail on the third is .125,

$$P(HTT) = P(H) \cdot P(T) \cdot P(T)$$
$$= (.5)(.5)(.5)$$
$$= .125$$

However, do not confuse the results in the probability tree with the property concerning "conditional probabilities." The probability of a head and then two tails occurring on three consecutive tosses is computed prior to any tosses taking place. If the first two tosses have already occurred, then at that point the probability of getting a tail on the third toss is still .5:

$$P(T/HT) = P(T)$$
$$= .5$$

## The Binomial Distribution

Some additional information can also be drawn from the probability tree of our example. For example, if the question is asked, "What is the probability of achieving exactly two tails on three tosses?" the answer can be found by observing the instances where two tails occurred. It can be seen that two tails in three tosses occurred three times each with a probability of .125. Thus, the probability of getting exactly two tails in three tosses is the sum of these three probabilities, or .375. The use of a probability tree can become very cumbersome, especially if we were to consider an example with twenty tosses. However, the example of tossing a coin exhibits certain properties that enable us to define it as a *Bernoulli process*. The properties of a Bernoulli process are:

*A Bernoulli process*

1. There are two possible outcomes for each trial (i.e., each toss of the coin). For example, outcomes could be success or failure, yes or no, heads or tails, good or bad, etc.

*Properties of a Bernoulli process*

2. The probability of the outcomes remains constant over time. In other words, the probability of getting a head on a coin toss remains the same regardless of the number of tosses.

3. The outcomes of the trials are independent. The fact that we get a head on the first toss does not affect the probabilities on subsequent tosses.

4. The number of trials is *discrete* and integer. The term *discrete* indicates values that are *countable,* and thus usually integer, for example, 1 car or 2 people rather than 1.34 cars or 2.51 people. Thus, there are 1, 2, 3, 4, 5, etc. tosses of the coin and not 3.36 tosses.

*Discrete trials*

Given that the properties of a Bernoulli process exist, then a *binomial probability distribution function* can be used to determine the probability of a number of successes in *n* trials. The binomial distribution is an example of a *discrete probability distribution,* since the values of the distribution (the number of successes) are discrete as are the number of trials. The formula for the binomial distribution is

$$P(r) = \frac{n!}{r!(n-r)!}\, p^r q^{n-r}$$

where

$p$ = probability of a success
$q = 1 - p$ = probability of a failure
$n$ = number of trials
$r$ = number of successes in $n$ trials

The terms $n!$, $(n - r)!$, and $r!$ are called *factorials.* Factorials are computed using the following formula.

$$m! = m(m-1)(m-2)(m-3) \ldots (2)(1).$$

$0!$ always equals one.

While the binomial distribution formula may look complicated, its actual use is not very difficult. For example, suppose we want to determine the probability of getting exactly 2 tails in 3 tosses of a coin. For this example, getting a head is a success, since it is the object of the analysis. The probability of a head, $p$, equals .5; therefore, $q = 1 - .5 = .5$. The number of tosses, $n$, is 3 and $r$, the number of tails, is 2. Substituting these values into the binomial formula will result in the probability of 2 tails in 3 coin tosses.

$$P(2 \text{ tails}) = P(r = 2) = \frac{3!}{2!(3-2)!}\, (.5)^2(.5)^{3-2}$$

$$= \frac{(3 \cdot 2 \cdot 1)}{(2 \cdot 1)(1)}\, (.25)(.5)$$

$$= \frac{6}{2}\, (.125)$$

$$P(r = 2) = .375$$

Notice that this is the same result achieved by using a probability tree in the previous section.

Now let us consider an example of more practical interest. An electrical manufacturer produces transistors. The transistors are inspected at the end of the production process at a quality control station. Out of every batch of transistors, 4 are selected at random and tested for defects. Given that 20% of all transistors are defective, what is the probability of the transistors containing exactly 2 defective transistors?

The two possible outcomes in this example are a good transistor and a defective transistor. Since defective transistors are the object of our analysis, a defective item is a success. The probability of a success is the probability of a defective transistor, or $p = .2$. The number of trials, $n$, equals 4. Substituting these values into the binomial formula:

$$P(r = 2 \text{ defectives}) = \frac{4!}{2!(4 - 2)!} \ (.2)^2(.8)^2$$

$$= \frac{(4 \cdot 3 \cdot 2 \cdot 1)}{(2 \cdot 1)(2 \cdot 1)} \ (.04)(.64)$$

$$= \frac{24}{4} \ (.0256)$$

$$= .1536$$

Thus, the probability of getting exactly two defective items out of 4 transistors is .1536.

Now, let us alter this problem to make it even more realistic. The manager has determined that 4 transistors should be tested for quality out of every large batch. If *2 or more* defective transistors are found, the whole batch will be rejected. The manager wants to know the probability of rejecting an entire batch of transistors, if, in fact, the batch has 20% defective items.

*Altering the example to make it more realistic*

From our previous use of the binomial distribution, we know that it gives us the probability of *an exact* number of *integer* successes. Thus, if we want the probability of 2 or more defective items, it is necessary to compute the probability of 2, 3, and 4 defective items. That is,

$$P(r \geq 2) = P(r = 2) + P(r = 3) + P(r = 4)$$

Substituting our values, $p = .2$, $n = 4$, $q = .8$, and $r = 2$, 3, and 4 into the binomial distribution results in the probability of 2 or more defective items:

$$P(r \geq 2) = \frac{4!}{2!(4 - 2)!}(.2)^2(.8)^2 + \frac{4!}{3!(4 - 3)!}(.2)^3(.8)^1$$

$$+ \frac{4!}{4!(4 - 4)!}(.2)^4(.8)^0$$

$$= .1536 + .0256 + .0016$$

$$= .1808$$

Thus, there is a .1808 probability that a batch of transistors will be rejected for poor quality.

Notice that the *collectively exhaustive* set of events for this example are 0, 1, 2, 3, and 4 defective transistors. Since the sum of the probabilities of a collectively exhaustive set of events equals 1.0,

$$P(r = 0, 1, 2, 3, 4) = P(r = 0) + P(r = 1) + P(r = 2)$$
$$+ P(r = 3) + P(r = 4) = 1.0$$

Recall that the results of the immediately preceding example show that

$$P(r = 2) + P(r = 3) + P(r = 4) = .1808$$

Given this result, we can compute the probability of "less than two defectives" as follows.

$$P(r < 2) = P(r = 0) + P(r = 1)$$
$$= 1.0 - [P(r = 2) + P(r = 3) + P(r = 4)]$$
$$= 1.0 - .1808$$
$$= .8192$$

It should be apparent at this point that our examples included very small values for *n* and *r*. This is so the examples could be worked out by hand. However, for problems that contain larger values for *n* and *r,* table A.2 in Appendix A can be used. For example, $P(r \geq 2)$ from our table is .1808, which is found as follows.

$$P(r \geq 2) = P(r = 2) + P(r = 3) + P(r = 4),$$
$$= .1536 + .0256 + .0016$$
$$= .1808$$

## Dependent Events

As stated earlier, if the occurrence of one event *does affect* the probability of the occurrence of another event, the events are *dependent*. The following example will demonstrate the presence of dependent events.

*An example of dependent events*

There are 2 buckets, each of which contains a number of colored balls. Bucket 1 contains 2 red balls and 4 white balls, while bucket 2 contains 1 blue ball and 5 red balls. A coin is tossed, the outcomes of which are a head or a tail. If a head results, a ball is drawn out of bucket 1. If a tail results from the coin toss, a ball will be drawn from bucket 2. These events are illustrated in figure 10.2.

---

**Figure 10.2 Dependent events.**

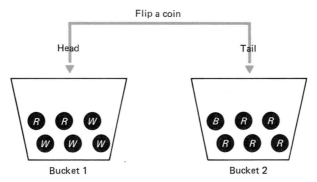

In this example the probability of drawing a *blue* ball is clearly dependent on whether a head or tail occurs on the coin toss. If a tail occurs, there is a 1/6 chance of drawing a blue ball from bucket 2. However, if a head results then there is no possibility of drawing a blue ball from bucket 1. In other words, the probability of the event "drawing a blue ball," is dependent upon the event "flipping a coin."

As in the case of statistical independence, dependent events also exhibit certain defining properties. In order to describe these properties, we will alter our previous example slightly, so that bucket 2 contains 1 white ball and 5 red balls. Our new example is shown in figure 10.3. The outcomes that can result from the events illustrated in figure 10.3 are shown in figure 10.4. When the coin is flipped, initially two outcomes are possible, a head or a tail. The probability of achieving a head is .50 and the probability of getting a tail is .50:

$$P(H) = .50$$
$$P(T) = .50$$

As we indicated previously these are referred to as the *marginal* probabilities. They are also called *unconditional* probabilities because they are the probabilities of the occurrence of a single event, and are not conditional on the occurrence of any other event(s). They are the same as the probabilities of independent events defined earlier, and like independent events, the marginal probabilities of a collectively exhaustive set of events *sum to one*.

Once the coin is tossed and a head or tail results, a ball is drawn from one of the buckets. If a head results, a ball is drawn from bucket 1. There is a 2/6 or .33 probability of drawing a red ball and a 4/6 or .67 probability

**Figure 10.3** Altered example.

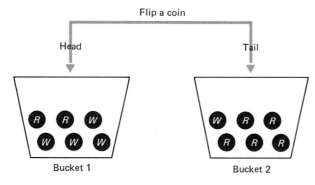

**Figure 10.4** Probability tree for dependent events.

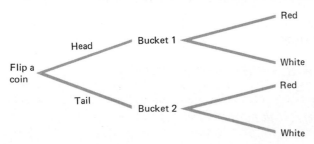

of drawing a white ball from bucket 1. Alternatively, if a tail results, a ball is drawn from bucket 2, which has a 5/6 or .83 probability of drawing a red ball and a 1/6 or .17 probability of drawing a white ball. These probabilities of drawing red or white balls are called *conditional* probabilities, since they are conditional on the outcome of the event of, "tossing a coin." Symbolically, these conditional probabilities are expressed as

*Conditional
probabilities*

$$P(R/H) = .33$$
$$P(W/H) = .67$$
$$P(R/T) = .83$$
$$P(W/T) = .17$$

The first term is verbally translated as "the probability of drawing a red ball given that a head results from the coin toss" and it equals .33. The other conditional probabilities are expressed similarly.

Conditional probabilities can also be defined by the following mathematical relationship. Given two dependent events, $A$ and $B$,

$$P(A/B) = \frac{P(AB)}{P(B)}$$

The term $P(AB)$ is the joint probability as noted previously.

This relationship can be manipulated (by multiplying both sides by $P(B)$) to yield

$$P(A/B) \cdot P(B) = P(AB)$$

Thus, the joint probability can be determined by multiplying the conditional probability of $A$ by the marginal probability of $B$.

Recall from our previous discussion of independent events that

$$P(AB) = P(A) \cdot P(B)$$

Substituting this result into the relationship for a conditional probability,

$$P(A/B) = \frac{P(A) \cdot P(B)}{P(B)}$$
$$= P(A)$$

which is consistent with the property for independent events.

Returning to our example, the joint events are the occurrence of a head and red ball, a head and a white ball, a tail and a red ball, and a tail and a white ball. The probabilities of these joint events are

$$P(RH) = P(R/H) \cdot P(H)$$
$$= (.33)(.5)$$
$$= .165$$
$$P(WH) = P(W/H) \cdot P(H)$$
$$= (.67)(.5)$$
$$= .335$$
$$P(RT) = P(R/T) \cdot P(T)$$
$$= (.83)(.5)$$
$$= .415$$

$$P(WT) = P(W/T) \cdot P(T)$$
$$= (.17)(.5)$$
$$= .085$$

The marginal, conditional and joint probabilities for this example are summarized in figure 10.5. Table 10.1 is a *joint probability table,* which summarizes the joint probabilities for the example.

*Joint probability table*

**Figure 10.5** Probability tree with marginal, conditional, and joint probabilities.

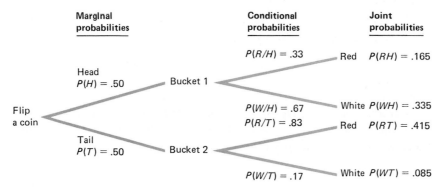

**Table 10.1** Joint Probability Table

| Flip a Coin | Draw a Ball | | Marginal Probabilities |
|---|---|---|---|
| | Red | White | |
| Head | $P(RH) = .165$ | $P(WH) = .335$ | $P(H) = .50$ |
| Tail | $P(RT) = .415$ | $P(WT) = .085$ | $P(T) = .50$ |
| Marginal Probabilities | $P(R) = .580$ | $P(W) = .420$ | 1.00 |

## Bayesian Analysis

The concept of conditional probability given statistical dependence forms the necessary foundation for an area of probability known as *Bayesian analysis.* The name is derived from the individual who pioneered this area of analysis, an eighteenth-century clergyman named Thomas Bayes.

*Improving marginal probabilities with additional information*

The basic principle of Bayesian analysis is that additional information (if available) can sometimes enable individuals to alter (improve) the marginal probabilities of the occurrence of an event. The altered probabilities are referred to as *revised* or *posterior* probabilities.

*Revised or posterior probabilities*

We will illustrate the concept of posterior probabilities with the following example. A production manager for a manufacturing firm is supervising the machine setup for a product to be produced. The machine operator sets up the machine. When a machine is set up correctly by an

*An example of Bayesian analysis*

operator there is a 10% chance that an item produced on the machine will be defective, while if the machine is set up incorrectly there is a 40% chance that an item will be defective. The production manager knows from past experience that there is a .50 probability that a machine will be set up correctly or incorrectly by an operator. In order to reduce the chance that an item produced on the machine will be defective, the manager has decided to have the operator produce a sample item. What the manager would like to know is the probability that the machine has been set up incorrectly if the sample item turns out to be defective.

The probabilities given in this problem statement can be summarized as follows.

$$P(C) = .50 \qquad P(D/C) = .10$$
$$P(IC) = .50 \qquad P(D/IC) = .40$$

where $C$ = correct, $IC$ = incorrect, and $D$ = defective.

*The posterior probability*    The *posterior probability* for our example is the conditional probability that the machine has been set up incorrectly, given that the sample item proves to be defective, or $P(IC/D)$. In Bayesian analysis once we are given the initial marginal and conditional probabilities, we can compute *Bayes' rule*    the posterior probability using *Bayes' rule* as follows.

$$P(IC/D) = \frac{P(D/IC)\ P(IC)}{P(D/IC)\ P(IC) + P(D/C)\ P(C)}$$
$$= \frac{(.40)(.50)}{(.40)(.50) + (.10)(.50)}$$
$$= .80$$

Previously the manager only knew that there was a 50% chance that the machine has been set up incorrectly. Now by producing a sample item and testing it, if it proves to be defective, the manager knows that there is a .80 probability that the machine was set up incorrectly. Thus, by gathering some additional information, the manager is able to revise the probability estimate regarding whether or not the machine is set up correctly. This will obviously improve the decision-making capabilities of the manager by allowing the manager to make a more informed decision on whether to have the machine set up again or not.

In general, given two events, $A$ and $B$, and a third event, $C$, that is conditionally dependent upon $A$ and $B$, Bayes' rule can be written as

$$P(A/C) = \frac{P(C/A)\ P(A)}{P(C/A)P(A) + P(C/B)P(B)}$$

## Expected Value

It is often possible to assign numerical values to the various outcomes that can result from an experiment. When these values occur in no particular order or sequence, they are referred to as *random variables*. A random *Random variables*    variable is a variable such that every value of the variable has a probability of occurrence associated with it. For example, if a coin is tossed three times, the number of heads obtained is a random variable. The possible values of the random variable are 0, 1, 2, and 3 heads. The values of the variable are random because there is no way of predicting which value (0, 1, 2, or 3) will result when the coin is tossed three times. If three tosses are made several times, the value (i.e., number of heads) that will result each of these times will have no sequence or pattern—they will be random.

As with variables defined in previous chapters in this text, random variables are typically represented symbolically by a letter, such as $x, y,$ or $z$. For example, consider a vendor who sells hot dogs outside a building every day. If the number of hot dogs the vendor sells is defined as a random variable, $x$, then $x$ will equal 0, 1, 2, 3, 4 . . . etc., hot dogs sold daily.

While the exact value of the random variables in the examples presented above are not known prior to the event taking place, it is possible to assign a probability to the occurrence of the possible values that can result. As an example, consider a production operation in which a machine breaks down periodically. From experience it has been determined that the machine will break down 0, 1, 2, 3, or 4 times per month. Although management does not know the exact number of breakdowns that will occur each month, they can determine the relative frequency probability of each number of breakdowns. These probabilities are shown below.

*Assigning probabilities to the possible values of a random variable*

*An example of expected value*

**Random Variable, $x$:**

| Number of Breakdowns | $P(x)$ |
|---|---|
| 0 | .10 |
| 1 | .20 |
| 2 | .30 |
| 3 | .25 |
| 4 | .15 |
| | 1.00 |

These probability values taken together form a *probability distribution*. That is, the probabilities are distributed over the range of possible values of the random variable $x$.

*A probability distribution*

The *expected value* of the random variable (number of breakdowns in any given month) is computed by multiplying each value of the random variable by its probability. The expected value of a random variable $x$, written symbolically as $E(x)$, is computed as follows.

*Computing the expected value*

$$E(x) = \sum_{i=1}^{n} x_i P(x_i)$$

where,

$n = $ the number of values of the random variable $x$

For our example the expected number of breakdowns per month is computed as

$$E(x) = (0)(.10) + (1)(.20) + (2)(.30) + (3)(.25) + (4)(.15)$$
$$= 0 + .20 + .60 + .75 + .60$$
$$= 2.15 \text{ breakdowns}$$

This means that, on the average, management can expect 2.15 break-downs every month.

*Mean of a probability distribution*

The expected value which is often referred to as the weighted average or *mean* of the probability distribution, is a measure of central tendency of the distribution. However, in addition to knowing the mean, it is often desirable to know how the values are dispersed around the mean (i.e., the degree to which the values are scattered about the mean). A measure of dispersion is the *variance*. The variance is computed by:

*Dispersion around the mean*

*Variance*

1. Squaring the difference between each value and the expected value.
2. Multiplying these resulting amounts by the probability of each value.
3. Summing the values compiled in step 2.

*The formula for computing variance*

The general formula for the variance, which we will designate as $\sigma^2$, is

$$\sigma^2 = \sum_{i=1}^{n} [x_i - E(x_i)]^2 P(x_i)$$

The computation of the *variance* ($\sigma^2$) is demonstrated within the context of the machine breakdown example, as follows:

| $x_i$ | $P(x_i)$ | $x_i - E(x)$ | $[x_i - E(x)]^2$ | $[x_i - E(x)]^2 \cdot P(x_i)$ |
|---|---|---|---|---|
| 0 | .10 | −2.15 | 4.62 | .462 |
| 1 | .20 | −1.15 | 1.32 | .264 |
| 2 | .30 | −0.15 | .02 | .006 |
| 3 | .25 | 0.85 | .72 | .180 |
| 4 | .15 | 1.85 | 3.42 | .513 |
| | 1.00 | | | 1.425 |

$$\sigma^2 = 1.425 \text{ breakdowns per month}$$

*Standard deviation*

The standard deviation is another widely recognized measure of dispersion. It is designated symbolically as $\sigma$ and is computed by taking the square root of the variance,

$$\sigma = \sqrt{1.425}$$
$$= 1.19 \text{ breakdowns per month}$$

A small standard deviation or variance, relative to the expected value, indicates that most of the values of the random variable distribution are bunched close to the expected value. However, a large relative value for the measures of dispersion indicates that the values of the random variable are widely dispersed from the expected value.

## The Normal Distribution

*A discrete random variable*

Previously we defined the term *discrete* to mean a value that is countable (and usually integer). When a random variable is defined as being discrete, the values a random variable can equal are finite and countable. The probability distributions that we have encountered so far have been examples of discrete distributions. The values of the random variables that these discrete distributions encompassed were always finite (i.e., there were *five* possible values of the random variable, breakdowns per month, in the example in the previous section on expected value). Since every value of the random variable had a unique probability of occurrence associated with it, a discrete probability distribution consisted of all the (finite) values of a random variable and their associated probabilities.

*A continuous random variable*

Alternatively, a *continuous* random variable can equal an infinite number of values within some interval. This is because continuous random variables equal values that are not specifically countable and are often fractional. The distinction between discrete and continuous random variables is sometimes made by saying that discrete relates to things that can be counted while continuous relates to things that are measured. A load of oil being transported by tanker may not consist of exactly 1 million barrels or 2 million barrels, but 1.35 million barrels. If we say that the barrels of oil being transported is a continuous random variable and the range of the random variable is between 1 and 2 million barrels, then it can be seen that there are an infinite number of (fractional) values that the random variable can take on between 1 and 2 million barrels. (Although the value 1.35 million corresponds to a discrete value of 1,350,000 barrels of oil, there are so many possible discrete values of the random variable that it essentially becomes continuous.) No matter how small an interval exists between two values in the distribution, there is always at least one value in between the values, and, in fact, an infinite number of values.

Since a continuous random variable can equal an extremely large or infinite number of values it is not possible to assign a unique probability to every value of the random variable. There would be an infinite (or very large) number of probabilities, each of which would be infinitely small. Therefore, we cannot assign a unique probability to each value of the random variable as we did in a discrete probability distribution. In a *continuous probability distribution* we can only refer to the probability that a value of the random variable is within some *range*. For example, we cannot determine the probability that exactly 1.35 million barrels of oil are transported, but we can determine the probability that between 1.35 and 1.40 million barrels are transported, or the probabilities that less than or more than 1.35 million barrels are shipped.

*Continuous probability distribution*

One of the most frequently used continuous probability distributions is the *normal distribution.* It is a popular continuous distribution because it has certain mathematical properties that make it easy to work with and it is a reasonable approximation of the continuous probability distributions of a number of natural phenomena that occur in the real world. Figure 10.6 is an illustration of the normal distribution.

*The normal distribution*

The normal distribution is a continuous curve that has the shape of a bell (i.e., it is symmetrical). The fact that the normal distribution is a continuous curve reflects the fact that it consists of an infinite or extremely large number of points (on the curve). The curve can be flatter or taller

*A bell-shaped curve*

depending on how much the values of the random variable the curve represents are dispersed from the center of the distribution. The center of the normal distribution is referred to as the *mean* ($\mu$), and it is analogous to the average of the distribution.

*The mean of a normal distribution*

---

**Figure 10.6** The normal curve.

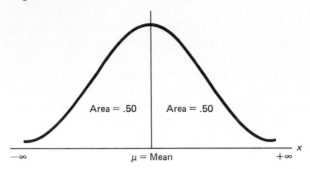

**Probability**

*Tails of the normal distribution*

Notice that the two ends (or tails) of the distribution in figure 10.6 extend from $-\infty$ to $+\infty$. However, since random variables do not often encompass an infinite range in reality, when the normal distribution is applied it is actually approximating the distribution of a random variable with finite limits. The *area* under the normal curve represents *probability*. As such, the entire area under the curve equals 1.0, since the sum of the probabilities of all values of a random variable in a probability distribution must equal 1.0. Fifty percent of the curve lies to the right of the mean and fifty percent lies to the left. Thus, the probability of a random variable $x$ having a value greater (or less) than the mean is .50.

*Area under the normal curve represents probability*

*An example of a normal distribution*

As an example of the application of the normal distribution, consider the Armor Carpet Store, which sells Super Shag carpet. From several years of sales records the store management has determined that the mean number of yards of Super Shag demanded by customers during a week is 4,200 yards, and the standard deviation is 1,400 yards. It is necessary to know both the mean and standard deviation in order to perform a probabilistic analysis using the normal distribution. The store management also assumes that the continuous random variable, yards of carpet demanded per week, is normally distributed (i.e., the values of the random variable have approximately the shape of the normal curve). The mean of the normal distribution is represented by the symbol $\mu$, while the standard deviation is represented by the symbol $\sigma$:

*The mean and standard deviation*

$$\mu = 4,200 \text{ yards}$$
$$\sigma = 1,400 \text{ yards}$$

The store manager desires to know the probability that the demand for Super Shag will exceed 6,000 yards for the upcoming week. The normal curve for this example is shown in figure 10.7. The probability that $x$ (the

**Figure 10.7** The normal distribution for carpet demand.

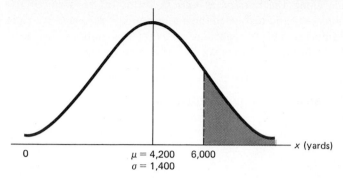

number of yards of carpet) will be equal to or greater than 6,000, expressed as

$$P(x \geq 6,000)$$

corresponds to the area under the normal curve to the right of the value 6,000, since the area under the curve (in fig. 10.7) represents probability. In a normal distribution, area or probability is measured by determining the *number of standard deviations the value of the random variable x is from the mean*. The number of standard deviations a value is from the mean is represented by Z and is computed using the following formula.

*Area measured by determining the number of standard deviations*

$$Z = \frac{x - \mu}{\sigma}$$

The number of standard deviations a value is from the mean gives us a consistent *standard* of measure for all normal distributions. In our example, the units of measure are yards, while in other problems the units of measure may be pounds, hours, feet, or tons. By converting these various units of measure into a common measure (number of standard deviations), a standard that is the same for all normal distributions is created.

*A standard of measure*

Actually the standard form of the normal distribution has a mean of zero ($\mu = 0$) and a standard deviation of one ($\sigma = 1$). The value of Z enables us to convert this scale of measure into whatever scale our problem requires.

Figure 10.8 shows the *standard* normal distribution with our example distribution of carpet demand above it. This illustrates the conversion of the scale of measure along the horizontal axis from yards to number of standard deviations.

*The standard normal distribution*

The horizontal axis along the bottom of figure 10.8 corresponds to the standard normal distribution. Notice that the area under the normal curve between $-1\sigma$ and $1\sigma$ represents 68% of the total area under the normal curve, or a probability of .68. Next observe the horizontal axis corresponding to our example. Recalling that the standard deviation for our example is 1,400 yards, the area between $-1\sigma$ (2,800 yards) and $1\sigma$

*Converting units of measure to the standard normal distribution*

(5,600 yards) is also 68% of the total area under the curve. Thus, if we measure distance along the horizontal axis in terms of the number of standard deviations *only* and disregard the actual units of measure, we can determine the same probability regardless of what the units of measure actually are. The formula for $Z$ makes this conversion for us.

**Figure 10.8** The standard normal distribution.

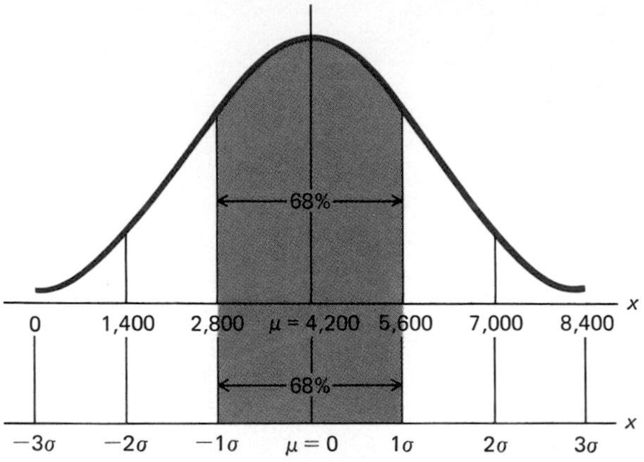

Returning to our example, recall that the manager of the carpet store desires to know the probability that the demand for Super Shag will be 6,000 yards or more for the upcoming week. Substituting the values, $x = 6,000$, $\mu = 4,200$, and $\sigma = 1,400$ yards into our formula for $Z$ we can determine the number of standard deviations the value 6,000 is from the mean.

$$Z = \frac{x - \mu}{\sigma}$$
$$= \frac{6,000 - 4,200}{1,400}$$
$$= 1.29 \text{ standard deviations}$$

The value $x = 6,000$ is 1.29 standard deviations from the mean, as shown in figure 10.9.

*Normal tables*    The area under the standard normal curve for values of $Z$ have already been computed in easily accessible *normal tables*. Such a table (A.1) is given in Appendix A. In table A.1, $Z = 1.29$ standard deviations corresponds to an area, or probability of .4015. However, this is the area between the mean, $\mu = 4,200$, and $x = 6,000$, since this is the number of standard deviations that was measured. Recall, though, that 50% of the area lies to the right of the mean. Thus, if we subtract .4015 from .5000, the area to the right of $x = 6,000$ results:

$$P(x \geq 6,000) = .5000 - .4015$$
$$= .0985$$

**Figure 10.9** Determination of the z value.

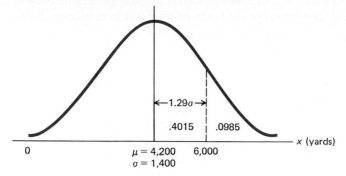

This means that there is a .0985(or 9.85%) probability that the demand for carpet will be 6,000 yards or more next week.

Now suppose that the carpet store manager wishes to consider several additional questions: (1) the probability that demand for carpet will be 5,000 yards or less, and (2) the probability that the demand for carpet will be between 3,000 yards and 5,000 yards. We will consider each of these questions separately. *Examples using normal tables*

First, we want to determine $P(x \leq 5,000)$. The area representing this probability is shown in figure 10.10. The area to the left of the mean in figure 10.10 equals .50. That leaves only the area between $\mu = 4,200$ and $x = 5,000$ to be determined. The number of standard deviations $x = 5,000$ is from the mean is

$$Z = \frac{x - \mu}{\sigma}$$
$$= \frac{5,000 - 4,200}{1,400}$$
$$= \frac{800}{1,400}$$
$$= .57 \text{ standard deviations}$$

**Figure 10.10** Normal distribution for $P$ ($x \leq 5,000$ yards).

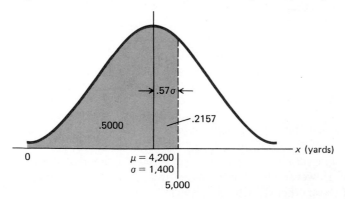

The value $Z = .57$ corresponds to a probability of .2157 in table A.1 in Appendix A. Thus, the area between 4,200 and 5,000 in figure 10.10 is .2157. To find our desired probability we simply add this amount to .5000,

$$P(x \leq 5,000) = .5000 + .2157$$
$$= .7157$$

Next, we want to determine $P(3,000 \leq x \leq 5,000)$. The area representing this probability is shown in figure 10.11. The shaded area in figure 10.11 is computed by finding two areas—the area between $x = 3,000$ and $\mu = 4,200$ and between $\mu = 4,200$ and $x = 5,000$ and summing them. We have already computed the area between 4,200 and 5,000 in the previous example and found it to be .2157.

The area between $x = 3,000$ and $\mu = 4,200$ is found by determining the number of standard deviations $x = 3,000$ is from the mean:

$$Z = \frac{3,000 - 4,200}{1,400}$$
$$= \frac{-1,200}{1,400}$$
$$= -.86$$

The negative sign is ignored as we find the area corresponding to the $Z$ value of .86 in table A.1. This value is .3051. Thus, our probability is found by summing .2157 and .3051,

$$P(3,000 \leq x \leq 5,000) = .2157 + .3051$$
$$= .5208$$

---

**Figure 10.11** Normal distribution with $P$ (3,000 yards $\leq x \leq$ 5,000 yards).

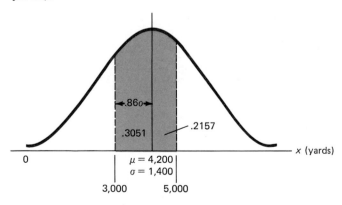

The normal distribution, although applied frequently in probability analysis, is just one of a number of continuous probability distributions. As we proceed through subsequent chapters, other continuous distributions will be identified. However, an acquaintance of the normal distribution will make the use of these other distributions much easier.

## Summary

In this chapter the basic principles and fundamentals of probability have been presented. However, the field of probability and statistics is quite large and complex and contains much more than what has been presented in this chapter. The purpose of this brief overview has been primarily to prepare the reader for the material to follow. The topics of decision analysis (chap. 11), game theory (chap. 12), Markov analysis (chap. 13), probabilistic inventory models (chap. 17), and to a certain extent CPM/PERT (chap. 19) are probabilistic in nature and require an understanding of the fundamentals of probability.

*An overview of probability*

## References

Chou, Ya-lun. *Statistical Analysis*. 2d ed. New York: Holt, Rinehart and Winston, 1975.

Cramer, H. *The Elements of Probability Theory and Some of Its Applications*. New York: John Wiley and Sons, 1955.

Dixon, W. J., and Massey, F. J. *Introduction to Statistical Analysis*. 3d ed. New York: McGraw-Hill, 1969.

Hays, W. L., and Winkler, R. L. *Statistics: Probability, Inference, and Decision*. New York: Holt, Rinehart and Winston, 1970.

Mendenhall, W., and Reinmuth, J. E. *Statistics for Management and Economics*. 2d ed. North Scituate, Mass.: Duxbury Press, 1974.

Neter, J.; Wasserman, W.; and Whitmore, G. A. *Fundamental Statistics for Business and Economics*. 4th ed. Boston: Allyn and Bacon, 1973.

Sasaki, K. *Statistics for Modern Business Decision Making*. Belmont, Calif.: Wadsworth Publishing Co., 1969.

Spurr, W. A., and Bonini, C. P. *Statistical Analysis for Business Decisions*. Homewood, Ill.: Richard D. Irwin, 1973.

## Problems

1. Distinguish between *deterministic* management science techniques and *probabilistic* techniques.

2. Indicate which of the following probabilities are objective and which are subjective. (Note that in some cases the probabilities may not be entirely one or another.)
   (a) The probability of snow tomorrow.
   (b) The probability of a fisherman catching a fish.
   (c) The probability of the prime interest rate rising in the upcoming year.
   (d) The probability that the Cincinnati Reds will win the World Series.
   (e) The probability that demand for a product will be a specific amount next month.

(f) The probability a political candidate will win an upcoming election.

(g) The probability a machine will break down.

(h) The probability of being dealt four aces in a poker hand.

3. A gambler in Las Vegas is cutting a deck of cards for $1,000. What is the probability that the card that comes up for the gambler is: (a) a face card, (b) a queen, (c) a spade, or (d) a jack of spades?

4. Another gambler in Las Vegas is at the crap table and rolls the dice. Define the following:
   (a) The experiment.
   (b) The possible events.

5. The Downhill Ski Resort in Colorado has accumulated information from records of the last 30 winters regarding the measurable snowfall. This information is organized as follows:

| Snowfall (inches) | Frequency |
|---|---|
| 0–19 | 2 |
| 20–29 | 7 |
| 30–39 | 8 |
| 40–49 | 8 |
| 50+ | 5 |
| | 30 |

   (a) Determine the probability of each event in this frequency distribution.
   (b) Are all of the events mutually exclusive in this distribution? Explain.

6. The employees in the textile industry can be segmented as follows:

| | Number |
|---|---|
| Female and union | 12,000 |
| Female and nonunion | 25,000 |
| Male and union | 21,000 |
| Male and nonunion | 42,000 |

   (a) Determine the probability of each event in this distribution.
   (b) Are the events in this distribution mutually exclusive? Explain.
   (c) What is the probability that an employee is male?
   (d) Is this experiment collectively exhaustive? Explain.

7. The quality control process at a manufacturing plant requires that each lot of finished units be sampled for defective items. Twenty units from each lot are inspected. If 5 or more defective units are found, the lot is rejected. If a lot is known to contain 10% defective items, what is the probability that the lot will be rejected? Accepted?

8. A manufacturing company has 10 machines in continuous operation during a work day. The probability that an individual machine will break down during the day is .10. Determine the probability that during any given day 3 machines will break down.

9. A polling firm is taking a survey regarding a proposed new law. Thirty percent of the voters are in favor of the law. If 10 people are surveyed, what is the probability of 4 indicating they are against passage of the new law?

10. Two law firms handle all the cases in a community dealing with consumer suits against companies in the area. The Abercrombie firm takes 40% of all suits, while the Olson firm handles the other 60%. The Abercrombie firm wins 70% of its cases and the Olson firm wins 60% of its cases.
    (a) Develop a probability tree showing all marginal, conditional, and joint probabilities.
    (b) Develop a joint probability table.
    (c) Using Bayes's rule, determine the probability that the Olson firm handled a particular case given that you know the case has been won.

11. The Senate consists of 100 senators, of which 34 are Republicans and 66 are Democrats. A bill to increase defense appropriations is before the Senate. Thirty-five percent of the Democrats are for the bill and 70 percent of the Republicans are for the bill. The bill requires a simple majority to pass. Using a probability tree determine the probability that the bill will pass.

12. A retail outlet receives radios from 3 electrical appliance companies. The outlet receives 20% of its radios from *A*, 40% from *B*, and 40% from *C*. The probability of a defective radio from *A* is .01, .02 from *B*, and .08 from *C*.
    (a) Develop a probability tree showing all marginal, conditional, and joint probabilities.
    (b) Develop a joint probability table.
    (c) What is the probability a defective radio that was returned came from Company *B*?

13. A metropolitan school system consists of three districts, north, south, and central. The north district contains 25% of all students, the south contains 40%, and the central district, 35%. A minimum competency test was given to all students and 10% of the north district students failed, 15% of the south students failed, and 5% of the central district students failed.
    (a) Develop a probability tree showing all marginal, conditional, and joint probabilities.
    (b) Develop a joint probability table.
    (c) What is the probability that a student selected at random failed the test?

14. A service station owner sells Goodroad tires, which are ordered from a local tire distributor. The distributor receives tires from 2 plants, *A* and *B*. When the owner of the service station receives an order from the distributor there is a .50 probability the order consists of tires from plant *A* or plant *B*. However, the distributor will not tell the owner which plant the tires came from. The owner knows that 20% of all tires produced at plant *A* are defective, while only 10% of the tires produced at *B* are defective. When an order arrives at the station, the owner is allowed to briefly inspect the order. The owner takes this opportunity to inspect one tire to see if it is defective. If the owner believes the tire came from plant *A* the order will be sent back. Using Bayes' rule, determine the posterior probability that a tire is from plant *A* given that the owner finds that it is defective.

15. A metropolitan school system consists of two districts, east and west. The east district contains 35% of all students and the west district contains the other 65%. A vocational aptitude test was given to all students and 10% of the east district students failed, while 25% of the west district students failed. Given a student from the system was found to have failed the test, what is the posterior probability that the student came from the east district?

16. The Ramshead Pub sells a large quantity of beer every Saturday. From past sales records the pub has determined the following probabilities for sales:

| Barrels | Probability |
|---------|-------------|
| 6 | .10 |
| 7 | .20 |
| 8 | .40 |
| 9 | .25 |
| 10 | .05 |
| | 1.00 |

Compute the expected number of barrels that will be sold on Saturday.

17. Based on past grade records, the following probabilities for grades in Management Science I have been determined.

| Grade | Probability |
|-------|-------------|
| A | .10 |
| B | .30 |
| C | .40 |
| D | .10 |
| F | .10 |

If the grades are assigned on a 4.0 scale where an A is a 4.0, a B a 3.0, etc., determine the expected grade and variance a student can expect in the course.

18. A market in Boston orders oranges from Florida. The oranges are shipped to Boston from Florida by either railroad, truck, or airplane, therefore, it can take an order 1, 2, 3, or 4 days to arrive in Boston once it is placed. The following probabilities have been assigned to the number of days to receive an order once it is placed (which is referred to as lead time).

| Lead Time | Probability |
|-----------|-------------|
| 1 | .20 |
| 2 | .50 |
| 3 | .20 |
| 4 | .10 |
| | 1.00 |

Compute the expected number of days to receive an order and the standard deviation.

19. An investment firm is considering two alternative investments, $A$ and $B$, under two possible future sets of economic conditions, good and poor. There is a .60 probability of good economic conditions occurring and a .40 probability of poor economic conditions occurring. The expected gains and losses under each economic conditions are given as follows.

| | Economic Conditions | |
|------------|---------------------|-----------|
| Investment | Good | Poor |
| A | $900,000 | −$800,000 |
| B | 120,000 | 70,000 |

Using the expected value of each investment alternative, which should be selected?

20. An investor is considering two investments, an office building and bonds. The possible returns from each investment and their probabilities are given as follows:

| Office Building | | Bonds | |
|-----------------|--------------|----------|---------------|
| Returns | Probabilities | Returns | Probabilities |
| $50,000 | .30 | $30,000 | .60 |
| 60,000 | .20 | 40,000 | .40 |
| 80,000 | .10 | | 1.00 |
| 10,000 | .30 | | |
| 0 | .10 | | |
| | 1.00 | | |

Using expected value and standard deviation as a basis for comparison discuss which of the two investments should be selected.

21. The Jefferson High School Band Boosters Club has organized a raffle. The prize is a $6,000 car. Two thousand tickets to the raffle are to be sold at $1 apiece. If a person purchases 4 tickets, what will be the expected value of the tickets?

22. The length of life of an electronic transistor is normally distributed with a mean of 500 hours and a standard deviation of 80 hours. Determine the probability that the transistor will last for more than 400 hours.

23. The grade point average of students at a university is normally distributed with a mean of 2.6 and a standard deviation of 0.6. A recruiter for a company is interviewing students for summer employment. What percentage of the students will have a grade point average of 3.5 or greater?

24. The weight of bags of fertilizers is normally distributed with a mean of 50 pounds and a standard deviation of 6 pounds. What is the probability that a bag of fertilizer will weigh between 45 and 55 pounds?

25. The monthly demand for a product is normally distributed with a mean of 700 units and a standard deviation of 200 units. What is the probability that demand will be greater than 900 units in a given month?

26. The Polo Development Firm is building a shopping center and has informed renters it will be ready in 19 months, and that they can occupy their rental space. If the expected time until the shopping center is completed is estimated to be 14 months with a standard deviation of 4 months, what is the probability that the renters will not be able to move in?

27. A warehouse distributor of carpet keeps 6,000 yards of deluxe shag carpet in stock during a month. The average demand for carpet from the stores that purchase the carpet from the distributor is 4,500 yards per month with a deviation of 900 yards. What is the probability that a customer's order will not be met during a month? (This is referred to as a stockout.)

# 11
## Decision Analysis

## Decision Making without Probabilities

Decision-Making Criteria
The Maximax Criterion
The Maximin Criterion
The Minimax Regret Criterion
The Hurwicz Criterion
The Equal Likelihood Criterion
Summary of Criteria Results

## Decision Making with Probabilities

Expected Value
Expected Opportunity Loss
Expected Value of Perfect Information
Decision Trees
Sequential Decision Trees

## Decision Analysis with Additional Information

Decision Trees with Posterior Probabilities
Computing Posterior Probabilities with Tables
The Expected Value of Sample Information

## Utility
## Summary

In the previous chapters in this text dealing with linear programming, models were formulated and solved in order to aid the manager in making a decision. The solutions to the models were represented by values for *decision* variables. However, these linear programming models were all formulated under the assumption that certainty existed. In other words, all of the model coefficients, constraint values, and solution values were known with certainty without any variability.

Alternatively, many realistic decision-making situations occur under conditions of *uncertainty*. For example, the demand for a product may not be 100 units next week, but either 50 or 200 units, depending upon the state of the market (which is uncertain). Given this type of decision situation where uncertainty exists, there are several decision-making techniques available to aid the decision maker.

*Decision making under conditions of uncertainty*

Decision situations can be categorized into two classes: decision-making situations where probabilities *cannot* be assigned to future occurrences and decision situations where probabilities *can* be assigned. In this chapter we will discuss each of these classes of decision situations separately and demonstrate the decision-making criterion most commonly associated with each.

*Categories of decision situations*

## Decision Making without Probabilities

Decision making involves situations where several alternative choices exist for the decision maker to select from. It is often possible to assign probabilities to these decision choices that aid the decision maker in selecting the one that has the best outcome. However, in some cases it is not possible for the decision maker to assign probabilities, and it is this type of decision-making situation that we will address first.

A decision-making situation includes several components—the decisions themselves *and* the actual events that will occur in the future, known as *states of nature*. At the time the decision is made, the decision maker is uncertain as to which state of nature will occur in the future, and thus has no control over them.

*States of nature*

For example, a distribution company is considering the purchase of a computer in order to increase the number of orders it can process, and thus increase its business. If economic conditions remain good, the company

*Examples of decision situations and states of nature*

will realize a large increase in profit, however, if the economy takes a downturn, the company will lose money. In this decision situation the decisions are to purchase the computer or to not purchase the computer. The states of nature are *good* economic conditions or *bad* economic conditions. The state of nature that occurs will determine the outcome of the decision, and it is obvious that the decision maker has no control over which state will occur.

As another example, consider a concessions vendor who must decide whether or not to stock coffee for the concession stands at a football game in November. If the weather is cold, most of the coffee will be sold; however, if the weather is warm, very little coffee will be purchased. The decision is to order or to not order coffee, while the states of nature are warm and cold weather.

*Payoff tables*    In order to analyze these types of decision situations so that the best decisions will result, they are organized into *payoff tables*. In general, a payoff table is a means of organizing and illustrating the payoffs from the different decisions given the various states of nature in a decision problem. A payoff table is constructed as shown in table 11.1.

**Table 11.1** Payoff Table

| Decision | States of Nature | |
| | a | b |
| --- | --- | --- |
| 1 | payoff 1a | payoff 1b |
| 2 | payoff 2a | payoff 2b |

*Decision outcomes*    Interpreting table 11.1, each decision, 1 or 2, will result in an outcome or *payoff* for the particular state of nature that will occur in the future. Payoffs are typically in terms of profit revenues, or cost (although they can be expressed by a variety of quantities). For example, if decision 1 is to purchase a computer and state of nature *a* is good economic conditions, payoff 1*a* could be $100,000 in profit.

In order to illustrate the development of a payoff table, the following example will be employed. An investor is going to purchase one of three types of real estate. The investor must decide between three alternative investments: an apartment building, an office building, and a warehouse. The future states of nature that will determine how much profit the investor will make are "good economic conditions" and "poor economic conditions." The profits that will result from each decision in the event of each state of nature are shown in table 11.2.

**Table 11.2** Payoff Table for the Real Estate Investments

| Decision (Purchase) | States of Nature | |
| --- | --- | --- |
| | Good Economic Conditions | Poor Economic Conditions |
| Apartment building | $ 50,000 | $ 30,000 |
| Office building | 100,000 | −40,000 |
| Warehouse | 30,000 | 10,000 |

## Decision-Making Criteria

Once the decision situation has been organized into a payoff table, there are several alternative criteria available for making the actual decision. These decision criteria, which will be presented in this section, include maximax, maximin, minimax regret, Hurwicz, and equal likelihood. On occasion these criteria will result in the same decision, however, they will often yield different decisions. As such, the decision maker must select the criterion or combination of criteria that suits his or her needs best.

## The Maximax Criterion

In the *maximax criterion* the decision maker selects the decision that will result in the maximum of the maximum payoffs. In fact, this is how this criterion derives its name (i.e., a maximum of a maximum). As such, the maximax criterion is very optimistic. The decision maker is assuming the most favorable state of nature will occur for each decision alternative. Thus, using this criterion the investor in our example would optimistically assume that good economic conditions will prevail in the future.

*A decision that will result in the maximum of the maximum payoffs*

The maximax criterion is applied in table 11.3. The decision maker first selects the maximum payoff for each decision. Notice that all three maximum payoffs occur under the state of nature, good economic conditions in this problem. Of these three maximum payoffs of $50,000, $100,000, and $30,000, the maximum is $100,000, thus, the corresponding decision is to purchase the office building.

*A maximax example*

**Table 11.3** Payoff Table with Maximax Decision

| Decision (Purchase) | States of Nature | |
| --- | --- | --- |
| | Good Economic Conditions | Poor Economic Conditions |
| Apartment building | $ 50,000 | $ 30,000 |
| Office building | 100,000 | −40,000 |
| Warehouse | 30,000 | 10,000 |

Maximum payoff

The decision to purchase an office building will result in the largest payoff of $100,000, however, such a decision completely ignores the possibility of a potential loss of $40,000. As such, the decision maker who uses the maximax criterion to make decisions assumes a very optimistic future concerning the states of nature.

Before presenting the next criterion, it should be pointed out that the maximax decision rule as presented above deals with *profit*. However, if the payoff table consisted of costs instead, the opposite selection would occur: the minimum of the minimum costs. In the subsequent decision criteria to be presented the same logic in the case of costs can also be employed.

## The Maximin Criterion

While the maximax criterion is very optimistic, the *maximin criterion* is pessimistic. In the maximin criterion the decision maker selects the decision that will contain the *maximum* of the *minimum* payoffs. For each decision alternative the decision maker perceives that the minimum payoff will occur. Of those minimum payoffs, the maximum is selected. The maximin criterion for our investment example is demonstrated in table 11.4

**Table 11.4** Payoff Table with Maximin Decision

| Decision (Purchase) | States of Nature | |
|---|---|---|
| | Good Economic Conditions | Poor Economic Conditions |
| Apartment building | $ 50,000 | $ 30,000 ← Maximum payoff |
| Office building | 100,000 | −40,000 |
| Warehouse | 30,000 | 10,000 |

The minimum payoffs for our example are $30,000, −$40,000, and $10,000. The maximum of these three payoffs is $30,000, thus the decision according to the maximin criterion is to purchase the apartment building. This decision is relatively conservative, since the alternatives considered included only the worst outcomes that could occur. The decision to purchase the office building determined by the maximax criterion included the possibility of a large loss (−$40,000). However, the worst that can occur from the decision to purchase the apartment building is *a gain of $30,000.* Alternatively, the largest possible gain from purchasing the apartment building is much less than purchasing an office building (i.e., $50,000 versus $100,000).

If table 11.4 contained costs instead of profits as the payoffs, the conservative approach would be to select the maximum cost for each decision. Then the decision that resulted in the minimum of these costs would be selected.

# The Minimax Regret Criterion

In our example, suppose the investor made the decision to purchase the warehouse. However, in the future the investor learns that good economic conditions prevail. Naturally, the investor would be disappointed that the office building was not purchased, since it would have resulted in the largest payoff ($100,000) under the state of nature, good economic conditions. In fact, the investor would *regret* the decision to purchase the warehouse and the *degree of his regret would be $70,000,* the difference between the investor's choice and the best choice.

*Regret resulting from a wrong decision*

This brief example demonstrates the principle underlying the decision criterion known as *minimax regret* or the *regret criterion.* In this decision criterion, the decision maker attempts to avoid regret by selecting the decision alternative that minimizes the maximum regret.

*A decision that avoids the greatest regret*

In the minimax regret criterion, first the maximum payoff is selected under each state of nature. For our example, the maximum payoff under good economic conditions is $100,000 and under poor economic conditions the maximum payoff is $30,000. All other payoffs under the respective states of nature are subtracted from these amounts as shown below.

*A minimax regret example*

|                | Good Economic Conditions |  |  | Poor Economic Conditions |  |  |
|---|---|---|---|---|---|---|
| $100,000 | − | 50,000 = $50,000 | $30,000 | − | 30,000 = $0 |
| 100,000 | − | 100,000 = 0 | 30,000 | − | (−40,000) = 70,000 |
| 100,000 | − | 30,000 = 70,000 | 30,000 | − | 10,000 = 20,000 |

These values represent the regret that would be experienced by the decision maker if a decision was made that would result in less than the maximum payoff. They are summarized in a modified version of the payoff table known as a *regret table,* shown in table 11.5. (This table is sometimes referred to as an opportunity loss table where the term *opportunity loss* is synonymous with "regret.")

*A regret table*

*Opportunity loss*

**Table 11.5** The Regret Table

| Decision (Purchase) | States of Nature | |
|---|---|---|
|  | Good Economic Conditions | Poor Economic Conditions |
| Apartment building | $50,000 | $ 0 |
| Office building | 0 | 70,000 |
| Warehouse | 70,000 | 20,000 |

In order to make the decision according to the minimax regret criterion, the maximum regret for *each decision* is determined. The decision corresponding to the minimum of these regret values is then selected. This process is illustrated in table 11.6.

*The minimax regret decision*

**Table 11.6** Regret Table with Minimax Regret Decision

| Decision (Purchase) | States of Nature | |
|---|---|---|
| | Good Economic Conditions | Poor Economic Conditions |
| Apartment building | $50,000 | $ 0 |
| Office building | 0 | 70,000 |
| Warehouse | 70,000 | 20,000 |

The minimum regret value

*The minimax regret logic*

According to the minimax regret criterion, the decision is to purchase the apartment building. The philosophy behind this particular decision is that of the three choices, the investor will experience the least amount of regret with this one. In other words, if the investor purchased either the office building or warehouse, $70,000 worth of regret could result; however, the purchase of the apartment building will result in, at most, $50,000 in regret.

## The Hurwicz Criterion

*A compromise between the maximax and maximin criteria*

The Hurwicz Criterion (named for its originator) strikes a compromise between the maximax and maximin criteria. The underlying principle of this decision criterion is that the decision maker is neither totally optimistic (as the maximax criterion assumes) or totally pessimistic (as the maximin criterion assumes). In the Hurwicz criterion the decision payoffs are weighted by a *coefficient of optimism,* a measure of the decision maker's optimism. The coefficient of optimism, which we will define as $\alpha$, is between zero and one (i.e., $0 \leq \alpha \leq 1.0$). If $\alpha = 1.0$, then the decision maker is said to be completely optimistic, and if $\alpha = 0.0$, then the decision maker is completely pessimistic. (Given this condition, if $\alpha$ is the coefficient of optimism, $1 - \alpha$ is the *coefficient of pessimism.*).

*Coefficient of optimism, $\alpha$*

*Coefficient of pessimism, $1 - \alpha$*

The Hurwicz criterion requires that for each decision alternative, the maximum payoff be multiplied by $\alpha$ and the minimum payoff be multiplied by $1 - \alpha$. For our investment example an $\alpha$ equaling 0.4 (i.e., the investor is slightly pessimistic) and, thus $1 - \alpha = 0.6$, would result in the following values:

**Decision**
Apartment building: $ 50,000(0.4) + 30,000(0.6) = $38,000
Office building: $100,000(0.4) - 40,000(0.6) = $16,000
Warehouse: $ 30,000(0.4) + 10,000(0.6) = $18,000

The Hurwicz criterion specifies that the decision alternative that corresponds to the maximum weighted value is selected, which for this example is $38,000. Thus, the apartment building is purchased.

It should be pointed out that when $\alpha = 0$, the Hurwicz criterion is actually the maximin criterion, and when $\alpha = 1.0$, it is the maximax

*Determining $\alpha$*

criterion. A limitation of the Hurwicz criterion is the determination of $\alpha$

by the decision maker. It can be quite difficult for a decision maker to accurately and objectively determine his or her degree of optimism. However, regardless of how the decision maker determines $\alpha$, it is still a completely *subjective* measure of the decision maker's degree of optimism. As such, the Hurwicz criterion is a completely subjective decision-making criterion.

## The Equal Likelihood Criterion

When the maximax criterion is applied to a decision situation, the decision maker implicitly assumes that the most favorable state of nature will occur for each decision. Alternatively, when the maximin criterion is applied, the least favorable states of nature are assumed. The *equal likelihood* (or LaPlace) *criterion* "weights" each state of nature equally, thus assuming that the states of nature are equally likely to occur.

*Weighting the occurrence of states of nature equally*

Since in our example there are two states of nature, we will assign a weight of .50 to each one. Next, we multiply these weights times each payoff for each decision as follows:

*An equal likelihood example*

**Decision**
Apartment building: $ 50,000(.5) + 30,000(.5) = $40,000
Office building: 100,000(.5) − 40,000(.5) = 30,000
Warehouse: 30,000(.5) + 10,000(.5) = 20,000

Like the Hurwicz criterion, we select the decision that has the maximum of these weighted values. Thus, since $40,000 is the highest weighted value, the decision for the investor is to purchase the apartment building.

Actually, when we apply the equal likelihood criterion we are assuming that there is a 50% chance or .50 *probability* that either state of nature will occur. Using this same basic logic, in many decision problems it is possible to weight the states of nature differently (i.e., unequal). In other words, different probabilities can be assigned to each state of nature indicating that there is a greater chance of the occurrence of one state as opposed to another state. The application of different probabilities to the states of nature is the principle behind the decision criteria to be presented next.

*The probability that states of nature will occur*

## Summary of Criteria Results

The equal likelihood criterion is the final decision criterion that will be presented. The decisions made in our example for each decision criterion are summarized as follows:

| Criterion | Decision (Purchase) |
| --- | --- |
| Maximax | Office building |
| Maximin | Apartment building |
| Minimax Regret | Apartment building |
| Hurwicz | Apartment building |
| Equal Likelihood | Apartment building |

The decision to purchase the apartment building is designated most often by the various decision criteria. However, notice that the decision to purchase the warehouse was never made in any of the criterion. This is because the payoffs for an apartment building under either future economic condition are always better than the payoffs for a warehouse. Thus, given any choice situation with these two alternatives (and any other choice, such as purchasing the office building) the decision to purchase the apartment will always be made over the decision to purchase a warehouse. As such, for all practical purposes the warehouse decision alternative could have been eliminated from consideration in each of our criterion. The decision alternative to purchase a warehouse is said to be *dominated* by the alternative to purchase an apartment building. In general, dominated decision alternatives can be removed from the payoff table and not considered in the various decision-making criteria. This reduces the complexity of the decision analysis somewhat. However, in our examples of the application of the decision criteria and all subsequent applications using this example, we will leave the dominated alternative in the payoff table for demonstration purposes.

*Dominant decision alternatives*

It often occurs that the decision criteria can result in a mix of decisions with no one decision being selected more than the others. The criterion or collection of criteria used and the resulting decision depend upon the characteristics and philosophy of the decision maker. For example, the extremely optimistic decision maker might eschew the majority of results above and make the decision to purchase the office building because the maximax criterion most closely reflects the decision-making philosophy of the decision maker.

*The appropriate criterion is dependent on the personality and philosophy of the decision maker*

## Decision Making with Probabilities

The decision-making criteria presented above were characterized by the fact that no information regarding the probable occurrence of states of nature was available. In other words, no *probabilities of occurrence* were assigned to the states of nature. An exception was the equal likelihood criterion. By assuming that each state of nature was equally likely and assigning a weight of .50 to each state of nature in our example, we were implicitly assigning a probability of .50 to the occurrence of each state of nature.

*Probabilities can be assigned to the occurrence of states of nature*

It is often possible for the decision maker to know enough about the future states of nature to assign probabilities to their occurrence. Given that probabilities can be assigned, there are several decision criteria available to aid the decision maker. We will present two of these criteria: *expected monetary value* and *expected opportunity loss* (although several others, including the *maximum likelihood criterion,* are available).

## Expected Value

In order to apply the concept of expected value as a decision-making criterion, it is first necessary for the decision maker to estimate the probability of occurrence of each state of nature. Once these estimates have been made, the *expected value* for each decision alternative is computed. Briefly reviewing, expected value is computed by multiplying each outcome (of a decision) by the probability of its occurrence and then summing these products (see chap. 10).

In our real estate investment example, let us suppose that, based on several economic forecasts, the investor is able to estimate the probability that good economic conditions will prevail to be .60, and the probability that poor economic conditions will result to be .40. This new information is shown in table 11.7.

*An expected value example*

**Table 11.7** Payoff Table with Probabilities for States of Nature

| | States of Nature | |
| | Good Economic Conditions .60 | Poor Economic Conditions .40 |
|---|---|---|
| Decision (Purchase) | | |
| Apartment building | $ 50,000 | $ 30,000 |
| Office building | 100,000 | −40,000 |
| Warehouse | 30,000 | 10,000 |

The expected value for each decision is computed as follows:

*Expected value computations*

$$EV(\text{Apartment}) = \$\ 50{,}000(.60) + 30{,}000(.40) = \$42{,}000$$
$$EV(\text{Office}) = \$100{,}000(.60) - 40{,}000(.40) = \$44{,}000$$
$$EV(\text{Warehouse}) = \$\ 30{,}000(.60) + 10{,}000(.40) = \$22{,}000$$

The best decision is the one with the greatest expected value. Since the greatest expected value is $44,000, the decision is to purchase the office building. This does not mean that if the investor purchases an office building that exactly $44,000 will result. One of the payoff values will occur (either $100,000 or −$40,000). The expected value means that if this decision situation occurred a large number of times, an *average* payoff of $44,000 would result.

*The decision with the greatest expected value*

*An average payoff*

## Expected Opportunity Loss

A decision criterion closely related to expected value is *expected opportunity loss*. Rather than multiplying the decision outcomes by the probabilities of their occurrence as we did for expected monetary value, in expected opportunity loss the probabilities are multiplied by the regret (i.e., opportunity loss) for each decision outcome.

Recall that the concept of regret has already been presented in our discussion of the *minimax regret criterion*. For our example, the regret values for each decision outcome were developed in table 11.6. Table 11.6 is repeated below in table 11.8, with the addition of the probabilities of occurrence for each state of nature.

**Table 11.8** Regret (Opportunity Loss) Table with Probabilities for States of Nature

| Decision (Purchase) | States of Nature | |
|---|---|---|
| | Good Economic Conditions .60 | Poor Economic Conditions .40 |
| Apartment building | $50,000 | $  0 |
| Office building | 0 | 70,000 |
| Warehouse | 70,000 | 20,000 |

The expected opportunity loss for each decision is computed as follows:

$$EOL(\text{Apartment}) = \$50,000(.60) + 0(.40) = \$30,000$$
$$EOL(\text{Office}) = \$0(.60) + 70,000(.40) = \$28,000$$
$$EOL(\text{Warehouse}) = \$70,000(.60) + 20,000(.40) = \$50,000$$

As in the minimax regret criterion, the best decision results from minimizing the regret, or in this case, minimizing the *expected* regret or opportunity loss. Since $28,000 is the minimum expected regret, the decision is to purchase the office building.

Notice that the recommended decisions derived from the expected value criterion and expected opportunity loss were the same—to purchase the office building. This is not a coincidence, as these two methods will always result in the same decision. Thus, it is repetitious to apply both methods to a decision situation when one of the two will suffice.

In addition, it should be noted that the decision from the expected value and expected opportunity loss criteria are totally dependent on the probability estimates determined by the decision maker. Thus, if inaccurate probabilities are used, then erroneous decisions can result. As such, it is important that the decision maker be as accurate as possible in determining the probabilities of each state of nature.

## Expected Value of Perfect Information

It is often possible to purchase additional information regarding future events, and thus make a better decision. For example, our real estate investor could hire an economic forecaster to perform an analysis of the economy in order to more accurately determine which economic condition will occur in the future. However, the investor (or any decision maker) would be foolish to pay more for this information than the extra profit that would be gained from having the information. As such, the information has some maximum value that represents a limit the decision maker would be willing to spend. This value of information can be computed as an expected value, hence, its name—the *expected value of perfect information* (also referred to as *EVPI*).

*The maximum amount a decision maker would pay for additional information*

In order to compute the expected value of perfect information, we first look at the decisions under each state of nature. If we could obtain information that assured us which state of nature was going to occur (i.e., perfect information), we could select the best decision for that state of nature. For example, in our real estate investment example, if we know for sure that good economic conditions will prevail, then the decision should be to purchase the office building. Similarly, if we know for sure that poor economic conditions will occur, then the decision is to purchase the apartment building. These hypothetical "perfect" decisions are summarized in table 11.9.

*The best decision under each state of nature*

**Table 11.9** Payoff Table with Decisions Given Perfect Information

| Decision (Purchase) | States of Nature | |
|---|---|---|
| | Good Economic Conditions .60 | Poor Economic Conditions .40 |
| Apartment building | $ 50,000 | $ 30,000 |
| Office building | 100,000 | −40,000 |
| Warehouse | 30,000 | 10,000 |

The probabilities of each state of nature (i.e., .60 and .40) tell us that good economic conditions will prevail 60% of the time and poor economic conditions 40% of the time (if this decision situation was repeated many times). In other words, even though perfect information will enable the investor to make the right decision, each state of nature will occur only a certain portion of the time. Thus, each of the decision outcomes obtained using perfect information must be weighted by those respective probabilities:

$$\$100,000(.60) + 30,000(.40) = \$72,000$$

The amount $72,000 is the expected value of the decision *given* perfect information, but not the expected value *of* perfect information. The expected value of perfect information is the maximum amount that would be paid to gain information that would result in a better decision than the decision made *without perfect information*. Recall that the expected value decision without perfect information was to purchase an office building and the expected value was computed as:

*The expected value given perfect information*

*The expected value without perfect information*

$$EV \text{ (Office)} = \$100,000(.60) - 40,000(.40) = \$44,000$$

The expected value of perfect information is computed by taking the difference between the expected value given perfect information ($72,000) and the expected value without perfect information ($44,000):

$$EVPI = \$72,000 - 44,000 = \$28,000$$

*The expected value of perfect information*

The expected value of perfect information, $28,000, is the maximum amount that the investor would pay to purchase perfect information from some other source, such as an economic forecaster. Of course, perfect information is rare and usually unobtainable. Typically, the decision maker would be willing to pay some amount less than $28,000, depending on how accurate (i.e., close to perfection) the decision maker believes the information to be.

*The EVPI equals the expected opportunity loss*

It is interesting to notice that the expected value of perfect information, $28,000 for our example, is the same as the *expected opportunity loss* for the decision selected using this latter criterion:

$$EOL \text{ (Office)} = \$0(.60) + 70,000(.40) = \$28,000$$

This is a logical occurrence that will always result, since regret reflects *the difference between the best decision under a state of nature and the decision actually made.* This is actually the same thing determined by the expected value of perfect information.

## Decision Trees

*A graphical diagram used for making decisions*

Another useful technique for analyzing a decision situation is a *decision tree*. A decision tree is a graphical diagram consisting of nodes and branches very similar to the probability tree shown in chapter 10 (fig. 10.1). However, rather than determining the probability of each branch (i.e., outcome) as in a probability tree, in a decision tree the expected value of each outcome is computed and a decision is made based on these expected values. The primary benefit gained from using a decision tree is that it provides an illustration (or picture) of the decision-making process. This makes it easier to correctly compute the necessary expected values and to understand the process of making the decision.

*A decision tree example*

We will demonstrate the basic fundamentals of decision tree analysis with our example of the real estate investor. The various decisions, probabilities, and outcomes of this example initially presented in table 11.7 are repeated in table 11.10 below. The decision tree for this example is shown in figure 11.1.

**Table 11.10** Payoff Table for Real Estate Investment Example

| Decision (Purchase) | States of Nature | |
|---|---|---|
| | Good Economic Conditions .60 | Poor Economic Conditions .40 |
| Apartment building | $ 50,000 | $ 30,000 |
| Office building | 100,000 | −40,000 |
| Warehouse | 30,000 | 10,000 |

**Figure 11.1** Decision tree for real estate investment example.

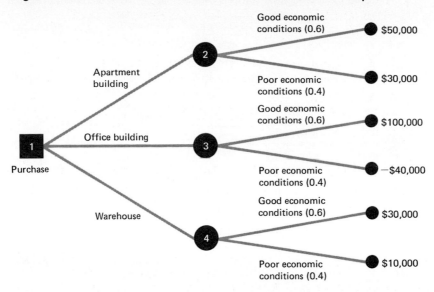

In figure 11.1, the circles (○) and squares (□) are referred to as *Decision nodes* *nodes*. The squares are decision nodes and the *branches* emanating from a decision node reflect the alternative decisions available at that point. For example, in figure 11.1, node 1 signifies a decision to purchase an apartment building, office building, or warehouse. The circles are "probability" nodes and the branches emanating from them indicate the probabilistic states of *Probability nodes* nature that can occur: good economic conditions or poor economic conditions.

The decision tree represents the sequence of events that occurs in a *The sequence of* decision situation. First, one of the three decision choices is selected at node *events in a decision* 1. Depending on the branch selected, either probability node 2, 3, or 4 will *situation* occur, and, hence, one of the states of nature will occur resulting in one of 6 possible payoffs.

The process of determining the best decision using a decision tree *Computing the* consists of computing the expected value at each probability node. This is *expected value at* accomplished by starting with the final outcomes (payoffs) and working *each probability node* backwards through the decision tree toward node 1. First, the expected value of the payoffs is computed at each probability node.

$EV$(node 2) = .60( 50,000) + .40( 30,000) = \$42,000
$EV$(node 3) = .60(100,000) + .40(−40,000) = \$44,000
$EV$(node 4) = .60( 30,000) + .40( 10,000) = \$22,000

These values are now shown as the *expected* payoffs from each of the *Selecting the branch* three branches emanating from node 1 in figure 11.2. Each of these three *with the greatest* expected values at nodes 2, 3, and 4 are the outcomes of the possible *expected value* decisions that can occur at node 1. Moving toward node 1, the branch is

**Figure 11.2** Decision tree with expected values at probability nodes.

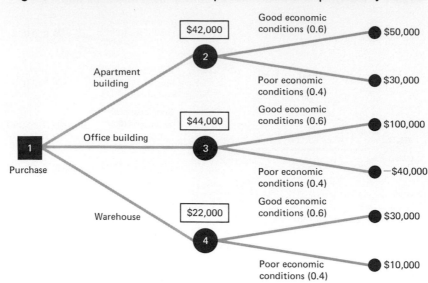

selected that comes from the probability node with the highest expected payoff. In figure 11.2, the branch corresponding to the highest payoff is from node 3 to node 1 with an outcome of $44,000. This represents the decision to purchase the office building. The decision to purchase the office building with an expected payoff of $44,000 is the same result we achieved using the expected value criterion presented earlier. In fact, when only one decision is made (i.e., there is not a series of decisions), then the decision tree will always result in the same decision and expected payoff as the expected value criterion. As a result, in these decision situations the decision tree is not very useful. However, when a sequence or series of decisions are required from the decision maker, the decision tree can be very useful.

## Sequential Decision Trees

*A decision situation requiring a series of decisions*

When a decision situation requires only a single decision, an expected value payoff table will yield the same result as a decision tree. However, a payoff table is usually *limited to* a single decision situation like our real estate investment example. If a decision situation requires a series of decisions, then a payoff table is not possible and a decision tree becomes the best method for decision analysis.

*A sequential decision tree example*

In order to demonstrate the use of a decision tree for a sequence of decisions, we will alter our real estate investment example to encompass a 10-year period during which several decisions must be made. In this new example the *first decision* facing the investor is whether to purchase an apartment building or land. If the investor purchases the apartment building, two states of nature are possible. The population of the town will grow (with a probability of .60) or the population will exhibit no growth (with a probability of .40). Both states of nature result in payoffs. Alternatively, if the investor chooses to purchase land, at a point 3 years in the future, another decision will be faced regarding the development of the land. The decision tree for this example, which contains all the pertinent data including decisions, states of nature, probabilities, and payoffs, is shown in figure 11.3.

**Figure 11.3** Sequential decision tree.

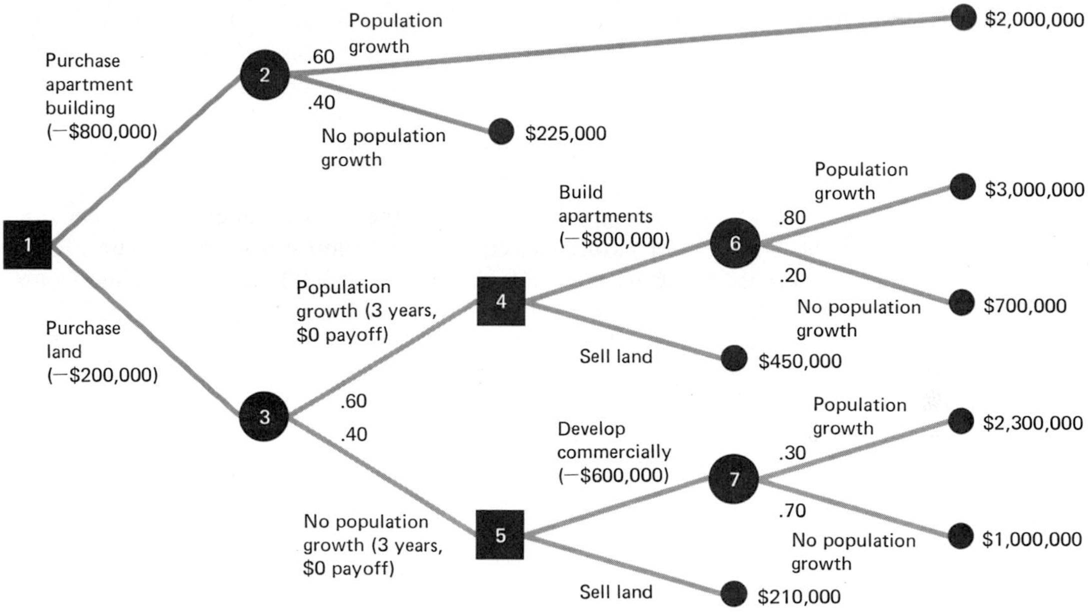

At decision node 1 in figure 11.3, the decision choices are to purchase an apartment building or to purchase land. Notice that the cost of each venture ($800,000 and $200,000, respectively) is shown in parentheses. If the apartment building is purchased, two states of nature are possible at probability node 2: the town can exhibit population growth with a probability of .60, or there can be no population growth or a decline with a probability of .40. If the state of nature, population growth, occurs, a payoff of $2,000,000 will accrue over a ten-year period. (Note that this whole decision situation encompasses a ten-year time frame.) However, if the state of nature, no population growth, occurs, a payoff of only $225,000 will result.

If the decision is made to purchase land, two states of nature are possible at probability node 3. These two states of nature and their probabilities are identical to those at node 2, however, the payoffs are different. If population growth occurs *for a three-year period,* no payoff will occur,

*Decision node 1*

*Probability node 2*

*Probability node 3*

but the investor will make another decision at node 4 regarding development of the land: apartments will be built at a cost of $800,000 or the land will be sold with a payoff of $450,000. Notice that the decision situation at node 4 can occur only if the state of nature, population growth, occurs first. If the state of nature, no population growth, occurs at node 3, there is no

payoff and another decision situation exists at node 5. The land can be developed commercially at a cost of $600,000 or the land can be sold for $210,000. (Notice that the sale of the land results in less profit if there is no population growth rather than population growth.)

If the decision is made at decision node 4 to build apartments, two states of nature are possible: population growth with a conditional probability of .80 or no population growth with a conditional probability of .20. The probability of population growth is higher (and the probability of no growth lower) than before because population growth for the first three years has already been exhibited by the branch from node 3 to node 4. The payoffs for these two states of nature at the end of the ten-year period are $3,000,000 and $700,000, as shown in figure 11.3.

If the investor decides to develop the land commercially at node 5, then two states of nature can occur. Population growth can occur with a probability of .30 with an eventual payoff of $2,300,000 accruing, or no population growth can occur with a probability of .70 and a payoff of $1,000,000. The probability of population growth is low (i.e., .30) because no population growth has already been exhibited by the branch from node 3 to node 5.

This decision situation encompasses several sequential decisions that can be analyzed using the decision tree approach outlined in our earlier (simpler) example. As before, we start at the end of the decision tree and work backwards toward a decision at node 1.

First we must compute the *expected values at nodes 6 and 7:*

$$EV(\text{node } 6) = .80(\$3,000,000) + .20(\$\ 700,000) = \$2,540,000$$
$$EV(\text{node } 7) = .30(\$2,300,000) + .70(\$1,000,000) = \$1,390,000$$

Both of these expected values (as well as all other nodal values) are highlighted in figure 11.4.

Now at decision nodes 4 and 5 we must make a decision. As with a normal payoff table we make the decision that results in the greatest expected value. At node 4 we have a choice of two values: $1,740,000, which is derived by subtracting the cost of building an apartment building ($800,000) from the expected payoff of $2,540,000, *or* $450,000, which is the expected value of selling the land computed with a probability of 1.0. As such, the decision is to build the apartment building, and the value of node 4 is $1,740,000.

This same process is repeated for node 5. The decisions at node 5 result in payoffs of $790,000 (i.e., $1,390,000 − 600,000 = $790,000) and $210,000. Since the value $790,000 is highest, the decision is made to develop the land commercially.

**Figure 11.4** Sequential decision tree with nodal expected values.

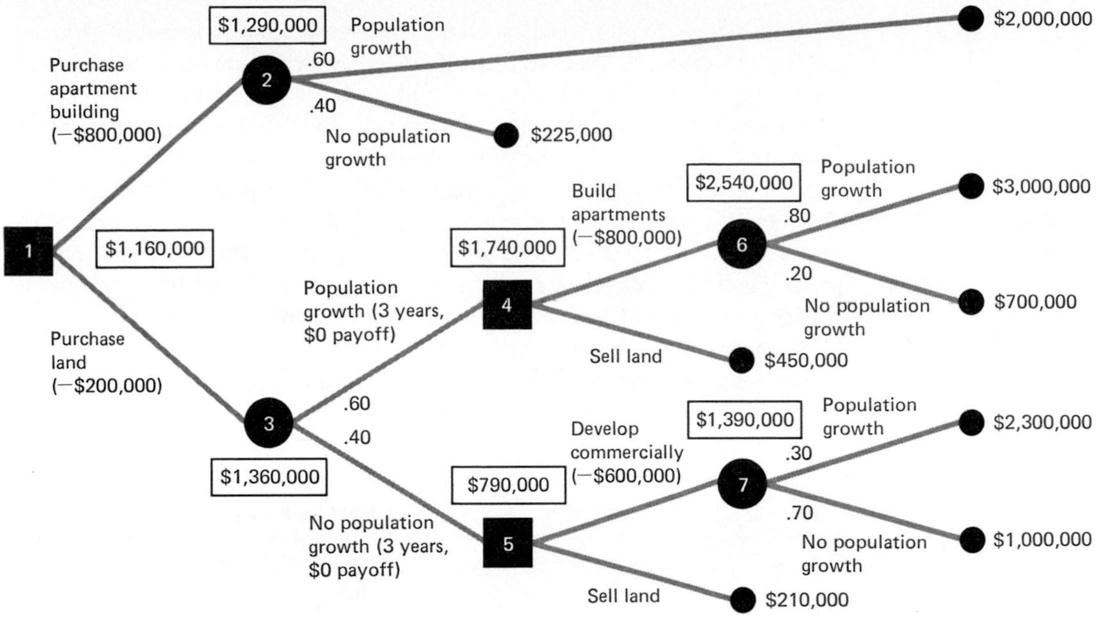

Next we must compute the expected values at *nodes 2 and 3:*

*Expected value at nodes 2 and 3*

$EV$(node 2) = .60($2,000,000) + .40($225,000) = $1,290,000
$EV$(node 3) = .60($1,740,000) + .40($790,000) = $1,360,000

(Note that the expected value for node 3 is computed from the decision values previously determined at nodes 4 and 5.)

Now we must make the final decision for node 1 and, as before, we select the decision with the greatest expected value *after the cost of each decision is subtracted out:*

*The final decision at node 1*

Purchase apartment
building:            $1,290,000 − 800,000 = $   490,000
Purchase land:     $1,360,000 − 200,000 = $1,160,000

Since the highest *net* expected value is $1,160,000, the decision is to purchase land, and the payoff of the decision is $1,160,000.

This example demonstrates the usefulness of decision trees for decision analysis. The fact that the decision tree provides a "picture" of the decision process greatly enhances the ability to observe the logic of decision making. In fact, decision trees can be used for decision problems more complex than the example above without too much difficulty.

*A picture of the decision process*

# Decision Analysis with Additional Information

Earlier in this chapter we discussed the concept of the *expected value of perfect information*. We noted that if perfect information could be obtained regarding which states of nature would occur in the future, the decision maker could obviously make better decisions. Although perfect information about the future is rare, it is often possible to gain some amount of additional information (that is not perfect) which will improve decisions.

*Bayesian analysis*

In this section we will present a process for using additional information in the decision-making process by applying *Bayesian* analysis, a probabilistic technique presented in chapter 10. In order to demonstrate this process, we will use the real estate investment example we have employed throughout this chapter. To briefly review this example, a real estate investor is considering three alternative investments, which will occur under two possible economic conditions (states of nature) as shown in table 11.11.

*An example*

**Table 11.11** Payoff Table for the Real Estate Investment Example

| Decision (Purchase) | States of Nature | |
| --- | --- | --- |
| | Good Economic Conditions .60 | Poor Economic Conditions .40 |
| Apartment building | $50,000 | $ 30,000 |
| Office building | 100,000 | −40,000 |
| Warehouse | 30,000 | 10,000 |

Recall that using the expected value criterion we found the best decision to be the purchase of the office building with an expected value of $44,000. We also computed the expected value of perfect information to be $28,000. Therefore, the investor would be willing to pay up to $28,000 for information about the states of nature, depending on how close to perfection the information would actually be.

*Purchasing additional information*

Now let us suppose that the investor has decided to hire a professional economic analyst who will provide additional information regarding the economic conditions that will occur in the future. The analyst is constantly involved in research of the economy and the results of this research is what the investor will be purchasing.

The economic analyst will provide the investor with a report with one of two outcomes. The report will be either positive, indicating good economic conditions are most likely to prevail in the future, or negative, indicating poor economic conditions will probably occur. Based on the past record of the economic analyst in forecasting future economic conditions, the investor has determined *conditional* probabilities of the different report outcomes given the occurrence of each state of nature in the future. (See chap. 10 for a discussion of conditional probabilities.) In order to express these conditional probabilities we will employ the following notation:

*Conditional probabilities*

*Probability notation*

$g$ = good economic conditions
$p$ = poor economic conditions
$P$ = positive economic report
$N$ = negative economic report

The conditional probability of each report outcome given the possible occurrence of each state of nature are:

$P(P/g) = .80$
$P(N/g) = .20$
$P(P/p) = .10$
$P(N/p) = .90$

For example, if the economic conditions in the future are actually good ($g$), the probability that a positive report ($P$) was given by the analyst, $P(P/g)$ is .80. The other three conditional probabilities are interpreted similarly. Notice that these probabilities indicate that the analyst is a relatively accurate forecaster of future economic conditions.

*Defining conditional probabilities*

The investor now has quite a bit of probabilistic information available. Not only are the conditional probabilities of the report outcome available, but the investor also has the *prior probabilities* that each state of nature will occur from table 11.11. These prior probabilities that good or poor economic conditions will occur in the future are

*Prior probabilities*

$P(g) = .60$
$P(p) = .40$

Given that the investor has the prior and conditional probabilities, the prior probabilities can be revised to determine *posterior probabilities* using Bayes' rule (as shown in chap. 10). If we have the conditional probability that a positive report was presented given that good economic conditions will prevail, $P(P/g)$, the posterior probability of good economic conditions given a positive report, $P(g/P)$, can be determined using Bayes' rule as follows.

*Revising prior probabilities*

*Posterior probabilities*

*Bayes' rule*

$$P(g/P) = \frac{P(P/g)\ P(g)}{P(P/g)\ P(g)\ +\ P(P/p)P(p)}$$
$$= \frac{(.80)(.60)}{(.80)(.60)\ +\ (.10)(.40)}$$
$$= .923$$

The prior probability that good economic conditions will occur in the future is .60. However, by obtaining the additional information of a positive report from the analyst, the investor can revise the prior probability of good conditions to a .923 probability that good economic conditions will occur. The remaining posterior (revised) probabilities are

$P(g/N) = .250$
$P(p/P) = .077$
$P(p/N) = .750$

Now that the investor has the revised probabilities of future economic conditions given each report outcome, the question is, "How is this probabilistic information used in the decision-making process?" The answer to this question can best be determined within the framework of a decision tree.

## Decision Trees with Posterior Probabilities

The original decision tree analysis of the real estate investment example without additional information is shown in figures 11.1 and 11.2. Using these decision trees, the appropriate decision was found to be the purchase of an office building with an expected value of $44,000. However, if the investor hires an economic analyst, then a decision regarding which piece of real estate to invest in will not be made until after the analyst presents the report. This provides an additional stage in the decision-making process, which is shown in the decision tree in figure 11.5.

**Figure 11.5** Decision tree with posterior probabilities.

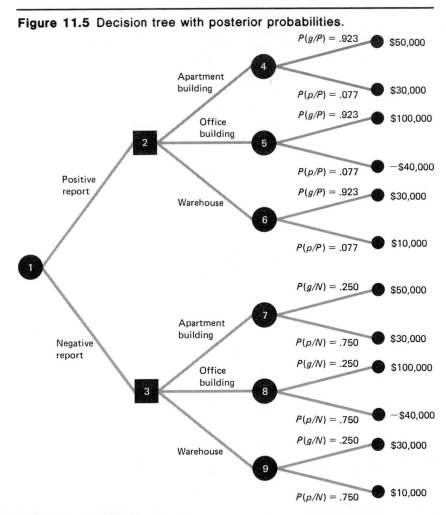

The decision tree shown in figure 11.5 is very similar to the decision trees in figures 11.1 and 11.2, except for two differences. The first difference is the existence of two new branches at the beginning of the decision tree that represent the two report outcomes that can occur. Notice that once either report outcome is presented then the decision alternatives, possible states of nature, and payoffs are the same as in figures 11.1 and 11.2.

*A decision tree with two new branches*

The second difference is that the probabilities of each state of nature occurring are no longer the prior probabilities given in figure 11.1, but the revised posterior probabilities computed in the previous section using Bayes's rule. For example, if a positive report results, then the upper branch in figure 11.5 (from node 1 to node 2) will be taken. If an apartment building is purchased (the branch from node 2 to node 4), the probability of good economic conditions is .923, while the probability of poor conditions is .077. These are the revised posterior probabilities of the economic conditions given that a positive report resulted. However, before we can perform an expected value analysis using this decision tree, one more piece of probabilistic information must be determined—the initial branch probabilities of a positive or negative economic report.

*Using posterior probabilities in the decision tree*

*Initial branch probabilities*

The probabilities of a positive report, $P(P)$, or negative report, $P(N)$, can be determined according to the following logic. Recall from chapter 10 that the probability of two dependent events, $A$ and $B$, both occurring is

$$P(AB) = P(A/B)\ P(B)$$

If we let event $A$ equal a positive report and event $B$ equal good economic conditions, then according to the above formula,

$$P(Pg) = P(P/g)\ P(g)$$

We can also determine the probability of a positive report and *poor* economic conditions the same way.

$$P(Pp) = P(P/p)\ P(p)$$

Next consider the two probabilities, $P(Pg)$ and $P(Pp)$. These are, respectively, the probability of a positive report and good economic conditions, and a positive report and poor economic conditions. These two sets of occurrences are *mutually exclusive,* since good and poor economic conditions cannot both occur simultaneously in the immediate future. Conditions will be either good or poor, but not both. This means that to determine the *probability of a positive report* we can add the mutually exclusive probabilities of a positive report with good economic conditions and a positive report with poor economic conditions, as follows.

*Mutually exclusive events*

$$P(P) = P(Pg) + P(Pp)$$

Now, substituting our relationships for $P(Pg)$ and $P(Pp)$ determined earlier in this formula, we have

$$P(P) = P(P/g)\ P(g) + P(P/p)\ P(p)$$

You might notice that this is the denominator of the Bayesian formula we used to compute $P(g/P)$ in the previous section. Using the conditional and prior probabilities which already exist, the probability of a positive report is

$$P(P) = P(P/g) \, P(g) + P(P/p) \, P(p)$$
$$= (.80)(.60) + (.10)(.40)$$
$$= .52$$

Likewise, the probability of a negative report is

$$P(N) = P(N/g) \, P(g) + P(N/p) \, P(p)$$
$$= (.20)(.60) + (.90)(.40)$$
$$= .48$$

Now we have all the information needed to perform a decision tree analysis. The decision tree analysis for our example is shown in figure 11.6. In order to demonstrate how the decision tree analysis is conducted, consider the result at node 4 first. The value $48,460 is the expected value of the purchase of an apartment building given both states of nature. This expected value is computed as follows.

$$EV \text{ (Apartment Building)} = \$50,000 \, (.923) + 30,000 \, (.077)$$
$$= \$48,460$$

The expected values at nodes 5, 6, 7, 8, and 9 were computed similarly. The investor will actually make the decision at nodes 2 and 3 as to which investment to make. It is assumed that the investor will make the best decision in each case. Thus, the decision at node 2 will be to purchase an office building with an expected value of $89,212, while the decision at node 3 will be to purchase an apartment building with an expected value of $35,000. These two results at nodes 2 and 3 are referred to as *decision*
*strategies*. They represent *a plan* of decisions to be made given either a positive or negative report from the economic analyst.

The final step in the decision tree analysis is to compute the expected value of the decision strategy given that an economic analysis is performed. This expected value, shown to be $63,190 at node 1 in figure 11.6, is computed as follows.

$$EV \text{ (strategy)} = \$89,212 \, (.52) + 35,000 \, (.48)$$
$$= \$63,190$$

This amount, $63,190, is the expected value of the investor's decision strategy given that a report forecasting future economic condition is generated by the economic analyst.

**Figure 11.6** Decision tree analysis.

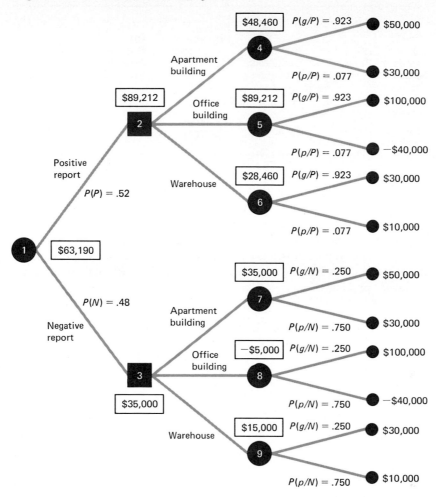

## Computing Posterior Probabilities with Tables

One of the difficulties that can occur with this type of decision analysis with additional information is that as the size of the problem increases (i.e., more decision alternatives and states of nature) the application of Bayes' rule to compute the posterior probabilities becomes more complex. In such cases, the posterior probabilities can be computed using tables. We will demonstrate this tabular approach with our real estate investment example. The table for computing posterior probabilities for a positive report and $P(P)$ is initially set up as shown in table 11.12.

*Using Bayes' rule for large decision problems*

*Computing posterior probabilities using a table*

**Table 11.12** Computation of Posterior Probabilities

| (1) States of Nature | (2) Prior Probabilities | (3) Conditional Probabilities | (4) Prior Probability × Conditional Probability: (2) × (3) | (5) Posterior Probabilities: (4) ÷ Σ (4) |
|---|---|---|---|---|
| Good conditions | $P(g) = .6$ | $P(P/g) = .80$ | $P(Pg) = .48$ | $P(g/P) = \dfrac{.48}{.52} = .923$ |
| Poor conditions | $P(p) = .4$ | $P(P/p) = .10$ | $P(Pp) = .04$ $\Sigma = P(P) = .52$ | $P(p/P) = \dfrac{.04}{.52} = .077$ |

The posterior probabilities for either state of nature (good or poor economic conditions) given a negative report are computed similarly.

As the size of the decision analysis increases, the steps of this tabular approach are followed the same way as in this relatively small problem. However, this approach is more systematic than the direct application of Bayes's rule, thus making it easier to compute the posterior probabilities for larger problems.

## The Expected Value of Sample Information

Recall that we previously computed the expected value of our real estate investment example (when we did not have any additional information) to be $44,000. With the additional information provided by the economic analyst we computed an expected value of $63,190 (using the decision tree analysis in fig. 11.6). The difference between these two expected values is called the *expected value of sample information (EVSI)*, and it is computed as follows.

*Computing the expected value of sample information*

$$EVSI = EV_{\text{with information}} - EV_{\text{without information}}$$

For our example, the expected value of sample information is

$$EVSI = \$63,190 - 44,000$$
$$= \$19,190$$

This means the real estate investor would be willing to pay the economic analyst up to $19,190 for an economic report that forecasted future economic conditions.

After we computed the expected value without additional information, we then computed the *expected value of perfect information,* which equaled $28,000. However, the expected value of the sample information was only $19,190. This is a logical result, since it is rare that absolutely *Less than perfect* perfect information can be determined. As such, since the additional in-*information* formation that is obtained is less than perfect, it will be worth less to the decision maker. We can determine how close to perfection our sample *Efficiency of sample* information is by computing the *efficiency of sample information* as fol-*information* lows.

$$\text{Efficiency} = \frac{EVSI}{EVPI}$$

$$= \frac{\$19,190}{28,000}$$

$$= .68$$

Thus, the economic report generated by the analysis is viewed by the investor to be 68% as efficient as perfect information. In general, a high efficiency rating indicates the information is very good and close to being perfect information, while a low rating indicates the additional information is not very good. For our example, the efficiency of .68 is relatively high, thus it is doubtful if the investor would seek additional information from another, or alternative, source. (However, this is usually dependent upon how much money the decision maker has available to purchase information.) If the efficiency had been lower, however, the investor might seek additional information elsewhere.

*Analyzing efficiency ratings*

## Utility

All of the decision-making criteria presented previously in this chapter have been based on monetary value. In other words, decisions were based on the potential dollar payoffs of the alternatives. However, there are certain decision situations in which individuals *do not* make decisions based on the expected dollar gain or loss.

*Decisions not based on dollar gains or losses*

For example, consider the individual who purchases automobile insurance. The decisions are to purchase or to not purchase and the states of nature are *an accident* and *no accident*. The payoff table for this decision situation including probabilities is shown in table 11.13.

*An insurance example*

**Table 11.13** Payoff Table for Auto Insurance Example

| | States of Nature | |
|---|---|---|
| Decision | No Accident .992 | Accident .008 |
| Purchase insurance | $500 | $ 500 |
| Do not purchase insurance | 0 | $10,000 |

The dollar outcomes in table 11.13 are the *costs* associated with each outcome. The insurance costs $500 whether there is an accident or no accident. If the insurance is not purchased and there is no accident, then there is no cost at all. However, if an accident does occur then the individual will incur a cost of $10,000.

The expected cost (*EC*) for each decision is

$$EC(\text{Insurance}) = .992(\$500) + .008(\$500) = \$500$$
$$EC(\text{No Insurance}) = .992(\$0) + .008(\$10,000) = \$80$$

Since the *lowest* expected cost is $80, the decision *should be* to not purchase insurance. However, individuals almost always purchase insurance (even when not legally required to do so). This is true of all types of insurance, such as accident, life, or fire.

*Foregoing a high expected value to avoid a disaster*

Why do people shun the greater *expected* dollar outcome in this type of situation? The answer is that people want to avoid a ruinous or painful situation. When faced with a relatively small dollar cost versus a disaster, people typically pay the small cost to avert the disaster. People who display

*Risk averters*

this characteristic are referred to as *risk averters* because they avoid risky situations.

Alternatively, people who go to the racetrack to wager on horseraces, travel to Atlantic City to play roulette, or speculate in the commodities market typically decide to take risks, even though the greatest *expected value* will occur from simply hanging on to their money. These individuals shun a greater expected value accruing from a sure thing, or keeping their money, in order to take a chance on receiving a "bonanza." Individuals

*Risk takers*

displaying this characteristic are referred to as *risk takers*.

For both risk averters and risk takers (as well as those individuals who are indifferent to risk), the decision criterion is something other than

*Utility*

the expected dollar outcome. This alternative criterion is known as *utility*. Utility is a measure of the satisfaction derived from money. In our examples

*A measure of satisfaction derived from money*

of risk averters and risk takers presented above, the utility derived from their decisions *exceeded* the expected dollar value.

As an example, reconsider the automobile insurance decision presented earlier. In this decision situation the utility to the decision maker of having insurance is much greater than the utility of not having insurance.

*The contrasting utility of money for individuals with different incomes*

As another example, consider two people, each offered $100,000 to perform some particularly difficult and strenuous task. However, one individual has an annual income of $10,000, while the other individual is a multimillionaire. It is reasonable to assume that a typical person with an annual income of only $10,000 would leap at the opportunity to earn $100,000, while the multimillionaire would reject the offer. Obviously, $100,000 has more *utility* (i.e., value) for one individual than the other.

In general, incremental amounts of money do not have the same intrinsic value to different people over the whole range of money values. For individuals with a great deal of wealth, more money does not usually have as much intrinsic value as it would to the individual who has little money. As such, while the actual dollar value is the same for all individuals, the value as measured by utility is different for individuals depending on how much present wealth they have. Thus, utility in this case is a measure of the pleasure or satisfaction an individual would receive from an incremental increase in wealth.

*Measuring utility*

In some decision situations an attempt is made to subjectively assign a value to a decision maker's utility. This value is typically measured in

*Utiles*

terms of units called *utiles*. For example, the $100,000 offered to the two individuals above may have a utility value of 100 utiles to the person with a low income and 0 utiles to the multimillionaire.

In our automobile insurance example, the *expected utility* of purchasing insurance could be 1,000 utiles, while the expected utility of not purchasing insurance is only 1 utile. These utility values are completely reversed from the expected *monetary* values computed from table 11.13, thus explaining the normal decision to purchase insurance.

As might be expected, it is usually very difficult to measure utility and measure the number of utiles derived from a decision outcome. It is a very subjective process in which the decision maker's psychological preferences must be determined. Thus, while the concept of utility is realistic and often more accurately portrays actual decision-making criteria than does expected monetary value, its application is difficult and, as such, is somewhat limited.

*Measuring utility is a subjective process*

## Summary

It has been the purpose of this chapter to demonstrate the concepts and fundamentals of decision making when uncertainty exists. Within this context several decision-making criteria were presented. In the case where probabilities could not be attached to the occurrence of outcomes, the maximax, maximin, minimax regret, equal likelihood, and Hurwicz decision criteria were demonstrated. In the case where probabilities could be assigned to the states of nature of a decision situation, the expected value criterion and decision trees were discussed.

All of the decision criteria presented in this chapter were demonstrated via rather simplified examples; however, actual decision-making situations are usually more complex. Nevertheless, the *process* of analyzing decisions presented in this chapter is the logical method that most decision makers would follow in order to make a decision.

In the examples presented in this chapter, the decision situations consisted of only one decision maker. However, many decisions are made in competitive situations where the decision of an antagonist will affect the decision of an individual. This type of competitive decision situation is the subject of *game theory,* the topic of the next chapter.

*Decision analysis illustrates the logical process of decision making*

## References

Baumol, W. J. *Economic Theory and Operations Analysis.* Englewood Cliffs, N.J.: Prentice-Hall, 1961.

Dorfman, R.; Samuelson, P. A.; and Solow, R. M. *Linear Programming and Economic Analysis.* New York: McGraw-Hill, 1958.

Holloway, C. A. *Decision Making Under Uncertainty.* Englewood Cliffs, N.J.: Prentice-Hall, 1979.

Kwak, N. K. *Mathematical Programming with Business Applications.* New York: McGraw-Hill, 1973.

Luce, R. D., and Raiffa, H. *Games and Decisions.* New York: John Wiley and Sons, 1957.

Von Neumann, J., and Morgenstern, O. *Theory of Games and Economic Behavior*. Princeton, N.J.: Princeton University Press, 1944.

Williams, J. D. *The Compleat Strategyst*. Rev. ed. New York: McGraw-Hill, 1966.

## Problems

1. A farmer in Iowa is considering leasing some extra land or investing in savings certificates at the local bank. If the weather conditions are good next year, having the extra land will allow the farmer to have an excellent harvest. However, if the weather is bad the farmer will lose money. Regardless of the weather conditions, the savings certificates will result in the same return. The return for each investment given each type of weather condition is given in the following payoff table.

| | Weather | |
|---|---|---|
| Decision | Good | Bad |
| Lease land | $90,000 | −40,000 |
| Savings certificate | 10,000 | 10,000 |

Select the best decision using:
   (a) The maximax criterion
   (b) The maximin criterion

2. The owner of the Burger Doodle Restaurant is considering two ways to expand operations: open a drive-up window or serve breakfast. The increased profits resulting from these proposed expansions depend on whether or not a competitor opens a franchise down the street. The profits resulting from each expansion in operations given both future competitive situations are given in the following payoff table.

| | Competitor | |
|---|---|---|
| Decision | Open | Not Open |
| Drive-up window | $−6,000 | $20,000 |
| Breakfast | 4,000 | 8,000 |

Select the best decision using:
   (a) The maximax criterion
   (b) The maximin criterion

3. Stevie Stone is a bellhop at the Royal Sundown Hotel in Atlanta. He has been offered a management position and although it would assure him of a job if a recession occurred, he would make less salary if good

economic conditions prevailed (because of the large tips he gets as a bellhop). His salary during the next 5 years for each job given each future economic condition is given in the following payoff table.

| Decision | Economic Conditions | |
| --- | --- | --- |
| | Good | Recession |
| Bellhop | $120,000 | $60,000 |
| Management | 85,000 | 85,000 |

Select the best decision using:
(a) The minimax regret criterion
(b) The Hurwicz criterion ($\alpha = 0.4$)
(c) The equal likelihood criterion

4. Given the following payoff table for three alternative investments, A, B, and C, under two future states of the economy, good and bad:

| Investment | Economic Conditions | |
| --- | --- | --- |
| | Good | Bad |
| A | $ 70,000 | $ 25,000 |
| B | 120,000 | −60,000 |
| C | 40,000 | 40,000 |

Determine the best decision using:
(a) The maximax criterion
(b) The maximin criterion
(c) The minimax regret criterion
(d) The Hurwicz criterion ($\alpha = 0.3$)
(e) The equal likelihood criterion

5. Brooke Bentley is a student in business administration and she is trying to decide which management science course to take next quarter, I, II, or III. Three professors in management science teach all three courses: "Steamboat" Fulton, "Death" Ray, and "Sadistic" Scott. Brooke can expect a different grade in each of the courses depending on who teaches it next quarter (which she does not presently know) as shown in the following payoff table.

| Course | Professor | | |
| --- | --- | --- | --- |
| | Fulton | Ray | Scott |
| I | B | D | D |
| II | C | B | F |
| III | F | A | C |

Determine the best course to take next quarter using:

(a) The maximax criterion

(b) The maximin criterion

6. A farmer in Georgia must decide which crop to plant next year on his land: corn, peanuts, or soybeans. The return from each crop will be determined by whether or not a new trade bill with Russia passes the Senate. The profit which the farmer will realize from each crop given the two possible results on the trade bill are shown in the following payoff table.

| | Trade Bill | |
| Crop | Pass | Fail |
| --- | --- | --- |
| Corn | $35,000 | $ 8,000 |
| Peanuts | 18,000 | 12,000 |
| Soybeans | 22,000 | 20,000 |

Determine the best crop to plant using:

(a) The maximax criterion

(b) The maximin criterion

(c) The minimax regret criterion

(d) The Hurwicz criterion ($\alpha = 0.3$)

(e) The equal likelihood criterion

7. A company must decide which of three products to make next year in order to plan and order proper materials. The cost per unit of producing each product will be determined by whether or not a new union labor contract passes or fails. The cost per unit for each product given both contract results are given in the following payoff table.

| | Contract Outcome | |
| Product | Pass | Fail |
| --- | --- | --- |
| 1 | $7.50 | $6.00 |
| 2 | 4.00 | 7.00 |
| 3 | 6.50 | 3.00 |

Determine which product should be produced using:

(a) The maximax criterion

(b) The maximin criterion

8. The owner of the Columbia Construction Company must decide between contract offers to build a housing development or a shopping
center or to lease all the company's equipment to another company.
The profit that will result from each alternative is determined by
whether material costs remain stable or increase. The profit from each
alternative given the two material cost outcomes are shown in the
following payoff table.

| | Material Costs | |
|---|---|---|
| Decision | Stable | Increase |
| Houses | $ 70,000 | $30,000 |
| Shopping center | 105,000 | 20,000 |
| Lease | 40,000 | 40,000 |

Determine the best decision using the following decision criterion:
(a) Maximax
(b) Maximin
(c) Minimax regret
(d) Hurwicz ($\alpha = 0.2$)
(e) Equal likelihood

9. An investor is considering investing in stocks, real estate, or bonds
under uncertain economic conditions. The payoff table of returns for
the investor's decision situation is:

| | Economic Conditions | | |
|---|---|---|---|
| Investment | Good | Stable | Poor |
| Stocks | $ 5,000 | $ 7,000 | $3,000 |
| Real estate | −2,000 | 10,000 | 6,000 |
| Bonds | 4,000 | 4,000 | 4,000 |

Determine the best investment using the following decision criteria:
(a) Equal likelihood
(b) Maximin
(c) Maximax
(d) Hurwicz ($\alpha = 0.3$)
(e) Minimax regret

10. A local real estate investor in Orlando is considering three alternative
investments: a motel, a theater, or a restaurant. The motel and restaurant will be adversely or favorably affected by the availability of
gasoline and the number of tourists, while the theater will be relatively
stable under any conditions. The following payoff table shows the profit
(or losses) resulting from each investment.

| Investment | Gasoline Availability | | |
|---|---|---|---|
| | Shortage | Stable | Surplus |
| Motel | −$8,000 | $15,000 | $20,000 |
| Restaurant | 2,000 | 8,000 | 6,000 |
| Theater | 6,000 | 6,000 | 5,000 |

Determine the best investment using the following decision criteria.
  (a) Maximax
  (b) Maximin
  (c) Minimax regret
  (d) Hurwicz ($\alpha = 0.4$)
  (e) Equal likelihood

11. A manufacturer is considering several capital investments. The manufacturer can either expand the physical plant, maintain the present size, or sell part of the physical plant. The success of each decision depends on the future demand for the manufacturer's product. The profit (or loss) to be realized for each decision is given in the following payoff table.

| Decision | Product Demand | | |
|---|---|---|---|
| | Increase | Stable | Decrease |
| Expand | $ 20,000 | $ 4,000 | −$10,000 |
| Status quo | 11,000 | 8,000 | −2,000 |
| Sell | −5,000 | −2,000 | 15,000 |

Determine the best decision for the manufacturer using any decision criterion you like; however, explain why you preferred the decision criterion you selected.

12. An investor is considering the purchase of some municipal bonds. The return will be determined by future economic conditions. The return under each condition and the associated probabilities are:

| Economic Conditions | | |
|---|---|---|
| Good .20 | Fair .70 | Poor .10 |
| $10,000 | $20,000 | −$7,000 |

Compute the expected value of the investment.

13. A machine shop owner is attempting to decide whether to purchase a new drill press, a lathe, or a grinder. The return from each will be determined by the success the owner has in getting a government

military contract. The profit (or loss) from each purchase and associated probabilities under each contract outcome are shown in the following payoff table.

| Purchase | Contract .40 | No Contract .60 |
|---|---|---|
| Drill press | $40,000 | −$8,000 |
| Lathe | 20,000 | 4,000 |
| Grinder | 12,000 | 10,000 |

Compute the expected value for each alternative purchase and select the best.

14. A concessions manager at the Tech vs. A & M football game is attempting to decide whether to have the vendors sell sun visors or umbrellas. There is a 30% chance of rain, 15% chance of overcast skies, and a 55% chance of sunshine according to the weather forecast in College Junction, where the game is to be held. The manager estimates the following profits will result from each decision given each set of weather conditions.

| | Weather Conditions | | |
|---|---|---|---|
| Decision | Rain .30 | Overcast .15 | Sunshine .55 |
| Sun Visors | −$500 | −$200 | $1,500 |
| Umbrellas | $2,000 | 0 | −$900 |

(a) Compute the expected value for each decision and select the best.
(b) Develop the opportunity loss table and compute the expected opportunity loss for each decision.

15. Given the following payoff table for three alternative investments (A, B, and C) and three states of the economy:

| | Economic Conditions | | |
|---|---|---|---|
| Decision | 1 0.3 | 2 0.5 | 3 0.2 |
| A | $1,000 | $2,000 | $500 |
| B | 800 | 1,200 | 900 |
| C | 700 | 700 | 700 |

(a) Compute the expected value for each decision and select the best one.
(b) Develop the opportunity loss table and compute the expected opportunity loss for each decision.
(c) Determine the expected value of perfect information (EVPI).

16. The Miramar Company is going to introduce one of three possible new products: a widget, a hummer, or a nimnot. The market conditions (favorable, stable, or unfavorable) will determine the profit (or loss) the company will receive as shown in the following payoff table.

| Product | Market Conditions | | |
|---|---|---|---|
| | Favorable<br>0.2 | Stable<br>0.7 | Unfavorable<br>0.1 |
| Widget | $120,000 | $70,000 | −$30,000 |
| Hummer | 60,000 | 40,000 | 20,000 |
| Nimnot | 35,000 | 30,000 | 30,000 |

(a) Compute the expected value for each decision and select the best one.
(b) Develop the opportunity loss table and compute the expected opportunity loss for each product.
(c) Determine how much the firm would be willing to pay to a market research firm to gain better information about future market conditions.

17. The financial success of the Downhill Ski Resort in the Blue Ridge Mountains is dependent upon the amount of snowfall during the winter months. If the snowfall averages more than 40 inches the resort will be successful; if the snowfall is between 20 and 40 inches a moderate financial return will be realized; and if snowfall averages less than 20 inches a financial loss will result. The financial return given each level of snowfall is:

| Snowfall | | |
|---|---|---|
| >40 inches<br>0.4 | 20 to 40 inches<br>0.2 | <20 inches<br>0.4 |
| $120,000 | 40,000 | −40,000 |

A large hotel chain has offered to lease the resort for the winter for $40,000. Compute the expected value to determine whether the resort should operate or lease. Explain your answer.

18. An investor must decide between two alternative investments, stocks and bonds. The return for each investment given two future economic conditions are given in the following payoff table.

| Investment | Economic Conditions | |
| | Good | Bad |
| --- | --- | --- |
| Stocks | $10,000 | −$4,000 |
| Bonds | 7,000 | 2,000 |

What probability for each economic condition would have to exist before the investor would be indifferent between stocks and bonds?

19. Fenton and Farrah Friendly, husband and wife car dealers, are going to open a new dealership. They have offers from a foreign compact car company, an American producer of large full-sized cars, and a truck company. The success of each type of dealership depends on how much gasoline will be available during the next few years. The profit from each type of dealership given the availabilities of gas are shown in the following payoff table.

| Dealership | Gasoline Availability | |
| | Shortage 0.6 | Surplus 0.4 |
| --- | --- | --- |
| Compact cars | $ 300,000 | $150,000 |
| Full-sized cars | −100,000 | 600,000 |
| Trucks | 120,000 | 170,000 |

Determine which type of dealership the couple should purchase.

20. The Blitzkrieg Banking House in Berlin speculates in the money market, and the status of the American dollar in trading determines the return from investments in other currencies. The banking house will invest in either the dollar, yen, or mark, and the return from each is shown in the following payoff table.

| Currency | Value of the Dollar | | |
| | Increases .30 | Stable .50 | Decline .20 |
| --- | --- | --- | --- |
| Dollar | $210,000 | 0 | $−170,000 |
| Yen | −10,000 | 20,000 | 80,000 |
| Mark | −40,000 | 35,000 | 150,000 |

Determine the best currency to invest in and the expected value of perfect information.

21. The Steak and Chop Butcher Shop purchases steak from a local meat packing house. The meat is purchased on Monday at a price of $2.00 per pound and the shop sells the steak for $3.00 per pound. Any steak left over at the end of the week is sold to a local zoo for $0.50 per pound. The possible demands for steak and the probability of each are as follows:

| Demand (lbs.) | Probability |
|---|---|
| 20 | .10 |
| 21 | .20 |
| 22 | .30 |
| 23 | .30 |
| 24 | .10 |
| | 1.00 |

The shop must decide how much steak to order in a week. Construct a payoff table for this decision situation and determine the amount of steak that should be ordered using expected value.

22. The Loebuck Grocery must decide how many cases of milk to stock each week in order to meet demand. The probability distribution of demand during a week is:

| Demand (cases) | Probability |
|---|---|
| 15 | .20 |
| 16 | .25 |
| 17 | .40 |
| 18 | .15 |
| | 1.00 |

Each case costs the grocer $10 and sells for $12. Unsold cases are sold to a local farmer (who mixes it with feed for livestock) for $2 per case. If a shortage exists, the grocer considers the ill will and lost profit cost to be $4 per case. The grocer must decide how many cases to order each week.
(a) Construct the payoff table for this decision situation.
(b) Compute the expected value of each alternative amount stocked and select the best decision.
(c) Construct the opportunity loss table and determine the best decision.
(d) Compute the expected value of perfect information.

23. Construct a decision tree for the decision situation described in problem 15 and indicate the best decision.

24. Construct a decision tree for the decision situation described in problem 19 and indicate the best decision.

25. Given the following sequential decision tree determine the optimal investment between A and B.

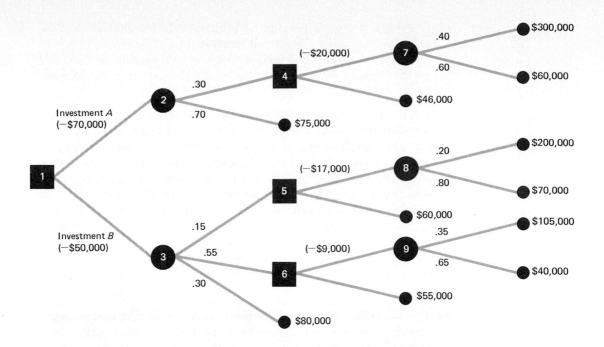

26. The Americo Oil Company is considering making a bid for a shale oil development contract to be awarded by the federal government. The company has decided to bid $110 million. The company estimates that it has a 60% chance of winning the contract at this bid. If the firm wins the contract, there are three alternative methods for getting the oil from the shale. It can develop a new method for oil extraction, use an existing (inefficient) process, or subcontract the processing out to a number of smaller companies (once the shale has been excavated). It will cost $45 million to develop and operate a new process. The present method will cost $20 million, and it will cost $9 million to distribute the shale to subcontractors. The results from these alternatives are given as follows:

**Develop new process**

| Outcomes: | | Probability | Profit ($1,000,000s) |
|---|---|---|---|
| | Success | .30 | $600 |
| | Moderate | .60 | 300 |
| | Failure | .10 | −100 |

**Use present process**

| Outcomes: | | Probability | Profit ($1,000,000s) |
|---|---|---|---|
| | Success | .50 | $300 |
| | Moderate | .30 | 200 |
| | Failure | .20 | −40 |

| **Subcontract** | | Probability | Profit ($1,000,000s) |
|---|---|---|---|
| | Moderate | 1.00 | $250 |

The cost of preparing the contract proposal is $2,000,000. If the company does not make a bid it will invest in an alternative venture with a guaranteed profit of $30 million. Construct a sequential decision tree for this decision situation and determine if the company should make a bid.

27. The machine shop owner in problem 13 is considering hiring a military consultant to ascertain if the shop will get the government contract or not. The consultant is a former military officer who uses various personal contacts to find out such information. By talking to other shop owners who have hired the consultant the owner has estimated there is a .70 probability that, given the contract is awarded to the shop, the consultant would give the owner a favorable report, and a .80 probability that the consultant would present an unfavorable report given that the contract is not awarded. Using decision tree analysis determine the decision strategy the owner should follow, the expected value of this strategy, and the maximum fee the owner should pay the consultant.

28. The Miramar Company in problem 16 is considering contracting a market research firm to do a survey to determine future market conditions. The results of the survey will indicate either positive or negative market conditions. There is a .60 probability that a positive report will result given that favorable conditions occur, a .30 probability of a positive report given stable conditions, and a .10 probability of a positive report given unfavorable conditions. There is a .90 probability that a negative report will result given that unfavorable conditions occur, a .70 probability given that stable conditions occur, and a .40 probability given that favorable conditions occur. Using decision tree analysis *and* posterior probability tables determine the decision strategy the company should follow, the expected value of the strategy, and the maximum amount the company should pay the market research firm for the survey results.

29. The Fentons in problem 19 are considering hiring a petroleum analyst to determine the future availability of gasoline. The analyst will report that either a shortage or surplus will occur. The probability that the analyst will indicate a shortage given that a shortage actually occurs is .90, while there is a .70 probability that the analyst will indicate a surplus given that a surplus actually occurs. Determine the decision strategy the Fentons should follow, the expected value of this strategy, and the maximum amount the Fentons should pay for the analyst's services.

30. Compute the efficiency of sample information for the Fenton car dealership in problem 29.

31. A young married couple has $5,000 to invest in either savings bonds or a real estate deal. The expected return on each investment given good and bad economic conditions are given in the following payoff table.

| | Economic Conditions | |
| | Good 0.6 | Bad 0.4 |
|---|---|---|
| Investment | | |
| Savings bonds | $ 1,000 | $1,000 |
| Real estate | $10,000 | −2,000 |

The expected value of investing in savings bonds is $1,000, while the expected value of the real estate investment is $5,200. However, the couple decided to invest in savings bonds. Explain the couple's decision in terms of the utility they might associate with each investment.

32. The purchase of all types of insurance by individuals is an example of a case where utility is the decision criterion rather than expected dollar value. As such, explain the concept of utility in regards to the purchase of insurance.

33. Many types of government expenditures reflect the concept of utility. Give three examples of government expenditures and how they are related to the concept of utility.

34. Discuss the concept of utility and risk taking as it relates to a gambler who wagers $10,000 on a 50 to 1 long shot in the Kentucky Derby.

# 12
Game Theory

In the previous chapter on decision analysis we discussed methods to aid the *individual* decision maker in making decisions. All of the decision situations analyzed in chapter 11 contained only a single decision maker. There were no *competitors* whose decisions might alter the decision maker's analysis of the decision situation. However, many situations do, in fact, contain several decision makers who compete with each other to receive the best outcome. These types of competitive decision-making situations are the subject of *game theory*. Although the topic of game theory encompasses a different type of decision situation than decision analysis, many of the fundamental principles and techniques of decision making are the same. Thus, game theory is, in effect, an extension of decision analysis rather than an entirely new topic area.

*Competitive decision makers*

As the name indicates, game theory relates to situations that everyone is familiar with that has played children or adult "games," such as card games or board games. In these games the conflicting participants often develop plans of action to win. Game theory encompasses similar situations where the competitive decision makers also develop plans of action in order to win. In addition, game theory consists of several mathematical techniques to aid the decision maker in selecting the plan of action that will result in the best outcome. In this chapter, we will discuss some of these techniques.

## Types of Game Situations

Competitive game situations can be subdivided into several categories. One classification is based on the number of competitive decision makers, called *players,* involved in the game. If the game situation consists of two players, it is referred to as a *two-person game*. Alternatively if more than two players exist, the game situation is known as an *n-person game*.

*Decision makers as game players*

*A two-person game*

Games are also classified according to the outcome of the game in terms of each player's gains and losses. If the sum of the players' gains and losses equals zero, the game is referred to as a *zero-sum game*. In a two-person game, one player's gains represents another's losses. For example, if one player gains $100, then the other player loses that same $100; the two values sum to *zero* (i.e., $+$100$ and $-$100$). Alternatively, if the sum of the player's gains and losses does not equal zero, it is known as a *non-zero-sum game*.

*A zero-sum game*

The *two-person, zero-sum game* is the game situation most frequently used to demonstrate the principles of game theory because it is the simplest mathematically. As such, we will confine our discussion of game theory to this form of game situation. The n-person game situation is quite complex, which not only prohibits us from demonstrating it, but also inhibits its actual application.

## The Two-Person, Zero-Sum Game

Examples of competitive situations that can be organized into two-person, zero-sum games include the following: (1) a union negotiating a new contract with management; (2) two armies participating in a war game; (3) two politicians in conflict over a proposed legislative bill, one attempting to secure its passage, the other attempting to defeat it; (4) a retail firm trying to increase its market share with a new product and a competitor attempting to minimize the firm's gains; and (5) a contractor negotiating with a government agent for a contract on a project.

In order to demonstrate a two-person, zero-sum game, we will use an example consisting of a professional athlete, Biff Rhino, who, with an agent, Jim Fence, is renegotiating Biff's contract with the Texas Buffaloes' general manager, Harry Sligo. The various outcomes of this game situation can be organized into a payoff table similar to the payoff tables used in decision

analysis in chapter 11. The payoff table for this example is shown in table 12.1.

**Table 12.1** Payoff Table for Two-Person, Zero-Sum Game

| Athlete/Agent Strategies | General Manager Strategies | | |
|---|---|---|---|
| | A | B | C |
| 1 | $50,000 | 35,000 | 30,000 |
| 2 | 60,000 | 40,000 | 20,000 |

The payoff table for a two-person game is organized so that the player who is maximizing the outcome of the game is on the left and the player who is minimizing the outcome is on the top. In table 12.1, the athlete and agent are attempting to maximize the athlete's contract, while the general manager hopes to minimize the athlete's contract. In a sense, the athlete is an offensive player in the game, while the general manager is a defensive player. In game theory it is assumed that the payoff table is known to both the offensive and defensive players, which is often an unrealistic assumption in real world situations, thus restricting the actual applications of this technique.

A strategy is a plan of action to be followed by a player. Each player in a game has two or more *strategies,* only one of which is selected by each player for each particular playing of a game. In table 12.1, the athlete and agent have two available strategies, 1 and 2, while the general manager has three strategies, *A, B,* and *C.* The values in the table are the payoffs or outcomes associated with each player's strategies.

For our example, the athlete has two strategies that correspond to different types of contracts, and the threat of a holdout and/or becoming a free agent. The general manager's strategies relate to alternative contract proposals that include such items as length of contract, residual payments, no cut/no trade clauses, and off-season promotional work. The outcomes are in terms of dollar value. If the athlete selects strategy 2 and the general manager selects strategy *C,* the outcome is a $20,000 gain for the athlete and a $20,000 loss for the general manager. This results in a "zero-sum" for the game (i.e., $+$20,000 $-$ 20,000 $=$ 0). The amount, $20,000, is known as the *value of the game.*

The purpose of the game for each player is to select the strategy that will result in the best possible payoff or outcome regardless of what the player's opponent does. The best strategy for each player is known as the *optimal strategy.* Next we will discuss the methods for determining the strategies of the game.

*Game strategies*

*Value of the game*

*Developing an optimal strategy*

## A Pure Strategy

When each player in the game adopts a single strategy as their optimal strategy, then a *pure strategy* game exists. In a pure strategy game the value of the game is the same for both the offensive player and the defensive player. Alternatively, a *mixed strategy* game is one in which the players would adopt a mixture of strategies if the game is played many times.

A pure strategy game can be solved according to the *minimax decision criterion.* According to this principle, each player plays the game in order to minimize the maximum possible losses. The offensive player will select the strategy that has the largest of the minimum payoffs (called the *maximin* strategy), and the defensive player will select the strategy that has the smallest of the maximum payoffs (called the *minimax* strategy). For our example involving the athlete's contract negotiation process, the athlete will select the maximin strategy between strategy 1 and 2, and the general manager will select the minimax strategy between strategies *A, B,* and *C.* We will first determine the athlete's decision, although in game theory the decisions are actually made *simultaneously.*

In order to determine the maximin strategy, the athlete first selects the minimum payoff for the strategies 1 and 2 as shown in table 12.2. The maximum of these minimum values indicates the optimal strategy and value of the game for the athlete.

*Each player adopts a single strategy*

*A mixed strategy*

*The minimax decision criterion*

*The offensive player strategy*

*The defensive player strategy*

*Decisions are made simultaneously*

*A pure strategy example*

**Table 12.2** Payoff Table with Maximin Strategy

| Athlete / Agent Strategies | General Manager Strategies | | |
|---|---|---|---|
| | *A* | *B* | *C* |
| 1 | $50,000 | 35,000 | 30,000 ← Maximum of minimum payoffs |
| 2 | | 60,000 | 40,000 | 20,000 |

*The athlete's strategy*

The value, $30,000, is the maximum of the minimum values for each of the athlete's strategies. Thus, the optimal strategy for the athlete is strategy 1. The logic behind this decision can be explained as follows. If the athlete selects strategy 1, the general manager could be expected to select strategy *C*, which would minimize the possible loss (i.e., a $30,000 contract is better than a $50,000 or $35,000 contract *for the manager*). Alternatively, if the athlete selected strategy 2, the general manager could be expected to select strategy *C* for the same reason (i.e., a $20,000 contract is better for the manager than a $60,000 or $40,000 contract). Now since the athlete has anticipated what the general manager would do for each strategy, it is realized that either a $30,000 or $20,000 contract can be obtained. As such, the athlete selects strategy 1 in order to get the larger possible contract of $30,000, given the actions of the general manager.

*The general manager's strategy*

Simultaneously, the general manager applies the minimax decision criterion to strategies *A, B,* and *C*. First, the general manager selects the maximum payoff for each strategy, *A, B,* and *C,* shown in table 12.3. The minimum of these maximum values determines the optimal strategy and value of the game for the general manager.

**Table 12.3** Payoff Table with Minimax Strategy

| Athlete / Agent Strategies | General Manager Strategies | | |
|---|---|---|---|
| | *A* | *B* | *C* |
| 1 | $50,000 | 35,000 | 30,000 ← Minimum of maximum values |
| 2 | 60,000 | 40,000 | 20,000 |

The value, $30,000, is the minimum of the maximum values for each of the general manager's strategies. Thus, the optimal strategy for the general manager is *C*. The logic of this decision is similar to that for the athlete. If the general manager selects strategy *A,* the athlete could be expected to select strategy 2 with a payoff of $60,000 (i.e., the athlete will choose the best contract between $50,000 and $60,000). If the general manager selects strategy *B,* then the athlete could be expected to select strategy 2 for a payoff of $40,000. Finally, if the general manager selects strategy *C,* then the athlete could be expected to select strategy 1 for a payoff of $30,000. Since the general manager has anticipated what the athlete could do for each strategy, it is realized that either a $60,000, $40,000, or $30,000 contract could possibly be awarded. Thus, the general manager selects strategy C, which will result in the minimum contract of $30,000. In general, the general manager considers the worst outcome that could result if a particular strategy is followed. Under the minimax criterion the general manager will select the strategy that insures the minimum of the maximum amounts that could be lost.

## Dominant Strategies

We could have reduced the choices of the general manager by noticing that strategy C *dominates* strategies A and B. Dominance occurs when all the payoffs for one strategy are better than the corresponding payoffs for another strategy. In table 12.3 the values $30,000 and $20,000 are both lower than the corresponding payoffs of $50,000 and $60,000 for strategy A and the corresponding payoffs of $35,000 and $40,000 for strategy B. Since strategy C dominates A and B, these two latter strategies can be eliminated from consideration altogether, as shown in table 12.4. Thus, strategy C could have been selected automatically without applying the minimax criterion. As such, it is always the most efficient approach to first examine the payoff table for dominance in order to possibly reduce its size.

*All payoffs for one strategy are better than all payoffs for an alternative strategy*

*Dominated strategies can be eliminated*

**Table 12.4** Payoff Table with Dominated Strategies Eliminated

| Athlete/Agent Strategies | General Manager Strategies | | |
| | A | B | C |
| --- | --- | --- | --- |
| 1 | $50,000 | 35,000 | 30,000 |
| 2 | 60,000 | 40,000 | 20,000 |

The fact that the optimal strategy for each player in this game resulted in the *same payoff* game value of $30,000 is what classifies it as a pure strategy game. In other words, strategy 1 is optimal for the athlete, strategy C is optimal for the general manager, and a contract for $30,000 will be awarded to the athlete. Since the outcome of $30,000 results from a pure strategy, it is referred to as an *equilibrium point* (or sometimes as a *saddle point*). A point of equilibrium is a value that is simultaneously the *minimum of a row* and a *maximum of a column,* as is the payoff of $30,000 in table 12.3.

*An equilibrium point*

It is important to realize that the minimax criterion results in the optimal strategy for each player as long as each player uses this criterion. If one of the players does not use this criterion, the solution will not be optimal. If we assume, however, that both players are logical and rational, then this criterion will be employed.

*The minimax criterion will result in the optimal strategies only if both players use it*

If an equilibrium point exists, it makes the determination of optimal strategies relatively easy, as no complex mathematical calculations are necessary. However, as we mentioned earlier, if a game does not consist of a pure strategy, then a mixed strategy exists. As such, we will discuss a mixed strategy game next.

## A Mixed Strategy

*Optimal strategy decisions that do not result in an equilibrium point*

*A mixed strategy example*

A mixed strategy occurs when each player selects an optimal strategy and they *do not result in an equilibrium point* (i.e., the same outcome) when the maximin and minimax decision criteria are applied.

In order to demonstrate a mixed strategy game, we will employ the following example. The Coloroid Camera Company (which we will refer to as Company I) is going to introduce a new instant camera into its product line, and it hopes to capture as large an increase in its market share as possible. Alternatively, the Camco Camera Company (which we will refer to as Company II) hopes to minimize Coloroid's market share increase. Coloroid and Camco dominate the camera market and any gain in market share for Coloroid will result in a subsequent identical loss in market share for Camco. The strategies for each company are based on their promotional campaigns, packaging, and cosmetic differences of the products. The payoff table, which includes the strategies and outcomes for each company (I = Coloroid and II = Camco) are shown in table 12.5.

**Table 12.5** Payoff Table for Camera Companies

| Camera Company I Strategies | Camera Company II Strategies | | |
|---|---|---|---|
| | A | B | C |
| 1 | 9 | 7 | 2 |
| 2 | 11 | 8 | 4 |
| 3 | 4 | 1 | 7 |

The values in table 12.5 are the *percentage* increases or decreases in market share for Company I.

*Eliminating dominated strategies*

The first item to check in the payoff table is for the existence of any dominant strategies. Doing so, we find that strategy 2 dominates strategy 1, and strategy *B* dominates strategy *A*. As such, strategies 1 and *A* can be eliminated from the payoff table, as shown in table 12.6.

**Table 12.6** Payoff Table with Strategies 1 and A Eliminated

| Company I Strategies | Company II Strategies | |
|---|---|---|
| | B | C |
| 2 | 8 | 4 |
| 3 | 1 | 7 |

Next, we apply the maximin decision criterion to the strategies for Company I, as shown in table 12.7. The minimum value for strategy 2 is 4%, while the minimum value for strategy 3 is 1%. The maximum of these two minimum values is 4%, thus strategy 2 is optimal for Company I.

*The maximin criterion for the offensive player*

**Table 12.7** Payoff Table with Maximin Criterion

| Company I Strategies | Company II Strategies | |
|---|---|---|
| | *B* | *C* |
| 2 | 8 | 4 ← Maximum of the minimum values |
| 3 | 1 | 7 |

Now the minimax decision criterion is applied to the strategies for Company II in table 12.8. The maximum value for strategy *B* is 8%, and the maximum value for strategy *C* is 7%. Of these two maximum values, 7% is the minimum, thus the optimal strategy for Company II is *C*.

*The minimax criterion for the defensive player*

**Table 12.8** Payoff Table with Minimax Criterion

| Company I Strategies | Company II Strategies | |
|---|---|---|
| | *B* | *C* |
| 2 | ⑧ | 4 |
| 3 | 1 | ⑦ ← Minimum of maximum values |

Table 12.9 combines the results of the application of the maximin and minimax criteria by the companies.

*The combined strategies*

**Table 12.9** Company I and II Combined Strategies

| Company I Strategies | Company II Strategies | |
|---|---|---|
| | *B* | *C* |
| 2 | 8 | 4 |
| 3 | 1 | ⑦ |

From table 12.9 we can see that the strategies selected by the companies do not result in an equilibrium point. As such, this is not a pure strategy game. In fact, this condition will not result in any strategy for either firm. Company I maximizes its market share percentage increase by selecting strategy 2. Company II selects strategy $C$ in order to minimize Company I's market share. However, as soon as Company I notices that Company II is using strategy $C$, it would switch to strategy 3 to increase its market share to 7%. This move would not go unnoticed by Company II, and they would immediately switch to strategy $B$ to reduce I's market share to 1%. This action by Company II would cause Company I to immediately switch to strategy 2 to maximize its market share increase to 8%. Given the action of Company I, Company II would switch to strategy $C$ to minimize Company I's market share increase to 4%. Now you will notice that the two companies are right back where they started from. They have completed a closed loop, as shown in table 12.10, which could continue indefinitely if the two companies persisted.

*Switching strategies*

*A closed loop*

**Table 12.10** Payoff Table with Closed Loop

| Company I Strategies | Company II Strategies | |
|---|---|---|
| | B | C |
| 2 | 8 | 4 |
| 3 | 1 | 7 |

*Methods for solving mixed strategy games*

There are several methods available for solving mixed strategy games, and we will present two of them, both of which are analytical—*the expected gain and loss method* and *linear programming*.

### Expected Gain and Loss Method

*Expected gains of one player equal the expected losses of the other*

The *expected gain and loss method* is based on the principle that in a mixed strategy game, a plan of strategies can be developed by each player so that the *expected gain* of the maximizing player or the *expected loss* of the minimizing player will be the same, regardless of what their opponent does. In other words, a player develops a plan of mixed strategies that will be employed regardless of what the opposing player will do (i.e., the player is indifferent to the opponent's actions). As might be expected from its name, this method is based on the concept of expected values.

*Computing the expected gain for Company I*

We will use our mixed strategy game for the two camera companies described in the previous section to demonstrate this method. First, we will compute the *expected gain* for Company I. Company I arbitrarily assumes that Company II will select strategy $B$. Given this condition, there is a probability of $p$ that Company I will select strategy 2 and a probability of $1 - p$ that Company I will select strategy 3. Thus, if Company II selects $B$, the expected gain for Company I is

*The expected gain if Company II selects strategy B*

$$8p + 1(1 - p) = 1 + 7p$$

Next, Company I assumes that Company II will select strategy $C$. Given strategy $C$, there is a probability of $p$ that Company I will select strategy 2 and a probability of $1 - p$ that Company I will select strategy 3. Thus, the expected gain given strategy $C$ is

*The expected gain if Company II selects strategy C*

$$4p + 7(1 - p) = 7 - 3p$$

Previously we noted that this method was based on the idea that Company I would develop a plan that would result in the same expected gain, regardless of the strategy that Company II selected. Thus, if Company I is indifferent to whether Company II selects strategy $B$ or $C$, we can simply equate the expected gain from each of these strategies:

*Equating expected gains*

$$1 + 7p = 7 - 3p$$

and

$$10p = 6$$
$$p = \frac{6}{10} = .60$$

Recall that $p$ is the probability of using strategy 2, or the *percentage of time* strategy 2 would be employed. Thus, Company I's plan is to use strategy 2 for 60% of the time, and to use strategy 3 the remaining 40% of the time. The expected gain (i.e., market share increase for Company I) can be computed using the payoff given either strategy $B$ or $C$, since the gain will be the same regardless. Using the payoffs from strategy $B$:

*The percentage of time each strategy is used by Company I*

*The expected gain for Company I*

$$EG(\text{Company I}) = .6(8) + .4(1)$$
$$= 5.2\%, \text{ market share increase}$$

In order to check this result we will compute the expected gain if strategy $C$ was used by Company II.

$$EG(\text{Company I}) = .6(4) + .4(7)$$
$$= 5.2\%, \text{ market share increase}$$

Now we must repeat this process for *Company II* to develop their mixed strategy, except that what was Company I's expected *gain* is now Company II's expected *loss*. First, we assume that Company I will select strategy 2. Thus, Company II will employ strategy $B$ $p$ percent of the time and $C$ $1 - p$ percent of the time. The expected *loss* given strategy 2 is

*Computing the expected loss for Company II*

*The expected loss if Company I selects strategy 2*

$$8p + 4(1 - p) = 4 + 4p$$

Next, we compute the expected loss for Company II given that Company I selects strategy 3,

*The expected loss if Company I selects strategy 3*

$$1p + 7(1 - p) = 7 - 6p$$

Equating these two expected losses for strategies 2 and 3 will result in values for $p$ and $1 - p$:

$$4 + 4p = 7 - 6p$$
$$10p = 3$$
$$p = \frac{3}{10} = .30$$

and

$$1 - p = .70$$

Since $p$ is the probability of employing strategy $B$, Company II will employ strategy $B$ 30% of the time, and thus strategy $C$ will be used 70% of the time. The actual expected loss given strategy 2 (which is the same for strategy 3) is computed as:

$$EL(\text{Company II}) = .30(8) + .70(4)$$
$$= 5.2\%, \text{ market share loss}$$

Let us summarize the mixed strategies for each company. For Company I:

Strategy 2: 60% of the time
Strategy 3: 40% of the time

For Company II:

Strategy $B$: 30% of the time
Strategy $C$: 70% of the time

The expected gain for Company I is a 5.2% increase in market share, while the expected loss for Company II is also a 5.2% market share. Thus, the mixed strategies for each company has resulted in an equilibrium point such that a 5.2% *expected* gain for Company I results in a simultaneous 5.2% *expected* loss for Company II.

It is also interesting to note that each company has improved its outcome over its original selections using the maximin and minimax strategies. Recall from table 12.9 that the payoff for Company I was only a 4% increase in market share, while by using the mixed strategy their expected gain is 5.2%. The outcome for Company II from the minimax strategy was a 7% loss, however, when using the mixed strategies the loss is only 5.2%. Thus, each company is in a better situation by using the mixed strategy approach.

This approach assumes that the game is repetitive and will be played over a period of time so that a strategy can be employed a certain percentage of that time. For our example, it can be logically assumed that the marketing of the new camera by Company I will require a lengthy time frame. Thus, each company could employ its mixed strategy.

## Linear Programming

The determination of mixed strategies using the expected gain (loss) method presented in the previous section can be more difficult as the size of the game increases beyond two strategies per player. In other words, we simply cannot multiply one outcome under a strategy by $p$ and the other by $1 - p$ if there are more than two outcomes per strategy. Given games of larger magnitude, *linear programming* is an alternative method for determining the mixed strategy probabilities and the value of the game. However, the formulation of the linear programming model for a game is slightly more complex than the models presented in chapters 2 through 5, and, as such, must be described in detail.

*The expected gain and loss method is limited to two strategies per player*

*Linear programming is used when more than two strategies exist*

The best way to present the linear programming approach to games is by example, thus we will use our camera companies example described in the previous section. The reduced payoff table for this game situation first shown in table 12.6 is repeated in table 12.11. Although this payoff table contains only two strategies per player, it will still serve to demonstrate how linear programming can be applied to games of any size. In addition, by using this example, which we have already analyzed using the expected gain (loss) method, we have the advantage of knowing the solution and understanding the logic in gaining that solution in advance.

*A linear programming example for a mixed strategy game*

**Table 12.11** Payoff Table for Camera Companies Example

| Company I Strategies | Company II Strategies | |
|---|---|---|
| | B | C |
| 2 | 8 | 4 |
| 3 | 1 | 7 |

This payoff table contains enough information for two linear programming models; one for Company I and one for Company II. The purpose of each model is to determine the mixed strategy for the respective companies, which you will recall are in the form of probabilities of occurrence for each strategy. Thus, for the Company I model, the decision variables can be defined as the probabilities of the occurrence of strategies 2 and 3:

*Developing a model for Company I*

*Decision variables*

$p_1$ = probability of the occurrence of strategy 2
$p_2$ = probability of the occurrence of strategy 3

Given these decision variables, we can now formulate several constraints based on the values of the outcomes in table 12.11. Recall that when we computed the expected gain for Company I previously, we multiplied each outcome for strategy 2 and 3 by $p$ and $1 - p$. In this case since $p_1$ and $p_2$ are synonymous with $p$ and $1 - p$, we can formulate a constraint for each strategy as follows:

*Model constraints*

$$8p_1 + 1p_2 \geq v$$
$$4p_1 + 7p_2 \geq v$$

*≥ inequalities*

In these two constraints the symbol $v$ represents the *value of the game*. Recall that the value of the game is the average gain for the offensive player and the identical average loss for the defensive player. We have used a $\geq$ inequality for these constraints because Company I is the maximizing (or offensive) player. In other words, Company I wants to maximize its expected gain and receive as high a value of $v$ as possible, if Company II selects a less than optimal strategy.

We can also develop one additional constraint to reflect the fact that the sum of the probabilities equals 1.0:

$$p_1 + p_2 = 1.0$$

*Simplifying the model constraints*

The model constraints in their present form can be simplified (for solution purposes) by dividing each coefficient in the constraints and the "quantity" values by $v$, as follows:

$$\frac{8p_1}{v} + \frac{1p_2}{v} \geq 1$$

$$\frac{4p_1}{v} + \frac{7p_2}{v} \geq 1$$

$$\frac{p_1}{v} + \frac{p_2}{v} = \frac{1}{v}$$

*Redefining the decision variables*

In order to further simplify the model and eliminate the $v$ symbols, we can redefine the model decision variables:

$$x_1 = \frac{p_1}{v}$$

$$x_2 = \frac{p_2}{v}$$

Substituting these new variables into the model constraints results in the following constraints.

$$8x_1 + 1x_2 \geq 1$$
$$4x_1 + 7x_2 \geq 1$$
$$x_1 + x_2 = 1/v$$

*Developing the objective function*

Now recall that this model reflects the actions of Company I, the maximizing player. As such, the *objective* of Company I is to *maximize the value of the game, $v$*. However, if we maximize $v$, we also minimize $1/v$. For example, if $v = 10$, then $1/v = 1/10$. If $v$ is increased to 100 (i.e., it is maximized), then $1/v = 1/100$ (i.e., it is minimized). Thus, the objective of Company I is to

maximize $Z = v$

We can also say

minimize $Z = 1/v$

Since $x_1 + x_2 = 1/v$, this objective function is equivalent to

minimize $Z = x_1 + x_2$

We can now summarize the linear programming model for Company I as

*The linear programming model for Company I*

minimize $Z = x_1 + x_2$
subject to
$$8x_1 + 1x_2 \geq 1$$
$$4x_1 + 7x_2 \geq 1$$
$$x_1, x_2 \geq 0$$

The solution of this model will yield values for $x_1$ and $x_2$, which must be converted back to their original form,

$$x_1 = \frac{p_1}{v}$$

$$x_2 = \frac{p_2}{v}$$

in order to determine the mixed strategy for Company I.

A similar model can be developed for the mixed strategy of Company II in the same way as the above model for Company I. The decision variables are defined as

*Developing a model for Company II*

$q_1$ = probability of the occurrence of strategy $B$
$q_2$ = probability of the occurrence of strategy $C$

*Decision variables*

The model constraints from table 12.11 are

*Model constraints*

$$8q_1 + 4q_2 \leq v$$
$$1q_1 + 7q_2 \leq v$$
$$q_1 + q_2 = 1.0$$

These constraints are $\leq$ inequalities, since Company II is the minimizing (or defensive player) and desires to achieve a value of the game less than $v$ if possible.

*$\leq$ inequalities*

As before, if we divide these constraints by $v$, we can simplify them:

*Simplifying the model constraints*

$$\frac{8q_1}{v} + \frac{4q_2}{v} \leq 1$$

$$\frac{1q_1}{v} + \frac{7q_2}{v} \leq 1$$

$$\frac{q_1}{v} + \frac{q_2}{v} = \frac{1}{v}$$

Next we redefine the model variables:

*Defining the objective function*

$$y_1 = \frac{q_1}{v}$$

$$y_2 = \frac{q_2}{v}$$

such that the model constraints are now

$$8y_1 + 4y_2 \leq 1$$
$$1y_1 + 7y_2 \leq 1$$
$$y_1 + y_2 = \frac{1}{v}$$

*Developing the objective function*

Since the objective of Company II is to minimize the value of the game, $v$, we can also maximize $1/v$. Thus, the objective function can be defined as

$$\text{maximize } Z = \frac{1}{v}$$

Since $1/v = y_1 + y_2$, the objective function can also be defined as

$$\text{maximize } Z = y_1 + y_2$$

*Summary of the Company I and Company II models*

The linear programming model for Company II is summarized below, along with the Company I model.

**Company I**
minimize $Z = x_1 + x_2$
subject to
$$8x_1 + 1x_2 \geq 1$$
$$4x_1 + 7x_2 \geq 1$$
$$x_1, x_2 \geq 0$$

**Company II**
maximize $Z = y_1 + y_2$
subject to
$$8y_1 + 4y_2 \leq 1$$
$$1y_1 + 7y_2 \leq 1$$
$$y_1, y_2 \geq 0$$

*Primal and dual models*

Inspecting each of these models closely, we can see that the Company I model is the *primal* form of the linear programming model and the Company II model is the *dual* form. Since we noted in chapter 6, "Post-optimality Analysis," that the solution to the primal provided complete information about the dual solution, it is necessary that only one of the models be solved in order to determine the mixed strategy for each company.

*The optimal simplex solution of the Company I model*

Solving the Company I model by the simplex method results in the optimal tableau shown in table 12.12.

**Table 12.12** Simplex Solution of the Company I Model

| $c_j$ | | | 1 | 1 | 0 | 0 |
|---|---|---|---|---|---|---|
| | basic variables | quantity | $x_1$ | $x_2$ | $s_1$ | $s_2$ |
| 1 | $x_1$ | 3/26 | 1 | 0 | −7/52 | 1/52 |
| 1 | $x_2$ | 2/26 | 0 | 1 | 2/26 | −2/13 |
| | $z_j$ | 5/26 | 1 | 1 | −3/52 | −7/52 |
| | $z_j - c_j$ | | 0 | 0 | −3/52 | −7/52 |

*Converting the solution into the original model form*

In order to determine the mixed strategy for Company I, we must convert the solution back to its original form. Recall that

$$\frac{p_1}{v} = x_1$$

$$\frac{p_2}{v} = x_2$$

$$\frac{1}{v} = Z$$

Since $Z = 5/26$,

$$Z = \frac{1}{v} = \frac{5}{26}$$

and

$$v = \frac{26}{5} = 5.2$$

Next, since $x_1 = 3/26$ and $x_2 = 2/26$, then

$$\frac{p_1}{v} = x_1$$

$$\frac{p_1}{26/5} = \frac{3}{26}$$

$$p_1 = .60$$

and

$$\frac{p_2}{v} = x_2$$

$$\frac{p_2}{26/5} = \frac{2}{26}$$

$$p_2 = .40$$

Thus, the mixed strategy for Company I is

*The mixed strategy for Company I*

$p_1 = .60 =$ percent of time strategy 2 is used
$p_2 = .40 =$ percent of time strategy 3 is used
$v = 5.2 =$ expected gain in percentage market share for Company I

As noted earlier, since the Company II model is the dual form, the mixed strategy for Company II can also be determined from the simplex solution of the primal shown in table 12.12. Observing the $z_j - c_j$ row, we can see that the dual solution values for $y_1$ and $y_2$ are

*The dual solution*

$$y_1 = \frac{3}{52}$$

$$y_2 = \frac{7}{52}$$

and

$$Z = \frac{5}{26}$$

*Converting the
solution into the
original model form*

Substituting these values into our original model terms will result in the mixed strategy solution. For the value of the game, $v$:

$$\frac{1}{v} = Z$$

$$v = \frac{26}{5}$$

For the values of $q_1$ and $q_2$:

$$\frac{q_1}{v} = y_1$$

$$\frac{q_1}{26/5} = \frac{3}{52}$$

$$q_1 = \frac{3}{10} = .30$$

and

$$\frac{q_2}{v} = y_2$$

$$\frac{q_2}{26/5} = \frac{7}{52}$$

$$q_2 = \frac{7}{10} = .70$$

*The mixed strategy
for Company II*

Thus, the mixed strategy for Company II is

$q_1 = .30 = $ percent of time strategy $B$ is used
$q_2 = .70 = $ percent of time strategy $C$ is used
$v = 5.2 = $ expected loss in percentage market share for
Company II

Note that both of these mixed strategies for Companies I and II are identical to those determined by the expected gain (loss) method in the previous section. Although the linear programming method seems much more laborious than the expected gain (loss) method, you must remember that the linear programming method is valuable for games of *greater magnitude than two strategies per player*. For the camera company example the expected gain (loss) method is more appropriate; however, for larger games linear programming is generally the preferred approach.

## Summary

Game theory provides a convenient framework for analyzing decision making among individuals in a competitive situation. The analysis of two-person games in this chapter provided an observation of the logic of decision

*Real-world
applications of game
theory are rare*

making among competing parties as encompassed in their determination of pure and mixed strategies. However, the incidence of application of game theory in the real world is rare.

In this chapter, the presentation of game theory was limited to two-person games. Unfortunately, there is no convenient and easy means for analyzing games with more than two competitive parties. For games with more than two players, the methods of analysis become quite complex, and thus difficult for the manager/decision maker to apply.

However, as a means for understanding the logic of decision making between competing individuals, game theory is very useful. The principles and fundamentals of game theory presented in this chapter provide valuable insight into the basics of strategic planning. As such, although one could not expect to apply game theory on a frequent basis, it does provide an understanding of the mechanics of decision making.

*Valuable as a means for understanding decision-making logic between competing individuals*

## References

Baumol, W. J. *Economic Theory and Operations Analysis*. Englewood Cliffs, N.J.: Prentice-Hall, 1961.

Dorfman, R.; Samuelson, P. A.; and Solow, R. M. *Linear Programming and Economic Analysis*. New York: McGraw-Hill, 1958.

Holloway, C. A. *Decision Making Under Uncertainty*. Englewood Cliffs, N.J.: Prentice-Hall, 1979.

Kwak, N. K. *Mathematical Programming with Business Applications*. New York: McGraw-Hill, 1973.

Luce, R. D., and Raiffa, H. *Games and Decisions*. New York: John Wiley and Sons, 1957.

Von Neumann, J., and Morgenstern, O. *Theory of Games and Economic Behavior*. Princeton, N.J.: Princeton University Press, 1944.

Williams, J. D. *The Compleat Strategyst*. Rev. ed. New York: McGraw-Hill, 1966.

## Problems

1. Given the following payoff table for two individuals competing in a game situation:

| Individual I Strategies | Individual II Strategies A | B |
|---|---|---|
| 1 | 100 | 80 |
| 2 | 60 | 70 |

(a) Determine the optimal strategey for each player.
(b) Is this a pure or mixed strategy game? Explain.

2. Given the following payoff table for two individuals competing in a game situation:

| Individual I Strategies | Individual II Strategies A | B |
|---|---|---|
| 1 | 50 | 40 |
| 2 | 30 | 60 |

Is this a pure or mixed strategy game? Explain.

3. In problems 1 and 2, do any *dominant* strategies exist? Explain.

4. The management of the Millstone Bread Company is involved in labor negotiations with the local bakers' union. The union has three alternative contracts reflecting their strategies in the labor negotiations, while the company has two contract proposals reflecting their strategies. The following payoff table shows the dollar value of each alternative contract proposal.

| Union Strategies | Management Strategies A | B |
|---|---|---|
| 1 | $200,000 | $170,000 |
| 2 | 300,000 | 220,000 |
| 3 | 160,000 | 180,000 |

(a) Do any dominant strategies exist in the payoff table?
(b) Determine the optimal pure strategy for both game players and the equilibrium point.
(c) Why is this a pure strategy game instead of mixed strategy game?

5. The Army is conducting war games in Europe. One simulated encounter is between the Blue and Red Divisions. The Blue Division is on the offensive, while the Red Division holds a defensive position. The results of the war game are measured in terms of troop losses. The following payoff table shows the troops losses on the part of the Red Division for each battle strategy available to each division.

| Blue Division Strategies | Red Division Strategies A | B | C |
|---|---|---|---|
| 1 | 1,800 | 2,000 | 1,700 |
| 2 | 2,300 | 900 | 1,600 |

Determine the optimal strategy for both divisions and the number of troop losses by the Red Division.

6. Given the following payoff table for two game players:

| Player I Strategies | Player II Strategies A | B | C |
|---|---|---|---|
| 1 | −250 | − 50 | 350 |
| 2 | 50 | 0 | 100 |
| 3 | 250 | − 100 | −350 |

(a) Determine the initial single strategy for each player.
(b) Show the closed loop that will result as the players change strategies.

7. The Baseball Players Association has voted to go on strike if a settlement is not reached with the owners within the next month. The players' representative, Melvin Mulehead, has two strategies (containing different free agent rules, pension formulas, etc.), while the owners' representative, Roy Stonewall, has three counterproposals. The financial gains in millions of dollars for each player strategy given each owner strategy are shown in the following payoff table.

| Player Strategies | Owner Strategies A | B | C |
|---|---|---|---|
| 1 | 15 | 9 | 11 |
| 2 | 7 | 20 | 12 |

(a) Determine the initial strategy for the players and owners.
(b) Is this a pure or mixed strategy game? Explain.

8. Given the following mixed strategy game for two players:

| Player I Strategies | Player II Strategies A | B |
|---|---|---|
| 1 | 8 | 15 |
| 2 | 30 | 12 |

(a) Determine the initial strategy for each player.
(b) Using the expected gain and loss method determine the mixed strategies for each player.

9. Mary Washington is the incumbent Congresswoman for a district in New Mexico and Franklin Truman is her opponent in the upcoming election. Since Truman is seeking to unseat Washington he is on the offensive, and she hopes to minimize his gains in the polls. The following payoff table shows the various percentage point gains in the polls for Truman given the various political strategies for each politician.

| Franklin Truman Strategies | Mary Washington Strategies A | B |
|---|---|---|
| 1 | 7 | 3 |
| 2 | 6 | 10 |

Determine the political strategies for each politician and the percentage gain in the polls by Franklin Truman.

10. Edgar Allan Melville is a successful novelist who is negotiating a contract for a new novel with his publisher, Potboiler Books, Inc. The novelist's various strategies encompass royalties, movie rights, advances, etc. The following payoff table shows the financial gains for the novelist from each contract strategy.

| Novelist Strategies | Publisher Strategies A | B | C |
|---|---|---|---|
| 1 | $ 80,000 | $120,000 | $ 90,000 |
| 2 | 130,000 | 90,000 | 80,000 |
| 3 | 110,000 | 140,000 | 100,000 |

(a) Does this payoff table contain any dominant strategies?
(b) Determine the strategy for the novelist and the publisher and the gains and losses for each.

11. Given the following payoff table for a mixed strategy game between two players:

| Player I Strategies | Player II Strategies A | B | C |
|---|---|---|---|
| 1 | 50 | 60 | 30 |
| 2 | 10 | 32 | 25 |
| 3 | 20 | 55 | 45 |

(a) Show why pure strategies do not exist.
(b) Identify the closed loop that will result as the players change strategies.
(c) Reduce the payoff matrix to two strategies per player using dominance.
(d) Determine the mixed strategy for each player and the expected gains and losses that result.

12. The United Dynamics Corporation is a contractor for the military. It is negotiating with the military to supply an electronic range finder for tanks. The corporation is attempting to gain the maximum selling price for the range finder and has developed strategies to do so. The selling prices are shown in the following table.

| United Dynamics Strategies | Military Strategies | |
|---|---|---|
| | A | B |
| 1 | $ 60,000 | $100,000 |
| 2 | 80,000 | 40,000 |

Determine the strategy for each party and the gains and losses for each.

13. Given the following payoff table for a mixed strategy game between two players:

| Player I Strategies | Player II Strategies | | | |
|---|---|---|---|---|
| | A | B | C | D |
| 1 | 40 | 30 | 20 | 80 |
| 2 | 90 | 50 | 60 | 65 |
| 3 | 80 | 75 | 52 | 90 |
| 4 | 60 | 40 | 35 | 50 |

Determine the strategy for each player and the gains and losses for each.

14. There are two major soft drink companies in the Southeast, the Cooler Cola Company and Smoothies Soft Drinks, Inc. Cooler Cola is presently the market leader, and Smoothie has developed several marketing strategies to gain a percentage of the market now belonging to Cooler Cola. The following payoff table shows the gains for Smoothie and losses for Cooler given the strategies of both companies.

| Smoothie Strategies | Cooler Cola Strategies | | |
|---|---|---|---|
| | A | B | C |
| 1 | 10 | 9 | 3 |
| 2 | 4 | 7 | 5 |
| 3 | 6 | 8 | −4 |

Determine the mixed strategy for each company and the expected market share gains for Smoothie and losses for Cooler Cola.

15. Tech is playing State in a basketball game. Tech employs two basic offenses, the shuffle and the overload, while State uses three defenses, the zone, the man-to-man, and a combination zone and man-to-man. The points Tech expects to score (estimated from past games) using each offense against each State defense are given in the following payoff table.

| Tech | | State Defenses | |
|------|------|------|------|
| Offenses | Zone | Man | Combination |
| Shuffle | 72 | 60 | 83 |
| Overload | 58 | 91 | 72 |

Determine the mixed strategy for each team and the points Tech expects to score. Interpret the strategy probabilities.

16. Given the following payoff table for two game players:

| Player I | | Player II Strategies | | |
|----------|------|------|------|------|
| Strategies | A | B | C | D |
| 1 | 6 | 25 | 18 | 10 |
| 2 | 12 | 14 | 19 | 11 |
| 3 | 20 | 15 | 7 | 9 |
| 4 | 15 | 30 | 21 | 16 |

A pure strategy is not possible for this game. Determine if a mixed strategy is possible using the expected gain and loss method. If not, explain why and identify an alternative solution approach.

17. Formulate a linear programming model for the mixed strategy game in problem 7.

18. Given the following mixed strategy game, formulate a linear programming model and solve using the simplex method to determine the mixed strategies. Compare the results with the results using the expected gain and loss method.

| Player I | Player II Strategies | |
|----------|------|------|
| Strategies | A | B |
| 1 | 6 | 10 |
| 2 | 8 | 4 |

19. Formulate a linear programming model for the mixed strategy game in problem 16 and determine the mixed strategies using the simplex method.

# 13
## Markov Analysis

Markov analysis, like the topic of decision analysis presented in chapter 11, is a probabilistic technique. However, Markov analysis is different in that it does not provide a recommended decision. Instead, Markov analysis provides probabilistic information about a decision situation that can aid the decision maker in making a decision. As such, Markov analysis is not an optimization technique, but rather a *descriptive* technique that results in probabilistic information.

*A descriptive technique*

Markov analysis is specifically applicable to systems that exhibit probabilistic movement from one state (or condition) of the system to another, over time. For example, the probability that a machine that will be running or broken down from one day to the next, or that a customer will change brands of cereal from one month to the next is the type of situation encompassed by Markov analysis. This latter type of example referred to as the "brand switching" problem will be used to demonstrate the principles of Markov analysis in the subsequent discussion.

*Systems that exhibit probabilistic movement from one state of the system to another*

## The Characteristics of Markov Analysis

Markov analysis can be used to analyze a number of different decision situations; however, one of its more popular applications has been the analysis of customer "brand switching." This is basically a marketing application that focuses on the loyalty of customers to a particular product brand, store, or supplier. Markov analysis provides information on the probability of customers switching from one brand to one or more other brands. As such, an example of the brand switching problem will be used to demonstrate Markov analysis.

*A brand switching example*

In this example, a small community has two gasoline service stations, Petroco and National. The residents of the community purchase gasoline at the two stations on a monthly basis. The marketing department of the Petroco company surveyed a number of the community residents and found that the customers were not totally loyal to one brand of gasoline or the other. Customers will change service stations as a result of advertising, service, etc. The marketing department found that if a customer traded with Petroco in any given month, there was only a .60 probability that the customer would trade with Petroco the next month and a .40 probability that the customer would trade with National the next month. Likewise, if a customer traded with National in a given month, there is a .80 probability that the customer will purchase gasoline from National in the next month and a .20 probability that the customer will purchase gasoline from Petroco. These probabilities are summarized in table 13.1.

**Table 13.1** Probabilities of Customer Movement per Month

| This Month | Next Month | |
|---|---|---|
| | Petroco | National |
| Petroco | .60 | .40 |
| National | .20 | .80 |

*Row probabilities sum to 1.0*

This example contains several important assumptions. *First,* notice that in table 13.1 the probabilities in each row sum to 1.0. This means that if a customer trades with Petroco in one month, the customer *must* trade with either Petroco or National the next month (i.e., the customer will not trade with both nor will the customer not purchase gasoline at all). *Second,* the probabilities in table 13.1 apply to every customer who purchases gasoline. *Third,* the probabilities in table 13.1 will not change over time. In other words, regardless of which future month the customer is in, the probabilities of trading with one of the service stations in the next month will be the values in table 13.1. The probabilities in table 13.1 will not change in the future if conditions remain the same. *Finally,* the events (i.e., trading with either station) are independent over time. The service station a customer is in during one month does not affect which station the customer will be in during a future month.

*The probabilities apply to everyone in the system*

*The probabilities are constant over time*

*Independent events*

*Markov states*

It is these properties that make this example a Markov process. In Markov terminology the service station a customer trades at in a given month is referred to as a *state of the system* (similar to states of nature in a decision analysis problem in chap. 11). Thus, this example contains two states of the system—a customer will purchase gasoline at either Petroco or National in any given month. The probabilities contained in table 13.1 of being in a particular state are known as *transition* probabilities. In other words, they are probabilities describing the transition by a customer from one state to another during one time period. As such, table 13.1 contains four transition probabilities.

*Transition probabilities*

Because the properties described above for our service station example define a Markov process, it will be beneficial to summarize them in Markov terminology.

*Summary of Markov properties*

*Property 1:* The transition probabilities for a given beginning state of the system sum to 1.0.

*Property 2:* The probabilities apply to all participants in the system.

*Property 3:* The transition probabilities are constant over time.

*Property 4:* The states are independent over time.

## Markov Analysis Information

Now that we have defined a Markov process and determined that our example contains the Markov properties, the next question is, "What information will Markov analysis provide?" The most obvious information available from Markow analysis is the probability of being in a state at some future time period, which is also the sort of information we can gain from a *decision tree*.

For example, suppose the service stations wanted to know the probability that a customer will trade with them in month 3 given that the customer trades with them this month (1). This analysis can be performed for each service station using decision trees as shown in figure 13.1 and 13.2. (Recall that the ending branch probabilities for independent events are obtained by multiplying the probabilities of the events as shown in chap. 10.)

*Decision tree analysis*

*Computing probabilities that a customer will trade with a station in a future month*

---

**Figure 13.1** Probabilities of future states given that a customer trades with Petroco this month.

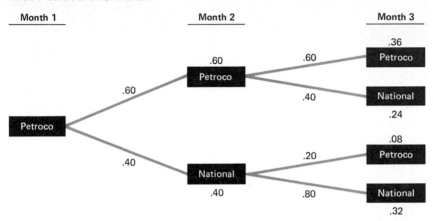

In order to determine the probability of a customer trading with Petroco in month 3 given that the customer initially traded with Petroco in month 1, we must add the two branch probabilities in figure 13.1 associated with Petroco:

.36 + .08 = .44, the probability of trading with Petroco in
      month 3

Likewise, in order to determine the probability of purchasing gasoline from National in month 3, the two branch probabilities in figure 13.1 associated with National are added:

.24 + .32 = .56, the probability of trading with National in
      month 3

This same type of analysis can be performed under the condition that a customer initially purchased gasoline from National, as shown in figure 13.2. Given that National is the starting state in month 1, then the probability of a customer purchasing gasoline from National in month 3 is

.08 + .64 = .72

and, the probability of trading with Petroco in month 3 is

.12 + .16 = .28

**Figure 13.2** Probabilities of future states given that a customer trades with National this month.

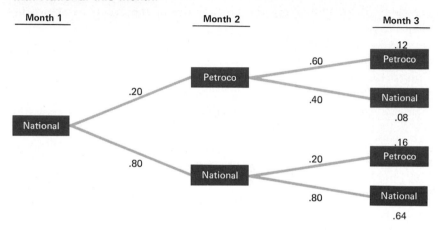

*Summary of month 3 probabilities for both starting states*

Notice that in the case of each starting state, Petroco and National, the probability of ending up in either state in month 3 sums to 1.0.

| | Probability of Trade in Month 3 | | |
|---|---|---|---|
| Starting State | Petroco | National | Sum |
| Petroco | .44 | .56 | 1.00 |
| National | .28 | .72 | 1.00 |

*Using matrix algebra instead of decision trees*

While the use of decision trees is perfectly logical for this type of analysis, it is time consuming and cumbersome. For example, if Petroco wanted to know the probability that a customer who trades with them in month 1 will trade with them in month 10, a rather large decision tree would have to be constructed. Alternatively, the same analysis performed above using decision trees can be done using *matrix algebra* techniques.

# The Transition Matrix

The probabilities of a customer moving from service station to service station within a one-month period as presented in table 13.1 can also be presented in the form of a rectangular array of numbers called a *matrix*, as shown below.

*A matrix*

$$T = \begin{array}{c} \\ \text{Petroco} \\ \text{National} \end{array} \begin{array}{cc} \textit{First Month} & \textit{Next Month} \\ \text{Petroco} & \text{National} \\ \begin{bmatrix} .60 & .40 \\ .20 & .80 \end{bmatrix} \end{array}$$

Since we previously defined these probabilities as "transition" probabilities, we will refer to the above matrix $T$, as a *transition matrix*. The present states of the system are listed on the left of the transition matrix, while the future states in the next time period are listed across the top. For example, there is a .60 probability that a customer who traded with Petroco in month 1 will trade with Petroco in month 2.

*Transition matrix*

Now we want to define several new symbols that we will use in our Markov analysis using matrix algebra. We will define the probability of a customer trading with Petroco in period $i$ given that a customer initially traded with Petroco as

*Markov probability notation*

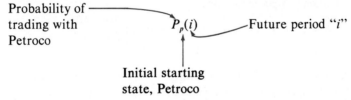

Alternatively, the probability of a customer trading with National in period $i$ given that a customer traded with Petroco initially is

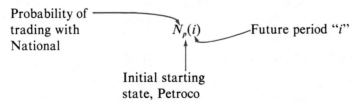

For example, the probability of a customer trading at National in month 2 given the customer initially traded with Petroco is written symbolically as

$$N_p(2)$$

The probabilities of a customer trading with Petroco and National in a future period $i$ given the customer traded initially with *National* are defined as

$$P_n(i) \text{ and } N_n(i)$$

(As a reminder in interpreting these symbols, always recall that the subscript refers to the starting state.)

*Petroco as the initial starting state*

If a customer is presently trading with Petroco in month 1, the following probabilities exist:

$$P_p(1) = 1.0$$
$$N_p(1) = 0.0$$

In other words, the probability of a customer trading at Petroco in month 1 given that the customer trades at Petroco is 1.0.

*Probabilities arranged in matrix form*

These probabilities can also be arranged in matrix form as follows.

$$[P_p(1) \quad N_p(1)] = [1.0 \quad 0.0]$$

*System starting conditions*

This matrix defines the starting conditions of our example system given that a customer initially trades at Petroco as in the decision tree in figure 13.1. In other words, a customer is originally trading with Petroco in month 1. We can determine the subsequent probabilities of a customer trading at Petroco or National in month 2 by multiplying the matrix above by the transition matrix as follows.

*Computing probabilities of a customer trading at either station in future months using matrix multiplication*

$$\text{Month 2: } [P_p(2) \quad N_p(2)] = [1.0 \quad 0.0] \begin{bmatrix} .60 & .40 \\ .20 & .80 \end{bmatrix}$$
$$= [.60 \quad .40]$$

(For those who have difficulty recalling, or are not familiar with matrix multiplication, appendix B explains matrix multiplication in detail.)

These probabilities of .60 of a customer trading at Petroco and .40 of a customer trading at National are the same as those computed in the decision tree in figure 13.1. We use the same procedure for determining the month 3 probabilities, except we now multiply the transition matrix by the month 2 matrix.

$$\text{Month 3: } [P_p(3) \quad N_p(3)] = [.60 \quad .40] \begin{bmatrix} .60 & .40 \\ .20 & .80 \end{bmatrix}$$
$$= [.44 \quad .56]$$

These are the same probabilities we computed using the decision tree analysis in figure 13.1. However, while it would be cumbersome to determine additional values using the decision tree analysis, we can continue to use the matrix approach as we have above.

$$\text{Month 4: } [P_p(4) \quad N_p(4)] = [.44 \quad .56] \begin{bmatrix} .60 & .40 \\ .20 & .80 \end{bmatrix}$$
$$= [.38 \quad .62]$$

The state probabilities for several subsequent months are shown as follows.

Month 5: $[P_p(5) \quad N_p(5)] = [.35 \quad .65]$
Month 6: $[P_p(6) \quad N_p(6)] = [.34 \quad .66]$
Month 7: $[P_p(7) \quad N_p(7)] = [.34 \quad .66]$
Month 8: $[P_p(8) \quad N_p(8)] = [.33 \quad .67]$
Month 9: $[P_p(9) \quad N_p(9)] = [.33 \quad .67]$

Notice an interesting characteristic regarding these values. As we go further and further into the future, the changes in the state probabilities become smaller and smaller. In fact, eventually there are no changes at all and every month in the future will result in the same probabilities. For this example, these state probabilities, which result after some future month, "$i$," are

*In future months the state probabilities begin to show no change*

$$[P_p(i) \quad N_p(i)] = [.33 \quad .67]$$

This characteristic of the state probabilities approaching a constant value after a number of time periods is shown for $P_p(i)$ in figure 13.3.

**Figure 13.3** The probability $P_p(i)$ for future values of "$i$."

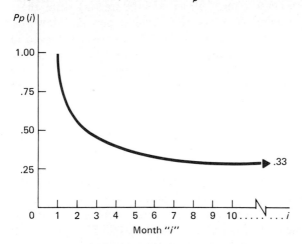

This same characteristic occurs for $N_p(i)$ as it approaches a value of .67. This is a potentially valuable result for the decision maker. In other words, the service station owner can now conclude that, if a customer initially traded with Petroco, after a certain number of months in the future, there is a .33 probability that the customer will trade with Petroco.

This same type of analysis can be performed given the starting condition that a customer initially trades with National in month 1. This analysis, shown below, corresponds to the decision tree in figure 13.2.

Given that a customer initially trades at the National station, then

*Computing future state probabilities when the initial starting state is National*

$$[P_n(1) \quad N_n(1)] = [0.0 \quad 1.0]$$

Using these initial starting-state probabilities we can compute future state probabilities as follows.

$$\text{Month 2: } [P_n(2) \quad N_n(2)] = [0.0 \quad 1.0] \begin{bmatrix} .6 & .4 \\ .2 & .8 \end{bmatrix}$$

$$= [.20 \quad .80]$$

$$\text{Month 3: } [P_n(3) \quad N_n(3)] = [.2 \quad .8] \begin{bmatrix} .6 & .4 \\ .2 & .8 \end{bmatrix}$$

$$= [.28 \quad .72]$$

These are the same values obtained using the decision tree analysis in figure 13.2. Subsequent state probabilities, computed similarly, are shown below.

*Summary of future state probabilities for National starting state*

$$\text{Month 4: } [P_n(4) \quad N_n(4)] = [.31 \quad .69]$$
$$\text{Month 5: } [P_n(5) \quad N_n(5)] = [.32 \quad .68]$$
$$\text{Month 6: } [P_n(6) \quad N_n(6)] = [.33 \quad .67]$$
$$\text{Month 7: } [P_n(7) \quad N_n(7)] = [.33 \quad .67]$$
$$\text{Month 8: } [P_n(8) \quad N_n(8)] = [.33 \quad .67]$$
$$\text{Month 9: } [P_n(9) \quad N_n(9)] = [.33 \quad .67]$$

*The probability of ending up in a state in the future is independent of the starting state*

As with the previous case where Petroco was the starting state, these state probabilities also become constant after several periods. However, notice that the eventual state probabilities (i.e., .33 and .67) achieved in this case where National is the starting state *are exactly the same* as the previous state probabilities when Petroco was the starting state. In other words, the probability of ending up in a particular state in the future is not dependent upon the starting state.

## Steady-State Probabilities

*Average probabilities that the system will be in a state in the future*

The probabilities of .33 and .67 in our example are referred to as *steady-state probabilities*. The steady-state probabilities are average probabilities that the system will be in a certain state after a large number of transition periods. This does not mean the system stays in one state. The system will continue to move from state to state in future time periods, however, the average *probabilities* of moving from state to state for all periods will remain constant in the long run future. In a Markov process after a number of periods have passed, the probabilities will approach steady state.

*Steady-state probabilities*

For our service station example, the steady-state probabilities are

.33 = probability of a customer trading at Petroco after a number of months in the future, regardless of where the customer traded in month 1.

.67 = probability of a customer trading at National after a number of months in the future, regardless of where the customer traded in month 1.

Notice that in the determination of the steady-state probabilities above, we considered each starting state separately. First, we assumed a customer was initially trading at Petroco and the steady-state probabilities were computed given this starting condition. Finally, we determined that the steady-state probabilities were the same regardless of the starting condition. However, it was not necessary to perform these matrix operations separately. We could have simply combined the operations into one matrix as follows:

*Combining state probabilities into one matrix*

$$\text{Month 2: } \begin{bmatrix} P_p(2) & N_p(2) \\ P_n(2) & N_n(2) \end{bmatrix} = \begin{bmatrix} 1 & 0 \\ 0 & 1 \end{bmatrix} \begin{bmatrix} .6 & .4 \\ .2 & .8 \end{bmatrix}$$

$$= \begin{bmatrix} .60 & .40 \\ .20 & .80 \end{bmatrix}$$

$$\text{Month 3: } \begin{bmatrix} P_p(3) & N_p(3) \\ P_n(3) & N_n(3) \end{bmatrix} = \begin{bmatrix} .60 & .40 \\ .20 & .80 \end{bmatrix} \begin{bmatrix} .60 & .40 \\ .20 & .80 \end{bmatrix}$$

$$= \begin{bmatrix} .44 & .56 \\ .28 & .72 \end{bmatrix}$$

$$\text{Month 4: } \begin{bmatrix} P_p(4) & N_p(4) \\ P_n(4) & N_n(4) \end{bmatrix} = \begin{bmatrix} .44 & .56 \\ .28 & .72 \end{bmatrix} \begin{bmatrix} .60 & .40 \\ .20 & .80 \end{bmatrix}$$

$$= \begin{bmatrix} .38 & .62 \\ .31 & .69 \end{bmatrix}$$

until eventually,

$$\text{Month 9: } \begin{bmatrix} P_p(9) & N_p(9) \\ P_n(9) & N_n(9) \end{bmatrix} = \begin{bmatrix} .33 & .67 \\ .33 & .67 \end{bmatrix}$$

## Direct Algebraic Determination of Steady-State Probabilities

In the previous section, it was necessary to compute the state probabilities for approximately 8 periods (i.e., months) before the steady-state probabilities were reached for both states. This required quite a few matrix computations. Alternatively, it is possible to solve for the steady-state probabilities directly without going through all of these matrix operations.

Notice that after eight periods in our previous analysis, the state probabilities did not change from period to period (i.e., from month to month). For example,

*At some point in the future the state probabilities remain constant from period to period*

Month 8: $[P_p(8) \quad N_p(8)] = [.33 \quad .67]$

Month 9: $[P_p(9) \quad N_p(9)] = [.33 \quad .67]$

The state
probabilities in
periods "i" and
"i + 1" are equal

Thus, we can also say that after a number of periods in the future (in this case 8), the state probabilities in period "i" equal the state probabilities in period "i + 1." For our example, this means that

$$[P_p(8) \quad N_p(8)] = [P_p(9) \quad N_p(9)]$$

In fact, it is not necessary to designate which period in the future is actually occurring. That is,

$$[P_p \quad N_p] = [P_p \quad N_p]$$

given steady-state conditions.

These probabilities are for some period "i" in the future once steady state has already been reached. To determine the state probabilities for period "i + 1," we would normally compute the following.

$$[P_p(i + 1) \quad N_p(i + 1)] = [P_p(i) \quad N_p(i)] \begin{bmatrix} .6 & .4 \\ .2 & .8 \end{bmatrix}$$

However, we have already stated that once steady state has been reached, then

$$[P_p(i + 1) \quad N_p(i + 1)] = [P_p(i) \quad N_p(i)]$$

and it is not necessary to designate the period. Thus our computation can be rewritten as

$$[P_p \quad N_p] = [P_p \quad N_p] \begin{bmatrix} .6 & .4 \\ .2 & .8 \end{bmatrix}$$

Developing a set of
equations from the
matrix operations

Performing matrix operations results in the following set of equations.

$$P_p = .6P_p + .2N_p$$
$$N_p = .4P_p + .8N_p$$

Recall that the transition probabilities for a row in the transition matrix (i.e., the state probabilities) must sum to 1.0:

$$P_p + N_p = 1.0$$

which can also be written as

$$N_p = 1.0 - P_p$$

Substituting this value into our first equation above ($P_p = .6P_p + .2N_p$) results in the following.

$$P_p = .6P_p + .2(1.0 - P_p)$$
$$P_p = .6P_p + .2 - .2P_p$$
$$P_p = .2 + .4P_p$$
$$.6P_p = .2$$
$$P_p = .2/.6 = .33$$

and

$$N_p = 1.0 - P_p$$
$$N_p = 1.0 - .33$$
$$N_p = .67$$

These are the steady-state probabilities we computed in our previous analysis,

$$[P_p \quad N_p] = [.33 \quad .67]$$

## Application of the Steady-State Probabilities

The steady-state probabilities not only indicate the probability of a customer trading at a particular service station in the long-term future, but also the *percentage of customers* who will trade at a service station during any given month in the long run. For example, if there are 3,000 customers in the community who purchase gasoline, then in the long run the following *expected* number will purchase gasoline at each station on a monthly basis.

$$\begin{aligned}
\textit{Petroco:} \quad P_p(3,000) &= .33(3,000) \\
&= 990 \text{ customers} \\
\textit{National:} \quad N_p(3,000) &= .67(3,000) \\
&= 2,010 \text{ customers}
\end{aligned}$$

Now suppose that Petroco has decided they are getting less than a reasonable share of the market and would like to increase their market share. In order to accomplish this objective, Petroco has improved their service substantially so that a survey indicated the transition probabilities had changed to the following.

$$T = \begin{array}{cc} & \begin{array}{cc} \text{Petroco} & \text{National} \end{array} \\ \begin{array}{c} \text{Petroco} \\ \text{National} \end{array} & \begin{bmatrix} .70 & .30 \\ .20 & .80 \end{bmatrix} \end{array}$$

In other words, the improved service has resulted in a smaller probability (.30) of customers who traded initially at Petroco from switching to National the next month.

Now we will recompute the steady-state probabilities based on this new transition matrix.

$$[P_p \quad N_p] = [P_p \quad N_p] \begin{bmatrix} .70 & .30 \\ .20 & .80 \end{bmatrix}$$

$$\begin{aligned}
P_p &= .7P_p + .2N_p \\
N_p &= .3P_p + .8N_p
\end{aligned}$$

Using the first equation and the fact that $N_p = 1.0 - P_p$, we have

$$\begin{aligned}
P_p &= .7P_p + .2(1.0 - P_p) \\
P_p &= .7P_p + .2 - .2P_p \\
.5P_p &= .2 \\
P_p &= .2/.5 = .4
\end{aligned}$$

and thus,

$$\begin{aligned}
N_p &= 1 - P_p \\
N_p &= 1 - .4 \\
N_p &= .6
\end{aligned}$$

This means that out of the 3,000 customers, Petroco will now get 1,200 customers (i.e., .40 × 3,000) in any given month in the long run. Thus, improvement in service will result in an increase of 210 customers per month (if the new transition probabilities remain constant for a long period of time in the future). The decision in this situation depends on the trade-off between the cost of the improved service and the increase in profit from the additional 210 customers. For example, if the improved service costs $1,000 per month, then the extra 210 customers must result in an increase in profit greater than $1,000 to justify the decision to improve service.

*Markov analysis results in information, not decisions*

This brief example demonstrates the usefulness of Markov analysis for decision making. While Markov analysis will not yield a recommended decision (i.e., a solution) it will provide "information" that will help the decision maker to make the decision.

## Applications of Markov Analysis

*A machine breakdown example*

Although the brand switching problem demonstrated in this chapter is probably the most popular example of Markov analysis, this technique does have other applications. One prominent application relates to machine or system breakdown. For example, a particular production machine could be assigned the states "operating" and "breakdown." The transition probabilities reflect the probability of a machine either breaking down or operating in the next time period (i.e., month, day, or year). This type of situation could also be applicable to a computer system, production operation, or electrical system.

As an example, consider a machine having the following transition matrix on a "daily" basis.

$$T = \begin{array}{c} \\ \text{Operate} \\ \text{Breakdown} \end{array} \begin{array}{c} Day\ 1 \qquad\qquad Day\ 2 \\ \text{Operate} \quad \text{Breakdown} \\ \begin{bmatrix} .90 & .10 \\ .70 & .30 \end{bmatrix} \end{array}$$

*Steady-state probabilities for the breakdown example*

The steady-state probabilities for this example are

.88 = steady-state probability of the machine operating
.12 = steady-state probability of the machine breaking down

*The cost of increased maintenance vs. profit from increased output*

Now if management decides that the long-run probability of a breakdown, .12, is excessive, they might consider increasing preventive maintenance, which would change the transition matrix for this example. The decision to increase maintenance would be based on the cost of the increase versus the increased production output gained from having fewer breakdowns.

Another example encompasses the movement of stock prices on a daily basis. For this type of problem, the states are the movement of a stock price up or down. The transition probabilities reflect the probability of a stock price moving up or down during the following day.

*A stock price movement example*

In our discussion of Markov analysis so far we have considered only examples that consisted of two states. This was partially a matter of convenience, as $2 \times 2$ matrices are easier to work with than matrices of a higher magnitude. However, examples that contain a larger number of states are analyzed in the same way as our previous examples. For example, consider the Carry-All Rental Truck Firm, which serves three states— Virginia, North Carolina, and Maryland. Trucks are rented on a daily basis and can be rented and returned in any of the three states. The transition matrix for this example is

*An example with three states*

$$
\begin{array}{cc}
\textit{Rented} & \textit{Returned} \\
& \begin{array}{ccc} \text{Virginia} & \text{Maryland} & \text{North Carolina} \end{array} \\
T = \begin{array}{c} \text{Virginia} \\ \text{Maryland} \\ \text{North Carolina} \end{array} & \left[ \begin{array}{ccc} .60 & .20 & .20 \\ .30 & .50 & .20 \\ .40 & .10 & .50 \end{array} \right]
\end{array}
$$

The steady-state probabilities for this example are determined using the same approach presented earlier, although the mathematical steps are more lengthy and complex. (These computations are shown in Appendix B.)

The steady-state probabilities for this example are

$$
\begin{array}{ccc}
\text{Virginia} & \text{Maryland} & \text{North Carolina} \\
[.471 & .244 & .285]
\end{array}
$$

Thus, in the long run, these are the percentages of Carry-All trucks that will terminate in the three states.

## Special Types of Transition Matrices

In some cases the transition matrix derived from a Markov problem is not in a form like the examples shown in this chapter. These matrices contain certain characteristics that alter the normal methods of Markov analysis. Although the actual detailed analysis of these special cases is beyond the scope of this chapter, we will give examples of them so that they can be easily recognized.

Consider the following transition matrix for states 1, 2, and 3.

$$
\begin{array}{cc}
& \begin{array}{ccc} 1 & 2 & 3 \end{array} \\
T = \begin{array}{c} 1 \\ 2 \\ 3 \end{array} & \left[ \begin{array}{ccc} .30 & .60 & .10 \\ .40 & .40 & .20 \\ 0 & 0 & 1.0 \end{array} \right]
\end{array}
$$

State 3 in this transition matrix is referred to as an *absorbing* or trapping state. Once state 3 is achieved there is a 1.0 probability that it will be achieved in succeeding time periods. Thus, the system in effect ends once state 3 is achieved. There is no movement from an absorbing state—the item is trapped in that state.

*The "bad debt" example*

A unique application of an absorbing state matrix is the debt example. In this example, the states are the months during which a customer will carry a debt. At any time, the customer may pay the debt (i.e., a bill) and thus achieve an absorbing state for payment. Alternatively, if the debt is carried longer then a specified number of periods (i.e., three months), the debt will be labeled "bad" and transferred to a bill collector. The state "bad debt" is also an absorbing state. Through various matrix manipulations (which we will not cover in this chapter), the amount of receipts during each month can be determined. Several of the references at the end of this chapter contain examples of the bad debt problem.

In the following transition matrix,

$$T = \begin{array}{c} \\ 1 \\ 2 \\ 3 \end{array} \begin{array}{ccc} 1 & 2 & 3 \\ \left[ \begin{array}{ccc} .40 & .60 & 0 \\ .30 & .70 & 0 \\ 1.0 & 0 & 0 \end{array} \right] \end{array}$$

*A transient state*

state 3 is a *transient* state. Once state 3 is achieved, the system will never return to that state. Both states 1 and 2 contain a 0.0 probability of going to state 3. The system will move out of state 3 to state 1 (with a 1.0 probability), but will never return to state 3.

*A cyclic transition matrix*

The following transition matrix is referred to as *cyclic*.

$$T = \begin{array}{c} \\ 1 \\ 2 \end{array} \begin{array}{cc} 1 & 2 \\ \left[ \begin{array}{cc} 0 & 1.0 \\ 1.0 & 0 \end{array} \right] \end{array}$$

The system will simply cycle back and forth between states 1 and 2 without ever moving out of the cycle.

## Summary

This chapter has presented an overview of an interesting and sometimes useful *probabilistic* technique, Markov analysis. We demonstrated one of the most popular applications of Markov analysis, the brand switching example and indicated other potential areas of application. However, realistic applications of Markov analysis have been somewhat limited. This is due in large part to the difficulty of finding decision problems that meet all the necessary properties for Markov analysis, especially transition probabilities that are constant over time.

*It is difficult to find problems that have all the Markov properties*

Markov analysis is useful for our purposes because it demonstrates a technique that does not result in a recommended actual decision in the form of an optimal solution. Instead, the analysis results in descriptive information that can be used to help make a decision. This same characteristic is exhibited by the topics presented in the next two chapters on queuing and simulation. These techniques do not optimize either, but rather provide information to aid the decision maker in making a decision.

## References

Feller, W. *An Introduction to Probability Theory and Its Applications.* Vol. I. 3d ed. New York: John Wiley and Sons, 1968.

Howard, R. A. *Dynamic Programming and Markov Processes.* Cambridge: M.I.T. Press, 1960.

Kemeny, J. G., and Snell, J. L. *Finite Markov Chains.* Princeton, N.J.: D. Van Nostrand Company, 1960.

Parzen, E. *Stochastic Processes.* San Francisco: Holden-Day, 1962.

Searle, S. R., and Hausman, W. H. *Matrix Algebra for Business and Economics,* New York: John Wiley and Sons, 1970.

## Problems

1. Given two products, *A* and *B,* the following table describes the probabilities of a customer changing products or purchasing the same product in a future period.

| This Period | Next Period | |
| | A | B |
| --- | --- | --- |
| A | .5 | .5 |
| B | .6 | .4 |

Determine the probabilities that a customer will purchase product *A* or *B* in period 3 in the future given that the customer purchased *A* or *B* in this (present) period by using decision trees. Summarize the resulting probabilities in a table.

2. Given the following transition matrix,

$$
\begin{array}{c} \textit{This Week} \end{array}
\begin{array}{c} \\ 1 \\ 2 \end{array}
\begin{array}{c} \textit{Next Week} \\ \begin{array}{cc} 1 & 2 \end{array} \\ \begin{bmatrix} .3 & .7 \\ .9 & .1 \end{bmatrix} \end{array}
$$

determine the probabilities of being in each state in week 3 in the future, given each starting state by using decision trees. Summarize the resulting probabilities in a table.

3. A town has three gasoline stations: Petroco, National, and Gascorp. The residents purchase gasoline on a monthly basis. The following transition matrix contains the probabilities of the brand of gasoline the customer will purchase next month.

|  |  | Next Month | |  |
| --- | --- | --- | --- | --- |
|  |  | Petroco | National | Gascorp |
|  | Petroco | .5 | .3 | .2 |
| This Month | National | .1 | .7 | .2 |
|  | Gascorp | .1 | .1 | .8 |

Determine the probabilities of a customer purchasing each brand of gasoline in month 3, given the customer purchases National in the present month, using a decision tree. Summarize the resulting probabilities in a table.

4. Discuss the properties that must exist for the transition matrix in problem 3 to be considered a Markov process.

5. The only grocery store in a community stocks milk from two dairies—Creamwood and Cheesedale. The following transition matrix shows the probabilities of a customer purchasing each brand of milk in the next week given that they purchased a particular brand in the present week.

|  |  | Next Week | |
| --- | --- | --- | --- |
|  |  | Creamwood | Cheesedale |
| This Week | Creamwood | .7 | .3 |
|  | Cheesedale | .4 | .6 |

Given that a customer purchases Creamwood milk in the present week use a decision tree to determine the probability that a customer will purchase Cheesedale in week 4.

6. Determine the state probabilities for period 3 requested in problem 1 using matrix multiplication methods.

7. Determine the state probabilities for week 3 requested in problem 2 using matrix multiplication methods.

8. Given the transition matrix in problem 3, determine the state probabilities for month 3, given that a customer initially purchases Petroco gas, by using matrix multiplication methods.

9. Determine the state probabilities requested in problem 5 using matrix multiplication methods.

10. A manufacturing firm has developed a transition matrix containing the probabilities a particular machine will operate or break down in the following week given its operating condition in the present week.

$$\text{This Week} \quad \begin{matrix} \text{Operate} \\ \text{Breakdown} \end{matrix} \begin{matrix} \overset{\text{Operate}}{} & \overset{\text{Breakdown}}{} \\ \begin{bmatrix} .4 & .6 \\ .8 & .2 \end{bmatrix} \end{matrix}$$

**Next Week**

(a) Assuming that the machine is operating in week 1, determine the probabilities that the machine will be operating or down in week 2, week 3, week 4, week 5, and week 6.

(b) Determine the steady-state probabilities for this transition matrix algebraically and indicate the percentage of future weeks in which the machine will break down.

11. A city is served by two newspapers—the Tribune and the Daily News. Each Sunday reader purchases one of the newspapers at a stand. The following transition matrix contains the probabilities of the newspaper a reader will buy in a week, given the newspaper purchased the previous Sunday.

$$\text{This Sunday} \quad \begin{matrix} \text{Tribune} \\ \text{Daily News} \end{matrix} \begin{matrix} \overset{\text{Tribune}}{} & \overset{\text{Daily News}}{} \\ \begin{bmatrix} .65 & .35 \\ .45 & .55 \end{bmatrix} \end{matrix}$$

**Next Sunday**

Determine the steady state probabilities for this transition matrix algebraically and explain their meaning.

12. The Hergeshiemer Department Store wants to analyze the payment behavior for customers who have accounts receivable outstanding. The store's credit department has determined the following bill payment pattern for credit customers from historical records.

$$\text{Present Month} \quad \begin{matrix} \text{Pay} \\ \text{Not Pay} \end{matrix} \begin{matrix} \overset{\text{Pay}}{} & \overset{\text{Not Pay}}{} \\ \begin{bmatrix} .9 & .1 \\ .8 & .2 \end{bmatrix} \end{matrix}$$

**Next Month**

(a) If a customer did not pay their bill in the present month, what is the probability that the bill will not be paid in any of the next 3 months?

(b) Determine the steady-state probabilities for this transition matrix and explain their meaning.

13. Define what a "steady state" means in a Markov process.

14. Discuss how Markov analysis can be used for decision making, since it is not considered to be an optimization technique.

15. A rural community has two television stations and, each Wednesday night the local viewers watch either the "Wednesday Movie" or a show called "Western Times." The following transition matrix contains the probabilities of a viewer watching one of the shows in a week, given they watched a particular show the preceding week.

|  |  | Next Week |  |
|---|---|---|---|
|  |  | Movie | Western |
| *Present Week* | Movie | $\begin{bmatrix} .75 \\ .45 \end{bmatrix}$ | $\begin{matrix} .25 \\ .55 \end{matrix}$ |
|  | Western |  |  |

(a) Determine the steady-state probabilities for this transition matrix algebraically.
(b) If the community contains 1,200 television sets, how many will be tuned to each show in the long run?
(c) If a prospective local sponsor wanted to pay for commercial time on one of the shows, which show would most likely be selected?

16. In problem 5, there were 600 gallons of milk sold weekly, regardless of the brand purchased.
(a) How many gallons of each brand of milk will be purchased in any given week in the long run?
(b) The Cheesedale dairy is considering a new advertising campaign costing $500 per week that would alter the brand switching probabilities as follows.

|  |  | Next Week |  |
|---|---|---|---|
|  |  | Creamwood | Cheesedale |
| *This Week* | Creamwood | $\begin{bmatrix} .6 \\ .2 \end{bmatrix}$ | $\begin{matrix} .4 \\ .8 \end{matrix}$ |
|  | Cheesedale |  |  |

If each gallon of milk sold results in $1.00 in profit for Cheesedale, should they institute the advertising campaign?

17. In problem 10 the manufacturing company is considering a preventive maintenance program that would change the operating probabilities as follows.

|  |  | Next Week |  |
|---|---|---|---|
|  |  | Operate | Breakdown |
| *This Week* | Operate | $\begin{bmatrix} .7 \\ .9 \end{bmatrix}$ | $\begin{matrix} .3 \\ .1 \end{matrix}$ |
|  | Breakdown |  |  |

Each week the machine operates, it earns the company $1,000 in profit. The preventive maintenance program would cost $8,000 per year. Should the company institute the preventive maintenance program?

18. In problem 11, each Sunday 20,000 newspapers are sold regardless of the publisher.
    (a) How many copies of the Tribune and the Daily News will be purchased in a given week in the long run?
    (b) The Daily News is considering a promotional campaign they estimate would change the weekly reader probabilities as follows.

$$
\begin{array}{c}
 & & \textit{Next Week} \\
 & & \text{Tribune} \quad\quad \text{Daily News} \\
\textit{This Week} \quad \begin{array}{l} \text{Tribune} \\ \text{Daily News} \end{array} & \begin{bmatrix} .5 & .5 \\ .3 & .7 \end{bmatrix}
\end{array}
$$

The promotional campaign will cost $150 per week. Each newspaper sold earns the Daily News $.05 in profit. Should they adopt the promotional campaign?

19. Explain the difference between an *absorbing* state and a *transient* state.

20. Determine the steady-state probabilities for the transition matrix in problem 3.

# 14
## Queuing Analysis

## The Single-Server Waiting Line System

The Queue Discipline
The Calling Population
The Arrival Rate
The Service Rate
The Single-Server Model
The Effect of Operating Characteristics on Managerial Decisions

## The Multiple-Server Waiting Line

## Additional Types of Queuing Systems

## Summary

Waiting in queues (or waiting lines) is one of the most common occurrences in everyone's life. Anyone who has gone shopping or to a movie has had the inconvenience of waiting in line to make purchases or buy a ticket. Not only do people spend a significant portion of their time waiting in lines but product queues also form in production plants, machinery waits in line to be serviced, etc. Since time is a valuable resource, the reduction of waiting time is an important topic of analysis.

*Waiting lines*

Like the topics of the preceding chapters on decision analysis and Markov Analysis, queuing analysis is also a probabilistic form of analysis, and not a deterministic technique. As such, the results of queuing analysis, referred to as "operating characteristics," are probabilistic. These operating statistics (such as the average time a person in line must wait to be served) are subsequently used by the manager of the operation containing the queue to make decisions.

*A probabilistic form of analysis*

A number of different queuing models exist to deal with different queuing systems. While we will eventually discuss many of these queuing variations, we will concentrate on two of the most common types of systems—the single-server system and the multiple-server system.

## The Single-Server Waiting Line System

The single server with a single waiting line is the simplest form of queuing system. As such, we will use it to demonstrate the basic fundamentals of a queuing system. As an example of this kind of system we will consider the Fast Shop Drive-In Market.

The Fast Shop Market consists of one checkout counter and one employee who operates the cash register at the checkout counter. The combination of the cash register and operator is the *server* (or service facility) in this queuing system, while the customers who line up at the counter to pay for their selections form the *waiting line,* or *queue.* The configuration of this example queuing system is shown in figure 14.1.

*A queuing example*

*Server*

*Queue*

**Figure 14.1** The Fast Shop Market queuing system.

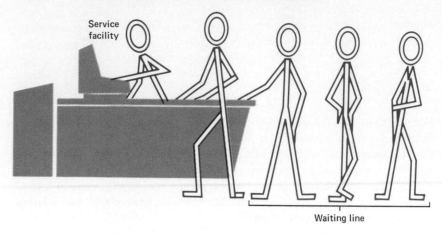

The most important factors in analyzing a queuing system such as the one in figure 14.1 are:

1. The queue discipline (in what order customers are served)
2. The nature of the calling population (where customers come from)
3. The arrival rate (how often customers arrive at the queue)
4. The service rate (how fast customers are served)

We will discuss each of these items as it relates to our example.

## The Queue Discipline

*The order in which customers are served*

The *queue discipline* is the order in which waiting customers are served. Customers at the Fast Shop Market are served on a "first-come, first-served" basis. That is, the first person in line at the checkout counter is served first. This is the most common type of queue discipline. However, other disciplines are possible. For example, a machine operator might stack in-process parts beside a machine so that the last part is on top of the stack and will be selected first. This queue discipline would be referred to as "last-in, first-out." Alternatively, the machine operator might simply reach into a box full of parts and select one at *random*. In this case the queue discipline is random. Often customers are scheduled for service according to a predetermined appointment, such as patients at a doctor's or dentist's office, or diners at a restaurant where reservations are required. In this case the customers are taken according to a prearranged schedule regardless of when they arrive at the facility. One final example of the many types of queue disciplines that can occur is when a number of customers are processed alphabetically according to their last name, such as occurs at school registration or at job interviews.

## The Calling Population

The *calling population* is the source of the customers to the market, which is assumed in this case to be infinite. In other words, there is such a large number of possible customers in the area where the store is located, which could come into the market, that the potential customers are assumed to be infinite. Alternatively, on occasion queuing systems have "finite" calling populations. For example, the repair garage of a trucking firm, which has 20 trucks, has a finite calling population. The queue is the number of trucks waiting to be repaired and the finite calling population is 20 trucks. However, queuing systems that have an assumed infinite calling population are more frequent.

*Source of arrivals to the queuing system*

## The Arrival Rate

The *arrival rate* is the average number of arrivals at the service facility during a specified period of time. For example, if 100 customers arrive at the store checkout counter during a 10-hour day, we could say the arrival rate is on average 10 per hour. However, although we may be able to determine a rate for arrivals by counting the number of paying customers at the market during a 10-hour day, we would not know exactly when these customers would arrive on the premises. In other words, during one hour no customers might arrive but during another hour, 20 customers might arrive. In general, these arrivals are assumed to be independent of each other and vary randomly over time.

*The number of arrivals during a time period*

Given these assumptions it is further assumed that arrivals at a service facility conform to some probability distribution. Although arrivals could be described by any distribution, it has been determined (through years of research and the practical experience of people in the field of queuing) that the number of arrivals per unit of time at a service facility can frequently be defined by a *Poisson distribution*. (Appendix C at the end of this text contains a more detailed presentation of the Poisson distribution.)

*Arrivals conform to a Poisson probability distribution*

## The Service Rate

The *service rate* is the average number of customers that can be served during a specified period of time. For our Fast Shop Market example, 30 customers can be checked out (served) in one hour. A service rate is similar to an arrival rate in that it is also a random variable. In other words, due to different sizes of customer purchases, the amount of change the cashier must determine, different forms of payment, etc., the number of persons that can be served varies over time. Only 10 customers might be checked out during one hour while 40 customers are checked out in the following hour.

*The average number served during a time period*

The description of arrivals in terms of a *rate* and service in terms of *time* is a convention that has developed in the literature of queuing theory. As in the case of an arrival rate, the service time is also assumed to be defined by a probability distribution. It has been determined by researchers in the field of queuing that service times can frequently be defined by an *exponential probability* distribution. (Appendix C at the end of this text contains a more detailed presentation of the exponential distribution.) However, in order to analyze a queuing system both arrivals and service must be in compatible units of measure. Thus, service time must be expressed as a service rate to correspond with an arrival rate.

## The Single-Server Model

*Characteristics
of the single-server
queuing system*

The Fast Shop Market checkout counter is an example of a single-server queuing system, which consists of the following characteristics:

1. An infinite calling population
2. A "first-come, first-served" queue discipline
3. Poisson arrival rate
4. Exponential service times

These assumptions have been used to develop a model of a single-server queuing system. However, the analytical derivation of even this simplest queuing model is relatively complex and lengthy. As such, we will refrain from deriving the model in detail and will present only the resulting queuing formulas. The reader must keep in mind, however, that these formulas are applicable only to queuing systems for which the above conditions exist.

Given that

$a$ = the arrival rate (average number of arrivals per time period)
$s$ = the service rate (average number served per time period)

*The service rate
exceeds the
arrival rate*

and that $a < s$ (customers are served at a faster rate than they arrive), the following formulas for the operating characteristics of a single-server model exist.

*The single-server
model queuing
formulas*

The probability that no customers are in the queuing system (either in the queue or being served):

$$P_0 = \left(1 - \frac{a}{s}\right)$$

The probability of $n$ customers in the queuing system:

$$P_n = \left(\frac{a}{s}\right)^n \cdot P_0$$
$$= \left(\frac{a}{s}\right)^n \left(1 - \frac{a}{s}\right)$$

The average number of customers in the queuing system (i.e., the customers being serviced and in the waiting line):

$$L = \frac{a}{s - a}$$

The average number of customers in the waiting line:

$$L_q = \frac{a^2}{s(s - a)}$$

The average time a customer spends in the total queuing system (i.e., waiting and being served):

$$W = \frac{1}{s - a}$$
$$= \frac{L}{a}$$

The average time a customer spends waiting in the queue to be served:

$$W_q = \frac{a}{s(s - a)}$$

The probability that the server is busy (i.e., the probability that a customer has to wait), known as the *utilization factor:*

$$U = \frac{a}{s}$$

The probability that the server is idle (i.e., the probability that a customer can be served):

$$I = 1 - U$$
$$= 1 - \frac{a}{s}$$

This last term, $1 - a/s$, is also equal to $P_0$. The probability of no customers in the queuing system is the same as the probability that the server is idle.

These various operating characteristics can be computed for the Fast Shop Market by simply substituting the average arrival and service rates into the above formulas. For example, if

*Computing the operating statistics for the queuing example*

$a = 24$ customers per hour arrive at checkout counter
$s = 30$ customers per hour can be checked out

then

$$P_0 = \left(1 - \frac{a}{s}\right)$$
$$= (1 - 24/30)$$
$$= .20 \text{ probability of 0 customers in the system}$$

$$L = \frac{a}{s - a}$$
$$= \frac{24}{30 - 24}$$
$$= 4 \text{ customers on the average in the queuing system}$$

$$L_q = \frac{a^2}{s\,(s - a)}$$
$$= \frac{(24)^2}{30\,(30 - 24)}$$
$$= 3.2 \text{ customers on the average in the waiting line}$$

$$W = \frac{1}{s - a}$$
$$= \frac{1}{30 - 24}$$
$$= .167 \text{ hours (10 minutes) average time in the system per customer}$$

$$W_q = \frac{a}{s\,(s - a)}$$
$$= \frac{24}{30\,(30 - 24)}$$
$$= .133 \text{ hours (8 minutes) average time in the waiting line per customer}$$

$$U = \frac{a}{s}$$
$$= \frac{24}{30}$$
$$= .80 \text{ probability that the server will be busy and the customer must wait}$$

$$I = 1 - U$$
$$= 1 - .80$$
$$= .20 \text{ probability that the server will be idle and the customer can be served}$$

Several important items concerning both the general model and this particular example will now be discussed in greater detail.

First, recall that the operating characteristics are "averages." Also, *Steady-state results* they are assumed to be *steady state* averages. In our discussion of Markov analysis (see chap. 13), it was indicated that the steady state was a constant average level that a system realized after a period of time. For a queuing system, the steady state is represented by the average operating statistics, also determined over a period of time.

Related to this condition is the fact that the utilization factor, $U$, must be less than 1.0

$$U < 1$$

or

$$\frac{a}{s} < 1.0$$

and

$$a < s$$

In other words, the ratio of the arrival rate to the service rate must be less than one, which also means *the service rate must be greater than the arrival rate* if this model is to be used. The server must be able to serve customers faster than they come into the store or the waiting line will grow to an infinite size, and the system will never reach a steady state.

## The Effect of Operating Characteristics on Managerial Decisions

We must now reflect on the operating characteristics as they relate to management decisions. The arrival rate of 24 customers per hour means that, on the average, a customer arrives every 2.5 minutes (i.e., $1/24 \times 60$ minutes). This indicates that the store is actually very busy. This is due to the fact that the customer purchases few items and expects quick service, since that is the nature of the store. Customers expect to spend a relatively large amount of time in a supermarket, since typically larger purchases are made. Alternatively, customers who trade at a drive-in market do so, at least partially, because it is quicker than a supermarket.

Given this condition, the store's manager feels that a customer waiting time of 8 minutes and a total time of 10 minutes in the queuing system (not including the actual shopping time) is excessive. As such, the manager wants to test several alternatives for reducing customer waiting time: (1) the addition of another employee to "sack" the purchases and (2) the addition of an additional checkout counter.

### Alternative I: The Addition of an Employee
The addition of an extra employee will cost the store manager $150 per week. With the help of the national office's marketing research group, the manager has determined that for each minute of customer waiting time that can be eliminated, a loss in sales of $75/week will be avoided (i.e., customers who leave prior to shopping because of the long line or customers who do not return).

If a new employee is hired, customers can be served within a shorter period of time. In other words, the *service rate*, which is the number of customers served per time period, will *increase*. The previous service rate was

$$s = 30 \text{ customers served/hour}$$

The addition of a new employee will increase the service rate to

$$s = 40 \text{ customers served/hour}$$

It will be assumed that the arrival rate will remain the same ($a = 24$ per hour), since the effect of the increased service rate will not increase arrivals but instead will minimize the loss of customers. (However, it is not illogical to also assume that an increase in service might increase arrivals.)

Given the "*a*" and "*s*" values, the operating characteristics can be recomputed as follows:

$$P_0 = \left(1 - \frac{a}{s}\right)$$
$$= \left(1 - \frac{24}{40}\right)$$
$$= .40 \text{ probability of 0 customers in the system}$$

$$L = \frac{a}{s - a}$$
$$= \frac{24}{40 - 24}$$
$$= 1.5 \text{ customers in the queuing system on the average}$$

$$L_q = \frac{a^2}{s\,(s - a)}$$
$$= \frac{(24)^2}{40\,(16)}$$
$$= .90 \text{ customers in the waiting line on the average}$$

$$W = \frac{1}{s - a}$$
$$= \frac{1}{40 - 24}$$
$$= .063 \text{ hours (3.75 minutes) average time per customer in the system}$$

$$W_q = \frac{a}{s\,(s - a)}$$
$$= \frac{24}{40\,(16)}$$
$$= .038 \text{ hours (2.25 minutes) average time in the waiting line per customer}$$

$$U = \frac{a}{s} = \frac{24}{40}$$

= 0.6 probability that the customer must wait

$$I = 1 - U$$

= 1 − .6 = .40 probability that the server be idle

It must be remembered that these operating characteristics are *averages* that will result over a period of time and that they are not absolutes. In other words, customers who arrive at the Fast Shop Market checkout counter will not find .90 customers in line. There could be no customers or some number of customers greater than .90, such as 1, 2, or 3. The value .90 is simply an average that will occur over time as are the other operating characteristics.

The average waiting time per customer has been reduced from 8 minutes to 2.25 minutes, a significant amount. The savings (due to the aversion of lost sales) is computed as follows.

*Deriving the savings resulting from the increased service rate*

8.00 minutes − 2.25 minutes = 5.75 minutes
5.75 minutes × \$75/minute = \$431.25

Since the extra employee costs management \$150 per week, the total savings will be

\$431.25 − 150 = \$281.25 per week

The store manager would probably consider this savings and the above operating statistics to be preferable to the previous condition where only one employee existed.

### Alternative II: The Addition of a New Checkout Counter

Next we will consider the manager's alternative of constructing a new checkout counter. The total cost of this project will be \$6,000 plus an extra \$200 per week for an additional cashier.

The new checkout counter will be opposite the present counter (such that the servers will have their backs to each other in an enclosed counter area). There will be several display cases and racks between the two lines so that customers waiting in line will not move back and forth between the lines. (Such movement, called *jockeying,* would not allow us to use our queuing formulas already developed.) We will assume that the customers will divide themselves equally between both lines so that the arrival rate for each line will be half of the prior arrival rate for a single checkout counter. Thus, the new arrival rate for each checkout counter is,

*Reducing the arrival rate*

$a$ = 12 customers per hour

and, the service rate will remain the same for each of the counters,

$s$ = 30 customers served per hour

Substituting this new arrival rate and the service rate into our queuing formulas results in the following operating characteristics.

$P_0 = .60$ probability of "0" customers in the system
$L = .67$ customers in the queuing system
$L_q = .27$ customers in the waiting line
$W = .055$ hours (3.33 minutes) per customer in the system
$W_q = .022$ hours (1.33 minutes) in the waiting line per customers
$U = 0.40$ probability that a customer must wait
$I = .60$ probability that the server will be idle

*Deriving the savings
resulting from the
decreased arrival
rate*

Using the same sales savings of $75 per week per minute reduction in waiting time, the store will save

8.00 minutes $-$ 1.33 minutes $=$ 6.67 minutes
6.67 minutes $\times$ $75/minute $=$ $500.00 per week

First we must subtract the $200 per week cost of the new cashier from this amount saved:

$500 $-$ 200 $=$ $300

Since the capital outlay of this project is $6,000, it will take 20 weeks ($6,000/$300 $=$ 20 weeks) to recoup the initial cost (ignoring the possibility of interest on the $6,000). Once the cost has been recovered, the store would make $18.75 ($300.00 $-$ 281.25) more by adding a new checkout counter rather than simply hiring an extra employee. However, we must not disregard the fact that during the 20-week cost recovery period, the $281.25 savings incurred by simply hiring a new employee would be lost.

Table 14.1 presents a summary of the operating characteristics for each alternative.

**Table 14.1** Operating Characteristics for Each Alternative System

| Operating Characteristics | Present System | Alternative I | Alternative II |
|---|---|---|---|
| $L$ | 4 customers | 1.5 customers | .67 customers |
| $L_q$ | 3.2 customers | .9 customers | .27 customers |
| $W$ | 10 minutes | 3.75 minutes | 3.33 minutes |
| $W_q$ | 8 minutes | 2.25 minutes | 1.33 minutes |
| $U$ | .80 | .60 | .40 |

For the store manager both of these alternatives seem preferable to the original conditions, which resulted in a lengthy waiting time of 8 minutes per customer. However, the manager might have a more difficult time selecting between the two alternatives. It might be appropriate to consider other factors besides waiting time. For example, the proportion of employee idle time is .40 with the first alternative and .60 with the second, which seems to be a significant difference. An additional factor is the "loss of space" resulting from a new checkout counter.

However, the final decision must be based on the manager's own experience and perceived needs. As we have noted previously, the results of queuing analysis provide information for decision making, but do not result in an actual recommended decision as an optimization model would.

Our two example alternatives illustrate the cost trade-off situation that is related to improved service. As the level of service is increased, the corresponding cost of this service also increases. For example, when we added an extra employee in alternative I, the service was improved but the cost of providing service also increased. Alternatively, when the level of service is increased, the costs associated with customer waiting decrease. The appropriate level of service to maintain should minimize the sum of these two costs as much as possible. This cost trade-off relationship is summarized in figure 14.2. As the level of service increases, the cost of service goes up while the waiting cost goes down. The sum of these costs results in a total cost curve, and the level of service that should be maintained is where this total cost curve is at a minimum. (However, this does not mean we can determine an exact optimal minimum cost solution, since the service and waiting characteristics we can determine are averages, and thus uncertain.)

*The cost trade-off related to improved service*

**Figure 14.2** Cost trade-offs for service levels.

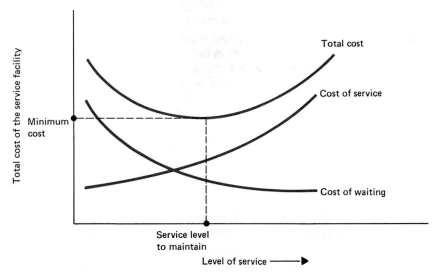

## The Multiple-Server Waiting Line

A slightly more complex queuing system than the single-server system is the case of a single waiting line being serviced by more than one server (i.e., multiple servers). As an example of this type of system we will consider the customer service department of the Biggs Department Store.

The customer service department of the store has a waiting room consisting of chairs placed along the wall of the area which, in effect, forms a single waiting line. Customers come to this area with questions or complaints or to clarify matters regarding credit card bills. The customers are served by three store representatives, each located in a partitioned stall. Customers are treated on a "first-come, first-served" basis. Figure 14.3 presents a schematic of this queuing system.

**Figure 14.3** Customer service queuing system.

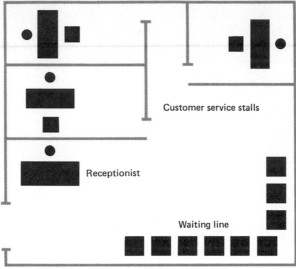

The store management desires to analyze this queuing system because excessive waiting times can result in irate customers, who will then often trade at other stores. Typically customers who come to this area have some problem and thus are impatient anyway. Waiting a long time only serves to increase their impatience.

*The characteristics of
the multiple-server
system*

First we will present the queuing formulas for a multiple-server queuing system. These formulas have been developed on the assumption of a *first-come, first-served queue discipline, Poisson arrivals, exponential service times,* and, *an infinite calling population,* just as the single-server model formulas were. The parameters of the multiple-server model are the arrival rate, "*a*," the service rate, "*s*," and the number of servers (often referred to as channels), "*c*":

$a$ = the arrival rate (average number of arrivals per time period)
$s$ = the service rate (average number served per time period) *per server* (channel)
$c$ = the number of servers

The formulas for the operating characteristics of the multiple-server model are given as follows.

The probability that there are no customers in the system (all servers are idle):

$$P_0 = \cfrac{1}{\left[\displaystyle\sum_{n=0}^{n=c-1} \frac{1}{n!}\left(\frac{a}{s}\right)^n\right] + \frac{1}{c!}\left(\frac{a}{s}\right)^c \left(\frac{cs}{cs-a}\right)}$$

The probability of n customers in the queuing system:

$$P_n = \frac{1}{c! c^{n-c}}\left(\frac{a}{s}\right)^n P_0, \text{ for } n > c$$

$$P_n = \frac{1}{n!}\left(\frac{a}{s}\right)^n P_0, \text{ for } n \le c$$

The average number of customers in the queuing system:

$$L = \frac{as \, (a/s)^c}{(c-1)! \, (cs-a)^2}P_0 + \frac{a}{s}$$

The average time a customer spends in the queuing system (waiting and being served):

$$W = \frac{L}{a}$$

The average number of customers in the queue:

$$L_q = L - \frac{a}{s}$$

The average time a customer spends in the queue waiting to be served:

$$W_q = W - \frac{1}{s}$$
$$= \frac{L_q}{a}$$

The probability that a customer arriving in the system must wait for service:

$$U = \frac{1}{c!}\left(\frac{a}{s}\right)^c \frac{cs}{cs-a}P_0$$

Notice in the formulas above that if $c = 1$ (i.e., one server), then they become the single-server formulas presented in the previous section.

Returning to our example, a survey of the customer service department for a 12-month period shows that the arrival rate and service rate are

$a = 10$ customers per hour arrive at the service department
$s = 4$ customers per hour can be served by *each* store representative

In addition, recall that this is a three-server queuing system, therefore,

$$c = 3 \text{ store representatives}$$

Using the multiple-server model formulas the operating characteristics of the service departments are computed as follows.

$$P_0 = \frac{1}{\left[ \sum_{n=0}^{n=c-1} \frac{1}{n!} \left( \frac{a}{s} \right)^n \right] + \frac{1}{c!} \left( \frac{a}{s} \right)^c \left( \frac{cs}{cs - a} \right)}$$

$$P_0 = \frac{1}{\left[ \frac{1}{0!} \left( \frac{10}{4} \right)^0 + \frac{1}{1!} \left( \frac{10}{4} \right)^1 + \frac{1}{2!} \left( \frac{10}{4} \right)^2 \right] + \frac{1}{3!} \left( \frac{10}{4} \right)^3 \frac{3(4)}{3(4) - 10}}$$

$$= .045 \text{ probability that no customers are in the service department}$$

$$L = \frac{as \, (a/s)^c}{(c - 1)! \, (cs - a)^2} P_0 + \frac{a}{s}$$

$$= \frac{(10) \, (4) \, (10/4)^3}{(3 - 1)! \, [3(4) - 10]^2} (.045) + \frac{10}{4}$$

$$= 6 \text{ customers (on the average) in the service department}$$

$$W = \frac{L}{a}$$

$$= \frac{6}{10}$$

$$= .60 \text{ hours (36 minutes) in the service department per customer on the average}$$

$$L_q = L - \frac{a}{s}$$

$$= 6 - \frac{10}{4}$$

$$= 3.5 \text{ customers (on the average) waiting to be served}$$

$$W_q = \frac{L_q}{a}$$

$$= \frac{3.5}{10}$$

$$= .35 \text{ hours (21 minutes) waiting in line per customer on the average}$$

$$U = \frac{1}{c!} \left( \frac{a}{s} \right)^c \frac{cs}{cs - a} P_0$$

$$= \frac{1}{3!} \left( \frac{10}{4} \right)^3 \frac{3(4)}{3(4) - 10} (.045)$$

$$= .703 \text{ probability that a customer must wait for service}$$

The department store's management has observed that customers have become frustrated with the relatively long waiting time of 21 minutes and the .703 probability of waiting. As such, they have decided to consider the addition of an extra service representative. The operating characteristics for this system must be recomputed with

$c = 4$ service representatives

Substituting this value along with $a$ and $s$ into our queuing formulas results in the following operating characteristics:

*Recomputed operating statistics with an additional server*

$P_0 = .073$ probability that no customers are in the service department

$L = 3.0$ customers (on the average) in the service department

$W = .30$ hours (18 minutes) in the service department per customer on the average

$L_q = .5$ customers (on the average) waiting to be served

$W_q = .05$ hours (3 minutes) waiting in line per customer on the average

$U = .31$, probability that a customer must wait for service

As in our previous example of the single-server system, the queuing operating characteristics provide input into the decision-making process, and the decision criteria are the waiting costs and service costs. The department store management would have to consider the cost of the extra service representative, as compared to the dramatic decrease in customer waiting time from 21 minutes to 3 minutes in order to make a decision.

## Additional Types of Queuing Systems

The *single queue with a single server* and the *single queue with multiple servers* are two of the most commonly applied and referred to queuing systems. However, in addition to these two categories of queuing systems, there are also two other general categories: *the single queue with single servers in sequence* and the *single queue with multiple servers in sequence*. Figure 14.4 presents a schematic of each of these two systems.

*Single- and multiple-servers in sequence*

An example of a queuing system that has a single queue leading into a sequence of single servers is the personnel office of a company where job applicants line up to apply for a specific job. All the applicants wait in one area and are called alphabetically. The application process consists of moving from one interview to the next in a single sequence to take tests, answer questions, fill out forms, etc. An alternative system of this type is an assembly line, where products queue up prior to being worked on by a sequenced line of machines.

*Examples of single-servers in sequence*

If, in the personnel office example above, an extra sequence of interviews were added, a queuing system with a single queue and multiple servers in sequence would exist. Likewise, if products were lined up in a

*Examples of multiple-servers in sequence*

**Figure 14.4** Single queues with single and multiple servers in sequence.

Queue                                    Servers

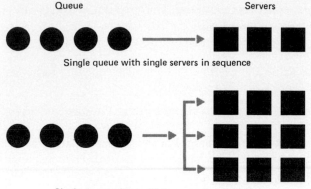

Single queue with single servers in sequence

Single queue with multiple servers in sequence

single queue prior to being worked on by machines in any one of 3 assembly lines, a *sequence of multiple servers* would exist.

*Other items that contribute to alternative queuing system forms*

In addition to the existence of the four general categories of queuing systems, other items that can contribute to the variety of possible queuing systems include:

Finite calling populations

*Balking*
*Reneging*

Queue systems in which customers can *balk* from entering the system or may leave the line if it is too long (i.e., renege)

Queues of limited capacity (such as a railhead with enough track for only 5 railroad cars)

Servers who provide service other than on a "first-come, first-served" basis

Service times that are not exponentially distributed

Arrival rates that are not Poisson distributed

*Jockeying*

Multiple servers, each preceded by a separate queue (such as a bank with several tellers, each with a queue); "*jockeying*" (i.e., movement between queues) can often result

## Summary

The various forms queuing systems can make queuing a potentially complex field of analysis. However, because of the frequency with which queues exist in our everyday life, the analysis of queues is an important and widely explored area of management science. While we have presented only the fundamentals of two basic types of queuing systems, a number of other analytical models have been developed to analyze the more complex queuing systems.

Some queuing situations, however, are so complex that it is impossible to develop an analytical model. When these situations occur, an alternative form of analysis is *simulation* in which the real life queuing system is simulated via a computerized mathematical model. The operating characteristics are determined by observing the simulated queuing system. This alternative technique, simulation, is the subject of our next chapter.

## References

Buffa, E. S. *Operations Management: Problems and Models*. 3d ed. New York: John Wiley and Sons, 1972.

Feller, W. *An Introduction to Probability Theory and Its Applications*. Vol. I. 3d ed. New York: John Wiley and Sons, 1968.

Hillier, F., and Lieberman, G. J. *Introduction to Operations Research*. 3rd ed. San Francisco: Holden-Day, 1980.

Lee, Sang M.; Moore, Laurence J.; and Taylor, Bernard W. *Management Science*. Dubuque, Iowa: Wm. C. Brown Company Publishers, 1981.

Morse, P. M. *Queues, Inventories, and Maintenance*. New York: John Wiley and Sons, 1958.

Saaty, T. L. *Elements of Queueing Theory*. New York: McGraw-Hill, 1961.

Shamblin, J. E., and Stevens, G. T., Jr. *Operations Research: A Fundamental Approach*. New York: McGraw-Hill, 1974.

Taha, H. A. *Operations Research: An Introduction*. New York: Macmillan Co., 1971.

## Problems

1. Identify 10 examples of queuing systems with which you are familiar in real life.

2. Define the following components of a queuing system:
   (a) queue discipline
   (b) calling population
   (c) arrival rate
   (d) service rate

3. A single-server queuing system with an infinite calling population, a first-come, first-served queue discipline, has an arrival rate of 50 customers per hour and a service rate of 70 customers per hour. Determine the following.
   (a) The probability of no customers in the queuing system.
   (b) The average number of customers in the queuing system.
   (c) The average number of customers in the waiting line.
   (d) The average time a customer is in the queuing system.
   (e) The probability that the server is busy.

4. A single-server queuing system with an infinite calling population and a first-come, first-served queue discipline has the following arrival and service rates:

$a = 16$ customers per hour
$s = 24$ customers per hour

Determine $P_0$, $P_3$, $L$, $L_q$, $W$, $W_q$, and $U$.

5. The ticket booth on the Tech campus is operated by one person, who is selling tickets for the annual Tech vs. State football game on Saturday. The ticket seller can serve 12 customers per hour on the average. On the average 10 customers arrive to purchase tickets every hour. Determine the average time a ticket buyer must wait and the portion of time the ticket seller is busy.

6. The Petroco Service Station has one pump for unleaded gas, which (with an attendant) can service 10 customers per hour. Cars arrive at the unleaded pump at a rate of 6 per hour. Determine the average queue length, the average time in the system for a car, and the average time a car must wait. If during a gasoline shortage the arrival rate increased to 12 cars per hour, what effect would it have on the average queue length?

7. The Dynaco Manufacturing Company produces a particular product in an assembly line operation. One of the machines on the line is a drill press that has a single assembly line feeding into it. A partially completed unit arrives at the press to be worked on every 7.5 minutes, on the average. The machine operator averages processing 10 parts per hour. Determine the average number of parts waiting to be worked on, the percentage of time the operator is working, and the percentage of time the machine is idle.

8. The management of Dynaco Manufacturing Company (problem 7) likes to have their operators working 90% of the time. What must the assembly line arrival rate be in order for the operator to be as busy as management would like?

9. The Peachtree Airport in Atlanta serves light aircraft. It has a single runway and one air traffic controller to land planes. It takes an airplane 12 minutes to land and clear the runway. Planes arrive at the airport at the rate of 4 per hour. Determine the following:
   (a) The number of planes that will stack up (on the average) waiting to land.
   (b) The average time a plane must wait in line before it can land.
   (c) The average time it takes a plane to clear the runway once it notifies the airport it is in the vicinity and wants to land.

(d) The FAA has a rule that an air traffic controller can be landing planes, on the average, a maximum of 45 minutes out of every hour. (There must be 15 minutes idle time available to relieve the tension.) Will this airport have to hire an extra air traffic controller?

10. The First American Bank of Rapid City presently has one outside drive-up teller. It takes the teller an average of 4 minutes to serve a bank customer. Customers arrive at the drive-up window at the rate of 12 per hour. The bank operations officer is currently analyzing the possibility of adding a second drive-up window at an annual cost of $20,000. It is assumed that arriving cars would be equally divided between both windows. The operations officer estimates that each minute reduction in customer waiting time will increase the bank's revenue by $2,000 annually. Should the second drive-up window be installed?

11. During registration at State University every quarter, students in the College of Business must have their courses approved by the college advisor. It takes the advisor an average of 2 minutes to approve each schedule, and students arrive at the advisor's office at the rate of 28 per hour.
   (a) Compute $L$, $L_q$, $W$, $W_q$, and $U$.
   (b) The dean of the college has received a number of complaints from students about the length of time they must wait to have their schedule approved. The dean believes a time of 10 minutes to wait and get a schedule approved is not unreasonable. Each assistant the dean assigns to the advisor's office will reduce the average time required to approve a schedule by 0.25 minutes, down to a minimum time of 1.0 minutes to approve a schedule. How many assistants should the dean assign to the advisor?

12. All trucks traveling on Interstate 40 between Albuquerque and Amarillo are required to stop at a weigh station. Trucks arrive at the weigh station at a rate of 200 per 8-hour day, and the station can weigh, on the average, 220 trucks per day.
   (a) Determine the average number of trucks waiting, the time at the weigh station for each truck, and the average waiting time (before being weighed) for each truck.
   (b) If the truck drivers find out they must remain at the weigh station longer than 15 minutes on the average, they will start taking a different route or travel at night, thus depriving the state of taxes. For each minute more than 15 minutes that trucks must remain at the weigh station, the state estimates it loses $10,000 in taxes per year. A new set of scales would have the same service capacity as the present set of scales, and it is assumed that arriving trucks would line up equally behind the 2 sets of scales. It will cost $50,000 per year to operate the new scales. Should the state install the new set of scales?

13. In problem 12, suppose passing truck drivers looked to see how many trucks were waiting to be weighed at the weigh station. If a driver sees that 4 or more trucks are at the weigh station line they will pass the station by and risk being caught and ticketed. What is the probability that a truck will pass the station by?

14. In the Fast Shop Market example in this chapter, the alternative II case consisted of the addition of a new checkout counter for the market. However, this alternative was analyzed using the single-server model. Why was the multiple-server model not used?

15. A queuing system has a single queue, an arrival rate of 40 customers per hour, 3 servers, and a service rate of 20 customers per server per hour. Determine $L$, $W$, $L_q$, and $U$.

16. The dean of the College of Business at State University (problem 11) is considering the addition of a second advisor in the college advising office to serve the line of students who wait at the office to have their schedules approved. This new advisor can serve the same number of students per hour as the present advisor. Determine $L$, $L_q$, $W$, and $W_q$ for this altered advising system. As a student, would you recommend adding the advisor?

17. The Cumberland River Carpet Mill has a warehouse with 2 loading docks, at which empty trucks are loaded with carpet to be shipped around the country. It takes the loaders at a dock an hour to load a truck. The empty trucks arrive every 45 minutes at a parking lot adjacent to the warehouse to wait until a dock is vacated. The warehouse is open 12 hours per day. Determine the following:
    (a) The average number of trucks waiting to be loaded.
    (b) The average number of trucks at the mill waiting and being loaded.
    (c) The average time a truck must wait in the parking lot.
    (d) The average time a truck is at the mill.

18. The Dynaco Manufacturing Company has an assembly line that feeds two drill presses. As partially completed products come off the line, they are lined up to wait for a vacant machine. The units arrive at the work station (containing both presses) at the rate of 100 per hour. Each press operator can process an average of 60 units per hour. Compute $L$, $L_q$, $W$, and $W_q$.

19. In problem 18 the Dynaco Company has found that if there are more than 3 units (average) waiting to be processed at any one work station, then they are tying up too much money in in-process inventory (i.e., units waiting to be processed). The company estimates that each unit (on the average) waiting to be processed costs $50 per day. Alternately, operating a third press would cost $150 per day. Should the company operate a third press at this work station?

20. The Freshfood Bakery bakes cakes in ovens and when they are done, they are transported from the ovens to be packaged by one of three wrappers. Each wrapper can wrap an average of 200 cakes per hour. The cakes are brought to the wrappers at the rate of 500 cakes per hour. It a cake has to wait longer than 5 minutes before being wrapped it will not be fresh enough to meet store standards. Does the bakery need to hire another wrapper?

21. The Riverview Clinic has 2 general practitioners that see patients daily. Patients arrive at the clinic at the rate of 6 per hour. Each doctor spends an average of 15 minutes with a patient. The patients wait in a waiting area until one of the 2 doctors is able to see them. However, since patients typically do not feel well when they come to the clinic, the doctors do not believe it is good practice to have a patient wait longer than an average of 15 minutes. Should this clinic add a third doctor, and if so, will this alleviate the waiting problem?

# 15
Simulation

## The Monte Carlo Process
The Use of Random Numbers

## Computer Simulation

## A Queuing Example
Model Experimentation
Continuous Probability Distributions

## Random Number Generators
Midsquare Method

## Optimization Using Simulation

## Validation of Simulation Results

## Simulation Applications
Queuing
Inventory Control
Production
Finance
Marketing
Public Service Operations
Environmental and Resource Analysis

## Simulation Languages

## Summary

Simulation represents a major divergence from the topics presented in the previous chapters of this text. These previous topics usually consisted of mathematical models and formulas that could be applied to certain types of problems. The solution approaches to these problems were, for the most part, analytical. However, not all real world problems can be solved by applying a specific type of technique and then solving it. Some problem situations are too complex to be represented by the concise techniques presented so far in this text. In such cases, *simulation* is an alternative form of analysis.

Analogue simulation is a form of simulation familiar to most people. In analogue simulation, an original physical system is replaced by an analogous physical system that is easier to manipulate. Much of the experimentation in manned space flight was conducted using physical simulation that recreated the conditions of space. For example, conditions of weightlessness were "simulated" using rooms filled with water. Other examples include wind tunnels, which simulate the conditions of flight, and treadmills, which simulate automobile tire wear in a laboratory instead of on the road.

*Analogue simulation*

Alternatively, this chapter will be concerned with *computerized mathematical simulation.* In this form of simulation, systems are replicated with mathematical models, which are analyzed with a computer. This form of simulation has become a very popular technique that has been applied to a wide variety of business problems.

*Computerized mathematical simulation*

One reason for its popularity is because it offers a means of analysis for very complex systems that cannot be analyzed using the other management science techniques in this text. However, because such complex systems are beyond the scope of this text, we will not present actual simulation models, but instead, simplified simulation models of systems that can also be analyzed analytically. We will begin with one of the simplest forms of simulation models, which encompasses the "Monte Carlo" process for simulating random variables.

*An alternative form of analysis for complex systems*

## The Monte Carlo Process

A characteristic of some systems, which makes them difficult to solve analytically, is that they consist of random variables represented by probability distributions. As a result, a large proportion of the applications of simulations are for probabilistic models.

A technique for
selecting numbers
randomly from a
probability
distribution

The term *Monte Carlo* has become synonymous with probabilistic simulation in recent years. However, in reality, Monte Carlo can be more narrowly defined as a technique for selecting numbers *randomly* from a probability distribution (i.e., "sampling") for use in a *trial* (computer) run of a simulation. As such, the Monte Carlo technique is not a type of simulation model but rather a mathematical process used within a simulation.

The name Monte Carlo is appropriate, since the basic principle behind the process is the same as one would find in the operation of a gambling casino in Monaco. In Monaco such devices as a roulette wheel, dice, and playing cards are used. These devices produce numbered results at random from well-defined populations. For example, a 7 resulting from thrown dice is a random value from a population of 11 possible numbers (i.e., 2 through 12). This same process is employed, in principle, in the Monte Carlo process used in simulation models.

## The Use of Random Numbers

The Monte Carlo process of selecting random numbers according to a probability distribution will be demonstrated using the following example. The manager of the Big T Supermarket must decide how many cases of milk to order each week. One of the primary considerations in the manager's decision is the amount of milk demanded each week. The number of cases of milk demanded is a random variable (which we will define as $x$), and ranges from 14 cases to 18 cases every week. From past records, the manager determined the frequency of cases of milk demanded for the past 100 weeks. From this frequency distribution, a probability distribution of demand can be developed, as shown in table 15.1

Generating values by
spinning a roulette
wheel

The purpose of the Monte Carlo process is to generate the random variable, demand, by "sampling" from the probability distribution, $P(x)$. The demand per week can be randomly generated according to the probability distribution by spinning a wheel that is partitioned into segments corresponding to the probabilities, as shown in figure 15.1.

**Table 15.1** Probability Distribution of Demand for Milk

| Cases Demanded Per Week | Frequency of Demand | Probability of Demand $P(x)$ |
|---|---|---|
| 14 | 20 | .20 |
| 15 | 40 | .40 |
| 16 | 20 | .20 |
| 17 | 10 | .10 |
| 18 | 10 | .10 |
| | 100 | 1.00 |

**Figure 15.1** A roulette wheel for demand.

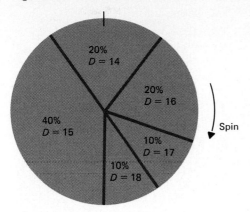

Since the surface area on the roulette wheel is partitioned according to the probability of each weekly demand value, the wheel replicates the probability distribution for demand if the values of demand occur in a random manner. In order to simulate demand for one week, the manager will spin the wheel, and the segment the wheel stops at will indicate demand for one week. Over a period of weeks (i.e., many spins of the wheel), the frequency with which demand values occur will approximate the probability distribution, *P(x)*. This method of generating values of a variable, *x,* by randomly selecting from the probability distribution—the wheel—is the Monte Carlo process.

By spinning the wheel, the manager artificially reconstructs the purchase of milk during a week. In this reconstruction, a long period of *real time* (i.e., a number of weeks) is represented by a short period of *simulated time* (i.e., several spins of the wheel).

*Real time*
*Simulated time*

Now let us slightly reconstruct our roulette wheel. In addition to partitioning the wheel into segments corresponding to the probability of demand, we will put numbers along the outer rim like a real roulette wheel. This reconstructed roulette wheel is shown in figure 15.2.

There are 100 total numbers (from 0 to 99) on the outer rim of the wheel, and they have been partitioned according to the probability of each demand value. For example, there are 20 numbers from 0 to 19 (i.e., 20% of the total 100 numbers) corresponding to a demand of 14 cases of milk. This now enables us to determine the value of demand by seeing which number the wheel stops at as well as looking at the segment of the wheel.

When the manager spins this new wheel, the actual demand for cases of milk will be determined by a number. For example, if the number 71 comes up on a spin, the demand is 15 cases per week, while the number 30

**Figure 15.2** Numbered roulette wheel.

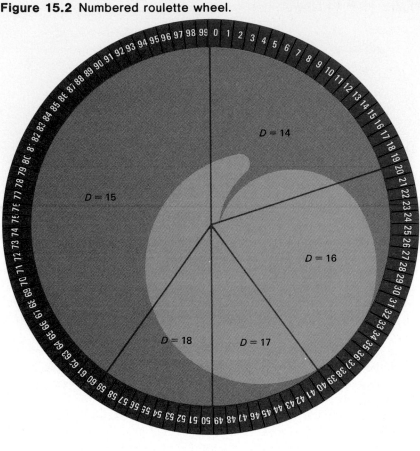

would indicate demand of 16. Since the manager does not know which number will come up at the marker prior to the spin and there is an equal chance of any of the 100 numbers occurring, the numbers occur at "random," that is, they are *random numbers*.

Obviously it is not generally practical to generate weekly demand for milk by spinning a wheel. Alternatively, the process of spinning a wheel can be replicated using random numbers alone.

*Using a random number table*

First, we will rearrange and transfer the ranges of random numbers for each demand value from the roulette wheel to tabular form, as shown in table 15.2. Next, instead of spinning the wheel to get a random number, we will select a random number from table 15.3, referred to as a *random number table*. (These random numbers have been generated by computer so that they are all *equally likely to occur* just as if we had spun a wheel. The development of random number tables will be discussed in more detail later in this chapter.) As an example, let us select the first number in table 15.3, 39. Looking again at table 15.2, we can see that the random number 39 falls in the range 20–59, which corresponds to a weekly demand of 15 cases of milk.

**Table 15.2** Generating Demand from Random Numbers

| Demand x | Ranges of Random Numbers r | |
|---|---|---|
| 14 | 0–19 | |
| 15 | 20–59 | r = 39 |
| 16 | 60–79 | |
| 17 | 80–89 | |
| 18 | 90–99 | |

By repeating this process of selecting random numbers from table 15.3 and then determining weekly demand from the random number, demand can be simulated for a period of time. For example, table 15.4 shows demand for a period of 15 consecutive weeks.

**Table 15.3** Random Number Table

```
39 65 76 45 45    19 90 69 64 61    20 26 36 31 62    58 24 97 14 97    95 06 70 99 00
73 71 23 70 90    65 97 60 12 11    31 56 34 19 19    47 83 75 51 33    30 62 38 20 46
72 18 47 33 84    51 67 47 97 19    98 40 07 17 66    23 05 09 51 80    59 78 11 52 49
75 12 25 69 17    17 95 21 78 58    24 33 45 77 48    69 81 84 09 29    93 22 70 45 80
37 17 79 88 74    63 52 06 34 30    01 31 60 10 27    35 07 79 71 53    28 99 52 01 41

02 48 08 16 94    85 53 83 29 95    56 27 09 24 43    21 78 55 09 82    72 61 88 73 61
87 89 15 70 07    37 79 49 12 38    48 13 93 55 96    41 92 45 71 51    09 18 25 58 94
98 18 71 70 15    89 09 39 59 24    00 06 41 41 20    14 36 59 25 47    54 45 17 24 89
10 83 58 07 04    76 62 16 48 68    58 76 17 14 86    59 53 11 52 21    66 04 18 72 87
47 08 56 37 31    71 82 13 50 41    27 55 10 24 92    28 04 67 53 44    95 23 00 84 47

93 90 31 03 07    34 18 04 52 35    74 13 39 35 22    68 95 23 92 35    36 63 70 35 33
21 05 11 47 99    11 20 99 45 18    76 51 94 84 86    13 79 93 37 55    98 16 04 41 67
95 89 94 06 97    27 37 83 28 71    79 57 95 13 91    09 61 87 25 21    56 20 11 32 44
97 18 31 55 73    10 65 81 92 59    77 31 61 95 46    20 44 90 32 64    26 99 76 75 63
69 08 88 86 13    59 71 74 17 32    48 38 75 93 29    73 37 32 04 05    60 82 29 20 25

41 26 10 25 03    87 63 93 95 17    81 83 83 04 49    77 45 85 50 51    79 88 01 97 30
91 47 14 63 62    08 61 74 51 69    92 79 43 89 79    29 18 94 51 23    14 85 11 47 23
80 94 54 18 47    08 52 85 08 40    48 40 35 94 22    72 65 71 08 86    50 03 42 99 36
67 06 77 63 99    89 85 84 46 06    64 71 06 21 66    89 37 20 70 01    61 65 70 22 12
59 72 24 13 75    42 29 72 23 19    06 94 76 10 08    81 30 15 39 14    81 33 17 16 33

63 62 06 34 41    79 53 36 02 95    94 61 09 43 62    20 21 14 68 86    84 95 48 46 45
78 47 23 53 90    79 93 96 38 63    34 85 52 05 09    85 43 01 72 73    14 93 87 81 40
87 68 62 15 43    97 48 72 66 48    53 16 71 13 81    59 97 50 99 52    24 62 20 42 31
47 60 92 10 77    26 97 05 73 51    88 46 38 03 58    72 68 49 29 31    75 70 16 08 24
56 88 87 59 41    06 87 37 78 48    65 88 69 58 39    88 02 84 27 83    85 81 56 39 38

22 17 68 65 84    87 02 22 57 51    68 69 80 95 44    11 29 01 95 80    49 34 35 36 47
19 36 27 59 46    39 77 32 77 09    79 57 92 36 59    89 74 39 82 15    08 58 94 34 74
16 77 23 02 77    28 06 24 25 93    22 45 44 84 11    87 80 61 65 31    09 71 91 74 25
78 43 76 71 61    97 67 63 99 61    30 45 67 93 82    59 73 19 85 23    53 33 65 97 21
03 28 28 26 08    69 30 16 09 05    53 58 47 70 93    66 56 45 65 79    45 56 20 19 47

04 31 17 21 56    33 73 99 19 87    26 72 39 27 67    53 77 57 68 93    60 61 97 22 61
61 06 98 03 91    87 14 77 43 96    43 00 65 98 50    45 60 33 01 07    98 99 46 50 47
23 68 35 26 00    99 53 93 61 28    52 70 05 48 34    56 65 05 61 86    90 92 10 70 80
15 39 25 70 99    93 86 52 77 65    15 33 59 05 28    22 87 26 07 47    86 96 98 29 06
58 71 96 30 24    18 46 23 34 27    85 13 99 24 44    49 18 09 79 49    74 16 32 23 02

93 22 53 64 39    07 10 63 76 35    87 03 04 79 88    08 13 13 85 51    55 34 57 72 69
78 76 58 54 74    92 38 70 96 92    52 06 79 79 45    82 63 18 27 44    69 66 92 19 09
61 81 31 96 82    00 57 25 60 59    46 72 60 18 77    55 66 12 62 11    08 99 55 64 57
42 88 07 10 05    24 98 65 63 21    47 21 61 88 32    27 80 30 21 60    10 92 35 36 12
77 94 30 05 39    28 10 99 00 27    12 73 73 99 12    49 99 57 94 82    96 88 57 17 91
```

**Table 15.4** Randomly Generated Demand for Fifteen Weeks

| Week | r | Demand (x) |
|------|-----|------------|
| 1 | 39 | 15 |
| 2 | 73 | 16 |
| 3 | 72 | 16 |
| 4 | 75 | 16 |
| 5 | 37 | 15 |
| 6 | 02 | 14 |
| 7 | 87 | 17 |
| 8 | 98 | 18 |
| 9 | 10 | 14 |
| 10 | 47 | 15 |
| 11 | 93 | 18 |
| 12 | 21 | 15 |
| 13 | 95 | 18 |
| 14 | 97 | 18 |
| 15 | 69 | 16 |
| | | $\Sigma = 241$ |

From table 15.4, the manager can compute the estimated average weekly demand:

$$\text{Estimated Average Demand} = \frac{241}{15}$$
$$= 16.1 \text{ cases per week}$$

*Comparing the simulation result with the analytical result*

The manager can then use this information to determine the number of cases of milk to order each week. However, although this example is convenient for illustrating how simulation works, the average demand could have more appropriately been calculated *analytically* using the formula for expected value. The *expected value* or average for weekly demand can be computed analytically from the probability distribution, $P(x)$.

$$E(x) = \sum_{i=1}^{n} P(x_i) \, x_i$$

where

$$x_i = \text{demand value ``}i\text{''}$$
$$P(x_i) = \text{probability of demand}$$
$$n = \text{the number of different demand values}$$

Therefore

$$E(x) = (.20)(14) + (.40)(15) + (.20)(16) + (.10)(17)$$
$$+ (.10)(18)$$
$$= 15.5 \text{ cases per week}$$

*The number of trials in a simulation*

While the analytical result of 15.5 cases is close to the simulated result of 16.1 cases, there is some difference. The margin of difference (.6 case) between the simulated value and the analytical value is a result of the number of periods over which the simulation was conducted. The results of any simulation study are subject to the number of times the simulation occurred (i.e., the number of *trials*). Thus, the more periods for which the simulation is conducted, the more accurate the result. For example, if demand was simulated for 1,000 weeks, in all likelihood, an average value exactly equal to the analytical value (15.5 cases of milk per week) would result.

Once a simulation is repeated enough times so that it reaches an average result that will remain constant, it is analogous to the *steady-state* result, a concept we discussed previously in our discussion of Markov analysis and queuing. For this example, 15.5 cases is the long run average or steady-state result, but we have seen that the simulation would have to be repeated at least more than 15 times (i.e., weeks) before this result is reached.

Comparing our simulated result with the analytical (expected value) result for this example points out one of the problems that can occur with simulation. It is often difficult to *validate* the results of a simulation model, i.e., to make sure the true steady-state average result has been reached. In this case we were able to compare the simulated result with the expected value (which is the true steady-state result) and we found there was a slight difference. As such, we logically deduced that 15 trials of the simulation were not sufficient to determine the steady-state average. However, simulation most often is employed when analytical analysis is not possible (which is one of the reasons simulation is generally useful). In these cases, there is no analytical standard of comparison, and validation of results becomes more difficult. We will discuss this problem of validation in more detail later in the chapter.

*Validating the simulation result*

## Computer Simulation

The simulation we performed manually in the previous section for our milk demand example was not too difficult. However, if we had performed the simulation for 1,000 weeks it would have taken several hours. Alternatively, this simulation could be done on the computer, and it would require only several seconds. Also, our simulation example was not very complex. As simulation models get progressively more complex, it becomes virtually impossible to perform them manually, thus making the computer a necessity.

*Computer vs. manual simulation*

Although we will not develop an actual computer model in a computer language for this example, we will demonstrate how a computerized simulation model is developed. Figure 15.3 is a diagram of the structure of a computerized simulation model for the supermarket example.

**Figure 15.3** Diagram of a computer simulation.

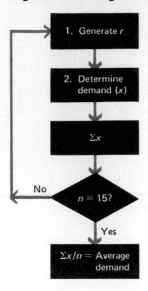

The first step in the computer model is to generate a random number, *r*. There are numerous subroutines available on practically every computer system that generate random numbers. Most are quite easy to use and require only a few "statements" to insert in a program. These random numbers are generated by mathematical processes (which we will discuss later in the chapter) as opposed to a physical process, such as a roulette wheel. For this reason, they are referred to as *pseudorandom numbers*.

*Pseudorandom numbers*

Once a random number is generated, a value for *x*, demand, is determined. This requires that computer statements be developed that will replicate the ranges of random numbers in table 15.2. Such statements typically take the form of, "If *r* is between 0 and 19, then *x* equals 14, otherwise go to the next statement, which specifies a range between 20 and 59, etc."

After each value for demand is determined, it is added to all previous values so that when the program is completed, the total sum of demand will exist.

At this point, demand has actually been simulated for one week. The program is constructed such that "*n*" number of weeks are counted and summed after each week is simulated. For our example, *n* equals fifteen weeks. At each simulation the computer checks to see if *n* has reached 15. If it has not, then the program is sent back to the beginning and another random number is generated and a value for demand is determined. However, if *n* does equal 15, the program is passed to the next stage. At the final stage of the program, the average weekly demand is computed by dividing the sum for demand by *n*.

This example simulation model is relatively simple. The computer program for this simulation would require only a few "statements" and only a few seconds to run. One reason for its simplicity is because it contains only one random variable, $x$. As the number of random variables increases as well as the items being computed, then the simulation model becomes more complex. In the following example we will discuss a slightly more complex simulation model with two random variables.

## A Queuing Example

In order to demonstrate the simulation of a queuing system, we will use a system similar to the Fast Shop Market example first introduced in chapter 14. In this system a drive-in market consisted of one cash register (the service facility) and a single queue of customers. In this example, we are going to make the assumption that the time intervals between customer arrivals and service times are *discrete* random variables defined by the probability distributions in tables 15.5 and 15.6 (which will exclude the use of the single-server queuing formulas developed in chapter 14).

*A simulation example with two random variables*

**Table 15.5** Distribution of Arrival Intervals

| Arrival Interval (minutes) x | Probability P(x) | Cumulative Probability | Random Number Range $r_1$ |
|---|---|---|---|
| 1.0 | .20 | .20 | 1–20 |
| 2.0 | .40 | .60 | 21–60 |
| 3.0 | .30 | .90 | 61–90 |
| 4.0 | .10 | 1.00 | 91–99,00 |

**Table 15.6** Distribution of Service Times

| Service Time (minutes) y | Probability P(y) | Cumulative Probability | Random Number Range $r_2$ |
|---|---|---|---|
| 0.5 | .20 | .20 | 1–20 |
| 1.0 | .50 | .70 | 21–70 |
| 2.0 | .30 | 1.00 | 71–99,00 |

Table 15.5 defines the interarrival time or how often customers arrive at the cash register. For example, there is a .20 probability of a customer arriving *one minute* after the previous customer. Table 15.6 defines the service time for a customer. Notice that cumulative probabilities have been included in tables 15.5 and 15.6. The cumulative probability provides a convenient (visual) means for determining the ranges of random numbers associated with each probability. For example, in table 15.5 the first random number range for $r_1$ is from 1 to 20, which corresponds to the cumulative

*Constructing the random number ranges using cumulative probabilities*

probability of .20 while the second range of random numbers is from 21 to 60 which corresponds to a cumulative probability of .60. However, although the cumulative probability goes up to 1.00, our random number table 15.3 only contains values from 0 to 99. Thus, the number 0 is used in the last random number range of each table in place of 100.

Table 15.7 illustrates the simulation of 10 customer arrivals to the cash register.

**Table 15.7** Simulation of the Fast Shop Queuing System

| Customer $r_1$ | Arrival Inter- val x | Arrival Clock | Enter Facil- ity Clock | Wait- ing Time | Length of Queue after Entry | $r_2$ | Ser- vice Time y | Depar- ture Clock | Time in System |
|---|---|---|---|---|---|---|---|---|---|
| 1 | — | — | 0.0 | 0.0 | 0.0 | 0 | 65 | 1.0 | 1.0 | 1.0 |
| 2 | 71 | 3.0 | 3.0 | 3.0 | 0.0 | 0 | 18 | 0.5 | 3.5 | .5 |
| 3 | 12 | 1.0 | 4.0 | 4.0 | 0.0 | 0 | 17 | 0.5 | 4.5 | .5 |
| 4 | 48 | 2.0 | 6.0 | 6.0 | 0.0 | 0 | 89 | 2.0 | 8.0 | 2.0 |
| 5 | 18 | 1.0 | 7.0 | 8.0 | 1.0 | 1 | 83 | 2.0 | 10.0 | 3.0 |
| 6 | 08 | 1.0 | 8.0 | 10.0 | 2.0 | 1 | 90 | 2.0 | 12.0 | 4.0 |
| 7 | 05 | 1.0 | 9.0 | 12.0 | 3.0 | 2 | 89 | 2.0 | 14.0 | 5.0 |
| 8 | 18 | 1.0 | 10.0 | 14.0 | 4.0 | 2 | 08 | 0.5 | 14.5 | 4.5 |
| 9 | 26 | 2.0 | 12.0 | 14.5 | 2.5 | 2 | 47 | 1.0 | 15.5 | 3.5 |
| 10 | 94 | 4.0 | 16.0 | 16.0 | 0.0 | 0 | 06 | 0.5 | 16.5 | .5 |
| | | | | | 12.5 | 8 | | | | 24.5 |

*Steps of the manual simulation process*

Now we will interpret the manual simulation process encompassed in table 15.7.

1. Customer 1 arrives at time 0, which is recorded on an *arrival clock*. Since there are no customers in the system, customer 1 enters the service facility (i.e., cash register) immediately, also at time 0. As such, the waiting time and queue length are 0.

2. Next, a random number, $r_2 = 65$, is selected from the second column in table 15.3. Observing table 15.6, we see that a random number of 65 results in a service time, y, of 1.0 minute. After checking out at the cash register, the customer departs at time 1.0 minute, having been in the total queuing system a total of 1.0 minute.

3. A new random number, $r_1 = 71$, is selected from table 15.3, which specifies that customer 2 arrives 3.0 minutes after customer 1, or at time 3.0 as shown on the arrival clock. Since customer 1 departed the service facility at time 1.0, customer 2 can be served immediately, and thus incurs no waiting time. As such, there is no waiting line.

4. Next a random number, $r_2 = 18$, is selected from table 15.3, which indicates that customer 2 will spend 0.5 minute being served and will depart at time 3.5.

This process of selecting random numbers and generating arrival intervals and service times continues in the same manner until 10 customer arrivals are simulated, as shown in table 15.7.

*Operating statistics from the simulation*

Once the simulation is complete, we can compute operating characteristics from the simulation results as follows.

$$\text{Average Waiting Time} = \frac{12.5 \text{ minutes}}{10 \text{ customers}}$$
$$= 1.25 \text{ minutes per customer}$$

$$\text{Average Queue Length} = \frac{8 \text{ customers}}{10 \text{ customers}}$$
$$= .80 \text{ customers}$$

$$\text{Average Time in the System} = \frac{24.5 \text{ minutes}}{10 \text{ customers}}$$
$$= 2.45 \text{ minutes per customer}$$

*Limitations of the simulation results*

However, as in our previous example, these results must be viewed with skepticism. Ten trials of the system do not insure steady-state results. In general, we can expect a considerable difference between the true average values and that which is estimated from only 10 random draws. For one thing, we cannot be sure that the random numbers we selected in this example replicated the actual probability distributions because we used so few random numbers. For example, of nine arrivals, five had interarrival times of 1.0 minute. This corresponds to a probability of .55 (i.e., 5/9), while the actual probability of an arrival interval of 1.0 minute is .20 (from table 15.5). As the number of random trials are increased, the probabilities in the simulation will more closely conform to the actual probability distributions. That is, if we simulated the queuing system for 1,000 arrivals, then we could more reasonably expect that 20% of the arrivals would have an interarrival time of one minute.

*Starting conditions of the simulation*

An additional factor that can affect the simulation results in this example is the starting conditions. By starting our queuing system with no customers at all in the system, we must simulate a length of time before the system replicates normal operating conditions. Of course in this example, it is logical to start simulating from when the market opens in the morning, especially if we simulate for an entire working day. Alternatively, some queuing systems start with items already in the system. For example, a production plant typically starts each day with partially completed products left over from the previous day waiting at each machine. In this case, it is necessary to begin the simulation with items already in the system.

By adding a second random variable to a simulation model, such as the one above, we have increased the complexity substantially and therefore the manual operations. To simulate the example in table 15.7 manually for 1,000 trials would require several hours. As such it would be imperative to perform this type of simulation on the computer. Such a model would require a number of mathematical computations to determine the various column values of table 15.7. This would result in a computer model of larger size than our model diagrammed in figure 15.3, since the number of statements in computer language would increase substantially. However, in the realm of computer models this would result in what would still be considered a relatively simple and easy model.

Notice that although the queuing system we used as an example in this section is relatively simple, it is different from the queuing models presented in chapter 14. The difference is that we used distributions other than the Poisson and exponential to describe arrivals and service in this example. This highlights the usefulness of simulation. In general, simulation allows us to analyze systems of many types (not just queuing) when analytical formulas are not readily available or are too difficult to develop. In many queuing situations that contain a number of complexities besides just different arrival and service distributions, analytical formulas cannot be developed at all. In such situations simulation is the only viable alternative.

## Model Experimentation

*Using the simulation model to test alterations in the system*

An additional benefit of simulation analysis is the ability to experiment with the model. For example, in our queuing example we could expand the model to include more service facilities, more queues, and different arrival and service times, and observe their effect on the results. In many analytical cases, such experimentation is limited by the availability of a particular formula. That is, by changing various parts of the problem we may create a problem to which we have no specific analytical formula to apply. Alternatively, simulation has no such limitations. The only limitation of simulation is one's ability to develop a computer program.

## Continuous Probability Distributions

The simulation examples we have presented so far in this chapter have consisted solely of discrete probability distributions. In our first example, the supermarket manager considered a probability distribution of discrete demand values. In the queuing example, the probability distributions were for discrete interarrival times and service times. However, while demand values are often discrete, time values as used in our queuing example are usually continuous. In other words, customers would arrive at the Fast Shop Market cash register at any time rather than exactly 1, 2, or 3 minutes after the last customer. In fact, applications of simulation models that reflect continuous distributions are more frequent than models that employ discrete distributions.

The reason we have considered only examples with discrete distributions is that the ranges of random numbers can be explicitly determined with a discrete distribution, and are thus easier to illustrate. However, when random numbers are being selected according to a continuous probability distribution, a continuous function must be used. For example, consider the following continuous probability function, $f(x)$, for time (minutes), $x$.

$$f(x) = \frac{x}{8}, 0 \leq x \leq 4$$

In order to determine the value of time, $x$, for a random number, $r$, this continuous function must be *integrated* over the range 0 to 4. This results in the following cumulative probability function.

*Integrating the continuous function*

$$F(x) = \frac{x^2}{16}$$

Cumulative probabilities are analogous to the discrete ranges of random numbers we used in previous examples. Thus, we let this function, $F(x)$, equal the random number, $r$,

$$r = \frac{x^2}{16}$$

and solve for $x$,

$$x = 4\sqrt{r}$$

By generating a random number, $r$, and substituting it into this function, a value for $x$, "time," is determined. (However, for a continuous function the range of random numbers must be between 0.0 and 1.00 to correspond to probabilities between 0.0 and 1.00.) For example, if $r = .25$, then

$$x = 4\sqrt{.25}$$
$$x = 2 \text{ minutes}$$

The purpose of presenting this example (although rather briefly) is to demonstrate the difference between discrete and continuous functions. This continuous function is relatively simple, and as functions get more complex, the more difficult it becomes to develop the equation for determining the random variable, $x$, from $r$. Even this simple example required some calculus, and more complex models would require even more higher order mathematics to develop.

## Random Number Generators

It should now be apparent from our previous discussion that in a probabilistic simulation, random numbers play a very important part. Both examples that were presented required random numbers. So far, the random numbers we have used have come from table 15.3, a table of random numbers. However, random numbers do not just come from tables, and their generation is not as simple as one might initially think. If random numbers are not truly random, then they can have a significant effect on the validity of the simulation results.

The random numbers selected from table 15.3 were generated using a *numerical technique*. As such, they are not true random numbers, but *pseudorandom numbers*. True random numbers can only be produced by a physical process, such as spinning a roulette wheel over and over. However, a physical process, such as spinning a roulette wheel, cannot be conveniently employed in a computerized simulation model. Thus, the need for a numerical method to artificially create random numbers.

In order to truly reflect the system being simulated, the artificially created random numbers must have the following characteristics.

1. The random numbers must be uniformly distributed. This means that each random number in the interval of random numbers (i.e., 0 to 1 or 0 to 100) has an equal chance of being selected. If this condition is not present, then the simulation results will be biased by the random numbers, which have a *more likely* chance of being selected.

2. The numerical technique for generating random numbers should be efficient. This means that the random numbers should not degenerate into constant values or recycle too frequently. In addition, they should not require too much (computer) time and cost to generate.

3. The sequence of random numbers should not reflect any pattern. For example, the sequence of numbers 0, 1, 2, 3, 4, 5, 6, 7, 8, 9, 0, 1, 2, 3, 4, 5, 6, 7, 8, 9, 0, 1, 2, 3, 4, 5, 6, 7, 8, 9, 0, etc., while uniform is not random.

In order to determine whether the random numbers that are to be used in a simulation contain these characteristics, they can be tested using any one of several statistical tests that are available.

## Midsquare Method

The midsquare method is an older random number technique, which, although it is still used, is not now considered to be as efficient as some other methods. However, it is a relatively simple method, and thus useful to illustrate how random numbers are developed in general. This method uses what is known as a *seed value* to generate a series of random numbers. The seed value is squared, and the middle digits of the squared number are used as the random number. This random number is then used as the seed and squared to generate the next random number. For example, a seed value of 1,345 would result in the following sequence of random numbers.

$$(1345)^2 = 1809025 \quad , \quad r = 0902$$
$$(0902)^2 = 813604 \quad , \quad r = 1360$$
$$(1360)^2 = 1849600 \quad , \quad r = 4960$$
$$(4960)^2 = \text{etc.}$$

These values could subsequently be employed as random numbers by taking only the first two digits (to create an interval of 0 to 99) or by making them decimal values (creating an interval of 0.0 to .99).

The midsquare method is unsatisfactory for several reasons. First, it requires the computer many manipulations to develop the middle digits of the value, and thus it is time consuming. Second, this method will degenerate when a sequence of zeros comes up as the middle digits, thus creating a series of zeros.

*Limitations of the mid-square method*

Other numerical methods exist, some of which are relatively sophisticated and very good (i.e., they meet our requirements). However, the search continues for methods that create absolutely random values in an easy and efficient manner.

## Optimization Using Simulation

Simulation is a management science technique that does not generally result in an optimal solution. Generally, a simulation model reflects the *operation of a system,* and the results of the model are in the form of operating statistics, such as averages. However, optimal solutions can sometimes be obtained for simulation models by employing *search techniques*.

*Search techniques*

A search technique is a method for searching sets of operating characteristics to a simulation model until the best set is found. Optimization in this manner requires a series of computer simulation runs, each with predetermined changes in the decision variables from run to run.

Our Big T Supermarket example of milk demand presented earlier in this chapter could be changed into an optimization model as follows. First, we would develop a cost function based on the profit from each case of milk sold and the loss due to each unsold case of milk spoiling. Given the fact that demand varies, the manager would simulate the system for various amounts of milk *ordered*. The manager would then determine the amount to order from the order quantity that resulted in the highest profit. In other words, the simulation would *search* through a sequence of order quantities and select the one with the greatest profit.

*An example of searching for the best solution*

## Validation of Simulation Results

A major problem with simulation is the difficulty that is often encountered in making sure the results of a simulation analysis are valid. In other words, does the model actually replicate what is going on in the real world? The user of simulation generally wants to be certain that the model is internally correct and that all the operations that are performed in the simulation are logical and mathematically correct. An old adage often associated with simulation is "garbage in, garbage out." In order to gain some assurances about the validity of simulation results several testing procedures are available.

*Testing simulation results to make sure the results are correct*

First, the simulation model can be run for short periods of time or for only a few simulation trials. This allows the results to be compared with manually derived solutions (such as we did in the examples in this chapter)

*Checking the simulation model manually*

in order to check for discrepancies. Another means of testing is to divide the model into parts and simulate each part separately. This reduces the complexity involved in seeking out errors in the overall model. In a similar vein the mathematical relationships in the simulation model can be simplified so that they can be tested easier to see if the model is operating correctly.

*Comparing the simulation results with real-world data* In order to determine if the model reliably represents the system being simulated, the simulation results can sometimes be compared with actual real-world data. Several statistical tests are available for performing this type of analysis. However, when a model is developed to simulate a *new or unique* system, there is no realistic way to ensure that the results are valid.

*Starting conditions* An additional problem in determining if a simulation model is a valid representation of the system under analysis relates to starting conditions. Should the system be simulated by assuming the system is empty (i.e., starting a queuing system with no customers in line) or should the simulation be started as close to possible to normal operating conditions? Another problem, we have already indicated, is the determination of how long the simulation should be run in order to reach true steady-state conditions, if indeed a steady-state exists.

In general, a standard, foolproof procedure for validation is simply not possible. In many cases, the confidence placed in a simulation model must be based on the expertise and experience of the user who develops the simulation model.

## Simulation Applications

Simulation can be applied to a number of problems that are too difficult to model and solve analytically. Some analysts feel that systems of complexity should be studied via simulation, whether they can be analyzed analytically or not, because it provides such an easy vehicle to experiment on the system. As a result, simulation has been applied to a wide range of problems. A *few* of the more prominent examples in the field of business have been made in the following areas.

### Queuing

A major area of application for simulation has been in the analysis of queuing systems. As indicated in chapter 14, the assumptions required to solve the operating characteristic formulas are relatively restrictive. For the more complex queuing systems (resulting from a relaxation of these assumptions), it is not possible to develop analytical formulas, and simulation is often the only available means of analysis.

## Inventory Control

Inventory control is a topic we will discuss in chapters 17 and 18. However, most people are aware that product demand is an essential component in determining the amount of inventory for a commercial enterprise to keep. Most of the mathematical formulas used to analyze inventory systems make the assumption that demand is certain (i.e., not a random variable). Since demand is rarely known with certainty, these inventory formulas do not reflect this uncertainty. When demand is a random variable, then simulation is one of the few means for analyzing inventory systems, such that demand uncertainty is reflected.

## Production

Various production problems have been simulated, such as production scheduling, production sequencing, assembly line balancing (of in-process inventory), plant layout, and plant location analysis. It is surprising how often various production processes can be viewed as queuing systems that can only be analyzed using simulation. Since machine breakdowns typically occur according to some probability distributions, maintenance-type problems are frequently analyzed using simulation.

## Finance

Capital budgeting problems include estimates of cash flows, which are often a result of many random variables. Simulation has been used to generate values of the various contributing factors to derive estimates of cash flows. Simulation has also been used to determine the inputs into a rate of return calculation where the inputs are random variables, such as market size, selling price, growth rate, and market share.

## Marketing

Marketing problems typically consist of numerous random variables, such as market size and type, and consumer preferences. Simulation can be used to ascertain how a particular market might react to the introduction of a product or to an advertising campaign for an existing product. Another area of application of simulation in marketing is the analysis of distribution channels to determine the most efficient distribution system.

## Public Service Operations

Recently the operation of police departments, fire departments, post offices, hospitals, court systems, airports, and other public systems have been analyzed using simulation. Typically such operations are so complex and contain so many random variables that no other technique can be employed for analysis except simulation.

### Environmental and Resource Analysis

Some of the more recent innovative applications of simulation have been directed at problems in the environment. Simulation models have been developed to ascertain the impact of man-made projects, such as nuclear power plants, reservoirs, highways, and dams, on the environment. In many cases, these models include measures to analyze the financial feasibility of such projects. Other models have been developed to simulate pollution conditions in geographic areas. In the area of resource analysis, numerous models have been developed in recent years to simulate energy systems and the feasibility of alternative energy sources.

## Simulation Languages

*Computer languages developed specifically to perform simulation operations*

The computer programming aspects of simulation can be quite difficult. Fortunately, generalized simulation languages have been developed to perform many of the functions of a simulation study. In fact, to varying degrees, these languages require limited knowledge of a scientific or business-oriented programming language. Some of these simulation languages are GPSS, GASP, DYNAMO, SIMSCRIPT, SIMULA, GERT, Q-GERT, and SLAM. These languages typically are more applicable to certain problems than others. For example, DYNAMO is useful when the random variables change over time (i.e., they are dynamic); GPSS and GASP are useful languages for queuing problems; GERT, Q-GERT, and SLAM are "network" simulation packages applicable to systems that can be represented as networks.

## Summary

*An important and widely used management science technique*

Simulation has become an increasingly important management science technique for analysis in recent years. Various surveys have shown simulation to be one of the most widely applied (to real-world problems) techniques presently available. Evidence of this popularity is the number of specialized simulation languages that have been developed by the computer industry and academia to deal with complex problem areas.

*The popularity of simulation*

The popularity of simulation is due in large part to the flexibility it allows in analyzing systems as opposed to more confining analytical techniques. In other words, the problem does not have to fit the model (or technique)—the simulation model can be constructed to fit the problem. Simulation is also very popular because it is an excellent experimental technique enabling systems and problems to be experimented within a laboratory-type setting.

*Limitations of simulation*

However, in spite of the versatility gained by using simulation, it still has limitations and must be used with caution. One limitation is that simulation models are typically unstructured, and they must be developed for a system or problem that is also unstructured. This is distinctly different from some of the structured techniques presented in this text that we simply applied to a specific type of problem. As a result, simulation models often require a certain amount of imagination and intuitiveness to develop that is not required by some of the other straightforward solution techniques we have presented. In addition, the validation of simulation models is an area of serious concern. In fact, it is often impossible to realistically validate simulation results to know if they accurately reflect the system under analysis. This problem has become an area of such concern that "output analysis" of simulation results is developing into a new field of study itself. A further limiting factor in simulation is the cost in money and time for model building. Because simulation models are developed for unstructured systems, they often take large amounts of manpower, time, money, and computer facilities to develop and run. For many business companies, this can be prohibitive.

## References

Greenberg, S. *GPSS Primer*. New York: Wiley-Interscience, 1972.

Hammersly, J. M., and Handscomb, D. C. *Monte Carlo Methods*. New York: John Wiley and Sons, 1964.

Markowitz, H. M.; Karr, H. W.; and Hausner, B. *SIMSCRIPT: A Simulation Programming Language*. Englewood Cliffs, N.J.: Prentice-Hall, 1963.

Meier, R. C.; Newell, W. T.; and Pazer, H. L. *Simulation in Business and Economics*. Englewood Cliffs, N.J.: Prentice-Hall, 1969.

Mize, J., and Cox, G. *Essentials of Simulation*. Englewood Cliffs, N.J.: Prentice-Hall, 1968.

Naylor, T. H.; Balintfy, J. L.; Burdinck, D. S.; and Chu, K. *Computer Simulation Techniques*. New York: John Wiley and Sons, 1966.

Pritsker, A. A. B. *Modeling and Analysis Using Q-GERT Networks*. 2d ed. New York: John Wiley and Sons, 1977.

Pritsker, A. A. B. *The GASP IV Simulation Language*. New York: John Wiley and Sons, 1974.

Schriber, T. S. *Simulation Using GPSS*. New York: John Wiley and Sons, 1974.

Tocher, K. D. "Review of Computer Simulation." *Operational Research Quarterly* 16 (June 1965):189–217.

Van Horne, R. L. "Validation of Simulation Results." *Management Science* 17 (January 1971):247–57.

Wyman, F. P. *Simulation Modeling: A Guide to Using SIMSCRIPT*. New York: John Wiley and Sons, 1970.

# Problems

1. Either 1, 2, 3, 4, or 5 customers come into the Fast Shop Market every hour, according to the following probability distribution.

| Customers/Hour | Frequency of Occurrence | Probability |
|---|---|---|
| 1 | 10 | .10 |
| 2 | 40 | .40 |
| 3 | 30 | .30 |
| 4 | 15 | .15 |
| 5 | 5 | .05 |
|   | 100 | 1.00 |

   (a) Generate the number of customers per hour that arrive at the market for 20 hours, using the random number table in this chapter (start with the fifth column from the left).

   (b) Compute the average number of customers that arrive per hour and compare this value with the expected value of the number of customers per hour computed from the probability distribution.

2. Cityside Realty gets either 2, 3, or 4 new listings for houses to sell every week, according to the following probability distribution.

| Listings/Week | Probability |
|---|---|
| 2 | .30 |
| 3 | .50 |
| 4 | .20 |
|   | 1.00 |

Simulate the listings per week for 6 months, using the random number table in this chapter, and compute the average listings per week.

3. The Hoylake Rescue Squad receives an emergency call every 1, 2, 3, 4, 5, or 6 hours according to the following probability distribution.

| Time Between Emergency Calls (hours) | Probability |
|---|---|
| 1 | .05 |
| 2 | .10 |
| 3 | .30 |
| 4 | .30 |
| 5 | .20 |
| 6 | .05 |
|   | 1.00 |

The squad is on duty 24 hours per day, 7 days per week.

  (a) Simulate the emergency calls for 3 days (note that this will require a "running" or cumulative hourly clock), using the random number table.

  (b) Compute the average time between calls and compare this value with the expected value of the time between calls from the probability distribution. Why are the results different?

  (c) How many calls were made during the 3-day period? Can you logically assume that this is an average number of calls per 3-day period? If not, how could you simulate to determine such an average?

4. The time between arrivals of cars at the Petroco Service Station is defined by the following probability distribution.

| Time Between Arrivals (minutes) | Probability |
| --- | --- |
| 1 | .15 |
| 2 | .30 |
| 3 | .40 |
| 4 | .15 |
| | 1.00 |

  (a) Simulate the arrival of cars at the service station for 20 arrivals and compute the average time between arrivals.

  (b) Simulate the arrival of cars at the service station for 1 hour using a different stream of random numbers than those used in part (a) and compute the average time between arrivals.

  (c) Compare the results obtained in parts (a) and (b).

5. The Dynaco Manufacturing Company produces a particular product from a process consisting of operations of 5 machines. The probability distribution of the number of machines that will break down in a week is given as follows.

| Machine Breakdowns per Week | Probability |
| --- | --- |
| 0 | .10 |
| 1 | .10 |
| 2 | .20 |
| 3 | .25 |
| 4 | .30 |
| 5 | .05 |
| | 1.00 |

  (a) Simulate the machine breakdowns per week for 20 weeks.

  (b) Compute the average number of machines that will break down per week.

6. Every time a machine breaks down at the Dynaco Manufacturing Company (problem 5), it requires either 1, 2, or 3 hours to fix it according to the following probability distribution.

| Repair Time (hours) | Probability |
|---|---|
| 1 | .30 |
| 2 | .50 |
| 3 | .20 |
| | 1.00 |

(a) Simulate the repair time for 20 weeks and compute the average weekly repair time.

(b) If the same random numbers that are used to simulate breakdowns per week are also used to simulate repair time per breakdown, will it affect the results determined in any way? Explain.

(c) If it costs $50 per hour to repair a machine (which includes lost productivity) when it breaks down, determine the average weekly breakdown cost.

(d) The Dynaco Company is considering a preventive maintenance program that would alter the probabilities of machine breakdowns per week as follows.

| Machine Breakdowns per Day | Probability |
|---|---|
| 0 | .20 |
| 1 | .30 |
| 2 | .20 |
| 3 | .15 |
| 4 | .10 |
| 5 | .05 |
| | 1.00 |

The weekly cost of the preventive maintenance program is $150. Using simulation, determine if the company should institute the preventive maintenance program.

7. The Stereo Warehouse in Georgetown sells stereo sets, which it orders from Fuji Electronics in Japan. However, because of shipping and handling costs, an order must be for five stereos. Because of the time it takes to receive an order, the warehouse outlet places an order every time the present stock of stereos drops to 3 stereos. It costs $100 to place an order. It costs the warehouse $400 in lost sales when a customer asks for a stereo and the warehouse is out of stock. It costs $40 per stereo to keep a stereo stored in the warehouse. If a customer cannot be sold a stereo when requested, the customer will not buy one when it comes in, but will go to a competitor. The following probability distribution for demand for stereos has been determined.

| Demand per Month | Probability |
|---|---|
| 0 | .04 |
| 1 | .08 |
| 2 | .28 |
| 3 | .40 |
| 4 | .16 |
| 5 | .02 |
| 6 | .02 |
| | 1.00 |

The time required to receive an order once it is placed has the following probability distribution.

| Time to Receive an Order (months) | Probability |
|---|---|
| 1 | .60 |
| 2 | .30 |
| 3 | .10 |
| | 1.00 |

The warehouse presently has 5 stereos in stock. Orders are always received at the beginning of the week.

(a) Simulate the Stereo Warehouse's ordering and sales policy for 20 months (use the first column of random numbers in the table given in this chapter). Compute the average monthly cost.

(b) In this model the monthly cost is determined by the size of the order and the level of stereos in stock before an order is made. Explain how the monthly cost could be determined by varying these model components.

8. The First American Bank is trying to determine if it should install one or two drive-in teller windows. The following probability distributions for arrival intervals and service times have been developed from historical data.

| Time Between Automobile Arrivals (minutes) | Probability |
|---|---|
| 1 | 0.20 |
| 2 | 0.60 |
| 3 | 0.10 |
| 4 | 0.10 |
| | 1.00 |

| Service Time (minutes) | Probability |
|---|---|
| 2 | 0.10 |
| 3 | 0.40 |
| 4 | 0.20 |
| 5 | 0.20 |
| 6 | 0.10 |
| | 1.00 |

In the two-server system we will assume that an arriving car will join the shortest queue. When the queues are of equal length, there is a 50–50 chance the driver will enter the queue for either window.

 (a) Simulate both the one- and two-teller systems. Compute the average queue length, waiting time, and percentage utilization for each system.

 (b) Discuss your results determined in part (a) and to what degree they could be used to make a decision about which system to employ.

9. The time between arrival of oil tankers at a loading dock at Prudhoe Bay is given by the following probability distribution.

| Time Between Ship Arrivals (days) | Probability |
|---|---|
| 1 | .05 |
| 2 | .10 |
| 3 | .20 |
| 4 | .30 |
| 5 | .20 |
| 6 | .10 |
| 7 | .05 |
|  | 1.00 |

The time required to fill a tanker with oil and prepare it for sea is given by the following probability distribution.

| Time to Fill and Prepare (days) | Probability |
|---|---|
| 3 | .10 |
| 4 | .20 |
| 5 | .40 |
| 6 | .30 |
|  | 1.00 |

 (a) Simulate the movement of tankers to and away from the single loading dock for the first 20 arrivals. Compute the average time between arrivals, average waiting time to load, and the average number of tankers waiting to be loaded.

 (b) Discuss any inhibitions you might have about using your results for decision making.

10. Discuss the difference between true random numbers and pseudorandom numbers.

11. Discuss the properties pseudorandom numbers must exhibit in order to be truly random.

12. The Saki automobile dealer in Minneapolis–St. Paul orders the Saki sport compact, which gets 50 miles per gallon of gasoline, from the manufacturer in Japan. However, the dealer never knows for sure how many months it will take to receive the order once it is placed. It can take 1, 2, or 3 months with the following probabilities.

| Months to Receive an Order | Probability |
|---|---|
| 1 | .50 |
| 2 | .30 |
| 3 | .20 |
| | 1.00 |

The demand per month is given by the following distribution.

| Demand per Month (cars) | Probability |
|---|---|
| 1 | .10 |
| 2 | .30 |
| 3 | .40 |
| 4 | .20 |
| | 1.00 |

The dealer orders when the number of cars on the lot gets down to a certain level. In order to determine the appropriate level of cars to use as an indicator of when to order, the dealer needs to know how many cars will be demanded during the time required to receive an order.

Simulate the demand for 30 orders and compute the average number of cars demanded during the time required to receive an order. At what level of cars in stock should the dealer place an order?

13. State University is playing Tech in their annual football game on Saturday. A sportswriter has scouted each team all season and accumulated the following data. The State team runs 4 basic plays—a sweep, pass, draw, and off tackle—while Tech uses 3 basic defenses—a wide tackle, an Oklahoma, and a blitz. The amount of yards State will gain for each play against each defense is shown in the following table.

| State Play | Tech Defense Wide Tackle | Oklahoma | Blitz |
|---|---|---|---|
| Sweep | −3 | 5 | 12 |
| Pass | 12 | 4 | −10 |
| Draw | 2 | 1 | 20 |
| Off Tackle | 7 | 3 | −3 |

The probability that State will run each of its 4 plays is given as follows.

| Play | Probability |
|------|-------------|
| Sweep | .10 |
| Pass | .20 |
| Draw | .20 |
| Off Tackle | .50 |

The probability of Tech using each of its defenses is as follows.

| Defense | Probability |
|---------|-------------|
| Wide Tackle | .30 |
| Oklahoma | .50 |
| Blitz | .20 |

The sportswriter estimates that State will run 40 plays during the game. The sportswriter believes that if State gains 300 yards or more it will win, while if Tech holds State to less than 300 yards it will win. Use simulation to determine who the sportswriter will predict to win the game.

14. Each quarter the students in the College of Business at State University must have their course schedule approved by the college advisor. The students line up in the hallway outside the advising office. The students arrive at the advising office according to the following probability distribution.

| Time Between Arrivals (minutes) | Probability |
|---------------------------------|-------------|
| 4 | .20 |
| 5 | .30 |
| 6 | .40 |
| 7 | .10 |
|   | 1.00 |

The time required by the advisor to examine and approve a schedule corresponds to the following probability distribution.

| Schedule Approval (minutes) | Probability |
|-----------------------------|-------------|
| 3 | .30 |
| 4 | .50 |
| 5 | .20 |
|   | 1.00 |

Simulate this course approval system for 90 minutes. Compute the average queue length and the average time a student must wait, and discuss these results.

15. A new airport is being planned for a large urban area. The FAA has estimated the air traffic that will flow through the airport. You have been hired as a management scientist to develop a computerized simulation model that will provide information for the actual physical design of the airport. Identify the items you believe should be incorporated into the simulation model, and discuss in general terms how the simulation model would be designed.

16
Forecasting

## Forecasting Methods

## Time Series Methods

The Moving Average
Weighted Moving Averages
Exponential Smoothing
Adjusted Exponential Smoothing
Forecast Reliability

## Regression Forecasting Methods

Simple Regression
Coefficient of Determination
Multiple Regression
Regression Analysis with the Computer

## Long-Range Forecast Methods

## Summary

A forecast is a prediction of what will occur in the future. Meteorologists forecast the weather, sportscasters predict the winners of football games, and managers of business firms attempt to predict how much of their product will be demanded in the future. In fact, managers are constantly trying to predict the future regarding a number of factors, in order to make decisions in the present that will insure the continued success of their firm. Often a manager will use judgment, opinion, or past experiences to forecast what will occur in the future. However, a number of mathematical methods are also available to aid the manager in making decisions. In this chapter, we will discuss two of the more traditional forecasting methods: time series analysis and regression. Although no technique will result in a totally accurate forecast (i.e., it is impossible to exactly predict the future), these forecasting methods can provide reliable guidelines for decision making.

*Predicting what will occur in the future*

## Forecasting Methods

There are a variety of forecasting methods, the applicability of which are dependent on the *time frame* of the forecast (i.e., how far in the future we are forecasting); the *existence of patterns* in the forecast (i.e., seasonal trends, peak periods, etc.); and the *number of variables* the forecast is related to. We will discuss each of these factors separately.

*Factors related to forecasting methods*

In general, forecasts can be classified according to three time frames: short range, medium range, and long range. *Short-range* forecasts typically encompass the immediate future and are concerned with the daily operations of a business firm, such as daily demand or resource requirements. As such, a short-range forecast would rarely exceed a couple of months into the future. A *medium-range* forecast typically encompasses anywhere from one to two months up to a year. This length of forecast is generally more closely related to a yearly production plan, and will reflect such items as peaks and valleys in demand and the necessity to secure additional resources for the upcoming year. A *long-range* forecast typically encompasses a period longer than one or two years. Long-range forecasts are related to management's attempt to plan new products for changing markets, build new facilities, or secure long-term financing.

*Time frame of the forecast*
*Short-range*

*Medium-range*

*Long-range*

These classifications should be viewed as relative generalizations. The line of demarcation between medium- and long-range forecasts is often quite arbitrary and not always distinct. For some firms, a medium-range forecast could be several years, and for other firms a long-range forecast could be in terms of months.

*Trend*

Forecasts will often exhibit patterns or trends. A *trend* is a long-term movement of the item being forecast. For example, the demand for electronic calculators has shown an upward "trend" during the last several

*Cycles*

years without any long downward movement in the market. A *cycle* represents movement up or down during a trend. For example, new housing starts have shown a long, generally upward trend, but with cycles of up and down periods corresponding to economic conditions (high inflation,

*Seasonal patterns*

interest rates, etc.). A *seasonal pattern* is a movement that occurs periodically and is repetitive. For example, every winter the demand for sleds increases dramatically.

While some forecasts are related solely to time, other forecasts are *dependent* upon several variables. For example, the demand for gasoline is a function of the number of automobiles, the price and availability of gasoline, and the availability of alternative sources of transportation. An accurate forecast of the demand for gasoline would have to take these variables into consideration.

These factors, discussed above, determine the type of forecasting method that can or should be employed. In this chapter we are going to discuss two general types of forecasting methods that reflect these factors, *time series analysis* and *regression*.

## Time Series Methods

*Forecasts related to time only*

Time series methods are statistical techniques, which are computed solely from historical data, accumulated over a period of time. As the name *time series* suggests, these methods relate the forecast to only one factor—*time*. Time series methods tend to be most useful for short-range forecasting, although they can be used for longer range forecasting. We will discuss two types of time series methods: *moving averages* and *exponential smoothing*.

### The Moving Average

*A moving average example*

In order to demonstrate the *moving average* forecasting method we will use the following example. The Instant Paper Clip Office Supply Company sells and delivers office supplies to various companies, schools, and agencies within a 30-mile radius of its warehouse. The office supply business is extremely competitive, and the ability to deliver orders promptly is an important factor in getting new customers and keeping old ones. (Offices typically do not order ahead of time when their inventory of supplies is getting low, but when they completely run out. As a result, they need their order immediately.) The manager of the company wants to be certain that enough drivers and delivery vehicles are available so that orders can be delivered promptly. Therefore, the manager wants to be able to "forecast" the number of orders that will occur during the next month (i.e., forecast the "demand" for deliveries).

From records of delivery orders, the manager has accumulated data for the past 10 months. These data are shown in table 16.1 and plotted in a graph in figure 16.1.

**Table 16.1** Orders for Ten-Month Period

| Month | Delivered Orders per Month |
| --- | --- |
| January | 120 |
| February | 90 |
| March | 100 |
| April | 75 |
| May | 110 |
| June | 50 |
| July | 75 |
| August | 130 |
| September | 110 |
| October | 90 |

**Figure 16.1** Graph of orders per month for Instant Paper Clip Office Supply Company.

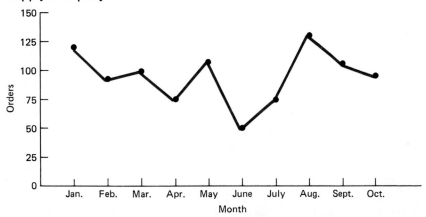

The moving average forecast is computed by dividing the sum of the values of the forecast variable, orders per month for a sequence of months, by the number of months in the sequence. A frequent moving average is for 3 time periods. A 3-month moving average for February in our example is computed by summing the number of orders for the 3-month sequence of January, February, and March, of which February is the middle month.

*Computing the moving average*

*A 3-month moving average*

$$\text{February moving average} = \frac{120 + 90 + 100}{3}$$
$$= 103.3 \text{ orders per month}$$

The March moving average is computed as

$$\text{March moving average} = \frac{90 + 100 + 75}{3}$$
$$= 88.3 \text{ orders per month}$$

Notice that this will result in no moving average for either January, the first month, or the last month, October. Only months that are in the middle of a sequence have moving averages.

The moving averages for the remaining months are shown in table 16.2. In addition, this table includes the 5-month moving average forecast in which a sequence of 5 months is employed.

**Table 16.2** Three- and Five-Month Moving Averages

| Month | Delivered Orders per Month | Three-Month Moving Average | Five-Month Moving Average | |
|-------|---------------------------|---------------------------|---------------------------|---|
| January | 120 | — | — | |
| February | 90 | 103.3 | — | |
| March | 100 | 88.3 | 99.0 | |
| April | 75 | 95.0 | 85.0 | |
| May | 110 | 78.3 | 82.0 | |
| June | 50 | 78.3 | 88.0 | |
| July | 75 | 85.0 | 95.0 | |
| August | 130 | 105.0 | 91.0 | ← |
| September | 110 | 110.0 ← | = | → November |
| October | 90 | — | — | Forecasts |

*The next period forecast*

For this example we are assuming that the manager of Instant Paper Clip is presently at the end of October. The forecast resulting from either the 3- or 5-month moving averages is typically for the next month in the sequence, which in this case is November. The forecast for November is 110 orders, using the 3-month moving average, and 91 orders, using the 5-month moving average. Thus, the moving average method has been used to generate a forecast for only the next immediate time period, in this example. (The actual forecast value is simply the last moving average computed in the sequence.)

*Forecasting into the future*

The moving average can also be used to forecast farther into the future than one period by determining if there is a pattern in the historical data. If there is a visible pattern (which would be most readily observed from a graph of the moving averages), then the last moving average value could be modified to reflect a more realistic forecast than simply projected as the next period forecast. In addition, evidence of a moving average pattern can enable the forecaster to project the pattern several periods into the future rather than just the next period.

*Smoothing the variability in the data*

Both moving average forecasts in table 16.2 tend to *smooth* out the variability occurring in the actual data. This smoothing effect can be observed in figure 16.2 in which the 3-month averages and 5-month averages

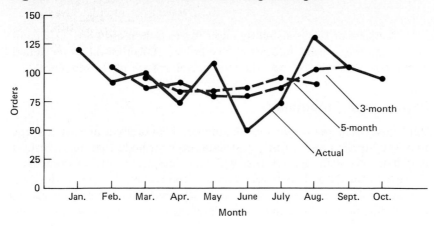

**Figure 16.2** Three- and five-month moving averages.

have been superimposed on our graph of the original data (fig. 16.1). The extremes in the actual orders per month have been reduced. This is beneficial if these extremes simply reflect random fluctuations in orders per month, since our moving average forecast will not be strongly influenced by them.

Notice that the 5-month moving average in figure 16.2 smooths out fluctuations to a greater extent than the 3-month moving average. However, the 3-month average more closely reflects the most recent data available to the office supply manager. (The 5-month average forecast considers data all the way back to June, while the 3-month average only goes back to August.)

The major disadvantage of the moving average method is that it does not react well to variations that occur *for a reason,* such as cycles and seasonal effects (although this method does reflect long-term trends). Those factors that cause actual changes are generally ignored. It is basically a "mechanical" method, which reflects historical data in a consistent fashion. However, the moving average method does have the advantage of being easy to use, quick, and inexpensive. In general, this method can provide a relatively good forecast for the *immediate future,* but an attempt should not be made to push the forecast too far into the distant future.

*Disadvantages of the moving average*

*Advantages of the moving average*

## Weighted Moving Averages

The moving average method can be adjusted to more closely reflect more recent fluctuations in the data and seasonal effects. This adjusted method is referred to as a *weighted moving average.* In this method, "weights" are assigned to the most recent data. For example, in our example we will assign a weight of 3 to the October data, while assigning weights of 2 and 1 to the September and August data. Next, the sum of the data values multiplied by the weights is divided by the sum of the weights to yield the forecast for November.

*Weighting recent data more heavily*

$$\text{Weighted 3-month average} = \frac{3(90) + 2(110) + 1(130)}{6}$$

$$= 103.3 \text{ orders per month}$$

Notice that this is a slightly lower forecast than our previously computed 3-month average forecast of 110 orders, reflecting the lower actual number of orders in October (the most recent month in the sequence).

## Exponential Smoothing

The *exponential smoothing* forecast method is actually a moving average that weights the most recently past data more strongly than more distant past data. As such, the forecast will react more strongly to immediate changes in the data. This is very useful *if* the recent changes in the data are the results of an *actual* change (i.e., seasonal pattern, etc.) instead of just random fluctuations (for which a simple moving average forecast would suffice).

Exponential smoothing consists of two forms: *simple exponential smoothing* and *adjusted exponential smoothing* (i.e., adjusted for trends, *Simple exponential* seasonal patterns, etc.). We will discuss the simple exponential smoothing *smoothing* case first, followed by the adjusted form.

In order to demonstrate simple exponential smoothing, we will return to the **Instant Paper Clip Office Supply Company example.**

The simple exponential smoothing forecast is computed using the following formula.

$$F_{t+1} = \alpha D_t + (1 - \alpha) F_t$$

where

$F_{t+1} =$ the forecast for the next period
$D_t =$ actual demand in the present period
$F_t =$ the previously determined forecast for the present period
$\alpha =$ a weighting factor referred to as the *smoothing constant*

*The smoothing*     The smoothing constant, $\alpha$, is between 0.0 and 1.0. It reflects the *constant,* $\alpha$    weight given to the most recent demand data. For example if $\alpha = .20$,

$$F_{t+1} = .20D_t + .80F_t$$

which means that our forecast for the next period is based on 20% of recent demand ($D_t$) and 80% of past demand (in the form of the forecast $F_t$, since $F_t$ is derived from previous demands and forecasts). If we go to one extreme $\alpha = 0.0$    and let $\alpha = 0.0$, then

$$F_{t+1} = 0D_t + 1F_t$$
$$= F_t$$

or the forecast for the next period is the same as this period. In other words, *we would not be reflecting the most recent demand at all.*

Alternatively, if $\alpha = 1.0$, then

$\alpha = 1.0$

$$F_{t+1} = 1D_t + 0F_t$$
$$= 1D_t$$

and we have considered only the most recent occurrence in our data (demand in the last period) and nothing else. Thus, we can conclude that the higher $\alpha$ is, the more sensitive to changes in recent demand the forecast will be. The most commonly used values of $\alpha$ are in the range from 0.01 to 0.30. However, the determination of $\alpha$ is usually judgmental and subjective. An inaccurate estimate can limit the usefulness of this forecasting technique.

Using $\alpha = .10$, we will compute the March (i.e., period 3) forecast for our example. From table 16.3, we can see that

*An exponential smoothing example*

Demand in February, $D_2 = 90$ orders
Forecast for February, $F_2 = 120$ orders

Notice that to begin the forecast we are using the actual January demand as the forecast for February (as a starting point). Alternatively, a subjective estimate could have been used. Thus, the forecast for March, $F_3$, is

*The March forecast*

$$F_3 = \alpha D_2 + (1 - \alpha) F_2$$
$$= (.10)(90) + (.90)(120)$$
$$= 117 \text{ orders}$$

The forecast for March ($F_3 = 117$) is subsequently used in the computation of the April forecast.

*The April forecast*

$$F_4 = \alpha D_3 + (1 - \alpha) F_3$$
$$= (.10)(100) + (.90)(117)$$
$$= 115.3 \text{ orders}$$

The remainder of the monthly forecasts are shown in table 16.3. The final forecast is for November and is the forecast of interest to the manager, assuming the manager is presently at the end of October.

$$F_{11} = .10(90) + .90(105.3)$$
$$= 103.9 \text{ orders for November}$$

Thus, the manager of the office supply company can "estimate" that there will be 103.9 delivery orders in November and make a decision regarding drivers and their trucks accordingly.

*Summary of monthly forecasts*

**Table 16.3** Exponential Smoothing Forecast

| Period | Month | Delivered Orders per Month, $D_t$ | Forecast, $F_{t+1}$ $\alpha = 0.10$ | $\alpha = 0.30$ | |
|---|---|---|---|---|---|
| 1 | January | 120 | – | – | |
| 2 | February | 90 | 120.0 | 120.0 | |
| 3 | March | 100 | 117.0 | 111.0 | |
| 4 | April | 75 | 115.3 | 107.7 | |
| 5 | May | 110 | 111.3 | 97.9 | |
| 6 | June | 50 | 111.2 | 101.5 | |
| 7 | July | 75 | 105.1 | 86.1 | |
| 8 | August | 130 | 102.1 | 82.8 | |
| 9 | September | 110 | 104.9 | 97.0 | |
| 10 | October | 90 | 105.4 | 100.9 | November |
| 11 | November | – | 103.9 ⟵ | 97.6 ⟵ | Forecasts |

Notice in table 16.3 that a forecast for $\alpha = 0.30$ was also computed. The November forecast using this smoothing constant is 97.6 orders.

$$F_{11} = .30(90) + .70(100.9)$$
$$= 97.6 \text{ orders for November}$$

The purpose of computing this alternative forecast is to demonstrate the ability of the forecast to react to demand changes. This can be observed in figure 16.3, which shows the two exponential smoothing forecasts for $\alpha = .10$ and .30 superimposed on the actual demand curve.

*The effect of a higher smoothing constant*    In figure 16.3, the forecast using the higher smoothing constant, $\alpha = .30$, reacts more strongly to changes in demand than does the forecast with $\alpha = .10$. However, both tend to smooth out the random fluctuations in the forecast. Notice that both forecasts lag behind the actual occurrences. For example, a pronounced change in demand in July (upward) is not really reflected in the forecast until September. If these changes mark a change in "trend" (i.e., a long-term upward or downward movement) rather *Forecast lag*    than just a random fluctuation, then the forecast will always lag behind

**Figure 16.3** Exponential smoothing forecasts with $\alpha = .10$ and $\alpha = .30$.

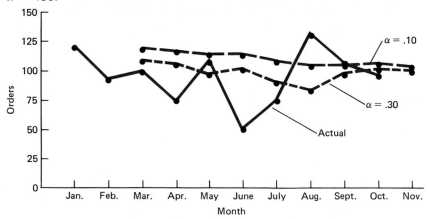

this trend. Observing figure 16.3, we can see that there is a general downward trend in delivered orders from January through June. Notice that both forecasts tend to be consistently higher than the actual demands, that is, the forecasts lag the trend. Simple exponential smoothing forecasts, however, can be adjusted for the effects of a trend.

## Adjusted Exponential Smoothing

The adjusted exponential smoothing forecast consists of the simple exponential smoothing forecast with a *trend adjustment* factor added to it. The formula for the adjusted forecast is

*Adjusting the forecast for trend*

$$\text{Adjusted } F_{t+1} = F_{t+1} + \left(\frac{1-\beta}{\beta}\right)T_{t+1}$$

where

$\beta$ = a smoothing constant for trend
$T$ = an exponentially smoothed trend factor.

Like $\alpha$, $\beta$ is a value between 0.0 and 1.0. It reflects the weight given to the most recent trend data. Also like $\alpha$, $\beta$ is often determined subjectively based on the judgment of the forecaster. A low $\beta$ reflects trend changes more than a high $\beta$. It is not uncommon for $\beta$ to equal $\alpha$ in this method.

*The smoothing constant for trend, $\beta$*

The exponentially smoothed trend factor is computed similarly to the computation of the simple exponentially smoothed forecast. It is, in fact, a forecast model for trend.

$$T_{t+1} = \beta(F_{t+1} - F_t) + (1 - \beta)T_t$$

where

$T_t$ = the last period trend factor

As an example, we will compute the adjusted forecast for March using the simple exponentially smoothed forecast for $\alpha = .10$, shown in table 16.3. The February trend, $T_2$, is assumed to equal zero, since we have no trend data for this month, and $\beta$ is given a value of 0.1. Thus, the trend factor is computed as

*The adjusted March forecast*

*Computing the trend factor*

$$\begin{aligned}
T_3 &= \beta(F_3 - F_2) + (1 - \beta)T_2 \\
&= 0.1(117.0 - 120) + (0.9)(0) \\
&= 0.1(-3) \\
&= -0.3
\end{aligned}$$

Using this trend factor, we next adjust our simple exponentially smoothed forecast for March.

$$\begin{aligned}
\text{Adjusted } F_3 &= F_3 + \left(\frac{1 - 0.1}{0.1}\right)T_3 \\
&= 117 + (9)(-0.3) \\
&= 114.3
\end{aligned}$$

This adjusted forecast as well as the other monthly adjusted forecasts for our office supply example are shown in table 16.4.

**Table 16.4** Adjusted Exponential Smoothing Forecast

| Period $t$ | Month | Delivered Orders per Month, $D_t$ | Forecast, $F_{t+1}$ $\alpha = 0.1$ | Adjusted Forecast $\beta = 0.1$ | |
|---|---|---|---|---|---|
| 1 | January | 120 | – | – | |
| 2 | February | 90 | 120.0 | 120.0 | |
| 3 | March | 100 | 117.0 | 114.3 | |
| 4 | April | 75 | 115.3 | 111.3 | |
| 5 | May | 110 | 111.3 | 104.1 | |
| 6 | June | 50 | 111.2 | 104.7 | |
| 7 | July | 75 | 105.1 | 93.7 | |
| 8 | August | 130 | 102.1 | 89.2 | |
| 9 | September | 110 | 104.9 | 95.8 | |
| 10 | October | 90 | 105.4 | 97.7 | November |
| 11 | November | – | 103.9 ← | 95.6 ← | Forecasts |

The adjusted exponential smoothing forecast for November ($F_{11}$) as shown in table 16.4 is 95.6 orders. Notice that the adjusted forecast is consistently lower than the simple exponential smoothing forecast. That is, the adjusted forecast does not "lag" the actual demand as much as the simple exponential smoothing forecast. This can also be observed in figure 16.4.

**Figure 16.4** Adjusted exponentially smoothed forecast.

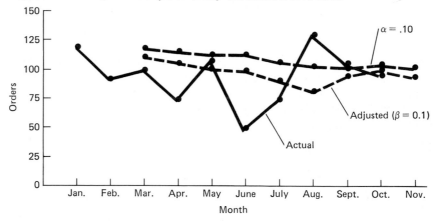

*Reaction to trends*

However, notice that while the adjusted forecast reacted better to the *downward trend* in the actual demand for delivered orders, it did not react as well to the sudden upward turn at the end of June. This characteristic demonstrates the usefulness of the adjusted forecast for *long-term trends* in the data, but not for situations that exhibit sudden and short movements up and down.

Since trends and seasonal patterns often tend to occur over a relatively long period of time, the adjusted exponential smoothing technique is sometimes used for medium-range forecasts. However, in general, time series methods are used primarily for short-range forecasts.

### Forecast Reliability

As we indicated in the introduction to this chapter, no forecast measure will result in a consistently perfect forecast. However, the person performing the forecast does hope it will be as accurate as possible and generally *reliable*. In order to test the forecast to see if it is accurately portraying what actually occurs, several reliability measures exist. We will discuss the *mean absolute deviation* as an example of a reliability test.

*Testing the forecast to see if it is accurate*

The *mean absolute deviation* (referred to as *MAD*) is a measure of the difference between the forecast and what actually occurred. It is computed as follows.

*The mean absolute deviation*

$$\text{MAD} = \frac{\Sigma|\text{actual} - \text{forecast}|}{\text{number of periods}}$$

For our office supply example, the deviations between actual and forecast demand using the simple exponential smoothing forecast ($\alpha = 0.10$) in table 16.3 are

$$\text{MAD} = \frac{17 + 40.3 + 1.3 + 61.2 + 30.1 + 27.9 + 5.2 + 15.3}{8}$$
$$= 24.8$$

Interpreting the significance of the MAD value is somewhat judgmental. In general, however, the lower the MAD value the better (i.e., a MAD value of zero means there is no forecast error). The MAD value for the adjusted forecast is 24.1. Although this is a slightly lower value than that obtained for the simple exponential smoothing forecast, it is not significant (due to the fact that the adjusted forecast did not react well to the sudden June rise in the data).

*Interpreting the MAD value*

## Regression Forecasting Methods

The time series techniques of exponential smoothing and moving average related a single variable being forecast (such as demand) to *time*. Alternatively, *regression* is a forecasting technique that measures the relationship of one variable to one or more other variables. In effect, regression attempts to relate forecasts to the factors that *cause* trends, cycles, and seasonal patterns. (Regression is sometimes referred to as a *causal* technique.) If it is possible to identify the factors that cause trends and to develop a mathematical relationship that reflects these causes, a very accurate forecast can often be determined. Because regression can often be

*A forecasting technique that measures the relationship of one variable to one or more other variables*

used to accurately forecast variables that reflect trends, it is frequently used as a medium-range forecast technique. We will explain regression within the context of the following example.

*A regression example*

The vice-president for operations of the Blue Sox Professional Baseball Team of the National League feels that the attendance at the team's home games is related to the amount spent on promotions by the team. Given that such a relationship exists, the vice-president would like to be able to use it to forecast the attendance of the team for various levels of promotional expenditures. In this example, the forecast for attendance will not be based solely on the pattern of the data over time, but on another variable, promotional expenditure.

Regression is a means for measuring the *relationship* of one variable, such as team attendance, to one or more other variables, such as promotional expenditures, won-lost record, or the fans' disposable income. The measure of this relationship is in the form of an equation, referred to as a *regression equation*. This regression equation can also be used to *forecast* the effect of one variable on another variable (i.e., the effect of promotional expenditure on attendance). Regression can be categorized as simple or multiple: *simple regression* reflects the relationship of *two* variables, and *multiple regression* encompasses *more than two variables*.

## Simple Regression

*Components of the regression equation*

Simple regression relates one dependent variable to one independent variable in the form of a linear equation.

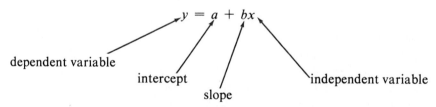

Returning to our example of the Blue Sox baseball team operation, the vice-president for operations has accumulated data (shown in table 16.5) on promotional expenditures (in constant, noninflated dollars) and home attendance for the past 10 years.

The data for promotional expenditures and team attendance is diagramed in figure 16.5.

*A scatter diagram*

The graph in figure 16.5 is referred to as a *scatter diagram*. While the points on the scatter diagram do not form an exact straight line, they do show a definite positive trend and seem to be linear in nature. As such, we will develop the regression equation from this data. The two components

**Table 16.5** Attendance and Promotional Expenditure Data

| Year | Promotional Expenditures ($10,000s) | Home Attendance (100,000s) |
|------|-------------------------------------|----------------------------|
| 1972 | 5.7 | 7 |
| 1973 | 5.5 | 10 |
| 1974 | 6.5 | 9 |
| 1975 | 9.0 | 12 |
| 1976 | 6.9 | 8 |
| 1977 | 8.1 | 14 |
| 1978 | 9.5 | 15 |
| 1979 | 10.2 | 17 |
| 1980 | 8.2 | 16 |
| 1981 | 10.6 | 18 |

**Figure 16.5** Scatter diagram.

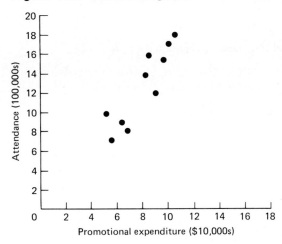

in the regression equation that must be computed are $a$, the intercept, and $b$, the slope. These two components are computed using the following formulas,

*The slope and intercept of the regression equation*

$$a = \bar{y} - b\bar{x}$$

$$b = \frac{\Sigma xy - n\bar{x}\bar{y}}{\Sigma x^2 - n\bar{x}^2}$$

where

$n$ = the number of pieces of data

$\bar{x} = \dfrac{\Sigma x}{n}$ = the mean of the $x$ data

$\bar{y} = \dfrac{\Sigma y}{n}$ = the mean of the $y$ data

Table 16.6 demonstrates how each of these values are computed.

**Table 16.6** Computations for Linear Regression Equation

| x (promotion) | y (attendance) | xy | $x^2$ |
|---|---|---|---|
| 5.7 | 7 | 39.9 | 32.5 |
| 5.5 | 10 | 55.0 | 30.3 |
| 6.5 | 9 | 58.5 | 42.3 |
| 9.0 | 12 | 108.0 | 81.0 |
| 6.9 | 8 | 55.2 | 47.6 |
| 8.1 | 14 | 113.4 | 65.6 |
| 9.5 | 15 | 142.5 | 90.3 |
| 10.2 | 17 | 173.4 | 104.0 |
| 8.2 | 16 | 131.2 | 67.2 |
| 10.6 | 18 | 190.8 | 112.4 |
| 80.2 | 126 | 1067.9 | 673.2 |

Recall that the linear regression equation is in the form

$$y = a + bx$$

*Computing the slope, b*

First we will compute the slope of this equation, *b*.

$$b = \frac{\Sigma xy - n\overline{x}\overline{y}}{\Sigma x^2 - n\overline{x}^2}$$

From the computations in table 16.6,

$$\overline{x} = \frac{80.2}{10} = 8.02$$

$$\overline{y} = \frac{126}{10} = 12.6$$

Therefore,

$$b = \frac{1,067.9 - (10)(8.02)(12.6)}{673.2 - (10)(8.02)^2}$$

$$= \frac{57.4}{30.2}$$

$$= 1.91$$

*Computing the intercept, a*

Next, given that we now know *b*, we can compute the intercept of our regression equation, *a*.

$$a = \overline{y} - b\overline{x}$$
$$= 12.6 - (1.91)(8.02)$$
$$= -2.72$$

*The regression equation*

Thus, our simple regression equation is

$$y = -2.72 + 1.91x$$

The line defined by this equation is superimposed on the scatter diagram of the data in figure 16.6.

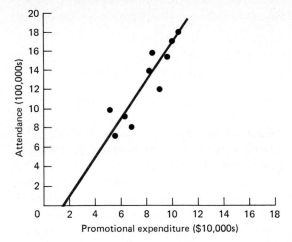

**Figure 16.6** Regression line.

In terms of our example, the calculated linear regression line appears to fit the data well, thus indicating attendance, *y,* is linearly related to promotional expenditure, *x.* Now the vice-president for operations can use the regression equation to forecast attendance for a specific expenditure on promotion. For example, if the baseball team spends $100,000 ($x = 10$) on promotion, the forecasted attendance is computed as

*Forecasting with the regression equation*

$$y = -2.72 + 1.91(10)$$
$$= 16.4$$

which is interpreted as 1,640,000 in attendance at the home games.

From figure 16.6 we can see that the regression line (and equation) is best suited for forecasting when long-term trends exist. In other words, because the regression equation is linear, it does not react to positive or negative trend changes in the data (i.e., it does not bend or change direction). It may flatten out or become steeper, but the line will not change direction if the data should change direction.

*Limitations of regression*

## Coefficient of Determination

In order for the regression equation to be a reliable forecast method, there must be a relatively strong relationship between the two variables in the equation, and any other factors affecting the forecast must remain constant (or nearly so). An indicator of the strength of the relationship of the variables in the regression equation, and thus the reliability of the forecast, is the *coefficient of determination.* The formula for the coefficient of determination is

*Testing the strength of the variable relationships*

$$r^2 = \left[ \frac{n\Sigma xy - \Sigma x\Sigma y}{\sqrt{[n\Sigma x^2 - (\Sigma x)^2][n\Sigma y^2 - (\Sigma y)^2]}} \right]^2$$

Although this equation looks formidable, all of the components (for our example) except $\Sigma y^2$ have already been determined in table 16.6. The value for $\Sigma y^2 = 1,728$. Thus, the coefficient of determination for our example is

$$r^2 = \left[ \frac{(10)(1,067.9) - (80.2)(126)}{\sqrt{[(10)(673.2) - (80.2)^2][(10)(1,728) - (126)^2]}} \right]^2$$

$$= (.89)^2$$

$$= .79$$

This value for the coefficient of determination means that 79% of the amount of variation in the attendance during the ten-year period of analysis is a result of promotional expenditure. The remaining 21% is due to other unexplained factors related to attendance. A value of 1.00 (or 100%) would indicate a completely total relationship between attendance and expenditures on promotion. Since 21% of the variation is a result of factors other than promotional expenditures, we can expect some amount of forecast error if the linear regression equation is used.

## Multiple Regression

The fact that the correlation of coefficient shows that 79% of the variation in attendance is related to promotional expenditures indicates that the remaining 21% is a result of other variables. These other variables could be the team's won-lost record, the fans' disposable income, or the growth in population of the city the team is located in. *Multiple regression* is a method that reflects the relationship between a number of variables. However, the computation of the multiple regression equation is quite a bit more complex than the simple regression equation. As a result, the only viable means for multiple regression analysis is the computer. This is beyond the indicated scope of this text, therefore, we will not pursue the topic of multiple regression.

## Regression Analysis with the Computer

The development of the simple regression equation and the coefficient of determination for our baseball promotion example was not too difficult because the amount of data was relatively small. However, manual computation of the components of the simple regression equations can become very time consuming and cumbersome as the amount of data increases. We have already indicated that the computation of the multiple regression equation is very complex, regardless of the amount of data.

Fortunately, several *computer packages* are available that perform both simple and multiple regression analysis. These packages are already programmed so that the user simply has to input the data.

The three most widely available packages are BMD (Biomedical Computer Programs), SPSS (Statistical Package for the Social Sciences), and SAS (Statistical Analysis System). At least one of these packages is typically available at most computer facilities. All three can be used for both simple and multiple regression.

## Long-Range Forecast Methods

Time series analysis is most useful (and reliable) for short-range forecasting, while regression analysis can be used for both short- and medium-range forecasting. However, neither method is generally appropriate for long-range forecasting.

Long-range plans by organizations represent some of their most important decisions. The growth of the organization, the introduction of new products, and the construction of new facilities are just a few of the items typically considered in long-range planning, which affect the continued life of the firm. However, analytical techniques (such as time series and regression) are, in general, not available for long-range forecasting. One reason is the lack of historical data that could be used in such models. The factors that affect the future are so diverse and complex that historical data is of little value for predictive purposes. These factors include technology, economic conditions, and political/social conditions. All three of these items are the subject of intense forecasting by many business firms.

*Technological forecasting* reflects an attempt to predict what types of technology will be available in the future. For example, several large electronic firms were able to successfully predict the development of microelectronics used in electronic products, such as calculators and computers, 10 to 15 years prior to the actual introduction of such products on the market. As a result, when these products were marketed, these companies were ready with the productive capabilities to effectively enter the market themselves. At the present many firms are deeply involved in attempting to forecast the type of energy sources that will be available in the future and the effect on business these sources will have.

*Technological forecasting*

*Economic forecasting* is concerned with predicting the state of the economy in the future. The possibility of recessions, economic growth, high and low interest rates, and periods of unemployment are all of vital importance to businesses. Although economic predictive models abound, their reliability is often suspect. One reason is that future economic conditions are so closely related to political and social factors.

*Economic forecasting*

*Political/social forecasting* is a relatively new and abstract form of forecasting. However, world politics have become so volatile that their effect on business firms has become immense. World trade is no longer

*Political/social forecasting*

subject strictly to economic conditions but also to political considerations. In addition, social conditions now change rapidly and can have dramatic effects on businesses. Such items as consumer awareness and protection and equal opportunity laws have had a significant impact on the economy in general. As a result, more and more firms are attempting to develop ways to predict such changes in order to lessen their effect.

The forecasting models that have been developed to reflect these longe-range factors (above) are qualitative in nature. They are typically based on expert opinion, judgment, surveys of all types, and research results. However, since long-range forecasting is often an attempt to predict future *events,* the reliability of such methods is limited.

## Summary

In this chapter we have presented several of the methods available for forecasting in the short-, medium-, and long-term future. Two of the most popular and traditionally applied forecasting techniques, time series and regression, were discussed in detail. However, these methods primarily serve to reflect the numerous forecasting methods that exist for each type of forecasting.

In general, the forecasts obtained from such methods are used as inputs to other decision models. For example, the development of probabilities of future states in a Markov model is a forecast. Another example of the use of forecasting results is in inventory models, the subject of our next two chapters. The primary factor in determining the amount of inventory a firm should order (i.e., prepare to have on hand) is the demand that will occur in the future—forecasted demand.

## References

Buffa, E. S., and Dyer, J. S. *Essentials of Management Science/Operations Research.* New York: John Wiley and Sons, 1978.

Benton, W. K. *Forecasting for Management.* Reading, Mass.: Addison-Wesley, 1972.

Box, G. E. P., and Jenkins, G. M. *Time Series Analysis, Forecasting and Control.* San Francisco: Holden-Day, 1970.

Huang, D. S. *Regression and Econometric Methods.* New York: John Wiley and Sons, 1970.

Monks, J. G. *Operations Management: Theory and Problems.* New York: McGraw-Hill, 1977.

Nelson, C. R. *Applied Time Series Analysis for Managerial Forecasting.* San Francisco: Holden-Day, 1973.

Tersine, R. J. *Production/Operations Management.* New York: Elsevier North Holland, 1980.

Wheelwright, S. C., and Makridakis. *Forecasting Methods for Management.* New York: John Wiley and Sons, 1973.

Younger, M. S. *A Handbook for Linear Regression.* North Scituate, Mass.: Duxbury Press, 1979.

# Problems

1. Distinguish between short-, medium-, and long-range forecasts.

2. Given the following demand data for a 6-period time frame,

| Period | Units Demanded per Period |
|--------|---------------------------|
| 1 | 50 |
| 2 | 60 |
| 3 | 70 |
| 4 | 50 |
| 5 | 80 |
| 6 | 110 |

(a) Compute a 3-period moving average forecast for periods 4 through 7.

(b) Plot the actual demand and the period forecasts graphically and compare the two.

3. Given the following demand data for a 10-period time frame,

| Period | Units Demanded per Period |
|--------|---------------------------|
| 1 | 25 |
| 2 | 18 |
| 3 | 17 |
| 4 | 40 |
| 5 | 34 |
| 6 | 32 |
| 7 | 41 |
| 8 | 50 |
| 9 | 53 |
| 10 | 26 |

(a) Compute a 3-period moving average forecast for periods 4 through 11.

(b) Compute a 5-period moving average forecast for periods 6 through 11.

(c) Plot the actual demand and the forecasts determined in parts (a) and (b) on the same graph and compare them.

4. For the data in problem 3, compute a weighted 3-period moving average for periods 4 through 11. Assign a weight of 3 to the most recent period, a weight of 2 to the next most recent period, and a weight of 1 to the most distant period in the moving average. Compare this forecast with the two obtained in parts (a) and (b) of problem 3. Which forecast appears to be the most accurate?

5. The Saki automobile dealer in Minneapolis–St. Paul wants to be able to accurately forecast demand for the Saki special compact car during the next month. Because the distributor is in Japan, if the proper number of cars are not ordered a month ahead it is difficult to send cars back or reorder. From past sales records the dealer has accumulated the following data for the past year.

| Month | Cars Demanded per Month |
|---|---|
| January | 6 |
| February | 7 |
| March | 5 |
| April | 4 |
| May | 8 |
| June | 10 |
| July | 12 |
| August | 16 |
| September | 14 |
| October | 10 |
| November | 16 |
| December | 18 |

(a) Compute a 3-month moving average forecast of demand for April through January (of the next year) and compare the forecasts with the actual demand for each month.

(b) Compute a 5-month moving average forecast for April through January and compare the forecast with the actual demand for each month.

(c) Compare the two forecasts in parts (a) and (b). Which one should the dealer use for January of the next year?

6. Carpet City is a carpet outlet in Fresno. The manager of the outlet needs to be able to accurately forecast the demand for Soft Shag carpet (the dealer's biggest seller). If the dealer does not order enough carpet from the carpet mill, then customers will buy their carpet from one of the dealer's many competitors. The dealer has collected the following demand data for the past 8 months.

| Month | Demand for Soft Shag Carpet (1,000 yards) |
|---|---|
| 1 | 8 |
| 2 | 12 |
| 3 | 7 |
| 4 | 9 |
| 5 | 15 |
| 6 | 11 |
| 7 | 10 |
| 8 | 12 |

(a) Compute a 3-month moving average forecast for months 4 through 9.

(b) Compute a weighted 3-month moving average forecast for months 4 through 9. Assign weights of 5, 3, and 1 to the months in sequence starting with the most recent month.

(c) Compare the two forecasts graphically. Which forecast appears to be most accurate?

7. The Fastgro Fertilizer Company distributes fertilizer to various lawn and garden shops. The company must base its quarterly production schedule on a forecast of how many tons of fertilizer will be demanded from it. The company has gathered the following data for the past 3 years from its sales records.

|  | Quarter | Demand for Fertilizer (tons) |
|---|---|---|
| Year 1: | 1 | 105 |
|  | 2 | 150 |
|  | 3 | 93 |
|  | 4 | 121 |
| Year 2: | 5 | 140 |
|  | 6 | 170 |
|  | 7 | 105 |
|  | 8 | 150 |
| Year 3: | 9 | 150 |
|  | 10 | 170 |
|  | 11 | 110 |
|  | 12 | 130 |

(a) Compute a 3-quarter moving average forecast for quarters 4 through 13 and compare the forecast graphically with the actual demand.

(b) Compute a 5-quarter moving average forecast for quarters 6 through 13 and compare the forecast graphically with the actual demand.

(c) Compute a weighted 3-quarter moving average forecast using weights of 3, 2, and 1 for the most recent, next recent, and most distant data respectively.

8. In problem 7 can you identify any *trends, cycles,* and/or *seasonal patterns* in the actual quarterly demand data?

9. Given the following demand data for a 5-month time frame,

| Period | Units Demanded per Period |
|---|---|
| 1 | 40 |
| 2 | 30 |
| 3 | 45 |
| 4 | 60 |
| 5 | 55 |

compute exponentially smoothed forecasts for periods 2 through 6 using $\alpha$ values of 0.10 and 0.30.

10. The dean of the College of Business at State University wants to forecast the number of students who desire to enroll in Management Science I next quarter in order to determine how many sections to schedule. The dean has accumulated the following enrollment data for the past eight quarters.

| Quarter | Students Enrolled in Management Science |
|---------|------------------------------------------|
| 1 | 400 |
| 2 | 450 |
| 3 | 350 |
| 4 | 420 |
| 5 | 500 |
| 6 | 575 |
| 7 | 490 |
| 8 | 650 |

Compute the exponential smoothed forecast ($\alpha = .20$) for the enrollment in Management Science next quarter.

11. The manager of the Petroco Service Station wants to forecast the demand for unleaded gasoline next month so the proper number of gallons can be ordered from the distributor. The owner has accumulated the following demand for unleaded gasoline from sales during the past 10 months.

| Month | Gallons of Gasoline Demanded |
|-------|------------------------------|
| October | 800 |
| November | 725 |
| December | 630 |
| January | 500 |
| February | 645 |
| March | 690 |
| April | 730 |
| May | 810 |
| June | 1,200 |
| July | 980 |

(a) Compute an exponential smoothed forecast using an $\alpha$ value of .10.
(b) Compute an adjusted exponential smoothed forecast ($\alpha = .10$, $\beta = .10$).
(c) Plot the actual data and the forecasts obtained in parts (a) and (b) graphically.

12. Compute an exponential smoothed forecast ($\alpha = .20$) for the monthly automobile demand data in problem 5. Graphically compare the exponential smoothed forecast and the 3-month moving average forecast obtained in problem 5 with the actual data. Does a trend appear to exist in the actual data? If so, which forecast seems to forecast the trend best?

13. Compute an exponential smoothed forecast ($\alpha = .10$) for the monthly carpet demand in problem 6.

14. Compute an exponential smoothed forecast ($\alpha = .30$) for the quarterly fertilizer demand in problem 7.

15. Compute an adjusted exponential smoothed forecast ($\alpha = .30$, $\beta = .10$) for the quarterly demand data for carpet in problem 7.

16. Compute an adjusted exponential smoothed forecast ($\alpha = .20$, $\beta = .10$) for the monthly automobile demand data in problem 5. Graphically plot the adjusted exponential smoothed forecast together with the simple exponential smoothed forecast obtained in problem 12 and the actual data. Which forecast do you believe would be most reliable?

17. Test the reliability of the 3-month moving average forecast of automobile demand in problem 5, using the mean absolute deviation. Next, test the reliability of the simple exponential smoothed forecast (problem 12) and the adjusted exponential smoothed forecast (problem 16) using the mean absolute deviation. Which forecast is indicated as being the most reliable?

18. Test the reliability of the exponential smoothed forecast for students enrolled in Management Science per quarter obtained in problem 10 using the mean absolute deviation.

19. Test the reliability of the two forecasts of gasoline demand in problem 11 using the mean absolute deviation and indicate the most reliable forecast.

20. Given the following data for a dependent variable, $y$, and an independent variable, $x$, develop the simple regression equation and superimpose the regression line on a scatter diagram of the data.

| x | y |
|---|---|
| 10 | 25 |
| 12 | 40 |
| 14 | 38 |
| 18 | 45 |
| 20 | 46 |
| 25 | 50 |
| 28 | 48 |
| 35 | 56 |
| 40 | 60 |
| 42 | 58 |

21. The job placement director at Tech believes that the salary offers for business administration graduates may be related to grade point averages. During the past 2 years the placement director has collected average salary and average grade point data as follows.

| Grade Point Average | Average Annual Salary Offers |
|---|---|
| 2.1 | $13,500 |
| 2.4 | 14,100 |
| 2.7 | 15,000 |
| 2.9 | 15,200 |
| 3.2 | 16,000 |
| 3.5 | 16,300 |

Determine the regression equation for this data and superimpose the regression line on a scatter diagram of the actual data.

22. The Williamsburg Tourism Association is constantly attempting to forecast the number of tourists who will visit their city. The association believes that the number of tourists is related to gasoline prices. The association has accumulated the following data on average monthly gasoline prices and the number of tourists visiting the city.

| Monthly Gasoline Prices (per gallon) | Tourists/Month (1,000s) |
|---|---|
| $1.05 | 10 |
| .90 | 17 |
| 1.17 | 9 |
| 1.21 | 8 |
| .95 | 14 |
| 1.30 | 12 |
| 1.08 | 11 |
| 1.40 | 7.5 |
| 1.10 | 12 |
| 1.06 | 13 |

(a) Develop the simple regression equation for this data.
(b) Compute the coefficient of determination for the regression equation.
(c) The tourist association estimates that the price of gasoline will be $1.25 next month. What will the expected number of tourists be next month?

23. The Fairface Cosmetics Firm believes its sales are directly related to the amount of money it spends on promotion. The firm has accumulated the following data on promotional expenditures and sales for the past 10 years.

| Annual Sales ($1,000s) | Annual Promotional Expenditures ($1,000s) |
|---|---|
| 95 | 12 |
| 106 | 15 |
| 84 | 10 |
| 65 | 8 |
| 110 | 20 |
| 105 | 21 |
| 120 | 25 |
| 90 | 14 |
| 96 | 15 |
| 115 | 18 |

(a) Develop a simple regression equation for this data.

(b) Plot the actual data on a scatter diagram and superimpose the regression line on it.

(c) For a promotional expenditure of $13,000, what level of sales would the firm expect?

(d) What limiting factors do you feel are associated with this forecast equation?

24. The Ali Baba Carpet Store wants to develop a means to forecast its carpet sales. The store owner believes that the store's sales are directly related to the number of new housing starts in town. As such, the store owner has gathered data from city hall on monthly house construction permits and from store records on monthly sales. These data are shown in the following table.

| Monthly Sales (1,000 yards) | Monthly Construction Permits |
|---|---|
| 5 | 21 |
| 10 | 35 |
| 4 | 10 |
| 3 | 12 |
| 8 | 16 |
| 2 | 9 |
| 12 | 41 |
| 11 | 15 |
| 9 | 18 |
| 14 | 26 |

(a) Develop a simple regression equation for this data.

(b) Compute the coefficient of determination. Does it appear that a relationship exists?

(c) What level of carpet sales can be expected next month if 30 housing construction permits were issued?

25. Compute the coefficient of determination for problem 23. Does it appear that a relationship exists?

# 17
Inventory Analysis with Certain Demand

## Economic Order Quantity

Carrying Cost
Ordering Cost
Total Inventory Cost
Computing Optimal $Q$
EOQ Analysis over Time
Assumptions of the EOQ Model

## The EOQ Model with a Reorder Point

## Noninstantaneous Receipt Model

## The EOQ Model with Shortages and Backordering

The Noninstantaneous Receipt Model with Shortages

## The Quantity Discount Model

## Summary

In all of the previous chapters, we have presented management science techniques that were applicable to decision-making problems in general. The topic of this chapter is slightly different in that a mathematical technique is developed that is applicable to a specific business function, inventory planning and control. However, to include the topic of inventory analysis is not inappropriate at all.

Inventory analysis is one of the most popular topics in management science. One reason is that almost all types of business organizations have inventory. Although we typically tend to think of inventory only in terms of stock on a store shelf, it can take on a variety of forms, such as partially finished products at different stages of a manufacturing process, raw materials, resources, labor, or cash. In addition, the purpose of inventory is not always to simply meet customer demand. For example, companies frequently stock large inventories of raw materials as a hedge against strikes. Whatever the form inventory takes or its purpose, it often represents a significant cost to a business firm. As such, it represents an important subject for the application of management science.

*All types of organizations have inventory*

In this chapter, we will present the classic economic order quantity models, which represent the most basic and fundamental form of inventory analysis. These models provide a means to determine how much to order (the order quantity) and when to place an order so that inventory-related costs are minimized. These models maintain the underlying assumption that demand is known with certainty and is constant. However, in chapter 18 we will present inventory models that do not include this assumption.

## Economic Order Quantity

The Armor Carpet Store stocks carpet in its warehouse and sells it through an adjoining showroom. The store keeps inventories of several brands of carpet, however, its biggest seller is Super Shag carpet. Since Super Shag is such an important product, the store does not allow the inventory of the carpet to run out, that is, the store always has Super Shag in stock.

*An inventory example*

The store incurs two costs associated with keeping this brand of carpet in inventory: the cost of holding the carpet in inventory and the cost of ordering the carpet from the carpet manufacturer. The manager of the store wants to know how much Super Shag should be ordered each time

*Carrying and ordering costs*

an order is placed in order to minimize the total sum of these costs. Our purpose will be to develop a model to help the manager make this decision. This model is known as the *classical EOQ* (economic order quantity) model. It will be developed with the assumptions that demand is known with certainty, that demand is constant over time, and that orders are made and received instantaneously with no shortages developing. (These assumptions will become more understandable as the model is developed.) In order to accomplish this, we will first analyze the two separate costs associated with inventory mentioned above.

## Carrying Cost

The *carrying cost* (also known as holding cost) is the cost incurred by the store for carrying the carpet in inventory. The total carrying cost generally includes some or all of the following items:

Direct storage costs (rent, heat, lights, maintenance, security, handling, recordkeeping, labor, etc., in the warehouse)

Deferred profit on investment (i.e., carpet in inventory does not produce a profit)

Interest on the investment in inventory

Product obsolescence

Depreciation, taxes, insurance

Carrying cost is usually expressed on a per unit basis for some period of time (although it is sometimes given as a percentage of average inventory). Traditionally the carrying cost is referred to on an annual basis (i.e., per year).

The manager of the Armor Carpet Store has determined that the carrying cost, which we will represent symbolically as $C_c$, is

$C_c =$ \$.75 per yard of carpet per year

However, this value represents only the cost/unit and not the *total annual carrying cost*. The total carrying cost is subject to the amount of inventory on hand during the year. The amount of inventory available to the store during the year is illustrated in figure 17.1.

In figure 17.1, $Q$ represents the size of the order to replenish inventory, which you will recall is what the manager wants to determine. The line connecting $Q$ to time, $t$, in our graph represents the rate at which inventory is depleted, *demand,* during the time period, $t$. Demand is assumed to be *known with certainty*, and thus constant, which explains why the line representing demand is straight. Also, notice that inventory never goes below zero, a condition the carpet store originally specified. In addition, when the inventory level does reach zero, it is assumed that an order immediately arrives after an infinitely small passage of time, referred to as *instantaneous receipt*. This is a simplifying assumption that we will maintain for the moment.

**Figure 17.1** Inventory usage.

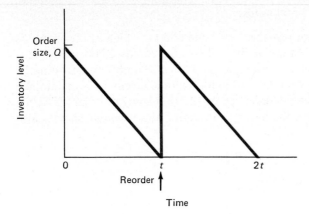

Referring to figure 17.1, we can see that the amount of inventory available is totally $Q$, the size of the order, for only an infinitely small period of time. $Q$ is always being depleted by demand. Alternatively, the amount of inventory is totally zero for an infinitely small period of time, since there is no inventory only at the specific time, $t$. As such, the amount of inventory available is somewhere in between these two extremes. A logical deduction is that the inventory available is the *average inventory level*, defined as

*Determining the average inventory level*

$$\text{Average inventory} = \frac{Q}{2}$$

In order to verify this relationship, specify any number of points—values of $Q$—over the entire time period, $t$, and divide by the number of points. For example, if $Q = 5{,}000$, the designated 6 points from 5,000 to 0 yards, as shown in figure 17.2, are summed and divided by 6.

**Figure 17.2** Levels of $Q$.

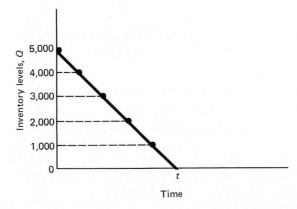

$$\text{Average inventory} = \frac{5,000 + 4,000 + 3,000 + 2,000 + 1,000 + 0}{6}$$

$$= 2,500 \text{ yards}$$

*Average annual inventory*

Alternatively, sum just the 2 extreme points (which also encompass the range of time, *t*) and divide by 2. This also equals 2,500 yards. This computation is the same, in principle, as adding $Q$ and 0 and dividing by 2, which equals $Q/2$. This relationship for average inventory is maintained regardless of the size of the order, $Q$, or the frequency of orders (i.e., the time period, *t*). As such, the average inventory of an *annual basis* is also $Q/2$, as shown in figure 17.3.

**Figure 17.3** Average inventory.

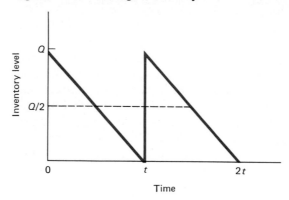

*Total annual carrying jcost*

Now that we know that the amount of inventory available *on an annual basis* is the average inventory, $Q/2$, we can determine the total annual carrying cost by multiplying the average number of yards in inventory by the carrying cost per yard per year, $C_c$:

$$\text{Total annual carrying cost} = C_c \frac{Q}{2}$$

## Ordering Cost

The second inventory cost the carpet store incurs is the *cost of placing an order*. The total ordering cost generally includes some or all of the following items:

*Items contributing to ordering cost*

The cost of processing an order, including all recordkeeping
Transportation costs to get the order from the supplier
The cost of unloading the order and placing it in inventory

Salaries of employees involved in the ordering process

All supplies used in ordering, including forms, postage, telephone, and computer time

Ordering cost is expressed on a per order basis. The manager of the Armor Carpet Store has determined that the cost of an order of Super Shag carpet, which we will represent symbolically as $C_o$, is

*Cost per order*

$$C_o = \$150 \text{ per order}$$

However, this value represents only the cost per order and not the *total ordering cost*. Since we previously developed a formula for finding the total carrying cost of an *annual* basis, we will also determine the total ordering cost per year. The total ordering cost is a result of the *number of orders* that will be made during the year. Since the manager will not order any more carpet to be put in inventory than will be demanded *and* we know demand with certainty, then the number of orders per year is defined as

*Determining the orders per year*

$$\text{Orders per year} = \frac{D}{Q}$$

where

$$D = \text{demand per year}$$

The total annual ordering cost per year can now be computed as the number of orders per year multiplied by the cost per order.

*Total annual ordering cost*

$$\text{Total annual ordering cost} = C_o\frac{D}{Q}$$

## Total Inventory Cost

The *total annual inventory cost* is computed by summing total annual carrying cost and total annual ordering cost.

*Summing the total annual carrying and ordering costs*

$$\text{Total annual inventory cost} = C_c\frac{Q}{2} + C_o\frac{D}{Q}$$

Total inventory cost, ordering cost, and carrying cost are shown graphically in figure 17.4.

*Graphically illustrating inventory costs*

We will analyze each one of the three cost curves shown in figure 17.4 separately. First observe the general upward trend of the total carrying cost curve. As the order size, $Q$ (listed on the vertical axis) increases, the total carrying cost (shown on the horizontal axis) increases. This is logical, since larger orders will result in more units carried in inventory. For our carpet store example, recall that the carrying cost per yard, $C_c$, is $0.75. Table 17.1 shows the total carrying cost computed for various (arbitrarily selected) increasing values of $Q$.

*As Q increases, carrying cost increases*

**Figure 17.4** Inventory cost model.

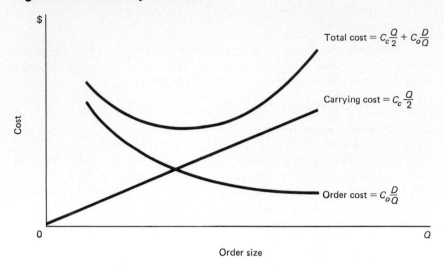

Order size

**Table 17.1** Total Annual Carrying Costs for Selected Order Sizes

| Q | Total Annual Carrying Cost $C_c \dfrac{Q}{2}$ |
|---|---|
| 1,000 | $ 375 |
| 2,000 | 750 |
| 3,000 | 1,125 |
| 4,000 | 1,500 |
| 5,000 | 1,875 |

Notice in table 17.1 that as $Q$ increases, so does total carrying cost, which is the trend shown by the carrying cost curve in figure 17.4.

*As Q increases, ordering cost decreases*

Next, observe the ordering cost curve in figure 17.4. As the order size, $Q$, increases, the ordering cost *decreases* (just the opposite effect that occurred with the carrying cost). This is also a logical result, since as orders become larger there will be fewer orders per year. For our carpet store example, recall that the cost per order, $C_o$, is $150. We are also going to assume that annual demand is for 10,000 yards of carpet. Table 17.2 shows the total ordering cost for the same example values of $Q$ we used in table 17.1.

Notice from table 17.2 that as $Q$ increases the total ordering cost declines, which the ordering cost curve reflects in figure 17.4.

Now we will combine the two costs for the selected values of $Q$ to get the total annual inventory costs as shown in table 17.3.

**Table 17.2** Total Annual Ordering Cost for Selected Order Sizes

| $Q$ | Total Annual Carrying Cost $C_o \dfrac{D}{Q}$ |
|---|---|
| 1,000 | $1,500 |
| 2,000 | 750 |
| 3,000 | 500 |
| 4,000 | 375 |
| 5,000 | 300 |

**Table 17.3** Total Annual Inventory Cost for Selected Order Sizes

| $Q$ | Total Annual Ordering Cost $C_o \dfrac{D}{Q}$ | + Total Annual Carrying Cost $C_c \dfrac{Q}{2}$ | = Total Annual Inventory Cost |
|---|---|---|---|
| 1,000 | $1,500 | $ 375 | $1,875 |
| 2,000 | 750 | 750 | 1,500 ◄──── Minimum total |
| 3,000 | 500 | 1,125 | 1,625   cost |
| 4,000 | 375 | 1,500 | 1,875 |
| 5,000 | 300 | 1,875 | 2,175 |

*Determining optimal Q graphically*

In table 17.3, the values in the total cost column represent points on the total cost curve in figure 17.4. The total cost curve first declines as $Q$ increases, and then begins to increase after a point as do the values in table 17.3. The best or *optimal* value of $Q$ is the one that results in the minimum total annual inventory cost. In table 17.3, the optimal value of $Q$ is 2,000, since $1,500 is the minimum total cost. This value of $Q$, which results in the total minimum inventory cost of $1,500, occurs at the point on our graph where the total cost curve is at its lowest, as shown in figure 17.5.

However, in this example encompassing tables 17.1, 17.2, and 17.3, we only considered increments of 1,000 yards of carpet as possible values of $Q$. As such, it was a *coincidence* that we happened to test a value for $Q$ (i.e., 2,000 yards) that turned out to correspond to the lowest point on the total cost curve. Some other value of $Q$ not considered could have just as easily been optimal. Of course, we could simply read the value of $Q$ directly off the inventory graph in figure 17.5 by locating the lowest point on the total cost curve. However, this is a rather time-consuming and cumbersome method, and depends on a completely accurate graph.

As such, some alternative mathematical method is necessary that includes all possible values of $Q$ (instead of a trial-and-error approach as we used in our example), and does not require graphical analysis.

**Figure 17.5** Optimal order size, $Q$.

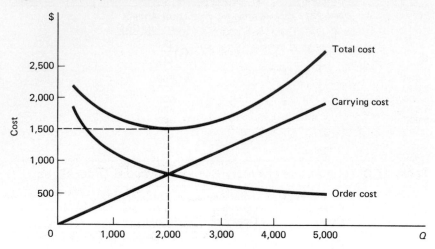

## Computing Optimal $Q$

Observing figure 17.5, we can see that the optimal value of $Q$ corresponding to the minimum total inventory cost not only occurs where the total cost curve is lowest, but also where *total ordering cost equals total carrying cost* (where the two cost curves intersect). This relationship is expressed mathematically as

*Equating ordering cost and carrying cost*

$$C_c \frac{Q}{2} = C_o \frac{D}{Q}$$

*Solving for Q*

Since $Q$ is the value the manager desires to know, it is the decision variable we will solve for. First, we multiply both sides of this equation by $Q$ which yields

$$C_c \frac{Q^2}{2} = C_o D$$

Next, we multiply both sides by 2 and divide both sides by $C_c$, which results in

$$Q^2 = \frac{2C_o D}{C_c}$$

Taking the square root of both sides,

$$Q^* = \sqrt{\frac{2C_o D}{C_c}}$$

*Optimal Q\*, the economic order quantity*

$Q^*$ signifies that this value of $Q$ is optimal and is referred to as the *economic order quantity* (EOQ).

Inventory Analysis with Certain Demand

The formula for the optimal value of $Q$ can also be derived using calculus. Notice that $Q*$ corresponds to the minimum point on the total cost curve in figure 17.5. At this point the slope of the total cost curve equals zero. Since the derivative of a curve (nonlinear function) equals the slope of the curve at any point, we can let the derivative of the total cost equation equal zero and solve for $Q$. This value of $Q$ corresponds to the minimum point on the total cost curve, thus it is optimal. This procedure for deriving the formula for $Q*$ is described in detail in chapter 23 (calculus-based techniques).

*Deriving Q\* using calculus*

For our carpet shop example, we will continue our assumption that demand for Super Shag is 10,000 yards per year. Also recall that carrying cost per yard, $C_c$, equals $0.75, and ordering cost, $C_o$, equals $150 per order. Substituting these values into our economic order quantity formula,

*Computing Q\**

$$Q* = \sqrt{\frac{2(\$150)(10,000)}{(\$0.75)}}$$
$$= 2,000 \text{ yards}$$

The total annual inventory cost is computed by using our economic order quantity, $Q*$, in our total cost formula:

*Computing the total minimum inventory cost*

$$\text{Total annual inventory cost} = C_c\frac{Q*}{2} + C_o\frac{D}{Q*}$$
$$= (\$0.75)\frac{(2,000)}{2} + (\$150)\frac{(10,000)}{2,000}$$
$$= \$750 + 750$$
$$= \$1,500 \text{ per year}$$

The number of orders that will be made annually can be computed as

*Computing the orders per year*

$$\text{Number of orders per year} = \frac{D}{Q*}$$
$$= \frac{10,000 \text{ yards}}{2,000 \text{ yards}}$$
$$= 5 \text{ orders per year}$$

Also, we can determine the time between orders as follows, assuming a year equals 365 days.

*Computing the time between orders*

$$\text{Time between orders} = \frac{365 \text{ days}}{\text{Number of orders per year}}$$
$$= \frac{365 \text{ days}}{5 \text{ orders}}$$
$$= 73 \text{ days between orders}$$

## EOQ Analysis over Time

One of the confusing aspects of inventory analysis can be the time frame encompassed by the analysis. Therefore, we will digress for just a moment to discuss this aspect of EOQ analysis.

*Developing the EOQ model on a monthly basis*

Recall that previously we developed the EOQ model "regardless of order size, $Q$, and time, $t$." Now we will verify this condition. In order to do so we will develop our EOQ model on a *monthly basis*. First, demand is equal to 833.3 yards per month (which we determined by dividing the annual demand of 10,000 yards by 12 months). Next, by dividing the carrying cost, $C_c$, of $0.75, which was on an annual basis, by 12, we get the monthly (per unit) carrying cost: $C_c = \$0.0625$. The ordering cost of $150 is not related to time. Summarizing,

$$D = 833.3 \text{ yards per month}$$
$$C_c = \$0.0625 \text{ per yard per month}$$
$$C_o = \$150 \text{ per order}$$

*Computing Q\**

Substituting these values into our EOQ formula,

$$Q^* = \sqrt{\frac{2C_oD}{C_c}}$$
$$= \sqrt{\frac{2(150)(833.3)}{(.0625)}}$$
$$= 2,000 \text{ yards}$$

*Q\* is the same regardless of the time frame*

This is the same optimal order size that we determined on an annual basis. Now we will compute total monthly inventory cost.

$$\text{Total monthly inventory cost} = C_c\frac{Q^*}{2} + C_o\frac{D}{Q^*}$$
$$= (\$.0625)\frac{(2,000)}{2} + (\$150)\frac{(833.3)}{(2,000)}$$
$$= \$125 \text{ per month}$$

In order to convert this monthly total cost to an annual cost, we multiply it by 12 (months).

$$\text{Total annual inventory cost} = (\$125)(12)$$
$$= \$1,500$$

This brief example demonstrates that regardless of the time period EOQ analysis encompasses, the economic order quantity ($Q^*$) is the same.

## Assumptions of the EOQ Model

*Simplifying assumptions*

In the development of the EOQ model we made several assumptions that tended to simplify the model. These assumptions were:

1. Demand for inventory was known with certainty and constant over time.
2. When the inventory level reached zero a new order was instantaneously placed and received (i.e., no shortages were allowed).

*Relaxing the second assumption*

We will maintain the first assumption throughout the remainder of this chapter. However, by relaxing the second assumption we can develop variations of the EOQ model, which can be applied to often more realistic inventory situations.

## The EOQ Model with a Reorder Point

One of the assumptions of our present EOQ model is that an order is received an infinitely short time after it is placed. However, a more realistic situation is that an order is placed and then after a reasonable period of time passes, it is received. The time required between the placement of an order and its receipt is referred to as the *reorder lead time*. For our carpet store example, once the manager places an order with the manufacturer for Super Shag carpet, it takes 10 days to receive the order. This lead time of 10 days is assumed to be constant.

*Reorder lead time*

The concept of lead time is illustrated graphically in figure 17.6. Notice that the order must now be made prior to the level of inventory falling to zero. Since demand for the carpet is consuming the inventory while the order is being shipped, the order must be made while there is enough *inventory in stock* to meet demand during the lead-time period. This level of inventory is referred to as the *reorder point* and is so designated in figure 17.6.

*Ordering with inventory in stock to meet lead time demand*

**Figure 17.6** Reorder point and lead time.

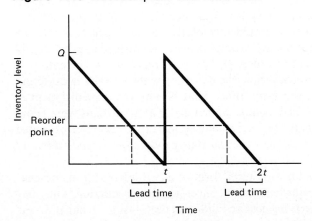

The reorder point is computed by multiplying the lead time, *L*, by the demand per day. If we assume that a year consists of 365 days, then the demand per day is *D*/365. Thus, the formula for the reorder point, *R*, is

$$R = L\frac{D}{365}$$

For our example, recall that *L* equals 10 days and demand is 10,000 yards of carpet per year. This will result in the following reorder point.

$$R = L\frac{D}{365}$$
$$= (10)\frac{(10,000)}{365}$$
$$= 274 \text{ yards}$$

*Q is independent of lead time*

A reorder point of 274 yards means that whenever inventory falls to 274 yards the order should be placed. During the 10-day period while the order is being shipped, the 274 yards will be completely depleted so that at exactly the same time the new order arrives the inventory level will reach zero. Notice, however, that the existence of a lead time does not affect the optimal order quantity at all. Thus, 2,000 units are still ordered regardless of the lead time and reorder point.

## Noninstantaneous Receipt Model

*Gradual receipt of an order*

The next assumption we will relax is that an order is received all at once. In many cases an order is received gradually over a period of time. This is what would occur if the carpet store was also able to produce carpet as well as sell it. The carpet would then go into inventory as it was produced.

*Production lot size model*

In fact, this form of inventory analysis is often referred to as the *production lot size* model because inventory is replenished directly from production.

This type of model is graphically illustrated in figure 17.7. Notice that inventory is not replenished instantaneously, but instead rises gradually

*Production rate exceeds demand rate*

to a point where the entire order, *Q*, has been received. As inventory is being replenished from production, the demand for the product is depleting the inventory stock at the same time. That is why the replenishment is gradual. However, replenishment could not occur at all if items were going out at a faster rate than they were coming in (i.e., if demand exceeded production). Thus, it must be assumed that *production exceeds demand* in this type of model.

Now we will develop an altered form of our EOQ model to compensate for the gradual replenishment of inventory by production. Our new model will consist of carrying cost and ordering cost, just as in our previous

*Ordering cost is unaffected*

EOQ model. The ordering cost is not affected by the gradual replenishment of inventory, since it is dependent only on the number of orders per year.

**Figure 17.7** Noninstantaneous receipt model.

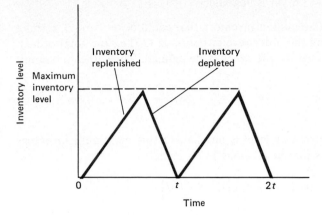

However, carrying cost is not the same, since this cost is dependent upon *average inventory*, which is different for this model.

*Determining average inventory*

For this form of inventory analysis it is necessary to reflect the rate of replenishment in the model. As such, we will define

$r$ = daily rate of replenishment of inventory (also known as the production rate)

Next, we must determine the maximum inventory level (as shown in fig. 17.7) in order to compute average inventory. First, we will compute the number of days required to receive the order (which is also the length of time of a production run) as follows.

*The number of days required to receive an order*

$$\text{Number of days to receive an order} = \frac{Q}{r}$$

For example, if $Q$ equals 1,000 yards of carpet and 150 yards of carpet are produced per day, it will take

$$\frac{1,000}{150} = 6.7 \text{ days to receive an order}$$

Next we need to know how many yards of carpet will be demanded during this period. As such, we must use the daily rate of demand, $d$, which is found by dividing annual demand by 365 days.

*Daily demand rate*

$$d = \frac{10,000}{365 \text{ days}}$$
$$= 27.4 \text{ yards demanded per day}$$

The number of yards of carpet demanded during the order receipt period is

*Demand during the order receipt period*

$$\text{Demand during order receipt} = \frac{Q}{r} \cdot d$$

and for our example, this amount is

6.7 (27.4) = 183.6 yards demanded

*The maximum inventory level*    The maximum amount of inventory that could be on hand if nothing was demanded during the order receipt period is $Q$ (i.e., the total order). However, $Q$ is depleted by the amount demanded. Thus, the maximum inventory level is

$$Q - \frac{Q}{r} \cdot d$$

*The average inventory level*    The average inventory level is one-half of this maximum inventory level (just like it was for our previous EOQ model).

$$\text{Average inventory level} = 1/2 \left( Q - \frac{Q}{r} d \right)$$
$$= \frac{Q}{2} \left( 1 - \frac{d}{r} \right)$$

*Total annual carrying cost*    Total carrying cost is computed by multiplying the per unit carrying cost, $C_c$, by average inventory.

$$\text{Total carrying cost} = C_c \frac{Q}{2} \left( 1 - \frac{d}{r} \right)$$

Notice that we can use annual carrying cost even though our equation uses daily demand and daily replenishment, because by dividing the two they form a ratio that is independent of time.

*Total annual inventory cost*    The total inventory cost model requires the addition of total carrying cost and total ordering cost, as in our previous EOQ model.

$$\text{Total annual inventory cost} = C_o \frac{D}{Q} + C_c \frac{Q}{2} \left( 1 - \frac{d}{r} \right)$$

*Equating total ordering cost and total carrying cost*    The total inventory cost is a function of two other costs, just as in our previous EOQ model. As such, the minimum inventory cost curve occurs when the total cost curve is lowest and where the carrying cost curve and ordering cost curve intersect (see fig. 17.4). Therefore, to find optimal $Q^*$, we equate total carrying cost with total ordering cost.

$$C_c \frac{Q}{2} \left( 1 - \frac{d}{r} \right) = C_o \frac{D}{Q}$$

*Optimal Q\**
$$C_c \frac{Q^2}{2} \left( 1 - \frac{d}{r} \right) = C_o D$$
$$Q^* = \sqrt{\frac{2 C_o D}{C_c (1 - d/r)}}$$

*Computing Q\**    For our example, if daily demand, $d$, is 27.4 yards; the daily production rate, $r$, is 150 yards; ordering cost, $C_o$, equals \$150; annual demand, $D$, is 10,000 yards (27.4 × 365 days); and carrying cost, $C_c$, is \$0.75, then the economic order quantity is computed as follows.

$$Q^* = \sqrt{\frac{2(150)(10,000)}{(0.75)(1 - 27.4/150)}}$$

$$= 2{,}212.2 \text{ yards per order}$$

The total annual cost is computed using the optimal order size, as follows.

*Computing total minimum inventory cost*

$$\text{Total annual inventory cost} = C_o \frac{D}{Q} + C_c \frac{Q}{2}(1 - d/r)$$

$$= 150\frac{(10,000)}{2,212.2} + (0.75)\frac{2,212.2}{2}$$

$$\left(1 - \frac{27.4}{150}\right)$$

$$= \$1{,}356.06 \text{ per year}$$

The number of orders per year (which corresponds to the number of annual production runs) is computed the same way as in our original model by using the formula

*Computing the number of orders per year*

$$\text{Number of orders per year} = \frac{D}{Q}$$

$$= \frac{10,000}{2,212.2}$$

$$= 4.52 \text{ orders (production runs)}$$

The length of time required to receive an order (the length of a production run) is one of the items we determined when we derived the average inventory level for this production model.

*Computing the number of days to receive an order*

$$\text{Number of days to receive an order} = \frac{Q}{r}$$

$$= \frac{2,212.2}{150}$$

$$14.75 \text{ days}$$

The maximum inventory level was also determined during our derivation of the average inventory level for this model as

*Computing the maximum inventory level*

$$\text{Maximum inventory level} = Q - \frac{Q}{r}d$$

$$= 2{,}212.2 - \frac{2,212.2}{150}(27.4)$$

$$= 1{,}808.2 \text{ yards}$$

In this example, inventory (carpet) that was subsequently sold was replenished by production. However, the noninstantaneous receipt model is also widely used when the inventory is not sold but used internally. For example, this model would be appropriate for a manufacturing company that produced a part or item that is subsequently used internally in another production process to produce a completed product, such as a furniture company that owned a sawmill to produce its own lumber that it would use to make furniture.

# The EOQ Model with Shortages and Backordering

*It can be more economical to allow shortages*

*Dividing the order receipt period*

Recall that the manager of the carpet store specified that there must be inventory of Super Shag available at all times (shortages could not exist). However, it is often more economical to allow shortages and backorder demand and incur the cost associated with not being able to meet demand, than keeping an excessive amount of inventory on hand to avoid shortages.

An inventory model with shortages is shown in figure 17.8. Notice that the time between order receipts has been divided into two other times: the time during which inventory is available, $t_1$, and the time during which there is a shortage, $t_2$, both *during 1 order cycle*. During the time shortages occur, the carpet store will be unable to meet demand and will *backorder* carpet. Typically, a cost is assigned to shortages. Shortage costs are primarily related to lost present and future sales due to customer dissatisfaction.

**Figure 17.8** Shortage model.

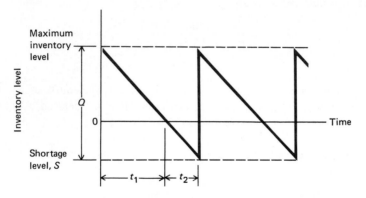

*Adding shortage cost to the EOQ model*

In order to develop an EOQ model that includes shortages, a shortage cost must be added to our total cost equation. The development of both carrying cost and shortage cost for this model is achieved using plane geometry, and as such is more complex than our previous EOQ model. Therefore, we will bypass the lengthy derivation of these cost equations and present them only in their final form.

Defining the shortage cost per unit as $C_s$ and the maximum shortage level as $S$ (as shown in fig. 17.8) the total shortage cost is computed as follows.

$$\text{Total shortage cost} = C_s \frac{S^2}{2Q}$$

The total carrying cost is defined as follows.

$$\text{Total carrying cost} = C_c \frac{(Q - S)^2}{2Q}$$

The total ordering cost is the same as in our previous EOQ model.

$$\text{Total ordering cost} = C_o\frac{D}{Q}$$

The total annual inventory cost is computed by summing all three of these costs.

$$\text{Total annual inventory cost} = C_s\frac{S^2}{2Q} + C_c\frac{(Q - S)^2}{2Q} + C_o\frac{D}{Q}$$

The total annual cost equation and all three of its component costs are illustrated graphically in figure 17.9.

---

**Figure 17.9** Cost model with shortages.

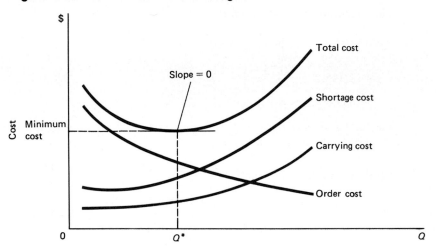

Notice in figure 17.9 that the lowest point on the total cost curve no longer occurs where all the component cost curves intersect. This means that we cannot simply equate all the individual cost equations in order to determine the economic order quantity, $Q^*$. However, an alternative method is to use *calculus,* as we indicated with the basic EOQ model.

*Optimal Q\* is no longer where all costs intersect*

The slope at any point on a curve can be found by taking the derivative of the equation of the curve at that point. At the lowest point of the total cost curve in figure 17.9, the slope equals zero. Therefore, if we take the derivative of our total cost equation and set it equal to the slope, zero, we can solve for $Q^*$. Doing so results in the following EOQ formula.

*Using calculus to compute Q\**

$$Q^* = \sqrt{\frac{2C_oD}{C_c}\left(\frac{C_s + C_c}{C_s}\right)}$$

The maximum shortage level can also be computed as

$$S = Q*\left(\frac{C_c}{C_c + C_s}\right)$$

*Computing Q\** For our carpet example, if we let $C_s$ (the shortage cost per yard of carpet per year) equal \$2.00, and all our other costs and demand remain the same ($C_c = \$0.75$, $C_o = \$150$, $D = 10,000$ yards), the economic order quantity is computed as follows.

$$Q* = \sqrt{\frac{2C_oD}{C_c}\left(\frac{C_s + C_c}{C_s}\right)}$$

$$= \sqrt{\frac{2(\$150)(10,000)}{(\$0.75)}\left(\frac{\$2 + \$0.75}{\$2}\right)}$$

$$= 2,345.2 \text{ yards per order}$$

*Computing the shortage level* The maximum shortage level is

$$S = Q*\left(\frac{C_c}{C_c + C_s}\right)$$

$$= 2,345.2\left(\frac{\$0.75}{\$2 + 0.75}\right)$$

$$= 639.6 \text{ yards per order}$$

*Computing total inventory cost* The total annual cost is computed using both the optimal order quantity, $Q*$, and the maximum shortage, $S$.

$$\text{Total annual inventory cost} = \frac{C_s S^2}{2Q} + C_c\frac{(Q - S)^2}{2Q} + C_o\frac{D}{Q}$$

$$= \frac{(\$2)(639.6)^2}{2(2,345.2)} + \frac{(\$0.75)(1,705.6)^2}{2(2,345.2)}$$

$$+ \frac{150(10,000)}{2,345.2}$$

$$= \$174.44 + 465.16 + 639.60$$

$$= \$1,279.20$$

*Computing the maximum inventory level* The maximum inventory level (shown in fig. 17.8) can be determined as follows.

$$\text{Maximum inventory level} = Q - S$$

$$= 2,345.2 - 639.6$$

$$= 1,705.6 \text{ yards}$$

*Computing the number of orders per year* The number of orders per year can be determined the same way as in our previous two models, by dividing total annual demand by the order quantity.

$$\text{Number of orders} = \frac{D}{Q}$$

$$= \frac{10,000}{2,345.2}$$

$$= 4.26 \text{ orders per year}$$

Given the number of orders per year, we can also compute the time between orders, $t$, by dividing the number of days per year by the number of orders per year.

*Computing the time between orders*

$$t = \frac{365}{4.26}$$
$$= 85.7 \text{ days between orders}$$

The time during which inventory exists ($t_1$ in fig. 17.8) and the time during which a shortage exists ($t_2$ in fig. 17.8) during each order cycle can be computed using the following formulas.

*Computing the times during which inventory and shortages exist*

$$t_1 = \frac{Q - S}{D}$$
$$= \frac{2,345.2 - 639.6}{10,000}$$
$$= .171 \text{ year}$$
$$= 62.4 \text{ days}$$

and

$$t_2 = \frac{S}{D}$$
$$= \frac{639.6}{10,000}$$
$$= .064 \text{ year}$$
$$= 23.3 \text{ days}$$

To determine the total days annually that inventory and shortages exist multiply $t_1$ and $t_2$ by orders per year, $D/Q$.

Notice that by allowing shortages, the total cost was reduced slightly from the total cost when shortages were not allowed (i.e., $1,500). Of course, the opposite occurrence is also feasible. However, cases can occur where the difference in cost can be significant. As such, the question of whether or not to allow shortages represents a major inventory decision.

*Comparing the EOQ models with and without shortages*

## The Noninstantaneous Receipt Model with Shortages

The two previous models we developed were for the noninstantaneous receipt of an order and for allowed shortages. Both of these inventory characteristics can be combined in one model. Such a model represents the final and most complex form of the classical EOQ model. Since it is even more complex to develop than the model with shortages, we will not pursue it further in this text. However, this model is available in other, more advanced texts including those listed in the references at the end of this chapter. The interested reader can pursue this model through these references.

*Combining the shortage and noninstantaneous receipt models*

# The Quantity Discount Model

*Receiving a discount for making a large order*

An additional variation of the classic EOQ model that does not include a relaxation of any of the original assumptions of the model is the case where a large order can result in a discount from the supplier. Quantity discount analysis requires that the carrying cost be defined as a percentage of the price of the item in inventory paid to the supplier. If we let price be represented symbolically as $P$, then our total annual inventory cost model becomes

*Including item price in the EOQ model*

$$\text{Total annual inventory cost} = C_o\frac{D}{Q} + C_cP\frac{Q}{2} + PD$$

The last term, $PD$ (price multiplied by demand), represents the total annual amount paid to the supplier for all ordered units of the product.

*Carrying cost as a percentage of price*

Now we will consider two options open to the manager of the carpet store. We will assume that the carrying cost per unit, $C_c$, is 10% of the price of a yard of carpet, and that the price without discount is $3.00 per yard. The first option is for the manager to purchase carpet from the supplier at the normal price. The second option is to purchase carpet at a price of $2.00 per yard (i.e., a $1.00 discount) if a minimum of 4,000 yards is ordered.

*Optimal Q\**

Considering the first option, we must compute the economic order quantity using a slightly altered version of our basic EOQ formula.

$$Q^* = \sqrt{\frac{2C_oD}{C_cP}}$$

*Computing the discount options*

For the first option, $C_c$ = 10% of the price, $P$ = $3.00, $D$ = 10,000 yards, $C_o$ = $150.

$$Q^* = \sqrt{\frac{2(150)(10,000)}{(.10)(3)}}$$
$$= 3,162.3 \text{ yards}$$

The total annual inventory cost for this optimal value of $Q^*$ is computed as follows.

$$\text{Total annual inventory cost} = C_o\frac{D}{Q} + C_cP\frac{Q}{2} + PD$$
$$= (150)\frac{10,000}{3,162.3} + (.10)(3)\frac{3,162.3}{2}$$
$$+ (3)(10,000)$$
$$= \$30,949 \text{ per year}$$

Next, we must consider the second option. However, in order to receive the discount, the order quantity must be at least 4,000 yards. Thus, we will let $Q$ = 4,000 yards and compute total cost with price equal to $2.00 per yard.

$$\text{Total annual inventory cost} = C_o\frac{D}{Q} + C_cP\frac{Q}{2} + PD$$

$$= (150)\frac{10,000}{4,000} + (.10)(2)\frac{4,000}{2}$$

$$+ (2)(10,000)$$

$$= \$20,775$$

Comparing the total cost of each option:

*Comparing the discount options*

|  | **Option 1** | **Option 2** |
|---|---|---|
| $Q$ | 3,162.3 yards | 4,000 yards |
| $P$ | \$3.00 | \$2.00 |
| Total annual cost | \$30,949 | \$20,775 |

As a result, the manager would select option 2 and receive the discount. Basically, this type of quantity discount analysis represents a trade-off between the added carrying costs for holding the extra amount (necessary to get the discount) in inventory and the reduced price.

## Summary

In this chapter the classical economic order quantity model has been presented. The basic form of the EOQ model included simplifying assumptions regarding order receipt, no shortages, and constant demand known with certainty. By relaxing some of these assumptions we were able to create increasingly complex *but* realistic models. These EOQ variations included the reorder point model, the noninstantaneous receipt model, and the model with shortages. However, all of these models maintained one assumption that was never relaxed—that demand was known with certainty and was constant. Although these EOQ models are quite useful in developing an inventory policy and are used extensively as approximations, they disregard the fact that demand is almost never known with certainty. Thus, to be truly realistic, this last assumption must also be dropped. As such, this is the topic of the next chapter—inventory analysis with uncertain demand.

*Certain demand is always assumed in this chapter*

## References

Buchan, J., and Koenigsberg, E. *Scientific Inventory Management*. Englewood Cliffs, N.J.: Prentice-Hall, 1963.

Buffa, E. S., and Taubert, W. J. *Production-Inventory Systems: Planning and Control*. Rev. ed. Homewood, Ill.: Irwin, 1972.

Churchman, C. W.; Ackoff, R. L.; and Arnoff, E. L. *Introduction to Operations Research*. New York: John Wiley and Sons, 1957.

Hadley, G., and Whitin, T. M. *Analysis of Inventory Systems*. Englewood Cliffs, N.J.: Prentice-Hall, 1963.

Johnson, L. A., and Montgomery, D. C. *Operations Research in Production Planning, Scheduling, and Inventory Control.* New York: John Wiley and Sons, 1974.

Lee, Sang M.; Moore, Laurence J.; and Taylor, Bernard W. *Management Science.* Dubuque, Iowa: Wm. C. Brown Company Publishers, 1981.

Magee, J. F., and Boodman, D. M. *Production Planning and Inventory Control.* 2d ed. New York: McGraw-Hill, 1967.

Shamblin, J. E., and Stevens, G. T., Jr. *Operations Research: A Fundamental Approach.* New York: McGraw-Hill, 1974.

Starr, M. K., and Miller, D. W. *Inventory Control: Theory and Practice.* Englewood Cliffs, N.J.: Prentice-Hall, 1962.

## Problems

1. Given the following annual demand, annual carrying cost, and cost per order, compute the economic order quantity and total minimum cost.

   $D = 15,000$ units per year
   $C_o = \$100$ per order
   $C_c = \$0.40$ per unit per year

2. Given the following annual demand, annual carrying cost, and cost per order, compute the economic order quantity and total minimum cost.

   $D = 750$ units per year
   $C_o = \$50$ per order
   $C_c = \$0.15$ per unit per year

3. An inventory system has an annual ordering cost of $200 per order, an annual per unit carrying cost of $0.75, and an annual demand of 5,000 units (assuming a 365-day year). Compute the following:
   (a) Economic order quantity
   (b) Minimum total annual inventory cost
   (c) Optimal number of orders per year
   (d) Optimal time between orders

4. For the inventory system in problem 3, illustrate the optimal order size, average inventory, and time between orders in a graph relating inventory and time. Next, illustrate the determination of the economic order quantity in a graph relating inventory cost and order size.

5. The Western Jeans Company purchases denim to make jeans from Cumberland Textiles Mills. The Western Company uses 35,000 yards of denim per year (365 days). The cost of ordering denim from the textile company is $500 per order. It costs Western $.35 per yard annually to hold a yard of denim in inventory. Determine the optimal number of yards of denim the Western Company should order, the minimum total annual inventory cost, the optimal number of orders per year (assuming a 365-day year), and the optimal time between orders.

6. The Metropolitan Book Company purchases paper from the Atlantic Paper Company. The company produces magazines and paperbacks that require 215,000 yards of paper per year (365 days). The cost per order for the magazine company is $1,200, while the cost of holding one yard of paper in inventory is $.08 per year. Determine the following:
   (a) Economic order quantity
   (b) Minimum total annual cost
   (c) Optimal number of orders per year
   (d) Optimal time between orders

7. The Atlantic Paper Company produces paper from wood pulp, which it purchases from the Adirondack Lumber Products Company. The paper company's customers' demand for paper requires 450,000 pounds of wood pulp per year (365 days). Each order of pulp costs Atlantic $700, while it costs $.30 per pound per year to carry a pound of pulp in inventory. It takes 8 days for Atlantic to receive an order from the Adirondack Company. Determine the following:
   (a) Economic order quantity
   (b) Minimum total annual inventory cost
   (c) Reorder point

8. The Midtown Bookstore and Newsstand orders paperbacks from the Metropolitan Book Company. The demand at the Midtown store for paperbacks is 300 per month. The cost per order is $50, while the cost per month of carrying a paperback on the shelf is $.02. Determine the optimal number of paperbacks to order per month, the total minimum monthly inventory cost and the total minimum annual inventory cost.

9. The Big Buy Supermarket stocks Munchies Cereal. The store's demand for Munchies is 4,000 boxes per year (365 days). It costs the store $60 per order of Munchies, and it costs $.80 per box per year to keep the cereal in stock. Once an order for Munchies is made, it takes 4 days to receive the order from a food distributor. Determine the following:
   (a) Optimal order size
   (b) Minimum total annual inventory cost
   (c) Reorder point

10. Illustrate the optimal order size, time between orders, and reorder point for the inventory policy in problem 9 graphically.

11. In problem 5 if it takes the Western Jeans Company 6 days to receive an order of denim, at what level of inventory should the company reorder?

12. Given the following demand and replenishment rates per day, annual carrying cost per unit, and order cost, determine the economic order quantity and minimum total annual inventory cost for a noninstantaneous receipt model (one year equals 365 days).

$d$ = 200 units per day
$r$ = 500 units per day
$C_o$ = $300 per order
$C_c$ = $0.80 per unit per year

13. Given an annual demand rate of 8,000 units and an annual replenishment rate of 12,000 units for a noninstantaneous receipt model, an annual carrying cost per unit of $1.15, and an order cost of $175 per order, determine the optimal order size and the minimum total annual inventory cost.

14. For the inventory system described in problem 13 graphically illustrate the optimal order size, the maximum inventory level, the time to receive an order, and the time between orders.

15. The Adirondack Lumber Products Company produces wood pulp in its mill and then stores it in warehouses until it is shipped to customers. The company's demand is 450,000 pounds of wood pulp per year. The company's mill is able to produce 600,000 pounds of wood pulp per year. Every time the mill starts a production run to produce wood pulp (i.e., an order) it costs $800. The annual carrying cost per pound is $0.80. Determine the following:
    (a) Optimal order size
    (b) Minimum total annual inventory cost
    (c) Maximum inventory level

16. The Petroco Oil Company refines oil into gasoline at its refinery in Corpus Christi and stores it in storage tanks until it is demanded by the company's distributors. The oil company refinery can produce 4,000 barrels of gasoline per day, and the demand for gasoline by the company's distributors is 3,500 barrels per day. The cost to make a production run is $2,000, and the annual carrying cost per barrel is $3. Determine the following:
    (a) Economic order quantity
    (b) Minimum total annual inventory cost
    (c) Maximum inventory level

17. The Wood Valley Dairy makes cheese, which it then supplies to stores in its area. The dairy can make 250 pounds of cheese per day, while the demand of the area stores is 180 pounds per day. Each time the dairy makes cheese it costs $125 to set up the production process. The annual cost of carrying a pound of cheese in a refrigerated storage area is $12. Determine the optimal order size and the minimum total annual inventory cost.

18. The Rainwater Brewery produces Rainwater Light Beer and stores it in barrels in its warehouse, which it supplies to its distributors as it's demanded. The demand for Rainwater is 1,500 barrels of beer per day. The Brewery can produce 2,000 barrels of Rainwater per day. It costs $6,500 to set up a production run for Rainwater. Once it is brewed, the beer is stored in a refrigerated warehouse at an annual cost of $50 per barrel. Determine the economic order quantity and the minimum total annual inventory cost.

19. Given the following information for an inventory system that allows shortages, compute the optimal order size and minimum total annual inventory cost.

$D$ = 25,000 units per year
$C_o$ = $300 per order
$C_c$ = $2 per unit per year
$C_s$ = $5 per unit per year

20. Consider the inventory system of the Western Jeans Company described in problem 5. Now assume that this company allows shortages and that the annual cost per unit of shortages is $2. Determine the optimal order size and minimum total annual inventory cost. Compare these results with those determined in problem 5 and indicate if shortages should be allowed.

21. Videoworld is a discount television store that sells color televisions. The annual demand for color television sets is 2,200. The cost per order from the manufacturer is $650. The carrying cost is $45 per set per year. The store has an inventory policy that allows shortages. The shortage cost per set is estimated to be $60. Determine the following:
    (a) Optimal order size
    (b) Maximum shortage level
    (c) Minimum total annual inventory cost

22. Graphically illustrate the optimal order size, maximum inventory level, and maximum shortage level for the inventory system described in problem 21.

23. Consider the inventory system of the Metropolitan Book Company as described in problem 6. Now assume that this company allows shortages and that the annual cost per shortage is $.12 per yard. Determine the optimal order size and minimum total annual inventory cost and compare these results with those determined in problem 6.

24. The Roadking Tire Store sells a brand of tire called the Roadrunner. The annual demand from the store's customers for Roadrunner tires is 3,700 per year. The cost to order tires from the tire manufacturer is $420 per order. The annual carrying cost is $1.75 per tire. The store allows shortages and the annual shortage cost per tire is $4. Determine the following:

(a) Optimal order size

(b) Maximum shortage level

(c) Minimum total annual inventory cost

25. The Laurel Creek Lawn Shop sells Fastgro Fertilizer. The annual demand for the fertilizer is 270,000 pounds. The cost to order the fertilizer from the Fastgro company is $105 per order. The annual carrying cost is $.25 per pound. The store operates with shortages, and the annual shortage cost is $.70 per pound. Compute the optimal order size, minimum total annual inventory cost, and the maximum shortage level.

26. A car dealer who sells compact cars has an annual demand of 1,200 cars. It costs the dealer $1,800 per order to order cars from the manufacturer in Dearborn, and $700 per year to carry a car in inventory on the dealer's lot. The dealer is trying to decide whether or not to allow shortages. The dealer estimates that the cost of not having a car on the lot when a customer wants to buy one is $1,200. Determine if the dealer should allow shortages and if so, how much of a shortage.

27. Assume that in problem 5 the carrying cost per yard of denim is 29% of the price per yard and that the price of denim from the Cumberland Mills is $1.20 per yard. Now suppose Western Company can get a discounted price of $1.00 per yard if it purchases 20,000 yards per order. Analyze both options and indicate what order policy the Western Jeans Company should follow.

28. Assume that in problem 7 the annual carrying cost per pound of wood pulp is 40% of the price per pound and that the price per pound of wood pulp is $.75. Now suppose the Atlantic Paper Company can get a discounted price of $0.60 per pound if it purchases a minimum of 60,000 pounds per order. Should Atlantic Paper Company purchase wood pulp at the normal price or at the discount?

29. Assume that in problem 9 the annual carrying cost is 80% of the price per box of Munchies and that the price per box is $1.00. Now suppose the Big Buy Supermarket can get a discounted price of $.95 per box if it purchases 2,000 boxes per order. Should the market purchase at the normal price or at the discount?

30. The Uptown Bar and Grill buys Old World draft beer from a local distributor by the barrel. The grill has an annual demand for the beer of 900 barrels, which it purchases from the distributor for a price of $205 per barrel. The annual carrying cost is 12% of the price, and the cost per order is $160. The distributor has offered to give the grill a reduced price of $190 per barrel if it will order a minimum of 300 barrels. Should the grill maintain its normal ordering policy or take the discount?

# 18
Inventory Analysis
with Uncertain
Demand

## The EOQ Model with Safety Stocks

Determination of the Safety Stock
Determining Safety Stocks Using Service Levels

## Determining the Order Quantity with Payoff Tables

## Simulation of Inventory

## Summary

This chapter is a logical extension of the topic of inventory analysis presented in the previous chapter. In chapter 17, several variations of a general technique (EOQ analysis) for inventory analysis were presented. These variations were created by selectively relaxing the general assumptions of the classical EOQ model. However, the assumption that demand was always constant and known with certainty was never dropped. Realistically, future demand can rarely be predicted with certainty. As such, it will be beneficial for us to look at several ways to compensate for uncertain demand when determining the order quantity.

## The EOQ Model with Safety Stocks

To begin our presentation of inventory analysis under conditions of uncertain demand, we will continue to work within the framework of the classic economic order quantity (EOQ) model developed in chapter 17. However, one of the problems in performing EOQ analysis with uncertain demand is that it is difficult to determine a *reorder point*. Recall that a reorder point is needed to prevent stockouts (i.e., shortages) when a period of time passes between the placement of an order and its receipt. The reorder point is a level of inventory remaining in stock that is equal to the demand occurring during the time required to receive an order (i.e., *lead time*). When demand is certain, this inventory will be depleted at a known rate so that the order arrives at the same time that the inventory level reaches zero.

*Determining a reorder point given uncertain demand*

As an example, consider the Armor Carpet Store introduced in chapter 17. Recall that the carpet store has a constant demand ($D$) of 10,000 yards of Super Shag carpet per year and a lead time ($L$) of 10 days. Thus, the reorder point, $R$, was computed as,

*A reorder point example*

$$R = L \frac{D}{365}$$
$$= \frac{(10)\,(10{,}000)}{365}$$
$$= 274 \text{ yards}$$

The manager of the carpet store will place the economic order quantity ($Q^*$) when the carpet in inventory reaches 274 yards, and this amount will be depleted by demand during the 10 days required to receive the order. However, although lead time may be constant, if demand is uncertain, then it is not possible to exactly predict the demand that will occur during these 10 days. Therefore, it is possible that even though we have a reorder point, shortages might occur anyway. As a hedge against stockouts when demand is uncertain, a buffer of extra inventory called a *safety stock* is often used.

*Safety stock*

The occurrence of stockouts when demand is uncertain is illustrated graphically in figure 18.1.

**Figure 18.1** Inventory model with uncertain demand.

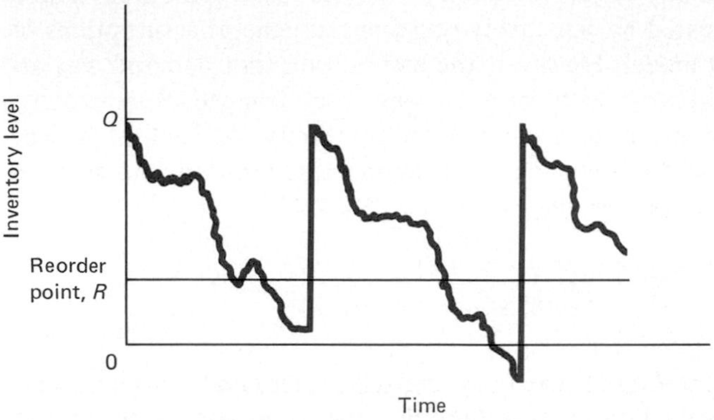

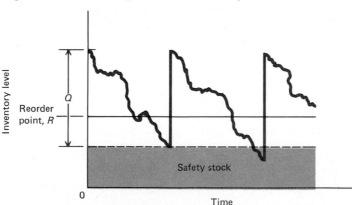

*A stockout*

In the second order cycle, a stockout occurs because demand exceeds the *expected* reorder point during the lead time. Now let us add a safety stock to our graph, as shown in figure 18.2. The reorder point is set so that the safety stock level is treated the same as the zero inventory level without a safety stock. In other words, we do not want inventory to go lower than the safety stock level. When it does, as in the second order cycle, demand is still met.

**Figure 18.2** Inventory model with safety stock.

**Inventory Analysis with Uncertain Demand**

Maintaining a safety stock is not cost free, however. A carrying cost is charged on the safety stock as it is on regular inventory. It is generally assumed that the frequency and amounts that actual demand is above the safety stock level equals the frequency and amounts with which it is below the safety stock level. Thus, the surpluses and deficits balance out over the year, so that on the average the safety stock is *unused*. This means that to determine the annual cost of the safety stock it is only necessary to multiply the annual carrying cost per unit by the safety stock level, $S_s$.

*A safety stock is not cost free*

*Determining the annual safety stock cost*

Total annual carrying cost of safety stock $= C_c S_s$

For our carpet store example, recall that $C_c =$ \$0.75 per yard. If we arbitrarily assume a safety stock of 300 yards, then the carrying cost is

$$\text{Total annual carrying cost of safety stock} = (\$0.75)(300)$$
$$= \$225$$

However, this cost must be weighed against the cost of having a stockout. As such, it is the objective of this form of inventory analysis to determine a safety stock level that minimizes the sum of the carrying cost *and* the stockout cost.

*The cost of a stockout vs. the cost of carrying a safety stock*

## Determination of the Safety Stock

Although demand is not known with certainty, we will assume that it can be described by a probability distribution. Based on the carpet store's records of demand, the manager has determined the following probability distribution for demand of carpet *during the lead time period*.

*Probabilistic demand*

| Demand during Lead Time | Probability |
|---|---|
| 500 | 0.10 |
| 600 | 0.20 |
| 700 | 0.40 |
| 800 | 0.20 |
| 900 | 0.10 |
| | 1.00 |

Using this distribution, we will compute the *expected demand* during lead time, as follows.

*Expected demand during lead time*

$$E(\text{Demand}) = .10(500) + .20(600) + .40(700) + .20(800)$$
$$+ .10(900)$$
$$= 700 \text{ yards}$$

We will use this average value of 700 yards of carpet as the *initial* reorder point. The amount by which our finally determined reorder point exceeds 700 yards will be the safety stock.

*The initial reorder point*

By using a reorder point of 700 yards and no safety stock, it is possible for the actual demand during lead time to exceed this amount by 100 yards 20% of the time (i.e., demand of 800 yards) and by 200 yards 10% of the time (i.e., demand of 900). Alternatively, if a reorder point of 800 yards including a safety stock of 100 yards is used, we could expect a stockout of 100 yards (i.e., demand of 900) only 10% of the time. If the reorder point is 900 yards including a safety stock of 200 yards, there would never be a stockout. The *expected shortages* for each of these possible reorder points with safety stock are computed in table 18.1.

*Computing expected shortages for each reorder point*

**Table 18.1** Computation of Expected Shortages per Reorder Point

| Reorder Point | Safety Stock | Actual Demand During Lead-Time | Resulting Shortage | Probability of Shortage | Expected Shortage per Demand | Total Expected Shortage per Reorder Point |
|---|---|---|---|---|---|---|
| 700 | 0 | 700 | 0 | .40 | 0 | |
| | | 800 | 100 | .20 | 20 | 40 |
| | | 900 | 200 | .10 | 20 | |
| 800 | 100 | 800 | 0 | .20 | 0 | |
| | | 900 | 100 | .10 | 10 | 10 |
| 900 | 200 | 900 | 0 | .10 | 0 | 0 |

From table 18.1, we see that a reorder point of 700 yards and no safety stock will result in an expected shortage of 40 yards. A reorder point of 800 yards, which includes a safety stock of 100 yards, will result in an average shortage of 10 yards. A reorder point of 900 yards, which includes a safety stock of 200 yards, will result in no shortages.

*Determining annual shortages*

In table 18.1, since the reorder points tested are for a single order, the expected shortages are *per order*. From this information, we need to determine annual shortages. This is accomplished by multiplying the average shortages per order by the number of orders per year. Recall that the number of orders per year is computed as

$$\text{Number of orders per year} = \frac{D}{Q}$$

Since demand is uncertain, we will use an *average demand* of 10,000 yards to compute both the order size, $Q$, and the number of orders per year. Recall that the carpet store manager (in chapter 17) had determined the following inventory costs for stocking Super Shag carpet.

Carrying cost, $C_c$ = \$0.75 per yard per year
Ordering cost, $C_o$ = \$150 per order

Thus, the economic order quantity and number of orders per year are

$$Q^* = \sqrt{\frac{2 \, C_o D}{C_c}}$$
$$= \sqrt{\frac{2(150)(10,000)}{0.75}}$$
$$= \quad 2,000 \text{ yards per order}$$

$$\text{Number of orders per year} = \frac{10,000}{2,000}$$
$$= 5$$

Now we can compute the average annual shortages and the cost of these shortages for each of the reorder points. Assuming a shortage cost, $C_s$, of $2.00 per yard, the shortage costs per reorder point are computed as follows.

$$\text{Total annual shortage cost} = \text{(Shortage cost per yard)(Number of orders)(Average shortage per order)}$$
$$= C_s \frac{D}{Q}\text{(Average shortage per order)}$$

*Total annual shortage costs for each safety stock*

Using the average shortages for each reorder point shown in table 18.1, the total annual shortage costs are:

Total annual shortage cost for safety stock of *0* yards = ($2)(5)(40)
$$= \$400$$
Total annual shortage cost for safety stock of *100* yards = ($2)(5)(10)
$$= \$100$$
Total annual shortage cost for safety stock of *200* yards = ($2)(5)(0)
$$= \$0$$

*Total annual carrying costs for each safety stock*

Next, we must compare the cost of these shortages to the carrying cost for each safety stock, $S_s$.

Total annual carrying cost of safety stock = $C_c S_s$
Total annual carrying cost for safety stock of *0* yards = ($0.75)(0)
$$= \$0$$
Total annual carrying cost for safety stock of *100* yards = ($0.75)(100)
$$= \$75$$
Total annual carrying cost for safety stock of *200* yards = ($0.75)(200)
$$= \$150$$

*Total annual safety stock cost for each safety stock*

Now that we have determined *both costs* of having a safety stock for each safety stock level, we can compute the total safety stock cost by summing the two.

Total safety stock cost for safety stock of *0* yards = $400 + $0
$$= \$400$$
Total safety stock cost for safety stock of *100* yards = $100 + 75
$$= \$175$$
Total safety stock cost for safety stock of *200* yards = $0 + 150
$$= \$150$$

*Selecting the minimum cost safety stock and reorder point*

The minimum total safety stock cost is $150, thus the manager would maintain a safety stock of 200 yards, which requires a reorder point of 900 yards.

This was a relatively simple example made so by the fact that we considered only 6 discrete values for demand during lead time (between 500 and 900 yards). It would have been more realistic to include all possible demand values between 500 and 900 yards in our probability distribution, since yards is a continuous unit of measure. In other words, demand during lead time would have been more appropriately defined by a continuous probability distribution. However, this would have greatly complicated this example. As such, by using discrete values for demand during lead time, we are, in effect, approximating actual occurrences.

## Determining Safety Stocks Using Service Levels

*Serving a specified percentage of customers during lead time*

An alternative way to determine a safety stock is to establish a safety stock level that will satisfy the demand of a specified percentage of total customers. This is an especially useful method for determining a safety stock when a shortage cost cannot be determined. For example, the manager of the carpet store might establish a reorder point of 1,000 yards of carpet, which would enable the store to meet the demand of 85% of the customers (with 15% not being able to buy the carpet because it is out of stock) *during the lead time period*. The percentage of customers the store is able to service during lead time (i.e., 85%) is referred to as the *service level*. By adding a safety stock to the reorder point, the store would be able to meet the demand of a larger percentage of the customers. In other words, the store is able to increase the service level by increasing the safety stock.

*Normal probability distribution*

In order to develop a safety stock for our carpet store example, we will assume that demand is uncertain, but that it can be described by a *normal probability distribution*. Figure 18.3 is a graph of the normal distribution of *carpet demand during lead time* (assuming a lead time of 10 days). The mean of this distribution is 300 yards with a standard deviation of 50 yards. (See chap. 10 for a discussion of the normal distribution.)

**Figure 18.3** Normal distribution of demand during lead time.

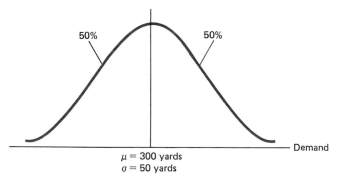

50%   50%

$\mu = 300$ yards
$\sigma = 50$ yards

Demand

*The average demand during lead time as the reorder point*

Since the average demand during lead time is 300 yards, as shown in figure 18.3, we will use this amount of inventory as the reorder point ($R = 300$ yards). However, this reorder point is simply an average, thus actual demand during the lead-time period will be more than 300 yards

Inventory Analysis with Uncertain Demand

50% of the time (i.e., 50% of the time customers will not be serviced) and less than 300 yards 50% of the time. Therefore, with a reorder point of 300 yards, the service level is 50% during the reorder lead time. In order to increase the service level we must add a safety stock.

*A 50% service level*

As an example, let us assume that the carpet store wants to establish a service level of 95%. This means that the reorder point must be set at the point labeled *R* in figure 18.4. Notice that 5% of the probability distribution lies above this point and 95% below this point, indicating that demand will exceed the reorder point (on the average) 5% of the time. The safety stock is the amount between the mean of 300 yards and the reorder point, *R*.

*A 95% service level*

**Figure 18.4** Normal distribution of demand during lead time with safety stock and reorder point.

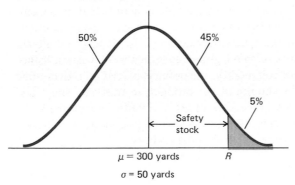

The distance from the mean to the reorder point in figure 18.4 is not only equal to the safety stock but is also equal to the number of standard deviations corresponding to 45% of the normal curve between the mean and this point. As such, we can make the following relationship.

*Computing the safety stock*

Safety stock $= Z\sigma$
where
$\quad Z =$ the number of standard deviations the reorder point is from the mean
$\quad \sigma =$ the standard deviation (50 yards)

A probability of .4500 in table A.1 of Appendix A corresponds to a $Z$ value of 1.645. Thus, the safety stock is computed as

$$\text{Safety stock} = Z\sigma$$
$$= (1.645)(50)$$
$$= 82.25 \text{ yards}$$

The new reorder point is equal to the previously computed average demand during lead time plus the safety stock.

*The new reorder point with safety stock*

$$R = 300 + 82.25$$
$$= 382.25 \text{ yards}$$

For practical purposes we can round this value off to a reorder point of 382 yards. Therefore, every time the inventory level falls to 382 yards, a new order is made (regardless of what the economic order quantity actually is).

## Determining the Order Quantity with Payoff Tables

*Decision analysis*

In chapter 11 on *decision analysis* we presented the concept of a *payoff table*. A payoff table presents the various outcomes of a decision under alternative probabilistic conditions (states of nature). In this section we will apply payoff tables (and thus decision analysis) to inventory analysis. In inventory analysis the decisions are the possible order quantities, and the probabilistic states of nature are the possible demands that can occur.

*Order quantities as decisions and demands as states of nature*

*A decision analysis example*

In order to demonstrate the application of decision analysis to inventory analysis we will use the following example. The Petals and Plants Flower Shop orders carnations from a greenhouse on a weekly basis. (Since carnations are a perishable commodity, the order is placed at a given time interval, which is typically the life of the product, in this case one week. Hence, the decision of when to place an order is already determined.) The manager of the flower shop developed the following probability distribution for demand of carnations per week from past records.

*Probability distribution of demand*

| Demand (dozens/week) | Probability |
|---|---|
| 9 | .15 |
| 10 | .40 |
| 11 | .25 |
| 12 | .20 |
| | 1.00 |

*Constructing the payoff table*

The carnations cost the flower shop $1.50 per dozen and sell for $3.00 per dozen. The manager has determined that the carrying cost is $0.50 per dozen per week and the shortage cost is $1.00 per dozen per week. The payoff table shown in table 18.2 consists of 4 alternative decisions representing the 4 order sizes and 4 possible states of nature reflecting the 4 possible demands for carnations.

**Table 18.2** Payoff Table of Order Size

| Decision (order size, $Q$) | States of Nature (demand, $D$) | | | |
|---|---|---|---|---|
| | 9 .15 | 10 .40 | 11 .25 | 12 .20 |
| 9 | | | | |
| 10 | | | | |
| 11 | | | | |
| 12 | | | | |

Each *payoff value* in table 18.2 will equal the profit that will result from that specific order size and demand. For example, if the flower shop orders 9 dozen carnations and sells 9 dozen, then the profit is computed as follows.

*Computing the payoff table values*

$$
\begin{aligned}
\text{Profit} &= (\text{Demand})(\text{Price}) - (\text{Order size})(\text{Cost}) \\
&\quad - (\text{Average inventory})(\text{Carrying cost}) \\
&= (9)(\$3) - (9)(\$1.50) - (9/2)(\$0.50) \\
&= \$11.25
\end{aligned}
$$

If we let $D$ = demand, $P$ = price per dozen, $Q$ = order size, $C$ = cost per dozen, $Q/2$ = average inventory, and $C_c$ = carrying cost, then the above profit equation can be represented by the following formula.

$$
\text{Profit} = DP - QC - \frac{Q}{2}C_c
$$

However, notice in this formula and the computation above for profit that *shortage cost* was not included. Since demand equaled the order size, a shortage did not exist. Any time order size exceeds or equals demand there is no shortage cost and the formula above for profit is applicable. If, on the other hand, *demand exceeds supply,* then the shortage cost must be included in the profit formula as follows.

*A shortage cost*

$$
\text{Profit} = QP - QC - \frac{Q}{2}C_c - \boxed{C_s(D - Q)}
$$

Shortage Cost

In this formula, shortage cost is computed by multiplying the amount demand exceeds the order size by the shortage cost. Also, notice that the first term in the profit equation has been changed from $DP$ to $QP$, since all that can be sold is what is ordered. If the order size is 9 dozen carnations but demand is for 10 dozen, the profit is computed as follows (recall, $C_s = \$1/\text{dozen}$).

$$
\begin{aligned}
\text{Profit} &= QP - QC - \frac{Q}{2}C_c - C_s(D - Q) \\
&= (9)(\$3.00) - (9)(\$1.50) - \frac{9}{2}(\$0.50) - (\$1.00)(10 - 9) \\
&= \$10.25
\end{aligned}
$$

Now we will summarize our profit formulas for both conditions of order size and demand.

*Summary of profit formulas*

*Order Size* $\geq$ *Demand*

$$
\text{Profit} = DP - QC - \frac{Q}{2}C_c
$$

*Demand* > *Order Size*

$$
\text{Profit} = QP - QC - \frac{Q}{2}C_c - C_s(D - Q)
$$

Using these formulas we are able to compute profit for all the combinations of order quantity and profit shown in table 18.2. These computed values are shown in table 18.3.

**Table 18.3** Payoff Table for Flower Shop Example

| Decision (order size, Q) | Demand (D) | | | |
|---|---|---|---|---|
| | 9 .15 | 10 .40 | 11 .25 | 12 .20 |
| 9 | $11.25 | 10.25 | 9.25 | 8.25 |
| 10 | 9.50 | 12.50 | 11.50 | 10.50 |
| 11 | 7.75 | 10.75 | 13.75 | 12.75 |
| 12 | 6.00 | 9.00 | 12.00 | 15.00 |

The values in table 18.3 represent *certain profit* for each of the possible combinations of order size and demand. However, each demand has a probability of occurrence reflecting the fact that demand is uncertain. Therefore, instead of a certain profit occurring for each order size, we will compute the *expected profit* based on the probability of each outcome (demand). The expected profit (*EP*) for each order size is computed by multiplying each profit for a specific order size by its corresponding probabilities and then summing these values.

*Computing the*
*expected profit for*
*each order size*

$$EP\ (9) = \$(11.25)(.15) + (10.25)(.40) + (9.25)(.25)$$
$$+ (8.25)(.20)$$
$$= \$9.75$$
$$EP\ (10) = \$(9.50)(.15) + (12.50)(.40) + (11.50)(.25)$$
$$+ (10.50)(.20)$$
$$= \$11.40$$
$$EP\ (11) = \$(7.75)(.15) + (10.75)(.40) + (13.75)(.25)$$
$$+ (12.75)(.20)$$
$$= \$11.45$$
$$EP\ (12) = \$(6.00)(.15) + (9.00)(.40) + (12.00)(.25)$$
$$+ (15.00)(.20)$$
$$= \$10.50$$

The greatest expected profit ($11.45) results from an order size of 11 dozen carnations, thus the optimal value of Q is 11. This means that if 11 dozen carnations are ordered every week for many weeks, an average profit of $11.45 per week will result during this period of time. The expected value does not mean that $11.45 will result every week. Since demand is uncertain, during some weeks there will be shortages and during some weeks there will be surpluses as well as weeks when demand is exactly 11 dozen. However, notice that shortages will occur on the average only 20% of the time (since the only demand greater than 11 dozen is 12 dozen, which occurs 20% of the time).

An additional item that could have been included in this payoff table example is a *salvage value* for items not sold. For example, if 11 dozen carnations are ordered but only 10 dozen are sold, then it is possible that the cost of the extra dozen not sold could be offset by selling them at a greatly reduced price (at the end of the week) to individual customers or to hospitals, churches, or schools. This reduced price is the salvage value.

*Including a salvage value*

We could have also analyzed the effect of alternative selling prices in this model by developing additional payoff tables. For example, a selling price of $4 per dozen carnations could be considered in another payoff table with the demand probabilities altered to reflect the effect on demand of the new price. The expected profit per week for the selling price of $4 would then be compared to the expected profit of $11.45 determined for the original price of $3 to see which price results in the greatest expected profit.

*Analyzing alternative selling prices*

## Simulation of Inventory

The final approach to inventory analysis under conditions of uncertain demand we will explore is simulation, a technique first presented in chapter 15. In chapter 15 it was noted that simulation is a method of analysis often employed when uncertainty exists. In fact, the first example in the simulation chapter was for the demand for milk at a grocery store, which was probabilistic.

In order to demonstrate how to use simulation for inventory analysis, we will use the same Petals and Plants Flower Shop example used in the previous section. All the inventory costs and the selling price and cost of carnations remain the same. The probability distribution for demand is the same, except that now we will develop corresponding ranges for random numbers, as shown in table 18.4.

*A simulation example*

*Developing random number ranges*

**Table 18.4** Random Number Ranges for Probability Distribution of Demand

| Demand (dozens/week) | Probability | Cumulative Probability | Random Numbers |
|---|---|---|---|
| 9 | .15 | .15 | 1–15 |
| 10 | .40 | .55 | 16–55 |
| 11 | .25 | .80 | 56–80 |
| 12 | .20 | 1.00 | 81–99, 00 |

Now instead of testing all four order size values (9, 10, 11, and 12) we must select one of them and simulate demand based on that order size. As an example, we will simulate demand for an order size (*Q*) of 10, as shown in table 18.5. The random numbers were selected from the first column of the random number table (table 15.3) in chapter 15.

*Simulating a single order size (Q = 10)*

**Table 18.5** Simulation of Demand for $Q = 10$

| Random Number | Demand | Sales DP or QP | | Cost QC | Carrying Cost $(Q/2)C_c$ | Shortage Cost $C_s(D - Q)$ | Profit |
|---|---|---|---|---|---|---|---|
| 39 | 10 | $30 | | $15 | $2.50 | $0 | $ 12.50 |
| 73 | 11 | | 30 | 15 | 2.50 | 1 | 11.50 |
| 72 | 11 | | 30 | 15 | 2.50 | 1 | 11.50 |
| 75 | 11 | | 30 | 15 | 2.50 | 1 | 11.50 |
| 37 | 10 | 30 | | 15 | 2.50 | 0 | 12.50 |
| 2 | 9 | 27 | | 15 | 2.50 | 0 | 9.50 |
| 87 | 12 | | 30 | 15 | 2.50 | 2 | 10.50 |
| 98 | 12 | | 30 | 15 | 2.50 | 2 | 10.50 |
| 10 | 9 | 27 | | 15 | 2.50 | 0 | 9.50 |
| 47 | 10 | 30 | | 15 | 2.50 | 0 | 12.50 |
| | | | | | | | $112.00 |

*Computing average profit for Q = 10*

The profit for each demand value in table 18.5 was computed using the same profit formulas developed in the previous section. For 10 simulations the total profit is $112.00, thus the average profit is

$$\text{Average profit} = \frac{\$112}{10}$$
$$= \$11.20$$

The expected profit computed from the payoff table in the previous section was $11.40, so our simulation result is very close to the steady-state value average using only 10 simulations. By increasing the number of simulations, the simulation result should approach the expected (steady state) value of $11.40.

*Replicating the payoff table example*

In order to replicate the payoff table example, we would have to repeat the simulation for order sizes of 9, 11, and 12 dozen flowers. This would result in an average profit for each order size with the optimal order size corresponding to the greatest average profit.

*Simulation is very useful as the problem increases in complexity*

This example is relatively simple and, as such, is probably better suited to solutions analytically. However, notice that we only considered 4 demand values and 4 order sizes. If we had considered perhaps 50 order sizes and 100 demands, then computerized simulation would have become a more inviting alternative. Going a step further, if demand was defined by a continuous probability distribution (such as yards of carpet), then simulation would be especially appropriate.

Computerized simulation becomes a necessity if more than one of the inventory model components is subject to uncertainty. For example, if *lead time* is also uncertain as well as *demand,* then during each order both order size and lead time vary. This is a situation very difficult to model and to solve mathematically, especially if lead time and demand can equal a large range of values. In order to simulate this type of situation one would typically simulate the inventory cost for a specific order size similar to the simulation in table 18.5, except that lead time would vary as well as demand.

## Summary

In this chapter we have presented four methods to compensate for conditions of uncertain demand in inventory analysis: safety stocks, safety stocks corresponding to service levels, payoff tables, and simulation. However, for very complex inventory models involving several components that are subject to uncertainty, computerized simulation becomes the only viable approach for analysis.

This concludes our two-chapter presentation of inventory analysis. The techniques for inventory analysis presented in these two chapters are not widely used to analyze other types of problems. However, many of the techniques presented in this text are used for inventory analysis (in addition to the methods we have presented in these chapters). The wide use of management science techniques for inventory analysis attests to the importance of inventory to all types of organizations.

*Conclusion of presentation of inventory*

## References

Buchan, J., and Koenigsberg, E. *Scientific Inventory Management*. Englewood Cliffs, N.J.: Prentice-Hall, 1963.

Buffa, E. S., and Taubert, W. J. *Production-Inventory Systems: Planning and Control*. Rev. ed. Homewood, Ill.: Irwin, 1972.

Churchman, C. W.; Ackoff, R. L.; and Arnoff, E. L. *Introduction to Operations Research*. New York: John Wiley and Sons, 1957.

Hadley, G., and Whitin, T. M. *Analysis of Inventory Systems*. Englewood Cliffs, N.J.: Prentice-Hall, 1963.

Johnson, L. A., and Montgomery, D. C. *Operations Research in Production Planning, Scheduling, and Inventory Control*. New York: John Wiley and Sons, 1974.

Magee, J. F., and Boodman, D. M. *Production Planning and Inventory Control*. 2d ed. New York: McGraw-Hill, 1967.

Shamblin, J. E., and Stevens, G. T., Jr. *Operations Research: A Fundamental Approach*. New York: McGraw-Hill, 1974.

Starr, M. K., and Miller, D. W. *Inventory Control: Theory and Practice*. Englewood Cliffs, N.J.: Prentice-Hall, 1962.

# Problems

1. An inventory system has an average yearly demand of 6,000 units and an ordering cost of $60 per order. The annual carrying cost is $2 per unit, while the shortage cost per unit is $1. The demand during lead time is defined by the following probability distribution.

| Demand During Lead Time | Probability |
|---|---|
| 100 | 0.10 |
| 200 | 0.20 |
| 300 | 0.40 |
| 400 | 0.20 |
| 500 | 0.10 |
| | 1.00 |

Determine the safety stock, reorder point, and minimum total safety stock cost.

2. An inventory system has an average annual demand of 1,200 units and an ordering cost of $200 per order. The annual carrying cost is $5 per unit, while the shortage cost per unit is $10. The demand during lead time is defined by the following probability distribution.

| Demand During Lead Time | Probability |
|---|---|
| 50 | .20 |
| 60 | .30 |
| 70 | .30 |
| 80 | .10 |
| 90 | .10 |
| | 1.00 |

Determine the safety stock, reorder point, and minimum total safety stock cost.

3. The Big Buy Supermarket stocks Munchies cereal. The average demand for Munchies is 4,000 boxes per year. It costs the store $90 per order of Munchies, $.30 per box per year to keep the cereal in inventory, and there is a shortage cost of $1 per box. The demand during lead time for boxes of cereal is defined by the following probability distribution.

| Demand During Lead Time | Probability |
|---|---|
| 75 | .05 |
| 100 | .20 |
| 125 | .40 |
| 150 | .25 |
| 175 | .10 |
| | 1.00 |

Determine the safety stock, reorder point, and minimum total safety stock cost.

4. The average annual demand for color television sets at Videoworld Discount Televisions is 2,200. The cost per order from the manufacturer is $650, while the carrying cost is $45, and the shortage cost is $60 per set. The demand during lead time for television sets is defined by the following probability distribution.

| Demand During Lead Time | Probability |
|---|---|
| 20 | .05 |
| 30 | .10 |
| 40 | .30 |
| 50 | .40 |
| 60 | .15 |
| | 1.00 |

Determine the safety stock, reorder point, and minimum total safety stock cost.

5. A car dealer who sells compact cars has an average annual demand of 1200 cars. It costs the dealer $1,800 per order to order cars from the manufacturer in Dearborn and $700 per year to carry a car in inventory on the lot. The shortage cost is $1,200 per car. The demand during lead time for cars is defined by the following probability distribution.

| Demand During Lead Time | Probability |
|---|---|
| 10 | .05 |
| 15 | .15 |
| 20 | .20 |
| 25 | .30 |
| 30 | .25 |
| 35 | .05 |
| | 1.00 |

Determine the safety stock, reorder point, and minimum total safety stock cost.

6. A local distributor of Rainwater beer in Memphis has an average annual demand for Rainwater of 40,000 barrels. It costs the distributor $1,500 for an order of beer from the brewery. The annual cost of carrying a barrel of beer in inventory is $1.50. The shortage cost is $3.00 per barrel. The demand during lead time for barrels of beer is defined by the following distribution.

| Demand During Lead Time | Probability |
| --- | --- |
| 500 | .05 |
| 600 | .05 |
| 700 | .10 |
| 800 | .25 |
| 900 | .30 |
| 1,000 | .15 |
| 1,100 | .10 |
| | 1.00 |

Determine the safety stock, reorder point, and minimum total safety stock cost.

7. Graphically illustrate the order size, safety stock, and reorder point for the inventory system in problem 1.

8. The demand during lead time for carpet at the Armor Carpet Store is normally distributed with a mean of 500 yards and a standard deviation of 80 yards. Determine a safety stock and reorder point that will result in an average service level of 80% during lead time.

9. The production process of the Western Jeans Company uses an average of 3,000 yards of denim (with a standard deviation of 600 yards) to make jeans during the time it takes to receive an order of denim from a textile mill. If the company wants to be able to operate during 95% of the lead-time period, what safety stock and reorder point should they have?

10. Graphically illustrate the average demand during lead time, service level, safety stock, and reorder point for the inventory system in problem 8.

11. The Atlantic Paper Company produces paper from wood pulp it orders from a lumber products company. The paper company uses an average of 8,000 pounds of wood pulp (with a standard deviation of 1,500 pounds) during the time required to receive an order. What safety stock and reorder point should Atlantic Paper Company maintain in order for their production process to be idle only 10% of the lead time?

12. The Uptown Bar and Grill serves Rainwater draft beer to its customers. The bar sells an average of 60 gallons of beer (with a standard deviation of 10 gallons) during the lead time to receive an order of beer from the local distributor. If the bar runs out of beer, the owner runs the risk of having a riot, therefore, the owner wants to maintain a 98% service level during lead time. What safety stock and reorder point should be used to meet this service level?

13. The Rainbow Paint Store in East Ridge sells an average of 110 gallons of paint (with a standard deviation of 35 gallons) during the lead time required to receive an order of paint from the manufacturer. However, since this is the only paint store in East Ridge, the owner is only interested in maintaining a 50% service level. What reorder point should be used to maintain this service level during lead time?

14. Suppose in problem 12 that the owner of the Uptown Bar and Grill has decided to use a reorder point of 75 gallons of beer. What level of service would this reorder point maintain?

15. The Uptown Bar and Grill orders either 5, 6, 7, or 8 barrels of beer each time it places an order with the distributor. Each barrel of beer costs $50 and sells for $100. The probability of demand for barrels of beer is

| Demand | Probability |
|--------|-------------|
| 5 | .10 |
| 6 | .30 |
| 7 | .40 |
| 8 | .20 |
| | 1.00 |

Using a payoff table approach, determine the number of barrels of beer that should be ordered.

16. The Petals and Plants Flower Shop orders roses from a greenhouse on a weekly basis. The manager of the flower shop has developed the following probability distribution for demand for dozens of roses per week.

| Demand (dozens/week) | Probability |
|----------------------|-------------|
| 6 | .10 |
| 7 | .20 |
| 8 | .30 |
| 9 | .30 |
| 10 | .10 |
| | 1.00 |

The roses cost the flower shop $3 per dozen and sell for $5 per dozen. The carrying cost is $0.60 per dozen per week and the shortage cost is $2 per dozen per week. Determine the number of dozens of roses that should be stocked per week using the payoff table approach. Given this order size how often will shortages occur?

17. The Loebuck Grocery orders milk from a dairy on a weekly basis. The manager of the store has developed the following probability distribution for demand per week (in cases).

| Demand (Cases) | Probability |
|---|---|
| 15 | .20 |
| 16 | .25 |
| 17 | .40 |
| 18 | .15 |
| | 1.00 |

The milk costs the grocery $10 per case and sells for $16 per case. The carrying cost is $0.50 per case per week and the shortage cost is $1 per case per week. Determine the number of cases of milk that should be ordered from the dairy each week using the payoff table approach.

18. The Steak and Chop Butcher Shop orders steak from a local meat packing house. The meat is purchased on Monday at a price of $2 per pound and it is sold for $3.50 per pound at the shop. The following probability distribution for the demand per week (in pounds) of steak has been developed.

| Demand (lbs.) | Probability |
|---|---|
| 20 | .10 |
| 21 | .20 |
| 22 | .30 |
| 23 | .30 |
| 24 | .10 |
| | 1.00 |

The carrying cost is $0.80 per pound per week and the shortage cost is $1.25 per pound per week. Determine the pounds of steak that should be ordered each week using the payoff table approach.

19. The Roadway Paving Company purchases asphalt from Bay Petroleum Products Company in Mobile. The number of tons of asphalt used by Roadway to pave roads and driveways annually is given by the following probability distribution.

| Demand (tons) | Probability |
|---|---|
| 4 | .20 |
| 5 | .30 |
| 6 | .40 |
| 7 | .10 |
| | 1.00 |

The asphalt costs the paving company $9,500 per ton, and the company sells it (converted from selling price per yard of road laid) for $15,000 per ton. The annual carrying cost is $1,600 per ton and the shortage cost is $4,000 per ton. Determine the number of tons that should be ordered each year using the payoff table approach.

20. The probability distribution of the cases of milk demanded each week at the Loebuck Grocery is given as follows.

| Demand Per Week (cases) | Probability |
|---|---|
| 14 | .20 |
| 15 | .40 |
| 16 | .20 |
| 17 | .10 |
| 18 | .10 |
| | 1.00 |

Using the random number table in chapter 15 (table 15.3) simulate demand for 15 weeks and compute the average demand.

21. Simulate the demand during lead time for the probability distribution in problem 4 for 20 reorder periods and compute the average demand during lead time.

22. Simulate the shortages per reorder period that will occur in problem 3 using the reorder point computed in the problem. Simulate for 20 reorder periods and compute the probability that a shortage will occur. How does this result compare with the percentage of time a shortage would occur determined in problem 3?

23. Determine the average weekly profit from beer in problem 15 using simulation and assuming an order size of 7 barrels of beer per week. Simulate for 20 weeks using the random number table (table 15.3) in chapter 15 and compute the average profit. How does this result compare with the results in problem 15?

24. Simulate the ordering system in problem 16 for 10 weeks using a weekly order size of 7 dozen roses and compute the average weekly profit. (Use table 15.3 in chap. 15.) Compare the results with those determined in problem 16 and indicate how the optimal order size would be determined.

25. A store has the following probability distribution of demand per week.

| Demand (units) | Probability |
|---|---|
| 0 | .10 |
| 1 | .15 |
| 2 | .30 |
| 3 | .25 |
| 4 | .20 |
| | 1.00 |

The lead time to receive an order (in weeks) is defined by the following distribution.

| Lead Time (weeks) | Probability |
|---|---|
| 1 | .35 |
| 2 | .45 |
| 3 | .20 |
| | 1.00 |

Assume an initial starting inventory level of 4 units, and that units are not back ordered. The carrying cost is $2 per unit per week, the shortage cost is $10 per unit per week, and the cost per order is $20. Simulate the weekly inventory cost for 20 weeks using a order size of 5 units and a reorder point of 3 units. Compute the average weekly inventory cost. How would the optimal order size be determined using simulation?

# 19
## Network Flow Models

A *network* is an arrangement of paths connected at various points through which an item (or items) move from one point to another. Networks that everyone are familiar with include highway systems, telephone networks, railroad systems, and television networks. For example, a railroad network consists of a number of fixed rail routes (paths) connected by terminals at various junctions of the rail routes. In chapter 7, the transportation problem illustrated in figure 7.1 is a network of transportation routes.

*An arrangement of paths connected at various points*

Network models have become a very popular management science technique for analysis in recent years for several reasons. First, networks are drawn as diagrams, which literally provide a *picture* of the system under analysis. This enables a manager to visually interpret the system, and thus enhances the manager's understanding. Second, a large number of real life systems can be modeled as networks, which are relatively easy to conceive and construct.

*Reasons for network models popularity*

In these next two chapters we will look at several different types of network models. In this chapter we will present a class of network models that are directed at the *flows of items* through a system. As such, they are referred to as *network flow models*. We will discuss the use of network flow models to analyze three types of problems: the shortest route problem, the minimal spanning tree problem, and the maximal flow problem. In chapter 20 we will present the network techniques of PERT and CPM, which are used extensively for project analysis.

## Network Components

Networks are illustrated as diagrams consisting of two main components: nodes and branches. *Nodes* represent junction points like an intersection of several streets. *Branches* connect the nodes and reflect the flow from one point in the network to another. Nodes are denoted in the network diagram by *circles* and branches are represented by *lines* connecting the nodes. Nodes typically represent localities, such as a city, an intersection, or an air or a railroad terminal, while branches are the roads connecting cities and intersections, and the railroad tracks or air routes connecting the terminals. For example, the different railroad routes between Atlanta, Georgia, and St. Louis, Missouri, and the intermediate terminals are shown in figure 19.1.

*Nodes*
*Branches*

*A network example*

**Figure 19.1** Network of railroad routes.

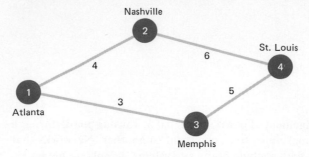

In the network shown in figure 19.1, there are four nodes and four branches. The node representing Atlanta is referred to as the *origin*, while any of the three remaining nodes could be the *destination*, depending on what we are trying to determine from the network. Notice that a numerical value has been assigned to each node. These numbers provide a more convenient means for identifying the nodes and branches than using literal names. For example, we can now refer to the origin (Atlanta) as node 1 and the branch from Atlanta to Nashville as branch 1–2.

*Values assigned to branches*

Typically, a value is assigned to each branch that represents a distance, length of time, or cost. Thus, the purpose of the network is to determine the shortest distance, length of time, or lowest cost between points in the network. In figure 19.1, the values 4, 6, 3, and 5 corresponding to the four branches represent the length of time in hours between the attached nodes. Thus, a traveler can see that to go to St. Louis through Nashville requires 10 hours and through Memphis requires 8 hours.

## The Shortest Route Problem

*The shortest distance between an originating point and several destination points*

The *shortest route problem* is to determine the shortest distance between an originating point and several destination points. For example, the Stagecoach Shipping Company transports oranges by six trucks from Los Angeles, California, to six cities in the West and Midwest. The different routes between Los Angeles and the destination cities and the length of time in hours required by a truck to transverse these routes are shown in figure 19.2.

*Minimizing travel time*

The shipping company manager wants to determine the best routes (in terms of the minimum travel time) for the trucks to take to reach their destinations. This problem can be solved using the shortest route solution technique. In order to apply this technique, it will be more convenient to represent the system of truck routes as a network, as shown in figure 19.3.

Now let us repeat our objective as it relates to figure 19.3. We want to determine the shortest routes from the origin (node 1) to the six destinations (nodes 2 through 7).

**Figure 19.2** Shipping routes from Los Angeles.

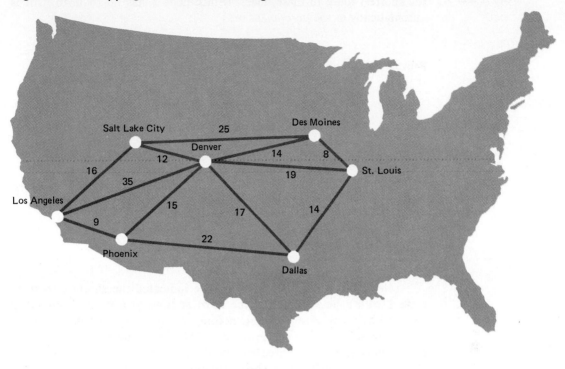

**Figure 19.3** Network of shipping routes.

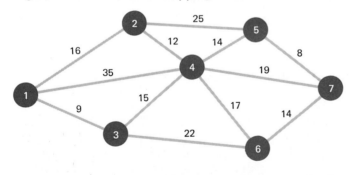

## The Shortest Route Solution Approach

We begin the shortest route solution technique by starting at node 1 (the origin) and determining the shortest time required to get to a directly connected (i.e., adjacent) node. The three nodes directly connected to node 1 are 2, 3, and 4, as shown in figure 19.4. Of these three nodes, the shortest time is 9 hours to node 3. As such, we have determined our first *shortest* route from node 1 to 3 (or from Los Angeles to Phoenix). We will now

*Determining the initial shortest route from node 1 to 3*

refer to nodes 1 and 3 as the *permanent set*, indicating that we have found the shortest route to these nodes. (Since node 1 has no route to it, it is automatically in the *permanent set*.)

---

**Figure 19.4** Network with node 1 in the permanent set.

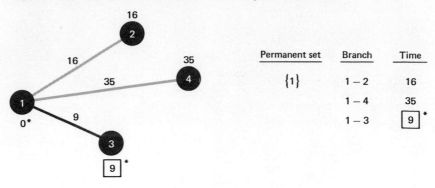

Notice that in figure 19.4 we have indicated the shortest route to node 3 with a heavy line and the shortest time to node 3 (9 hours) is enclosed by a box. Also the table accompanying figure 19.4 describes the process of selecting the shortest route. The permanent set is shown containing only node 1. The three branches from node 1 are 1–2, 1–4, and 1–3, with this last branch having the minimum time of 9 hours.

*Determine all nodes
directly connected to
the permanent set
nodes*

Next we will repeat the steps used to determine the shortest route to node 3 above. First, we must *determine all the nodes directly connected to the nodes in the permanent set* (nodes 1 and 3). Nodes 2, 4, and 6 are all directly connected to nodes 1 and 3, as shown in figure 19.5.

---

**Figure 19.5** Network with nodes 1 and 3 in the permanent set.

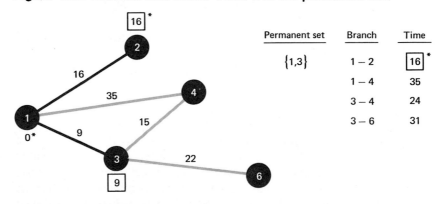

The next step is to determine the shortest route to the three nodes (2, 4, and 6) directly connected to the permanent set nodes. There are two branches starting from node 1 (1–2 and 1–4) and two branches from node 3 (3–4 and 3–6). The branch with the shortest time is to node 2 with a time of 16 hours. As such, node 2 becomes part of the permanent set. Notice in our computations accompanying figure 19.5 that the time to node 6 (branch 3–6) is 31 hours. This value was determined by adding the branch 3–6 time of 22 hours to the shortest route time of 9 hours at node 3.

*Node 2 joins the permanent set*

The permanent set now consists of nodes 1, 2, and 3 as we move to the next step. This indicates that we have now found the shortest route to nodes 1, 2, and 3. The first thing we must do is to determine the nodes directly connected to the permanent set nodes. Node 5 is the only *adjacent* node not presently connected to the permanent set, so it is connected directly to node 2. In addition, node 4 is now connected directly to node 2 (since node 2 has joined the permanent set). These additions are shown in figure 19.6.

*The redefined permanent set*

**Figure 19.6** Network with nodes 1, 2, and 3 in the permanent set.

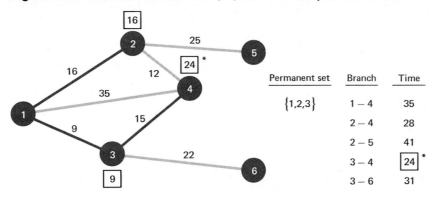

| Permanent set | Branch | Time |
|---|---|---|
| {1,2,3} | 1 — 4 | 35 |
| | 2 — 4 | 28 |
| | 2 — 5 | 41 |
| | 3 — 4 | 24 * |
| | 3 — 6 | 31 |

There are five branches leading from the permanent set nodes (1, 2, and 3) to their directly connected nodes as shown in the table accompanying figure 19.6. The branch representing the route with the shortest time is 3–4, with a time of 24 hours. Thus, we have determined the shortest route to node 4, and it joins the permanent set. Notice that the shortest time to node 4 (24 hours) reflects the route from node 1 through node 3 and then to node 4. The other routes to node 4 directly from node 1 and through node 2 are longer, and as such we will not consider them any further as possible routes to node 4.

*Node 4 joins the permanent set*

To summarize, the shortest routes to nodes 1, 2, 3, and 4 have all been determined and these nodes now form the permanent set.

Next we repeat the process of determining the nodes directly connected to the permanent set nodes. These directly connected nodes are 5, 6, and 7, as shown in figure 19.7. Notice in figure 19.7 that we have eliminated the branches from nodes 1 and 2 to node 4, since we have determined that the route with the shortest time to node 4 does not include these branches.

---

**Figure 19.7** Network with nodes 1, 2, 3, and 4 in the permanent set.

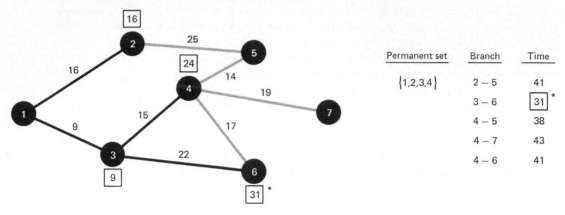

| Permanent set | Branch | Time |
|---------------|--------|------|
| {1,2,3,4}     | 2 – 5  | 41   |
|               | 3 – 6  | 31 * |
|               | 4 – 5  | 38   |
|               | 4 – 7  | 43   |
|               | 4 – 6  | 41   |

*Node 6 joins the permanent set*   From the table accompanying figure 19.7, we can see that of the branches leading to nodes 5, 6, and 7, branch 3–6 has the shortest *cumulative* time of 31 hours. Thus, node 6 is added to our permanent set. This means that we have now found the shortest route to nodes 1, 2, 3, 4, and 6.

Repeating our process, the nodes directly connected (adjacent) to our permanent set are nodes 5 and 7, as shown in figure 19.8. (Notice that branch 4–6 has been eliminated, since the best route to node 6 goes through node 3 instead of node 4.)

*Node 5 joins the permanent set*   Of the branches leading from the permanent set nodes to node 5 and 7, branch 4–5 has the shortest cumulative time of 38 hours. Thus, node 5 joins the permanent set. We have now determined the routes with shortest times to nodes 1, 2, 3, 4, 5, and 6 (as denoted by the darkened branches in fig. 19.8).

*Node 7 joins the permanent set*   The only remaining node directly connected to the permanent set is node 7, as shown in figure 19.9. Of the three branches connecting node 7 to the permanent set, branch 4–7 has the shortest time of 43 hours. Therefore, node 7 joins the permanent set.

*Summary of the shortest routes*   The routes with the shortest times from the origin (node 1) to each of the other six nodes and the travel times are summarized in figure 19.10 and table 19.1.

**Figure 19.8** Network with nodes 1, 2, 3, 4, and 6 in the permanent set.

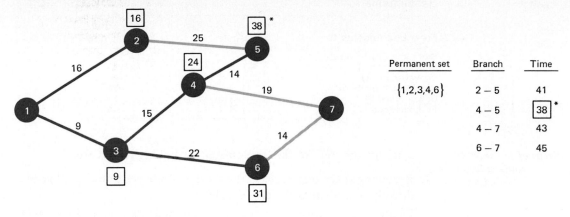

| Permanent set | Branch | Time |
|---|---|---|
| {1,2,3,4,6} | 2 – 5 | 41 |
| | 4 – 5 | 38 * |
| | 4 – 7 | 43 |
| | 6 – 7 | 45 |

**Figure 19.9** Network with nodes 1, 2, 3, 4, 5, and 6 in the permanent set.

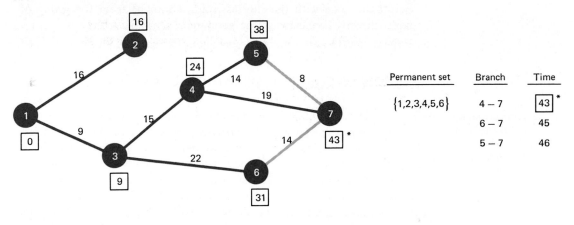

| Permanent set | Branch | Time |
|---|---|---|
| {1,2,3,4,5,6} | 4 – 7 | 43 * |
| | 6 – 7 | 45 |
| | 5 – 7 | 46 |

**Figure 19.10** Network with optimal routes from Los Angeles to all destinations.

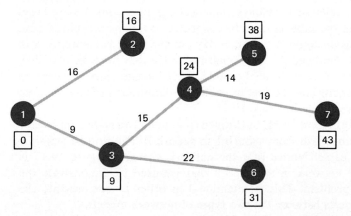

**Table 19.1** Routes with Shortest Times from Origin to All Destinations

| From Los Angeles to: | Route | Total Hours |
|---|---|---|
| Salt Lake City (node 2) | 1-2 | 16 |
| Phoenix (node 3) | 1-3 | 9 |
| Denver (node 4) | 1-3-4 | 24 |
| Des Moines (node 5) | 1-3-4-5 | 38 |
| Dallas (node 6) | 1-3-6 | 31 |
| St. Louis (node 7) | 1-3-4-7 | 43 |

*Steps of the shortest route solution method*

Briefly, the steps of the shortest route solution method are:

1. Beginning at the origin, select the shortest route node among all nodes directly connected to the origin node.
2. Establish a *permanent set* with the origin node and the node selected in step 1.
3. Determine all nodes directly connected to the permanent set nodes.
4. Select the node with the shortest route (branch) from the group of nodes directly connected to the permanent set nodes.
5. Repeat steps 3 and 4 until all nodes join the permanent set.

## The Minimal Spanning Tree Problem

*Connecting all nodes so that the total branch lengths are minimized*

In the shortest route problem presented in the previous section, the objective was to determine the shortest routes between the origin and the destination nodes in the network. In our example, we determined the best route from Los Angeles to each of the six destination cities. The *minimal spanning tree problem* is similar to the shortest route problem, except that the objective is to connect all the nodes in the network so that the total branch lengths are minimized. The resulting network *spans* (connects) all the points in the network at a minimum total distance (or length).

*A minimal spanning tree example*

In order to demonstrate the minimal spanning tree problem, we will consider the following example. The Metro Cable Television Company is going to install a television cable system in a community consisting of seven suburbs. Each of the suburbs must be connected to the main cable system. The cable television company wants to lay out the main cable network in a way that will minimize the total length of cable that must be installed. The possible paths available to the cable television company (by consent of the town council) and the feet of cable (in thousands of feet) required by each path are shown in figure 19.11.

Interpreting figure 19.11, the branch from node 1 to node 2 represents the available cable path from suburb 1 to suburb 2. The branch length is 16,000 feet of cable. Notice that the network shown in figure 19.11 is identical to the network in figure 19.2 that we used to demonstrate the shortest route problem. This is intentional in order to demonstrate the difference in results between the two types of network models.

**Figure 19.11** Network of possible cable TV paths.

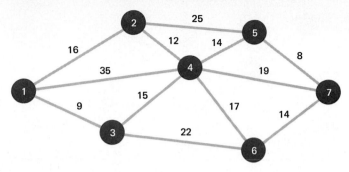

## The Minimal Spanning Tree Solution Approach

The solution approach to the minimal spanning tree problem is actually easier than the shortest route solution method. In the minimal spanning tree solution approach, it is not necessary to start at the origin; we can start at any node in the network. However, it is usually conventional to start with node 1. Beginning at node 1, the node closest to node 1 (i.e. the shortest branch) is selected to join our spanning tree. The shortest branch from node 1 is to node 3, with a length of 9,000 feet. This branch is highlighted in figure 19.12.

*Start with any node in the network*

*Determining the initial spanning tree for nodes 1 and 3*

**Figure 19.12** Spanning tree with nodes 1 and 3.

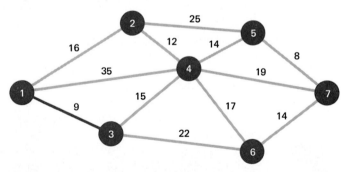

Now we have a *spanning tree* consisting of two nodes: 1 and 3. The next step is to select the closest node not presently in the spanning tree. The node closest to either node 1 or 3 (the nodes in our present spanning tree) is node 4, with a branch length of 15 (thousand) feet. The addition of node 4 to our spanning tree is shown in figure 19.13.

*Node 4 joins the spanning tree*

Next we repeat the process of selecting the closest node to our present spanning tree (nodes 1, 3, and 4). The closest node not presently connected to the nodes in our spanning tree is node 2. The length of the branch from node 4 to node 2 is 12 (thousand) feet. The addition of node 2 to the spanning tree is shown in figure 19.14.

*Node 2 joins the spanning tree*

**Figure 19.13** Spanning tree with nodes 1, 3, and 4.

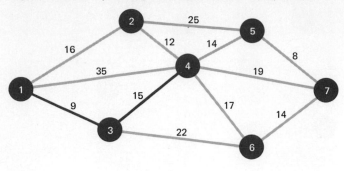

**Figure 19.14** Spanning tree with nodes 1, 2, 3, and 4.

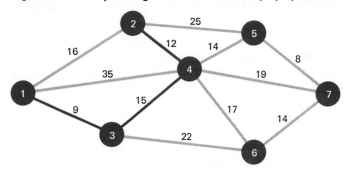

**Figure 19.15** Spanning tree with nodes 1, 2, 3, 4, and 5.

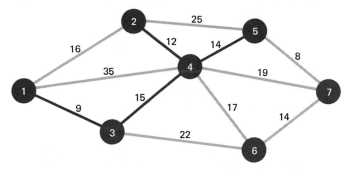

*Node 5 joins the spanning tree*

Our spanning tree now consists of nodes 1, 2, 3, and 4. The node closest to this spanning tree is node 5, with a branch length of 14 (thousand) feet to node 4. Thus, node 5 joins our spanning tree, as shown in figure 19.15.

The spanning tree now contains nodes 1, 2, 3, 4, and 5. The closest node not currently connected to the spanning tree is node 7. The branch connecting node 7 to node 5 has a length of 8 (thousand) feet. Figure 19.16 shows the addition of node 7 to the spanning tree.

*Node 7 joins the spanning tree*

**Figure 19.16** Spanning tree with nodes 1, 2, 3, 4, 5, and 7.

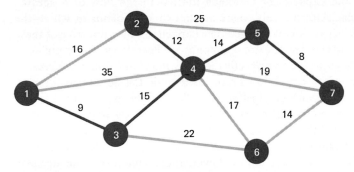

Now our spanning tree includes nodes 1, 2, 3, 4, 5, and 7. The only remaining node not connected to the spanning tree is node 6. The node in the spanning tree closest to node 6 is node 7, with a branch length of 14 (thousand) feet. The complete spanning tree, which now includes all seven nodes, is shown in figure 19.17.

*Node 6 joins the spanning tree*

**Figure 19.17** Minimal spanning tree for cable TV network.

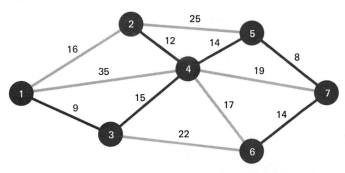

The spanning tree shown in figure 19.17 requires the minimum amount of television cable to connect the seven suburbs—72,000 feet. This same minimal spanning tree could have been obtained by starting at any of the six nodes other than node 1.

*The minimum total branch lengths*

Notice the difference between the minimal spanning tree network shown in figure 19.17 and the shortest route network in figure 19.10. The shortest route network represents the shortest paths between the origin and all the destination nodes (i.e., six different routes). Alternatively, the minimal spanning tree network shows how to connect all seven nodes so that the total distance (length) is minimized.

*The difference between the minimal spanning tree network solution and shortest route network solution*

# The Maximal Flow Problem

*Maximizing the total flow from a source to a destination*

In the shortest route problem we were concerned with determining the shortest route for trucks to get from the origin (Los Angeles) to six destinations. In the minimal spanning tree problem we wanted to find the shortest connected network for laying television cable. In neither of these problems was the capacity of a branch limited to the flow of a specific number of items. Alternatively, there are network problems in which the branches of the network have limited flow capacities. The objective of these networks is to maximize the total amount of flow from an origin to a destination. These problems are referred to as *maximal flow problems*.

Examples of maximal flow problems include the flow of water, gas, or oil through a network of pipelines; the flow of forms through a paper processing system (such as a government agency); the flow of traffic through a road network; and the flow of products through a production line system. In each of these examples, the branches of the network would have limited and often different flow capacities. Given these conditions the decision maker wants to determine the maximum flow that can be obtained through the system.

*A maximal flow example*

An example of a maximal flow problem is illustrated by the network of a railway system between Omaha and St. Louis shown in figure 19.18. The Scott Tractor Company ships tractor parts from Omaha to St. Louis by railroad. However, the company can only secure (by contract) a limited number of railroad cars on each branch during a week.

**Figure 19.18** Network of railway system.

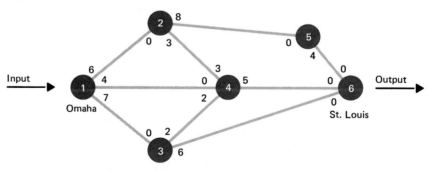

Given these limiting conditions, the company wants to know the maximum number of railroad cars of tractor parts that can be shipped from Omaha to St. Louis during a week. The number of railroad cars available to the tractor company on each rail branch is indicated by the number on the branch to *the immediate right of every node* (which represent rail junctions). For example, six cars are available from node 1 (Omaha) to node 2, 8 cars are available from node 2 to node 5, 5 cars are available from node 4 to node 6 (St. Louis), etc. The number on each

**Network Flow Models**

branch to the *immediate left* of each node is the number of cars available for shipping in the opposite direction. For example, from node 2 to node 1 there are zero cars available. As such, the branch from node 1 to node 2 is referred to as a *directed* branch, since flow is possible in only one direction (from node 1 to node 2, but not from 2 to 1). Notice that flow is possible in both directions on the branches from nodes 2 to 4 and nodes 3 to 4. These are referred to as *undirected branches*.

*A directed branch*

*Undirected branches*

## The Maximal Flow Solution Approach

The first step in determining the maximum possible flow of railroad cars through the rail system is to *choose any path from origin to destination arbitrarily* and ship as much as possible on that path. In figure 19.19 we will select the path 1–2–5–6 arbitrarily. The maximum number of railroad cars that can be sent through this route is 4. We are limited to 4 cars, since that is the maximum amount available on the branch between nodes 5 and 6. This path is shown in figure 19.19.

*Determine the maximum flow for any path through the system*

*The maximum flow for path 1–2–5–6*

**Figure 19.19** Maximal flow for path 1-2-5-6.

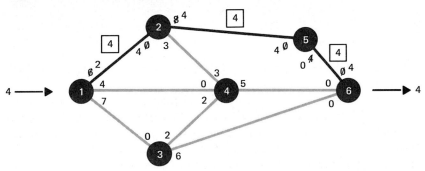

Notice that the capacities remaining on the branches from node 1 to node 2 and from node 2 to node 5 are 2 and 4 cars respectively, while no cars are available from node 5 to node 6. These values were computed by subtracting the flow of 4 cars from the number available. The actual flow of 4 cars along each branch is shown enclosed in a box. Notice that the present input of 4 cars into node 1 and the output of 4 cars out of node 6 are also designated.

*Recomputing branch capacities*

The final adjustment on this path is to add the designated flow of 4 cars to the values at the immediate left of each node on our path, 1–2–5–6. These are the flows in the opposite direction. Thus, the value of 4 is added to the zeros at nodes 2, 5, and 6. This may seem incongruous (to designate flow in a direction not possible), however, it is the means used in this solution approach to compute the *net flow* along a branch. (If, for example, a later iteration showed a flow of 1 car from node 5 to node 2, then the net

*Determining branch flows in the opposite direction*

flow in the correct direction would be computed by subtracting this flow of 1 in the wrong direction from the previous flow of 4 in the correct direction. A net flow of 3 in the correct direction results.)

*The maximum flow for path 1–4–6*

We have now completed one iteration of the solution process and must repeat the steps above. Again, we select a path arbitrarily. This time we will select path 1–4–6, as shown in figure 19.20. The maximum flow along this path is 4 cars, which is subtracted at each of the nodes. This increases the total flow through the network to 8 cars (by adding the flow of 4 along 1–4–6 to the flow previously determined in figure 19.19).

**Figure 19.20** Maximal flow for path 1-4-6.

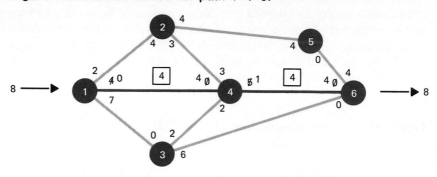

As a final step, the flow of 4 cars is added to the flow along the path in the opposite direction at nodes 4 and 6.

*The maximum flow for path 1–3–6*

Now we must select another path arbitrarily. This time we will choose the path 1–3–6 with a maximum possible flow of 6 cars. This flow of 6 is subtracted from the branches along the path from 1–3–6 and added to the branches in the opposite direction, as shown in figure 19.21. The flow of 6 for this path is added to the previous flow of 8, which results in a total flow of 14 railroad cars.

**Figure 19.21** Maximal flow for path 1-3-6.

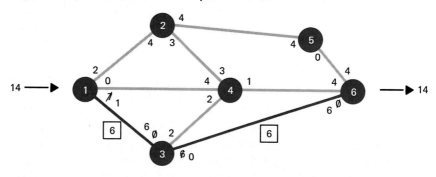

The next path we will select is 1–3–4–6. Notice that at this point there are a restricted number of paths that we can take. For example, we cannot take the branch from node 3 to node 6 out of node 3, since zero flow capacity is available. Likewise any path including the branch from node 1 to node 4 is not possible.

*The maximum flow for path 1–3–4–6*

The available flow capacity along the path 1–3–4–6 is 1 car, as shown in figure 19.22. This increases the total flow from 14 cars to 15 cars.

**Figure 19.22** Maximal flow for path 1-3-4-6.

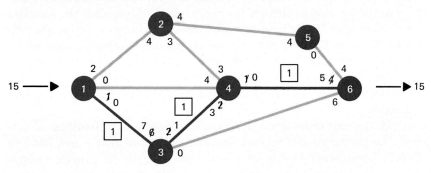

The resulting network is shown in figure 19.23. Close observation of the network in figure 19.23 shows that there are no more paths with available flow capacity. All paths out of nodes 3, 4, and 5 show zero available capacity, which prohibits any further paths through the network.

*The maximal flow solution*

This completes the maximal flow solution for our example problem. The maximum flow is 15 railroad cars. The flows that will occur along each branch are highlighted in boxes in figure 19.23.

**Figure 19.23** Maximal flow for railway network.

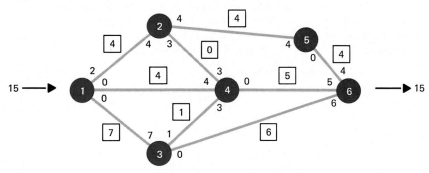

# Summary

In this chapter we have introduced the management science technique of network analysis. We specifically concentrated on a class of networks referred to as network flow models. These included the shortest route network, the minimal spanning tree network, and the maximal flow network. These networks are all concerned with the flow of an item (or items) through an arrangement of paths (or routes).

Solution approaches were demonstrated for each of the three network types presented in this chapter. At times it may have seemed tiresome to go through the various steps of these solution methods when the solutions could have more easily been found by simply looking closely at the networks. However, as the size of networks increase, intuitive solution by observation becomes more difficult, thus creating the need for a solution procedure. Of course, like the other techniques in this text, when a network gets extremely large and complex, computerized solution becomes the best approach.

In the next chapter we are going to continue our discussion of networks by presenting the network analysis techniques known as CPM and PERT. These network techniques are used primarily for project analysis and are not only the most popular types of network analysis, but also two of the most widely applied management science techniques.

# References

Ford, L. R., Jr., and Fulkerson, D. R. *Flows in Networks*. Princeton, N.J.: Princeton University Press, 1962.

Hillier, F. S., and Lieberman, G. J. *Operations Research*. 2d ed. San Francisco: Holden-Day, 1974.

Hu, T. C. *Integer Programming and Network Flows*. Reading, Mass.: Addison-Wesley, 1969.

Lee, Sang M.; Moore, Laurence J.; and Taylor, Bernard W. *Management Science*. Dubuque, Ia.: Wm. C. Brown Company Publishers, 1981.

Trueman, R. E. *An Introduction to Quantitative Methods for Decision Making*. 2d ed. New York: Holt, Rinehart and Winston, 1977.

# Problems

1. Given the following network with the distances between nodes (in miles), determine the shortest route from node 1 to each of the other four nodes (2, 3, 4, and 5).

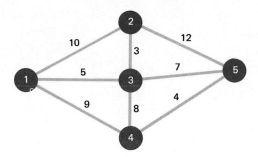

2. Given the following network with the distances between nodes (in miles), determine the shortest route from node 1 to each of the other four nodes (2, 3, 4, and 5).

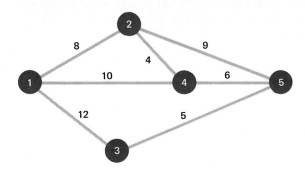

3. Given the following network with distances between nodes (in miles), determine the shortest route from node 1 to each of the other six nodes (2, 3, 4, 5, 6, and 7).

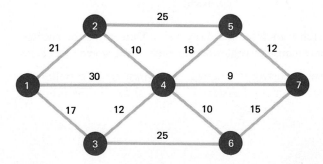

4. The Roanoke, Virginia, distributor for Rainwater Beer delivers beer by truck to stores in six other Virginia cities as shown in the following network. The mileage between each city is shown above each branch.

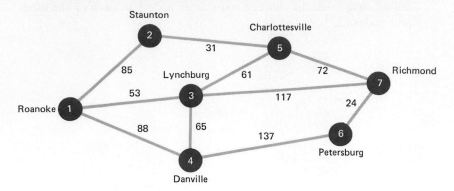

Determine the shortest truck route from Roanoke to each of the other six cities in the network.

5. The Burger Doodle restaurant franchises in Los Angeles are supplied from a central warehouse in Inglewood. The location of the warehouse and its proximity in minutes of travel time to the franchises is shown in the following network.

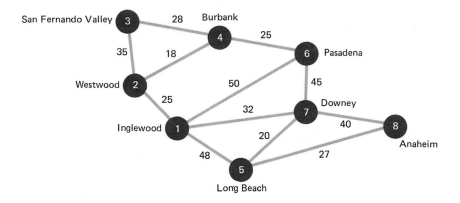

Trucks supply each franchise on a daily basis. Determine the shortest route from the warehouse at Inglewood to each of the seven franchises.

6. The Petroco gasoline distributor in Jackson, Mississippi, supplies service stations in six other southeastern cities, as shown in the following network.

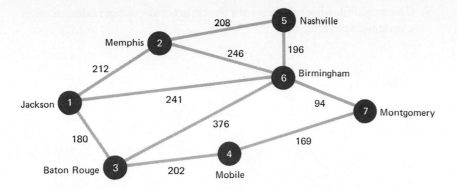

The distance in miles is shown on each branch. Determine the shortest route from Jackson to the six other cities in the network.

7. A steel mill in Gary supplies steel to manufacturers in seven other midwestern cities via truck as shown in the following network.

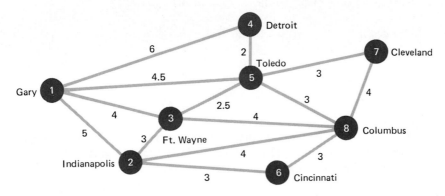

The travel time between each city in hours is shown on each branch. Determine the shortest route from Gary to each of the other seven cities in the network.

8. Given the following network with the distances between nodes, develop a minimal spanning tree.

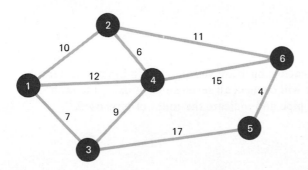

9. Given the following network with the distances between nodes, develop a minimal spanning tree.

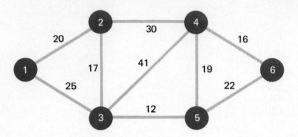

10. Given the following network with the distances between nodes, develop a minimal spanning tree.

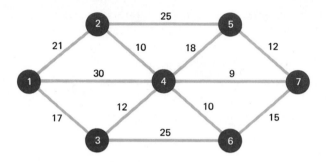

11. The community of Preston Forest is going to install a new sewer system to connect several suburbs. The network of possible sewage lines between the seven suburbs is shown as follows.

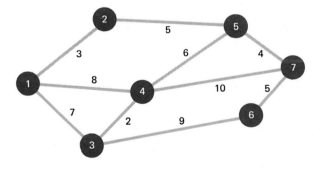

The miles between each suburb are shown on each branch. Determine a sewer system that will connect all seven suburbs using the minimum number of miles of pipe and indicate the miles of pipe used.

12. Several oil companies are jointly planning to build an oil pipeline to connect several southwestern and midwestern cities as shown in the following network.

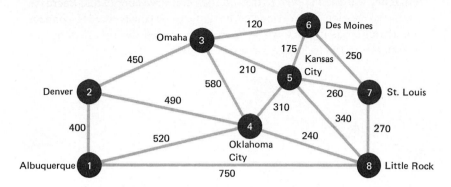

The miles between each city are shown on each branch. Determine a pipeline system that will connect all eight cities using the minimum number of miles of pipe and indicate the number of miles of pipe used.

13. A major hotel chain is constructing a new resort hotel complex in Greenbranch Springs, West Virginia. The resort is in a heavily wooded area, and the developers want to preserve as much of the natural beauty as possible. As such, the developers want to connect all the various facilities in the complex with a combination walking and riding path that will minimize the amount of pathway that will have to be cut through the woods. The following network shows possible connecting paths between all the facilities and their distance in yards.

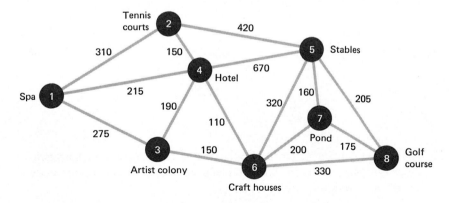

Determine the path that will connect all the facilities with the minimum amount of construction and indicate the total length of the pathway.

14. The town council of Whitesville has decided to construct a bicycle path to connect the various suburbs of the town with the shopping center, downtown area, and the local college. The council hopes the local citizenry will use the bike path, and thus conserve energy and decrease traffic congestion. The various paths that can be constructed to connect the major areas in the town with their associated distances (in miles) are shown in the following network.

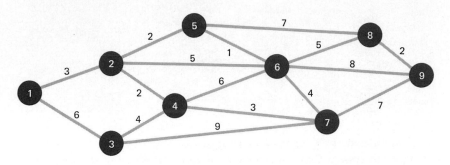

Determine the bicycle path that will connect all the areas of the town with the minimum construction of pathway. Indicate the total length of the path.

15. Given the following network with the flow capacities along each branch, determine the maximum flow from source node 1 to destination node 6 and the flow along each branch.

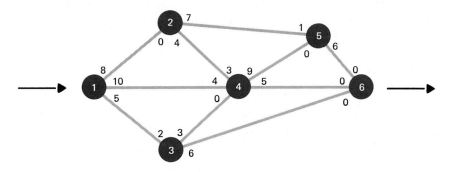

16. Given the following network with the flow capacities along each branch, determine the maximum flow from source node 1 to destination node 7 and the flow along each branch.

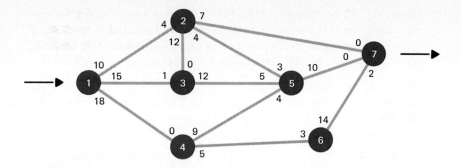

17. Given the following network with the flow capacities along each branch, determine the maximum flow from source node 1 to destination node 6 and the flow along each branch.

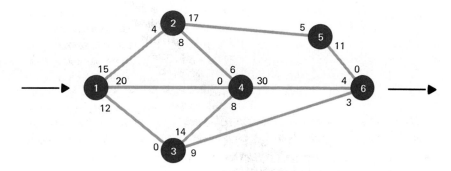

18. A new stadium complex is being planned for Denver, and the Denver traffic engineer is attempting to determine if the city streets between the stadium complex and the interstate highway can accommodate the expected traffic of 21,000 cars when a game is over. The various traffic arteries between the stadium (node 1) and the interstate (node 8) are shown in the following network.

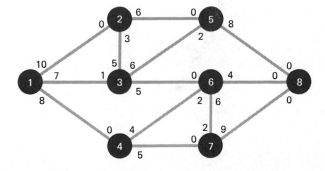

The flow capacities on each street are determined by the number of available lanes, the use of traffic police and lights, and the number of lanes that can be opened or closed in either direction. The flow capacities are given in 1,000s of cars. Determine the maximum traffic flow the streets can accommodate and the traffic along each street. Will the streets be able to handle the expected flow after a game?

19. The FAA has granted a license to a new airline, Omniair, and awarded it several routes between Los Angeles and Chicago with the flights per day for each route shown in the following network.

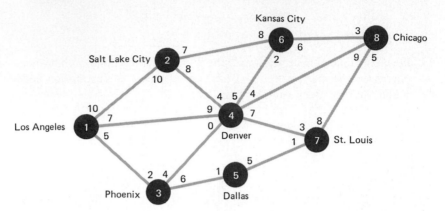

Determine the maximum number of flights the airline can schedule per day from Chicago to Los Angeles and indicate the flights along each route.

20. The National Express Parcel Service has various truck and air routes established around the country over which they ship parcels. The holiday season is approaching, which means a dramatic increase in the number of packages that will be sent. The service wants to know the maximum flow of packages it can accommodate (in tons) from station 1 to station 7. The network of routes with the flow capacities (in tons of packages per day) along each route is shown as follows.

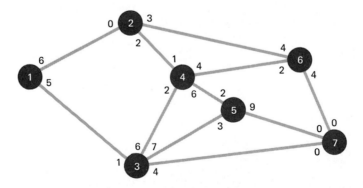

Determine the maximum tonnage of packages that can be transported per day from station 1 to station 7 and indicate the flow along each branch.

# 20
CPM and PERT
Network Analysis

CPM and PERT Network Analysis

One of the most popular uses of networks is for project analysis. Such projects as the construction of a building, the development of a drug, or the installation of a computer system can be developed as networks. These networks illustrate the way in which the parts of the project are organized, and they can be used to determine the time duration of the projects. The network techniques that are used for project analysis are CPM and PERT. CPM stands for *Critical Path Method,* while PERT is an acronym for *Project Evaluation and Review Technique.* These two techniques are basically identical except that PERT is a probabilistic technique, while CPM is deterministic (i.e., nonprobabilistic).

CPM and PERT were developed at approximately the same time (although independently) during the late 1950s. The fact that they have been so frequently and widely applied in such a short period of time attests to their value as management science techniques.

## The CPM Network

The network flow models in the previous chapter consisted of nodes and branches. The *branches* represented routes (or paths) over which items flowed from one point in the network to another point, which were represented by *nodes.* A CPM network also consists of branches and nodes, however, the branches reflect *activities* of a project or operation, while nodes represent the beginning and termination of activities referred to as *events.*

*Branches*

*Nodes*

*Activities and events*

As an example of a CPM network, we will consider the project of constructing a house. The network for building a house is shown in figure 20.1.

*A network example*

**Figure 20.1** Network for building a house.

This network consists of three activities: designing the house, obtaining financing, and actually building the house. These activities are represented in the network by arrows (directed branches). The circles (nodes)

*Precedence relationships*

in figure 20.1 reflect events. For example, node 1 is the event "start designing the house," while node 2 is an event representing the "end of designing the house" and the "beginning of obtaining financing."

The use of directed branches (arrows) in this network indicates that there is a *precedence relationship* between the three activities. In other words, the activity "designing the house" must precede the activity "obtain financing," which in turn precedes the activity "build the house." These precedence relationships must be strictly followed. That is, an activity in this network cannot begin until the preceeding activity has been totally *Node realization* completed. In network terminology we say that when an activity is completed at a node, that node has been *realized*.

*Planning and scheduling*
The purpose of developing a network is to aid in *planning* and *scheduling* a project. The network for building a house in figure 20.1 will indicate to the home builder which activities are included in building a house and the order in which the activities must be undertaken. However, scheduling implies that there are times associated with the activities. As such, we will designate estimated times for the duration of the activities in our home-building network, as shown in figure 20.2.

**Figure 20.2** Network for building a house with activity times.

*Project duration*
In the network in figure 20.2, the home builder has estimated that financing can be obtained after month 2, the house can be started after month 3, and the entire project will be completed in 9 months. Based on this schedule, the home builder can plan when to vacate a present dwelling and move into the new house.

## Concurrent Activities

*Activities that occur at the same time*
Our home building example consists of only three activities occuring one after the other. However, it is often possible and usually likely that a project will include several activities that can occur at the same time (concurrently). In order to demonstrate concurrent activities, we will expand our home-building project network as shown in figure 20.3.

The expanded network in figure 20.3 contains the following differences relative to our previous project network shown in figure 20.1. First, the activities for designing the house and obtaining financing have been combined into activity 1 ⇒ 2 (where 1 and 2 are the nodes encompassing this activity). Next, an activity for ordering and receiving building materials will follow the first activity. *In addition,* an activity for laying the foundation will also follow the first activity. In other words, the home builder can have the foundation laid *and* order the materials *concurrently*. Neither of these activities depend on each other, but instead on the completion of the house design and financing.

**Figure 20.3** Expanded network for building a house showing concurrent activities.

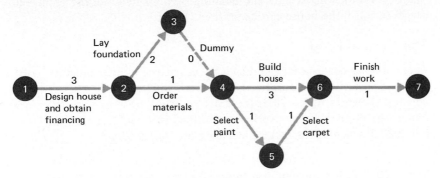

When the activities for laying the foundation (2 ⇒ 3) and ordering materials (2 ⇒ 4) are completed, then activities 4 ⇒ 5 and 4 ⇒ 6 can begin simultaneously. However, before discussing these activities further, we will look more closely at activity 3 ⇒ 4, referred to in the network as a *dummy*.    *A dummy activity*

A dummy activity is inserted in the network to show a precedence relationship, but it does not represent any actual passage of time. The activities could actually be represented in the network as shown in figure 20.4.

**Figure 20.4** Concurrent activities.

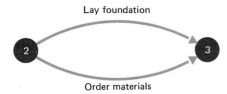

However, in a CPM network, two or more activities are not allowed to share the same starting and ending nodes. (The reason will become apparent later when we develop a schedule for the network.) As a result, a *dummy* activity (3 ⇒ 4) is inserted to give two activities separate end nodes. Notice, though, that a time of zero months has been assigned to activity 3 ⇒ 4. Thus, the dummy activity, while not representing the passage of time, does show that activity 2 ⇒ 3 must be completed prior to any activities beginning at node 4.

*Two or more activities cannot share the same start and end nodes*

Returning to the network (fig. 20.3) at node 4, we see that two activities start at this point. Activity 4 ⇒ 6 is the actual building of the house, and activity 4 ⇒ 5 is the search for and selection of the paint for the exterior and interior of the house. Activity 4 ⇒ 6 and activity 4 ⇒ 5 can both begin simultaneously and take place concurrently. Following the selection of the paint (activity 4 ⇒ 5) and the realization of node 5, the carpet can be selected (since the carpet color is dependent on the paint color). This activity can also occur concurrently with the building of the house (activity 4 ⇒ 6). Finally once the building is completed and the paint and carpet selected, the house can be finished (activity 6 ⇒ 7).

## The Critical Path

*Network paths* In our simpler network for building a house (before we expanded it), there was a single path with a duration of nine months. However, in the expanded network shown in figure 20.3, there are several paths. In fact, there are four paths through the network, as identified in table 20.1 and shown in figure 20.5 which can be determined by close observation.

**Table 20.1** Paths through the House-Building Network

| Path | Events |
| --- | --- |
| A: | 1 ⇒ 2 ⇒ 3 ⇒ 4 ⇒ 6 ⇒ 7 |
| B: | 1 ⇒ 2 ⇒ 3 ⇒ 4 ⇒ 5 ⇒ 6 ⇒ 7 |
| C: | 1 ⇒ 2 ⇒ 4 ⇒ 6 ⇒ 7 |
| D: | 1 ⇒ 2 ⇒ 4 ⇒ 5 ⇒ 6 ⇒ 7 |

**Figure 20.5** Alternative paths in the network.

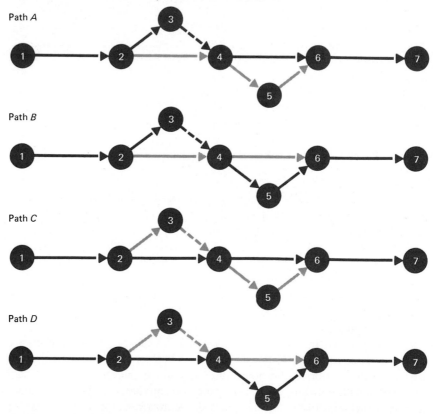

Path A

Path B

Path C

Path D

**CPM and PERT Network Analysis**

The minimum time in which the project can be completed (i.e., the house be built) is equal to the length of time required by the longest path in the network. The longest path is referred to as the *critical path*. In order to better understand the relationship between the minimum project time and the longest network path, we will determine the length of each of the four paths shown in figure 20.5.

*The longest path in the network*

By summing the activity times (shown in fig. 20.3) along each of the four paths, we can compute the length of each path as follows.

*Determining the length of each path*

Path *A:* $1 \Rightarrow 2 \Rightarrow 3 \Rightarrow 4 \Rightarrow 6 \Rightarrow 7$
$\phantom{Path A:} 3 + 2 + 0 + 3 + 1 = 9$ months
Path *B:* $1 \Rightarrow 2 \Rightarrow 3 \Rightarrow 4 \Rightarrow 5 \Rightarrow 6 \Rightarrow 7$
$\phantom{Path B:} 3 + 2 + 0 + 1 + 1 + 1 = 8$ months
Path *C:* $1 \Rightarrow 2 \Rightarrow 4 \Rightarrow 6 \Rightarrow 7$
$\phantom{Path C:} 3 + 1 + 3 + 1 = 8$ months
Path *D:* $1 \Rightarrow 2 \Rightarrow 4 \Rightarrow 5 \Rightarrow 6 \Rightarrow 7$
$\phantom{Path D:} 3 + 1 + 1 + 1 + 1 = 7$ months

Since path *A* is the longest path, it is also the critical path, thus the minimum completion time of the project is 9 months. Now let us analyze the critical path more closely. From figure 20.3 we can see that event 2 will not occur until 3 months have passed. It is also relatively easy to see that event 3 will not occur until the passage of 5 months. However, the realization of event 4 is dependent upon two activities leading into node 4. Activity $3 \Rightarrow 4$ is completed after 5 months (adding the dummy activity time of zero to the time until node 3 occurs of 5 months), but activity $2 \Rightarrow 4$ is completed at the end of month 4. Thus, we have two possible realization times for node 4 — 5 months and 4 months. Recall, however, that a node represents the event of the next activity occurring. Since no activity starting at node 4 can occur until *all* preceding activities have been finished, node 4 cannot be realized until *both* activities leading into it have been completed. Thus, the soonest node 4 can be realized is 5 months.

*Analyzing the critical path*

Now let us consider the activities leading from node 4. Using the same logic as above, we can see that node 6 will be realized after either 8 months (5 months at node 4 plus the 3 months required by activity $4 \Rightarrow 6$), or after 7 months (5 months at node 4 plus the two months required by activities $4 \Rightarrow 5$ and $5 \Rightarrow 6$). Since all activities ending at node 6 must be completed before node 6 can be realized, the soonest node 6 can be realized is 8 months. Adding the time for activity $6 \Rightarrow 7$ of 1 month to the time at node 6 results in the project duration of 9 months. Recall that this is the time of the longest path in the network, or the critical path.

This brief analysis demonstrates the concept of a critical path and the determination of the minimum completion time of a project. Now we will look more closely at how each event in the network can be scheduled individually.

## Event Scheduling

*Earliest event time*

Recall from our analysis of the critical path in the previous section that at each event we determined the soonest time that event could be realized. For example, at node 4 we found that the *earliest* time it could be realized was 5 months. This time is referred to as the *earliest event time,* and it will be expressed symbolically on the network as $ET$. The earliest times for every event in our house-building network are shown in figure 20.6.

---

**Figure 20.6 Network with earliest event times.**

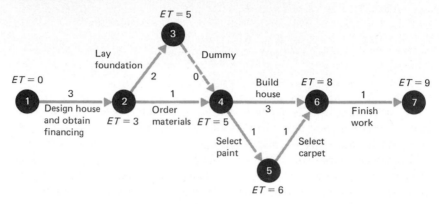

*A forward pass*

In order to determine the earliest time at every node, we make what is known as a *forward pass* through the network. That is, we start at the origin and move forward through the network. The earliest time at a node is at the point in time when all activities ending at that node have been completed—the time when the node is realized. The earliest time at the final node in the network is always the project completion time, or the critical path time.

Observing node 2 in figure 20.6, the earliest time of this event is 3 months. The only activity leading into node 2 has a duration of 3 months. Adding this amount to the earliest time of the immediately preceeding node (zero at node 1) results in the earliest time of 3 months. At node 3, again there is only one activity to be considered. Thus, the earliest time at node 3 is the activity time of 2 plus the earliest time of node 2, which equals 5 months.

At node 4, two activities terminate, thus the earliest time will be based on when *both* activities are completed. Activity $2 \Rightarrow 4$ is completed at 4 months, but activity $3 \Rightarrow 4$ is completed at 5 months. As such, 5 months is the earliest time event 4 can be realized. The remaining earliest event times are determined similarly.

*A formula for computing earliest event times*

In general, the earliest event time at a node, $j$, is computed as follows.

$$ET_j = \text{Maximum } (ET_i + t_{ij})$$

where $i$ is the starting node number of all activities ending at node $j$ and $t_{ij}$ is the time for activity $i \Rightarrow j$.

As an example, we will compute the earliest time at node 6 (i.e., $j = 6$).

$$ET_6 = \text{Maximum } (ET_5 + t_{56,} ET_4 + t_{46})$$
$$= \text{Maximum } (6 + 1, 5 + 3)$$
$$= \text{Maximum } (7, 8)$$
$$= 8 \text{ months}$$

which is the earliest time at node 6, as shown in figure 20.6.

## Latest Event Times

A companion to the earliest event time is the *latest event time.* The latest event time is the latest time an activity can start without delaying the completion of the project beyond the project critical path time. For our example, the project completion time (and earliest event time) at node 7 is 9 months. Thus, the objective of determining latest event times is to see how long each activity can be delayed without the project exceeding 9 months.

While a forward pass through the network was made to determine the earliest event times, the latest event times are computed using a *backward pass.* We start at the end of the network at node 7 and work backwards, computing the latest time at each event (node). Since we want to determine how long each activity in the network can be delayed *without extending the project time,* the latest time at node 7 cannot exceed the earliest time. Therefore, the latest time at node 7 (referred to as LT) is 9 months. This and all other latest event times are shown in figure 20.7.

*A backward pass*

---

**Figure 20.7** Network with latest event times.

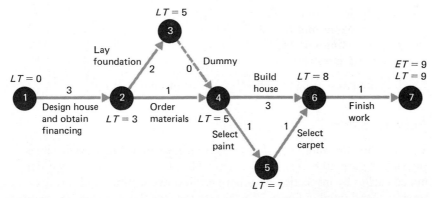

Moving backwards through the network, the latest time at node 6 is 8 months, computed by subtracting the activity $6 \Rightarrow 7$ time of 1 month from the latest time at node 7 (9 months). If event 6 is realized at any time later than 8 months, it can be seen that the overall project time will be increased beyond 9 months. For example, if node 6 is realized at month 9, then activity $6 \Rightarrow 7$ will not be completed until *month 10*.

Next we compute the latest event time at node 5 the same way as we did at node 6. Subtracting the activity $5 \Rightarrow 6$ time of 1 month from the latest time at node 6 (8 months) results in a latest event time of 7 months at node 5.

At node 4 we have a choice as to the selection of the latest time. We can either subtract the activity $4 \Rightarrow 6$ time of 3 months from the latest time at node 6 (8 months), which results in a latest event time of 5 months, or we can subtract the activity $4 \Rightarrow 5$ time of 1 month from the latest time at node 5, which results in a latest event time of 6 months. The latest time at node 4 can be either 5 months or 6 months. In such a case, we select the minimum latest event time, which is 5 months. The reason can be seen if we use a latest time of 6 months at node 4.

If activity $4 \Rightarrow 6$ starts at 6 months, then it will be completed after 9 months, which in turn will result in the project being completed after 10 months. This is an obvious violation of our rule not to exceed the project (critical path) time. Alternatively, a latest event time of 5 months at node 4 will enable the project to be completed on time.

The remaining latest event times at nodes 3, 2, and 1 are determined similarly.

*A formula for computing the latest event times*

In general, the latest event time at node $i$ is computed as follows,

$$LT_i = \text{Minimum } (LT_j - t_{ij})$$

where $j$ is the ending node number of all activities starting at node $i$ and $t_{ij}$ is the time for activity $i \Rightarrow j$.

As an example, we will compute the latest time at node 4 (i.e., $i = 4$).

$$
\begin{aligned}
LT_4 &= \text{Minimum } (LT_6 - t_{46}, LT_5 - t_{45}) \\
&= \text{Minimum } (8 - 3, 7 - 1) \\
&= \text{Minimum } (5, 6) \\
&= 5 \text{ months}
\end{aligned}
$$

which is the latest time at node 4 as shown in figure 20.7.

## Activity Slack

*Earliest and latest event times are equal on the critical path*

The network for building a house with earliest and latest event times is shown in figure 20.8. The critical path ($1 \Rightarrow 2 \Rightarrow 3 \Rightarrow 4 \Rightarrow 6 \Rightarrow 7$) we determined earlier by inspection with both earliest event times and latest event times is highlighted in figure 20.8. Notice that for the events on the critical path the earliest event times and latest event times are equal. This means that these events on the critical path must start at an exact time and cannot be delayed at all. If the start of any activity on the critical path is delayed,

**Figure 20.8** Network with earliest and latest event times.

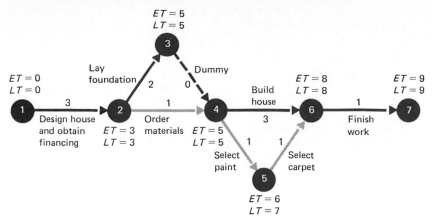

then the overall project time will be increased. As a result, we now have an alternative way to determine the critical path besides simply inspecting the network. The events on the critical path can be determined by seeing at which nodes the earliest event times equal the latest event times. Observing figure 20.8, the nodes 1, 2, 3, 4, 6, and 7 all have earliest event times and latest event times that are equal, thus they are on the critical path.

A difficulty sometimes incurred when determining the critical path solely using the earliest and latest event times is that while the events on the critical path can be identified, it is possible to confuse the critical path activities with some activities not on the critical path. For example, in figure 20.8, the three nodes, 2, 3, and 4, all have equal earliest and latest event times. As such, we might inadvertently designate the critical path as including activity 2 ⇒ 4 rather than going through node 3 as the critical path actually does. As a result, care must be taken in identifying the critical path.

There is, however, a way to tell exactly which activities are on the critical path. This alternative approach uses a concept known as *activity slack*. Slack is the time an activity can be delayed without affecting the overall project duration. In effect, it is *extra time* available for completing an activity. The slack for each activity in our example network is shown in figure 20.9.

As an example of how slack is computed, we will look specifically at activity 2 ⇒ 4 in figure 20.9. The earliest time this activity can start is at 3 months (i.e., the earliest event time at node 2). The latest this activity can be completed is at 5 months (the latest event time at node 4). This leaves 2 months available to complete the activity. Since the activity requires only 1 month to complete, there is an extra month left over. This extra month is slack. If we delayed the start of activity 2 ⇒ 4 for one month, it could still be completed by month five, thus, not delaying the project completion time.

*Activity slack*

*Extra time available for completing an activity*

**Figure 20.9** Network with slack.

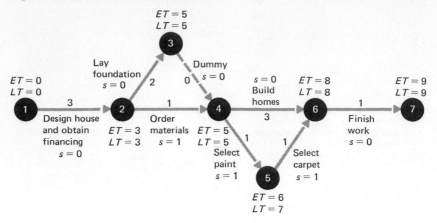

Alternatively, activity 2 ⇒ 3 does not have any slack at all. The reason is that the earliest this activity can start is at month 3 (the earliest event time at node 2). The latest it can be completed is at month 5 (the latest event time at node 3). Thus, 2 months are available for completion of this activity. Since activity 2 ⇒ 3 requires 2 months, there is no extra time left over. Now recall that activity 2 ⇒ 3 is on the critical path. Careful inspection of figure 20.9 shows that there is no slack on any of the activities on the critical path (1 ⇒ 2 ⇒ 3 ⇒ 4 ⇒ 6 ⇒ 7). All other activities not on the critical path do have slack. Therefore, as a general rule, the critical path encompasses those activities in the network that have no slack. In general, activity slack can be determined as follows.

*Activities on the critical path have no slack*

Slack for activity $i ⇒ j$ = Latest time (activity $j$) − earliest time (activity $i$)
    − activity time for activity $i ⇒ j$

*A formula for computing activity slack*

As an example, consider activity 5 ⇒ 6. The slack is computed as follows.

$$\text{Slack for activity } 5 ⇒ 6 = LT_6 - ET_5 - t_{56}$$
$$= 8 - 6 - 1$$
$$= 1 \text{ month}$$

*Shared stock*

Before ending our discussion of slack, an additional aspect should be mentioned. Notice that activities 4 ⇒ 5 and 5 ⇒ 6 in figure 20.9 both have slack equaling 1 month. However, the start of *both activities* cannot be delayed for a month. Activity 4 ⇒ 5 can be delayed 1 month *or* activity 5 ⇒ 6 can be delayed 1 month, but not both. If activity 4 ⇒ 5 is started at month 6 instead of month 5, then it will be completed at month 7, which will not allow the start of activity 5 ⇒ 6 to be delayed. The opposite is also true. If 4 ⇒ 5 is started at month 5, activity 5 ⇒ 6 can be delayed 1 month. As a result the slack on these two activities is referred to as *shared slack*. This means that the *sequence of activities, 4 ⇒ 5 ⇒ 6,* can be delayed 1 month jointly without delaying the project.

# PERT Analysis

In the CPM network for building a house presented in the previous section, all of the activity time estimates were a single value. By using only a single activity time estimate, we are, in effect, assuming that activity times are known with certainty (i.e., they are deterministic). For example, in figure 20.9, the time estimate for activity 2 ⇒ 3, laying the foundation, is shown to be 2 months. Since only this one value is given, we must assume that the activity time does not vary (or varies very little) from 2 months. However, in reality, it is rare that activity time estimates can be made with certainty. This is especially true since projects that are networked tend to be unique, and as such, there is little historical evidence that can be used as a basis to predict future occurrences. As an alternative to CPM, PERT (Project Evaluation and Review Technique) uses *probabilistic activity times*.

*Probabilistic activity times*

In order to demonstrate the PERT technique, we will employ a new example. (We could use the house-building network of the previous section, however, it will be useful to use a little larger and more complex network in order to provide more experience with different types of projects.) The Southern Textile Company has decided to install a new computerized order-processing system. In the past, orders for the cloth material the company produced were processed manually, which contributed to delays in delivering orders, and as a result, lost sales. The company wants to know how long it will take to install the new system.

*A PERT example*

The network for the installation of the new order-processing system is shown in figure 20.10. We will briefly describe the activities.

**Figure 20.10** Network for installation of order-processing system.

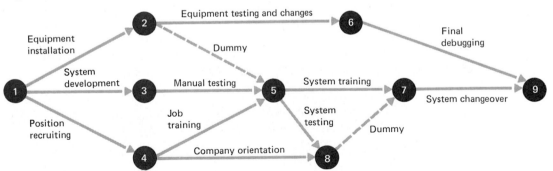

The network begins with three concurrent activities: the new computer equipment is installed (activity 1 ⇒ 2); the computerized order-processing system is developed (activity 1 ⇒ 3); and people are recruited to operate the system (activity 1 ⇒ 4). Once people are hired, they are trained for the job (activity 4 ⇒ 5), and other personnel in the company, such as marketing, accounting, and production personnel, are informed about the new system (activity 4 ⇒ 8). Following the development of the system (activity 1 ⇒ 3), it is tested manually to make sure it is logical (activity 3 ⇒ 5). Following activity 1 ⇒ 2, the new equipment is tested and corrected (activity 2 ⇒ 6), and the newly trained personnel begin training on the computerized system (activity 5 ⇒ 7). Also, event 5 begins the testing of the system on the computer to check for errors (activity 5 ⇒ 8). The final activities include a trial run and changeover to the system (activity 7 ⇒ 9) and final debugging of the computer system (activity 6 ⇒ 9).

*Three time estimates for each activity*

At this stage in a CPM network we would assign a single-time estimate to each network activity. However, in a PERT network we determine *three time estimates* for each activity, which will enable us to estimate the mean and variance for a *beta distribution* of the activity times. We are assuming that the activity times can be described by a beta distribution for several reasons. First, the beta distribution mean and variance can be approximated with three estimates. Second, the beta distribution is continuous, but it has no predetermined shape (such as the bell shape of the normal curve). It will take on the shape (i.e., be skewed) that is indicated by the time estimates given. This is beneficial, since typically we would have no prior knowledge of the shapes of the distributions of activity times in a unique project network. Third, although other types of distributions have been shown to be no more or less accurate than the beta, it has become traditional to use the beta distribution for PERT analysis.

*The beta distribution*

*The most likely, optimistic and pessimistic activity times*

The three time estimates for each activity are the most likely time, the optimistic time, and the pessimistic time. The *most likely time* is the time that would most frequently occur if the activity were repeated many times. The *optimistic time* is the shortest possible time within which the activity could be completed if everything went right. The *pessimistic time* is the longest possible time the activity would require to be completed assuming everything went wrong. In general, the person most familiar with an activity would make these estimates to the best of their knowledge and ability (i.e., the estimate is "subjective," see chap. 10 on probability).

*The mean and variance of a beta distribution*

These three time estimates can subsequently be used to estimate the mean and variance of a *beta distribution*. If we let

a = optimistic time estimate
m = most likely time estimate
b = pessimistic time estimate

then the mean and variance are computed as follows.

$$\text{Mean (expected time): } t = \frac{a + 4m + b}{6}$$
$$\text{Variance: } v = \left(\frac{b - a}{6}\right)^2$$

These formulas provide a reasonable estimate of the mean and variance of the beta distribution, a distribution that is continuous and can take on various shapes (i.e., skewness).

The three time estimates, mean, and variance for all the activities in our network shown in figure 20.10 are given in table 20.2.

**Table 20.2** Activity Time Estimates for Figure 20.10

| Activity | Time Estimates (weeks) | | | Mean Time | Variance |
|---|---|---|---|---|---|
| | $a$ | $m$ | $b$ | $t$ | $v$ |
| 1 ⇒ 2 | 6 | 8 | 10 | 8 | 4/9 |
| 1 ⇒ 3 | 3 | 6 | 9 | 6 | 1 |
| 1 ⇒ 4 | 1 | 3 | 5 | 3 | 4/9 |
| 2 ⇒ 5 | 0 | 0 | 0 | 0 | 0 |
| 2 ⇒ 6 | 2 | 4 | 12 | 5 | 25/9 |
| 3 ⇒ 5 | 2 | 3 | 4 | 3 | 1/9 |
| 4 ⇒ 5 | 3 | 4 | 5 | 4 | 1/9 |
| 4 ⇒ 8 | 2 | 2 | 2 | 2 | 0 |
| 5 ⇒ 7 | 3 | 7 | 11 | 7 | 16/9 |
| 5 ⇒ 8 | 2 | 4 | 6 | 4 | 4/9 |
| 8 ⇒ 7 | 0 | 0 | 0 | 0 | 0 |
| 6 ⇒ 9 | 1 | 4 | 7 | 4 | 1 |
| 7 ⇒ 9 | 1 | 10 | 13 | 9 | 4 |

*Computing the activity mean and variance*

As an example of the computation of the individual activity mean times and variance, we will consider activity 1 ⇒ 2. The three time estimates ($a = 6$, $m = 8$, $b = 10$) are substituted in our formulas as follows.

$$t = \frac{a + 4m + b}{6}$$

$$= \frac{6 + 4(8) + 10}{6}$$

$$= 8 \text{ weeks}$$

$$v = \left(\frac{b - a}{6}\right)^2$$

$$= \left(\frac{10 - 6}{6}\right)^2$$

$$= 4/9 \text{ weeks}$$

The other values for the mean and variance in table 20.2 are computed similarly. All of the means and variances for the activities in our example network are shown in figure 20.11.

Once the expected activity times are computed for each activity, we can determine the critical path the same way we did in the CPM network, except that we use the expected activity times, "$t$." Recall that in the CPM network we identified the critical path containing those activities with zero slack. This requires the determination of earliest and latest event times, as shown in figure 20.12.

**Figure 20.11** Network with mean activity times and variances.

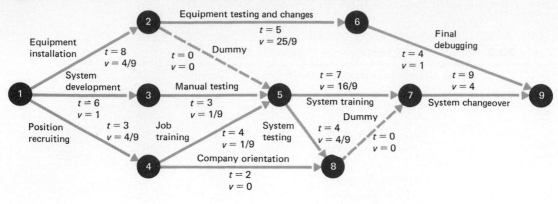

**Figure 20.12** Network with earliest and latest event times and slack.

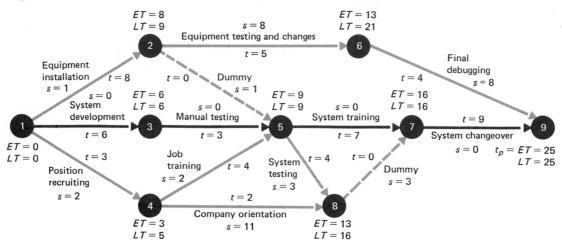

*The critical path and expected project completion time*

Observing figure 20.12, we can see that the critical path encompasses activities $1 \Rightarrow 3 \Rightarrow 5 \Rightarrow 7 \Rightarrow 9$, since these activities have no available slack. We can also see that the *expected* project completion time ($t_p$) is 25 weeks. However, it is also possible to compute the variance for project completion

*Project variance*

time. To determine the project variance, *the variances for those activities on the critical path are summed*. Using the variances computed in table 20.2 and the critical path activities shown in figure 20.12, the variance for project duration ($v_p$) is computed as follows.

| Critical Path Activity | Variance |
|---|---|
| $1 \Rightarrow 3$ | 1 |
| $3 \Rightarrow 5$ | 1/9 |
| $5 \Rightarrow 7$ | 16/9 |
| $7 \Rightarrow 9$ | 4 |
| | 62/9 |

$$v_p = 62/9$$
$$= 6.9 \text{ weeks}$$

The PERT method assumes that the activity times are statistically independent, which allows us to sum the individual expected activity times and variances in order to get an expected *project* time and variance. In addition, it is further assumed that the network mean and variance are normally distributed. Given these assumptions, we can interpret the expected project time ($t_p$) and variance ($v_p$) as the mean ($\mu$) and variance ($\sigma^2$) of a normal distribution:

*Assuming the project time is normally distributed*

$$\mu = 25 \text{ weeks}$$
$$\sigma^2 = 6.9 \text{ weeks}$$

In turn, we can use these statistical parameters to make various probabilistic statements about the project.

## Probability Analysis of the PERT Network

Recall from our discussion of the normal distribution in chapter 10 that probabilities can be determined by computing the number of standard deviations ($Z$) a value is from the mean, as illustrated in figure 20.13

---

**Figure 20.13** Normal distribution of network duration.

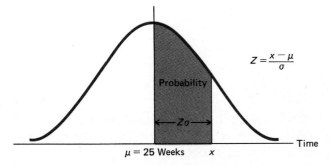

The value, $Z$, is computed using the following formula.

$$Z = \frac{x - \mu}{\sigma}$$

This value is then used to find the corresponding probability in table A.1 of Appendix A.

*Determining the*
*probability that the*
*project will be*
*completed within a*
*specific time*

For example, suppose the textile company manager told customers that the new order-processing system would be completely installed in 30 weeks. What is the probability that it will, in fact, be ready by that time? This probability is illustrated as the shaded area in figure 20.14.

**Figure 20.14** Probability the network will be completed in 30 weeks or less.

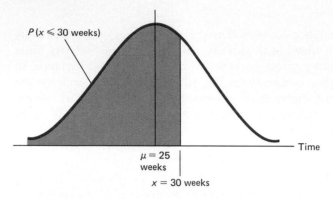

To compute the $Z$ value for a time of 30 weeks, we must first compute the standard deviation ($\sigma$) from the variance, $\sigma^2$.

$$\sigma^2 = 6.9$$
$$\sigma = \sqrt{6.9}$$
$$\sigma = 2.63$$

Next we substitute this value for the standard deviation, the mean, and our proposed time project completion time (30 weeks) into the following formula.

$$Z = \frac{x - \mu}{\sigma}$$
$$= \frac{30 - 25}{2.63}$$
$$= 1.90$$

A $Z$ value of 1.90 corresponds to a probability of .4713 in table A.1 in Appendix A. This means that there is a .9713 (.5000 + .4713) probability of completing the project in 30 weeks or less.

Alternatively, suppose one customer has become so frustrated with delayed orders that she has told the textile company that if it does not have the new ordering system working within 22 weeks then she will trade elsewhere. The probability of the project being completed within 22 weeks is computed as follows.

$$Z = \frac{22 - 25}{2.63}$$

$$= \frac{-3}{2.63}$$

$$= -1.14$$

A $Z$ value of 1.14 (the negative is ignored) corresponds to a probability of .3729 in table A.1 of Appendix A. Thus, there is only a .1271 probability that the customer will be retained, as illustrated in figure 20.15.

**Figure 20.15** Probability the network will be completed in 22 weeks or less.

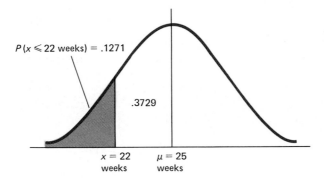

$P(x \leqslant 22 \text{ weeks}) = .1271$

.3729

$x = 22$ weeks $\quad \mu = 25$ weeks

## Summary

In this chapter we have discussed two of the most popular management science techniques—CPM and PERT networks. Their popularity is due primarily to the fact that a network forms a picture of the system under analysis that is easy for a manager to interpret. Sometimes it is difficult to explain a set of mathematical equations to a manager, but a network can often be easily explained.

It was shown that CPM and PERT differ in how the activity times are determined. In a CPM network, single (certain) activity times are used, while in a PERT network probabilistic activity times are used. At first glance, it is tempting to use only the PERT approach, as it seems more realistic to assume probabilistic activity times. However, PERT is subject to several difficulties. First, it is often difficult to generate three accurate activity time estimates for the beta distribution. There is a strong tendency for the estimator to be conservative and to give an optimistic time that is too high. Second, the PERT statistical results have sometimes been attacked as not always theoretically correct. In general, such reservations have not deterred from the popularity of PERT, as most people feel its usefulness far outweighs any theoretical drawbacks. (For a more thorough explanation of these theoretical difficulties the reader should consult the references at the end of this chapter.)

*Limitations of CPM and PERT*

# References

Lee, Sang M.; Moore, Laurence J.; and Taylor, Bernard W. *Management Science*. Dubuque, Ia.: Wm. C. Brown Company Publishers, 1981.

Levy, F.; Thompson, G.; and Wiest, J. "The ABC's of the Critical Path Method;" *Harvard Business Review* 41, no. 5 (October 1963).

Moder, J., and Phillips, C. R. *Project Management with CPM and PERT*. 2d ed. New York: Van Nostrand Reinhold, 1970.

O'Brian, J. *CPM in Construction Management*. New York: McGraw-Hill, 1965.

Wiest, J. D., and Levy F. K. *A Management Guide to PERT/CPM*. 2d ed. Englewood Cliffs, N.J.: Prentice-Hall, 1977.

# Problems

1. Construct the CPM network described by the following set of activities, compute the length of each path in the network, and indicate the critical path.

| Activity | Time (weeks) |
|----------|--------------|
| 1-2 | 5 |
| 1-3 | 4 |
| 2-4 | 3 |
| 3-4 | 6 |

2. Construct the CPM network described by the following set of activities, compute the length of each path in the network, and indicate the critical path.

| Activity | Time (weeks) |
|----------|--------------|
| 1-2 | 3 |
| 1-3 | 7 |
| 2-4 | 2 |
| 3-4 | 5 |
| 3-5 | 6 |
| 4-6 | 1 |
| 5-6 | 4 |

3. Construct the CPM network described by the following set of activities, compute the length of each path in the network, and indicate the critical path.

| Activity | Time (months) |
|----------|---------------|
| 1-2 | 4 |
| 1-3 | 7 |
| 2-4 | 8 |
| 2-5 | 3 |
| 3-5 | 9 |
| 4-5 | 5 |
| 4-6 | 2 |
| 5-6 | 6 |
| 3-6 | 5 |

4. Identify all of the paths in the following network, compute the length of each, and indicate the critical path (activity times are in weeks).

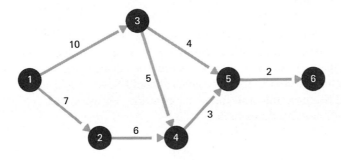

5. For the network in problem 4, determine the earliest event time, latest event time, and slack for each activity. Indicate how the critical path would be determined from this information.

6. Given the following network with activity times in months, determine the earliest event time, latest event time, and slack for each activity. Indicate the critical path and the project duration.

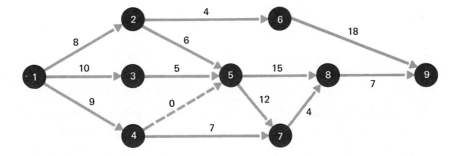

7. Given the following network with activity times in weeks, determine the earliest event time, latest event time, and slack for each activity. Indicate the critical path and the project duration.

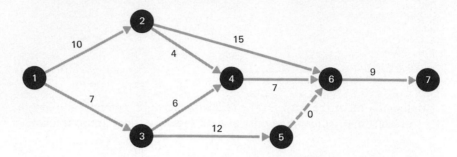

8. In one of the little-known battles of the Civil War, General Tecumseh Beauregard lost the Third Battle of Bull Run because his preparations were not complete when the enemy attacked. However, if the critical path method had been available, the general could have done a better planning job. Suppose that the following planning network had been available (with activity times in days).

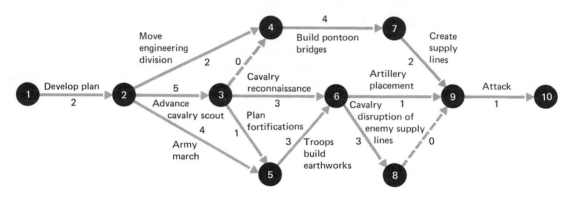

Determine the earliest event times, latest event times, and activity slack for the network. Indicate the critical path and the time between the general's receipt of battle orders to the time the battle began.

9. A group of developers are building a new shopping center. A consultant for the developers has constructed the following CPM network of the project and assigned the indicated activity times (in weeks).

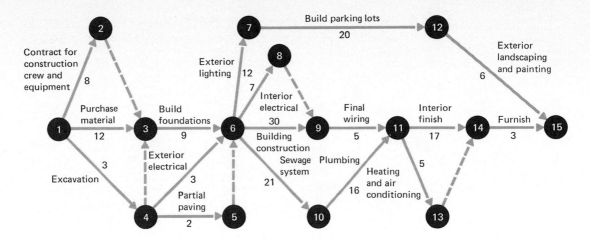

Determine the earliest event times, latest event times, activity slack, critical path, and duration for the project.

10. A farm owner is going to erect a maintenance building with a connecting electrical generator and water tank. The activities, activity descriptions, and estimated durations are given in the following table. (Notice that the activities are not defined by node numbers, but instead by activity descriptions. This is an alternative form of expressing activities and precedence relationships often used in CPM.)

| Activity | Activity Description | Activity Predecessor | Activity Duration (weeks) |
|---|---|---|---|
| a | Excavation | – | 2 |
| b | Erect building | a | 6 |
| c | Install generator | a | 4 |
| d | Install tank | a | 2 |
| e | Install maintenance equipment | b | 4 |
| f | Connect generator and tank to building | b, c, d | 5 |
| g | Paint on a finish | b | 3 |
| h | Checkout facility | e, f | 2 |

Construct the network for this project, identify the critical path, and determine the project duration time.

11. Given the following network and PERT activity time estimates, determine the expected time and variance for each activity and indicate the critical path

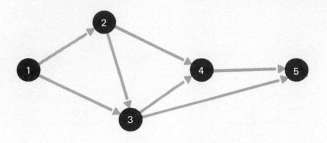

| Activity | Time Estimates (weeks) | | |
|----------|-----|-----|-----|
| | a | m | b |
| 1-2 | 5 | 8 | 17 |
| 1-3 | 7 | 10 | 13 |
| 2-3 | 3 | 5 | 7 |
| 2-4 | 1 | 3 | 5 |
| 3-4 | 4 | 6 | 8 |
| 3-5 | 3 | 3 | 3 |
| 4-5 | 3 | 4 | 5 |

12. Given the following network and PERT activity time estimates, determine the expected time and variance for each activity and indicate the critical path.

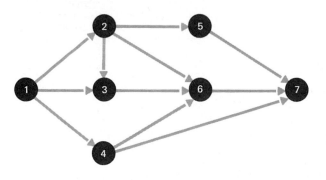

| Activity | Time Estimates (weeks) | | |
|----------|-----|-----|-----|
| | a | m | b |
| 1-2 | 6 | 10 | 15 |
| 1-3 | 2 | 7 | 16 |
| 1-4 | 4 | 8 | 11 |
| 2-3 | 3 | 10 | 15 |
| 2-5 | 7 | 9 | 20 |
| 2-6 | 4 | 12 | 15 |
| 3-6 | 3 | 6 | 9 |
| 4-6 | 5 | 9 | 16 |
| 5-7 | 3 | 20 | 35 |
| 4-7 | 4 | 12 | 16 |
| 6-7 | 2 | 9 | 14 |

13. Given the following **PERT** activity time estimates for the network in problem 6:

| Activity | Time Estimates (months) | | |
|---|---|---|---|
| | a | m | b |
| 1-2 | 4 | 8 | 12 |
| 1-3 | 6 | 10 | 15 |
| 1-4 | 2 | 10 | 14 |
| 2-5 | 3 | 6 | 9 |
| 2-6 | 1 | 4 | 13 |
| 3-5 | 3 | 6 | 18 |
| 4-5 | 0 | 0 | 0 |
| 4-7 | 2 | 8 | 12 |
| 5-8 | 9 | 15 | 22 |
| 5-7 | 5 | 12 | 21 |
| 7-8 | 5 | 6 | 12 |
| 6-9 | 7 | 20 | 25 |
| 8-9 | 3 | 8 | 20 |

Determine the following:
 (a) Expected activity times
 (b) Earliest event times
 (c) Latest event times
 (d) Activity slack
 (e) Critical path
 (f) Expected project duration and variance

14. Given the following **PERT** activity time estimates for the network in problem 8:

| Activity | Time Estimates (days) | | |
|---|---|---|---|
| | a | m | b |
| 1-2 | 1 | 2 | 6 |
| 2-4 | 1 | 3 | 5 |
| 2-3 | 3 | 5 | 10 |
| 2-5 | 3 | 6 | 14 |
| 3-4 | 0 | 0 | 0 |
| 3-5 | 1 | 1.5 | 2 |
| 3-6 | 2 | 3 | 7 |
| 4-7 | 2 | 4 | 9 |
| 5-6 | 1 | 3 | 5 |
| 7-9 | 1 | 2 | 3 |
| 6-9 | 1 | 1 | 5 |
| 6-8 | 2 | 4 | 9 |
| 8-9 | 0 | 0 | 0 |
| 9-10 | 1 | 1 | 1 |

Determine the following:
 (a) Expected activity times
 (b) Earliest event times
 (c) Latest event times
 (d) Activity slack
 (e) Critical path
 (f) Expected project duration and variance

15. The Nevada Highway Department has developed the following PERT network and activity time estimates for a highway construction project.

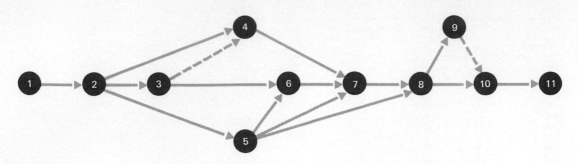

| Activity | Time Estimates (months) | | |
|---|---|---|---|
| | a | m | b |
| 1-2 | 1 | 3 | 5 |
| 2-4 | 3 | 4 | 5 |
| 2-3 | 4 | 6 | 10 |
| 2-5 | 3 | 5 | 7 |
| 3-4 | 0 | 0 | 0 |
| 3-6 | 2 | 4 | 8 |
| 4-7 | 1 | 2 | 5 |
| 6-7 | 2 | 2 | 2 |
| 5-6 | 1 | 1 | 1 |
| 5-7 | 4 | 7 | 16 |
| 5-8 | 6 | 8 | 16 |
| 7-8 | 1 | 4 | 7 |
| 8-9 | 2 | 3 | 4 |
| 8-10 | 1 | 2 | 3 |
| 9-10 | 0 | 0 | 0 |
| 10-11 | 1 | 1 | 1 |

Determine the following:
(a) Expected activity times
(b) Earliest and latest event times
(c) Activity slack
(d) Critical path
(3) Expected project duration and variance

16. The Stone River Textile Mill has been inspected by OSHA and was found to be in violation of a number of safety regulations. The OSHA inspectors reported that the mill needed to alter some existing machinery to make it safer (i.e., safety guards, etc.); purchase some new machinery to replace older, dangerous machinery; and relocate some machinery to make safer passages and unobstructed entrances and exits. In addition, OSHA gave the mill only 35 weeks to make the changes or be fined $300,000.

The mill determined that the following activities in a PERT network would have to be completed, and then estimated the indicated activity times.

| Activity | Description | Time Estimates (weeks) | | |
|---|---|---|---|---|
| | | a | m | b |
| 1-2 | Order new machinery | 1 | 2 | 3 |
| 1-3 | Plan new physical layout | 2 | 5 | 8 |
| 1-4 | Determine safety changes in existing machinery | 1 | 3 | 5 |
| 2-6 | Equipment receipt | 4 | 10 | 25 |
| 2-5 | Hire new employees | 3 | 7 | 12 |
| 3-7 | Plant alterations | 10 | 15 | 25 |
| 4-8 | Make changes in existing machinery | 5 | 9 | 14 |
| 5-6 | Dummy | 0 | 0 | 0 |
| 6-7 | Dummy | 0 | 0 | 0 |
| 7-8 | Dummy | 0 | 0 | 0 |
| 6-9 | Train new employees | 2 | 3 | 7 |
| 7-9 | Install new machinery | 1 | 4 | 6 |
| 8-9 | Relocate old machinery | 2 | 5 | 10 |
| 9-10 | Employee safety orientation | 2 | 2 | 2 |

Construct the PERT network for this project and determine the following:
(a) Expected activity times
(b) Earliest and latest event times and activity slack
(c) Critical path
(d) Expected project duration and variance
(e) The probability that the mill will be fined $300,000

17. The student center at State University has unexpectedly found out that the famous rock group Thunder and Lightning has had a cancellation and can appear at State. However, the concert will be scheduled for a date only 18 days in the future, therefore, the center must prepare quickly. The center has determined the following activities of a PERT network and estimated the activity times.

| Activity | Description | Time Estimates (days) | | |
|---|---|---|---|---|
| | | a | m | b |
| 1-2 | Secure auditorium | 2 | 4 | 7 |
| 1-3 | Hire preliminary concert act | 4 | 5 | 8 |
| 2-3 | Print tickets | 1 | 2 | 4 |
| 2-4 | Local hotel and transportation arrangements | 3 | 5 | 10 |
| 2-5 | Employee union negotiations | 1 | 3 | 8 |
| 5-6 | Hire stagehands | 2 | 4 | 7 |
| 5-7 | Hire ushers | 1 | 3 | 5 |
| 4-9 | Arrange press conference | 2 | 3 | 4 |
| 6-9 | Set up stage | 2 | 3 | 6 |
| 7-9 | Assign ushers | 1 | 2 | 3 |
| 3-9 | Advertising and promotion | 2 | 6 | 12 |
| 3-8 | Sell tickets | 1 | 5 | 12 |
| 8-9 | Dummy | 0 | 0 | 0 |

Construct a PERT network and determine the following:
(a) Expected activity times
(b) Earliest and latest event times
(c) Critical path
(d) Expected project duration and variance
(e) The probability that the concert preparations will be completed in time

18. On May 21, 1927, Charles Lindbergh landed at LeBourget Field in Paris, completing his famous transatlantic solo flight. However, the preparation period prior to his flight was quite hectic and time was very critical, since several other famous pilots of the day were also planning a transatlantic flight. Once Ryan Aircraft was contacted to build the *Spirit of St. Louis,* it took only a little over 2½ months to construct the plane and fly it to New York for the takeoff. If CPM/PERT had been available to Charles Lindbergh, it no doubt would have been useful in helping him plan this project. Therefore, let us use our imagination and assume that a CPM/PERT network was developed for the flight with the estimated activity times as follows.

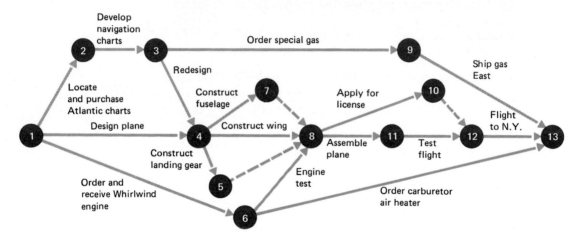

| Activity | Time Estimates (days) | | |
|---|---|---|---|
| | a | m | b |
| 1-2 | 1 | 3 | 5 |
| 1-4 | 4 | 6 | 10 |
| 1-6 | 20 | 35 | 50 |
| 2-3 | 4 | 7 | 12 |
| 3-4 | 2 | 3 | 5 |
| 4-7 | 8 | 12 | 25 |
| 4-8 | 10 | 16 | 21 |
| 4-5 | 5 | 9 | 15 |
| 3-9 | 6 | 8 | 14 |
| 6-8 | 1 | 2 | 2 |
| 6-13 | 5 | 8 | 12 |
| 8-10 | 5 | 10 | 15 |
| 8-11 | 4 | 7 | 10 |
| 9-13 | 5 | 7 | 12 |
| 11-12 | 5 | 9 | 20 |
| 12-13 | 1 | 3 | 7 |

Determine the expected project duration and variance and the probability of completing the project in 67 days.

19. For the PERT network in problem 13, determine the probability that the network duration will exceed 50 months.

20. In the Third Battle of Bull Run for which a PERT network was developed in problem 14, if preparations would have been ready in 15 days, General Beauregard would have won. What would have been the probability of General Beauregard winning the battle?

# 21
Dynamic
Programming

In chapter 19, "Network Flow Models," we analyzed networks in *stages* in order to determine the shortest route through the network. That is, we determined the shortest route (from several routes) up to a particular node, then determined the shortest route from this node to another node, and so on, until we reached the last node in the network. This process of analyzing a network in sequential stages instead of all at once is a potentially useful solution approach that can be applied to topics other than networks. Dynamic programming is a solution approach that encompasses the principle of solving problems in *stages*.

*A solution approach rather than a specific technique*

Dynamic programming is a rather unique approach that you will find to be quite different from the other techniques presented in this text. One difference is that dynamic programming is a solution *approach* and not a technique (such as the simplex method in linear programming). In fact, dynamic programming will often use other techniques within its overall solution approach. However, because it is an approach and not a technique, it is not limited to certain classes of problems as a technique often is. As such, dynamic programming is applicable to a wide variety of problems. In this chapter we will present the basic fundamentals of the dynamic programming solution approach through several popular examples of dynamic programming.

## The Dynamic Programming Solution Approach

*Breaking down a problem into stages*

The solution approach encompassed by dynamic programming is to break down a problem into smaller subproblems called *stages,* and then solve these stages sequentially. The outcome of a decision (i.e., the solution) at one stage will affect the decision made at the next stage in the sequence. However, this process is very difficult to visualize from a written description, therefore, we will demonstrate the dynamic programming solution approach within the context of an example problem.

*A dynamic programming example*

The Wood Valley Cosmetics Company has subdivided its sales area into three regions—north, east, and south. The company has 3 salespeople it wants to allocate to these 3 regions. However, the company wants to allocate the salespeople in a manner that will result in the maximum dollar sales. In order to achieve this objective in the most efficient manner, the company will not restrict the number of salespeople that can be assigned to any one region. In the extreme case, all 3 salespeople could be assigned to any one region.

The sales returns that will be generated in each region from each possible combination of salespeople are shown in table 21.1.

**Table 21.1** Sales Return for Combinations of Salespeople Per Region

| Decision Alternatives Salespeople / Territory | Return for Each Territory ($1,000s) | | |
|---|---|---|---|
| | North | East | South |
| 0 | $ 0 | $ 0 | $ 2 |
| 1 | 7 | 9 | 6 |
| 2 | 12 | 15 | 10 |
| 3 | 20 | 18 | 16 |

Interpreting table 21.1, there will be no sales in the north and east regions if no salespeople are assigned to these regions. However, in the southern region $2,000 in sales will result without any salespeople from direct customer-to-company orders. If all 3 salespeople are assigned to the eastern region, sales of $18,000 will occur. Alternatively, if all 3 salespeople are allocated to the southern region, $16,000 in sales will result. An allocation of 2 salespeople to the northern region and 1 salesperson to the southern region will result in sales of $18,000.

*A mathematical model of the problem*

The objective of this problem is to maximize total sales subject to the limited number of salespeople available to allocate to the three regions. We can express this problem statement mathematically as

maximize $R_1 + R_2 + R_3$
subject to
$D_1 + D_2 + D_3 \leq 3$

where

$R_1, R_2,$ and $R_3 =$ the *returns* (i.e., sales) from each of the 3 regions
$D_1, D_2,$ and $D_3 =$ the *decision* to assign a number of salespeople to each of the 3 regions

As we noted at the beginning of this section, the dynamic programming solution approach is to subdivide a problem into smaller subproblems called *stages*. The stages of our example problem correspond to the 3 regions that we can allocate salespeople to. We will solve for the best solutions at each stage (i.e., region), which will, in turn, be used as an input into the next stage of the problem.

### Stage 1—Allocation to the Southern Region

*The final decision of a sequence of decisions*

We will *arbitrarily* select the southern region as the *first stage* of our problem. The decision at the first stage is how many salespeople to allocate to this region. In dynamic programming we assume that the stage 1 decision is actually the final decision of a sequence of decisions. Therefore, if we consider the other 2 regions to also be stages, then the decision at stage 1 is based on how many salespeople *might have already been allocated to the other 2 regions*. That is, there may be either 0, 1, 2, or 3 salespeople available to allocate to the southern region, depending on how many might have been allocated previously to the other 2 regions. The possible stage 1 allocations are shown in table 21.1.

**Table 21.2** Stage 1 (Southern Region): Decision Alternatives for Each State

| State 1 ($S_1$): Salespeople Available | Decision 1 ($D_1$): Salespeople to Allocate | Return 1 ($R_1$): Amount of Sales |
|---|---|---|
| 0 | 0 | $ 2 |
| 1 | 0 | 2 |
|   | 1 | 6 |
| 2 | 0 | 2 |
|   | 1 | 6 |
|   | 2 | 10 |
| 3 | 0 | 2 |
|   | 1 | 6 |
|   | 2 | 10 |
|   | 3 | 16 |

Observing table 21.2, if no (zero) salespeople are available (which means all 3 salespeople have been allocated to the other two regions), then the *decision* at stage 1 is to allocate zero salespeople to the southern region. This will result in a return of $2,000. If 1 salesperson is available then either 0 or 1 salesperson can be allocated with corresponding returns of $2,000 or $6,000. If 2 salespeople are available, then 0, 1, or 2 salespeople can be allocated to the southern region, and if 3 salespeople are available, 0, 1, 2, or 3 salespeople can be allocated.

*The possible decisions at stage 1*

Notice in table 21.2 the use of symbolic notation that is common to dynamic programming: $S_1$, $D_1$, and $R_1$. $S_1$ represents the *state of the system* at stage 1. The states of the system for this problem are the number of salespeople available to allocate to each region. As can be seen from table 21.2, a stage contains several possible state values. $D_1$ represents the decision at stage 1, while $R_1$ is the return at stage 1 for each decision.

*System state at each stage*

The next step in the dynamic programming solution approach is to determine the *best decision for each possible state*. The best decision at each state is the one that results in the *greatest return*. The best decisions in terms of the number of salespeople to allocate given each state (salespeople available) for stage 1 are shown in table 21.3

*The best decision for each possible state*

**Table 21.3** Stage 1: Optimal Decisions for Each State

| State 1 ($S_1$): Salespeople Available | Decision 1 ($D_1$): Salespeople to Allocate | Return 1 ($R_1$): Amount of Sales |
|---|---|---|
| 0 | 0 | $ 2* |
| 1 | 0 | 2 |
|   | 1 | 6* |
| 2 | 0 | 2 |
|   | 1 | 6 |
|   | 2 | 10* |
| 3 | 0 | 2 |
|   | 1 | 6 |
|   | 2 | 10 |
|   | 3 | 16* |

In table 21.3, the best decision for each state and the return are shaded and designated by an asterisk(*). There is only one possible decision if no salespeople are available, therefore it must be the best decision. If 1 salesperson is available, then the best decision is to allocate 1 salesperson to the southern region, while if 2 or 3 salespeople are available, 2 or 3 should be allocated respectively. *These decisions for the various states at stage 1 will subsequently be used as input for the next set of decisions at stage 2.*

*Stage 1 decisions will be used as inputs to determine stage 2 decisions*

## Stage 2—Allocation to the Eastern Region

Now that the best decisions for stage 1 have been determined, we move to stage 2 in the solution approach, which we will arbitrarily designate as the allocation of salespeople to the eastern region.

The stage 2 decision choices and states are basically the same as those in stage 1. However, the best decision for each state is not determined in the same way. The states and decisions for stage 2 are shown in table 21.4.

**Table 21.4** Stage 2 (Eastern Region): Decision Alternatives for Each State

| State 2 ($S_2$): Salespeople Available | Decision 2 ($D_2$): Salespeople to Allocate | Return 2 ($R_2$): Amount of Sales | State 1 ($S_1$): Salespeople Available at Stage 1 | Return ($R_1$) for Best State 1 Decision | Total Return: $R_1 + R_2$ |
|---|---|---|---|---|---|
| 0 | 0 | $ 0 | 0 | $ 2 | $ 2 |
| 1 | 0 | 0 | 1 | 6 | 6 |
|   | 1 | 9 | 0 | 2 | 11 |
| 2 | 0 | 0 | 2 | 10 | 10 |
|   | 1 | 9 | 1 | 6 | 15 |
|   | 2 | 15 | 0 | 2 | 17 |
| 3 | 0 | 0 | 3 | 16 | 16 |
|   | 1 | 9 | 2 | 10 | 19 |
|   | 2 | 15 | 1 | 6 | 21 |
|   | 3 | 18 | 0 | 2 | 20 |

The states $(S_2)$ for stage 2 are the same as those for stage 1. In other words, we will assume that *depending on what might occur at stage 3* (the northern region) either 0, 1, 2, or 3 salespeople can be allocated to the eastern region. Given the possible states for stage 2, the decision alternatives at each state are also the same as in stage 1. For example, if there are 2 salespeople available to be allocated in the eastern region (i.e., 2 left over not previously allocated), then *either 0, 1, or 2 can be allocated.* The returns (labeled $R_2$) for each of these possible decisions are $0, $9,000, and $15,000 (from table 21.1). This summarizes the items in the first three columns of table 21.4.

The next (fourth) column in table 21.4 reflects the number of salespeople remaining to be allocated (at stage 1) *given the allocation at this stage (2).* For example, if 0 salespeople are available at stage 2, then this would leave 0 salespeople available to be allocated at stage 1 (as shown in column 4). If 1 salesperson is available at stage 2 and 0 salespeople are allocated at stage 2, then *this leaves 1 salesperson available to be allocated at stage 1.* Alternatively, if the 1 salesperson available at stage 2 is allocated at stage 2, this leaves 0 salespeople available at stage 1. Thus, we can see that the salespeople available at stage 1 is a function of both *the salespeople available at stage 2 and the decision at stage 2.*

This relationship between the stages of a problem is referred to as a *transition function.* The transition function defines how the stages of a dynamic programming model are interrelated. Given a stage, $n$, the functional relationship between the states in this stage and the previous stage states can be expressed mathematically as

$$S_{n-1} = S_n - D_n$$

where (you will recall) $S_n$ and $D_n$ are the state and decision, respectively, at stage $n$.

For example, if the state at stage 2 $(S_2)$ equals 3 available salespeople *and* the decision is to allocate 2 salespeople, then the remaining state at stage 1 is determined as

$$S_{n-1} = S_n - D_n$$
$$S_1 = S_2 - D_2$$
$$S_1 = 3 - 2$$
$$S_1 = 1 \text{ salesperson}$$

This result can be seen in table 21.4. For $S_2 = 3$ (the available salespeople), if 2 are allocated, then only 1 salesperson is available to be allocated at stage 1.

The fifth column in table 21.4 shows the return for *the best decision* given a state at stage 1 $(S_1)$. This requires that we observe both stages simultaneously. For example, we saw above that if 3 salespeople are available at stage 2, a decision to allocate 2 salespeople will result in 1 salesperson available at stage 1. Looking at table 21.3 (stage 1), the best decision *given 1 salesperson* $(S_1 = 1)$ is to allocate 1 salesperson, which results in a return of $6,000.

Now we must add this $6,000 to the return at stage 2 of $15,000, which will result in a total return of $21,000 for this combination of decisions—the allocation of 2 salespeople to the eastern region and 1 salesperson to the southern region. This value is shown in the last column of table 21.4. This total accumulated return is referred to as the *recursive return*. The recursive return function is the return at stage $n$ plus the previous summed returns for a decision. Mathematically it is expressed as

$$\text{Total Recursive Return} = R_n + R_{n-1} + R_{n-2} + \ldots + R_1$$

Next we select the decision that results in the *best total return* for each state at stage 2. These four best decisions are shaded and marked by an asterisk in table 21.5.

**Table 21.5** Stage 2: Optimal Decision for Each State

| State 2 ($S_2$): Salespeople Available | Decision 2 ($D_2$): Salespeople to Allocate | Return 2 ($R_2$): Amount of Sales | State 1 ($S_1$): Salespeople Available at Stage 1 | Return ($R_1$) for Best State 1 Decision | Total Return: $R_1 + R_2$ |
|---|---|---|---|---|---|
| 0 | 0 | $ 0 | 0 | $ 2 | $ 2* |
| 1 | 0 | 0 | 1 | 6 | 6 |
|  | 1 | 9 | 0 | 2 | 11* |
| 2 | 0 | 0 | 2 | 10 | 10 |
|  | 1 | 9 | 1 | 6 | 15 |
|  | 2 | 15 | 0 | 2 | 17* |
| 3 | 0 | 0 | 3 | 16 | 16 |
|  | 1 | 9 | 2 | 10 | 19 |
|  | 2 | 15 | 1 | 6 | 21* |
|  | 3 | 18 | 0 | 2 | 20 |

The optimal decisions for each state at both stage 2 and stage 1 have now been determined. This is referred to as *stage optimization*.

## Stage 3—Allocation to the Northern Region

We now have only one remaining stage (3) to consider—the allocation of salespeople to the northern region. Stage 3 actually reflects the first decision regarding the allocation of salespeople that will be made. In other words, at stage 3 we assume that all 3 salespeople are available to be allocated. This is shown in table 21.6.

Notice in table 21.6 that we are assuming that all 3 salespeople are available for allocation. The decision is how many of these three salespeople to allocate to this region. The returns ($R_3$) for each of the possible decisions ($D_3$) are from table 21.1. The states for stage 2 ($S_2$) are determined from the transition function between 2 and 3.

$$S_2 = S_3 - D_3$$

**Table 21.6** Stage 3 (Northern Region): Decision Alternatives for Each State

| State 3 ($S_3$):Salespeople Available | Decision 3 ($D_3$): Salespeople to Allocate | Return 3 ($R_3$): Amount of Sales | State 2 ($S_2$): Salespeople Available at Stage 2 | Return ($R_1 + R_2$) for Best State 2 Decision | Total Return: ($R_1 + R_2$) + $R_3$ |
|---|---|---|---|---|---|
| 3 | 0 | $ 0 | 3 | $21 | $21 |
|   | 1 | 7 | 2 | 17 | 24 |
|   | 2 | 12 | 1 | 11 | 23 |
|   | 3 | 20 | 0 | 2 | 22 |

For example, since $S_3 = 3$, if we allocate one salesperson ($D_3 = 1$), then $S_2$ equals 2 salespeople as shown in the fourth column of table 21.6. The optimal return for each one of these states is selected from table 21.5. If 2 salespeople are available at stage 2 (which means 1 salesperson is allocated at stage 3), the best decision is to allocate 2 with a return of $17,000. This amount, added to the stage 3 return of $7,000, results in a recursive return value of $24,000. All four decisions and their recursive returns are determined similarly at stage 3, as shown in table 21.6.

The optimal decision at stage 3 is the one that results in the maximum total recursive return. Since the maximum total return is $24,000, the best decision is to allocate 1 salesperson to the northern region, as shown in table 21.7.

*The optimal stage 3 decision*

**Table 21.7** Stage 3: Optimal Decision for State 3

| State 3 ($S_3$): Salespeople Available | Decision 3 ($D_3$): Salespeople to Allocate | Return 3 ($R_3$): Amount of Sales | State 2 ($S_2$): Salespeople Available at Stage 2 | Return 2 ($R_1 + R_2$) for Best State 2 Decision | Total Return: ($R_1 + R_2$) + $R_3$ |
|---|---|---|---|---|---|
| 3 | 0 | $ 0 | 3 | $21 | $21 |
|   | 1 | 7 | 2 | 17 | 24* |
|   | 2 | 12 | 1 | 11 | 23 |
|   | 3 | 20 | 0 | 2 | 22 |

The optimal decision to allocate 1 salesperson to the northern region (stage 3) corresponds to a stage 2 decision to allocate 2 salespeople to the eastern region. Now returning to table 21.5, we see that if 2 salespeople are available at stage 2 ($S_2 = 2$) and 2 salespeople are allocated (the optimal decision for this state), then 0 salespeople are allocated to the southern region. Summarizing this decision sequence:

*The sequence of optimal decisions*

*Summarizing the decision sequence*

| Stage (region) | Allocation of Salespeople | Return (sales) |
|---|---|---|
| 1. South | 0 | $2,000 |
| 2. East | 2 | $15,000 |
| 3. North | 1 | 7,000 |
| Totals | 3 Salespeople | $24,000 Sales |

The steps of the sequential decision process of this dynamic programming problem are illustrated in figure 21.1. The nodes at each stage in figure 21.1 correspond to the possible decisions at each stage. Notice that at stage 1 in figure 21.1 there are 10 nodes reflecting the 10 possible decisions shown in table 21.2. As such, it is beneficial to analyze figure 21.1 in conjunction with the tables representing each of the three stages of our problem

---

**Figure 21.1** Decision network and optimal allocation for salesperson allocation example.

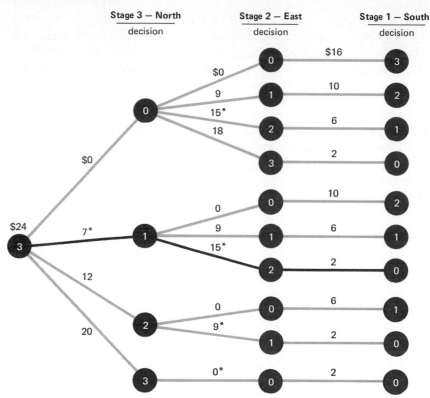

This completes our analysis of the dynamic programming solution approach within the context of our example problem of allocating salespeople to sales regions. However, these solution steps are generally the same for all dynamic programming problems. As such, we will review the steps of the dynamic programming solution approach in general terms.

# Review of the Solution Steps
# for Dynamic Programming

The main principle encompassed by dynamic programming is the subdivision of a problem into smaller subproblems referred to as *stages*. In effect, the subdivision of a problem into stages transforms a decision into a sequential process. This concept is illustrated abstractly (for a three-stage problem like our example) in figure 21.2.

*Stages transform a decision into a sequential process*

**Figure 21.2** Subdivision of a problem into sequential stages.

The diagram in figure 21.2 illustrates the interrelationship between each stage with the arrows reflecting information flowing from left to right, from one stage to the next. However, the stages are numbered oppositely from right to left. This coincides with the solution sequence in which stage 1 solutions are considered first, then stage 2, and so on. We consider stages in reverse order because it enables us to observe the *last decision* (i.e., stage 1) in terms of all possible outcomes.

*Information flows from left to right*

At each stage *states* are identified. Often dynamic programming (like linear programming) is concerned with the allocation of scarce resources. As such, the *states* at a stage are often the different resource levels available at that stage. For example, in our problem of allocating salespeople to regions, the states were the possible number of salespeople (i.e., the resource) available at that stage.

*States as resource levels*

Given each state, a number of *decisions* are possible, each of which results in a *return*. The stage, decision, and return are all illustrated in figure 21.3.

*Decision returns*

**Figure 21.3** The stage decision process.

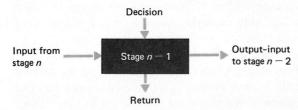

For each state, the best decision is determined as the one that results in the greatest return. These states and decisions are then related to the next stage in the solution process with a *transition function*. Figure 21.4 illustrates how the transition function connects the three stages of our example problem.

**Figure 21.4** The transition between problem stages.

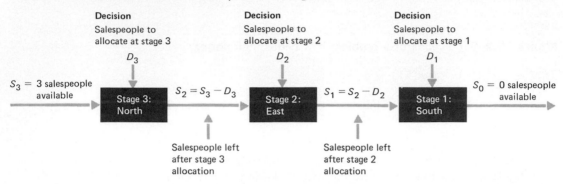

For example, if at stage 2 one of the states is the availability of 2 salespeople and we make a decision to allocate 1 salesperson at stage 2, then we can allocate either 0 or 1 salesperson at stage 1. The decision we make at stage 2 is based on the total return resulting from our decision at stage 2 and the best corresponding decision (either 0 or 1 salesperson) at stage 1. In other words, we make the *best combination* of decisions for the two stages. The total return is determined by using a *recursive return function* that computes the return from a *sequence of optimal decisions*.

At the last stage of our problem all resources are considered to be available. That is, we are theoretically on the threshold of making our sequence of decisions and all the resources are available to us. As such, there is typically only one state at this final level of resources—the maximum level.

Since we have already determined the returns that can be obtained for *all* combinations of decisions up to (but not including) the final stage, we can determine the return for a sequence of decisions given any decision at the final stage. This is accomplished by computing the recursive return from the decision at the final stage and the *previous best decisions* from the states, which will result from this decision at the final stage.

For our example problem, we had all 3 salespeople available to us to allocate at stage 3, the final stage. Any number of salespeople we decided to allocate at stage 3 would leave a number of salespeople available to be allocated in the other regions. If we allocate 2 salespeople at stage 3, we have 1 salesperson left to allocate in the other two stages. The number of salespeople we actually do allocate at stage 3 is determined by the return from the sequence of best decisions that the decision at stage 3 triggers.

We have now presented the dynamic programming solution approach within the context of an example problem and in general terms. Next we will apply dynamic programming to two traditional examples: the *knapsack problem* and the *stagecoach problem*.

## The Knapsack Problem

The *knapsack problem* is a traditional example of dynamic programming that is concerned with how many of each of several different kinds of items to put in a knapsack in order to maximize the return from the items. The knapsack typically has some capacity in terms of weight or size. The general framework of the knapsack problem is applicable to a variety of different types of allocation problems. *An allocation problem*

In order to demonstrate the dynamic programming solution approach to the knapsack problem, we will use the following example. Russian travelers who visit the United States and Europe on a frequent basis (such as athletes, musicians, and dancers) are allowed to return with a limited number of consumer items not generally available in Russia. The items are carried into Russia in a duffel bag, the weight of which cannot exceed 5 pounds (i.e., the total weight of the items cannot exceed 5 pounds). Once the traveler is inside Russia, the items are sold on the black market at a highly inflated price. *A knapsack example*

The three most popular items in Russia (and that are not considered security risks by the police) are denim jeans, radio/tape cassette players, and tape cassette sets of a popular rock group. The black market profit (in American dollars) and weight of each of these items is shown in table 21.8.

**Table 21.8** Black Market Items

| Item | Weight (lbs.) | Profit ($) |
|---|---|---|
| 1. Denim Jeans | 2 | $90 |
| 2. Radio/Tape Players | 3 | 150 |
| 3. Tape Cassette Sets | 1 | 30 |

The objective of the traveler is to determine the combination of items to put in the duffel bag that will maximize the total return from selling them on the black market, but not exceed the capacity limit of 5 pounds. (Failure to obey the 5-pound limit will result in revocation of the travel permit.) We can express this problem statement mathematically, as follows. *The objective of the traveler*

*A mathematical model of the problem*

maximize $R_1D_1 + R_2D_2 + R_3D_3$
subject to
$$W_1D_1 + W_2D_2 + W_3D_3 \leq 5 \text{ pounds}$$
where,

$R_1$, $R_2$, and $R_3$ = the *return* (profit) from each item
$D_1$, $D_2$, and $D_3$ = the *decision* to include a number of each item
$W_1$, $W_2$, and $W_3$ = the *weight* of each item

The first step in the dynamic programming solution approach is to divide the problem into stages. This problem can conveniently be divided into three stages representing the three consumer items to put into the duffel bag.

## Stage 1—Denim Jeans

*States of the problem*   We will arbitrarily select the number of pairs of denim jeans to include in the duffel bag as stage 1. At stage 1 there are 5 states corresponding to the number of pounds that might be available at this stage. As such the states go from 0 to 5 pounds, as shown in table 21.9. Notice that state 1 ($S_1$) consists only of integer weights (i.e., 0, 1, 2, 3, 4, and 5 pounds). Since the consumer items only have integer weights (i.e., 2, 3, and 1 pound) regardless of which or how many items are selected at stages 2 and 3, the remaining weight available at stage 1 must also be an integer.

**Table 21.9** Stage 1 (Denim Jeans): Decision Alternatives

| State 1 ($S_1$): Available weight | Decision 1 ($D_1$): Number of Items | Weight (lbs.) of Items | Return ($R_1$) |
|---|---|---|---|
| 5 | 2 | 4 | $180 |
| 4 | 2 | 4 | 180 |
| 3 | 1 | 2 | 90 |
| 2 | 1 | 2 | 90 |
| 1 | 0 | 0 | 0 |
| 0 | 0 | 0 | 0 |

Interpreting table 21.9, the first column represents the possible values that $S_1$ can assume. After making decisions regarding the number of the other types of items to pack, we will have either 0, 1, 2, 3, 4, or 5 pounds available for denim jeans. The actual decision ($D_1$) is constrained by the weight limitation.

For example, if $S_1$ = 5 pounds (i.e., 5 pounds are available), then we can only pack 2 pairs of jeans, which would result in 4 pounds of weight. One more pair of jeans would result in 6 pounds, which would exceed the 5-pound limit, as shown by the third column in table 21.9. The return ($R_1$) for each decision (i.e., quantity of jeans to pack) is given in the last column. For example, 2 pairs of jeans will result in a profit of $180.

*Only optimal decisions are considered at stage 1*   We have also simplified our stage 1 decision model (table 21.9) by excluding some of the possible decisions. Since we will eventually consider only the optimal decisions at stage 1, all other nonoptimal decisions have been deleted. For example, if $S_1 = 5$ pounds, then there actually would be 3 possible decisions; pack 0, 1, or 2 pairs of jeans. However, since we want to maximize the return, we would obviously pack the greatest number of items possible (2 pairs). In other words, the optimal decisions at this stage are all the maximum number of items possible. *Thus, only the optimal decision for each state 1 value is contained in table 21.9.* (This could have also been done in our salesperson allocation problem, however, we were more detailed for explanatory purposes.)

## Stage 2—Radio/Tape Cassette Players

The number of radio/tape players is arbitrarily selected as stage 2. The possible states, decisions, and returns for this stage are contained in the first four columns of table 21.10.

**Table 21.10** Stage 2 (Radio/Tape Players): Decision Alternatives

| State 2 $(S_2)$: Available Weight | Decision 2 $(D_2)$: Number of Items | Weight (lbs.) of Items | Return $(R_2)$ | State 1 $(S_1)$: Available Weight at Stage 1 | Best State 1 Decision | Return $(R_1)$ for Best State 1 Decision | Total Return: $R_1 + R_2$ |
|---|---|---|---|---|---|---|---|
| 5 | 1 | 3 | $150 | 2 | 1 | $ 90 | $240* |
|   | 0 | 0 | 0 | 5 | 2 | 180 | 180 |
| 4 | 1 | 3 | 150 | 1 | 0 | 0 | 150 |
|   | 0 | 0 | 0 | 4 | 2 | 180 | 180* |
| 3 | 1 | 3 | 150 | 0 | 0 | 0 | 150* |
|   | 0 | 0 | 0 | 3 | 1 | 90 | 90 |
| 2 | 0 | 0 | 0 | 2 | 1 | 90 | 90* |
| 1 | 0 | 0 | 0 | 1 | 0 | 0 | 0* |
| 0 | 0 | 0 | 0 | 0 | 0 | 0 | 0* |

Notice that in table 21.10 we are considering all possible decisions for each state (as opposed to considering only the optimal decisions at stage 1). This is because the optimal decision for each state 2 value may not be the maximum number of items (i.e., radio/tape players), since the best return will be a function of the decision at this stage *and* the previous stage (1).

The weight available at stage 1 is determined by the transition function between stages 1 and 2.

*The transition function*

$$S_1 = S_2 - D_2 W_2$$

For example, if $S_2 = 4$ pounds, and $D_2 = 1$ radio/tape player, then $W_2$ automatically equals 3 pounds, and

$$S_1 = 4 - (1)(3)$$
$$= 1 \text{ pound}$$

which is the amount shown in the $S_1$ column for this decision in table 21.10.

The best decision for each of the values in the $S_1$ column is determined from table 21.9. For example, if $S_1 = 1$, then the best decision from table 21.9 is $D_1 = 0$.

*The recursive returns at stage 2*

The recursive returns are computed by summing the returns from the combination of best decisions at stages 1 and 2. For example, if 5 pounds are available at stage 2 ($S_2 = 5$) and 1 radio/tape player is packed, the return is $150. Given the 2 pounds remaining at stage 1 ($S_1 = 2$) the best decision is to pack 1 pair of denim jeans with a return of $90. The total recursive return is the sum of these two returns, $240.

The optimal decision for each state in table 21.10 is shaded and marked by an asterisk.

## Stage 3—Tape Cassette Sets

The number of tape cassette sets is selected as stage 3. The states, decisions, and returns for this stage are shown in table 21.11.

**Table 21.11** Stage 3 (Tape Cassette Sets): Decision Alternatives

| State 3 ($S_3$): Available Weight | Decision 3 ($D_3$): Number of Items | Weight (lbs.) of Items | Return ($R_3$) | State 2 ($S_2$): Available Weight at Stage 2 | Best State 2 Decision | Return ($R_1 + R_2$) for Best State 2 Decision | Total Return: ($R_1 + R_2$) + $R_3$ |
|---|---|---|---|---|---|---|---|
| 5 | 5 | 5 | $150 | 0 | 0 | $ 0 | $150 |
|   | 4 | 4 | 120 | 1 | 0 | 0 | 120 |
|   | 3 | 3 | 90 | 2 | 0 | 90 | 180 |
|   | 2 | 2 | 60 | 3 | 1 | 150 | 210 |
|   | 1 | 1 | 30 | 4 | 1 | 180 | 210 |
|   | 0 | 0 | 0 | 5 | 1 | 240 | 240* |

*The optimal decision at stage 3*

Since stage 3 theoretically represents the first decision that will be made by the Russian traveler, then the total weight of 5 pounds is available. The values in table 21.11 for stage 3 are determined in the same way as our stage 2 values. The optimal decision is to pack 0 tape cassette sets, which will result in all 5 pounds being available at stage 2. The best decision given that $S_2 = 5$ is to pack 1 radio/tape player. This leaves 2 pounds for stage 1 (i.e., $S_1 = 2$), and given this state the best decision (from table 21.9) is to pack 1 pair of denim jeans.

*Summarizing the optimal decision sequence*

Summarizing our solution,

| Item | Decision | Weight | Return |
|---|---|---|---|
| Denim Jeans | 1 | 2 lbs. | $ 90 |
| Radio/Tape Players | 1 | 3 lbs. | $150 |
| Tape Cassette Sets | 0 | 0 | 0 |
|  |  | 5 lbs. | $240 |

# The Stagecoach Problem

The *stagecoach problem* is a network routing problem in which a stage-coach traveler in the nineteenth century wants to determine the shortest route between two cities given that several alternative routes exist. In order to demonstrate the stagecoach problem, we will use an example similar to the one introduced in chapter 19, "Network Flow Models," to demonstrate the *shortest route problem.*

*A network routing problem*

In this example, the Stagecoach Shipping Company transports oranges by truck from Los Angeles to six other cities in the West and Midwest. The routes and travel time (in hours) for each branch are shown in figure 21.5. For our purposes in this chapter, we will assume that the manager of the company wants to determine the shortest route (in terms of travel time) from Los Angeles to St. Louis (i.e., from node 1 to node 7).

*A stagecoach example*

By carefully observing the network of routes in figure 21.5, it can be seen that there is a maximum of 3 legs for each possible journey from nodes 1 to 7. For example, a truck could go from nodes 1 to 2 to 5 to 7, which encompasses three *branches* in the network. As such, we will decompose this problem into three dynamic programming stages representing the legs of the journey.

## Stage 1—The Last Leg of the Journey

The last leg of the journey is selected as stage 1 in the stagecoach problem. Observing figure 21.5, there are two possible branches the truck can take on the last leg. That is, there are two branches that end at node 7. These two branches are 5 ⇒ 7 and 6 ⇒ 7. The *state* at stage 1 is the location of the truck as it is about to take the last leg of the journey. Thus, the two states are nodes 5 and 6, as shown in table 21.12.

*The branches that end at node 7*

**Figure 21.5** Network of travel routes.

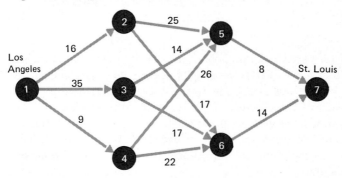

**Table 21.12** Stage 1 (Last Leg): Decision Alternatives

| State 1 ($S_1$):<br>Location of Truck | Decision 1 ($D_1$):<br>Route to Take | Return 1 ($R_1$):<br>Time of Route |
|---|---|---|
| 5 | 5 ⇒ 7 | 8 |
| 6 | 6 ⇒ 7 | 14 |

*State 1*  In table 21.12, the state ($S_1$) represents the two locations the truck could be at as the end of the journey (node 7) approaches. The decision ($D_1$) is the branch to take from the state 1 locations to the ending node. There is only one decision from each state 1 node to node 7 because only one branch exists. As such, each of the two decisions is optimal. The time for each in hours is the return shown in the last column of table 21.12.

## Stage 2—The Second Leg

The second leg of the journey is designated as stage 2. The state 2 nodes are the possible locations of the truck as it approaches our state 1 nodes. Observing figure 21.5, nodes 2, 3, and 4 all connect directly to our state 1 nodes of 5 and 6. Thus, nodes 2, 3, and 4 represent the state 2 locations of the truck, as shown in table 21.13.

**Table 21.13** Stage 2 (Second Leg): Decision Alternatives

| State 2 ($S_2$):<br>Location of Truck | Decision 2 ($D_2$): Route to Take | Return 2 ($R_2$):<br>Time of Route | State 1 ($S_1$):<br>Locations of Truck at Stage 1 | Return 1 ($R_1$) from State 1 Route | Total Return:<br>$R_1 + R_2$ |
|---|---|---|---|---|---|
| 2 | 2 ⇒ 5 | 25 | 5 | 8 | 33 |
|   | 2 ⇒ 6 | 17 | 6 | 14 | 31* |
| 3 | 3 ⇒ 5 | 14 | 5 | 8 | 22* |
|   | 3 ⇒ 6 | 17 | 6 | 14 | 31 |
| 4 | 4 ⇒ 5 | 26 | 5 | 8 | 34* |
|   | 4 ⇒ 6 | 22 | 6 | 14 | 36 |

In table 21.13 if the truck is at node 2, it has two alternative branches it can take: 2 ⇒ 5 or 2 ⇒ 6. The returns of 25 and 17 hours are shown for each. Similarly, if the truck is at node 3 or 4, there are also two possible branches from each of these nodes. If, for example, the truck takes the branch from 2 ⇒ 6, it must go from 6 ⇒ 7 at stage 1. This combination of branches represents the transition function between states 1 and 2. The recursive return is the sum of the times for these two branches: $17 + 14 = 31$ hours.

*The recursive return at stage 2*

The optimal decision (i.e., route) is designated for each state 2 location by an asterisk (and is also shaded).

## Stage 3—The First Leg

The first leg of the journey, designated as stage 3, is shown in table 21.14. The location of the truck is at the start of the journey, which is represented by node 1. Node 1 connects directly (i.e., with one branch) with the three state 2 nodes at stage 2: 2, 3, and 4.

**Table 21.14** Stage 3 (First Leg): Decision Alternatives

| State 3 ($S_3$): Location of Truck | Decision 3 ($D_3$): Route to Take | Return 3 ($R_3$): Time of Route | State 2 ($S_2$): Location of Truck at Stage 2 | Return 2 ($R_1 + R_2$) from State 2 Route | Total Return: ($R_1 + R_2$) + $R_3$ |
|---|---|---|---|---|---|
| 1 | 1 ⇒ 2 | 16 | 2 | 31 | 47 |
|   | 1 ⇒ 3 | 35 | 3 | 22 | 57 |
|   | 1 ⇒ 4 | 9 | 4 | 34 | 43* |

The total recursive return shows that the minimum time of 43 hours is achieved by going from node 1 to node 4. Looking back to table 21.13, the optimal branch from node 4 is to node 5. Next, observing table 21.12, the optimal branch from node 5 is to node 7. Thus, the shortest route is 1 ⇒ 4 ⇒ 5 ⇒ 7 with a minimum time of 43 hours, as shown in figure 21.6. (Notice that the dynamic programming approach used in this example represents an alternative method for solving the shortest route problem as shown in chap. 19.)

*The optimal network route*

**Figure 21.6** The optimal shortest route.

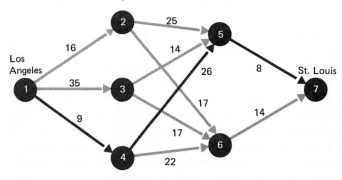

## Applications of Dynamic Programming

The examples we have presented in this chapter to demonstrate the dynamic programming solution approach reflect popular applications of dynamic programming. However, for the most part, these examples were very similar and not very complex. Alternatively, dynamic programming can be applied

*Dynamic programming has been applied to a wide variety of problems*

to a wide variety of complex problems. Dynamic programming has been applied to problems in capital investment analysis, inventory control, job-shop scheduling, plant maintenance, sales planning, energy development, and many other problem areas.

*Problems with more than one state variable*

All three examples in this chapter contained only one *state variable*. That is, the states at each stage represented only one type of item, such as weight, available salespeople, or travel time. Alternatively, dynamic programming can encompass problems with more than one state variable. For example, in our knapsack problem, the consumer items taken into Russia could have been subject to volume as well as weight.

*Probabilistic dynamic programming*

Our examples can also be referred to as *deterministic* dynamic programming problems. The possible outcomes at each stage were deterministic. We could specifically determine the optimal decision for each state at a stage. Alternatively, in some dynamic programming problems, when a decision is made at stage $n$, a probability distribution of states will occur at stage $n-1$.

*Problems in which time increments are the stages*

One of the most popular applications of dynamic programming is to classes of problems in which *time* is one of the essential components. In such problems the time increments are the stages of the dynamic programming model. For example, consider a company that plans to invest in plant expansion over the next five years. During each year several projects compete for limited investment funds. For this problem the stages would be the years, the states are the available funds, and the decisions are the projects to select.

## Summary

Dynamic programming is a very flexible solution technique that can be applied to a wide variety of problems. The example problems presented in this chapter represent only a small sample of the types of problems to which dynamic programming is applicable. However, the solution approach of decomposing problems into smaller subproblems called stages and solving these stages sequentially allows solution of very complex problems that could not be easily solved otherwise. In fact, many of the more complex problems that are encountered in the topic areas covered by other chapters in this text can be solved with dynamic programming.

*Limitations of dynamic programming*

A limitation of dynamic programming is that it is an *approach,* and not a *technique* (such as linear programming). As a result, dynamic programming often requires a great deal of ingenuity, expertise, and insight in developing the model, including the stages, transition function, states, and recursive function. An additional limiting factor is the proliferation of symbolic (mathematical) notation that often accompanies more complex dynamic programming models. A concerted effort was made to avoid a great deal of symbolic notation in this chapter in order that the basic principles of the dynamic solution approach could be more easily understood. However, anyone seeking a more advanced presentation of dynamic programming would confront this often confusing notation. This, in turn, has resulted in the limited application of dynamic programming for solving problems to which it would be very beneficial. In effect, many potential users of dynamic programming are initially "scared off" by the perceived complexity of dynamic programming resulting from this extensive notation.

## References

Bellman, R. *Dynamic Programming*. Princeton, N.J.: Princeton University Press, 1957.

Bellman, R., and Dreyfus, S. E. *Applied Dynamic Programming*. Princeton, N.J.: Princeton University Press, 1962.

Dallenbach, H. G., and George, J. A. *Introduction to Operations Research Techniques*. Boston: Allyn and Bacon, 1978.

Howard, R. A. *Dynamic Programming and Markov Processes*. New York: John Wiley and Sons, 1960.

Lee, Sang M.; Moore, Laurence J.; and Taylor, Bernard W. *Management Science*. Dubuque, Iowa: Wm. C. Brown Company Publishers, 1981.

Loomba, N. P., and Turban, E. *Applied Programming for Management*. New York: Holt, Rinehart and Winston, 1974.

Nemhauser, G. L. *Introduction to Dynamic Programming*. New York: John Wiley and Sons, 1966.

Wagner, H. M. *Principles of Operations Research*. Englewood Cliffs, N.J.: Prentice-Hall, 1969.

## Problems

1. The Barnes and Ewing Pharmaceutical Firm has divided its sales area into two regions: east and west. The company has 3 salespeople it wants to allocate to these 2 regions in a manner that will result in the maximum dollar sales. The company will not restrict the number of salespeople that can be assigned to any one region. The sales returns that will be generated in each region from each possible combination of salespeople are shown in the following table.

| Salespeople per Region | Return per Region ($1,000s) | |
|---|---|---|
| | East | West |
| 0 | $ 0 | $ 1 |
| 1 | 8 | 6 |
| 2 | 20 | 23 |
| 3 | 31 | 36 |

   (a) Express this problem as a mathematical model and explain how it would be solved using the dynamic programming approach.
   (b) Determine the optimal number of salespeople to assign to each region using the dynamic programming approach.

2. The Universal Encyclopedia Company has divided its sales area into 3 regions: East, Midwest, and West. The company has 4 sales representatives, which it desires to allocate to these 3 regions in a manner that will result in the maximum dollar sales. The company will not restrict the number of sales representatives that can be assigned to any one region. The sales returns that will be generated in each region from each possible combination of sales representatives are shown in the following table.

| Sales Representatives per Region | Returns per Region ($1,000s) | | |
|---|---|---|---|
| | East | Midwest | West |
| 0 | $ 0 | $ 0 | $ 0 |
| 1 | 22 | 17 | 25 |
| 2 | 51 | 48 | 45 |
| 3 | 65 | 71 | 58 |
| 4 | 82 | 90 | 75 |

Determine the optimal number of sales representatives to assign to each region in order to maximize the total sales returns.

3. The captain of a whaling ship in the nineteenth century allowed each member of the crew to carry a bag full of items to trade with natives of south sea islands, however, the bag of items could not exceed 5 pounds in weight. One crew member, Ishmael, is going to take mirrors and pocket knives to trade. The profit (in gold) and the weight of each trade item are shown in the following table.

| Item | Weight (lbs.) | Profit($) |
|---|---|---|
| 1. Mirrors | 1 | $20 |
| 2. Knives | 2 | 24 |

Determine the optimal number of each item Ishmael should carry in his bag in order to maximize his total profit using the dynamic programming solution approach.

4. A member of the diplomatic staff for the East German Embassy in Washington, D.C., makes several trips per month to East Berlin to carry classified documents. On each trip the diplomat carries several black market items back to sell for a high profit. In order to not arouse suspicion, the diplomat limits the weight of the items to 7 pounds, so that they can be conveniently hidden in a briefcase. The items that the diplomat smuggles are denim jackets, perfume, and bourbon. The weight and profit of each item are shown in the following table.

| Item | Weight (lbs.) | Profit($) |
|---|---|---|
| 1. Denim Jackets | 3 | $120 |
| 2. Bourbon | 2 | 90 |
| 3. Perfume | 1 | 70 |

Determine the optimal number of each item the diplomat should smuggle in a briefcase in order to maximize profit.

5. A cargo plane is leaving Philadelphia for Spokane. The plane has a (remaining) weight capacity of 5 tons. A company wishes to transport several pieces of heavy machinery on the plane. The weights and values of the 3 types of machinery are given as follows.

| Item | Weight | Value ($1,000s) |
|---|---|---|
| A | 2 tons | $65 |
| B | 3 tons | 80 |
| C | 1 ton | 30 |

Determine how many of each piece of machinery to ship on the cargo plane in order to maximize the value of the shipment.

6. A company has budgeted $5 million for the coming fiscal year to be allocated among its plants in Akron, Baltimore, and Chicago. The $5 million is to be allocated in $1 million block amounts, with a maximum of $4 million going to any one plant. The expected annual return from each level of capital investment at each plant is given as follows.

| Capital Investment ($ millions) | Expected Annual Cash Return ($ millions) | | |
|---|---|---|---|
| | Akron | Baltimore | Chicago |
| 0 | $0 | $ 0 | $ 0 |
| 1 | 2 | 3.5 | 4 |
| 2 | 6 | 5 | 7 |
| 3 | 8 | 7 | 10 |
| 4 | 9 | 9 | 11 |

Using dynamic programming, determine the optimal allocation of capital among the 3 plants.

7. In problem 6, determine the optimal allocation of capital among the 3 plants if only $4 million is available for investment.

8. Illustrate the optimal solution in problem 2 using a decision network as shown in figure 21.1.

9. The Rountown Bus Company has purchased 6 additional buses, which it plans to use on 3 routes. However, the bus line has not decided how many of the new buses to assign to each of the 3 routes. They have developed estimates of additional profit per day that would result for the various routes as follows.

| Number of Buses Assigned | Profit per week ($) | | |
|---|---|---|---|
| | Route A | Route B | Route C |
| 0 | $ 0 | $ 0 | $ 0 |
| 1 | 350 | 100 | 225 |
| 2 | 450 | 250 | 300 |
| 3 | 500 | 450 | 475 |
| 4 | 525 | 650 | 600 |
| 5 | 450 | 700 | 650 |
| 6 | 400 | 750 | 650 |

Use dynamic programming to determine the optimal number of buses to assign to each route.

10. In problem 9, determine the optimal assignment of buses to routes if only 5 buses are available.

11. The police department of a city must determine the optimum allocation of 5 new officers to 4 precincts. The police department has developed estimates of the number of crimes per 8-hour period that can be expected to occur, given the various assignments of officers to precincts.

| Number of Allocated Officers | Crimes per 8-hour Period | | | |
|---|---|---|---|---|
| | North Precinct | South Precinct | East Precinct | West Precinct |
| 0 | 40 | 35 | 32 | 27 |
| 1 | 27 | 31 | 25 | 23 |
| 2 | 18 | 23 | 20 | 19 |
| 3 | 12 | 15 | 17 | 16 |
| 4 | 10 | 10 | 12 | 14 |
| 5 | 8 | 9 | 10 | 12 |

Use dynamic programming to determine the optimal allocation of officers to precincts that will minimize the total number of crimes per 8-hour period.

12. The Pyrotec Company has 4 machines on which it can produce 3 products (A, B, and C). All 4 machines can be set up to produce any of the 3 products. However, when a machine is set up to produce 1 of the 3 products, a production run of 1 week is always used. Each week the company must determine how many machines to schedule for each of the 3 products. The expected return from each product (which is based on a weekly demand forecast) is shown in the following table.

| Machines Scheduled | Forecasted Profit ($) | | |
|---|---|---|---|
| | Product A | Product B | Product C |
| 0 | $ 0 | $ 0 | $ 0 |
| 1 | 1,000 | 1,500 | 500 |
| 2 | 1,900 | 2,500 | 1,600 |
| 3 | 2,700 | 3,200 | 2,800 |
| 4 | 3,400 | 3,500 | 4,000 |

Use dynamic programming to determine the optimal number of machines to schedule for production of each of the 3 products for the coming week.

13. The Reserve Milling Company, a large industrial firm, has plants in Lincoln, Dubuque, and Terre Haute. Recently a competing firm went bankrupt, and Reserve purchased 5 large machines from the sale of equipment by the bank. The company wants to determine the optimal allocation of the new machines to its 3 plants. The expected profit the machines will earn at the plants are shown in the following table.

| Machines Allocated | Profit per Plant ($1,000s) | | |
|---|---|---|---|
| | Lincoln | Dubuque | Terre Haute |
| 0 | $ 0 | $ 0 | $ 0 |
| 1 | 40 | 35 | 50 |
| 2 | 65 | 52 | 60 |
| 3 | 72 | 66 | 70 |
| 4 | 80 | 92 | 80 |
| 5 | 105 | 115 | 90 |

Determine the optimal allocation of machines to plants that will maximize profit using dynamic programming.

14. The Rainwater Brewery ships beer by truck from Indianapolis to Columbus. The possible routes a truck can take and the mileage of each are shown in the following network.

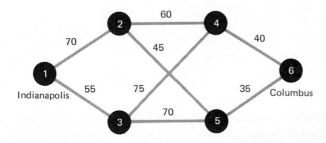

Determine the shortest route from Indianapolis to Columbus using dynamic programming.

15. A traveler during the 1800s wishes to determine the shortest stagecoach route from San Francisco to New York. The traveler would have to travel by 4 different stagecoaches in the overall journey. The different routes and their time in hours from San Francisco to New York are shown in the following network.

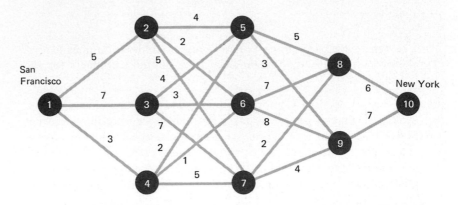

Using dynamic programming determine the optimal route from San Francisco to New York.

16. The Black Diamond Coal Company transports coal from a railyard in Charleston, West Virginia, to the port of Norfolk, Virginia. The following network shows the various rail routes and the time (in hours) between these 2 cities.

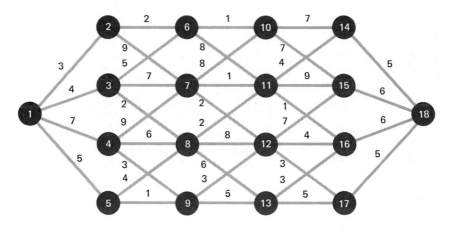

Determine the optimal (shortest) route from Charleston to Norfolk using dynamic programming.

**22**
Break-Even
Analysis

## Components of Break-Even Analysis
Volume
Costs
Profit
The Break-Even Point
Variations in Volume

## Profit Analysis
Price
Variable Costs
Fixed Costs

## Summary

The objective of most business enterprises is to make as much profit as possible (as we have already indicated in previous chapters). The topic of this chapter, break-even analysis, is often referred to as *profit analysis*. The purpose of break-even analysis is to determine the number of units of a product (i.e., volume) to produce that will equate total revenue with total cost. At this point, referred to as the break-even point, profit is zero. As such, the break-even point gives the manager a point of reference in determining how many units will be needed to insure a profit.

*Profit analysis*

*The product volume that equates total revenue and total cost*

Because break-even analysis deals with a topic of direct concern to managers—profit—and because it is a relatively easy form of analysis to learn (as will be seen in this chapter), it is a popular management science technique. However, an additional reason for studying this topic, especially at this point in the text, is that the more complex forms of break-even analysis require solutions using calculus techniques. As such, it provides a useful introduction to classical optimization techniques to be introduced in the next chapter.

## Components of Break-Even Analysis

The three components of break-even analysis are volume, cost, and profit. However, each of these three factors is a function of several other components. As a result, we will analyze each of these components of break-even analysis individually.

### Volume

Volume is the level of production by a company. Volume can be expressed as the *number of units* produced (i.e., quantity), *dollar* volume, or as a *percentage* of total capacity available.

*The level of production*

### Costs

The production of a product typically encompasses two costs: *fixed costs* and *variable costs*. Fixed costs are generally independent of the volume of units produced. That is, fixed costs will remain constant regardless of how

*Fixed costs*

many units of product are produced within a given range. Various individual costs, which taken together result in total fixed costs, include:

Rent on plant and equipment
Taxes
Insurance
Management and staff salaries
Advertising
Interest on investment
Depreciation on plant and equipment
Heat and light
Janitorial services

*Variable costs per unit*

Variable costs are determined on a per unit basis. As such, total variable costs depend on the number of units produced. Examples of variable costs include:

Raw materials and resources
Direct labor
Packaging
Material and product handling
Maintenance
Freight

*Total variable costs*

Total variable costs are a function of the *volume* and the *variable cost per unit*. This relationship can be expressed mathematically as

Total variable cost $= vc_v$
where
$c_v$ = variable cost per unit
$v$ = volume (number of units)

*Total cost*

The total cost of an operation is computed by summing total fixed cost and total variable cost as follows.

Total cost $=$ Total fixed cost $+$ Total variable cost

or,

$TC = c_f + vc_v$
where
$c_f$ = fixed cost

*Computing total cost*

As an example, consider the Western Clothing Company, which produces denim jeans. The company incurs the following monthly costs to produce denim jeans.

Fixed costs $= c_f = \$10,000$
Variable cost $= c_v = \$8$ per pair

If we arbitrarily let the volume, $v$, equal 400 pairs of denim jeans, the total cost is

$$TC = c_f + vc_v$$
$$= \$10,000 + (400)(8)$$
$$= \$13,200$$

Since this equation for total costs as well as fixed costs and variable costs are all linear equations, we can also illustrate these relationships graphically as shown in figure 22.1.

---

**Figure 22.1** Cost relationships for the break-even model.

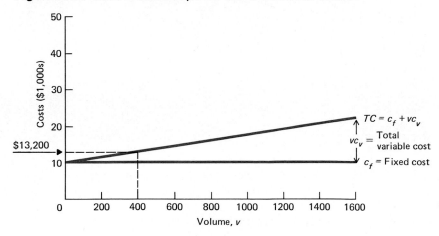

In figure 22.1, the fixed cost, $c_f$, has a constant value of $10,000, regardless of the volume. The total cost line, $TC$, represents the sum of the variable cost and fixed cost. The total cost line increases because variable cost increases as the volume increases. Our example volume of 400 pairs of jeans, which results in $13,200 in total cost, is also designated in figure 22.1.

## Profit

The third component in our break-even model is *profit*. Profit is the difference between *total revenue* and total cost. Total revenue is the volume multiplied by the price per unit.

*Total revenue*

Total revenue = $vp$
where
   $p$ = price per unit

*Computing total revenue*

For our clothing company example, if denim jeans sell for $23 per pair and we sell 400 pair per month, then the total monthly revenue is

$$\begin{aligned} \text{Total revenue} &= vp \\ &= (400)(23) \\ &= \$9,200 \end{aligned}$$

The graph of total revenue for our example is shown in figure 22.2.

**Figure 22.2** Revenue relationship for the break-even model.

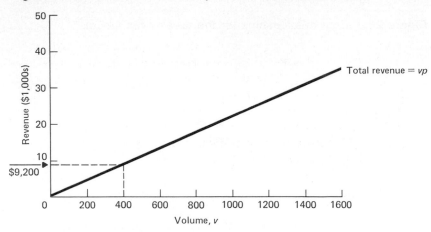

We have already determined total cost to be

$$\text{Total cost} = c_f + c_v$$

*Total profit equals revenue minus cost*

Given that we have now developed relationships for total revenue and total cost, profit ($Z$) can be computed as follows.

$$\begin{aligned} \text{Total profit} &= \text{total revenue} - \text{total cost} \\ Z &= vp - [c_f + vc_v] \\ Z &= vp - c_f - vc_v \end{aligned}$$

## The Break-Even Point

*Computing total profit*

In our clothing company example, we have determined total revenue and total cost to be $9,200 and $13,200, respectively. As such, there is no actual profit, but instead, a loss of $4,000.

$$\begin{aligned} \text{Total profit} &= \text{total revenue} - \text{total cost} \\ &= \$9,200 - 13,200 \\ &= -\$4,000 \end{aligned}$$

We can verify this result by using our total profit formula,

$$Z = vp - c_f - vc_v$$

and the values $v = 400$, $p = \$23$, $c_f = \$10,000$, and $c_v = \$8$.

**Break-Even Analysis**

$$Z = vp - c_f - vc_v$$
$$= (400)(23) - 10,000 - (400)(8)$$
$$= \$9,200 - 10,000 - 3,200$$
$$= -\$4,000$$

Obviously the clothing company does not want to operate with a monthly loss of $4,000, since it would probably eventually result in bankruptcy. If we assume that price is static because of market conditions and that fixed costs and the variable cost per unit are not subject to change, then the only part of our model that can be varied is *volume*. Thus, in order to avoid a loss, *the company must produce more units*. This may not be immediately obvious, since costs increase as well as profit if more items are produced. However, we can observe what occurs from figure 22.3, which is actually a composite graph of figures 22.1 and 22.2.

**Figure 22.3** Break-even model.

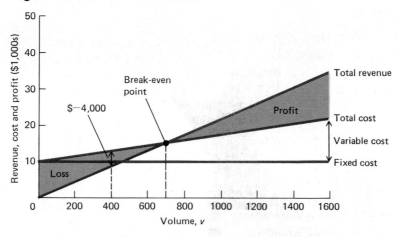

Notice in figure 22.3 that a volume of 400 pairs of denim jeans results in a loss of $4,000. This loss occurs because the total cost line is above the total revenue line at the point representing 400 pairs of jeans. However, as volume is increased, the loss area in figure 22.3 decreases until a point is reached where the 2 lines intersect, which indicates that total revenue equals total cost. The volume, $v$, that corresponds to this point is the *break-even volume*. The break-even volume in figure 22.3 is 666.7 pairs of denim jeans.

We can also determine the break-even volume mathematically (and more conveniently). At the break-even point where total revenue equals total cost, the profit, $Z$, equals zero. Thus, if we let profit, $Z$, equal zero in our total profit equation and solve for $v$, we can determine the break-even volume.

*Computing break-even volume*

$$Z = vp - c_f - vc_v$$
$$0 = v(23) - 10{,}000 - v(8)$$
$$0 = 23v - 10{,}000 - 8v$$
$$15v = 10{,}000$$
$$v = 666.7 \text{ pairs of jeans}$$

In other words, if the company produces 666.7 pairs of jeans, the profit (and loss) will be zero, and the company will *break even*. This gives the company a point of reference from which to determine how many pairs of jeans to produce in order to gain a profit (subject to any capacity limitations). For example, a volume of 800 pairs of denim jeans will result in the following monthly profit.

$$Z = vp - c_f - vc_v$$
$$= \$(800)(23) - 10{,}000 - (800)(8)$$
$$= \$2{,}000$$

*A break-even formula*   In general, the break-even volume can be determined using the following formula.

$$Z = vp - c_f - vc_v$$
$$0 = v(p - c_v) - c_f$$
$$v(p - c_v) = c_f$$
$$v = \frac{c_f}{p - c_v}$$

For our example,

$$v = \frac{c_f}{p - c_v}$$
$$= \frac{10{,}000}{23 - 8}$$
$$= 666.7 \text{ pairs of jeans}$$

## Variations in Volume

When we first introduced the break-even component, volume, we mentioned that it could be expressed in three forms: quantity volume, dollar volume, and volume as a percentage of available capacity. The general break-even formula we have already developed was for *quantity volume*. Now we will alter the general break-even formula to reflect these other two ways of expressing volume.

*Break-even sales volume*   First we will consider volume expressed in terms of dollar sales. This is achieved by multiplying the break-even quantity volume by the price, $p$.

Break-even sales volume $= pv$

Thus, for our example,

$$pv = \$(23)(666.7)$$
$$= \$15,334$$

Next we will consider volume expressed as a percentage of total capacity. This value is determined by dividing the break-even quantity volume by the maximum operating capacity, $k$.

*Break-even volume as a percentage of total capacity*

Break-even volume as a percentage of capacity $= \dfrac{v}{k}$

If in our example the maximum capacity, $k$, equals 1,000 pairs of denim jeans, then the break-even volume as a percentage of total capacity is

$$\frac{v}{k} = \frac{666.7}{1,000}$$
$$= 66.7\%$$

Both of these variations of break-even volume are illustrated in figure 22.4.

**Figure 22.4** Break-even point in terms of sales volume and percentage of capacity.

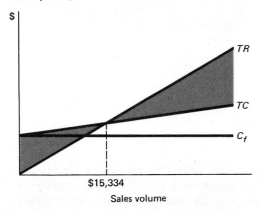
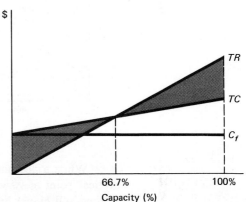

## Profit Analysis

We have now developed a general relationship for determining the break-even volume. This relationship has enabled us to see how the level of profit (and loss) is directly affected by changes in volume. However, when we developed this model, we assumed that both fixed and variable (per unit) costs as well as selling price were constant. All three of these items, though, can affect profit if changed. Thus, we will now observe the effect of these items on our general break-even relationship.

*The effect of parameter changes on profit*

## Price

*The effect of a price increase*

The first item in our break-even relationship we will analyze is price. As an example, we will increase the price for denim jeans from $23 to $30. As expected, this will increase the total revenue, and therefore reduce the break-even point from 666.7 pairs of jeans to 454.5 pairs of jeans.

$$v = \frac{c_f}{p - c_v}$$
$$= \frac{10,000}{30 - 8}$$
$$= 454.5 \text{ pairs of denim jeans}$$

The effect of the price change on break-even volume is illustrated in figure 22.5

**Figure 22.5** Break-even model with a change in price.

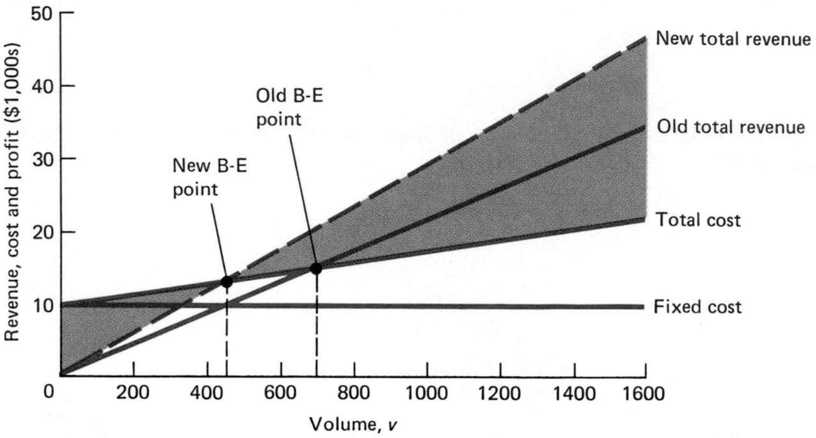

While a decision to increase price looks inviting from a strictly analytical point of view, it must be remembered that the lower break-even volume and higher profit area are *possible,* but not guaranteed. A higher price can also make it more difficult to *sell* the product. As such, a change in price often must be accompanied by corresponding increases in costs, such as advertising or packaging and possibly costs to enhance quality. (However, even such direct changes as these may have little effect on product demand, since price is often sensitive to numerous factors, such as the type of market, monopolistic elements, product differentiation, etc.)

## Variable Costs

*The effect of an increase in variable costs*

In our consideration of an increase in price, we mentioned the possibility of better quality to offset a potential loss of sales due to the price increase. For example, suppose the stitching on the denim jeans was changed to make them more attractive and stronger. This would result in an increase in variable costs of \$4 per pair of jeans, thus raising the variable costs per unit, $c_v$, to \$12 per pair. This change (in conjunction with our previous price change to \$30) results in a new break-even volume.

$$v = \frac{c_f}{p - c_v}$$
$$= \frac{10,000}{30 - 12}$$
$$= 555.5 \text{ pairs of denim jeans}$$

This new break-even volume and the change in the total cost line occurring as a result of the variable cost change are shown in figure 22.6.

**Figure 22.6** Break-even model with a change in variable cost.

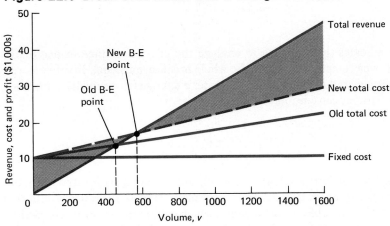

## Fixed Costs

Next we will consider an increase in advertising as an additional expenditure needed to offset the sales lost due to a price increase. An increase in advertising is an addition to fixed costs. For example, if the clothing company increases its monthly advertising budget by \$3,000, then the total fixed cost, $c_f$, becomes \$13,000. The break-even volume using this fixed cost, as well as the increased variable cost per unit of \$12 and the increased price of \$30, is computed as follows.

*The effect of an increase in fixed costs*

$$v = \frac{c_f}{p - c_v}$$
$$= \frac{\$13,000}{30 - 12}$$
$$= 722.2 \text{ pairs of denim jeans}$$

This new break-even volume representing changes in price, fixed costs, and variable costs is illustrated in figure 22.7. Notice that the break-even volume is now higher than the original volume of 666.7 pairs of jeans, as a result of the increased costs necessary to offset the potential loss in sales.

**Figure 22.7** Break-even model with a change in fixed cost.

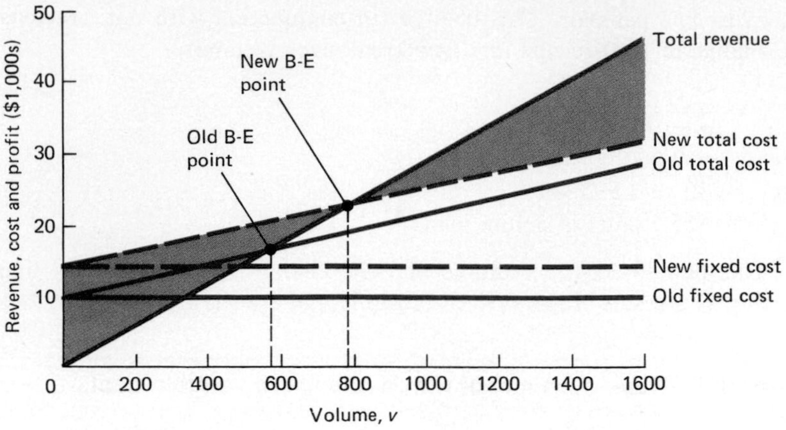

This indicates the necessity to analyze the effect a change in one of the break-even components has on the whole break-even model. In other words, it is not generally appropriate to consider a change in one model component alone without considering the overall effect.

## Summary

Break-even analysis is a very applicable aid to managers for decision making in the short run. It is basically a simple type of analysis using data that is generally available to the manager, which enhances its usefulness. Besides the brief application used in this chapter to demonstrate break-even analysis, it can also be used for product planning (i.e., whether to add a new product or delete an old product, determining the appropriate price for a product, and when to purchase new equipment and operating facilities, among other applications).

*Break-even analysis is used to introduce calculus-based techniques*

As we indicated in the introduction, an additional reason for studying break-even analysis at this point in the text, is that it provides an excellent vehicle for introducing calculus-based solution techniques, the topic of the next chapter. The break-even model in this chapter included only linear relationships. However, break-even analysis can be extended to include nonlinear profit and cost relationships, which requires a calculus solution. As such, we will use the extension of break-even analysis as the introductory material for the next chapter on calculus-based techniques.

# References

Lee, S. M., and Moore, L. J. *Introduction to Decision Science.* New York: Petrocelli/Charter, 1975.

Levin, R. I., and Kirkpatrick, C. A. *Quantitative Approaches to Management.* 3d ed. New York: McGraw-Hill, 1975.

Loomba, N. P. *Management: A Quantitative Perspective.* New York: Macmillan, 1978.

Monks, J. G. *Operations Management: Theory and Problems.* New York: McGraw-Hill, 1977.

# Problems

1. The Willow Furniture Company produces tables. The fixed monthly cost of production is $8,000, while the variable cost per table is $65. The tables sell for $180 apiece. For a monthly volume of 300 tables determine the total cost, total revenue, and profit.

2. The Retread Tire Company recaps tires. The fixed annual cost of the recapping operation is $60,000. The variable cost of recapping a tire is $9. The company charges $25 to recap a tire. For an annual volume of 12,000 tires, determine the total cost, total revenue, and profit.

3. The Rolling Creek Textile Mill produces cotton denim. The fixed monthly cost is $21,000, while the variable cost per yard of denim is $0.45. The mill sells a yard of denim for $1.30. For a monthly volume of 18,000 yards of denim, determine the total cost, total revenue, and profit.

4. Determine the monthly break-even volume for the Willow Furniture Company operation described in problem 1.

5. Determine the annual break-even volume for the Retread Tire Company operation described in problem 2.

6. Determine the monthly break-even volume for the Rolling Creek Textile Mill operations described in problem 3.

7. The Evergreen Fertilizer Company produces fertilizer. The fixed monthly cost is $25,000, while the variable cost per pound of fertilizer is $0.15. The fertilizer sells for $0.40 per pound. Determine the monthly break-even volume for the company.

8. Graphically illustrate the break-even volume for the Retread Tire Company determined in problem 5.

9. Graphically illustrate the break-even volume for the Evergreen Fertilizer Company determined in problem 7.

10. Determine the break-even sales volume for the Willow Furniture Company described in problem 1.

11. Determine the break-even sales volume for the Retread Tire Company described in problem 2.

12. Determine the break-even sales volume for the Evergreen Fertilizer Company described in problem 7.

13. If the maximum operating capacity of the Retread Tire Company described in problem 2 is 8,000 tires annually, determine the break-even volume as a percentage of capacity.

14. If the maximum operating capacity of the Rolling Creek Textile Mill described in problem 3 is 25,000 yards of denim per month, determine the break-even volume as a percentage of capacity.

15. If the maximum operating capacity of the Evergreen Fertilizer Company described in problem 7 is 120,000 pounds of fertilizer per month determine the break-even volume as a percentage of capacity.

16. If the Retread Tire Company changes its price to recap a tire from $25 to $31, what effect will it have on the break-even volume determined in problem 5?

17. If the Evergreen Fertilizer Company changes its price of fertilizer from $0.40 per pound to $0.60 per pound, what effect will it have on the break-even volume determined in problem 7?

18. If Evergreen Fertilizer Company changes its production process to add a weed killer to the fertilizer in order to make it sell better, the variable cost per pound will be increased from $0.15 to $0.22. What effect will this change have on the break-even volume computed in problem 17?

19. If the Evergreen Fertilizer Company increases its advertising expenditures by $14,000 per year, what effect will it have on the break-even volume computed in problem 18?

20. The Pastureland Dairy makes cheese, which it sells at local supermarkets. The fixed monthly cost of production is $4,000, while the variable cost per pound of cheese is $0.21. The cheese sells for $0.75 per pound. The dairy presently produces and sells 9,000 pounds of cheese per month. However, it is considering raising the price of its cheese to $0.95 per pound, which would decrease its sales to 5,700 pounds per month. Should the dairy raise the price?

# 23
## Problem Analysis
## with Calculus

**Differential Calculus**
Profit Analysis
**Inventory Analysis**
**Summary**

The functional relationships (i.e., formulas and equations) we have developed in previous chapters have been predominantly *linear*. These linear functions related a set of variables, some of which were referred to as decision variables. In general, problems were solved in order to determine values for these decision variables. Because these variables were contained in linear relationships, many of the solution techniques that have been presented in this text involved the solution of sets of linear equations.

Alternatively, many realistic management problems consist of one or more *nonlinear relationships*. When nonlinear functions exist in a problem, traditional linear solution methods are no longer applicable. The solution techniques for problems that include nonlinear relationships generally embody the branch of mathematics known as *differential calculus*. In this chapter we will look at some of the types of management problems that require solutions using calculus and demonstrate the general calculus-based solution approach. However, the objectives of this chapter do not encompass the actual teaching of calculus. Rather, it will be assumed that (1) the reader of this chapter is already familiar with the basic fundamentals of calculus or (2) the reader is interested in obtaining a general awareness of the class of problems requiring calculus solutions without desiring to know how to actually solve the problems.

*Nonlinear relationships*

*Differential calculus*

## Differential Calculus

There are two basic forms of calculus: *differential calculus* and *integral calculus*. Differential calculus involves taking the derivative of a mathematical function, while integral calculus encompasses the integration of a mathematical function. In this chapter we will concentrate on differential calculus, although integral calculus is also often used to analyze certain types of management science problems.

The principal concept of differential calculus is that the slope of a curve at any point equals the *derivative of the mathematical function* that defines the curve. An additional mathematical principle is that the slope of a curve at its highest or lowest point equals zero. Combining these two fundamental principles tells us that at the maximum and minimum points of a curve, the *derivative of the curve equals zero*. These fundamentals of calculus are illustrated in figure 23.1.

*The derivative of a function equals the slope of the curve defined by that function*

**Figure 23.1** Determining maximum and minimum points on a curve.

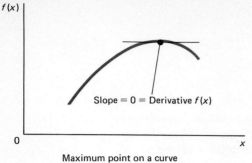

Maximum point on a curve

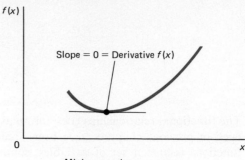

Minimum point on a curve

The relationship that equates the derivative to zero at the maximum or minimum point on a curve is very important for our purposes, since it has been repeatedly demonstrated that the objective of solving management problems is often to *maximize* or *minimize* a function or value. For example, in figure 23.1, if the curve on the left represents profit, then the maximum profit occurs where the slope of the curve equals zero.

*Setting the derivative of a function equal to zero and solving for the variables in the derivative*

The ability to set the derivative of a curve (i.e., a nonlinear mathematical function) equal to zero at the maximum or minimum point of the curve enables us to solve for the variables contained in the derivative. In other words, we can solve for the value of a variable (such as the quantity of a product) that will maximize (or minimize) the value of some mathematical function (such as a profit equation). However, these concepts are relatively difficult to perceive in the abstract and, like other topics in this text, are more easily understood within the context of an example. One of the easiest models to which the principles of differential calculus can be applied is an extension of the general *break-even model* presented in chapter 22. In this extension of the break-even model (known as the profit model) profit is represented by a curve instead of a line.

*The break-even model*

## Profit Analysis

*The total profit equation*

Recall from chapter 22 that in our break-even model total profit was computed as follows.

$$\text{Total profit} = \text{total revenue} - \text{total cost}$$
$$Z = vp - [c_f + vc_v]$$
$$= vp - c_f - vc_v$$

where

$$Z = \text{profit}$$
$$v = \text{volume}$$
$$p = \text{price}$$
$$c_f = \text{fixed cost}$$
$$c_v = \text{variable cost}$$
$$\text{total revenue} = vp$$
$$\text{total cost} = c_f + vc_v$$

Given this formula, if we set profit, $Z$, equal to zero, then we can determine the break-even volume.

*The break-even volume formula*

$$0 = vp - c_f - vc_v$$
$$v = \frac{c_f}{p - c_v}$$

The example we used in the preceding chapter to illustrate the break-even model was for the production of denim jeans by the Western Clothing Company. Each pair of jeans sold for \$23 and had a variable cost ($c_v$) of \$8 per pair. The fixed cost per month was \$10,000. This resulted in a break-even volume of

*Computing the break-even volume*

$$v = \frac{c_f}{p - c_v}$$
$$= \frac{\$10,000}{\$23 - 8}$$
$$= 666.7 \text{ pairs of jeans}$$

However, one important but somewhat unrealistic assumption of the break-even model as constructed above is that demand is independent of price (i.e., *volume remains constant* regardless of the price for the product). A more realistic situation would be for the volume to vary as price increased or decreased. For example, let us suppose that the dependency of volume on price is defined by the following linear function.

*Volume as a function of price*

$$v = 1,500 - 24.6p$$

This linear relationship is illustrated in figure 23.2

**Figure 23.2** Linear relationship of volume to price.

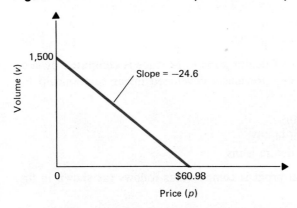

This figure demonstrates the fact that as price increases, volume decreases up to a particular price level (\$60.98) that will result in no sales volume.

Now we will substitute our new relationship for volume ($v$) back into our original profit equation.

$$Z = vp - c_f - vc_v$$
$$= (1{,}500 - 24.6p)p - c_f - (1{,}500 - 24.6p)c_v$$
$$= 1{,}500p - 24.6p^2 - c_f - 1500c_v + 24.6pc_v$$

Substituting the values for fixed cost ($c_f = \$10{,}000$) and variable cost ($c_v = \$8$) into this new profit function results in the following equation.

$$Z = 1{,}500p - 24.6p^2 - 10{,}000 - 1{,}500(8) + 24.6p(8)$$
$$= 1{,}696.8p - 24.6p^2 - 22{,}000$$

This equation for profit is now a nonlinear function that relates profit to price, as shown in figure 23.3.

Observing figure 23.3, the greatest profit will occur at the point where the profit curve is at its highest point. At this point the slope of the curve equals zero, as shown in figure 23.4.

Recall our previous statement that the slope of a curve at any point is equal to the derivative of the mathematical function that defines the curve. The derivative of our profit function is determined as follows (for a review of the rules of differentiation see Appendix D).

$$Z = 1{,}696.8p - 24.6p^2 - 22{,}000$$
$$\frac{\partial Z}{\partial p} = 1{,}696.8 - 49.2p$$

Given this derivative, the slope of the profit curve at its highest point is defined by the following relationship.

$$0 = 1{,}696.8 - 49.2p$$

Now we can solve this relationship for the optimal price, $p$, which will maximize total profit.

$$0 = 1{,}696.8 - 49.2p$$
$$49.2p = 1{,}696.8$$
$$p = 1{,}696.8/49.2$$
$$p = \$34.49$$

The optimal volume of denim jeans to produce is computed by substituting this price into our previously developed linear relationship for volume.

$$v = 1{,}500 - 24.6p$$
$$= 1{,}500 - 24.6(34.49)$$
$$= 651.6 \text{ pair of denim jeans}$$

The maximum total profit is computed as follows (as shown in fig. 23.5).

$$Z = \$1{,}696.8p - 24.6p^2 - 22{,}000$$
$$= \$1{,}696.8(34.49) - 24.6(34.49)^2 - 22{,}000$$
$$= \$7{,}259.45$$

**Problem Analysis with Calculus**

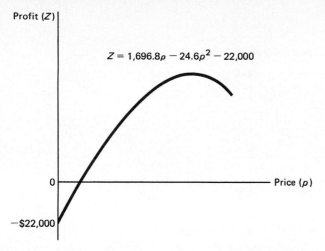

**Figure 23.3** The nonlinear profit function.

Profit ($Z$)

$Z = 1{,}696.8p - 24.6p^2 - 22{,}000$

0 — Price ($p$)

−$22,000

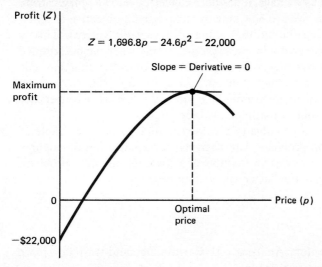

**Figure 23.4** Maximum profit for the profit function.

Profit ($Z$)

$Z = 1{,}696.8p - 24.6p^2 - 22{,}000$

Slope = Derivative = 0

Maximum profit

0 — Price ($p$)

Optimal price

−$22,000

The maximum profit, optimal price, and volume are shown graphically in figure 23.5.

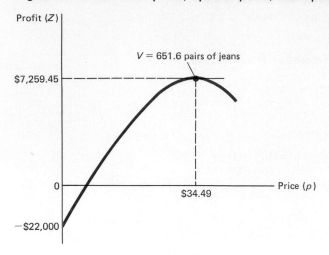

**Figure 23.5** Maximum profit, optimal price, and optimal volume.

An important concept we have yet to mention is that by extending the break-even model as we have, it has been converted into an *optimization* model. In other words, we are now able to maximize an objective function (profit) by determining the optimal value of a variable (price). This is exactly the same thing we did in linear programming when we determined the value of decision variables, which optimized an objective function. For this reason, the use of calculus to find optimal values for variables is often

*Classical optimization*

referred to as *classical optimization*. The term *classical* is used because calculus is one of the oldest mathematical techniques.

*A cost minimization example*

The application of calculus to break-even analysis is an example of a *profit maximization* problem. Alternatively, the application of calculus to *inventory analysis* provides an example of a *cost minimization* problem. As such, we will pursue this latter application next.

## Inventory Analysis

*The EOQ model*

In chapter 17 ("Inventory Analysis with Certain Demand") we developed the following inventory cost model.

$$\text{Total annual inventory cost} = C_c\frac{Q}{2} + C_o\frac{D}{Q}$$

where

$C_c$ = carrying cost per unit
$Q$ = economic order quantity
$C_o$ = cost per order
$D$ = demand

$C_c\dfrac{Q}{2}$ = annual carrying cost

$C_o\dfrac{D}{Q}$ = annual ordering cost

**Problem Analysis with Calculus**

The relationship of ordering cost, carrying cost, and total annual inventory cost is illustrated in figure 23.6.

**Figure 23.6** Optimal order quantity.

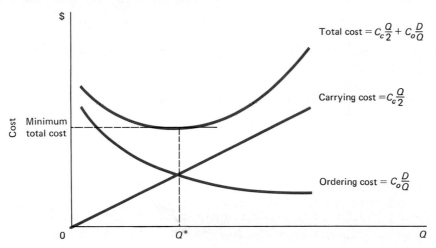

The minimum total cost occurs at the lowest point on the total cost curve in figure 23.6, which corresponds to the optimal order quantity, $Q*$. Since the order cost curve and carrying cost curve intersect at the point where the total cost curve is at a minimum, we can determine $Q*$ by equating these two equations.

*Computing optimal Q by equating the cost equations*

$$C_c \frac{Q}{2} = C_o \frac{D}{Q}$$

$$Q^2 = \frac{2C_o D}{C_c}$$

$$Q* = \sqrt{\frac{2C_o D}{C_c}}$$

However, we can also determine the optimal order quantity by using differential calculus. Recall from our break-even example that the slope at any point on a curve is equal to the derivative of the equation defining that curve, *and* the slope at the highest or *lowest* point of a curve equals zero. For our economic order quantity model this means that we must take the derivative of the total cost curve and set it equal to zero. The derivative of the total cost curve is computed as follows.

*Determining optimal Q using calculus*

*Differentiating the total cost function*

$$\text{Total Cost} = C_c \frac{Q}{2} + C_o \frac{D}{Q}$$

$$\frac{\partial TC}{\partial Q} = \frac{C_c}{2} - \frac{C_o D}{Q^2}$$

Now setting this derivative of total cost equal to zero and solving for $Q$ will result in the optimal order quantity corresponding to the minimum total cost.

$$\frac{\partial TC}{\partial Q} = \frac{C_c}{2} - \frac{C_o D}{Q^2}$$

$$0 = \frac{C_c}{2} - \frac{C_o D}{Q^2}$$

$$\frac{C_c}{2} = \frac{C_o D}{Q^2}$$

$$Q^2 C_c = 2 C_o D$$

$$Q^2 = \frac{2 C_o D}{C_c}$$

$$Q* = \sqrt{\frac{2 C_o D}{C_c}}$$

This is exactly the same result we got previously when we equated the ordering and carrying cost equations. Either method for determining $Q*$ is acceptable, and neither one could be said to be more advantageous or efficient than the other. However, there are more complex inventory models for which calculus is the *only* solution method. The addition of a shortage cost to the basic economic order quantity model results in such a model that requires a calculus solution.

In chapter 18 the following inventory cost equation was developed for the case where shortages are allowed.

$$\text{Total annual inventory cost} = C_s \frac{S^2}{2Q} + C_c \frac{(Q-S)^2}{2Q} + C_o \frac{D}{Q}$$

where

$C_s$ = shortage cost per unit
$S$ = the maximum shortage level
$\dfrac{C_s S^2}{2Q}$ = the annual shortage cost

The relationship of shortage cost, carrying cost, ordering cost, and total cost is illustrated in figure 23.7.

*Calculus is the only*
*method for*
*determining optimal*
*Q in the shortage*
*model*

Notice in figure 23.7 that the lowest point on the total cost curve does not occur where the ordering, shortage, and carrying cost curves intersect. This means that the only possible method of solution is to compute the derivative of the total cost curve. However, this is not quite as easy as it was for our model without shortages. The total cost equation without shortages contained only *one variable*, $Q$ ($C_o$, $D$, and $C_c$ are parameters that have constant values). On the other hand, notice that the total cost equation with shortages allowed contains *two variables, Q and S*. This

means that if we take the derivative of the total inventory cost equation (with respect to either variable) and set it equal to zero, we will have one equation in terms of two unknowns—a situation that does not allow us to independently solve for either variable.

**Figure 23.7** Minimum cost point for inventory model with shortages.

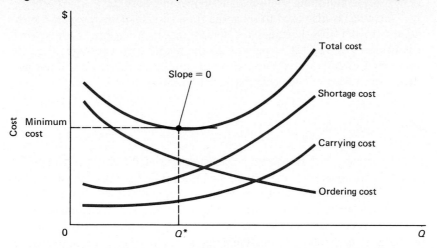

For the shortage model, both $S$ and $Q$ must be solved for. This means that we must take the derivative of the total inventory cost equation with respect to both of these variables. First we will determine the derivative of the inventory cost equation *with respect to Q*.

*Differentiating the cost function with respect to Q*

$$\frac{\partial TC}{\partial Q} = \frac{-C_o D}{Q^2} + \frac{C_c}{2} - \frac{S^2}{2Q^2}(C_c + C_s)$$

Next, we will compute the derivative of the cost equation *with respect to S*.

*Differentiating the cost function with respect to S*

$$\frac{\partial TC}{\partial S} = -C_c + \frac{C_c S}{Q} + \frac{C_s S}{Q}$$

Each of the derivatives must now be set equal to zero.

*Setting the derivatives equal to zero*

$$0 = \frac{-C_o D}{Q^2} + \frac{C_c}{2} - \frac{S^2}{2Q^2}(C_c + C_s)$$

$$0 = -C_c + \frac{C_c S}{Q} + \frac{C_s S}{Q}$$

This gives us two equations that can be solved simultaneously for the values of $Q$ and $S$. We will not go through the detailed mathematical steps required for the simultaneous solution of these equations, presenting instead only the final results.

*Solving simultaneous equations for Q and S*

$$Q^* = \sqrt{\left(\frac{2DC_o}{C_c}\right)\left(\frac{C_s + C_c}{C_s}\right)}$$

$$S^* = Q^*\left(\frac{C_c}{C_c + C_s}\right)$$

Of course, $Q^*$ is the primary value we are looking for, and it corresponds to the minimum total cost, as shown in figure 23.7.

Calculus is also used to solve the final version of the economic order quantity model with shortages and noninstantaneous receipt of units. Since it is basically solved the same way as the model with shortages (i.e., determining two derivatives that are solved simultaneously), we will not pursue the derivation of the economic order quantity here.

## Summary

In this chapter we have demonstrated the use of differential calculus to solve several types of management science problems: break-even analysis and inventory analysis. These problems reflect two of the most traditional and frequent management science applications of calculus. In general, these applications demonstrate the necessity of using calculus to solve problems that consist of nonlinear functional relationships (i.e., curves instead of straight lines).

One of the topics we have devoted a large portion of this text to is *linear* programming. However, an alternative form of mathematical programming, which contains nonlinear, as well as linear relationships, is *nonlinear programming*. This form of mathematical programming that incorporates solution methods based on calculus is the subject of our next chapter.

## References

Childress, R. L. *Mathematics for Managerial Decisions*. Englewood Cliffs, N.J.: Prentice-Hall, 1974.

Haeussler, E. F., and Paul, R. S. *Introductory Mathematical Analysis*. 2d ed. Reston, Va.: Reston, 1976.

Loomba, N. P., and Turban, E. *Applied Programming for Management*. New York: Holt, Rinehart and Winston, 1974.

Shockley, J. E. *The Brief Calculus*. 2d ed. New York: Holt, Rinehart and Winston, 1976.

Weber, Jean E. (Draper and Klingman's). *Mathematical Analysis*. 3d ed. New York: Harper and Row, 1976.

# Problems

1. The Hickory Cabinet and Furniture Company makes chairs. The fixed cost per month of making chairs is $7,500, while the variable cost per chair is $40. Price is related to volume according to the following linear equation.

$$v = 400 - 1.2p$$

Develop the nonlinear profit function for this company and determine the price that will maximize profit, the optimal volume, and the maximum profit per month.

2. Illustrate the profit curve developed in problem 1 graphically. Indicate the optimal price and maximum profit per month.

3. The Rainwater Brewery produces beer. The annual fixed cost is $150,000 and the variable cost per barrel is $16. Price is related to volume according to the following linear equation.

$$v = 75,000 - 1,153.8p$$

Develop the nonlinear profit function for the brewery and determine the price that will maximize profit, the optimal volume, and the maximum profit per year.

4. The Rolling Creek Textile Mill makes denim. The monthly fixed cost is $8,000 and the variable cost per yard of denim is $0.35. Price is related to volume according to the following linear equation.

$$v = 17,000 - 5,666p$$

Develop the nonlinear profit function for the textile mill and determine the optimal price, volume, and the maximum profit per month.

5. The Grady Tire Company recaps tires. The weekly fixed cost is $2,500 and the variable cost per tire is $9. Price is related to volume according to the following linear equation.

$$v = 200 - 4.75p$$

Develop the nonlinear profit function for the tire company and determine the optimal price, the optimal volume, and the maximum profit per week.

6. Suppose Grady Tire Company (problem 5) has determined that their variable cost per tire decreases as volume increases (due to rubber discounts for higher order sizes). Variable cost is related to volume according to the following linear function.

$$c_v = 6 + .03v$$

Assume the company charges $25.00 to recap a tire. Develop the nonlinear profit function for the tire company and determine the optimal volume and maximum profit.

7. For an inventory system with an order cost of $50 per order, a carrying cost of $2 per unit, and a demand of 800 units annually, develop the total cost function, differentiate this function, and solve for the optimal value of $Q$.

8. Consider an inventory system with the following values for the inventory parameters.

   $C_s$ = $2 per unit
   $C_c$ = $3 per unit
   $C_o$ = $250 per order
   $D$ = 1,500 units per year

   Develop the total inventory cost function and outline the steps for computing the optimal order size.

9. Explain why it is necessary to use differential calculus to determine the optimal order size for an inventory model with shortages and why it is not necessary to use differential calculus to determine the optimal order size for the inventory model without shortages.

10. In this chapter differential calculus was applied to nonlinear profit and cost functions in order to determine optimal values for decision variables (i.e., price and order size). Identify another topic area in this text consisting of a profit or cost function that calculus could be applied to.

# 24
Nonlinear
Programming

A substantial proportion of this text has been devoted to linear programming. Chapters 2 through 9 relate directly to linear programming techniques. This emphasis is due in large part to the popularity and applicability of linear programming in the real world and in part to the very efficient methods of solution that have been developed for linear programming problems. However, not all problems that can be classified as *mathematical programming* consist solely of linear relationships. Some problems encompass the general form of a mathematical programming model with an objective function and constraints, but these relationships are not linear. Such problems are referred to as *nonlinear programming,* which is the topic of this chapter.

*Mathematical programming models with nonlinear relationships*

In the preceding chapter, the profit analysis model and inventory models contained a nonlinear function. It was demonstrated that the solution approach for problems with nonlinear relationships required the application of calculus. As might be expected, the solution approaches for nonlinear programming problems are also based on calculus methods. As such, the topic of nonlinear programming represents a convergence of the topics of mathematical programming and calculus. Unlike linear programming, however, the solution methods for nonlinear programming are not very efficient and are very complex. As a result, the topic of nonlinear programming is too broad and advanced for more than a cursory introduction within the limits of one textbook chapter. Therefore, we will simply introduce the basic principles underlying nonlinear programming and offer some insight into how the solution to such problems is approached.

## Constrained Optimization

In the preceding chapter the profit analysis model was developed as an extension of the break-even model. To briefly review, the total profit function is

*The total profit equation*

$$Z = vp - c_f - vc_v$$
where
$v$ = volume
$p$ = price
$c_f$ = fixed cost
$c_v$ = variable cost

The demand function (i.e., volume as a function of price) for our example presented in chapter 23 is

$$v = 1,500 - 24.6p$$

*The nonlinear profit function* By substituting this demand function into our total profit equation, a non-linear function was developed.

$$Z = 1,500p - 24.6p^2 - c_f - 1,500c_v + 24.6pc_v$$

By substituting values for $c_f$ ($10,000) and $c_v$ ($8) into this function, we obtained

$$Z = 1,696.8p - 24.6p^2 - 22,000$$

You will recall that we then differentiated this function, set it equal to zero, and solved for $p$ ($34.49). This value of $p$ corresponded to the maximum point on the profit curve (where the slope equaled zero).

*Unconstrained optimization*     This type of model is referred to as an *unconstrained optimization* problem. It consists of a single nonlinear objective function and *no* constraints, hence the name "unconstrained." However, if we add one or more *Constrained optimization* constraints to this model, it then becomes known as a *constrained optimization model,* which is more commonly referred to as *nonlinear programming.* The reason we designate this type of model as being a form of mathematical programming is because all types of mathematical programming are actually constrained optimization models. That is, they all have the general form of an objective function that is *subject to one or more constraints.* In linear programming there is an objective function and constraints, but they happen to be linear. Nonlinear programming has the same general form as linear programming, except that either the objective function or constraint(s) or both are nonlinear.

*Solving nonlinear programming problems is very complex*     Nonlinear programming does differ from linear programming, however, in one other critical aspect: the solution of nonlinear programming problems is much more complex. In linear programming there is a guaranteed procedure that will lead to a solution in any linear programming problem that has been correctly formulated, whereas in nonlinear programming no such procedure exists. The reason for this complexity can be illustrated by a graph of our profit analysis model. Figure 24.1 shows the nonlinear profit curve for our example model.

As stated previously, the solution is found by taking the derivative of the profit function, setting it equal to zero, and solving for $p$ (price). This results in an optimal value for $p,$ which corresponds to the maximum profit, as shown in figure 24.1.

*A nonlinear programming model*     Now we will transform this unconstrained optimization model into a nonlinear programming model by adding the constraint,

$$p \leq \$20$$

In other words, we are restricting price to a maximum of $20 (as a result of market conditions). This constraint results in a feasible solution space, as shown in figure 24.2

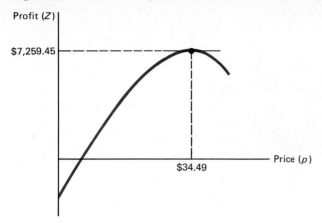

**Figure 24.1** Nonlinear profit curve for the profit analysis model.

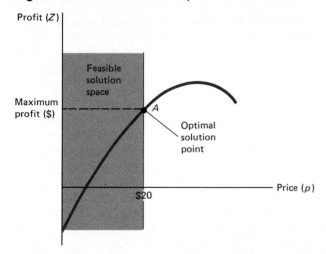

**Figure 24.2** A constrained optimization model.

As in a linear programming problem, the solution is on the boundary of the feasible solution space formed by the constraint. Thus, in figure 24.2, point $A$ is the optimal solution. It corresponds to the maximum value of the portion of the objective function that is still feasible. However, the difficulty with nonlinear programming is that this is not always the case. For example, consider the addition of the following constraint to our original nonlinear objective function.

$$p \leq \$40$$

This constraint creates a feasible solution space, as shown in figure 24.3.

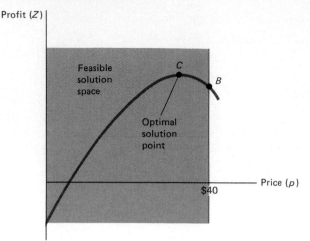

**Figure 24.3** Constrained optimization model with a solution point not on the constraint boundary.

<table>
<tr><td></td></tr>
</table>

The difficulty of locating the solution point for a nonlinear programming problem

In figure 24.3 the solution is no longer on the *boundary* of the feasible solution space as it would be in linear programming. Point $C$ represents a greater profit than point $B$, and it is also in the feasible solution space. This means that we cannot simply look at points on the solution space boundary to find the solution, but we must also consider other points on the surface of the objective function. This greatly complicates the process of finding a solution to a nonlinear programming problem. This difficulty is aggravated as the number of variables and constraints increases and if the nonlinear functions are of a higher order. When one contemplates a model in space made up of intersecting cones, ellipses, and undulating surfaces as well as planes, and the solution not even being on the boundary of the solution space, the difficulties of solution can be imagined.

There are a number of different solution approaches to nonlinear programming problems. As we have already indicated they typically represent a convergence of the principles of calculus and mathematical programming. However, as noted above, the solution techniques can be very complex. As such, we will confine the following discussion of nonlinear programming solution methods to the simplest cases.

## The Substitution Method

Substituting the constraint equation into the objective function

The least complex method for solving nonlinear programming problems is referred to as *substitution*. This method is restricted to models that contain only equality constraints, and typically only one of these. The method involves solving the constraint equation for one variable in terms of another. This new expression is then substituted in the objective function. This effectively eliminates the constraint. In other words, a constrained optimization model is transformed into an unconstrained model.

For an example of the substitution method it is only necessary to return to our profit analysis model. This model is actually a nonlinear programming model that we solved by the substitution method. The demand function is a constraint. Thus, the nonlinear programming model is formulated as

*An example of the substitution method*

maximize $Z = vp - c_f - vc_v$
subject to
$$v = 1,500 - 24.6p$$

The objective function is nonlinear in this model, since both $v$ (volume) and $p$ (price) are variables, and multiplying them (i.e., $vp$) creates a curvilinear relationship.

The constraint has already been solved for one variable ($v$) in terms of another ($p$), thus, we can substitute this expression directly into the objective function. This results in the following *unconstrained* function.

$$Z = 1,500p - 24.6p^2 - c_f - 1,500c_v + 24.6pc_v$$

*A nonlinear objective function*

By substituting in the constant values for $c_f$ ($10,000) and $c_v$ ($8), we obtain

$$Z = 1,696.8p - 24.6p^2 - 22,000$$

Next, we solve this problem by differentiating the function, $Z$, and setting it equal to zero as we did in chapter 23.

$$\frac{\partial Z}{\partial p} = 1,696.8 - 49.2p$$
$$0 = 1,696.8 - 49.2p$$
$$49.2p = 1,696.8$$
$$p = \$34.49$$

Since we have become very familiar with this example, we will present another example as a further illustration of a nonlinear programming problem and of the substitution method. This example is a modified version of our Colonial Pottery Company example first introduced in chapter 2. Recall that the company produced bowls ($x_1$) and mugs ($x_2$), which had unit profits of $4 and $5 respectively. The linear objective function was formulated as

*The Colonial Pottery Company example*

maximize $Z = \$4x_1 + 5x_2$

However, now we will assume that the profit contribution for each product *declines* as the quantity produced of each increases. Thus, for bowls the per unit profit contribution is now expressed according to the relationship,

*Relating profit to quantity produced*

$$\$4 - .1x_1$$

For mugs, the profit contribution per unit is

$$\$5 - .2x_2$$

(These relationships occur because the production costs for each product increase as the number of units sold increases.)

These profit relationships are on a per unit basis. Thus, the total profit contribution from each product is determined by multiplying these relationships by the number of units produced. For bowls, the profit contribution is

$$(4 - .1x_1)x_1$$

or

$$4x_1 - .1x_1^2$$

and for mugs,

$$(5 - .2x_2)x_2$$

or

$$5x_2 - .2x_2^2$$

*A nonlinear objective function*

Total profit is the sum of these two terms.

$$Z = \$4x_1 - .1x_1^2 + 5x_2 - .2x_2^2$$

*Adding a labor constraint*

In the original linear programming model there were constraints for labor and pounds of clay. In this model, we will consider only the labor constraint, and we will treat it as an equality rather than an inequality.

$$x_1 + 2x_2 = 40 \text{ hours}$$

The complete nonlinear programming model can be summarized as

maximize $Z = \$4x_1 - .1x_1^2 + 5x_2 - .2x_2^2$
subject to
$x_1 + 2x_2 = 40$

*Substituting the constraint into the objective function*

The first step in the substitution method is to solve the constraint equation for one variable in terms of another. We will arbitrarily solve for $x_1$, as follows.

$$x_1 = 40 - 2x_2$$

Now everywhere $x_1$ appears in the nonlinear objective function, we will substitute the expression $40 - 2x_2$.

$$
\begin{aligned}
Z &= 4(40 - 2x_2) - .1(40 - 2x_2)^2 + 5x_2 - .2x_2^2 \\
&= 160 - 8x_2 - .1(1{,}600 - 160x_2 + 4x_2^2) + 5x_2 - .2x_2^2 \\
&= 160 - 8x_2 - 160 + 16x_2 - .4x_2^2 + 5x_2 - .2x_2^2 \\
&= 13x_2 - .6x_2^2
\end{aligned}
$$

*Differentiating the objective function*

This is an unconstrained optimization function that we can solve by differentiating it and setting it equal to zero.

$$\frac{\partial Z}{\partial x_2} = 13 - 1.2x_2$$
$$0 = 13 - 1.2x_2$$
$$1.2x_2 = 13$$
$$x_2 = 10.8 \text{ mugs}$$

To determine $x_1$, we can substitute $x_2$ into the constraint equation.

$$x_1 + 2x_2 = 40$$
$$x_1 + 2(10.8) = 40$$
$$x_1 = 18.4 \text{ bowls}$$

Substituting the values of $x_1$ and $x_2$ into the original objective function results in the following total profit.

$$Z = \$4x_1 - .1x_1^2 + 5x_2 - .2x_2^2$$
$$= \$4(18.4) - .1(18.4)^2 + 5(10.8) - .2(10.8)^2$$
$$= \$70.40$$

Both of the examples presented in this section for solving nonlinear programming problems exhibit the limitations of this approach. The objective functions were not very complex (i.e., the highest order of a variable was a power of 2 in the second example), there were only two variables, and the single constraint in each example was restricted to an equation. This method becomes very difficult if the constraint becomes complex. An alternative solution approach that is not quite as restricted is the method of Lagrange multipliers.

## The Method of Lagrange Multipliers

The method of Lagrange multipliers is a general mathematical technique that can be used for solving constrained optimization problems consisting of a nonlinear objective function and one or more linear or nonlinear constraint equations. In this method, the constraints as multiples of a Lagrange multiplier, $\lambda$, are subtracted from the objective function.

In order to demonstrate this method, we will use our modified pottery company example developed in the preceding section. This model was formulated as

*A Lagrange example*

$$\text{maximize } Z = 4x_1 - .1x_1^2 + 5x_2 - .2x_2^2$$
subject to
$$x_1 + 2x_2 = 40$$

The first step is to transform the nonlinear objective function into a *Lagrangian function*. This is accomplished by first transforming the constraint equation as follows.

*The Lagrangian function*

$$x_1 + 2x_2 - 40 = 0$$

Next this expression is multiplied by $\lambda$, the *Lagrangian multiplier,* and subtracted from the objective function to form the Lagrangian function.

$$L = 4x_1 - .1x_1^2 + 5x_2 - .2x_2^2 - \lambda(x_1 + 2x_2 - 40)$$

Since the constraint equation now equals zero, the subtraction of the constraint, multiplied by $\lambda$, from the objective function does not affect the value of the function. (We will explain the exact meaning of $\lambda$ after a solution is determined.)

Now we must determine the partial derivatives of the Lagrangian function with respect to each of the three variables, $x_1$, $x_2$, and $\lambda$.

$$\frac{\partial L}{\partial x_1} = 4 - .2x_1 - \lambda$$

$$\frac{\partial L}{\partial x_2} = 5 - .4x_2 - 2\lambda$$

$$\frac{\partial L}{\partial \lambda} = -x_1 - 2x_2 + 40$$

These three equations are all set equal to zero and solved simultaneously to determine the values of $x_1$, $x_2$, and $\lambda$.

$$4 - .2x_1 - \lambda = 0$$
$$5 - .4x_2 - 2\lambda = 0$$
$$-x_1 - 2x_2 + 40 = 0$$

To solve these equations simultaneously, we will multiply the first equation by $-2$ and add it to the second equation, which will eliminate $\lambda$.

$$-8 + .4x_1 + 2\lambda = 0$$
$$\underline{5 - .4x_2 - 2\lambda = 0}$$
$$-3 + .4x_1 - .4x_2 = 0$$

This new equation and the original third equation above represent two equations with two unknowns ($x_1$ and $x_2$). Thus, we will multiply the third equation above by .4 and add it to the new equation in order to eliminate $x_1$.

$$-.4x_1 - .8x_2 + 16 = 0$$
$$\underline{.4x_1 - .4x_2 - 3 = 0}$$
$$-1.2x_2 + 13 = 0$$

Solving this resulting equation for $x_2$:

$$-1.2x_2 + 13 = 0$$
$$-1.2x_2 = -13$$
$$x_2 = 10.8 \text{ mugs}$$

Substituting this value back into previous equations will result in the values of $x_1$ and $\lambda$.

$$-x_1 - 2x_2 + 40 = 0$$
$$-x_1 - 2(10.8) = -40$$
$$x_1 = 18.4 \text{ bowls}$$
$$5 - .4x_2 - 2\lambda = 0$$
$$5 - .4(10.8) = 2\lambda$$
$$\lambda = .35$$

Substituting the values for $x_1$ and $x_2$ into the original objective function results in the total profit.

$$Z = \$4x_1 - .1x_1{}^2 + 5x_2 - .2x_2{}^2$$
$$= \$4(18.4) - .1(18.4)^2 + 5\,(10.8) - .2(10.8)^2$$
$$= \$70.40$$

This result can also be obtained by using the Lagrangian function, $L$, and $\lambda$.

$$L = \$4x_1 - .1x_1{}^2 + 5x_2 - .2x_2{}^2 - \lambda\,(x_1 + 2x_2 - 40)$$
$$= \$4(18.4) - .1(18.4)^2 + 5(10.8) - .2(10.8)^2 - 0.35(0)$$
$$= \$70.40$$

Summarizing, $x_1 = 18.4$ bowls, $x_2 = 10.8$ mugs, $Z = \$70.40$, and *The optimal solution* $\lambda = .35$. This is the same answer obtained previously using the substitution method. However, unlike the substitution method, the Lagrange multiplier approach can solve nonlinear programming problems with more complex constraint equations and *inequality constraints*. In addition, it can encompass problems with more than two variables. We will not pursue any examples, though, that demonstrate these complexities. The Lagrange multiplier method must be altered to compensate for inequality constraints and more variables, and the resulting mathematics are very difficult. In fact, while the Lagrange multiplier method is more flexible than the substitution method, it can practically solve only small problems. As the problem size expands, the mathematics become overwhelmingly difficult. As a result, several computerized approaches have been developed, which we will discuss later in the chapter.

## The Meaning of $\lambda$

The Lagrange multiplier, $\lambda$, in nonlinear programming problems is analogous to the dual variables in a linear programming problem. It reflects the approximate change in the objective function resulting from a unit change in the quantity (right-hand-side) value of the constraint equation. For our example, we will increase the quantity value in the constraint equation from 40 to 41 hours of labor (and recall from above that $\lambda = .35$).

$\lambda$ *is analogous to the dual variable*

$$x_1 + 2x_2 = 41$$

or

$$x_1 + 2x_2 - 41 = 0$$

This will result in the following Lagrangian function.

$$L = 4x_1 - .1x_1^2 + 5x_2 - .2x_2^2 - \lambda(x_1 + 2x_2 - 41)$$

Solving this problem in the same way we did for the original model results in the following solution.

$$x_1 = 18.68$$
$$x_2 = 11.16$$
$$\lambda = .27$$
$$Z = \$74.75$$

*λ as the marginal value of labor*

This value for $Z$ is \$.35 greater than the previous $Z$ value of \$74.40. Thus, a one-unit increase in the right-hand side of the constraint equation results in a $\lambda$ increase in the objective function. More specifically, a unit increase in a resource (labor) resulted in a \$.35 increase in profit. As such, we would be willing to pay \$.35 for one additional hour of labor. This is the same interpretation as that of a dual variable given in chapter 6.

In general, if $\lambda$ is positive, the optimal objective function value will increase if the quantity (absolute) value in the constraint equation is increased and decrease if the quantity (absolute) value is decreased. Alternatively, if $\lambda$ is negative, the optimal objective function value will increase if the quantity (absolute) value is decreased and decrease if the quantity value is increased.

## Nonconvex and Nonconcave Functions

*Nonlinear objective functions that are not totally convex or concave*

In all of the examples in this chapter and the preceding chapter, the nonlinear objective functions were either completely convex or concave. That is, shapes of the curves formed by the functions were either upright or inverted "bowls," as shown in figure 24.4. This means that there could be only one maximum or minimum point on the curve, and thus only one possible solution point. However, this is not always the case, as the objective function can define an undulating curve that contains both convex and concave portions. Such a curve is shown in figure 24.5.

When this type of nonlinear function exists in a problem, simply taking the derivative of the function will not automatically identify the optimal solution (i.e., there are several points on the curve where the slope equals zero). As a result, several additional calculus steps must be performed in order to exactly determine the optimal solution. These steps encompass the use of higher order derivatives. Since these steps are necessary for more complex nonlinear functions that we have not demonstrated in this chapter, we will not pursue this topic. However, Appendix E presents the basic principles for determining optimality for nonlinear functions.

**Figure 24.4** Convex and concave functions.

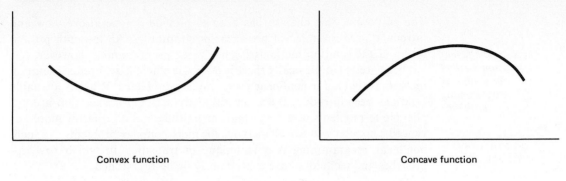

Convex function                                   Concave function

**Figure 24.5** A curve with concave and convex portions.

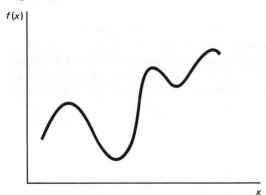

## Advanced Solution Methods for Nonlinear Programming

Most of the modern-day solution methods for nonlinear programming problems are iterative search procedures that have been developed rather recently. These procedures, which are referred to as *gradient search methods,* are conducted almost exclusively on the computer. These methods are analogous to climbing the highest peak in a mountain range where the unknown peak of the highest mountain is sought by successively searching from peak to peak. The search starts at point $A$ then goes to point $B$, when $B$ appears to be the highest point in the immediate vicinity of $A$. The search is continued until the summit (optimal solution) is reached where there can be no additional improvement in the objective function. There are a number of these search techniques that have been documented and used. The interested reader is referred to the references (especially Luenberger) at the end of this chapter for a more thorough presentation of these techniques.

*Gradient search methods*

## Summary

*There is no efficient solution method for nonlinear programming problems*

The purpose of this chapter has been to provide a general overview and introduction to the topic of nonlinear programming. An in-depth presentation of the solution methods for nonlinear programming, however, has not been presented. Basically there is no single efficient generalized solution method available for nonlinear programming problems. What is available (and has been introduced) are several analytical approaches that are applicable to problems of a very small magnitude and alternative more advanced computerized search methods for more complex problems. As such, nonlinear programming is a technique in transition in which new approaches and techniques are continuously being researched.

## References

Gottfried, B. S., and Weisman, J. *Introduction to Optimization Theory.* Englewood Cliffs, N.J.: Prentice-Hall, 1973.

Hillier, F. S., and Lieberman, G. J. *Operations Research.* 3rd ed. San Francisco: Holden-Day, 1980.

Kuhn H. W., and Tucker, A. W. "Non-Linear Programming." In *Proceedings of the Second Berkeley Symposium on Mathematical Statistics and Probability*, edited by Jerzy Neyman, pp. 481–92. Berkeley: University of California Press, 1951.

Loomba, N. P., and Turban, E. *Applied Programming for Management.* New York: Holt, Rinehart & Winston, 1974.

Luenberger, David G. *Introduction to Linear and Non-Linear Programming.* Reading, Mass.: Addison-Wesley, 1973.

McMillan, Claude, Jr. *Mathematical Programming.* 2d ed. New York: John Wiley & Sons, 1975.

Taha, Hamdy A. *Operations Research, An Introduction.* 2d ed. New York: Macmillan Co., 1976.

## Problems

1. Explain why the addition of one or more constraints to a problem with a nonlinear objective function complicates the process of finding a solution to the problem.

2. Explain the *substitution* method for solving nonlinear programming problems and its limitations as a solution approach.

3. The Rainwater Brewery produces beer, which it sells to distributors in barrels. The brewery incurs a monthly fixed cost of $12,000, and the variable cost per barrel is $17. The brewery has developed the following profit function and demand constraint.

maximize $Z = vp - \$12{,}000 - 17v$
subject to
$$v = 800 - 15p$$

Solve this nonlinear programming model for the optimal price $(p)$ using the substitution method.

4. The Colonial Pottery Company has developed the following nonlinear programming model to determine the optimal number of bowls $(x_1)$ and mugs $(x_2)$ to produce each day.

maximize $Z = \$7x_1 - .3x_1^2 + 8x_2 - .4x_2^2$
subject to
$$4x_1 + 5x_2 = 100 \text{ hours}$$

Determine the optimal solution to this model using the substitution method.

5. The Evergreen Fertilizer Company produces two types of fertilizers, Fastgro and Super Two. The company has developed the following nonlinear programming model to determine the optimal number of bags of Fastgro $(x_1)$ and Super Two $(x_2)$ to produce each day in order to maximize profit given a constraint for available potassium.

maximize $Z = \$30x_1 - 2x_1^2 + 25x_2 - .5x_2^2$
subject to
$$3x_1 + 6x_2 = 300 \text{ pounds}$$

Determine the optimal solution to this model using the substitution method.

6. The Rolling Creek Textile Mill produces denim and brushed cotton cloth. The company has developed the following nonlinear programming model to determine the optimal number of yards of denim $(x_1)$ and brushed cotton $(x_2)$ to produce each day in order to maximize profit subject to a labor constraint.

maximize $Z = \$10x_1 - .02x_1^2 + 12x_2 - .03x_2^2$
subject to
$$.2x_1 + .1x_2 = 40 \text{ hours}$$

Determine the optimal solution to this model using the substitution method.

7. Solve problem 4 using the method of Lagrange multipliers.

8. Solve problem 5 using the method of Lagrange multipliers.

9. Solve problem 6 using the method of Lagrange multipliers.

10. The Riverwood Paneling Company makes two kinds of wood paneling, Colonial and Western. The company has developed the following nonlinear programming model to determine the optimal number of sheets of Colonial paneling $(x_1)$ and Western paneling $(x_2)$ to produce in order to maximize profit subject to a labor constraint.

maximize $Z = \$25x_1 - .8x_1^2 + 30x_2 - 1.2x_2^2$
subject to
$$x_1 + 2x_2 = 40$$

Determine the optimal solution to this model using the method of Lagrange multipliers.

11. Interpret the meaning of $\lambda$, the Lagrange multiplier, in problem 10.

12. Explain the difficulties in determining an optimal solution when the nonlinear objective function in a model is not completely convex or concave.

# 25
# The Manager and Management Science

Management Information Systems and Implementation

## Management Information Systems

Data Collection and Organization
The Computer System
Decision-Making Information
Management Decisions

## Implementation

The Causes of Implementation Problems
Strategies for Achieving Successful Implementation

## The Cost of Management Science

## Management Science in the Organization

## Summary

In all of the preceding chapters in this text we have presented management science *techniques*. These techniques do not actually make decisions, but rather they provide information that can aid the manager in making decisions. However, we have not yet discussed how this information generated from management science techniques is assimilated into the business organization. In other words, where in the organization is this information generated and how does it get to the manager? In most organizations the vehicle for accumulating, organizing, and distributing information is a *management information system*. As such, management information systems will be the first topic we will present in this chapter.

Even though information is provided in most organizations through a management information system, this does not ensure that this information will be used in an effective manner upon receipt by the manager. The manager may simply ignore the information altogether. When the information generated from management science techniques is not used by the recipient, we say the technique results are not *implemented*. Failure to implement model results can be a serious problem in organizations, and as such, it will be the second topic we will discuss in this chapter.

## Management Information Systems

A *management information system* (also known as *MIS*) is a system specifically designed to channel large quantities and numerous types of information through an organization. In a management information system data is collected, organized, and processed in order to provide managers with information that will aid them in making decisions. Often this information is in the form of management science solutions or descriptive results. Such a system also serves to provide a communication system that links the various units (or departments) of an organization so that decisions will be cooperative.

*A system designed to channel information through an organization*

A general framework of a management information system is illustrated in figure 25.1. In order to provide an understanding of how a management information system is constructed and how it operates, we will explain each component in figure 25.1 separately.

*An MIS framework*

**Figure 25.1** A management information system.

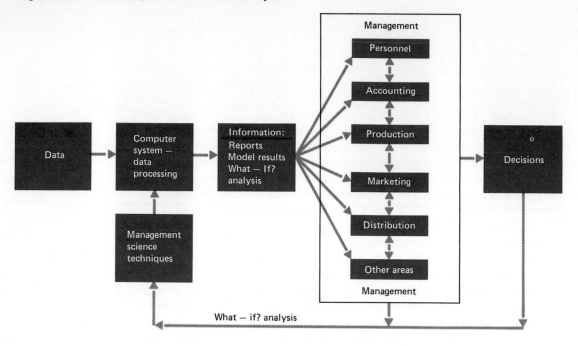

## Data Collection and Organization

*A data base*

The first stage in a management information system is the development of a *data base*, which is an organized collection of numerical information. Items such as prices, production output and rates, number of orders, available resources, capacities, and labor (rates) are examples of pieces of information that form a data base.

For a management information system to be efficient and effective the data base must contain relevant and quality information, the right types of information, and enough information. In addition, for a data base to be efficient, the information must be properly organized. Since most modern organizations have access to such a large quantity and variety of information, an efficient and organized data base requires the use of a computer.

## The Computer System

*MIS is generally computerized*

Modern management information systems generally imply a computerized system. The vast amounts of data available to organizations make the computer an essential component of most management information systems (although manual systems do exist for smaller organizations).

*Hardware*

Essentially a computer is an electrical machine that performs arithmetic operations very rapidly. The actual machine as well as any ancillary equipment, such as printers, keypunch machines, and terminals, is referred to as *hardware*. Alternatively, the mathematical and written codes that instruct the computer how to perform operations are referred to as *software*. *Software* In order for the computer to perform a specific task, a *program* must be developed by the operator and fed into the computer to tell it what to do. Certain programs can be purchased from outside sources, such as a computer consulting firm or manufacturer, or programs can be written by an individual, such as a manager or management scientist. Programs are written in computer languages such as FORTRAN, COBOL, or BASIC (among others).

In figure 25.1 *management science* models are shown as being an input into the computer system. The computer system actually serves to combine the data base with the management science models in order to generate the types of results demonstrated in this text. All of the management science techniques presented in this text can be developed as computer programs. The computer can solve management science problems very rapidly and usually at a low cost. In fact, *prewritten* software packages exist for most of the techniques. For example, there are perhaps several dozen prewritten programs available just for the solution of linear programming problems.

## Decision-Making Information

The computer in a management information system processes data and generates information to be used by the different units in the organization to make decisions. The flow of information from the computer system to *Information flows* the organizational units is illustrated in figure 25.1. Although information is shown flowing to each department, this does not mean that each piece of information generated by the system goes to each department. These channels represent *possible* information flows that can occur, but not necessarily all at once.

The information flowing from the computer to the different departments can take several forms. It can be in the form of *reports*, which *Types of* summarize and organize the data, such as accounts receivables, orders, *information flows* work force, inventory levels, resource levels, market information, or production output. These reports can provide recent information or historical information that might be relevant for decisions in the present or future. Reports typically do not reflect any form of management science analysis, but are simply collections of data organized in a useful and easily interpretable manner. They can be generated at the request of management or on a regular basis as a matter of policy. For example, the manager of the production area might *request* a report on the frequency of machine breakdowns during a particular month, while a report on monthly production output would be provided on a regular basis without request.

Information can also take the form of *management science model* *Management science* *results or solutions*. Like reports, this information can be generated upon *model results* request or on a regular basis. The more frequent case is that the information is at the request of a manager who wants the solution to a specific problem.

However, it is important to point out that the management information system generally cannot formulate the management science model itself. This must be accomplished by the manager, a management scientist, or a management science staff skilled in management science techniques. (The development of these skills has been the purpose of this text.) The computer system can only provide the solution to the model that represents the problem.

*What-if? analysis*

Another form information can take reflects the interaction between the manager and the computer system or, as it is more commonly referred to, *what-if? analysis*. That is, the computer system generates the results of a management science model and the manager asks the computer, "What if something were changed in the model?" For example, the computer might generate an economic order quantity ($Q$) based on data provided in the EOQ model. The manager might then speculate that the order cost will change, and ask the computer for new results based on this change. Such experimentation with possible changes educates the manager regarding the possible courses of action that can be taken as a result of occurrences in the future. The manager can also test possible decisions to see their potential results before actually making them.

*Interactive feedback*

As shown in figure 25.1, what if? analysis takes the form of *interactive feedback* with the computer. In other words, such information occurs only at the request of management. Computer hardware and software exists that can perform this type of analysis very efficiently. With the use of *remote terminals* and *interactive computer programs* managers can work directly with the computer, bypassing intermediate personnel or procedures. A remote terminal is a piece of computer equipment much like a typewriter that is usually connected to the main computer by telephone lines. It is approximately the size of a portable typewriter sitting on top of a student's desk. The user types the request for the desired information directly into the terminal, which does not actually perform the operations but passes it to the computer. The desired information is returned to the terminal via a teletype, which prints out the information. More modern terminals contain video screens on which the results are printed out like a television.

*Interactive computer programs*

The use of the terminal can be enhanced by interactive programs. These programs are developed to determine the necessary input data from the manager in the form of questions. The computer actually carries on a *dialogue* with the manager. For example, if the manager is performing inventory analysis, the computer might ask the question (which would be printed out on the terminal teletype or screen):

WHAT IS THE ORDER COST PER UNIT, $C_o$?
The manager would then type in the order cost,
$C_o = 200$
and the computer would type out the optimal order quantity on the teletype (or video screen):
$Q = 500$

One final aspect of this portion of a management information system is the interaction between departments. Notice in figure 25.1 the information flows between the departments. Information rarely affects only one unit in an organization. For example, inventory information (and decisions) not only affect the production operation but also the marketing department (the ability to promise customers immediate delivery), the distribution department (the availability of units of product affects shipping loads), and accounting (the inventory on hand represents both an investment and a cost). The fact that the information between areas must be coordinated in order to develop cooperative decisions is the function of top management that pervades all departments, as shown in figure 25.1.

*Departmental interaction*

## Management Decisions

The final stage in the management information system shown in figure 25.1 reflects the actual decisions made by management. Based on the information contained in reports, the solution results from management science models, and what-if? analysis, managers make decisions. However, these decisions are not an end in themselves; the decisions and their results in the form of *feedback* provide additional data for the data base. As such, a management information system is an ongoing, dynamic system that continuously updates itself.

This completes our analysis of the management information system in figure 25.1. Although the sophistication of management information systems can vary dramatically, they are generally developed similarly to the system shown in figure 25.1. However, regardless of the type of management information system a business firm employs, *the generation of information does not ensure use of the information*. This problem is the next topic to be presented in this chapter, implementation.

*Having information does not ensure its use*

## Implementation

A major consideration in a management information system is ensuring that the manager uses the information provided as efficiently as possible to make decisions. If the information is not used or is ignored altogether, then it represents a total loss. In other words, there is only the cost of providing the information and not any benefit received from it.

The application of information generated from management science models is referred to as *implementation*. However, implementation is not always achieved, and as such poses a potential problem for the top management of an organization. The problem of implementing management science results has received a great deal of attention in recent years. Management information systems have become more sophisticated, and the number and types of management science techniques have increased. However, there is evidence that these advancements have not been accompanied

*Ensuring that the manager uses the information provided to make more efficient decisions*

by a corresponding increase in implementation. The results of management science techniques are not being used to the fullest extent possible and thus their total potential is not being realized. As a result, in this section we will explore some of the causes of failure to implement management science generated information and some possible remedies.

## The Causes of Implementation Problems

When the problem of implementation first began to be noticed by managers and management scientists, the causes that were identified were somewhat superficial. These causes included (among others) the following:

The personality and training of managers

Ill-defined problems and improper model formulation

Models that are too sophisticated (and complicated) for the problems to be solved

A lack of understanding of management and decision-making processes by the management scientist

A lack of understanding of management science techniques by managers

Too much time required to develop models for decisions that must be made immediately

Models that do not reflect the realism of the actual problem

The appropriate data is not always available in the management information system

An improperly designed management information system

A resistance to use new tools of analysis (such as a management science technique) on the part of the manager

These are generally typical of the causes that have often been advanced for problems in implementing the results of management science models. However, although these are often the causes of a problem, there are usually opinions based in many cases on practical experiences. As a result they tend to be generalizations that are inappropriate to apply to the problem of implementation as a whole.

As is the case with many types of problem analysis, attempts to explain the problems of implementation eventually passed from generalization to directed research. Such research typically identified the problem *Factors related to* as being rooted in the relationship of the management science staff to the *implementation* surrounding organization. Some of these more subtle factors relating to *problems* implementation problems are:

The support for management science in the organization

The success of prior uses of management science

The "political" opposition to and support for management science

The amount of power and influence the management science staff has in the organization

The size of the management science staff and the amount of resources it
    commands

The climate for innovation and change within the organization

The time frame for decision making

The location of the responsibility for implementation

Management's experience with management science techniques

These factors are only a few of the many factors that have been
identified as being related to successful or unsuccessful implementation.
One thing that all of these factors demonstrate rather conclusively is that
there is no one cause or set of causes for implementation failure. As a
result, it is difficult to propose a specific strategy for ensuring successful
implementation. In effect, an implementation strategy must be tailored to
fit the particular organization.

## Strategies for Achieving Successful Implementation

There are numerous strategies that have been proposed for attaining successful implementation, as might be expected because of the many causes
of the problem that have been identified. However, a common thread run-
ning through the various proposals for achieving success is that the imple- *Implementation as a*
mentation process must be viewed as a *continuous, ongoing process.* This *continuous, ongoing*
means that implementation encompasses not only the final decision but also *process*
problem formulation, model development, and construction and model testing.

In this framework, the experiences gained from implementation pro- *Implementation*
vide feedback to different stages in the management science modeling pro- *experiences provide*
cess. Thus, the model evolves through the implementation process. The *feedback to the*
basic premise underlying this approach is that successful implementation *modeling process*
is dependent upon success at each stage of the modeling process. If the
management problem is not formulated properly, if the model is constructed
improperly, if the results are not realistic or applicable, then implementation will never occur.

Within this framework management involvement in the management *Management*
science process enhances the possibility of successful implementation. This *involvement in the*
means that the manager must be an active participant in the development *management science*
and use of the management science model. If this interaction takes place, *process*
then there is a better chance that the model will be designed with the
proposed use more closely in mind, and the model will not be too sophisticated for the user.

Another strategy to achieve successful implementation is to create a *Implementation*
situation where the manager is conducive to *change.* This is based on the *creates changes for*
notion that behavioral change on the part of the manager is a major factor *the manager*
in implementation. For the manager a *lack of change* promotes stability
and continuity leading to feelings of comfort and safeness. Management
and labor functions tend to become routinized and habitual in this envi-

ronment. When change becomes imminent it is resisted, since it is perceived as a threat to the normal safe routine of the manager. In this scenario the management science technique is a potential change, since it often represents a new and different way of doing things.


*Overcoming the resistance to change*

In order to overcome this resistance to change, an organized process must be established to overcome the resistance to change, introduce the management science model, and create a new feeling of routine that will reinforce the use of the model. There are several ways to achieve these steps, but basically they require a joint effort by both the manager and the management scientist. However, regardless of the means used, the important point is that the information generated from management science models cannot simply be *dumped* on the manager without some prior preparation.

## The Cost of Management Science

*The cost in time and resources of developing management science models*

An often overlooked but important aspect of management science is the cost in time and required resources to develop and use management science models. The financial cost, manpower requirements, staff skills, and computer cost required to develop and use management science can sometimes be high. As such, any consideration of using management science techniques should also include an estimate of the benefits and costs involved.

The easiest costs to estimate are the direct manpower requirements necessary to develop a model, however, not even this cost is easy to forecast. These costs include the cost of the management science personnel and the cost of teaching management personnel the techniques. A more difficult cost to determine results from is the disruption of normal operating conditions that can result in temporarily decreased output and productivity, lost sales, and disrupted schedules.

The benefits accruing from a management science model are measured in terms of increased productivity, profits, efficiency, or reduced cost or time. Failure to implement the result of a management science model results in little or no benefit.

## Management Science in the Organization

*The location of the management science staff in the organization*

The location of management science within the organization structure, the size of the management science staff, the existence of a staff at all, and the status of the management scientist are all factors affecting the degree of successful implementation of management science results. Many large and medium-sized business firms have management science departments or

staffs concerned exclusively with problem solving and model development. Although those staffs can be quite large containing as many as thirty members, their success is primarily dependent on quality.

The management science staff can exist at several locations within the organization structure. It can be contained at the top management level, the corporate level, or the operational level. Some firms have management science groups at each level of the organization. The officer the management science staff reports to is basically determined by the location of the staff in the organization. There does not, however, appear to be a typical organizational location for a management science staff.

This discussion of the management science staff should not indicate that management science does not exist in firms where there is no management science staff or department. In many instances a member (or several members) of the management staff will be well versed in management science and apply management science techniques to their problems. This will become more frequent in the future as a result of the increased training in management science techniques being provided in college business programs. Undergraduate business majors will be more prepared in the future to apply management science techniques to business problems. Although the managers/management scientists of the future will be constrained by a lack of time and resources, they will have the advantage of being directly involved in the problem situation, which can enhance implementation.

## Summary

The purpose of this concluding chapter has been to indicate how management science is made available to the manager through management information systems and some of the problems that can occur to prevent the implementation of the management science results that are obtained. An attempt has been made to convey the fact that even though management science techniques have tremendous potential for solving business problems, their actual use is dependent upon an efficient management information system and a concerted emphasis on implementation. Although the documented successes of management science are many and more successes will be forthcoming in the future, there is a need for continued refinement of MIS and implementation. It would be negligent not to realize the full potential offered by management science techniques because obstacles to their assimilation by management into the organization could not be overcome. However, as this chapter has indicated, the problems have been recognized and solutions will continue to be sought in the future.

# References

Churchman, C., and Shainblatt, A. A. "The Researcher and the Manager: A Dialectic of Implementation." *Management Science* 11, no. 4 (February 1965): 869–87.

Davis, G. B. *Management Information Systems: Conceptual Foundations, Structure and Development.* New York: McGraw-Hill, 1974.

Davis, K. R., and Taylor, B. W. "Addressing the Implementation Problem: A Gaming Approach." *Decision Sciences* 7, no. 4 (October 1976): 677–87.

Gaither, N. "The Adoption of Operations Research Techniques by Manufacturing Organizations." *Decision Sciences* 6, no. 4, (October 1975): 797–813.

Grayson, C. J., Jr. "Management Science and Business Practice." *Harvard Business Review* 51, no. 4 (July–August 1973): 41–48.

Harvey, A. "Factors Making for Implementation Success and Failure." *Management Science* 16, no. 6 (February 1970): B312–21.

Lee, Sang M.; Moore, Laurence J.; and Taylor, Bernard W. *Management Science.* Dubuque, Iowa: Wm. C. Brown Company Publishers, 1981.

McLeod, R., Jr. *Management Information Systems.* Chicago: SRA, 1979.

Murdick, R. G., and Ross, J. E. *Introduction to Management Information Systems.* Englewood Cliffs, N.J.: Prentice-Hall, 1977.

Rubenstein, A. H.; Radnor, M.; Baker, N. R.; Heiman, D. K.; and McColly, J. B. "Some Organizational Factors Related to Effectiveness of Management Science Groups in Industry." *Management Science* 13, no. 8 (April 1967): B508–18.

Schultz, R. L., and Slevin, D. P., eds. *Implementing Operations Research/ Management Science.* New York: Elsevier, 1975.

Sprague, R. H., and Watson, H. J. "MIS Concepts." *Journal of Systems Management* (January and February 1975).

# Problems

1. What is a *management information system*?
2. Explain the function of a *data base* in a management information system.
3. Why are management information systems typically computerized?
4. Explain what the term *what-if? analysis* means.
5. Explain what an interactive computer program does.
6. What is the function of information *feedback* in a management information system?
7. Define what *implementation* means.
8. List and discuss the three biggest causes of an implementation problem as you perceive them.
9. Why must implementation be viewed as a *continuous* process?
10. What effect does *change* have on the implementation process?
11. Describe some of the costs associated with management science.
12. Discuss the relationship of management science to the organization as a whole and its effect on successful implementation.

Appendix A
**Tables**

**Table A.1** Normal Curve Areas

| Z | .00 | .01 | .02 | .03 | .04 | .05 | .06 | .07 | .08 | .09 |
|---|-----|-----|-----|-----|-----|-----|-----|-----|-----|-----|
| 0.0 | .0000 | .0040 | .0080 | .0120 | .0160 | .0199 | .0239 | .0279 | .0319 | .0359 |
| 0.1 | .0398 | .0438 | .0478 | .0517 | .0557 | .0596 | .0636 | .0675 | .0714 | .0753 |
| 0.2 | .0793 | .0832 | .0871 | .0910 | .0948 | .0987 | .1026 | .1064 | .1103 | .1141 |
| 0.3 | .1179 | .1217 | .1255 | .1293 | .1331 | .1368 | .1406 | .1443 | .1480 | .1517 |
| 0.4 | .1554 | .1591 | .1628 | .1664 | .1700 | .1736 | .1772 | .1808 | .1844 | .1879 |
| 0.5 | .1915 | .1950 | .1985 | .2019 | .2054 | .2088 | .2123 | .2157 | .2190 | .2224 |
| 0.6 | .2257 | .2291 | .2324 | .2357 | .2389 | .2422 | .2454 | .2486 | .2517 | .2549 |
| 0.7 | .2580 | .2611 | .2642 | .2673 | .2704 | .2734 | .2764 | .2794 | .2823 | .2852 |
| 0.8 | .2881 | .2910 | .2939 | .2967 | .2995 | .3023 | .3051 | .3078 | .3106 | .3133 |
| 0.9 | .3159 | .3186 | .3212 | .3238 | .3264 | .3289 | .3315 | .3340 | .3365 | .3389 |
| 1.0 | .3413 | .3438 | .3461 | .3485 | .3508 | .3531 | .3554 | .3577 | .3599 | .3621 |
| 1.1 | .3643 | .3665 | .3686 | .3708 | .3729 | .3749 | .3770 | .3790 | .3810 | .3830 |
| 1.2 | .3849 | .3869 | .3888 | .3907 | .3925 | .3944 | .3962 | .3980 | .3997 | .4015 |
| 1.3 | .4032 | .4049 | .4066 | .4082 | .4099 | .4115 | .4131 | .4147 | .4162 | .4177 |
| 1.4 | .4192 | .4207 | .4222 | .4236 | .4251 | .4265 | .4279 | .4292 | .4306 | .4319 |
| 1.5 | .4332 | .4345 | .4357 | .4370 | .4382 | .4394 | .4406 | .4418 | .4429 | .4441 |
| 1.6 | .4452 | .4463 | .4474 | .4484 | .4495 | .4505 | .4515 | .4525 | .4535 | .4545 |
| 1.7 | .4554 | .4564 | .4573 | .4582 | .4591 | .4599 | .4608 | .4616 | .4625 | .4633 |
| 1.8 | .4641 | .4649 | .4656 | .4664 | .4671 | .4678 | .4686 | .4693 | .4699 | .4706 |
| 1.9 | .4713 | .4719 | .4726 | .4732 | .4738 | .4744 | .4750 | .4756 | .4761 | .4767 |
| 2.0 | .4772 | .4778 | .4783 | .4788 | .4793 | .4798 | .4803 | .4808 | .4812 | .4817 |
| 2.1 | .4821 | .4826 | .4830 | .4834 | .4838 | .4842 | .4846 | .4850 | .4854 | .4857 |
| 2.2 | .4861 | .4864 | .4868 | .4871 | .4875 | .4878 | .4881 | .4884 | .4887 | .4890 |
| 2.3 | .4893 | .4896 | .4898 | .4901 | .4904 | .4906 | .4909 | .4911 | .4913 | .4916 |
| 2.4 | .4918 | .4920 | .4922 | .4925 | .4927 | .4929 | .4931 | .4932 | .4934 | .4936 |
| 2.5 | .4938 | .4940 | .4941 | .4943 | .4945 | .4946 | .4948 | .4949 | .4951 | .4952 |
| 2.6 | .4953 | .4955 | .4956 | .4957 | .4959 | .4960 | .4961 | .4962 | .4963 | .4964 |
| 2.7 | .4965 | .4966 | .4967 | .4968 | .4969 | .4970 | .4971 | .4972 | .4973 | .4974 |
| 2.8 | .4974 | .4975 | .4976 | .4977 | .4977 | .4978 | .4979 | .4979 | .4980 | .4981 |
| 2.9 | .4981 | .4982 | .4982 | .4983 | .4984 | .4984 | .4985 | .4985 | .4986 | .4986 |
| 3.0 | .4987 | .4987 | .4987 | .4988 | .4988 | .4989 | .4989 | .4989 | .4990 | .4990 |

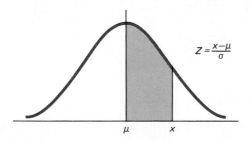

$$Z = \frac{x - \mu}{\sigma}$$

**Table A.2** The Binomial Distribution for Selected Values of $n$

| | | | | | | $p$ | | | | | |
|---|---|---|---|---|---|---|---|---|---|---|---|
| $r$ | .01 | .02 | .03 | .04 | .05 | .10 | .15 | .20 | .30 | .40 | .50 |
| | | | | | $n = 1$ | | | | | | |
| 0 | .9900 | .9800 | .9700 | .9600 | .9500 | .9000 | .8500 | .8000 | .7000 | .6000 | .5000 |
| 1 | .0100 | .0200 | .0300 | .0400 | .0500 | .1000 | .1500 | .2000 | .3000 | .4000 | .5000 |
| | | | | | $n = 2$ | | | | | | |
| 0 | .9801 | .9604 | .9409 | .9216 | .9025 | .8100 | .7225 | .6400 | .4900 | .3600 | .2500 |
| 1 | .0198 | .0392 | .0582 | .0768 | .0950 | .1800 | .2550 | .3200 | .4200 | .4800 | .5000 |
| 2 | .0001 | .0004 | .0009 | .0016 | .0025 | .0100 | .0225 | .0400 | .0900 | .1600 | .2500 |
| | | | | | $n = 3$ | | | | | | |
| 0 | .9704 | .9412 | .9127 | .8847 | .8574 | .7290 | .6141 | .5120 | .3430 | .2160 | .1250 |
| 1 | .0294 | .0576 | .0847 | .1106 | .1354 | .2430 | .3251 | .3840 | .4410 | .4320 | .3750 |
| 2 | .0003 | .0012 | .0026 | .0046 | .0071 | .0270 | .0574 | .0960 | .1890 | .2880 | .3750 |
| 3 | .0000 | .0000 | .0000 | .0001 | .0001 | .0010 | .0034 | .0080 | .0270 | .0640 | .1250 |
| | | | | | $n = 4$ | | | | | | |
| 0 | .9606 | .9224 | .8853 | .8493 | .8145 | .6561 | .5220 | .4096 | .2401 | .1296 | .0625 |
| 1 | .0388 | .0753 | .1095 | .1416 | .1715 | .2916 | .3685 | .4096 | .4116 | .3456 | .2500 |
| 2 | .0006 | .0023 | .0051 | .0088 | .0135 | .0486 | .0975 | .1536 | .2646 | .3456 | .3750 |
| 3 | .0000 | .0000 | .0001 | .0002 | .0005 | .0036 | .0115 | .0256 | .0756 | .1536 | .2500 |
| 4 | .0000 | .0000 | .0000 | .0000 | .0000 | .0001 | .0005 | .0016 | .0081 | .0256 | .0625 |
| | | | | | $n = 5$ | | | | | | |
| 0 | .9510 | .9039 | .8587 | .8154 | .7738 | .5905 | .4437 | .3277 | .1681 | .0778 | .0312 |
| 1 | .0480 | .0922 | .1328 | .1699 | .2036 | .3280 | .3915 | .4096 | .3602 | .2592 | .1562 |
| 2 | .0010 | .0038 | .0082 | .0142 | .0214 | .0729 | .1382 | .2048 | .3087 | .3456 | .3125 |
| 3 | .0000 | .0001 | .0003 | .0006 | .0011 | .0081 | .0244 | .0512 | .1323 | .2304 | .3125 |
| 4 | .0000 | .0000 | .0000 | .0000 | .0000 | .0004 | .0022 | .0064 | .0284 | .0768 | .1562 |
| 5 | .0000 | .0000 | .0000 | .0000 | .0000 | .0000 | .0001 | .0003 | .0024 | .0102 | .0312 |
| | | | | | $n = 6$ | | | | | | |
| 0 | .9415 | .8858 | .8330 | .7828 | .7351 | .5314 | .3771 | .2621 | .1176 | .0467 | .0156 |
| 1 | .0571 | .1085 | .1546 | .1957 | .2321 | .3543 | .3993 | .3932 | .3025 | .1866 | .0938 |
| 2 | .0014 | .0055 | .0120 | .0204 | .0305 | .0984 | .1762 | .2458 | .3241 | .3110 | .2344 |
| 3 | .0000 | .0002 | .0005 | .0011 | .0021 | .0146 | .0415 | .0819 | .1852 | .2765 | .3125 |
| 4 | .0000 | .0000 | .0000 | .0000 | .0001 | .0012 | .0055 | .0154 | .0595 | .1382 | .2344 |
| 5 | .0000 | .0000 | .0000 | .0000 | .0000 | .0001 | .0004 | .0015 | .0102 | .0369 | .0938 |
| 6 | .0000 | .0000 | .0000 | .0000 | .0000 | .0000 | .0000 | .0001 | .0007 | .0041 | .0156 |
| | | | | | $n = 7$ | | | | | | |
| 0 | .9321 | .8681 | .8080 | .7514 | .6983 | .4783 | .3206 | .2097 | .0824 | .0280 | .0078 |
| 1 | .0659 | .1240 | .1749 | .2192 | .2573 | .3720 | .3960 | .3670 | .2471 | .1306 | .0547 |
| 2 | .0020 | .0076 | .0162 | .0274 | .0406 | .1240 | .2097 | .2753 | .3177 | .2613 | .1641 |
| 3 | .0000 | .0003 | .0008 | .0019 | .0036 | .0230 | .0617 | .1147 | .2269 | .2903 | .2734 |
| 4 | .0000 | .0000 | .0000 | .0001 | .0002 | .0026 | .0109 | .0287 | .0972 | .1935 | .2734 |
| 5 | .0000 | .0000 | .0000 | .0000 | .0009 | .0002 | .0012 | .0043 | .0250 | .0774 | .1641 |
| 6 | .0000 | .0000 | .0000 | .0000 | .0000 | .0000 | .0001 | .0004 | .0036 | .0172 | .0547 |
| 7 | .0000 | .0000 | .0000 | .0000 | .0000 | .0000 | .0000 | .0000 | .0002 | .0016 | .0078 |

|  | | | | | | $p$ | | | | | |
|---|---|---|---|---|---|---|---|---|---|---|---|
| $r$ | .01 | .02 | .03 | .04 | .05 | .10 | .15 | .20 | .30 | .40 | .50 |

$n = 8$

| 0 | .9227 | .8508 | .7837 | .7214 | .6634 | .4305 | .2725 | .1678 | .0576 | .0168 | .0039 |
| 1 | .0746 | .1389 | .1939 | .2405 | .2793 | .3826 | .3847 | .3355 | .1977 | .0896 | .0312 |
| 2 | .0026 | .0099 | .0210 | .0351 | .0515 | .1488 | .2376 | .2936 | .2965 | .2090 | .1094 |
| 3 | .0001 | .0004 | .0013 | .0029 | .0054 | .0331 | .0839 | .1468 | .2541 | .2787 | .2188 |
| 4 | .0000 | .0000 | .0001 | .0002 | .0004 | .0046 | .0185 | .0459 | .1361 | .2322 | .2734 |
| 5 | .0000 | .0000 | .0000 | .0000 | .0000 | .0004 | .0026 | .0092 | .0467 | .1239 | .2188 |
| 6 | .0000 | .0000 | .0000 | .0000 | .0000 | .0000 | .0002 | .0011 | .0100 | .0413 | .1094 |
| 7 | .0000 | .0000 | .0000 | .0000 | .0000 | .0000 | .0000 | .0001 | .0012 | .0079 | .0312 |
| 8 | .0000 | .0000 | .0000 | .0000 | .0000 | .0000 | .0000 | .0000 | .0001 | .0007 | .0039 |

$n = 9$

| 0 | .9135 | .8337 | .7602 | .6925 | .6302 | .3874 | .2316 | .1342 | .0404 | .0101 | .0020 |
| 1 | .0830 | .1531 | .2116 | .2597 | .2985 | .3874 | .3679 | .3020 | .1556 | .0605 | .0176 |
| 2 | .0034 | .0125 | .0262 | .0433 | .0629 | .1722 | .2597 | .3020 | .2668 | .1612 | .0703 |
| 3 | .0001 | .0006 | .0019 | .0042 | .0077 | .0446 | .1069 | .1762 | .2668 | .2508 | .1641 |
| 4 | .0000 | .0000 | .0001 | .0003 | .0006 | .0074 | .0283 | .0661 | .1715 | .2508 | .2461 |
| 5 | .0000 | .0000 | .0000 | .0000 | .0000 | .0008 | .0050 | .0165 | .0735 | .1672 | .2461 |
| 6 | .0000 | .0000 | .0000 | .0000 | .0000 | .0001 | .0006 | .0028 | .0210 | .0743 | .1641 |
| 7 | .0000 | .0000 | .0000 | .0000 | .0000 | .0000 | .0000 | .0003 | .0039 | .0212 | .0703 |
| 8 | .0000 | .0000 | .0000 | .0000 | .0000 | .0000 | .0000 | .0000 | .0004 | .0035 | .0176 |
| 9 | .0000 | .0000 | .0000 | .0000 | .0000 | .0000 | .0000 | .0000 | .0000 | .0003 | .0020 |

$n = 10$

| 0 | .9044 | .8171 | .7374 | .6648 | .5987 | .3487 | .1969 | .1074 | .0282 | .0060 | .0010 |
| 1 | .0914 | .1667 | .2281 | .2770 | .3151 | .3874 | .3474 | .2684 | .1211 | .0403 | .0098 |
| 2 | .0042 | .0153 | .0317 | .0519 | .0746 | .1937 | .2759 | .3020 | .2335 | .1209 | .0439 |
| 3 | .0001 | .0008 | .0026 | .0058 | .0105 | .0574 | .1298 | .2013 | .2668 | .2150 | .1172 |
| 4 | .0000 | .0000 | .0001 | .0004 | .0010 | .0112 | .0401 | .0881 | .2001 | .2508 | .2051 |
| 5 | .0000 | .0000 | .0000 | .0000 | .0001 | .0015 | .0085 | .0264 | .1029 | .2007 | .2461 |
| 6 | .0000 | .0000 | .0000 | .0000 | .0000 | .0001 | .0012 | .0055 | .0368 | .1115 | .2051 |
| 7 | .0000 | .0000 | .0000 | .0000 | .0000 | .0000 | .0001 | .0008 | .0090 | .0425 | .1172 |
| 8 | .0000 | .0000 | .0000 | .0000 | .0000 | .0000 | .0000 | .0001 | .0014 | .0106 | .0439 |
| 9 | .0000 | .0000 | .0000 | .0000 | .0000 | .0000 | .0000 | .0000 | .0001 | .0016 | .0098 |
| 10 | .0000 | .0000 | .0000 | .0000 | .0000 | .0000 | .0000 | .0000 | .0000 | .0001 | .0010 |

$n = 15$

| 0 | .8601 | .7386 | .6333 | .5421 | .4633 | .2059 | .0874 | .0352 | .0047 | .0005 | .0000 |
| 1 | .1303 | .2261 | .2938 | .3388 | .3658 | .3432 | .2312 | .1319 | .0305 | .0047 | .0005 |
| 2 | .0092 | .0323 | .0636 | .0988 | .1348 | .2669 | .2856 | .2309 | .0916 | .0219 | .0032 |
| 3 | .0004 | .0029 | .0085 | .0178 | .0307 | .1285 | .2184 | .2501 | .1700 | .0634 | .0139 |
| 4 | .0000 | .0002 | .0008 | .0022 | .0049 | .0428 | .1156 | .1876 | .2186 | .1268 | .0417 |
| 5 | .0000 | .0000 | .0001 | .0002 | .0006 | .0105 | .0449 | .1032 | .2061 | .1859 | .0916 |
| 6 | .0000 | .0000 | .0000 | .0000 | .0000 | .0019 | .0132 | .0430 | .1472 | .2066 | .1527 |
| 7 | .0000 | .0000 | .0000 | .0000 | .0000 | .0003 | .0030 | .0138 | .0811 | .1771 | .1964 |
| 8 | .0000 | .0000 | .0000 | .0000 | .0000 | .0000 | .0005 | .0035 | .0348 | .1181 | .1964 |
| 9 | .0000 | .0000 | .0000 | .0000 | .0000 | .0000 | .0001 | .0007 | .0116 | .0612 | .1527 |
| 10 | .0000 | .0000 | .0000 | .0000 | .0000 | .0000 | .0000 | .0001 | .0030 | .0245 | .0916 |
| 11 | .0000 | .0000 | .0000 | .0000 | .0000 | .0000 | .0000 | .0000 | .0006 | .0074 | .0417 |
| 12 | .0000 | .0000 | .0000 | .0000 | .0000 | .0000 | .0000 | .0000 | .0001 | .0016 | .0139 |
| 13 | .0000 | .0000 | .0000 | .0000 | .0000 | .0000 | .0000 | .0000 | .0000 | .0003 | .0032 |
| 14 | .0000 | .0000 | .0000 | .0000 | .0000 | .0000 | .0000 | .0000 | .0000 | .0000 | .0005 |

| $p$ | | | | | | | | | | | |
|---|---|---|---|---|---|---|---|---|---|---|---|
| $r$ | .01 | .02 | .03 | .04 | .05 | .10 | .15 | .20 | .30 | .40 | .50 |

n = 20

| $r$ | .01 | .02 | .03 | .04 | .05 | .10 | .15 | .20 | .30 | .40 | .50 |
|---|---|---|---|---|---|---|---|---|---|---|---|
| 0 | .8179 | .6676 | .5438 | .4420 | .3585 | .1216 | .0388 | .0115 | .0008 | .0000 | .0000 |
| 1 | .1652 | .2725 | .3364 | .3683 | .3774 | .2702 | .1368 | .0576 | .0068 | .0005 | .0000 |
| 2 | .0159 | .0528 | .0988 | .1458 | .1887 | .2852 | .2293 | .1369 | .0278 | .0031 | .0002 |
| 3 | .0010 | .0065 | .0183 | .0364 | .0596 | .1901 | .2428 | .2054 | .0716 | .0123 | .0011 |
| 4 | .0000 | .0006 | .0024 | .0065 | .0133 | .0898 | .1821 | .2182 | .1304 | .0350 | .0046 |
| 5 | .0000 | .0000 | .0002 | .0009 | .0022 | .0319 | .1028 | .1746 | .1789 | .0746 | .0148 |
| 6 | .0000 | .0000 | .0000 | .0001 | .0003 | .0089 | .0454 | .1091 | .1916 | .1244 | .0370 |
| 7 | .0000 | .0000 | .0000 | .0000 | .0000 | .0020 | .0160 | .0545 | .1643 | .1659 | .0739 |
| 8 | .0000 | .0000 | .0000 | .0000 | .0000 | .0004 | .0046 | .0222 | .1144 | .1797 | .1201 |
| 9 | .0000 | .0000 | .0000 | .0000 | .0000 | .0001 | .0011 | .0074 | .0654 | .1597 | .1602 |
| 10 | .0000 | .0000 | .0000 | .0000 | .0000 | .0000 | .0002 | .0020 | .0308 | .1171 | .1762 |
| 11 | .0000 | .0000 | .0000 | .0000 | .0000 | .0000 | .0000 | .0005 | .0120 | .0710 | .1602 |
| 12 | .0000 | .0000 | .0000 | .0000 | .0000 | .0000 | .0000 | .0001 | .0039 | .0355 | .1201 |
| 13 | .0000 | .0000 | .0000 | .0000 | .0000 | .0000 | .0000 | .0000 | .0010 | .0146 | .0739 |
| 14 | .0000 | .0000 | .0000 | .0000 | .0000 | .0000 | .0000 | .0000 | .0002 | .0049 | .0370 |
| 15 | .0000 | .0000 | .0000 | .0000 | .0000 | .0000 | .0000 | .0000 | .0000 | .0013 | .0148 |
| 16 | .0000 | .0000 | .0000 | .0000 | .0000 | .0000 | .0000 | .0000 | .0000 | .0003 | .0046 |
| 17 | .0000 | .0000 | .0000 | .0000 | .0000 | .0000 | .0000 | .0000 | .0000 | .0000 | .0011 |
| 18 | .0000 | .0000 | .0000 | .0000 | .0000 | .0000 | .0000 | .0000 | .0000 | .0000 | .0002 |

n = 25

| $r$ | .01 | .02 | .03 | .04 | .05 | .10 | .15 | .20 | .30 | .40 | .50 |
|---|---|---|---|---|---|---|---|---|---|---|---|
| 0 | .7778 | .6035 | .4670 | .3604 | .2774 | .0718 | .0172 | .0038 | .0001 | .0000 | .0000 |
| 1 | .1964 | .3079 | .3611 | .3754 | .3650 | .1994 | .0759 | .0236 | .0014 | .0000 | .0000 |
| 2 | .0238 | .0754 | .1340 | .1877 | .2305 | .2659 | .1607 | .0708 | .0074 | .0004 | .0000 |
| 3 | .0018 | .0118 | .0318 | .0600 | .0930 | .2265 | .2174 | .1358 | .0243 | .0019 | .0001 |
| 4 | .0001 | .0013 | .0054 | .0137 | .0269 | .1384 | .2110 | .1867 | .0572 | .0071 | .0004 |
| 5 | .0000 | .0001 | .0007 | .0024 | .0060 | .0646 | .1564 | .1960 | .1030 | .0199 | .0016 |
| 6 | .0000 | .0000 | .0001 | .0003 | .0010 | .0239 | .0920 | .1633 | .1472 | .0442 | .0053 |
| 7 | .0000 | .0000 | .0000 | .0000 | .0001 | .0072 | .0441 | .1108 | .1712 | .0800 | .0143 |
| 8 | .0000 | .0000 | .0000 | .0000 | .0000 | .0018 | .0175 | .0623 | .1651 | .1200 | .0322 |
| 9 | .0000 | .0000 | .0000 | .0000 | .0000 | .0004 | .0058 | .0294 | .1336 | .1511 | .0609 |
| 10 | .0000 | .0000 | .0000 | .0000 | .0000 | .0001 | .0016 | .0118 | .0916 | .1612 | .0974 |
| 11 | .0000 | .0000 | .0000 | .0000 | .0000 | .0000 | .0004 | .0040 | .0536 | .1465 | .1328 |
| 12 | .0000 | .0000 | .0000 | .0000 | .0000 | .0000 | .0001 | .0012 | .0268 | .1140 | .1550 |
| 13 | .0000 | .0000 | .0000 | .0000 | .0000 | .0000 | .0000 | .0003 | .0115 | .0760 | .1550 |
| 14 | .0000 | .0000 | .0000 | .0000 | .0000 | .0000 | .0000 | .0001 | .0042 | .0434 | .1328 |
| 15 | .0000 | .0000 | .0000 | .0000 | .0000 | .0000 | .0000 | .0000 | .0013 | .0212 | .0974 |
| 16 | .0000 | .0000 | .0000 | .0000 | .0000 | .0000 | .0000 | .0000 | .0004 | .0088 | .0609 |
| 17 | .0000 | .0000 | .0000 | .0000 | .0000 | .0000 | .0000 | .0000 | .0001 | .0031 | .0322 |
| 18 | .0000 | .0000 | .0000 | .0000 | .0000 | .0000 | .0000 | .0000 | .0000 | .0009 | .0143 |
| 19 | .0000 | .0000 | .0000 | .0000 | .0000 | .0000 | .0000 | .0000 | .0000 | .0002 | .0053 |
| 20 | .0000 | .0000 | .0000 | .0000 | .0000 | .0000 | .0000 | .0000 | .0000 | .0000 | .0016 |
| 21 | .0000 | .0000 | .0000 | .0000 | .0000 | .0000 | .0000 | .0000 | .0000 | .0000 | .0004 |
| 22 | .0000 | .0000 | .0000 | .0000 | .0000 | .0000 | .0000 | .0000 | .0000 | .0000 | .0001 |

| $p$ | | | | | | | | | | | |
|---|---|---|---|---|---|---|---|---|---|---|---|
| $r$ | .01 | .02 | .03 | .04 | .05 | .10 | .15 | .20 | .30 | .40 | .50 |

| | | | | | | $n = 30$ | | | | | |
|---|---|---|---|---|---|---|---|---|---|---|---|
| 0 | .7397 | .5455 | .4010 | .2939 | .2146 | .0424 | .0076 | .0012 | .0000 | .0000 | .0000 |
| 1 | .2242 | .3340 | .3721 | .3673 | .3389 | .1413 | .0404 | .0093 | .0003 | .0000 | .0000 |
| 2 | .0328 | .0988 | .1669 | .2219 | .2586 | .2277 | .1034 | .0337 | .0018 | .0000 | .0000 |
| 3 | .0031 | .0188 | .0482 | .0863 | .1270 | .2361 | .1703 | .0785 | .0072 | .0003 | .0000 |
| 4 | .0002 | .0026 | .0101 | .0243 | .0451 | .1771 | .2028 | .1325 | .0208 | .0012 | .0000 |
| 5 | .0000 | .0003 | .0016 | .0053 | .0124 | .1023 | .1861 | .1723 | .0464 | .0041 | .0001 |
| 6 | .0000 | .0000 | .0002 | .0009 | .0027 | .0474 | .1368 | .1795 | .0829 | .0115 | .0006 |
| 7 | .0000 | .0000 | .0000 | .0001 | .0005 | .0180 | .0828 | .1538 | .1219 | .0263 | .0019 |
| 8 | .0000 | .0000 | .0000 | .0000 | .0001 | .0058 | .0420 | .1106 | .1501 | .0505 | .0055 |
| 9 | .0000 | .0000 | .0000 | .0000 | .0000 | .0016 | .0181 | .0676 | .1573 | .0823 | .0133 |
| 10 | .0000 | .0000 | .0000 | .0000 | .0000 | .0004 | .0067 | .0355 | .1416 | .1152 | .0280 |
| 11 | .0000 | .0000 | .0000 | .0000 | .0000 | .0001 | .0022 | .0161 | .1103 | .1396 | .0509 |
| 12 | .0000 | .0000 | .0000 | .0000 | .0000 | .0000 | .0006 | .0064 | .0749 | .1474 | .0806 |
| 13 | .0000 | .0000 | .0000 | .0000 | .0000 | .0000 | .0001 | .0022 | .0444 | .1360 | .1115 |
| 14 | .0000 | .0000 | .0000 | .0000 | .0000 | .0000 | .0000 | .0007 | .0231 | .1101 | .1354 |
| 15 | .0000 | .0000 | .0000 | .0000 | .0000 | .0000 | .0000 | .0002 | .0106 | .0783 | .1445 |
| 16 | .0000 | .0000 | .0000 | .0000 | .0000 | .0000 | .0000 | .0000 | .0042 | .0489 | .1354 |
| 17 | .0000 | .0000 | .0000 | .0000 | .0000 | .0000 | .0000 | .0000 | .0015 | .0269 | .1115 |
| 18 | .0000 | .0000 | .0000 | .0000 | .0000 | .0000 | .0000 | .0000 | .0005 | .0129 | .0806 |
| 19 | .0000 | .0000 | .0000 | .0000 | .0000 | .0000 | .0000 | .0000 | .0001 | .0054 | .0509 |
| 20 | .0000 | .0000 | .0000 | .0000 | .0000 | .0000 | .0000 | .0000 | .0000 | .0020 | .0280 |
| 21 | .0000 | .0000 | .0000 | .0000 | .0000 | .0000 | .0000 | .0000 | .0000 | .0006 | .0133 |
| 22 | .0000 | .0000 | .0000 | .0000 | .0000 | .0000 | .0000 | .0000 | .0000 | .0002 | .0055 |
| 23 | .0000 | .0000 | .0000 | .0000 | .0000 | .0000 | .0000 | .0000 | .0000 | .0000 | .0019 |
| 24 | .0000 | .0000 | .0000 | .0000 | .0000 | .0000 | .0000 | .0000 | .0000 | .0000 | .0006 |
| 25 | .0000 | .0000 | .0000 | .0000 | .0000 | .0000 | .0000 | .0000 | .0000 | .0000 | .0001 |

**Table A.3** Values of $e^a$ and $e^{-a}$

| $a$ | $e^a$ | $e^{-a}$ | $a$ | $e^a$ | $e^{-a}$ | $a$ | $e^a$ | $e^{-a}$ |
|---|---|---|---|---|---|---|---|---|
| 0.00 | 1.000 | 1.000 | 2.10 | 8.166 | 0.122 | 4.10 | 60.340 | 0.017 |
| 0.10 | 1.105 | 0.905 | 2.20 | 9.025 | 0.111 | 4.20 | 66.686 | 0.015 |
| 0.20 | 1.221 | 0.819 | 2.30 | 9.974 | 0.100 | 4.30 | 73.700 | 0.014 |
| 0.30 | 1.350 | 0.741 | 2.40 | 11.023 | 0.091 | 4.40 | 81.451 | 0.012 |
| 0.40 | 1.492 | 0.670 | 2.50 | 12.182 | 0.082 | 4.50 | 90.017 | 0.011 |
| 0.50 | 1.649 | 0.607 | 2.60 | 13.464 | 0.074 | 4.60 | 99.484 | 0.010 |
| 0.60 | 1.822 | 0.549 | 2.70 | 14.880 | 0.067 | 4.70 | 109.95 | 0.009 |
| 0.70 | 2.014 | 0.497 | 2.80 | 16.445 | 0.061 | 4.80 | 121.51 | 0.008 |
| 0.80 | 2.226 | 0.449 | 2.90 | 18.174 | 0.055 | 4.90 | 134.29 | 0.007 |
| 0.90 | 2.460 | 0.407 | 3.00 | 20.086 | 0.050 | 5.00 | 148.41 | 0.007 |
| 1.00 | 2.718 | 0.368 | 3.10 | 22.198 | 0.045 | 5.10 | 164.02 | 0.006 |
| 1.10 | 3.004 | 0.333 | 3.20 | 24.533 | 0.041 | 5.20 | 181.27 | 0.006 |
| 1.20 | 3.320 | 0.301 | 3.30 | 27.113 | 0.037 | 5.30 | 200.34 | 0.005 |
| 1.30 | 3.669 | 0.273 | 3.40 | 29.964 | 0.033 | 5.40 | 221.41 | 0.005 |
| 1.40 | 4.055 | 0.247 | 3.50 | 33.115 | 0.030 | 5.50 | 244.69 | 0.004 |
| 1.50 | 4.482 | 0.223 | 3.60 | 36.598 | 0.027 | 5.60 | 270.43 | 0.004 |
| 1.60 | 4.953 | 0.202 | 3.70 | 40.447 | 0.025 | 5.70 | 298.87 | 0.003 |
| 1.70 | 5.474 | 0.183 | 3.80 | 44.701 | 0.022 | 5.80 | 330.30 | 0.003 |
| 1.80 | 6.050 | 0.165 | 3.90 | 49.402 | 0.020 | 5.90 | 365.04 | 0.003 |
| 1.90 | 6.686 | 0.150 | 4.00 | 54.598 | 0.018 | 6.00 | 403.43 | 0.002 |
| 2.00 | 7.389 | 0.135 | | | | | | |

## Table A.4 Squares and Square Roots (1–500)

| n | $n^2$ | $\sqrt{n}$ | n | $n^2$ | $\sqrt{n}$ | n | $n^2$ | $\sqrt{n}$ |
|---|---|---|---|---|---|---|---|---|
| 1 | 1 | 1.000 | 51 | 2601 | 7.141 | 101 | 10201 | 10.049 |
| 2 | 4 | 1.414 | 52 | 2704 | 7.211 | 102 | 10404 | 10.099 |
| 3 | 9 | 1.732 | 53 | 2809 | 7.280 | 103 | 10609 | 10.148 |
| 4 | 16 | 2.000 | 54 | 2916 | 7.348 | 104 | 10816 | 10.198 |
| 5 | 25 | 2.236 | 55 | 3025 | 7.416 | 105 | 11025 | 10.246 |
| 6 | 36 | 2.449 | 56 | 3136 | 7.483 | 106 | 11236 | 10.295 |
| 7 | 49 | 2.645 | 57 | 3249 | 7.549 | 107 | 11449 | 10.344 |
| 8 | 64 | 2.828 | 58 | 3364 | 7.615 | 108 | 11664 | 10.392 |
| 9 | 81 | 3.000 | 59 | 3481 | 7.618 | 109 | 11881 | 10.440 |
| 10 | 100 | 3.162 | 60 | 3600 | 7.745 | 110 | 12100 | 10.488 |
| 11 | 121 | 3.316 | 61 | 3721 | 7.810 | 111 | 12321 | 10.535 |
| 12 | 144 | 3.464 | 62 | 3844 | 7.874 | 112 | 12544 | 10.583 |
| 13 | 169 | 3.605 | 63 | 3969 | 7.937 | 113 | 12769 | 10.630 |
| 14 | 196 | 3.741 | 64 | 4096 | 8.000 | 114 | 12996 | 10.677 |
| 15 | 225 | 3.872 | 65 | 4225 | 8.062 | 115 | 13225 | 10.723 |
| 16 | 256 | 4.000 | 66 | 4356 | 8.124 | 116 | 13456 | 10.770 |
| 17 | 289 | 4.123 | 67 | 4489 | 8.185 | 117 | 13689 | 10.816 |
| 18 | 324 | 4.242 | 68 | 4624 | 8.246 | 118 | 13924 | 10.862 |
| 19 | 361 | 4.358 | 69 | 4761 | 8.306 | 119 | 14161 | 10.908 |
| 20 | 400 | 4.472 | 70 | 4900 | 8.366 | 120 | 14400 | 10.954 |
| 21 | 441 | 4.582 | 71 | 5041 | 8.426 | 121 | 14641 | 11.000 |
| 22 | 484 | 4.690 | 72 | 5184 | 8.485 | 122 | 14884 | 11.045 |
| 23 | 529 | 4.795 | 73 | 5329 | 8.544 | 123 | 15129 | 11.090 |
| 24 | 576 | 4.898 | 74 | 5476 | 8.602 | 124 | 15376 | 11.135 |
| 25 | 625 | 5.000 | 75 | 5625 | 8.660 | 125 | 15625 | 11.180 |
| 26 | 676 | 5.099 | 76 | 5776 | 8.717 | 126 | 15876 | 11.224 |
| 27 | 729 | 5.196 | 77 | 5929 | 8.774 | 127 | 16129 | 11.269 |
| 28 | 784 | 5.291 | 78 | 6084 | 8.831 | 128 | 16384 | 11.313 |
| 29 | 841 | 5.385 | 79 | 6241 | 8.888 | 129 | 16641 | 11.357 |
| 30 | 900 | 5.477 | 80 | 6400 | 8.944 | 130 | 16900 | 11.401 |
| 31 | 961 | 5.567 | 81 | 6561 | 9.000 | 131 | 17161 | 11.445 |
| 32 | 1024 | 5.656 | 82 | 6724 | 9.055 | 132 | 17424 | 11.489 |
| 33 | 1089 | 5.744 | 83 | 6889 | 9.110 | 133 | 17689 | 11.532 |
| 34 | 1156 | 5.830 | 84 | 7056 | 9.165 | 134 | 17956 | 11.575 |
| 35 | 1225 | 5.916 | 85 | 7225 | 9.219 | 135 | 18225 | 11.618 |
| 36 | 1296 | 6.000 | 86 | 7396 | 9.273 | 136 | 18496 | 11.661 |
| 37 | 1369 | 6.082 | 87 | 7569 | 9.327 | 137 | 18769 | 11.704 |
| 38 | 1444 | 6.164 | 88 | 7744 | 9.380 | 138 | 19044 | 11.747 |
| 39 | 1521 | 6.244 | 89 | 7921 | 9.433 | 139 | 19321 | 11.789 |
| 40 | 1600 | 6.324 | 90 | 8100 | 9.486 | 140 | 19600 | 11.832 |
| 41 | 1681 | 6.403 | 91 | 8281 | 9.539 | 141 | 19881 | 11.874 |
| 42 | 1764 | 6.480 | 92 | 8464 | 9.591 | 142 | 20164 | 11.916 |
| 43 | 1849 | 6.557 | 93 | 8649 | 9.643 | 143 | 20449 | 11.958 |
| 44 | 1936 | 6.633 | 94 | 8836 | 9.695 | 144 | 20736 | 12.000 |
| 45 | 2025 | 6.708 | 95 | 9025 | 9.746 | 145 | 21025 | 12.041 |
| 46 | 2116 | 6.782 | 96 | 9216 | 9.797 | 146 | 21316 | 12.083 |
| 47 | 2209 | 6.855 | 97 | 9409 | 9.848 | 147 | 21609 | 12.124 |
| 48 | 2304 | 6.928 | 98 | 9604 | 9.899 | 148 | 21904 | 12.165 |
| 49 | 2401 | 7.000 | 99 | 9801 | 9.949 | 149 | 22201 | 12.206 |
| 50 | 2500 | 7.071 | 100 | 10000 | 10.000 | 150 | 22500 | 12.247 |

| $n$ | $n^2$ | $\sqrt{n}$ | $n$ | $n^2$ | $\sqrt{n}$ | $n$ | $n^2$ | $\sqrt{n}$ |
|---|---|---|---|---|---|---|---|---|
| 151 | 22801 | 12.288 | 206 | 42436 | 14.352 | 261 | 68121 | 16.155 |
| 152 | 23104 | 12.328 | 207 | 42849 | 14.387 | 262 | 68644 | 16.186 |
| 153 | 23409 | 12.369 | 208 | 43264 | 14.422 | 263 | 69169 | 16.217 |
| 154 | 23716 | 12.409 | 209 | 43681 | 14.456 | 264 | 69696 | 16.248 |
| 155 | 24025 | 12.449 | 210 | 44100 | 14.491 | 265 | 70225 | 16.278 |
| 156 | 24336 | 12.490 | 211 | 44521 | 14.525 | 266 | 70756 | 16.309 |
| 157 | 24649 | 12.529 | 212 | 44944 | 14.560 | 267 | 71289 | 16.340 |
| 158 | 24964 | 12.569 | 213 | 45369 | 14.594 | 268 | 71824 | 16.370 |
| 159 | 25281 | 12.609 | 214 | 45796 | 14.628 | 269 | 72361 | 16.401 |
| 160 | 25600 | 12.649 | 215 | 46225 | 14.662 | 270 | 72900 | 16.431 |
| 161 | 25921 | 12.688 | 216 | 46656 | 14.696 | 271 | 73441 | 16.462 |
| 162 | 26244 | 12.727 | 217 | 47089 | 14.730 | 272 | 73984 | 16.492 |
| 163 | 26569 | 12.767 | 218 | 47524 | 14.764 | 273 | 74529 | 16.522 |
| 164 | 26806 | 12.806 | 219 | 47961 | 14.798 | 274 | 75076 | 16.552 |
| 165 | 27225 | 12.845 | 220 | 48400 | 14.832 | 275 | 75625 | 16.583 |
| 166 | 27556 | 12.884 | 221 | 48841 | 14.866 | 276 | 76176 | 16.612 |
| 167 | 27889 | 12.922 | 222 | 49284 | 14.899 | 277 | 76729 | 16.643 |
| 168 | 28224 | 12.961 | 223 | 49729 | 14.933 | 278 | 77284 | 16.673 |
| 169 | 28561 | 13.000 | 224 | 50176 | 14.966 | 279 | 77841 | 16.703 |
| 170 | 28900 | 13.038 | 225 | 50625 | 15.000 | 280 | 78400 | 16.733 |
| 171 | 29241 | 13.076 | 226 | 51076 | 15.033 | 281 | 78961 | 16.763 |
| 172 | 29584 | 13.114 | 227 | 51529 | 15.066 | 282 | 79524 | 16.792 |
| 173 | 29929 | 13.152 | 228 | 51984 | 15.099 | 283 | 80089 | 16.822 |
| 174 | 30276 | 13.190 | 229 | 52441 | 15.132 | 284 | 80656 | 16.852 |
| 175 | 30625 | 13.228 | 230 | 52900 | 15.165 | 285 | 81225 | 16.881 |
| 176 | 30976 | 13.266 | 231 | 53361 | 15.198 | 286 | 81796 | 16.911 |
| 177 | 31329 | 13.304 | 232 | 53824 | 15.231 | 287 | 82369 | 16.941 |
| 178 | 31684 | 13.341 | 233 | 54289 | 15.264 | 288 | 82944 | 16.970 |
| 179 | 32041 | 13.379 | 234 | 54756 | 15.297 | 289 | 83521 | 17.000 |
| 180 | 32400 | 13.416 | 235 | 55225 | 15.329 | 290 | 84100 | 17.029 |
| 181 | 32761 | 13.453 | 236 | 55696 | 15.362 | 291 | 84681 | 17.058 |
| 182 | 33124 | 13.490 | 237 | 56169 | 15.394 | 292 | 85264 | 17.088 |
| 183 | 33489 | 13.527 | 238 | 56644 | 15.427 | 293 | 85849 | 17.117 |
| 184 | 33856 | 13.564 | 239 | 57121 | 15.459 | 294 | 86436 | 17.146 |
| 185 | 34225 | 13.601 | 240 | 57600 | 15.491 | 295 | 87025 | 17.175 |
| 186 | 34596 | 13.638 | 241 | 58081 | 15.524 | 296 | 87616 | 17.204 |
| 187 | 34969 | 13.674 | 242 | 58564 | 15.556 | 297 | 88209 | 17.233 |
| 188 | 35344 | 13.711 | 243 | 59049 | 15.588 | 298 | 88804 | 17.262 |
| 189 | 35721 | 13.747 | 244 | 59536 | 15.620 | 299 | 89401 | 17.291 |
| 190 | 36100 | 13.784 | 245 | 60025 | 15.652 | 300 | 90000 | 17.320 |
| 191 | 36481 | 13.820 | 246 | 60516 | 15.684 | 301 | 90601 | 17.349 |
| 192 | 36864 | 13.856 | 247 | 61009 | 15.716 | 302 | 91204 | 17.378 |
| 193 | 37249 | 13.892 | 248 | 61504 | 15.749 | 303 | 91809 | 17.406 |
| 194 | 37636 | 13.928 | 249 | 62001 | 15.779 | 304 | 92416 | 17.435 |
| 195 | 38025 | 13.964 | 250 | 62500 | 15.811 | 305 | 93025 | 17.464 |
| 196 | 38416 | 14.000 | 251 | 63001 | 15.842 | 306 | 93636 | 17.492 |
| 197 | 38809 | 14.035 | 252 | 63504 | 15.874 | 307 | 94249 | 17.521 |
| 198 | 39204 | 14.071 | 253 | 64009 | 15.905 | 308 | 94864 | 17.549 |
| 199 | 39601 | 14.106 | 254 | 64516 | 15.937 | 309 | 95481 | 17.578 |
| 200 | 40000 | 14.142 | 255 | 65025 | 15.968 | 310 | 96100 | 17.606 |
| 201 | 40401 | 14.177 | 256 | 65536 | 16.000 | 311 | 96721 | 17.635 |
| 202 | 40804 | 14.212 | 257 | 66049 | 16.031 | 312 | 97344 | 17.663 |
| 203 | 41209 | 14.247 | 258 | 66564 | 16.062 | 313 | 97969 | 17.691 |
| 204 | 41616 | 14.282 | 259 | 67081 | 16.093 | 314 | 98596 | 17.720 |
| 205 | 42025 | 14.317 | 260 | 67600 | 16.124 | 315 | 99225 | 17.748 |

| n | $n^2$ | $\sqrt{n}$ | n | $n^2$ | $\sqrt{n}$ | n | $n^2$ | $\sqrt{n}$ |
|---|---|---|---|---|---|---|---|---|
| 316 | 99856 | 17.776 | 371 | 137641 | 19.261 | 426 | 181476 | 20.639 |
| 317 | 100489 | 17.804 | 372 | 138384 | 19.287 | 427 | 182329 | 20.663 |
| 318 | 101124 | 17.832 | 373 | 139129 | 19.313 | 428 | 183184 | 20.688 |
| 319 | 101761 | 17.860 | 374 | 139876 | 19.339 | 429 | 184041 | 20.712 |
| 320 | 102400 | 17.888 | 375 | 140625 | 19.364 | 430 | 184900 | 20.736 |
| 321 | 103041 | 17.916 | 376 | 141376 | 19.390 | 431 | 185761 | 20.760 |
| 322 | 103684 | 17.944 | 377 | 142129 | 19.416 | 432 | 186624 | 20.784 |
| 323 | 104329 | 17.972 | 378 | 142884 | 19.442 | 433 | 187489 | 20.808 |
| 324 | 104976 | 18.000 | 379 | 143641 | 19.467 | 434 | 188356 | 20.832 |
| 325 | 105625 | 18.027 | 380 | 144400 | 19.493 | 435 | 189225 | 20.856 |
| 326 | 106276 | 18.055 | 381 | 145161 | 19.519 | 436 | 190096 | 20.880 |
| 327 | 106929 | 18.083 | 382 | 145924 | 19.544 | 437 | 190969 | 20.904 |
| 328 | 107584 | 18.110 | 383 | 146689 | 19.570 | 438 | 191844 | 20.928 |
| 329 | 108241 | 18.138 | 384 | 147456 | 19.595 | 439 | 192721 | 20.952 |
| 330 | 108900 | 18.165 | 385 | 148225 | 19.595 | 440 | 193600 | 20.976 |
| 331 | 109561 | 18.193 | 386 | 148996 | 19.646 | 441 | 194481 | 21.000 |
| 332 | 110224 | 18.220 | 387 | 149769 | 19.672 | 442 | 195364 | 21.023 |
| 333 | 110889 | 18.248 | 388 | 150544 | 19.697 | 443 | 196249 | 21.047 |
| 334 | 111556 | 18.275 | 389 | 151321 | 19.723 | 444 | 197136 | 21.071 |
| 335 | 112225 | 18.303 | 390 | 152100 | 19.748 | 445 | 198025 | 21.095 |
| 336 | 112896 | 18.330 | 391 | 152881 | 19.773 | 446 | 198916 | 21.118 |
| 337 | 113569 | 18.357 | 392 | 153664 | 19.798 | 447 | 199809 | 21.142 |
| 338 | 114244 | 18.384 | 393 | 154449 | 19.824 | 448 | 200704 | 21.166 |
| 339 | 114921 | 18.411 | 394 | 155236 | 19.849 | 449 | 201601 | 21.189 |
| 340 | 115600 | 18.439 | 395 | 156025 | 19.874 | 450 | 202500 | 21.213 |
| 341 | 116281 | 18.466 | 396 | 156816 | 19.899 | 451 | 203401 | 21.236 |
| 342 | 116964 | 18.493 | 397 | 157609 | 19.924 | 452 | 204304 | 21.260 |
| 343 | 117649 | 18.520 | 398 | 158404 | 19.949 | 453 | 205209 | 21.283 |
| 344 | 118336 | 18.547 | 399 | 159201 | 19.974 | 454 | 206116 | 21.307 |
| 345 | 119025 | 18.574 | 400 | 160000 | 20.000 | 455 | 207025 | 21.330 |
| 346 | 119716 | 18.601 | 401 | 160801 | 20.024 | 456 | 207936 | 21.354 |
| 347 | 120409 | 18.627 | 402 | 161604 | 20.049 | 457 | 208849 | 21.377 |
| 348 | 121104 | 18.654 | 403 | 162409 | 20.074 | 458 | 209764 | 21.400 |
| 349 | 121801 | 18.681 | 404 | 163216 | 20.099 | 459 | 210681 | 21.424 |
| 350 | 122500 | 18.708 | 405 | 164025 | 20.124 | 460 | 211600 | 21.447 |
| 351 | 123201 | 18.734 | 406 | 164836 | 20.149 | 461 | 212521 | 21.470 |
| 352 | 123904 | 18.761 | 407 | 165649 | 20.174 | 462 | 213444 | 21.494 |
| 353 | 124609 | 18.788 | 408 | 166464 | 20.199 | 463 | 214369 | 21.517 |
| 354 | 125316 | 18.814 | 409 | 167281 | 20.223 | 464 | 215296 | 21.540 |
| 355 | 126025 | 18.841 | 410 | 168100 | 20.248 | 465 | 216225 | 21.563 |
| 356 | 126736 | 18.867 | 411 | 168921 | 20.273 | 466 | 217156 | 21.587 |
| 357 | 127449 | 18.894 | 412 | 169744 | 20.297 | 467 | 218089 | 21.610 |
| 358 | 128164 | 18.920 | 413 | 170569 | 20.322 | 468 | 219024 | 21.633 |
| 359 | 128881 | 18.947 | 414 | 171396 | 20.346 | 469 | 219961 | 21.656 |
| 360 | 129600 | 18.973 | 415 | 172225 | 20.371 | 470 | 220900 | 21.679 |
| 361 | 130321 | 19.000 | 416 | 173056 | 20.396 | 471 | 221841 | 21.702 |
| 362 | 131044 | 19.026 | 417 | 173889 | 20.420 | 472 | 222784 | 21.725 |
| 363 | 131769 | 19.052 | 418 | 174724 | 20.445 | 473 | 223729 | 21.748 |
| 364 | 132496 | 19.078 | 419 | 175561 | 20.469 | 474 | 224676 | 21.771 |
| 365 | 133225 | 19.104 | 420 | 176400 | 20.493 | 475 | 225625 | 21.794 |
| 366 | 133956 | 19.131 | 421 | 177241 | 30.518 | 476 | 226576 | 21.817 |
| 367 | 134689 | 19.157 | 422 | 178084 | 20.542 | 477 | 227529 | 21.840 |
| 368 | 135424 | 19.183 | 423 | 178929 | 20.566 | 478 | 228484 | 21.863 |
| 369 | 136161 | 19.209 | 424 | 179776 | 20.591 | 479 | 229441 | 21.886 |
| 370 | 136900 | 19.235 | 425 | 180625 | 20.615 | 480 | 230400 | 21.908 |

| $n$ | $n^2$ | $\sqrt{n}$ | $n$ | $n^2$ | $\sqrt{n}$ | $n$ | $n^2$ | $\sqrt{n}$ |
|---|---|---|---|---|---|---|---|---|
| 481 | 231361 | 21.931 | 491 | 241081 | 22.158 | 496 | 246016 | 22.271 |
| 482 | 232324 | 21.954 | 492 | 242064 | 22.181 | 497 | 247009 | 22.293 |
| 483 | 233289 | 21.977 | 493 | 243049 | 22.203 | 498 | 248400 | 22.315 |
| 484 | 234256 | 22.000 | 494 | 244036 | 22.226 | 499 | 249001 | 22.338 |
| 485 | 235225 | 22.022 | 495 | 245025 | 22.248 | 500 | 250000 | 22.360 |
| | | | | | | | | |
| 486 | 236196 | 22.045 | | | | | | |
| 487 | 237169 | 22.068 | | | | | | |
| 488 | 238144 | 22.090 | | | | | | |
| 489 | 239121 | 22.113 | | | | | | |
| 490 | 240100 | 22.135 | | | | | | |

Appendix B
# Matrix
# Multiplication

The dimensions of a matrix relate to the number of rows and columns contained in the matrix. A matrix is typically referred to in terms of its dimensions expressed as $m$ rows and $n$ columns. For example, the following are examples of a $2 \times 3$, $3 \times 2$, and $1 \times 2$ matrix.

$$2 \times 3 \text{ matrix: } \begin{bmatrix} a_1 & a_2 & a_3 \\ b_1 & b_2 & b_3 \end{bmatrix}$$

$$3 \times 2 \text{ matrix: } \begin{bmatrix} a_1 & a_2 \\ b_1 & b_2 \\ c_1 & c_2 \end{bmatrix}$$

$$1 \times 2 \text{ matrix: } \begin{bmatrix} a_1 & a_2 \end{bmatrix}$$

The symbols $(a, b, c)$ within each matrix above represent values, either integer or fractional (i.e., probabilities).

*Multiplying two matrices* In order to multiply two matrices, the number of columns, $n$, in the first matrix must equal the number of rows, $m$, in the second matrix. For example, it is possible to multiply a $2 \times 3$ matrix and a $3 \times 2$ matrix, since the number of columns in the first, 3, equals the number of rows in the second, also 3.

$$\begin{bmatrix} a_1 & a_2 & a_3 \\ b_1 & b_2 & b_3 \end{bmatrix} \qquad \begin{bmatrix} c_1 & c_2 \\ d_1 & d_2 \\ e_1 & e_2 \end{bmatrix}$$

It is not possible to multiply two matrices of the dimensions, for example, of $1 \times 2$ and $3 \times 3$.

Two matrices of compatible dimensions are multiplied together by multiplying the values in the rows of the first matrix times the values in the columns of the second matrix and summing each of these sets of values. The dimensions of the resulting matrix will be the number of rows in the first matrix and the number of columns in the second matrix. As examples, we will use several of the matrices used in Markov analysis in chapter 13.

First, consider the multiplication of a $2 \times 2$ matrix by a $1 \times 2$ matrix. This will result in a $1 \times 2$ matrix.

$$\begin{bmatrix} a_1 & a_2 \end{bmatrix} \begin{bmatrix} b_1 & b_2 \\ c_1 & c_2 \end{bmatrix} = \begin{bmatrix} (a_1b_1 + a_2c_1) & (a_1b_2 + a_2c_2) \end{bmatrix}$$

*Examples of matrix multiplication* For our gasoline service station example in chapter 13:

$$\begin{bmatrix} .6 & .4 \end{bmatrix} \begin{bmatrix} .6 & .4 \\ .2 & .8 \end{bmatrix}$$

$$\begin{bmatrix} (.6)(.6) + (.4)(.2) & (.6)(.4) + (.4)(.8) \end{bmatrix}$$
$$\begin{bmatrix} .44 & .56 \end{bmatrix}$$

Next consider the multiplication of two $2 \times 2$ matrices, which will result in another $2 \times 2$ matrix.

$$\begin{bmatrix} a_1 & a_2 \\ b_1 & b_2 \end{bmatrix} \begin{bmatrix} c_1 & c_2 \\ d_1 & d_2 \end{bmatrix} = \begin{bmatrix} (a_1c_1 + a_2d_1) & (a_1c_2 + a_2d_2) \\ (b_1c_1 + b_2d_1) & (b_1c_2 + b_2d_2) \end{bmatrix}$$

For our service station example from chapter 13:

$$\begin{bmatrix} .44 & .56 \\ .28 & .72 \end{bmatrix} \begin{bmatrix} .60 & .40 \\ .20 & .80 \end{bmatrix}$$

$$\begin{bmatrix} (.44)(.60) + (.56)(.20) & (.44)(.40) + (.56)(.80) \\ (.28)(.60) + (.72)(.20) & (.28)(.40) + (.72)(.80) \end{bmatrix}$$

$$\begin{bmatrix} .38 & .62 \\ .31 & .69 \end{bmatrix}$$

Notice in the above case that the values in the first row are multiplied by the values in the first column and then summed. Next the values in the first row are multiplied by the values in the second column and summed. This results in the first row of the new matrix. This process is then repeated using the second row of the first matrix.

Now consider the multiplication of two $3 \times 3$ matrices. *A $3 \times 3$ matrix*

$$\begin{bmatrix} a_1 & a_2 & a_3 \\ b_1 & b_2 & b_3 \\ c_1 & c_2 & c_3 \end{bmatrix} \begin{bmatrix} d_1 & d_2 & d_3 \\ e_1 & e_2 & e_3 \\ f_1 & f_2 & f_3 \end{bmatrix} = \begin{bmatrix} (a_1d_1 + a_2e_1 + a_3f_1) & (a_1d_2 + a_2e_2 + a_3f_2) & (a_1d_3 + a_2e_3 + a_3f_3) \\ (b_1d_1 + b_2e_1 + b_3f_1) & (b_1d_2 + b_2e_2 + b_3f_2) & (b_1d_3 + b_2e_3 + b_3f_3) \\ (c_1d_1 + c_2e_1 + c_3f_1) & (c_1d_2 + c_2e_2 + c_3f_2) & (c_1d_3 + c_2e_3 + c_3f_3) \end{bmatrix}$$

As an example consider the squaring of the $3 \times 3$ matrix used in our truck rental example in chapter 13:

$$\begin{bmatrix} .6 & .2 & .2 \\ .3 & .5 & .2 \\ .4 & .1 & .5 \end{bmatrix} \begin{bmatrix} .6 & .2 & .2 \\ .3 & .5 & .2 \\ .4 & .1 & .5 \end{bmatrix}$$

$$\begin{bmatrix} (.6)(.6)+(.2)(.3)+(.2)(.4) & (.6)(.2)+(.2)(.5)+(.2)(.1) & (.6)(.2)+(.2)(.2)+(.2)(.5) \\ (.3)(.6)+(.5)(.3)+(.2)(.4) & (.3)(.2)+(.5)(.5)+(.2)(.1) & (.3)(.2)+(.5)(.2)+(.2)(.5) \\ (.4)(.6)+(.1)(.3)+(.5)(.4) & (.4)(.2)+(.1)(.5)+(.5)(.1) & (.4)(.2)+(.1)(.2)+(.5)(.5) \end{bmatrix}$$

$$\begin{bmatrix} .50 & .24 & .26 \\ .41 & .33 & .26 \\ .47 & .18 & .35 \end{bmatrix}$$

Appendix C
# The Poisson and Exponential Distributions

# The Poisson Distribution

*The Poisson distribution formula* The formula for a Poisson distribution is

$$P(x) = \frac{a^x e^{-a}}{x!}$$

where

$a = $ the average arrival rate (i.e., arrivals during a specified period of time)

$x = $ the number of arrivals during the specified time period

$e = 2.71828$

$x! = $ the factorial of a value, $x$ (i.e., $x! = x(x - 1)(x - 2)$ . . . (3)(2)(1)

*An example of the Poisson distribution* As an example of this distribution consider an average arrival rate of 5 customers per hour to a service facility ($a = 5$). The probability that exactly two customers will arrive at the service facility is found by letting $x = 2$ in the above Poisson formula.

$$P(x = 2) = \frac{5^2 e^{-5}}{2!}$$

$$= \frac{25 \, (.007)}{(2)(1)}$$

$$= .084$$

The value for $e^{-5}$ was found by using table A.3, a table with selected $e^{-a}$ values, in Appendix A. The value, .084, is the probability of exactly two customers arriving at the service facility.

*A distribution of customer arrivals* By substituting values of $x$ into the Poisson formula, a distribution of customer arrivals during a 1-hour period can be developed, as shown in figure C.1. However, remember that this distribution is for an arrival rate of 5 customers per hour. Other values of $a$ will result in different distributions than the one in figure C.1.

---

**Figure C.1** Poisson Distribution for $a = 5$.

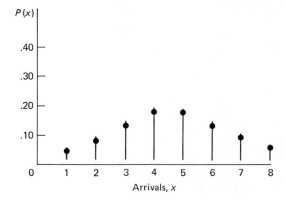

666          Appendix C

# The Exponential Distribution

The formula for the exponential distribution is

$$f(t) = se^{-st} \qquad t \geq 0$$

where

*The exponential distribution formula*

$s$ = the average number of customers served during a specified period of time.

$t$ = service time

$e$ = 2.71828

The *probability* that a customer is served within a specified time period can be determined by using the exponential distribution in the following form

$$P(T \leq t) = 1 - e^{-st}$$

If, for example, the service rate is 6 customers served per hour, then the probability that a customer will be served within 10 minutes (0.17 hours) is computed as follows.

*An exponential distribution example*

$$
\begin{aligned}
P(T \leq .17) &= 1 - e^{-6(.17)} \\
&= 1 - e^{-1.0} \\
&= 1 - .368 \\
&= .632
\end{aligned}
$$

Thus, the probability of a customer being served within 10 minutes is .632. Figure C.2 is the exponential probability distribution for this service rate ($s$ = 6).

---

**Figure C.2** Exponential distribution for $s$ = 6.

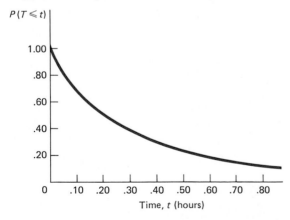

Appendix D
# Rules of
# Differentiation

Given a function defined by the following notation,

$$y = f(x)$$

then the derivative of this function is expressed as $\dfrac{dy}{dx} = f'(x)$.

The following is a set of rules for determining the derivatives of several different types of functions.

Rule 1: The derivative of a constant equals zero. In functional notation, if

$$y = k$$

where $k$ is a constant, then the derivative is

$$\frac{dy}{dx} = 0$$

For example, if $y = 10$, then $\dfrac{dy}{dx} = 0$.

Rule 2: The derivative of a variable equals one. In functional notation, if

$$y = x$$

then the derivative is

$$\frac{dy}{dx} = 1$$

Rule 3: For a variable raised to a power, $n$,

$$y = x^n$$

the derivative is

$$\frac{dy}{dx} = nx^{n-1}$$

For example, if $y = x^3$, the derivative is

$$\frac{dy}{dx} = 3x^2$$

We can also verify rule 2 using this formula. For a variable, $x$, the power ($n$) is one.

$$y = x^1$$

The derivative of this function is

$$\frac{dy}{dx} = 1x^0$$
$$= 1$$

which is the result we determined for rule 2.

*Rule 4:* For a function multiplied by a constant,

$$\frac{dy}{dx} = k \cdot f'(x)$$

For example, if $f(x) = x^4$ and $k = 10$ (i.e., $f(x) = 10x^4$), the derivative is

$$\frac{dy}{dx} = 10\,[4x^3]$$
$$= 40x^3$$

*Rule 5:* For two functions that are added (or subtracted),

$$y = f(x) + g(x)$$

the derivative is the sum (or difference) of the derivatives of the two functions.

$$\frac{dy}{dx} = f'(x) + g'(x)$$

For example, if $y = x^3 + 3x^4$, the derivative is

$$\frac{dy}{dx} = 3x^2 + 12x^3$$

*Rule 6:* For two functions that are multiplied,

$$y = f(x) \cdot g(x)$$

the derivative is the product of the first function multiplied by the derivative of the second, plus the second function times the derivative of the first.

$$\frac{dy}{dx} = f(x)g'(x) + f'(x)g(x)$$

For example, if $f(x) = x^3$ and $g(x) = 4x^4$, the derivative is

$$\frac{dy}{dx} = (x^3)(16x^3) + (3x^2)(4x^4)$$
$$= 16x^6 + 12x^6$$
$$= 28x^6$$

*Rule 7:* For two functions that are divided,

$$y = \frac{f(x)}{g(x)}$$

the derivative is determined by multiplying the denominator times the derivative of the numerator minus the numerator multiplied by the denominator squared.

$$\frac{dy}{dx} = \frac{g(x)f'(x) - g'(x)f(x)}{[g(x)]^2}$$

For example, if $f(x) = x^3$ and $g(x) = 5x^2$, the derivative is

$$\frac{dy}{dx} = \frac{(5x^2)(3x^2) - (x^3)(10x)}{[5x^2]^2}$$

$$= \frac{15x^4 - 10x^4}{25x^4}$$

$$= \frac{1}{5}$$

In chapter 23 the nonlinear functions that were included in our examples of the break-even model and inventory models were either *concave* or *convex*. In a convex function a straight line connecting any two points on the curve will be entirely *above* the curve. Alternatively, for a concave function, a straight line connecting any two points on the curve will be entirely *below* the curve. Examples of convex and concave functions are illustrated in figure E.1.

**Figure E.1** Convex and concave functions

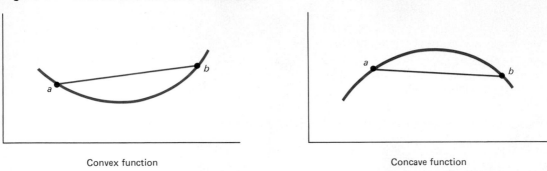

Convex function            Concave function

If either a convex or concave function exists in a problem, there will be only one minimum (or one maximum) point on the curve. The values of the variable corresponding to these maximum and minimum points can be computed by determining the first derivative of the nonlinear function and setting it equal to zero (as demonstrated in chaps. 23 and 24). This is a rather simple procedure, made so because the nonlinear function is either convex or concave. However, it is possible for a nonlinear function to be neither totally convex or concave, but instead a curve that contains several minimum and/or maximum points. Such a curve is shown in figure E.2.

**Figure E.2** A nonlinear function with several maximum and minimum points.

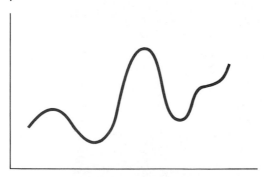

When this type of nonlinear function exists in a problem, we must go beyond the first derivative of the function and apply additional calculus steps.

The nonlinear function in figure E.2 contains two minimum points and two maximum points. These points are referred to as *extreme points*. Extreme points are further classified as *local* or *global* and *maximum* or *minimum*. The points *a, b, c,* and *d* in figure E.3 are relative extreme points. Points *a* and *c* are relative maximums, while points *b* and *d* are relative minimums. Since point *c* is the maximum of the two relative maximum points, it is known as the global (or absolute) maximum, while point *a* is a local maximum. Similarly, since point *b* is the minimum of the two relative minimum points, it is known as the global (or absolute) minimum, while point *d* is a local minimum. In nonlinear programming it is these global maximum and minimum points we are most interested in, since they correspond to items like maximum profit or minimum cost.

*Extreme points*

*Relative maximums and minimums*

*Global maximums and minimums*

**Figure E.3** A nonlinear function with global maximum and minimum points.

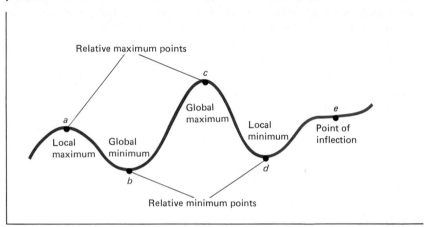

In our example problems in chapter 23, it was unnecessary to worry whether a maximum point on the curve was a *global* maximum (or whether a minimum point was a global minimum). Since they were either convex or concave, there was only one maximum or minimum point, so it had to be the global point. Thus, it was only necessary to compute the first derivative and solve for the values of the variables. However, for the function in figure E.3 by simply determining the first derivative at points *a, b, c,* and *d*, we do not actually determine the global points. To find the global maximum or minimum point, we must apply several additional calculus steps, which we will outline in the following discussion.

First, we must determine the first derivative and set it equal to zero as we have done in the past. This enables us to solve for the value of the variable corresponding to a relative extreme point. This is referred to as a

*necessary condition* for identifying relative extreme points. However, determining whether we have a relative maximum or minimum requires that

we take the *second derivative* of the function.

The second derivative of a nonlinear function is determined by applying the rules of differentiation to the first derivative. The symbolic notation for the second derivative of a function, $y$, with respect to a variable, $x$, is

$$\frac{\partial^2 y}{\partial x^2}$$

Once the second derivative is determined, the value of the variable, $x$, determined from the first derivative is substituted into the second derivative function. If the resulting value of the second derivative is greater than zero, the point (defined by the variable values) is a relative minimum. If the value of the second derivative is less than zero, the point is a relative maximum. (If the second derivative value equals zero, the point is *generally*

known as a *point of inflection*, which is a point on the curve where it flattens out, but is neither a maximum or minimum. Point $e$ in fig. E.3 is

a point of inflection.) This step is referred to as a *sufficient condition*.

In order to determine if a relative maximum or minimum point is a global point, the value of the variable at this point must be substituted into the original function ($y$) and solved (for $y$). All other relative points are treated similarly and then compared to determine which one is global. This comparison should also include the *end points* of the function.

These steps are summarized as follows.

1. Determine the first derivative $\frac{\partial y}{\partial x}$ of a function, $y$, with respect to the variable, $x$. Set it equal to zero and solve for the value of the variable, $x$. This is called a *necessary condition.*

2. Determine the second derivative, $\frac{\partial^2 y}{\partial x^2}$ of the function, and substitute the value of $x$ determined in step 1 into this second derivative. If

   $\frac{\partial^2 y}{\partial x^2} \geq 0$, a relative minimum exists

   $\frac{\partial^2 y}{\partial x^2} < 0$, a relative maximum exists.

3. Substitute the variable values computed at all relative maximum (or minimum) points into the original function and compare the results to all other relative points to see which is the global point (i.e., the maximum or minimum).

As an example, consider our first example of the profit analysis model in chapter 24. We will go through the above steps for the function.

*The profit model example*

$$Z = 1,696.8p - 24.6p^2 - 22,000$$

1. Determine the first derivative, set it equal to zero, and solve.

$$\frac{\partial z}{\partial p} = 1,696.8 - 49.2p$$

$$0 = 1,696.8 - 49.2p$$
$$p = 34.49$$

2. Determine the second derivative.

$$\frac{\partial^2 Z}{\partial p^2} = -49.2$$

Since no values can be substituted into this relationship, we perform our test.

$$\frac{\partial^2 Z}{\partial p^2} = -49.2 < 0$$

As such, a relative maximum exists.

3. Since this solution point, $p = \$34.49$, is the only solution available, it is the global maximum.

These basic principles of calculus are the foundation on which some of the more complex extensions of the Lagrangian solution method are based. However, the calculus steps we have presented in this appendix are for functions with a single variable. As more variables are introduced into a nonlinear programming, these steps must be extended somewhat, although the basic approach remains the same.

# Glossary

## a

**absorbing state**   a state in a Markov transition matrix that the system cannot move from once it has been achieved (also known as a trapping state).

**activities**   in a CPM/PERT project network, the branches reflecting project operations.

**activity slack**   in a CPM/PERT network, the extra time an activity start can be delayed without exceeding the critical path project time.

**adjusted exponential smoothing**   the exponential smoothing forecasting technique adjusted for trend changes and seasonal patterns.

**analytical**   containing or pertaining to mathematical analysis using formulas or equations.

**a priori probability**   one of the two types of objective probabilities. Given a set of outcomes for an activity, it is the ratio of the number of specific (desired) outcomes to the total number of outcomes.

**arrival rate**   the number of arrivals at a service facility (within a queuing system) during a specified period of time.

**artificial variable**   a variable that is added to an "=" or "≥" constraint so that initial solutions in a linear programming problem can be obtained at the origin.

**assignment model**   a type of linear programming model similar to a transportation model, except that the supply at each source is limited to one unit and the demand at each destination is limited to one unit.

## b

**backorder**   a customer order that cannot be filled from existing inventory and is filled when inventory is replenished.

**backward pass**   a means for determining the latest event times in a CPM/PERT network.

**balanced transportation model**   a model in which supply equals demand.

**basic feasible solutions**   any solution in linear programming that satisfies the model constraints.

**basic variables**   variables that have values (other than zero) at a basic feasible solution point in a linear programming problem.

**Bayes' law**   a method for altering marginal probabilities, given additional information. The altered probabilities are referred to as revised or posterior probabilities.

**Bernoulli process**   a probability experiment that contains the following properties: (1) two outcomes for each trial, (2) the probabilities remain constant, (3) the outcomes are independent, and (4) the number of trials is discrete.

**beta distribution**   a probability distribution used in network analysis to determine activity times.

**binomial distribution**   a probability distribution in which the Bernoulli properties exist.

**branch**   in a network diagram, a line that represents the flow of items from one point (i.e., node) to another.

**branch and bound method**   a solution approach that partitions a total set of feasible solutions into smaller subsets, which are then evaluated systematically. This technique is used extensively to solve integer programming problems.

**break-even analysis**   the determination of the number of units that must be produced and sold to equate total revenue with total cost.

**break-even point**   the volume of units that equates total revenue with total cost.

## c

**calculus**   a branch of mathematics concerned with the rate of change of functions. The two basic forms of calculus are differential calculus and integral calculus.

**calling population**   the source of customers to a waiting line.

**carrying cost**   the cost incurred by a business for holding items in inventory.

**classical optimization**   the use of calculus to find optimal values for variables.

**classical probability** an a priori probability.

**closed path** in a transportation tableau, a path along which transported items can be reallocated.

**coefficient of determination** a measure of the strength of the relationship of the variables in a regression equation.

**coefficient of optimism** a measure of a decision maker's optimism.

**collectively exhaustive events** all of the possible events of an experiment.

**computer program** a set of instructions written by an operator to tell a computer what operations to perform.

**concave** a curve shaped like an inverted bowl.

**conditional probability** the probability that one event will occur, given that another event has already occurred.

**constrained optimization** a model with a single objective function and one or more constraints.

**constraint** a mathematical relationship that represents limited resources or minimum levels of activity in a mathematical programming model.

**continuous distribution** a probability distribution in which the random variables can equal an infinite number of values within an interval.

**convex** a curve shaped like an upright bowl.

**critical path** the longest path through a CPM/PERT network. It indicates the minimum time in which a project can be completed.

**critical path method (CPM)** a network technique used for project planning and scheduling, which consists of deterministic activity times.

**cycle** movement up or down during a trend in a forecast.

# d

**data** pieces of information

**data base** an organized collection of numerical information.

**decision analysis** the analysis of decision situations in which certainty cannot be assumed.

**decision tree** a graphical diagram for analyzing a decision situation.

**decision variable** a variable, the value of which represents a potential decision on the part of the manager.

**degeneracy (in a simplex tableau)** a series of loops in the simplex solution to a linear programming problem that does not allow the solution to improve in subsequent simplex iterations.

**degeneracy (in a transportation tableau)** a transportation tableau that does not have the required "$m + n - 1$" cell allocations.

**dependent events** the occurrence of one event affects the probability of the occurrence of another event.

**derivative** in calculus, a transformation of a mathematical function to a form, which equals the slope of the function.

**deterministic** the assumption is made that there is no uncertainty.

**deviational variables** in a goal programming model constraint, variables that reflect the possible deviation from a goal level.

**differential** the derivative of a function.

**directed branch** a branch in a network in which flow is possible in only one direction.

**discrete distribution** a probability distribution that consists of values for the random variable that are countable and usually integer.

**dominant strategies** the outcomes of a strategy for a player in a game are consistently better than another strategy (or strategies).

**dual** an alternative form of a linear programming model that contains useful information regarding the value of the resources, which form the constraints of the model.

**dual constraints** the constraints of the dual of a linear programming model. There is a dual constraint corresponding to each variable in the primal model.

**dual variables** the variables of the dual of a linear programming model. There is a dual variable corresponding to each constraint in the primal model.

**dummy activity** a branch in a CPM/PERT network, which reflects a precedence relationship but does not constitute any passage of time.

**dynamic programming** a solution approach in which problems are solved in stages.

**dynamic programming state** the possible resource levels available at each stage of a dynamic programming problem.

# e

**earliest event time** in a CPM/PERT network, the earliest time an event can be started without exceeding the critical path project time.

**economic forecast** a prediction of the state of the economy in the future.

**economic order quantity (EOQ)** the optimal order size that corresponds to total minimum inventory cost.

**efficiency of sample information** an indicator of how close to perfection sample information is; it is computed by dividing the expected value of sample information by the expected value of perfect information.

**empirical** consisting of (or based on) data or information gained from an experiment and observation.

**equal likelihood criterion** a method for making a decision in which all states of nature are weighted equally.

**equilibrium point** the outcome of a game that results from a pure strategy.

**event** the possible result of a probability experiment.

**events** in a CPM/PERT project network, the nodes that reflect the beginning and termination of activities.

**expected monetary value** the expected (average) monetary outcome of a decision, computed by multiplying the outcomes by their probabilities of occurrence and summing these multiples.

**expected opportunity loss** the expected opportunity loss as the result of an incorrect decision by the decision maker.

**expected value** an *average* value computed by multiplying each value of a random variable by its probability of occurrence.

**expected value of perfect information (EVPI)** the value of information that a decision maker would be willing to pay in order to make a better decision.

**expected value of sample information** the difference between the expected value of a decision situation with information and without additional information.

**experiment** in probability, a particular action, such as tossing a coin.

**exponential distribution** a probability distribution often used to define the service times in a queuing system.

**exponential smoothing** a time series forecasting method similar to a moving average, except the more recent data is weighted more heavily than past data.

**extreme points** the maximum and minimum points on a curve (also known as relative extreme points).

## f

**factorials** for a value of $n$, the factorial is $n! = n(n - 1)(n - 2) \ldots (2)(1)$.

**feasible solution** a solution that does not violate any of the restrictions or constraints in a model.

**feedback** decision results that are fed back into the management information system to be used as data.

**fixed costs** costs that are independent of the volume of units produced.

**forecast** a prediction of what will occur in the future.

**forecast reliability** a measure of how closely a forecast reflects reality.

**forecast time frame** how far in the future the forecast encompasses.

**forward pass** a method for determining earliest event times in a CPM/PERT network.

**frequency distribution** the organization of events into classes, which shows the frequency with which the events occur.

**functional relationship** an equation that relates a dependent variable to one or more independent variables.

## g

**game players** the competing decision makers in a game situation.

**game strategy** a plan of action to be followed by a player.

**game theory** an area of management science encompassing decision situations in which one or more decision makers compete for the best outcome.

**global maximum** the absolute maximum extreme point on a curve.

**global minimum** the absolute minimum extreme point on a curve.

**goal constraint** a constraint in a goal programming model that contains deviational variables.

**goal programming** a linear programming technique that considers more than one objective in the model.

**goals** the alternative objectives in a goal programming model.

**gradient search methods** computerized approaches for solving complex nonlinear programming problems.

## h

**hardware** the computer machine and ancillary equipment.

**Hurwicz criterion** a method for making a decision in a decision analysis problem. The decision is a compromise between total optimism and total pessimism.

## i

**implementation** the actual use of model results.

**implicit enumeration** a method for solving integer programming problems in which obviously infeasible solutions are eliminated and the remaining solutions are systematically evaluated to see which one is best.

**independent events** the occurrence of one event does not affect the probability of the occurrence of another event.

**inequality** a mathematical relationship that contains a "$\geq$" or "$\leq$" sign.

**infeasible problem** a linear programming problem with no feasible solution area, thus there is no solution.

**information flow** the flow of information from one point to another in an organizational management information system.

**instantaneous receipt** when an inventory level reaches zero an order arrives immediately after the passage of an infinitely small amount of time.

**integer programming** a form of linear programming that consists of only integer solution values for the model variables.

**interactive computer program** programs developed to determine input data from a manager in the form of questions.

**inventory analysis** the analysis of the problems of inventory planning and control, with the objective of minimizing inventory related costs.

# j

**joint probability** the probability of several of the events occurring jointly in an experiment.

# k

**knapsack problem** a dynamic programming problem concerned with how many of each of several different kinds of items to put in a knapsack in order to maximize the return from the items.

# l

**Lagrange multiplier** a value, $\lambda$, which reflects the approximate change in the objective function resulting from a unit change in the right-hand side quantity of a constraint equation.

**Lagrange multipliers method** a solution approach for nonlinear programming problems in which the constraints, as multiples of a constant, are subtracted from the objective function.

**Lagrangian function** the transformed objective function in a nonlinear programming problem being solved with Lagrange multipliers.

**LaPlace criterion** a method for making a decision in which all states of nature are weighted equally (more commonly known as the equal likelihood criterion).

**latest event time** in a CPM/PERT network, the latest time an event can be started without exceeding the critical path project time.

**linear programming** a management science technique in which an objective is sought subject to restrictions where all the mathematical relationships are linear.

**linear (simple) regression** a form of regression that reflects the relationship of two variables.

**long-range forecast** a forecast which typically encompasses a period of time longer than one or two years.

# m

**management information system (MIS)** a system in an organization for accumulating, organizing, and distributing information.

**management science** the application of mathematical techniques and scientific principles to management problems in order to help managers make better decisions.

**Markov analysis** a probabilistic technique applicable to systems that exhibit probabilistic movement from one state of the system to another over time.

**maximal flow problem** a network problem in which the objective is to maximize the total amount of flow from a source to a destination.

**maximax criterion** a method for making a decision in a decision analysis problem. The decision will result in the maximum of the maximum payoffs.

**maximin criterion** a method for choosing a decision in a decision analysis problem. The decision that will result is the maximum of the minimum payoffs.

**maximization problem** a linear programming problem in which an objective, such as profit, is maximized.

**mean absolute deviation (MAD)** a measure of the difference between a forecast and what actually occurred.

**medium-range forecast** a forecast that encompasses anywhere from one or two months up to a year.

**midsquare method** a numerical method for generating a series of random numbers.

**minimal spanning tree problem** a network problem in which the objective is to connect all the nodes so that the total branch lengths are minimized.

**minimax regret criterion** a method for making a decision in a decision analysis problem. The decision will minimize the maximum regret.

**minimization problem** a linear programming problem in which an objective, such as cost, is minimized.

**minimum cell cost method**   a method for determining the initial solution to a transportation model.

**mixed integer model**   an integer linear programming model that can contain a solution with both integer and noninteger values.

**mixed strategy game**   a game in which the players adopt a mixture of strategies.

**model**   an abstract (mathematical) representation of an existing problem situation.

**modified distribution method (MODI)**   a method for solving a transportation model that is a modified version of the stepping-stone method.

**Monte Carlo process**   a technique used in simulation for selecting numbers randomly from a probability distribution.

**most likely time**   one of the three time estimates used in a beta distribution to determine an activity time. It is the time that would most frequently occur if the activity were repeated many times.

**moving average**   a time series forecasting method computed by dividing values of a forecast variable by a sequence of time periods.

**multiple optimum solutions**   the existence of more than one best solution to a linear programming problem. All such alternative solutions achieve the same objective function value.

**multiple regression**   a form of regression that reflects the relationship of more than two variables.

**multiple-server queuing system**   a single waiting line that feeds into two or more servers in parallel.

**mutually exclusive events**   a probability experiment where only one of the events can occur at a time.

## n

**necessary condition**   a mathematical condition that must exist for a point on a curve to be a global maximum or minimum.

**network**   an arrangement of paths connected at various points (drawn as a diagram) through which an item (or items) move from one point to another.

**network flow models**   networks that are directed at the flow of items through a system.

**node**   in a network diagram, a point that represents a junction or intersection. It is represented by a circle.

**nonbasic variables**   the variables that equal zero at a basic feasible solution point in a linear programming problem.

**noninstantaneous receipt**   the gradual receipt of inventory over time when a company produces its own inventory.

**nonlinear programming**   a form of mathematical programming in which the objective function or constraints (or both) are nonlinear functions.

**normal distribution**   a continuous probability distribution that has the shape of a bell.

**northwest corner method**   a method for determining the initial solution to a transportation model.

**n-person game**   a game situation in which more than two decision makers compete.

## o

**objective function**   a mathematical relationship that represents the objective of a problem solution.

**objective probability**   a probability that is the relative frequency that a specific outcome in an experiment has been observed to occur in the long run.

**opportunity cost table**   a table derived in the solution to an assignment problem.

**optimal solution**   the one best solution to a problem.

**optimistic time**   one of the three time estimates used in a beta distribution to determine an activity time. It is the shortest possible time within which an activity could be completed if everything went right.

**order cycle**   the time period during which a maximum inventory level is depleted and a new order is received to bring inventory back to its maximum level.

**ordering cost**   the cost a business incurs when it makes an order to replenish its inventory.

## p

**parameter**   a constant value that is generally a coefficient of a variable in a mathematical equation.

**payoff table**   a table used to show the payoffs that can result from decisions under various states of nature.

**penalty cost**   the penalty (or regret) suffered by the decision maker when a wrong decision is made.

**permanent set**   in a shortest route network problem, a set of nodes to which the shortest route from the start node has been determined.

**pessimistic time**   one of the three time estimates used in a beta distribution to determine an activity time. It is the longest possible time an activity would require to be completed, assuming everything went wrong.

**pivot column**   the column in a simplex tableau that corresponds to the entering nonbasic variable.

**pivot row**   the row in the simplex tableau that corresponds to the leaving basic variable.

**poisson distribution**   a probability distribution often used to define arrivals at a service facility in a queuing system.

**political/social forecast**   a prediction of political and social changes that may occur in the future.

**postoptimality analysis**   the analysis of the optimal simplex solution in order to gain additional information, i.e., duality and sensitivity analysis.

**precedence relationship**   a specified sequence of activities and events that is represented by a CPM/PERT network.

**primal**   the original form of a linear programming model.

**priority goal**   the priority of a goal reflects its importance as compared to other goals in a goal programming model.

**probabilistic techniques**   management science techniques that reflect information that is uncertain and give probabilistic solutions.

**probability distribution**   a distribution showing the probability with which all events in an experiment occur.

**probability tree**   a diagram showing the probabilities of the various outcomes of an experiment.

**production lot size model**   an inventory model in which the business produces its own inventory at a gradual rate (also known as the noninstantaneous receipt model).

**prohibited route**   in a transportation model, a route (i.e., variable) to which no allocation can be made.

**project evaluation and review technique (PERT)**   a network technique used for project planning and scheduling, which consists of probabilistic activity times.

**pseudorandom numbers**   random numbers generated by a mathematical process rather than a physical process.

**pure strategy game**   a game in which each player adopts a single strategy as their optimal strategy.

## q

**quantity discount model**   an inventory model in which a discount is received for large orders.

**queue**   a waiting line.

**queue discipline**   the order in which customers waiting in line are served.

**queuing analysis**   the probabilistic analysis of waiting lines.

## r

**random numbers**   numbers that are equally likely to be drawn from a large population of numbers.

**random number table**   a table containing random numbers derived from some artificial process, such as a computer program.

**random variable**   a variable that can be assigned a numerical value reflecting the outcomes of an event. Since these values occur in no particular order, they are said to be random.

**recursive return function**   the return from stage $n$ of a dynamic programming problem plus the *previous* returns at previous stages.

**regression**   a statistical technique for measuring the relationship of one variable to one or more other variables. This method is used extensively in forecasting.

**regression equation**   the transformation of historical data into an equation that is used to forecast.

**regret**   a value representing the regret a decision maker suffers when a wrong decision is made.

**relative frequency probability**   another name for an objective (a posteriori) probability. It is the relative frequency that a specific outcome has been observed to occur in the long run.

**relaxed solution**   a solution to an integer programming model in which the integer restrictions are relaxed.

**remote terminal**   a piece of computer equipment much like a typewriter that is connected to the computer by telephone lines, which can be used to operate a computer from a distance.

**reorder lead time**   the time required between the placement of an order and its receipt into inventory.

**reorder point**   the inventory level at which an order is placed and which will be depleted during the reorder lead time.

**rim requirements**   the supply and demand values along the outer row and column of a transportation tableau.

**risk averter**   a person who avoids risky situations.

**risk taker**   a person who takes risks in order to achieve a large return.

**row operations**   an algebraic method for solving simultaneous linear equations.

## s

**safety stock**   a buffer of extra inventory to guard against a stockout (i.e., running out of inventory).

**satisfactory solution** in a goal programming model, a solution that satisfies the goals in the best way possible.

**scatter diagram** a diagram used in forecasting that shows historical data points.

**scientific method** a method for solving problems that includes the following steps: (1) observation, (2) problem definition, (3) model construction, (4) model solution, and (5) implementation.

**search techniques** methods for searching through the solutions generated by a simulation model to find the best one.

**seasonal pattern** a movement that occurs periodically and is repetitive in a forecast.

**sensitivity analysis** the analysis of changes in the parameters of a linear programming problem.

**sequential decision tree** a decision tree that analyzes a series of sequential decisions.

**service level** the percentage of customers a business is able to service from inventory in stock during the reorder period.

**service rate** the average number of customers that can be served from a queue in a specified period of time.

**shadow prices** the price one would be willing to pay to obtain one more unit of a resource in a linear programming problem.

**shared slack** in a CPM/PERT network, slack that is shared between several adjacent activities.

**shortest route problem** a network problem in which the objective is to determine the shortest distance between an originating point and several destination points.

**short-range forecast** a forecast of the immediate future, which is concerned with daily operations.

**simple regression** a form of regression that reflects the relationship of two variables.

**simplex method** a tabular approach to solving linear programming problems.

**simplex tableau** the table in which the steps of the simplex method are conducted. Each tableau represents a solution.

**simulated time** the quickened representation of real time in a simulation model.

**simulation** the replication of a real system with a mathematical model that can be analyzed with a computer.

**simulation language** a computer programming language developed specifically for performing simulation.

**single-server waiting line** a waiting line that contains only one service facility at which customers can be served.

**slack variable** a variable added to a $\leq$ inequality constraint to make the constraint an equation. It represents unused resources.

**slope** the rate of change in a mathematical function.

**smoothing constant** a weighting factor used in the exponential smoothing forecasting technique.

**software** the mathematical and written codes that instruct the computer how to perform mathematical operations.

**stagecoach problem** a network routing problem of determining the shortest route between two places that can be solved using dynamic programming or network flow models.

**stages** the smaller subproblems of a dynamic programming problem.

**standard deviation** a measure of dispersion around the mean of a probability distribution.

**standard form of a linear programming model** a maximization model with all "$\leq$" constraints or a minimization model with all "$\geq$" constraints.

**states of nature** in a decision situation, the possible events that will occur in the future.

**steady state** a constant value, which a system achieves after an extended period of time.

**steady-state probability** a constant probability of ending up in a state in the future, regardless of the starting state.

**stepping-stone method** a method for solving a transportation model.

**stockout** running out of inventory.

**subjective probability** a probability that is based on personal experience, knowledge of a situation, or intuition without the benefit of a priori or a posteriori evidence.

**substitution method** a method for solving nonlinear programming problems that contain only one equality constraint. The constraint is solved for one variable in terms of another and substituted in the objective function.

**surplus variable** a surplus variable is subtracted from a $\geq$ inequality constraint in a linear programming problem and reflects the excess above a minimum resource requirement level.

**system** a set or arrangement of items related in such a way as to form an organic whole (i.e., an organization of things).

**t**

**technological forecast** a prediction of what types of technology may be available in the future.

**time series methods** statistical forecasting techniques that are computed solely from historical data accumulated over a period of time.

**total revenue** volume of units produced multiplied by price per unit.

**transient state** a state in a Markov transition matrix that will never be returned to once it has been left for the first time.

**transition function** a mathematical relationship that relates the stages of a dynamic programming problem.

**transition matrix** a matrix containing the transition probabilities for the states of a Markov system.

**transition probability** a probability that describes the transition from one Markov state to another in one time period.

**transportation model** a type of linear programming problem in which a product is transported from a number of sources to a number of destinations at the minimum cost.

**transportation tableau** the table in which the solution of a transportation model is determined.

**trend** a long-term movement of an item being forecast.

**two-person game** a game situation in which two decision makers compete.

## U

**unbalanced transportation model** a transportation model in which supply exceeds demand or demand exceeds supply.

**unbounded problem** a linear programming problem that does not contain a completely closed-in feasible solution area, thus allowing the objective function to increase infinitely.

**unconstrained optimization** a model with a single objective function and no constraints.

**undirected branch** a branch in a network in which flow is possible in both directions.

**utiles** the units in which utility is measured.

**utility** a numerical measure of the satisfaction a person derives from money.

**utilization factor** the probability that a server in a queuing system is busy.

## V

**validation** the process of making sure model solution results are correct (valid).

**value of the game** the value of one player's gain and another's loss in a game situation.

**variable** a mathematical symbol within a model that can take on different values.

**variable costs** costs that are determined on a per unit basis.

**variance** a measure of how much values in a probability distribution vary from the mean.

**Vogel's approximation method (VAM)** a method that uses opportunity costs for determining the initial solution to a transportation model.

## W

**weighted moving average** a time series forecasting method in which the most recent data is weighted.

**what-if? analysis** a form of interaction between the computer and manager in which the computer is asked to determine the result if various changes are made in the model.

## Z

**zero-one integer model** an integer programming model that can consist of solution values of 0 or 1 only.

**zero-sum game** in a game situation, when the sum of the players' gains and losses equals zero.

# Index